Economics of Intellectual Property and R&D

An International Approach

World Scientific Lecture Notes in Economics and Policy

ISSN: 2630-4872

The World Scientific Lecture Notes in Economics and Policy series is aimed to produce lecture note texts for a wide range of economics disciplines, both theoretical and applied at the undergraduate and graduate levels. Contributors to the series are highly ranked and experienced professors of economics who see in publication of their lectures a mission to disseminate the teaching of economics in an affordable manner to students and other readers interested in enriching their knowledge of economic topics. The series was formerly titled World Scientific Lecture Notes in Economics.

Published:

Vol. 28: *Economics of Intellectual Property and R&D: An International Approach*
by Walter G. Park

Vol. 27: *Lecture Notes on Environmental and Resource Economics: A Theoretical Introduction*
by Aart de Zeeuw

Vol. 26: *Agricultural Economics and Policy*
by David Zilberman, Ruiqing Miao and Jian Rong

For the complete list of volumes in this series, please visit
www.worldscientific.com/series/wslnep

World Scientific Lecture Notes in Economics and Policy – Vol. 28

Economics of Intellectual Property and R&D

An International Approach

Walter G. Park

American University, USA

World Scientific

NEW JERSEY • LONDON • SINGAPORE • BEIJING • SHANGHAI • HONG KONG • TAIPEI • CHENNAI • TOKYO

Published by

World Scientific Publishing Co. Pte. Ltd.
5 Toh Tuck Link, Singapore 596224
USA office: 27 Warren Street, Suite 401-402, Hackensack, NJ 07601
UK office: 57 Shelton Street, Covent Garden, London WC2H 9HE

Library of Congress Cataloging-in-Publication Data
Names: Park, Walter author
Title: Economics of intellectual property and r&d : an international approach / Walter G. Park, American University, USA.
Description: Hackensack, NJ : WORLD SCIENTIFIC, 2026. | Series: World scientific lecture notes in economics and policy, 2630-4872 ; volume 28 | Includes bibliographical references and index.
Identifiers: LCCN 2026001720 | ISBN 9789819826124 hardcover | ISBN 9789819827152 paperback | ISBN 9789819826131 ebook | ISBN 9789819826148 ebook other
Subjects: LCSH: Intellectual property--Economic aspects | Intellectual property (International law)--Economic aspects | Artificial intelligence--Law and legislation | Research and development projects | Economic development
Classification: LCC K1401 .P37 2026
LC record available at https://lccn.loc.gov/2026001720

British Library Cataloguing-in-Publication Data
A catalogue record for this book is available from the British Library.

For any available supplementary material, please visit
https://www.worldscientific.com/worldscibooks/10.1142/14670#t=suppl

Desk Editors: Eshak Nabi Akbar Ali/Yulin Jiang

Typeset by Stallion Press
Email: enquiries@stallionpress.com

Preface

This book is an introduction to the economics of intellectual property rights (IPRs), with an emphasis on the *international* dimensions. Domestic perspectives tend to focus on market structure, antitrust, regulation, and public finance, among other topics. While the book addresses some of these, its primary focus is on the global institutions and regimes governing IPRs and on the cross-border flows of intellectual property through international trade and investment. An international focus is particularly relevant given current debates over artificial intelligence governance, pandemic preparedness, and digital trade agreements.

The book is intended for master's and upper-level undergraduate courses in business, economics, public policy, law, and related social sciences. It can also be used as a supplemental or recommended reading in doctoral courses. Often, an intuitive overview helps doctoral students "see the forest for the trees" and supports their advanced research. No specific prerequisites are required; essential background is provided in the chapters and in the Appendices.

Beyond the classroom, the book may also serve as a useful reference for researchers in government, think tanks, and advocacy groups, as well as creative artists, engineers, lawyers, IP professionals, and journalists seeking a non-technical treatment of the field.

The volume is designed for a semester-long course. I recommend covering Chapters 1–6 in order and Chapter 13 last. Chapters 1–6 present the core foundations of IPRs, including the North–South workhorse model of international IPRs. Chapter 13 serves as a capstone that builds on earlier chapters. In between, Chapters 7–12 address applications in creative industries, public health, agriculture, IP markets, and artificial intelligence. These chapters may be covered in any order, although Chapter 11 (legal debates around AI) may be covered before Chapter 12 (applications of AI in innovation). Key learning outcomes are to analyze the debates in international IPRs, identify and explain the core concepts and arguments, and develop an evidence-based perspective on the rules and policies that govern international IP.

This book grew out of my lecture notes and workshop materials developed over the past 12 years. Updating them sometimes took longer than preparing the originals, given the need to track sources and make sense of the twists and turns in the debates. It was an interesting writing experience. I am used to preparing slides after I write a paper or chapter, but here, the slides came first. I converted their bullet points into prose, retaining some where they best captured the gist of the arguments.

I am extraordinarily thankful to the Series Editor-in-Chief, Professor Felix Muñoz-García, for this opportunity and for his encouragement and guidance. I am also grateful to Dr. Zvi Ruder, Senior Executive Publisher, Yulin Jiang, Desk Editor, and Eshak Nabi Akbar Ali, Book Editor, for their support and stewardship of this project. I am deeply indebted to my co-authors and collaborators for sharing their knowledge and expertise. For reasons of space, I cannot cite them all; their influence is evident throughout. Of course, I remain solely responsible for any errors or omissions.

Lastly, I would like to acknowledge Eduardo Lederman-Rawet, Sarah Al-Masri, Sabine Kanter-Huchting, and Maggie McFarlane for their capable research assistance. I am especially grateful to Eduardo for his heroic help with document preparation, which allowed me to focus on the writing. As a teaching assistant and research assistant, he has been an excellent deputy instructor.

About the Author

Walter G. Park is a Professor of Economics at American University in Washington, D.C. His research focuses on intellectual property systems, R&D analysis, productivity and business cycles, and multinational firms. His articles have appeared in *Economic Inquiry*, *Journal of International Business Studies*, *Research Policy*, and *Review of World Economics*, among others. He has received research grants from the American Consortium on European Studies, European Patent Office, Government of India, Motion Picture Association of America, and the U.S. Patent and Trademark Office, among others. Park is the editor of the *Handbook of Innovation and Intellectual Property Rights* (Edward Elgar, 2024) and serves on the advisory editorial board of *Research Policy*. He has been a special sworn employee at the U.S. Bureau of Economic Analysis, and has consulted for the Center for Global Development, Industry Canada, Organization for Economic Cooperation and Development, World Bank, and the World Intellectual Property Organization, among others. He holds a Ph.D. in Economics from Yale University, an M.Phil. in Economics from Oxford University, and a B.A. in Economics and Statistics from the University of Toronto.

Contents

Preface v

About the Author vii

1 Essentials of Intellectual Property Rights 1

1.1 Introduction 1
1.2 Why IPR is a Global Matter 3
1.3 Types of Intellectual Property Rights 4
1.3.1 Patents 5
1.3.2 Copyrights 7
1.3.3 Trademarks 8
1.3.4 Trade Secrecy 10
1.3.5 Industrial Designs 11
1.3.6 Plant Variety Protection 11
1.3.7 Geographical Indications 12
1.4 How IPR Fits into the Economy 13
1.5 IP Institutions 15
1.5.1 The World Intellectual Property Organization (WIPO) 16
1.5.2 The World Trade Organization (WTO) 17
1.6 Global Processes 21
1.6.1 How an Invention Becomes a Patent 21
1.6.2 Patenting Costs 29

2 Data and Measurement **35**
2.1 Introduction 35
2.2 Trends in Innovation 36
2.2.1 R&D 36
2.2.2 Patents and Trademarks 42
2.2.3 Copyrights 46
2.3 Quantifying IP Regimes 48
2.3.1 Types of Indexes 50
2.3.2 Trends in IP Protection 52
2.3.3 Enforcement in Practice 59
2.3.4 IP Provisions and Country Characteristics 61
2.4 Comparative North–South Analyses 63
2.4.1 Explanatory Factors 66
2.4.2 Policy Implications 68
Appendix 2A. Data Sources 68
Appendix 2B. Quantitative Methods 70
Appendix 2C. Empirical Methods 73
2C.1 Regression Analysis 74
2C.2 Interpreting Results 75
2C.3 Empirical Strategies 78
2C.4 For Further Reading 79

3 R&D and Economic Growth **81**
3.1 Introduction 81
3.2 Production Possibility Frontier 82
3.3 Determinants of Economic Growth 84
3.4 R&D Decisions 87
3.4.1 Firm Value 89
3.4.2 Time-Cost Tradeoffs 91
3.4.3 Market Failures and Innovation 95
3.5 R&D Spillovers 97
3.5.1 Spillover Example 98
3.5.2 Public Sector R&D 102
3.5.3 Evidence on International R&D Spillovers 105

4 Economic Theories of IPR **111**
4.1 Introduction 111
4.2 Rationale for IPR 112
4.2.1 Illustrative Example: Drug Development 115

4.2.2 The Case of Trademarks 117
4.2.3 Qualifications 117
4.3 Conceptual Tools 120
4.4 Market Power 126
4.4.1 Case 1: Monopoly 127
4.4.2 Case 2: Competitive Industry 127
4.4.3 Limitations of the Illustration 130
4.5 Imitation and Commercialization 130
4.6 Optimal IPR 131
4.6.1 Patent Life, Breadth, and Costly Imitation 134
4.6.2 Product Innovations and Process Innovations 136
4.7 Patent Value and Quality 139
4.7.1 Patent Value 139
4.7.2 Patent Quality 146
Appendix 4A. Prizes for Innovations 149

5 North–South Models of Innovation 151
5.1 Introduction 151
5.2 North–South Framework 152
5.2.1 Partial Equilibrium 152
5.2.2 General Equilibrium Analysis 156
5.3 Critiques of North–South Models 162
5.4 Empirical Studies on North–South Innovation 165
5.4.1 Non-linearities 165
5.4.2 Economic Complexity 172
5.4.3 Natural Experiment 174
5.5 Harmonization 177
5.5.1 Equilibrium Protection 180
5.5.2 Optimal Protection 183
5.6 Utility Models 184
5.6.1 Evidence 188

6 North–South Models of Technology Transfer 191
6.1 Introduction 191
6.2 Types (or Modes) of Technology Transfer 192
6.3 Trends 194

6.4 Previous Research . . . 195
6.4.1 Trade as a Channel of Technology Transfer . . . 195
6.4.2 FDI as a Channel of Technology Transfer . . . 197
6.4.3 Licensing as a Channel of Technology Transfer . . . 199
6.4.4 Cross-Cutting Themes . . . 201
6.5 International Technology Transfer and Patent Rights . . . 202
6.5.1 Conceptual Framework for Patented Works . . . 203
6.5.2 Evidence . . . 209
6.5.3 Summary . . . 214
6.6 International Technology Transfer and Copyrights . . . 214
6.6.1 Core Copyright and Complementary Industries . . . 216
6.6.2 Conceptual Framework for Copyrighted Works . . . 219
6.6.3 Evidence . . . 225
Appendix 6A. Transfer Pricing and Profit-Shifting . . . 232
6A.1 Implications for North–South Technology Transfers . . . 235

7 Creative Works **237**
7.1 Introduction . . . 237
7.2 Creative Markets . . . 237
7.2.1 Copyrights Review . . . 238
7.2.2 Economics Review . . . 240
7.3 Copyrights and Technological Development . . . 241
7.4 Effects of Piracy . . . 242
7.4.1 Empirical Evidence . . . 244
7.5 Case Studies . . . 247
7.5.1 Case of Bollywood . . . 247
7.5.2 Case of Italian Opera . . . 249
7.6 Limitations and Exceptions . . . 251
7.6.1 L&E Regimes and Rationale . . . 252
7.6.2 Costs and Benefits of L&E . . . 254
7.6.3 Empirical Work . . . 256

7.7 Publishing Industry 258
7.7.1 Select Debates 259
7.7.2 Are Scholars Hindered by the Cost of Books and Journals? 262
7.7.3 On Profit Margins and Circular Flow 262
7.7.4 Related Controversy 263

8 Public Health 265
8.1 Introduction 265
8.2 Nature of Pharmaceutical Innovation 266
8.3 Case Study: HIV/AIDS 267
8.4 Parallel Imports 269
8.4.1 International Price Discrimination 271
8.4.2 Differential Pricing Example 271
8.4.3 Role of Price Controls 274
8.4.4 TRIPS-Plus Free Trade Agreements 276
8.5 Compulsory Licensing 277
8.5.1 Compulsory License and Consumer Access to Patented Products 278
8.5.2 Compulsory Licensing and Innovation 281
8.6 Generic Competition 283
8.6.1 Evergreening 284
8.6.2 Data Exclusivity 288
8.7 Neglected Tropical Diseases 290
8.8 TRIPS Waiver and COVID-19 292
8.8.1 Vaccine Nationalism 295
8.9 Select Evidence on Pharmaceutical Innovation and Tech Transfers 296
Appendix 8A. Traditional Medicines 298
8A.1 Determinants of Traditional Medicine 298
8A.2 Case of Modern Day Taiwan 300
8A.3 Should Traditional Medicines be Granted IPRs? 301

9 Agriculture 303
9.1 Introduction 303
9.2 Agriculture and Economic Development 304

9.3 Agriculture and IPR 305
9.3.1 Trends 308
9.3.2 Case Studies 309
9.4 Community Plant Variety Office 310
9.5 Impacts on Agricultural Productivity 313
9.5.1 Selected Evidence 314
9.6 Genetically Modified Organisms 317
9.6.1 GMO and IPR 321
9.7 Market Concentration in Seed Markets 323
9.7.1 Data on Seed Market Concentration 325
9.7.2 Effects of Market Concentration 327
9.7.3 Implications for Developing Countries 330
9.7.4 Mitigating Market Concentration 330
9.8 Open Biotechnology 331
9.8.1 Open Innovation 332
9.8.2 Open Source Biotech 335
9.8.3 Examples in Agriculture and Biotechnology . . . 336
9.8.4 Policy Issues 337

10 Organization and Markets 341
10.1 Introduction 341
10.2 Case Study: Tale of Two Tech Companies 342
10.3 Patent Thickets 344
10.4 Defensive Patenting 345
10.5 Standard Essential Patents 346
10.5.1 Network Effects 347
10.5.2 Standards 349
10.5.3 Relevance to IP 350
10.6 Standard Setting Organizations 352
10.6.1 A FRAND to Lean on 353
10.6.2 Declarations of SEPs 354
10.6.3 Select Challenges 354
10.6.4 Implications for North–South Relations 355
10.7 Patent Hold-Up and Royalty Stacking 356
10.7.1 Digression: Quality-Adjusted Prices 357
10.7.2 Quality-Adjusted Prices in Practice 358
10.7.3 Policy Effect 359
10.7.4 Effects of Royalty Stacking: Case Study 360
10.7.5 Summary and Explanations 362

10.8 Secondary Patent Markets . . . 363
10.8.1 Innovation Resilience . . . 363
10.8.2 Secondary Market Deals . . . 365
10.8.3 Prior Research on Secondary Patent Markets . . . 368
10.8.4 Index of Secondary Patent Market Exposure . . . 369
10.9 Real Options Theory and Uncertainty . . . 371
10.9.1 Conceptual Framework . . . 372
10.9.2 Some Evidence . . . 378
10.9.3 Reflections . . . 382

11 Artificial Intelligence and IP **385**
11.1 Introduction . . . 385
11.2 State of AI . . . 386
11.2.1 Nature of the AI Market . . . 389
11.2.2 Trends in AI Patenting . . . 392
11.3 Copyright Issues . . . 394
11.3.1 Guiding Principles . . . 396
11.4 Patent Issues . . . 404
11.4.1 AI as Inventor . . . 405
11.4.2 Inventive Step . . . 408
11.5 Privacy . . . 413
11.5.1 Selected Empirical Studies on Impacts of Privacy . . . 415
11.5.2 Examples of Data-Saving Innovations . . . 419
11.6 Enablement Requirement and AI Training . . . 420
11.6.1 Source Codes and Algorithms . . . 420
11.6.2 Case Study: EPO Guidelines on AI Training . . . 421
Appendix 11A. Primer on Artificial Intelligence . . . 423
11A.1 Key AI Concepts . . . 424
11A.2 AI Interfaces . . . 424
11A.3 How the Sausage is Made . . . 425
11A.4 AI Frameworks and Development Tools . . . 425
11A.5 The Hardware of AI . . . 426
11A.6 The AI Computing Ecosystem . . . 426
11A.7 Glossary of AI Terminology . . . 428
11A.8 For Further Reading . . . 429

12 Artificial Intelligence, Innovation, and Diffusion **431**
12.1 Introduction . . . 431
12.2 Innovation . . . 432

12.3 Technology Transfer . . . 437
12.3.1 Why Trade-Related? . . . 438
12.3.2 Case of Digital Services Trade . . . 440
12.4 Productivity . . . 443
12.4.1 A Word on Automation . . . 452
12.4.2 Singularity . . . 454
12.5 North–South Gaps . . . 456
12.5.1 AI, Technological Progress, and Catch-Up . . . 460
12.5.2 Policy Implications . . . 466
12.6 Bottlenecks . . . 467
12.6.1 Market Concentration . . . 467
12.6.2 Bottleneck 1: Compute Resources . . . 471
12.6.3 Bottleneck 2: Environment . . . 472

13 Lessons for Economic Growth and Development 475
13.1 Introduction . . . 475
13.2 Recap on Framework . . . 476
13.2.1 Economic Development . . . 477
13.3 IP Effects: Varying Factors . . . 479
13.3.1 Product Market Competition . . . 479
13.3.2 Firm Productivity Advantages . . . 481
13.4 Stages of Economic Development . . . 486
13.4.1 Case Study . . . 487
13.4.2 Conceptual Framework . . . 488
13.4.3 Empirical Testing . . . 491
13.5 Lessons for the Developing World . . . 496
13.6 Lessons for IP Reforms . . . 498
13.7 Docket I: IP Flexibilities . . . 501
13.7.1 Contributions from Other Sources . . . 503
13.8 Docket II: Capacity Building . . . 508
13.8.1 AI in Developing Countries . . . 510
13.9 Future Directions . . . 513

Bibliography 517

Index 537

Chapter 1

Essentials of Intellectual Property Rights

1.1 Introduction

Market economies function on the price system and on a system of well-defined property rights. In many regions, this includes the provision of property rights over intangible assets, such as the products of knowledge: inventions, creative works, designs, and brands, among others. The system of intellectual property laws governs the production, consumption, and exchange of knowledge goods and services, locally and globally.

The purpose of this book is to survey academic research on the economics of intellectual property rights and to draw implications for international economic growth, development, and policy. Economic growth is the branch of economics concerned with the determinants and mechanisms of productivity increase, including the technical efficiency of economic systems. Economic development is broader in scope: it addresses the structural foundations of living standards and examines growth in conjunction with distributional and institutional factors.

Both growth and development are intrinsically tied to technological change. Access to medical innovations, educational content, and advanced industrial tools plays a vital role in alleviating poverty and promoting both social and economic advancement. Moreover, the process of technological change is global in scope. Economic transformation rarely occurs in isolation: methods and tools for solving problems flow across borders, and in many cases, cross-national teams collaborate on solutions to common challenges.

Central to these processes, intellectual property (IP) has a critical influence on the technological changes that affect national and international growth and development. How the IP system is designed and operates influences product development, technological adoption and diffusion, the creative arts, human capital, and public health outcomes.

This book is organized around intellectual property rights (IPRs) and the institutions that govern them. Before turning to their economic implications, the book first introduces the basic forms of IPRs and the legal and institutional frameworks in which they operate. While this is not a law textbook focused on doctrinal details, a high-level overview provides adequate background for understanding the academic research on the economics of IP.

Economists have developed a wide array of theories and models, but this book distills them to their essential elements. The book aims to help educated professionals in the field follow the literature and effectively apply the models.

The analysis also examines data and evidence, which sometimes present conflicting findings. The book examines how and why such conflicts arise. Policy issues and debates present similar complexity, requiring careful examination of the assumptions and underlying conceptual frameworks.

This book has the following three key features:

- International perspective with focus on developed and developing country issues;
- Economic perspectives on technology and laws;
- Survey and interpretation of research:
  - ❑ Theory and evidence, emphasizing intuitive understanding;
  - ❑ Policy applications: health, agriculture, education, technology markets, artificial intelligence, and more.

These features reflect the book's intended audience and approach. It serves two roles. First, it helps non-economists, particularly professionals involved in developing innovations or facilitating IP protection, better understand the economic debates surrounding intellectual property. Second, it helps economists better understand how IP policies and institutions work, especially empirical researchers whose work informs policy recommendations.

Traditional economics textbooks devote minimal attention to intellectual property rights, and when they do, coverage tends to be superficial, often limited to a brief treatment within monopoly theory. Thus, a more in-depth understanding of how IP systems work will enable economics scholars to construct better theoretical models and undertake more informed empirical research.

Naturally, a book like this cannot cover all topics, issues, or research methodologies in the field. The goal is to provide readers with enough of a foundation to pursue their interests in intellectual property and economic development.

This opening chapter provides an overview of intellectual property rights, introduces key definitions and institutions, and discusses the key economic linkages. It also outlines the basic processes involved in securing patent protection, which is the predominant IP mechanism examined in research on innovation, growth, and development.

1.2 Why IPR is a Global Matter

Why did intellectual property become an international concern? At first glance, one might assume that IP protection should remain a matter of domestic policy. Yet, intellectual property rights (IPRs) have emerged as a global issue for several interrelated reasons:

1. Although IPR laws are enacted and enforced at the national level, the markets for knowledge-based goods and services are increasingly global (Figure 1.1).[1]

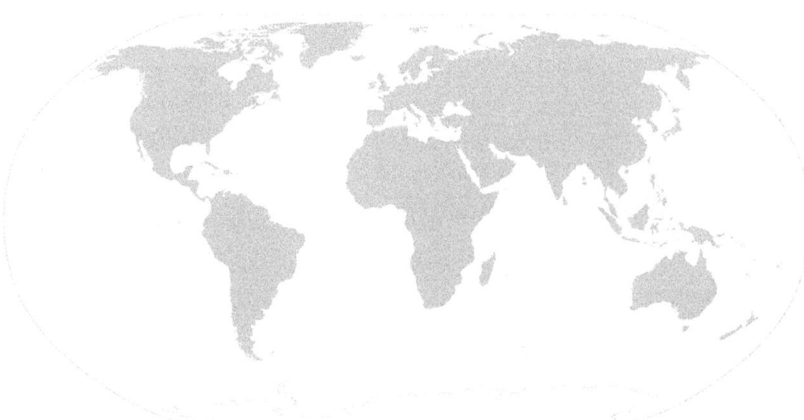

Figure 1.1. IP and the world economy

[1]https://commons.wikimedia.org/wiki/File:World_Map_Blank.svg

2. International cooperation or coordination is often necessary to prevent discriminatory IP policies, mercantilist strategies, and free-riding across borders.
3. Critics argue that global IP systems contribute to the economic exploitation of developing countries by wealthier nations, particularly through the misappropriation of traditional knowledge and unequal access to patented technologies.

Though IP laws are national in scope, their influence is international in terms of innovation incentives and impact on technological progress. In countries where IP laws are absent or weakly enforced, innovators not only lose earnings to infringement in those markets, but also face the risk that infringing goods re-enter their own domestic markets to compete against their products. Furthermore, confining innovators to domestic or local markets limits the scale of innovation incentives. Restricted market access reduces innovation ambitions, whereas access to global markets enables innovators to pursue ambitious projects and develop world-class technologies.

Intellectual property is also an international issue because nations have competing interests. Countries may prefer to prevent royalty payments from flowing abroad while simultaneously seeking to maintain technological advantages over other nations.

At the same time, many in the developing world view global IP regimes with suspicion, seeing them as remnants of colonialism. From this perspective, strong IP enforcement can prevent technological catch-up by restricting access to technology. As developing countries accumulate technical capabilities, they can learn to navigate the IP system more effectively. However, these gains may trigger new forms of exclusion, such as market access restrictions imposed by developed countries. This highlights the need for neutral, multilateral IP legal frameworks to balance competing interests across the development spectrum.

1.3 Types of Intellectual Property Rights

- Patents (Inventions)
- Copyrights (Creative Expressions)
- Trademarks (Names, Brand Symbols)
- Trade Secrecy (Method, Process, Know-How)
- Industrial Designs (Product Shapes)

- Plant Varieties and Plant Breeder Rights (Agriculture)
- Geographical Indications (Product Identification)

Intellectual property rights (IPRs) take many forms, encompassing product designs; inventions in manufacturing, services, and agriculture; creative works in the visual and performing arts; brand names and geographical indications; and confidential business information such as trade secrets. Prior to 1995, certain IPRs did not exist in many countries, and most were not strongly protected, particularly in the developing world. Since 1995, however, developing countries have undertaken the most significant increases in IPR standards. While their legal standards still lag behind those of high-income countries, they have borne the heaviest burden of adjustment.

1.3.1 *Patents*

Patents protect inventions. They grant the inventor the exclusive right to make, use, or sell an invention for a limited time. By delineating property rights, the patent system also facilitates the trading of knowledge assets. Patents and other IP rights are granted by the appropriate authorities (e.g., patent office or industrial property office) in a country. Patent rights are territorial in that the rights, privileges, and obligations apply only within the country or region. Patents do not automatically extend to other countries. The inventor would need to seek a patent in each of the countries or regional areas in which protection is desired.

It is essential to understand that a patent typically covers not the entire product, but rather the inventions that contribute to its creation, functionality, or operation. This is because the technological domain is rarely coextensive with a product domain.[2] For instance, no patent exists for the entire smartphone (see Figure 1.2).[3] Thousands of patents protect a single product like the Apple iPhone.[4] Each of these patents protects a specific technology, function, or design feature, such as the Touchscreen technology, Face ID and biometric authentication, Slide-to-unlock interface, Wireless communication methods, and battery management. Thus, patents are for

[2]See Menell *et al.* (2023).

[3]Image of iPhone is from https://freerangestock.com/. Figure 1.2 is a riff on Carly Rae Jepsen's iconic song "Call Me, Maybe."

[4]The same goes for disposable baby diapers, which are protected by numerous patents, covering various technological components such as absorbent materials and fastening mechanisms. See https://www.brighterstridesaba.com/blog/diaper-facts-and-statistics.

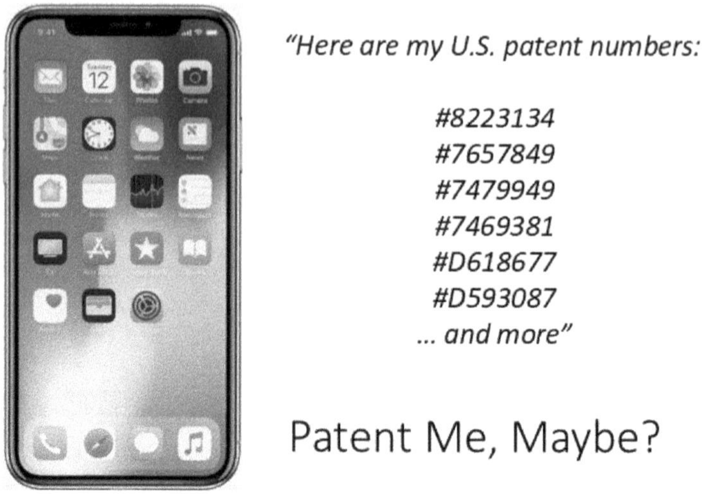

Figure 1.2. Product Domain vs. Technological Domain

the technological components that comprise the product or for the underlying methods of production.

Occasionally, however, a patent might cover a product if it is a pioneering invention, like the Wright Brothers' Airplane Patent, which at the time (1906) was the only working flight design. Another example is the Gillette safety razor (1904) or the first ballpoint pen (1945). Once their patents expired, competitors for all these innovations entered the market and produced differentiated inventions.

However, in the pioneering case of Alexander Graham Bell's invention, Bell's patent was not for the entire telephone but for the "Improvement in Telegraphy." It covered the method of transmitting sound using electrical signals over a wire. Bell invented a specific but key component of a telephone, but not every aspect of it. Like the modern smartphone, the telephone was protected by multiple patents.[5]

In modern times, a situation where a patented invention may come close to covering an entire product is the case of pharmaceutical drugs. A patent can be issued for a new chemical entity (NCE) or an active pharmaceutical ingredient (API), which may effectively cover the entire drug.[6]

[5]For a history of Bell and his labs, see Gertner (2012).

[6]For example, the anti-cholesterol drug Lipitor contains the active ingredient (atorvastatin), which is patented by Pfizer. With few other compositions of matter substitutes, this patent effectively blocks competitors from making the same drug until the patent expires.

Why this discussion of technological domain versus product domain matters is that patents do not create monopolies *per se*. A monopoly describes a situation where only one seller of a product operates in the market. As long as a patent does not cover the entire product, there can be other suppliers of a good. Producers may all require the same invention(s) to make their goods, in which case they will pay licensing fees for the right to use the invention. The result is that multiple goods can compete for the consumer's attention. The above discussion is also relevant because it helps explain why cross-licensing is common among many companies; namely, where a company licenses one of its patents to another company, and vice versa. This is because no one company may own all the technologies it needs to produce its goods, and so it engages in the trading of IP rights.

1.3.2 *Copyrights*

Copyrights protect creative works, like books, music, films, and computer programs. They give creators the exclusive rights to reproduce, distribute, display their work or perform their work in public. Chapters 6 and 7 provide an extensive treatment of the economic impacts of copyrights and discuss further aspects of copyright laws, including limitations and exceptions.

The author of a work is usually the first owner of the work, but the author can assign the copyright to other parties. For works created for hire, the employer is the owner of the copyright, but the author may have the "moral" right of attribution and integrity. *Moral rights* protect the non-economic interests of authors. The right of integrity gives the creator the right to prevent distortion or modification of the work that can harm the author's reputation. So, while the author is the original creator, ownership can change hands through sales, inheritance, contracts, and employment.

Another important distinction is author's rights versus *neighboring rights*. These are also known as "related rights," which cover works created by entrepreneurs, be they performances, broadcasts, phonograms, or sound recordings. Neighboring rights are rights of performers, phonogram producers, and broadcasting organizations. They reward a different kind of skill set, namely, organizational and entrepreneurial skills. They contribute to the public dissemination of a work. These rights exist alongside copyrights.[7]

[7] As examples, a songwriter has a copyright to a song and a singer has the neighboring right to the performance of the song; or a filmmaker has a copyright to a film, while a television broadcasting network has the neighboring right in its broadcast of the film.

1.3.3 *Trademarks*

A trademark protects business names, brand names, logos, slogans, musical sounds, and color marks. While laws do not permit the trademarking of a color in general, they allow it as a combination with a distinctive shape or sign. The laws also cover three-dimensional marks such as figures, packaging, or the distinctive shape of the good; for example, the *Toblerone* chocolate bar, which features a triangular shape. The trademarked shape must not be functional. It cannot be essential to the working of a product (e.g., the basic shape of eyeglasses).

Trademarks can be renewed indefinitely, as long as the owner pays the required renewal fees periodically (typically every ten years). In principle, a trademark right can last perpetually, though in practice, it may lapse or become generic. This is where trademarks differ from copyrights and patents. The latter incentivize creative and innovative work, whereas trademarks serve to identify the source of products and help consumers distinguish among them. The incentive for firms to invest in branding and product quality comes not from a fixed-term reward, but from the ability to exclude others from misusing the brand.

Automatic expiration of trademarks is not necessary to advance the public interest because the underlying goal is to prevent consumer confusion. As long as a brand remains in active commercial use, it continues to serve its economic function. By contrast, when patents and copyrights expire and enter the public domain, ideas and expressions can be reused or recombined. But with trademarks, no comparable social gain arises from allowing the public to use a still-distinctive brand name. Doing so would undermine source identification, confuse consumers, and erode firms' incentives to maintain quality.

However, if a trademarked name becomes generic — whereby it is commonly used to refer to a general class of products — trademark protection is lost. Many once-distinctive trademarked names have entered our vernacular: Xerox, Kleenex, Nylon, Aspirin, Escalator, Zipper, Kerosene, Thermos, Dumpster, Frisbee, Popsicle, and Windbreaker.

Trademarks are especially recognizable through visual means like a company's logo, as a way to encapsulate the essence of the company's brand and business. Companies spend time and effort designing their logos, and through trademark protection have exclusive rights to the use of their logos.

Figure 1.3. Logos

Figure 1.3 shows some well-known company logos.[8] Amazon's yellow swoosh looks like a smile, and the swoosh joins the letters a and z, meaning that this store has everything from a to z. At the center of the Tostitos logo are two people enjoying a Tostitos chip with a bowl of salsa. The pink parts of the Baskin-Robbins logo form the number 31, a reference to the 31 flavors of ice cream it sells. BMW stands for Bavarian Motor Works. Its logo is shaped like an aircraft propeller, as the company started out as an aircraft manufacturer, and the checkered blue and white are the colors of the Bavarian flag. The VAIO (Visual Audio Intelligence Organizer) corporation is a spin-off of Sony Ltd. VAIO was later acquired by Nojima Co. of Japan. The first two letters of the VAIO logo represent the basic analogue signal. The last two letters are a 1 and 0, representing the digital signal. Lastly, the FEDEX logo signifies speed and efficiency. Notice the arrow in the white space between E and x.

[8] Sources of logos: https://freebiesupply.com/logos/fedex-express-logo/, https://upload.wikimedia.org/wikipedia/commons/c/ca/Tostitos_brand_logo.png, https://commons.wikimedia.org/wiki/File:BMW.svg, https://freebiesupply.com/logos/baskin-robbins-logo/, https://en.wikipedia.org/wiki/Vaio, https://freebiesupply.com/logos/amazon-logo/.

1.3.4 *Trade Secrecy*

Trade secret laws protect against the unauthorized disclosure of three categories of information: (1) technical information, such as blueprints, formulas, and industrial processes; (2) confidential business information, such as customer lists, financial information, and business plans; and (3) know-how, regarding information about methods, steps and procedures, for achieving successful outcomes. A famous example of a trade secret is the formula for Coca-Cola. As Lippoldt and Schultz (2014) point out in its survey of 37 nations, the legal expectations are that companies or individuals make reasonable efforts to maintain secrecy, that commercial value exists as a result of secrecy, and that the secret information is not an absolute secret but is information within the organization or unit that is not readily publicly accessible. Trade secrecy does not protect against company information that is fairly disclosed or enters the public domain fairly.

Trade secrecy protection is important for firms that need to disclose information to public authorities for purposes of product registration or obtaining regulatory approval. It is also important to a company that chooses not to patent an innovation. It may find more commercial value in keeping the innovation a trade secret.[9] But then a firm risks having a rival independently develop the innovation and then patent it. The firm would not be able to seek damages.

That a company has the option to keep an innovation a trade secret should not imply that secrecy is necessarily a substitute for patenting. Protection for trade secrets can complement the patenting endeavor. First, not all innovative information is patentable. Second, during the experimental stages of research, prior to a breakthrough that leads to a patent, risks of unauthorized leakage could deter investments in research.[10]

Trade secrecy laws can play a role in global technology transfers. Firms that undertake foreign direct investment (FDI) or license their IP in foreign countries often need to engage with local partners and distributors. This may require that they reveal or share some sensitive business information.

---

[9]See Klein and Sener (2024) for an analysis of a firm's choice between secrecy and patenting.

[10]See Png (2017), who examines trade secrecy laws by U.S. states and finds a positive association between trade secret protection and research and development. See also Schultz (2024), who points out that during the COVID-19 pandemic, trade secrecy protection enabled private companies to collaborate and develop treatments. It provided the necessary security for companies to share information without the fear of losing advantages to rivals.

Again, risks of misappropriation of information would make firms quite reluctant to do business abroad.

1.3.5 *Industrial Designs*

The protection of industrial designs relates to a product's aesthetic appearance (shape, pattern, color) but not its function. Examples abound. In consumer electronics, unique designs include the shape of the Sony PlayStation controller or the shape of the Apple iPhone. In transportation, they include the Vespa Scooter or the Tesla Cybertruck. Other recognizable designs include the Hermes Birkin bag or Mattel's Hot Wheels car. Product designs are valuable because consumers exhibit a preference for them. They could choose any dress shirt for functionality, but prefer an elegantly designed shirt. So, industrial design protection incentivizes companies to invest in unique product aesthetics. The free copying of designs would mislead consumers and diminish the value of designer products, and undermine the investments that companies made to design their products.

Laws protecting industrial designs evolved because these "designs" do not fit neatly under copyright, trademark, and patent protection. Copyrights protect the artistic expressions, but not the appearance (shape) of the platform used in the expression. Trademarks protect those product aspects that identify a brand, but not the aesthetic product features in the abstract. Patents protect the functionality of a product, so if a design affects how a product works, it might be eligible for a patent, but if it is purely aesthetic, it will not.

1.3.6 *Plant Variety Protection*

Plant variety protection (PVP) or plant breeders' rights (PBR) protect plant science innovations such as higher-yielding crops, crops that are resistant to diseases, or crops with enhanced nutritional content. The new plant variety must meet the DUS criteria: distinct, uniform, and stable. Distinctiveness refers to being distinguishable from existing varieties. Uniformity refers to the consistency in the plant variety's characteristics when propagated (i.e., exhibiting the same traits). Stability refers to the maintenance of distinctiveness through successive generations; for instance, if a rose has a specific fragrance, so should its offspring. These properties matter for determining whether the innovation can be reproduced. Mere discoveries of plant varieties are excluded from PVP. A breeder's intervention is required.[11] Compared to a patent, PVPs have a narrower scope of protectable matter, and they do not need to meet the more difficult standard of being inventive. Chapter 9 is devoted to agricultural innovations and plant variety protection.

Under a PVP, the plant breeder has exclusive rights to the propagating material, like seeds and cuttings, and in some cases to harvested material, such as cut flowers and fruit. Plant varieties are typically not patentable, but some countries or regions allow for the patenting of genetically modified plants, but the protection covers the gene modifications, not the plant variety itself. Examples include Monsanto's Roundup Ready Soybeans, a CRISPR-edited crop,[12] and genetically modified rice that is drought resistant. In addition, the U.S. permits plant patents for asexually reproduced plants (through cloning or using tissue culture, where a small piece of plant tissue is grown in a sterile controlled environment). An example is the Honeycrisp Apple, known for its crisp texture and juicy sweet flavor.

1.3.7 *Geographical Indications*

Geographical indications (GI) are IP rights that identify the specific region from which a good originates, and which associate or attribute qualities of the good to its geographical origin; for example, Parmesan Cheese, Darjeeling tea, Bordeaux wine, Champagne, Blue Mountain Coffee, Tequila, and Idaho potatoes. A GI signals an authenticity about the good.

GIs are a fusion of globalization and localization. The good is sold in global markets but is marketed as an indigenous product. It can motivate and underwrite local economic development, while satisfying the global consumer's taste for authentic traditional goods. A key goal of GI protection is to prevent imitators from free-riding off the reputation of the origin of the good. Consumers are unable to determine the quality of the goods. Hence, the asymmetry of information can prevent market transactions from occurring.

Figure 1.4 shows the GIs in force as of 2022.[13]

Overall, China has the most GIs in force. By region, Europe accounts for more than half, followed by Asia, which accounts for a little more than

---

[11] See Campi (2024).

[12] CRISPR (Clustered Regularly Interspaced Short Palindromic Repeats) is a gene-editing tool for enhancing desired traits.

[13] *Source*: WIPO (2023), Table 5.7, p. 161.

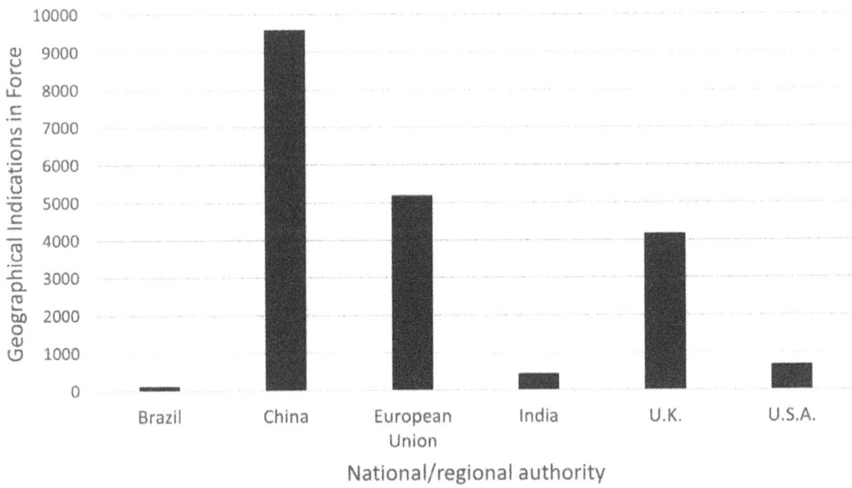

Figure 1.4. Geographical Indications in Force for Selected Countries and Regions, 2022

one-third. Among the EU, Hungary and Germany are the two leading countries with the most GIs in force. Brazil and India account for relatively few GIs. High-income countries account for 43%, while upper-middle-income countries account for over 46%. Low-income countries account for just 10.6%, making GIs an important North–South matter.[14] Some policy debates concern whether protections should be extended to cover GIs for all types of products.[15]

1.4 How IPR Fits into the Economy

The extensive literature on economic growth and development identifies knowledge and technology as central drivers of economic transformation.[16] In turn, the principal determinants of knowledge accumulation and technological progress include as follows:

- Legal regime and other institutions governing intellectual property rights (IPR);
- Public Support and related policies;

[14] See Cardoso *et al.* (2022).
[15] See International Trade Center (2009).
[16] See Jones and Vollrath (2024) for an introduction.

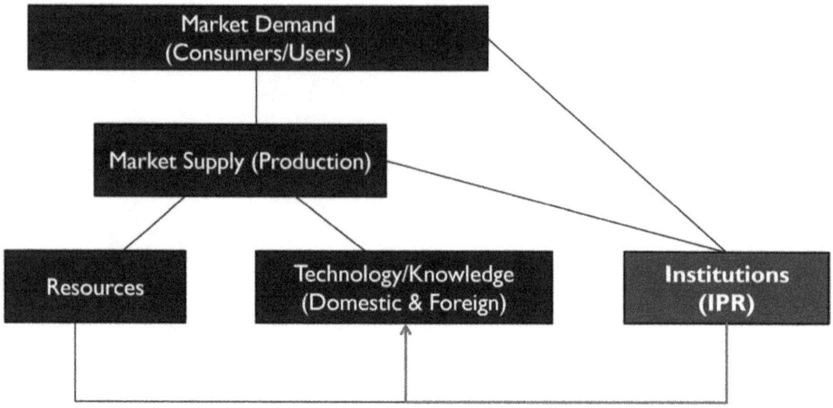

Figure 1.5. An Economic Development Framework

- Market structure, incentives, and opportunities (local, regional, and global);
- Resources (capital, financial, and existing stock of know-how).

While a portion of knowledge capital is produced by governments, universities, and other non-profit institutions, the majority of technological activity takes place within market systems.

Figure 1.5 offers a bird's-eye view of how intellectual property rights relate to the market system and their ultimate impact on economic development. Addressing the impact of IPRs on the national economy is a complex undertaking. Essentially, IPRs affect consumers' access to creative and inventive works, as well as business incentives for innovation and the production and distribution of goods. Economic growth and development depend significantly on private sector development, particularly the productive capacity of firms on the supply side.

Firm productivity depends on available resources — including skilled and unskilled workers and capital — and on technologies that determine the efficiency of resource utilization. Intellectual property rights affect both the inputs used in production, such as new and improved capital goods, and the technological processes or methods of production. Technological changes, in turn, influence resource productivity and incentives to expand and maintain productive capacity.

IPRs also exert an "umbrella effect" on the broader market environment. They influence the legal and institutional context in which firms operate, enter into contracts, and commercialize their outputs.

Much of the research focuses on the relationship between IPRs and domestic innovation and technology transfer, which makes foreign innovations available to local markets. Both domestic and foreign innovation affect productivity and regional or national growth. For developing economies, technology transfer is likely to be the key linkage through which IPRs influence economic outcomes. While these economies are emerging as innovation centers, their innovation systems remain less advanced than those of developed countries. Hence, technology transfer plays a relatively more important role in providing access to existing foreign innovations and enabling their absorption or adaptation to local economic conditions.

Figure 1.5 shows that IPRs affect knowledge accumulation and technological development. Their effects can be positive or negative and vary depending on circumstances, as the remaining twelve chapters of this book will demonstrate. At the same time, it is important to acknowledge other factors that influence innovation outcomes, since intellectual property does not operate in isolation. These include public sector R&D, government grants, and policies such as R&D subsidies, depreciation allowances, and tax treatment of R&D and income from intangible assets.

The broader market environment also matters significantly: the size of markets at local, regional, or global levels; the nature of competition, whether highly competitive or heavily concentrated; and the availability of adequate resources. Critical factors include access to machinery and equipment, necessary human capital, finance and venture capital, and the existing knowledge base.

1.5 IP Institutions

Intellectual property rights (IPRs) are shaped and administered by a set of national and international institutions that govern the scope, registration, and enforcement of IP laws. Two central institutions in the global IP landscape are the World Trade Organization (WTO) and the World Intellectual Property Organization (WIPO).[17] This section discusses their roles, the major treaties and agreements they oversee, and the global systems for managing IP protection.

[17] Their logos are shown in Figure 1.6 and are from https://wto.org/ and https://www.wipo.int/portal/en.

Figure 1.6. World Trade Organization and World Intellectual Property Organization

1.5.1 *The World Intellectual Property Organization (WIPO)*

WIPO is a specialized United Nations agency based in Geneva that serves as a central forum for international cooperation on intellectual property matters. It administers key global treaties on IP law and facilitates cross-border protection, including the following:

- *The Paris Convention (1883)*: This agreement pertains to industrial property, such as patents and trademarks. It mandates *national treatment*, whereby each member state grants foreign nationals the same IP protections as it does its own citizens. It also establishes *priority rights*, allowing applicants to use the filing date of their first patent application across member countries, provided they apply within 12 months (for patents) or 6 months (for industrial designs and trademarks).
- *The Berne Convention (1886)*: This agreement protects literary and artistic works. Like the Paris Convention, it provides for national treatment, but it goes further by stipulating *automatic protection*, eliminating the need for formal registration. This contrasts with opt-in systems such as *Creative Commons*, where creators must explicitly specify terms of reuse.
- *WIPO Internet Treaties*: These include the *WIPO Copyright Treaty (WCT)* and the *WIPO Performances and Phonograms Treaty (WPPT)*,

which address IP issues in the digital environment. The WCT extends protection to software and databases, while the WPPT covers digital sound recordings and certain online transmission rights. Both treaties contain provisions against the circumvention of technological protection measures.

Beyond treaties, WIPO provides services that simplify international IP protection:

- *The Patent Cooperation Treaty (PCT)* system allows inventors to file a single international patent application, which then enters the national phases in designated countries.
- WIPO also oversees *global registration systems* for trademarks and industrial designs, which make cross-border protection more accessible.
- *The Patent Law Treaty (PLT)* is another harmonization initiative administered by WIPO. Unlike substantive patent treaties, the PLT focuses on procedural simplification. It standardizes filing procedures, provides for extensions to meet deadlines, allows restoration of rights, and reduces formalities, so as to help lower the administrative burdens on applicants and patent offices alike. Although not an incentive mechanism *per se*, it indirectly supports innovation by helping to improve consistency about processes.

However, WIPO lacks the authority to enforce its treaties upon member states. Its role is primarily facilitative. The international body that has enforcement and dispute resolution powers is the WTO.

1.5.2 *The World Trade Organization (WTO)*

The World Trade Organization (WTO) oversees major agreements:

1. General Agreement on Tariffs and Trade (GATT)
2. General Agreement on Trade in Services (GATS)
3. Agreement on Trade-Related Investment Measures (TRIMS)
4. Agreement on Trade-Related Aspects of Intellectual Property Rights (TRIPS)

Unlike WIPO, the WTO provides for a dispute settlement mechanism that enables member states to resolve trade disputes through a structured legal process. When a panel or appellate ruling favors one party, the decision is binding under WTO rules. The losing party is expected to comply with the ruling and modify its practices or policies within a reasonable time frame. If it fails to do so, the prevailing party may request authorization from the WTO to impose retaliatory trade measures. Now, the WTO does not have the authority to impose sanctions directly. Instead, sanctions are a tool that member countries can use if another member does not comply with WTO rulings.[18]

Established in 1995, the Trade-Related Aspects of Intellectual Property Rights (TRIPS) integrates IPRs into the domain of international trade, where disparities in IP are treated as potential non-tariff barriers. The key features of TRIPS include as follows:

- Minimum standards for IP protection;
- Enforcement obligations, including procedures and remedies;
- Dispute settlement mechanisms, allowing members to file complaints and pursue trade sanctions against violators;
- Flexibilities and transition periods for developing and least-developed countries.

TRIPS also embodies normative goals.

1. **Article 7:** "The protection and enforcement of intellectual property rights should contribute to the promotion of technological innovation and to the transfer and dissemination of technology, to the mutual advantage of producers and users of technological knowledge and in a manner conducive to social and economic welfare, and to a balance of rights and obligations."
2. **Article 66.2:** "Developed country Members shall provide incentives to enterprises and institutions in their territories for the purpose of promoting and encouraging technology transfer to least-developed country Members in order to enable them to create a sound and viable technological base."

It is important to remember that TRIPS only set minimum standards. It "allows Members to provide more extensive protection of intellectual property if they so wish. Members are left free to determine the appropriate method of implementing the provisions of the Agreement within their own legal system and practice."

To be mutually advantageous to both rights holders and users — as emphasized in Article 7 — the TRIPS Agreement includes not only IP rights

[18] https://www.wto.org/english/thewto_e/whatis_e/tif_e/disp1_e.htm.

but also provisions for limitations and exceptions. It requires developing countries to strengthen their IPR regimes and obliges developed countries to facilitate international technology transfer, as outlined in Article 66.2.

1.5.2.1 TRIPS-Plus Agreements

Since TRIPS sets only minimum standards, developed countries have sought to increase the strength of intellectual property protection by entering into bilateral and regional free trade agreements (FTAs) with their trading partners — particularly developing countries — to include provisions that exceed TRIPS requirements. These so-called **TRIPS-plus** agreements, such as CAFTA-DR, the U.S.–Jordan FTA, and the Comprehensive and Progressive Agreement for Trans-Pacific Partnership (CPTPP), often impose stricter IP obligations. They may extend patent terms, restrict the use of compulsory licensing, lengthen data exclusivity periods, or delay the entry of generic competitors. Critics argue that these agreements disproportionately benefit developed countries and upset the balance TRIPS sought to establish between protection and access.

Morin and Surbeck (2020) examine the evolution of TRIPS-plus provisions in regional and preferential trade agreements. One of their important investigations is the average number of such provisions per agreement over time. Since the entry into force of the TRIPS Agreement in 1995, the inclusion of TRIPS-plus provisions has increased steadily. Most of these provisions concern patents, copyrights, and trademarks, which constitute the bulk of TRIPS-plus provisions. By contrast, other forms of intellectual property, such as industrial designs and geographical indications, figure less prominently in TRIPS-plus trade agreements.

Table 1.1 provides a summary of the global institutions and agreements that have been discussed.

1.5.2.2 TRIPS Reviews

Interestingly, Article 71.1 of the TRIPS Agreement calls for regular review and reassessment that could lead to its amendment:

> "The Council for TRIPS shall review the implementation of this Agreement after the expiration of the transitional period referred to in paragraph 2 of Article 65. The Council shall, having regard to the experience gained in its implementation, review it two years after that date, and at identical intervals thereafter. The Council may

Table 1.1. Key International Institutions and Treaties in Intellectual Property

Institution	Treaty/Instrument	Focus Area	Key Features
WIPO	Paris Convention	Industrial Property	National treatment, priority rights.
WIPO	Berne Convention	Copyrights	Automatic protection, no registration.
WIPO	WCT, WPPT	Digital, Performers' Rights	Anti-circumvention, digital content.
WIPO	PCT System	Patents	Centralized filing, international breadth.
WIPO	PLT	Patent Procedures	Harmonized procedures and filing formalities.
WTO	TRIPS	All IP types	Minimum standards, enforcement, dispute settlement.
WTO+	TRIPS-plus FTAs	Trade-Related IP	Stronger-than-TRIPS provisions, limited flexibilities.

> also undertake reviews in the light of any relevant new developments which might warrant modification or amendment of this Agreement."

The purpose of these reviews is to determine whether the Agreement continues to meet the developmental, technological, and public policy needs of all WTO members. In practice, however, Article 71.1 has not been robustly implemented. Although the TRIPS Council has convened discussions on public health, enforcement, and TRIPS-plus issues, these have not amounted to systematic reviews as envisioned. Several developing countries and civil society organizations have called for a formalized review process, particularly in light of emerging technologies, the COVID-19 pandemic, and the expanding influence of TRIPS-plus provisions. Commentators have criticized the WTO for failing to utilize Article 71.1 as a core mechanism for feedback and reform.[19] The lack of full compliance with Article 71.1 contributes to a perception that the TRIPS regime remains top-down and insufficiently responsive to the needs of IP users.

[19]See https://docs.wto.org/dol2fe/Pages/SS/directdoc.aspx?filename=q:/IP/C/W712.pdf&Open=True.

1.6 Global Processes

This section explains the processes for obtaining and enforcing patent rights globally. In economic analyses, patent protection receives the most attention primarily because industrial inventions are closely tied to economic variables such as investment, technological progress, and productivity growth. Copyrights also relate to technological progress and knowledge accumulation, through their influence on education, research, libraries, museums, performances, and broadcasting. Thus, the main IP focus of this book will be patents, followed by copyrights. Other forms of IP will be treated less extensively, such as trade secrets, trademarks, utility models, and plant variety protection. In reviewing how the processes work, this section provides definitions of terms used in later chapters.

1.6.1 *How an Invention Becomes a Patent*

The logic of why patent systems exist is discussed in later chapters. This section focuses on the administrative details. The patent is both a scientific and a legal document. It is a scientific document in that it contains a full description of the underlying technology, enabling those persons skilled in the art to make and use the invention. Insufficient technical disclosure is a ground for disqualifying a patent right. In this regard, an underlying bargain exists. In exchange for patent protection, the inventors must disclose their new knowledge. Thus, patents help to diffuse new knowledge. There is no trade-off between technology creation and knowledge diffusion. The patent system should facilitate both. Rather, as will be discussed later, a trade-off exists between technology creation and the diffusion (or supply) of output embodying the new knowledge, because the patent holder has exclusive rights to use, sell, or license the patented invention, and so the output based on the invention will not be supplied competitively. But as far as knowledge goes, the patent system does not restrict knowledge access. It does the opposite of trade secrecy: it reveals knowledge. The patent system can restrict use of the knowledge, but not typically the access.[20]

[20]However, a few might quibble over how "access" is defined. If it means access to information, then patents promote knowledge sharing. But if it regards the ability to implement, experiment with, or improve upon a patented technology, then patents can be restrictive because unauthorized use is not permitted. And how knowledge can be applied might be limited even when information is freely available. Nonetheless, if "access" is about acquiring knowledge rather than acting on it, what has been stated holds. But the practical impact of patents on access to knowledge can still be debated depending on specific cases.

The patent document also acts as a legal title (or deed) to a piece of intellectual territory, within which others may not trespass and utilize without a license. Possession of this territory is temporary (for example, a statutory length of 20 years from the filing date), ownership rights must be renewed (through payment of renewal fees), and, like real estate, this intellectual territory can be sold or transferred. This territory of ideas must also be industrially applicable (not consisting of abstract ideas, such as scientific theories, mathematical knowledge, or organizational methods). The boundaries of the intellectual territory given to the patent holder are identified by the "claims" in the granted patent; each of these claims describes what the invention does or can do. The number and breadth of claims implicitly define the extent of the territory.[21]

How do patent systems work? It is convenient to describe them in roughly the chronological order in which inventors apply for and enforce their patent rights. Box 1 presents an outline of the procedures from the patent application stage to the patent enforcement stage. The outline is not meant to be exhaustive but to give an idea of the activities and decisions involved.

Box 1. An Outline of Patenting Procedures

(A) Patent Application

1. Pre-Application Choice: Patent vs. Trade Secrecy

• If choose to patent ⟹	Decide on national filing only or international
• If international ⟹	Separate National Filings (country by country)? PCT Filing? EPO Filing? EPO/PCT Filings? Other Combination of Filings?

(Continued)

[21]Patent applicants who seek broader protection may often try to insert more claims. A kind of negotiating process may take place in which the patent examiner deletes certain patent claims (especially those that seem to extend beyond the scope of the invention or cross into the territory of prior patent holders). Applicants may risk rejection of a patent if their applications contain too many claims (especially if the claims are not part of a unifying inventive theme). They may be required to file separate patent applications instead.

2. Pre-Grant Determinations:
- Priority Date of Application
- Publication of Application (18 months from date of application)
- Patentable Matter (whether subject matter is restricted)
- Patentability (search/exam for novelty, nonobviousness, utility)
- Duration (length) and Scope (breadth) of Patent Protection

3. Post-Grant Processes:
- Oppositions (by third parties) or reviews about patent validity
- Conditions on patent grant (e.g., working, compulsory licensing)
- Patent renewal or maintenance fees; vary by country

(B) Patent Enforcement

1. Enforcement Routes:	2. Statutory Provisions:
• Litigation • Arbitration • Settlement	• Preliminary Injunctions • Contributory Infringement • Burden of Proof Reversals • Doctrine of Equivalents • Discovery

PCT denotes Patent Cooperation Treaty, EPO European Patent Office.

(a) Patent Application

The inventor must first decide whether to seek patent protection or keep the invention a trade secret. By choosing the latter course of action, the inventor risks being imitated and not being able to claim damages, as pointed out earlier, but some nations do provide some form of trade secrecy protection (which prohibits the obtaining of company secrets by illegal means). However, trade secret protection does not protect against another inventor independently developing the invention or reverse engineering it.

If the inventor decides to patent, another decision to make is whether to patent nationally only (i.e., in the domestic market only) or internationally (in more than one country). If the inventor decides to patent internationally, there are a number of routes in which to seek worldwide protection. One way is simply to file a patent in each country of interest. Obtaining a patent in one country does not automatically grant protection in other countries (unless there exists some specific agreement between countries, as in the case where one country registers patents obtained in another country).[22]

Filing patents in each country of interest may be efficient if the inventor is interested in obtaining protection only in a few countries; however, if the inventor is interested in a much broader geographic coverage, separate national filing is cumbersome. Hence, an alternative way is to seek a regional patent. A European Patent Office (EPO) patent is one such regional patent. Through a single, centralized filing with the EPO, the applicant can try to obtain a patent in several EPO member states. An international patenting route is the Patent Cooperation Treaty (or PCT) system, administered by the World Intellectual Property Organization (WIPO). An inventor can file a single PCT application and designate as many member states of WIPO as desired. Since EPO states are also member states of WIPO, if PCT applicants are also designating a number of EPO countries, the PCT patent has a provision whereby the patent applicant can designate the entire EPO as a block (treated as one member state unit), thus cutting down on those fees that vary with the number of states designated. In that case, the applicant is filing an EPO-PCT patent.[23]

Having decided upon the route for applying for a patent, the inventor goes through the appropriate review and examination. A crucial determination to be made early on is priority: who gets to apply for a patent for a particular invention? Is another application pending? In the vast majority of countries, the first to apply gets priority.[24] If someone else has priority,

[22]This occurred when some African countries granted patent rights to inventors who obtained a patent in the U.K.

[23]These regional patent filings (i.e., EPO or PCT) consist of two stages. In the first stage, the single, centralized filing takes place, which establishes a priority date. Several months later, the applicant undergoes a second stage (known as the "validation" or national phase), where the applicant must eventually file the application in the separate national jurisdictions, meeting local legal requirements and paying local fees. The advantage of the regional patent is in establishing priority and obtaining some extension of time to improve upon the patent application and invention, assess market conditions, and, where applicable, translate the application into the different native languages of the countries designated in the regional patent application. For more details about the European patent system, see Chapter 6 of Guellec and van Pottelsberghe (2007).

[24]Before the *America Invents Act (AIA)* of 2011, priority in the U.S. was awarded to the first party to invent. The AIA does provide an exception, however, through a derivation proceeding under which a first inventor can obtain priority if substantial evidence exists that the applicant who filed first had derived the claimed invention from the first inventor and that the earlier application that claimed it was filed without authorization.

the inventor loses the right to seek a patent for that invention. For inventors filing patents internationally, the Paris Convention allows inventors (of signatory states) up to 12 months to file an application in other signatory countries after first filing in a signatory country. The inventor thus reserves that initial filing date for 12 months for purposes of establishing the priority date and for indicating who filed first. All relevant matters are referred to that filing date (or to the earliest date of priority) for official purposes.

Patent applications are generally published after the earliest filing date (priority date), even if the patent has not yet been granted. The published applications are also available to the public after 18 months, even if the patents are rejected or abandoned.[25] While early publication contributes to quicker knowledge diffusion, it has competing effects on the incentives for patenting. On the one hand, it enables rivals to build on the knowledge, potentially creating competing patented inventions or compelling the parties into cross-licensing agreements. On the other hand, the information in the application can be used by potential competitors to distance themselves from the applicant's technological turf, and thereby avoid infringement and costly litigation, or avoid unwanted cross-licensing arrangements.[26]

Another important part of the patent application process is the determination of patentability. First, the laws generally indicate subject matters that are not patentable, as certain subjects are not novel, non-obvious, and industrially useful. For example, methods for medical treatment may not be patentable in some jurisdictions because they do not yield industrially applicable output. Or, subject matters may be declared unpatentable if they are considered contrary to public order, morality, health, and national security.

During the determination of patentability, a crucial conclusion is arrived at concerning novelty. The invention must not be in the pool of existing (prior) knowledge. By that criterion, an invention could lose novelty if it is publicly disclosed before a patent application for it is filed. Some countries provide a grace period, allowing the invention to remain novel if the patent application is made within 12 months of public disclosure (for example, at an exhibition or public demonstration).

[25]The U.S. AIA does allow applicants to request non-publication if the application is classified under national security or will not be filed in another country. See *U.S. Code of Federal Regulations*, 37 CFR 1.213(a).

[26]Hegde and Luo (2018) examined the advantages of early disclosure in expediting licensing deals. Analyzing data on the biomedical industry, the study found that early publication infuses the market with greater information and transparency.

Novelty, non-obviousness, and industrial applicability are determined after search and examination by patent examiners. If, at the end of the process, a patent is granted, a determination of patent scope is also made. The scope of protection refers to the size of the protected intellectual territory (i.e., how many claims are accepted or how broadly they are written). If the scope of protection is extensive, competitors must develop inventions sufficiently different to avoid infringing on the patent holder's rights.[27] Economists have debated whether technological change is better served by a broad or narrow scope (see Chapter 4). On the one hand, a broad scope gives more market power to an inventor and might be a strong inducement to invent; on the other hand, it makes it more difficult for competitors to develop new follow-on inventions.

Upon grant, inventors may face opposition from third parties. In the EPO, third-party oppositions occur for a limited time after a patent is granted. Similarly, in Japan, post-grant oppositions can take place, although before 2004, oppositions were permitted before the grant. The U.S. has a system of post-grant review that allows third parties to challenge the validity of a recently granted patent on various grounds (lack of novelty, obviousness, or insufficient disclosure). Alternatively, in the U.S., an *Inter Partes Review* can occur after 9 months from the date of grant. This involves challenging the grant based on prior art. The advantage of a system of oppositions and reviews is that it helps spread the burden of fully determining patent validity to competitors. A disadvantage is that an expensive obstacle is placed in the path of a patent applicant. Rivals could especially try to delay, if not prevent, the applicant from getting a patent or commercializing the invention.

After a patent is granted, patent holders may also face conditions regarding working and licensing. Working requirements are essentially conditions that the patent holder must practice or exploit the invention by a certain period, or else forfeit the patent right or be mandated to license the technology to others willing to exploit the invention. Compulsory licensing reduces the patent holder's exclusive rights. But countries do have provisions for imposing it in cases of public interest, emergencies, or anti-competitive

[27]Patent claims are listed in the patent's *specifications*. Of course, if the patent applicant drafts claims too broadly, the patent could get rejected since broad claims are likely to step on some prior invention's technological space, in which case the claimed invention is not novel. But if the patent claims are drafted too narrowly, the applicant's competitors are more easily able to invent around the invention.

behavior; for example, public health crises (e.g., pandemics like COVID-19), national emergencies (like HIV/AIDS crises), or the lack of access due to high drug prices or monopolistic conditions. Under TRIPS, Article 31, compulsory licenses are allowed provided that efforts to negotiate a voluntary license are made first unless there is an emergency, and that adequate remuneration is made to the patent owner. A compulsory license must be primarily for domestic use, not for exporting (except in special cases involving medicines, and where importing countries lack manufacturing capacity).[28]

Some countries allow for compulsory licensing in the case of blocking patents. These are patents that contain enough overlapping or related subject matter that manufacturing one item would involve infringing the other. They usually arise when one patent is an improvement over the other; for example, a second patent covers a major technological improvement but cannot be worked without infringing the first patent. The solution to this dilemma is to have improvers and pioneers approach each other with licensing agreements. Otherwise, if voluntary private bargaining cannot resolve the blocking problem, the authorities in some countries will impose compulsory cross-licensing. Blocking also tends to arise in situations where the scope of protection is too narrow, allowing inventors to patent too closely to one another in "technology space."[29]

Finally, after the grant, to keep the patent right in force, the patent holder must pay renewal (or maintenance) fees. The dates and frequency of renewal vary across countries. Most patentees do not renew continuously until the patent term ends. More than half of the patents granted expire voluntarily within 8-10 years from the date of application.[30] This arises if the value of holding a patent is less than the cost of maintaining it because of technological obsolescence, among other factors.

---

[28] Agricultural patents are also subject to compulsory licensing if food security is endangered.

[29] In the popular game *Monopoly*, a situation analogous to "blocking patents" can arise. If two or more players each own some of the same colored lots (e.g., blue), then none can build houses. One of them must have all two or three of the same colored lots. Thus, the colored lots are analogous to technologies. Some products cannot be made unless all of their technological components are put to use. If different patent owners own different components, the entire product might not be created unless the gridlock is broken by either private negotiation or compulsory license.

[30] See https://www.maxval.com/blog/patent-renewal-rates-under-different-renewal-period-schemes/.

(b) Patent Enforcement

During the duration of patent protection, the inventor may be required to defend or enforce its patent rights. If infringement occurs, and the patent right has not expired, the patent rights holder must largely seek redress through the court system (not through the patent offices). Depending on what enforcement mechanisms are available, the patent rights holder can pursue litigation, arbitration, or outside settlement. Litigation, however, is costly and lengthy. Combatants often settle or defer to an arbitration board. Jury trials are relatively infrequent because of the high costs of getting expert testimony and acquiring documents, among other things. How adequate enforcement mechanisms are, and how well they work, affect the inventor's ex ante incentive to innovate (and the imitator's incentive to imitate). Poor enforcement mechanisms have the effect of devaluing patent rights and discouraging patenting. New ideas are more apt to be kept as trade secrets.

While litigation, arbitration, and settlement offer different enforcement routes should infringement occur, patent holders may also have recourse to a number of statutory provisions that can aid in enforcement:

- *Preliminary injunctions* are pre-trial actions that require the accused infringer to cease the production or use of the patented product or process during the trial. Preliminary injunctions are a means of protecting the patentee from infringement until a final decision is made in a trial.
- *Contributory infringement* refers to actions that do not in themselves infringe a patent right but cause or otherwise contribute to infringement by others. Examples include the supplying of materials or machinery parts that are essential to the use of a patented invention. Thus, the rights holder can make a third party liable for contributory infringement as a way to deter infringement.
- *Burden of proof reversals* in patent process cases put the onus on the accused to prove innocence (that is, to show that the process used is not the patented one). Under a burden-of-proof reversal, if a certain product is produced by another party, it is assumed that it was produced with the patented process, unless proven otherwise. Given the difficulty patentees have in proving that others are infringing on their patented processes (since there are often several ways of producing the same product), the shift in burden can be a powerful enforcement mechanism.
- The *doctrine of equivalents* would find the accused infringer liable if she uses the essence of the patented invention but does not literally infringe

the patent. This doctrine is especially helpful if the imitator makes modest changes to an invention and claims on a technicality not to have infringed. According to the doctrine, inventions that substantially perform the same function, in substantially the same way, and produce the same result, are the same inventions. Therefore, a modified invention that exhibits these characteristics infringes upon the original invention.

- *Discovery* permits the accuser to obtain evidence from the accused, such as documentation. Pre-trial discovery, by compelling parties to exchange information in their possession, helps to facilitate settlement as parties develop a consensus about the likely outcome of a trial.

1.6.2 *Patenting Costs*

The emphasis thus far has been on patent rights — the *rights* of inventors. However, obtaining these rights can be quite expensive. Excluding the costs of research and development, the acquisition of a right can involve legal representation, fees to authorities that review and grant rights, and fees to maintain those rights until they expire or are sold or abandoned. There may also be costs associated with commercialization, such as obtaining marketing approval, or with enforcement, such as litigation. The relevance of all this is that the patent system likely favors large, wealthier players, such as large multinational companies, to obtain patent protection not only in one country but in many others where the inventor wishes to market the invention or to deter infringement.

On the other hand, if the cost of patenting is too low, the system could be overwhelmed with many filings of low-value patents with trivial technological benefits. Excessive patent rights or overlapping claims to technological innovations and creations could create a situation of an "anti-commons" where the rights of some inventors *block* the exercise of rights of others, including the rights of users, so that the inventions are underutilized and innovation is stifled.[31] How to make the global system more equitable and affordable, without sacrificing quality or utilization, should warrant further attention.

The costs of patenting vary with the route in which a patent is sought. Suppose the inventor wishes to obtain patent protection in ten countries, all

[31] The tragedy of the anti-commons arises when a resource has too many owners. Each can exclude others from accessing the resource, causing it to be underutilized. See Heller and Eisenberg (1998). What constitutes an "excessive" quantity of patent rights or the number of owners is not easily determinable. Another term used is *Patent Thickets*, which will be addressed in Chapters 8 and 10.

of which are contracting states of the PCT and half of which are contracting states of the EPO. The inventor can file: (i) a separate application in each of the ten countries; (ii) one PCT application, which designates six states: the EPO (as a unit) and the five non-EPO countries; (iii) an EPO application that designates five contracting states and a PCT application that designates five non-EPO states; or (iv) an EPO application that designates some of the five EPO contracting states, a PCT application that designates some of the five non-EPO states, and the rest as separate national patent applications. Hence, there are several possible permutations, each of which yields a different stream of patenting costs, depending on the mixture of national and regional fees.[32]

Table 1.2 provides a sample of the patent procurement and maintenance fees for a selection of countries, some developed and some developing, and for the EPO and WIPO. The unit of analysis here is a patent, 25 pages in length, including 5 pages of drawings and containing 15 claims.[33] The table

Table 1.2. Patenting Costs by Destination

	Official & Agent Fees		Translation Fees		Maintenance Fees	
Destination	**2010**	**2023**	**2010**	**2023**	**2010**	**2023**
U.S.	11,617	8,826	0	0	8,870	11,994
PCT	8,159	4,143	0	0	0	0
EPO	18,668	12,696	1,642	2,248	2,249	3,098
Japan	11,279	5,142	6,583	645	18,888	2,583
Germany	7,354	5,579	4,346	1,619	26,737	17,326
U.K.	6,832	7,585	0	0	15,321	10,313
China	6,778	5,284	2,677	978	13,144	12,916

Note: Fees are in constant 2015 U.S. dollars. EPO denotes European Patent Office, PCT Patent Cooperation Treaty.

Source: Global IP Estimator.

[32]A survey by Berger (2005) finds that most companies (74%) file first at their respective national patent offices, 18% file first at the EPO, and 8% first file a PCT patent. Also, most companies use the PCT-EPO route; that is, they designate the EPO as one of the states in their PCT application. Only 39% of their EPO applications were directly filed with the European Patent Office.

[33]Different assumptions can be made about the number of claims, but the ranking of costs across countries will not be affected too greatly. The source of the fee data is Global IP Estimator (https://www.quantifyip.com/).

shows the fees for the years 2010 and 2023. The fees are in real 2015 U.S. dollars. The translation costs are from the perspective of English-speaking applicants or applicants whose country of residence has English as an official language. The maintenance fees (based on renewal fees) are for 20 years of protection, except in the case of the EPO and WIPO (to be explained below), and are not in present discounted value terms. Of course, many patent holders do not renew their patents for the full term of 20 years, but for purposes of comparison across countries, the full term is used.

Official Fees include filing, examination, granting fees, and prosecution fees. Agent fees include attorney fees and in-house, and miscellaneous charges. Maintenance fees refer to patent renewal fees or annuities and are the non-discounted sum across 20 years of protection.[34] As these filing fees are from the perspective of English-speaking applicants, the cost of translating patent applicants is zero in destinations like the U.S. and U.K. (or Australia, Canada, and New Zealand). Otherwise, the translation costs can be quite burdensome for non-English speaking applicants or English-speaking applicants in patent offices where English is not the official language of business.

Post-grant, the rights holder may also experience costs of enforcement, such as litigation, which can be enormous. Litigation costs are revealed through sample surveys. Table 1.3 presents data for patent litigation in the U.S.[35]

Table 1.3 shows that the median patent litigation cost varies with what is at stake. For each risk level, the median cost has gone down, but what is

Table 1.3. Median Litigation Costs in the U.S.

Patent Infringement, All Varieties	2013 ($)	2019 ($)	2022 ($)
Less than 1 Million at Risk	700,000	700,000	600,000
$1–10 Million at Risk	2,000,000	1,500,000	1,000,000
$10–25 Million at Risk	3,325,000	2,700,000	3,000,000
More than $25 Million at Risk	5,500,000	4,000,000	3,625,000

Note: Inclusive of pre-trial and post-trial, and appeal where applicable.

Source: American Intellectual Property Law Association.

[34]No maintenance fees are associated with a PCT patent since WIPO does not grant patents, but only receives international patent applications.

[35]Data come from the American Intellectual Property Law Association (AIPLA) *Report of the Economic Survey 2019*, https://www.aipla.org/.

Table 1.4. Select Litigation Costs in the Rest-of-the-World

Country	First Instance
Australia	$1–5 Million Australian dollars
China	300–1,000 K Renminbi (RMB)
France	€150–250 K Euros
Italy	€70–120 K Euros
Norway	€200–400 K Euros
Switzerland	30–60 K CHF (Swiss francs)
U.K.	£100–500 K Pounds
Japan	¥15–25 Million Yen
S. Korea	$50K–$1 Million U.S. dollars

Source: Legal500.

not observed is the skew and the range in costs, and how those have shifted over time. Litigation costs are relatively lower elsewhere in the world, as shown in Table 1.4.[36]

The first instance refers to the first court that hears a trial and issues an initial decision; for example, a judgment on patent validity or infringement.[37] The above costs of litigation are not comprehensive. It is difficult to quantify fully the average or median costs since they depend on the complexity of a case, the extent of expert testimony needed, and the duration of proceedings.

Note that the costs of patenting discussed thus far are associated with one patent. For firms that file a portfolio of patents in multiple countries, the costs can add up. Earlier, the high cost was mentioned and how the international patent system likely favors applicants with deep financial resources, like large companies. But many of these patent offices do offer fee discounts to small inventors, small-medium enterprises (SMEs), and universities. However, the discounts do not typically apply to the maintenance fees, except in Japan and China. The smaller firms are burdened in another way, which is that at the time of application, many have uncertain expectations about the value of the invention or the value of obtaining a patent right (as opposed to relying on trade secrecy). Amid this uncertainty, smaller

[36] Data are from https://www.legal500.com/. See also Park (2010), for some cross-country data before 2013.

[37] A court of second instance would hear any appeals.

firms may be liquidity-constrained and unable to borrow against future profits from patents to pay for the upfront costs. These financial constraints are further compounded by the high costs of patent litigation shown in Table 1.3, which disadvantages smaller companies against the larger ones.

According to Table 1.2, patent procurement fees have mostly gone down between 2010 and 2023. Official and agent fees have fallen except in the U.K. Translation costs have fallen except at the EPO, and maintenance fees have also declined, and substantially for Japan. Renewal fees in the U.S. and EPO have risen. The determination of fees is based largely on the operating needs of the patent offices. The fees are their main source of revenue and respond to their budgetary situations. The decline in fees is likely attributable to the rise of electronic filing, improved database management systems, the harmonization of formalities and procedural requirements, and the global liberalization of patent professional services. In many countries, rules have been relaxed somewhat to permit patent agents (or patent attorneys) to represent non-nationals in filing and prosecuting patents. However, patent representation is still largely country-specific due to regulatory constraints. The PCT system does allow patent agents to file international applications through WIPO, but national phase entries must still be handled by local patent agents. Enough liberalization and mutual recognition of professional representation, though, has occurred to make a difference in patent cost reduction.

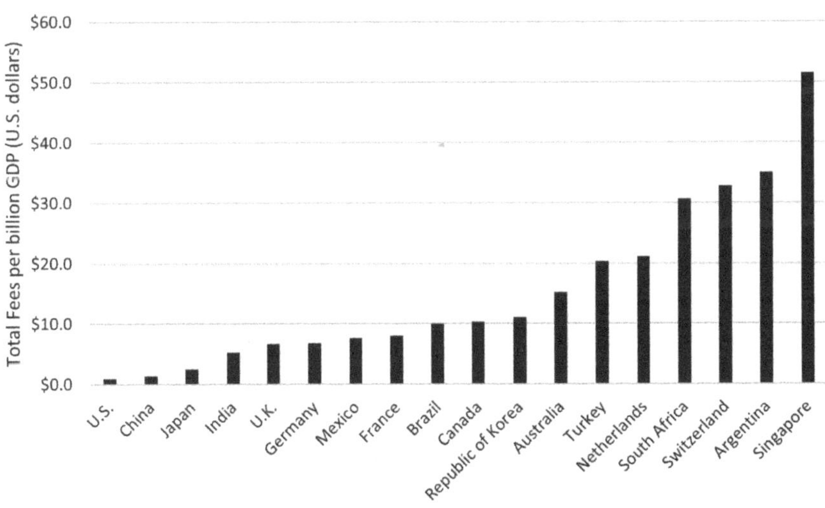

Figure 1.7. Patenting Costs Relative to Market Size, 2023

Figure 1.7 shows the costs of patenting relative to gross domestic product (GDP) by country. GDP is used here as a proxy for market size and patenting costs are the sum of all the fees discussed so far. Seen from this perspective, patenting in the U.S. is relatively the cheapest; that is, the costs of patenting in the U.S. seem to be a bargain considering the market size that a patent in the U.S. covers. Among the countries shown, patenting is relatively most expensive in Singapore and Argentina.

In conclusion, the costs of acquiring intellectual property rights should be considered alongside the strength and flexibility of the IP system and the value of IP when assessing their impact on international economic development.

Chapter 2

Data and Measurement

2.1 Introduction

This chapter is data-oriented. It discusses common measures of innovation and creativity and presents some trends in the data. It also discusses how to quantify the IP regulatory regimes and provides examples of indices that have been constructed to measure the strength of a country's IP regime over time.

The chapter contains three Appendices. The first summarizes data sources on measures of innovation and IP laws and institutions. The second provides the essential tools of calculus used in prior theoretical research, and the third provides the essentials of econometrics used in prior empirical research. Readers already familiar with these tools can skip Appendices 2B and 2C. Though the book is geared to be non-technical, it proves helpful in understanding the literature by having an intuitive grasp of the tools used by researchers to derive their findings.

On measures of innovation, it is useful to conceptualize an *input* side and an *output* side. Investments in research and development (R&D) or creative pursuits are considered inputs into producing knowledge. The knowledge outputs are typically in the form of tangible goods, such as books and journal articles, or their electronic counterparts, or sculptures, drawings, and digital art, or machinery, equipment, and chemical formulas, among others.

Patents are often used as measures of inventions. Patent counts, in particular, are used to measure the quantity of inventions. Of course, patent counts do not cover the universe of inventions because some inventors choose not to patent (and thereby publicly disclose the details of their inventions). They, therefore, keep their inventions a secret. Some inventions may not be economically valuable to warrant the cost of filing for a patent and maintaining the property right over time. Moreover, not all knowledge goods are patentable, such as abstract concepts like mathematical formulas or algorithms, discoveries or laws of nature (such as photosynthesis) or products of nature (like minerals) as these are due to nature and not to human ingenuity and creation, and ethically questionable inventions (such as genetically engineered human embryos).

To the extent that the inventor files for a patent for the same invention in multiple countries, this is evidence of global technology transfer, as inventive knowledge is spread throughout the world.

2.2 Trends in Innovation

2.2.1 *R&D*

According to the OECD (2015), research and development (R&D) expenditures "comprise creative and systematic work undertaken in order to increase the stock of knowledge — including knowledge of humankind, culture and society — and to devise new applications of available knowledge."[1] For some activity to be regarded as R&D, it must satisfy five core criteria: novelty, creativity, planned and budgeted, uncertainty (as the investment into knowledge creation is not guaranteed), and transferable (or reproducible).

This section shows the overall levels of *real* R&D spending (that is, controlling for inflation) for selected countries, and the breakdown by funding and performance, by industrial sector, or by government activity.[2] In what follows, the focus is on the leading R&D nations within the OECD.[3] For comparison, China (a non-OECD member state) is included.

[1]See OECD (2015, p. 44).

[2]The source of data is the OECD's *Main Science and Technology Indicators*, available on the web. See Appendix 2A for details.

[3]OECD member-states include the following countries: Australia, Austria, Belgium, Canada, Chile, Colombia, Costa Rica, Czechia, Denmark, Estonia, Finland, France, Germany, Greece, Hungary, Iceland, Ireland, Israel, Italy, Japan, S. Korea, Latvia, Lithuania, Luxembourg, Mexico, Netherlands, New Zealand, Norway, Poland, Portugal, Slovak Rep., Slovenia, Spain, Sweden, Switzerland, Turkey, U.K., and U.S.

Table 2.1. Real Gross Expenditures on R&D

Country	**1991 ($)**	**2000 ($)**	**2010 ($)**	**2022 ($)**
China	13.4	40.7	213.1	686.7
Germany	68.1	79.1	97.7	131.8
Japan	111.8	133.3	153.2	180.4
U.K.	30.9	34.9	41.1	90.2
U.S.	256.1	359.4	443.5	761.6
OECD	648.3	861.7	1,113.5	1,707.2

Note: Figures are in billions of constant 2015 dollars.

Table 2.1 shows the overall national level of spending in select countries, including for the OECD group as a whole.

The U.S. accounts for the largest share of total R&D spending among OECD member-states, namely 45%. R&D spending in China grew the largest over the thirty-year period (1991–2022). While German national R&D doubled and U.K. and U.S. R&D tripled over this period, Chinese R&D grew over 50-fold!

Figure 2.1 shows the R&D spending in terms of gross domestic product. This helps to adjust for overall country size and indicates the intensity of research and share of national resources invested in growing knowledge capital.

As of 2022, the U.S. spends about 3.5% of its GDP on research and development, and Japan just under 3%. China spends 2% of its GDP on R&D, below the OECD average, but its rate of R&D spending has been growing since 2000.

Table 2.2 shows how gross expenditures on R&D are financed and who performs the R&D. Both funding and performance differ. It could be one sector (say, the government) that funds the research, but another sector (say, the private sector) that conducts the research and development.

In general, the business or private sector conducts and funds most of a country's research and development. The government or public sector is the second biggest source of funding for research, while the higher education sector (namely, universities) is the second leading performer of research — except in China. The private non-profit research sector is virtually absent in China. Observe how a significant share of U.K. R&D is funded from abroad. This is the result of an international collaborative research environment in

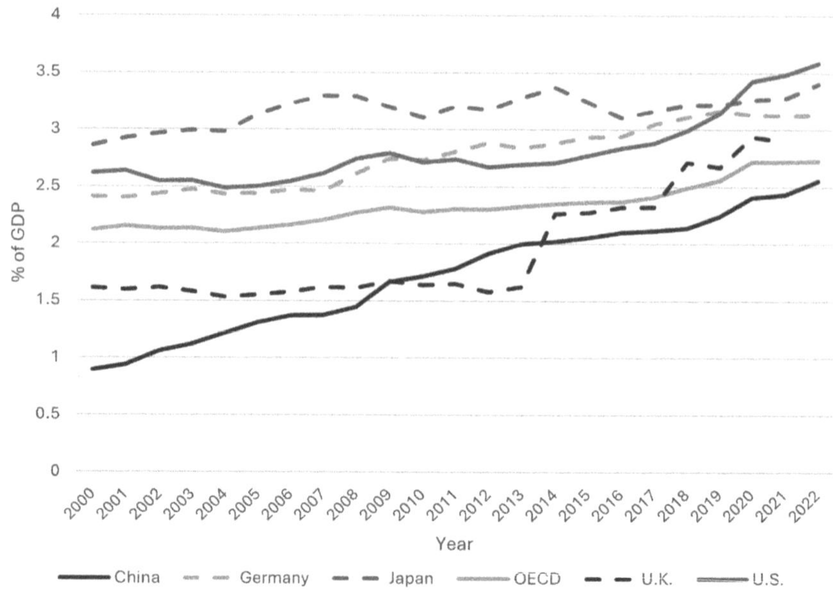

Figure 2.1. Gross Expenditures on R&D as a Percentage of GDP

Table 2.2. Distribution of Gross Expenditures on R&D by Funding and Performance

	Funding				Performance			
Country	**BUS (%)**	**GOV (%)**	**EDU (%)**	**ROW (%)**	**BUS (%)**	**GOV (%)**	**EDU (%)**	**NPF (%)**
China	72.3	22.8	3.9	1.0	72.4	19.3	8.3	—
Germany	65.8	29.3	0.3	4.5	68.5	14.0	17.4	2.4
Japan	76.6	16.5	6.4	0.5	77.0	8.5	12.8	1.7
U.K.	47.9	28.2	7.2	16.7	66.8	7.9	23.5	1.8
U.S.	63.7	26.7	6.1	3.5	72.0	11.2	12.7	4.0
OECD	62.2	27.4	5.4	5.0	69.2	10.7	17.5	2.6

Notes: Shares are averages of 2000–2022. BUS denotes business, GOV government, EDU higher education, ROW rest-of-the-world, and NPF private non-profit.

the U.K. The U.K. has received significant funding from the European Union through the EU's *Horizon Europe* projects.

Table 2.3 shows the distribution of private sector or business R&D across industrial sectors.

Industrial R&D is heterogeneous across countries. For Japan and China, the computer, electronic, and optical industries occupy the largest shares of private sector research and development. In the U.S. and U.K., services R&D has the largest share. This sector conducts research on production

Table 2.3. Distribution of Business R&D by Sector

Country	PHRM (%)	COMP (%)	AERO (%)	SERV (%)	ICT (%)
China	3.8	16.7	2.3	6.6	3.7
Germany	7.5	13.6	3.9	12.3	5.5
Japan	9.4	22.1	0.3	11.1	4.1
U.K.	1.1	3.6	—	72.4	18.3
U.S.	14.6	20.9	7.0	33.8	20.1

Notes: Shares are averages of 2000–2022. PHRM denotes pharmaceuticals, COMP computer, electronic and optical industry, AERO aerospace, SERV service, and ICT information and communication services.

processes, new services, and improved customer experiences in fields such as banking and health care. The U.S. has the highest level of pharmaceutical R&D in the world and the highest share of pharmaceutical R&D among OECD nations. This fact will figure prominently in later chapters about the role and significance of IP protection in this industry.

While Table 2.3 showed the composition of business R&D by sector, Table 2.4 shows the ratio of R&D to sales (as a percentage) for major patenting companies operating in the U.S. by industry.[4]

The firms in the pharmaceuticals-related industries tend to have the highest R&D to sales ratio, followed by those in the semiconductor industry. Software companies also have a high rate of R&D investment. Note the growth of R&D to sales in the media industry. This is related to the growth in digitization — new streaming platforms and services, and the creation of immersive virtual and augmented reality experiences. Energy and utility companies have the lowest R&D spending relative to their sales.

Table 2.5 shifts attention to the public sector and shows the distribution of public sector R&D across different activities.

The U.S. government has the largest share of spending on defense-related R&D. The U.K. government spends about one-fifth of its public R&D on defense. The U.S. spends nearly 30% of its public R&D on health and the environment, and the U.K. government spends nearly a quarter of its R&D in this category of spending. The Japanese government spends most of its R&D on economic development programs. Unlike the U.S. government, those in Germany, Japan, and the U.K. spend a significant share

[4]These are domestic and foreign companies that are among the top 1,000 patenting firms in the U.S.

Table 2.4. R&D as a Percentage of Sales in the U.S., by Industry Group

Industry Group	1990–2000	2001–2011	2012–2023
Automobiles and Components	0.92	1.64	1.59
Capital Goods	2.14	2.02	2.01
Commercial and Professional Services	0.40	0.61	0.65
Consumer Durables and Apparel	0.16	0.52	0.92
Consumer Services	0.10	0.27	0.96
Diversified Financials	0.33	0.08	0.07
Energy	0.07	0.03	0.03
Food, Beverage and Tobacco	0.15	0.17	0.43
Health Care Equipment and Services	2.89	2.74	2.16
Household and Personal Products	0.42	0.96	1.19
Materials	1.58	1.28	1.20
Media and Entertainment	0.70	2.91	11.99
Pharmaceuticals, Biotechnology & Life Sciences	10.83	13.60	15.43
Semiconductors and Semiconductor Equip.	10.75	14.76	14.66
Software and Services	7.10	7.98	10.80
Technology Hardware and Equipment	5.80	6.08	5.93
Utilities	0.04	0.04	0.02
Total	2.32	2.70	3.83

Source: Calculations from S&P 500 Capital IQ database.

of their public R&D on general university funds. These are R&D funds from general grant universities, which receive support from a central government ministry of education.[5]

[5]The U.S. does not have a designated GUF since its academic research funding operates differently than in other OECD nations. The U.S. has an agency-based funding model. Funding at universities is disbursed from federal agencies like the *National Science Foundation (NSF)* or *National Institutes of Health (NIH)*, which give grants for specific research projects.

Table 2.5. Government Budget Allocations for R&D

Country	DEF (%)	ECON (%)	HLTH (%)	EDU (%)	SPACE (%)	NOR (%)	GUF (%)
Germany	5.0	21.2	9.5	4.1	4.8	16.2	39.2
Japan	3.6	31.3	7.7	1.0	6.0	18.4	31.8
U.K.	20.3	11.3	23.8	4.2	2.2	15.2	22.7
U.S.	45.4	6.5	29.8	1.1	8.8	8.3	—
OECD	21.5	17.7	19.0	2.8	6.1	13.6	19.1

Notes: Shares are averages of 2000–2022. DEF denotes defense, ECON economic development, HLTH health and environment, EDU education and society, SPACE space programs, NOR non-oriented research programs, and GUF general university funds.

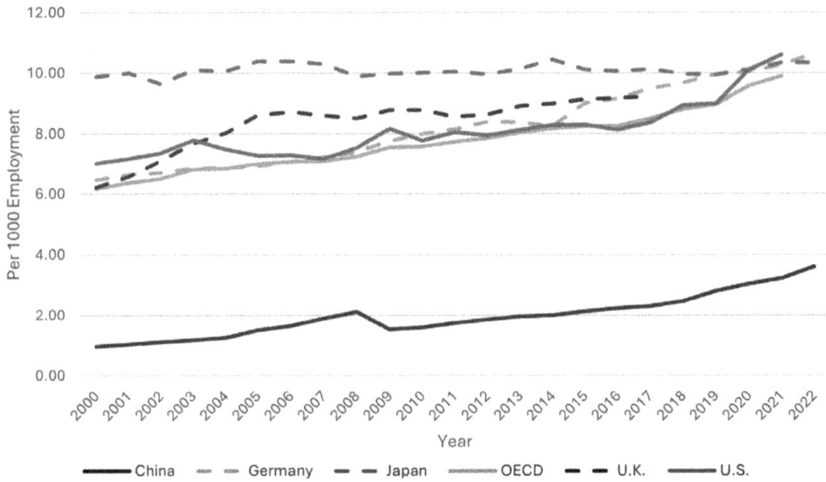

Figure 2.2. Full-Time Equivalent Researchers per Thousand Employees

In addition to R&D expenditures, human capital is required to execute research projects and develop innovations. Each R&D conducting nation has R&D personnel, which includes researchers, technicians, and other support staff, administrative and clerical. In Figure 2.2, the focus is on the researchers (the scientists and engineers who perform the R&D) and their share of total employment in a country.

During the past twenty years, the share of researchers in total employment has grown in the top R&D nations. As of 2022, the top OECD R&D countries have between 8–10 researchers for every 1,000 employees working full-time. China lags somewhat with about four researchers per thousand employees. This is likely due to its large population size and its still heavily labor-intensive manufacturing base.

2.2.2 *Patents and Trademarks*

The next set of data is on the outputs of R&D activity or creative activity, namely patent applications, trademark applications, and copyright registrations.

Figure 2.3 shows the count of all patents and trademark applications filed during a ten-year period. The solid lines are applications made by resident companies and agents. These include domestic companies and agents as well as foreign companies or agents that have a residential presence, such as a subsidiary or affiliate of a foreign multinational parent company. Non-resident filings are applications filed by companies or agents based abroad, or from outside a country. Non-resident filings are an important indicator of international technology transfer. They reflect the efforts of foreign applicants to secure IP protection outside their home markets — typically a signal of intent to commercialize an invention or brand abroad.

Figure 2.4 breaks down residential patenting by five leading countries over time. The rapid growth in Chinese patents is quite stark from 1985 to 2023 (see the right scale). It is important to remember that these are raw counts of applications. They do not control for the quality of inventions. The filings show active participation in the IP system, but the quantity differences are not reflective of patent value or quality (which will be addressed

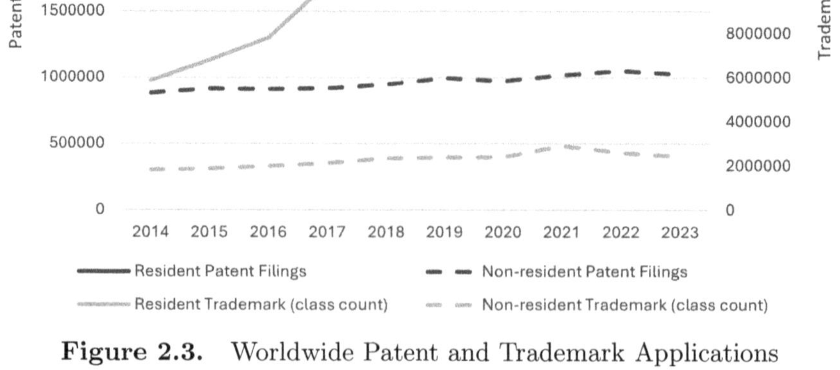

Figure 2.3. Worldwide Patent and Trademark Applications

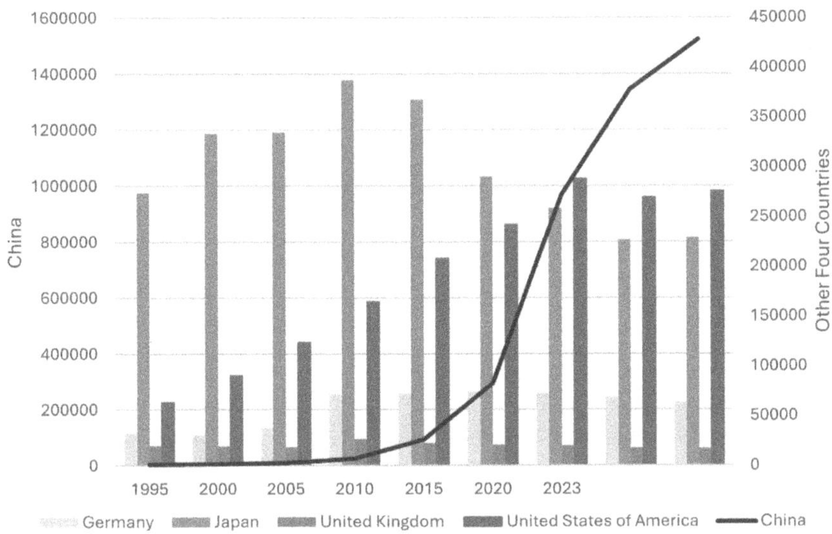

Figure 2.4. Patenting by Residents

in Chapter 4). Note that early in the period, Japan had far more residential patent applications than the U.S. did, but from 2015, the U.S. has had more. Again, these differences do not reflect quality, but they reflect some changes in legal practice. Earlier, Japanese companies would file one patent per claim, but later in the period, they would bundle more claims in one patent. Recall from Chapter 1 that a claim is a specific attribute or inventive aspect that is claimed as intellectual *property* in the patent.[6] Due to allowing for multiple claims in a patent, Japanese filings fell, but not necessarily because of a decline in inventiveness.

Figure 2.5 breaks down the foreign patenting by the five leading countries. Again, patenting abroad is highly suggestive of global technology transfers. Companies file abroad because they are exporting their IP-related products to foreign markets or are engaging in foreign direct investment and therefore seek protection against infringement or copying. But, of course, they may file for protection abroad, not necessarily to manufacture or license abroad, but merely to exclude competitors from doing so. This is an example where the invention is not *worked*. Some local IP regimes may impose a *working requirement* to mandate that the technology not just be

[6]The claim could be over some composition of matter, some apparatus, or some method of production.

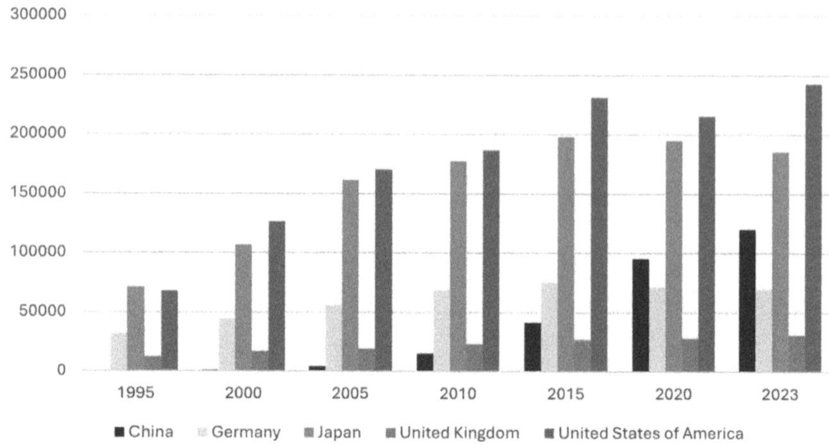

Figure 2.5. Patenting Abroad

Table 2.6. Trademark Applications, Resident Filings and Filings Abroad

Country	Applications	1995 (%)	2000 (%)	2005 (%)	2010 (%)	2015 (%)	2020 (%)	2023 (%)
Germany	Total	112,516	179,990	422,286	622,026	608,617	729,254	665,856
	Share Resident	14.5	30.9	13.9	10.5	10.1	10.6	9.7
	Share Abroad	85.5	69.1	86.1	89.5	89.9	89.4	90.3
Japan	Total	155,764	109,530	157,686	188,452	189,557	237,199	192,985
	Share Resident	87.9	72.5	51.3	42.1	40.1	43.5	46.8
	Share Abroad	12.1	27.5	48.7	57.9	59.9	56.5	53.2
U.K.	Total	40,933	42,156	206,669	310,675	393,769	388,653	328,485
	Share Resident	38.4	45.8	12.0	10.5	13.4	18.7	21.7
	Share Abroad	61.6	54.2	88.0	89.5	86.6	81.3	78.3
U.S.	Total	173,411	326,751	500,438	631,262	773,670	835,805	827,130
	Share Resident	42	29.2	19.9	21.1	22.1	22.0	21.7
	Share Abroad	58	70.8	80.1	78.9	77.9	78.0	78.3

Source: WIPO IP Statistics Data Center.

protected but used for the benefit of consumers and other producers. Based on the metric of foreign patenting, the U.S. is the leading source of global technology transfers, followed by Japan.

Table 2.6 repeats the above analysis for trademark filings — that is, broken down by resident filings and filings abroad. Four leading countries are shown. The data for China are fewer.

Again, trademark filings abroad are significant for capturing global flows. Companies seek to protect their brands and trade names abroad. The share abroad is much larger than the shares at home (residential filings).

That is because the same trademark can be filed in multiple countries — wherever the company or agent intends to market.

In practice, companies or agents seeking IP protection do not simply apply to a local or foreign country's IP authority. They have a choice as to the route by which they seek protection, as discussed in the previous chapter. They can file first with an international authority. For example, for patent rights, they can file at the World Intellectual Property Office (WIPO), making a *Patent Cooperation Treaty (PCT)* filing. Other international authorities offering similar processes include the African Intellectual Property Organization (AIPO) and the African Regional Intellectual Property Organization (ARIPO).

Table 2.7 shows where patent applications come from and where they go. The vast majority of U.S. and Japanese patent applicants file in their home office first before subsequently filing in other destinations. This matrix tends to contain a "dominant diagonal."[7] For applications in the U.S., most applicants apply directly to the USPTO rather than indirectly via the PCT route, but for applications in Japan, applicants file indirectly to the JPO (Japanese Patent Office) via the PCT. Similarly, filings at the EPO arrive mostly via the PCT, except for German applicants who have a greater share of direct filings at the EPO (55.2%) than an indirect filing via the PCT (44.8%). Patents sought in Africa predominantly arrive via the PCT. Thus, the PCT system has helped to facilitate cross-national patenting. Its single filing system is cost-effective for applicants, and it gives them a longer time to decide where to seek patent protection.[8]

Table 2.8 is important because of the heterogeneity in the frequency of patenting and dependence on patents by fields of technology and by industry. This will be emphasized in later chapters. The data below are for the five leading countries that have been profiled thus far.

By technological field, computer technology stands out, as it accounts for the largest share of patenting during 1990–2010 and 2011–2023. Its share grew by 50% over these two periods, and digital communication's share has

[7]That is, in a matrix with source countries in the columns and destination countries in the rows, the diagonal shows the local applications (where source = destination, which can only be the home country). There is a home bias in that most inventors file locally rather than across borders. Canada is one of the exceptions, as Canadians file more patents in the U.S. than in Canada. See https://www150.statcan.gc.ca/n1/ pub/36-28-0001/2022003/article/00005-eng.htm.

[8]The PCT system provides applicants 30 months to decide whether to enter the national phase — i.e., choose the countries in which to protect their invention — and this extended time allows inventors to better assess the commercial viability of their inventions before committing further resources to protecting them.

Table 2.7. Breakdown of Routes of International Patenting

Patent (First) Filings, broken down by Route of Filing					
	Source				
Destination	**U.S.** (%)	**Japan** (%)	**U.K.** (%)	**Germany** (%)	**China** (%)
U.S. Patent Office (USPTO):					
Total	279,291	81,720	13,447	29,468	35,293
Share of Direct Filings	88.3	60.9	49.1	50.6	60.7
Share of PCT Filings	11.7	39.1	50.9	49.4	39.3
Japanese Patent Office (JPO):					
Total	24,739	244,189	1,966	6,138	6,385
Share of Direct Filings	37.3	89.7	26.1	29.3	28.3
Share of PCT Filings	62.7	10.3	73.9	70.7	71.7
European Patent Office (EPO):					
Total	43,907	21,755	5,506	25,625	11,747
Share of Direct Filings	30.2	29.0	35.3	55.2	20.0
Share of PCT Filings	69.8	71.0	64.7	44.8	80.0
African Intellectual: Property Organization (AIPO):					
Total	97	18	16	13	23
Share of Direct Filings	12.0	9.1	5.6	25.2	40.4
Share of PCT Filings	88.0	90.9	94.4	74.8	59.6
African Regional Intellectual: Property Organization (ARIPO):					
Total	239	31	43	46	38
Share of Direct Filings	2.3	3.9	1.4	1.3	10.4
Share of PCT Filings	97.7	96.1	98.6	98.7	89.6

Note: Data are averages of 2015–2023.
Source: WIPO.

doubled. These reflect recent technological trends in the global economy, shaped by the internet, AI, and computer hardware and software. The shares of pharmaceuticals, biotechnology, and electrical machinery have been fairly stable over the two periods, while the shares of telecommunication and audio-visual have declined. The shares of organic and basic materials chemistry have also declined.

2.2.3 *Copyrights*

For a last look at the trends in innovation and creativity, turn to copyright activity. The data are not as widely available as for patents. This is largely

Table 2.8. Patent Publications by Selected Field of Technology

Field of Technology	1990–2010 (%)	2011–2023 (%)
Electrical Mach., Apparatus, Energy	6.13	6.96
Audio-Visual Technology	5.38	3.00
Telecommunications	3.52	1.98
Digital Communication	2.57	5.00
Computer Technology	6.58	9.76
Semiconductors	4.17	2.87
Optics	5.07	2.57
Measurement	4.28	5.58
Medical Technology	3.93	4.54
Organic Fine Chemistry	3.39	2.17
Biotechnology	2.14	2.15
Pharmaceuticals	3.50	3.23
Basic Materials Chemistry	2.87	2.76
Materials, Metallurgy	2.16	2.47
Chemical Engineering	2.30	2.87
Environmental Technology	1.39	1.87
Machine Tools	2.63	3.38
Engines, Pumps, Turbines	2.73	2.15
Transport	3.92	4.04
Civil Engineering	3.25	3.45
Other	28.09	27.20
Total	17,674,859	29,714,900

Note: Sample is U.S., U.K., Germany, Japan, and China.
Source: Calculations based on data from WIPO.

because copyright protection is automatic. Creators need not register their copyrights.[9] Given that copyright registrations are optional, the data in Table 2.9 provide a limited window into the kinds of creative activity that have been observed.

The data are based on registrations in the U.S. By far, the dominant share of registered works is non-dramatic literary works, which include computer programs (as works of "expression"), followed by performing arts.

[9]However, registration does offer advantages in keeping a public record of the work, deterring copying, and aiding in licensing. It may also be useful in infringement cases by establishing some presumption of validity.

Table 2.9. Copyright Registrations in the U.S.

Types of Work	1990	1995	2000	2005	2010	2015	2019	2023
Nondramatic Literary	179,671	195,999	169,793	191,439	247,139	175,493	185,903	169,192
Performing Arts	185,315	163,622	138,935	133,742	124,504	80,135	147,497	92,914
Serials	111,539	88,577	69,190	55,534	89,230	55,122	26,124	26,534
Sound Recordings	37,527	34,008	34,290	49,934	77,947	42,977	83,658	54,563
Visual Arts	76,718	99,550	85,839	82,517	97,181	89,229	88,762	69,030
Total Basic Registrations	590,770	577,756	498,047	515,269	636,001	442,956	547,741	441,346

Source: U.S. Copyright Office, Annual Reports. Includes published and unpublished works.

Serials (e.g., magazines, newspapers) have trended downwards, while registrations in sound recordings have fluctuated but trended upwards. Later chapters will discuss how these creative works relate to economic development and productivity.

2.3 Quantifying IP Regimes

Quantifying the overall strength of an IP system is not an easy task. It is subject to measurement errors. Moreover, IP laws can be very detailed and complex. Typically, the Acts or Statutes provide key definitions of legal terms, describe what protections are available or what activities are not permissible, delineate what the rights and privileges are, and also what the limitations and exceptions on rights are. They describe the enforcement options and remedies against infringement. All of that information is a lot to assess about a system. The objective of an index is to map those legal provisions and features onto a quantitative rating system; for example, a unidimensional scale from 0 (weakest) to 5 (strongest). Users of the index can then express more concretely which national system is stronger than that of another, or whether a nation's laws have strengthened over time. The rating method minimizes the use of subjective assessments, opinions, or testimonials.

However, because all the laws and details are reduced to a single number, the index is necessarily simplistic, overlooking the nuances and qualifications of laws and rulings. Like the use of gross domestic product (GDP) to measure a nation's income or level of development, a single dollar amount of a country's per-capita GDP cannot fully capture the quality of life or the non-marketable but valuable activities.

The chief utility of an index is that it helps facilitate empirical research and inform policy. Scholars can use it to study the impacts of intellectual property reforms on various outcomes of interest, such as research and development (R&D), innovation, diffusion of innovations, international technology transfers via trade, foreign direct investment, licensing, and joint ventures, and other indicators, such as wages and prices, inequality, and market structure. The research project can be turned around so that the index is the outcome of interest; that is, scholars can try to understand what motivates policymakers to adopt or reform their IP systems. Does it depend on the national level of development, cultural attitudes and social norms, or pressure from trading partners? This section describes some examples of IP indexes created and the principles underlying their construction.

The quantitative process begins with identifying the legal provisions that provide strong protection for IP and then choosing selectively those that should comprise an index. Some general principles that guide the selection are, first, that an IP index should capture the strength of national IPR laws, not necessarily the quality or efficiency of IP protection. From a social welfare point of view, stronger IPRs create both costs and benefits, so that the optimal level of IPR protection need not be the one associated with maximal strength. Thus, the index is composed of features measuring the strength of intellectual property rights rather than factors that contribute to the quality or efficiency of IPR systems. Subsequently, it is up to empirical research to determine if shifts in the strength of IP protection yield benefits to or impose costs on social well-being.

Second, the index should focus on substantive law, rather than procedural law. Procedural laws govern matters associated with the acquisition of rights, such as notarization, signatures, and other legal formalities, filing procedures, priority determination, renewal payments, and the use of local agent representation (i.e., patent attorneys or agents) for certain tasks. Substantive law, on the other hand, defines the actual rights, entitlements, and obligations of the holders of IP.

A third guiding principle in choosing legal features is that indexes should not be exhaustive but selective; that is, those legal features should be chosen that yield maximum variability across countries and time.[10] Adding information to the index that marginally adds variability also dilutes the

[10]For example, incorporating the ability to copyright artistic and literary works adds no variability in the strength of copyrights across countries because all countries that have copyright laws tend to protect these kinds of works.

contribution of the rest of the features in the index. That is, if three legal factors represent the strength of court actions, adding a fourth factor necessarily reduces the weight of the first three factors. The marginal value of adding such a factor needs to be weighed against the marginal reduction in the value of the previous factors.

Lastly, a common pitfall in creating an index is to judge whether a country's measured protection level is too low or too high according to the country's level of economic development, the a priori assumption being that richer countries should have stronger levels of IP protection. In general, this is the case, but there are instances where it is not (some rich countries have weak IP systems, and some poor economies have strong systems). In such cases, other factors are not held constant (for example, richer economies with weak IP systems may have good educational systems to compensate, or poorer economies with strong IP systems may follow poor fiscal and monetary policies which offset the effects of IPRs). In all of these cases, it should be understood that the IPR indexes are not measures of economic development. They may be important determinants of development, but are not themselves indicators of it. The approach in constructing these IP indexes should be to let the chips fall where they may, with minimal (if any) reliance upon a priori views about the economic consequences of IPRs.

2.3.1 *Types of Indexes*

Two types of measures exist: (a) experience-based measures and (b) statutory measures. Both have advantages and drawbacks. Experience-based measures are based on surveys of expert opinion, reports, or cases. For example, Mansfield (1994) surveyed executives from 94 U.S. manufacturing firms to rate the IPR systems of 16 countries on the basis of whether protection was adequate for engaging in a variety of technology transfer activities. Sherwood (1997) rated the adequacy of a broad range of IPRs (patents, trade secrecy, trademarks, and copyrights) in 18 countries. The World Economic Forum (WEF), Economist Intelligence Unit (EIU), and the Institute for Management Development (IMD) have all surveyed business leaders in various countries as to whether they regard intellectual property as well-protected, with answers ranging from 1 (strongly disagree) to 7 (strongly agree), or 1 to 5, 1 to 10, and so forth. The average rating across all respondents in a country gives the index for that country.[11]

[11] Appendix 2A describes the sources of data.

Surveys of experience have the obvious advantage of conveying laws in actual practice, as the actual provision of rights may deviate somewhat from rules, or barriers may exist to implementing rules.[12] The drawback with surveys of expert opinion is that they are usually available for a cross-section of only a small number of countries. The surveys are intensive, and it is not surprising to see a limited time-series dimension. The opinions are subjective, even if they are based on experience, and the intensity of opinions is difficult to compare among different experts without a common anchor for the perceptions. Also, except for a few indexes, views on the different IPRs (such as copyrights, patents, and trademarks) are lumped together when they are distinct types of rights. Lastly, based on responses to questions such as "are IPR laws adequate?" it is difficult to ascertain whether a weak system is due to the lack of laws or to poor enforcement or implementation of the laws.

Statutory measures construct an index based on whether various features of IPR systems exist. For example, the strength of IPR protection in country i at time t could equal:

$$\theta_{it} = \omega_1 \theta_{it}^1 + \ldots + \omega_J \theta_{it}^J$$

where $\theta^1, \ldots, \theta^J$ are the different components or provisions of an IP system, and $\omega_1, \ldots, \omega_J$ their corresponding weights. The weights add up to 1 (or 100%). Ginarte and Park (1997) and Park (2008a) follow this approach to construct an index of patent rights, as discussed in the next sub-section. They assign equal weights to each of these components, finding that adjusting the weights did not substantially change the ranking of countries in terms of the strength of their patent laws. Rapp and Rozek (1990) use a similar approach to derive an index of patent protection, except that their measure is for one year, namely 1984.

One drawback with statutory measures is that there are likely to be deviations between actual practice and what the laws on the books state.[13]

[12] For example, deterrence against infringement may be obstructed by the lack of funding for enforcement activities, such as detection and prosecution.

[13] Deviations of actual practice from statutory rules will depend on the exact legal provision. For instance, if a law states that a certain class of inventions, say lifeforms, is not patentable, it would be highly unusual to find patents on lifeforms to be in force. On the other hand, copyright laws allow for fair use — that is, the limited use of copyrighted material without requiring permission from the rights holder — but its application in practice may be subjective and not always consistent. For example, the courts may be too strict about permitting fair use, allowing for material to be used in education, but not in a *YouTube* clip.

Most prominently, a country may allow for extensive judicial and administrative enforcement mechanisms in its law but fail to invest resources in actual enforcement, leading to an effectively weak system. But one should not downplay the importance of statutory provisions. Having laws on the books constitutes an explicit obligation on the part of the state, or the international order, to provide certain rights (much like a written contract). Though in practice the enforcement of laws may not always be effective, the presence of laws on the books forms the basis for a grievance against another party or for seeking redress. Statutes and precedent provide guidance for judges and other officials as to how to apply the law.

A second drawback is that IP indexes to date are aggregated at the country level. This is fine as a first step since IP laws are territorial and apply at the national level. But in practice, different industries or sectors within a country may vary as to their dependence on IP protection for innovative activity and for commercialization.[14] These industries or sectors may be affected differently by different features or provisions in IP law. Future work that incorporates these heterogeneities would improve the precision of IP indexes and allow for richer analyses of the impacts of IP protection.[15]

2.3.2 *Trends in IP Protection*

This section discusses some indexes of IP and what they can tell us about the global trends in IP protection. The information needed to construct a statutory index is available through national laws on IPRs. The World Intellectual Property Office (WIPO) provides electronic access to national regulations and statutes on IPRs by member country. The TRIPS Council of the World Trade Organization (WTO) receives notifications of implementations of IP legislation from member-states. In addition to these sources, publishers such as Matthew Bender and Thomson-Reuters provide commentaries on statutory laws and case laws around the world — publications such as *World Patent Law & Practice* or *International Copyright Law & Practice.* Another rich legal database is *TAPED* which traces digital trade provisions in trade agreements, including provisions relevant for intellectual property protection as well as for developments in artificial intelligence. Appendix 2A provides a detailed list of these sources.

[14]A few exceptions exist. For example, an index of pharmaceutical IP has been created by Liu and La Croix (2015).

[15]Differences in industrial dependence on IP will be one of the themes in the book.

Table 2.10. Patent Rights Index

Components	Description	Point Value
Duration of Protection	Fraction of 20 years	0–1
Coverage	Fraction of subject matter protected	0–1
Enforcement Mechanisms	Fraction of available provisions	0–1
International Agreement Memberships	Proportion of agreements joined	0–1
Restrictions	Fraction of restrictions not imposed	0–1
Total Score		0–5

Table 2.10 summarizes how an index of patent rights has been created in Ginarte and Park (1997) and Park (2008a).

As an overview, the *Patent Rights Index* (PRI) ranges from zero (weakest) to five (strongest), covering more than one hundred countries from 1960 to 2015 quinquennially.[16] The value of the index is obtained by aggregating five components, as described in Table 2.10: duration, membership in international treaties, coverage, enforcement mechanisms, and restrictions. The duration component measures the years of patent protection allowed relative to the international standard of 20 years. The membership component indicates the extent to which countries are signatories to major international treaties on patent rights. The coverage component refers to the subject matter that is patentable.[17] Enforcement mechanisms refer to the availability of enforcement procedures, such as preliminary injunctions and burden-of-proof reversal for process patents.[18] Restrictions are limits or conditions on the use of patent rights, such as working requirements and compulsory licensing. Each of these five components is scored out of one. Hence, the PRI ranges from zero to five. The PRI is granular; that is, it is a continuous variable rather than a discrete one (such as 1 = low, 2 = medium, and 3 = high).

[16]The PRI is used interchangeably with GP-Index, referring to the Ginarte and Park (1997) index and updates.

[17]Such as pharmaceutical products, surgical products, or food.

[18]These were discussed in Chapter 1.

Table 2.11. Index of Copyrights

Components	Description	Point Value
Coverage/Duration	Percentage of duration per type of work	0–1
Enforcement Mechanisms	Fraction of available provisions	0–1
International Agreement Memberships	Proportion of agreements joined	0–1
Usage	Degree of private use not permitted	0–1
Total Score		0–4

Table 2.11 shows the analogous schema for an index of copyrights.[19]

The drivers of copyright strength are the duration and coverage of protection, limitations and exceptions (e.g., compulsory licensing, provisions on fair use and fair dealing), enforcement mechanisms, and membership in international copyright agreements. For example, copyright protection is stronger if protection is over a longer period, covers more types of works, and has limited exceptions for private use, if strong enforcement mechanisms are widely available, and if the country adheres to various international agreements on copyrights. Each measure is assigned a value from 0 to 1, which equals the share of conditions a country satisfies. The overall score is a sum of these four values and so ranges from zero (lowest) to four (highest).

Table 2.12 outlines the index of trademark rights.[20]

For trademark protection, the list of subject matter contains service marks, collective marks, certification marks, colors, shapes, and protection for well-known marks. Countries vary over whether these types of marks can be granted trademark protection. Service marks are words, names, symbols, or devices that identify services. Certification marks are words, names, symbols, or devices that certify the origin (e.g., region) of particular types of goods, such as Champagne. These marks help identify the type of product.

[19] Details can be found in Ivus and Park (2022).
[20] Details can be found in Reynolds (2003).

Table 2.12. Index of Trademark Rights

Components	Description	Point Value
Coverage	Fraction of subject matter protected	0–1
International Treaty Memberships	Proportion of agreements joined	0–1
Enforcement Procedures	Fraction of procedures provided	0–1
Total Score		0–3

Collective marks identify trade associations or membership in some cooperative or other organization. The association (or its independent members) may be responsible for some product(s). The collective mark should tie the product(s) to the reputation of the collective. Well-known marks are those with an international reputation. Laws that protect such marks prohibit other agents from registering a mark that would benefit from (or free ride on) the reputation of an existing brand, name, or symbol.

The procedures component represents how procedural elements affect the enforcement of trademark laws. For example, trademark laws have either civil or criminal remedies for offenses. Trademarks can also be subject to restrictions. Marks that are already in bona fide public use cannot become protected property, such as "fresh-brewed coffee." Trademarks that become generic terms (such as aspirin) become part of the public domain, to be used freely by anyone. The licensing of trademarks may also be subject to conditions, such as a quality standard on the goods produced by the licensee. Such standards may be in the public interest, but they may also reduce the demand for a license and, consequently, the potential earnings of a licensor. The assignment of trademarks may also be subject to restrictions; for example, a trademark may not be transferred without, or independently of, the underlying business. IP laws may also impose linking requirements, whereby a foreign trademark must be linked to a domestic (locally-owned) producer. Lastly, trademark laws may have use-or-lose provisions; that is, a loss of rights due to failure to exploit the trademark right adequately. Trademark rights may not be renewed unless proof of use is established.

Table 2.13 shows the evolution of patent rights, copyrights, and trademark rights across countries.

Table 2.13. Evolution of IP Indexes Pre/Post-TRIPS

	Patent Rights Index		Copyright Index		Trademark Index	
Year	**Mean**	**C.V.**	**Mean**	**C.V.**	**Mean**	**C.V.**
1990	1.91	0.53	1.55	0.52	1.32	0.36
1995	2.52	0.44	1.90	0.48	1.56	0.31
2000	2.96	0.34	2.15	0.43	1.77	0.29
2005	3.23	0.28	2.26	0.42	1.81	0.29
2010	3.32	0.27	2.46	0.41	—	—
2015	3.38	0.27	2.48	0.41	—	—

Notes: CV = coefficient of variation (standard deviation over mean). Based on Ginarte and Park (1997), Reynolds (2003), and Park (2005).

These various indexes show a significant strengthening of IP protection between 1990 and 2015, especially in the wake of the TRIPS agreement of 1995. Recall that the scale of the patent rights index is 0–5. In 1990, the mean value of the index was just 1.9. By 2015, it is 3.38. The patent rights index is averaged for 122 countries. The coefficient of variation, CV, is the ratio of the standard deviation of the index to the mean. It captures the variation in values across countries and time. The CV has fallen steadily from 1990 to 2015. This is indicative of a convergence in patent protection over time, as many countries that previously had no patent system or offered weak protection raised their standards to the minimum standards of protection required by TRIPS.

A similar strengthening and convergence of copyright and trademark laws can be seen. The copyright index's mean and coefficient of variation were calculated for 119 countries, and those for the trademark index were calculated for 74 countries. The trademark index of Reynolds (2003) has only been extended to 2005. More recently, Chen *et al.* (2024) developed an index of trademark strength by the level of applicant friendliness within a country's trademark system. Its components are based on international agreements, legislation, enforcement, and administration. This index also shows a rise in the mean level of trademark protection from 1990 to 2020 and a decline in the coefficient of variation after TRIPS came into effect.

The correlation between this index and the Reynolds Index over the period 1990–2005 is relatively high, at 0.73.

Since the indexes of IP shown thus far were measured until 2015, more recent trends in IP protection can be seen from the International IP Indexes calculated by the U.S. Chamber of Commerce's *Global Intellectual Property Center* or GIPC, which began computing its indexes in 2012. Its indexes combine statutory provisions, survey opinion, and policies relevant to IP protection.[21] In 2012, only 11 countries were sampled. In 2015, 19 more countries were added. In 2020, the sample consisted of 53 countries, and by 2024, 55 countries were in the sample. The GIPC has separate indexes for patent rights, copyrights, and trademark rights, as well as an aggregate index for all of them. The GIPC permits an investigation of IP strength beyond 2015 and allows for a comparison with the previous indexes of patent rights, copyrights, and trademark rights. The GIPC indexes are all scaled from zero to one (highest).

Table 2.14 shows the rise in average strength and convergence of patent and copyright protection across countries, except for trademark protection, which appears to have fallen and become more varied across countries.

Table 2.14. USCC GIPC Version: International Intellectual Property Indexes

	GIPC Pat		GIPC Copy		GIPC TM		GIPC Overall	
Year	**Mean**	**C.V.**	**Mean**	**C.V.**	**Mean**	**C.V.**	**Mean**	**C.V.**
2015	0.55	0.52	0.49	0.53	0.70	0.22	0.54	0.43
2020	0.60	0.43	0.48	0.50	0.62	0.28	0.57	0.41
2024	0.60	0.44	0.51	0.48	0.63	0.30	0.58	0.40

Note: GIPC Pat is the sub-index for patent rights, GIPC Copy for copyrights, and GIPC TM for trademarks. CV denotes the coefficient of variation.

Source: U.S. Chamber of Commerce (USCC), Global Intellectual Property Center (GIPC).

[21] In the ninth edition, the GIPC index consists of 50 indicators across nine categories, covering patents, copyrights, trademarks, trade secrets, design rights, commercialization of IP assets and market access, enforcement, systemic efficiency, and membership in international treaties. Each indicator is scored from zero to one. The overall index value is an average of the indicators.

Table 2.15. Correlations between GIPC Index and Previous Indexes

	Indexes of Rights		
	Patents (Year 2015)	**Copyrights (Year 2015)**	**Trademarks (Year 2005)**
GIPC Pat (Year 2020)	0.670		
GIPC Pat (Year 2024)	0.660		
GIPC Copy (Year 2020)		0.649	
GIPC Copy (Year 2024)		0.670	
GIPC TM (Year 2020)			0.356
GIPC TM (Year 2024)			0.328

Note: GIPC = Global Intellectual Property Center.

This may be driven by several societal, legal, and market factors. Increasing genericization, legal challenges, inconsistent enforcement, and changes in legislation would contribute to this development.

The question is whether the GIPC indexes could fill in the gaps from the pre-2020 indexes, despite the fact that they are all constructed somewhat differently. Could the GIPC indexes, for example, be used to "nowcast" the previous statutory indexes (that is, predict in retrospect what the statutory indexes would reveal in 2020–2024). Table 2.15 shows a high correlation between the patent rights index (PRI) in 2015 and the GIPC's patent index in 2020, as well as between the PRI in 2015 and the GIPC patent index in 2024. Analogous correlations are found with the copyright indexes. However, the trademark index of Reynolds in 2005 does not correlate well with the GIPC trademark indexes in 2020 and 2024, largely because of the much longer time gap. Much has changed since 2005. The Chen *et al.* index of trademark strength in 2020 does have a high correlation of 0.67 with the GIPC trademark index in 2020, and a correlation of 0.54 with the GIPC trademark index in 2024.

Table 2.16 shows the global strengthening of patent protection and overall IP protection by income group. The grouping of countries by income is based on the World Bank's classification, which follows the *Atlas of Global Development* method that measures income thresholds in U.S. dollars and

Table 2.16. Breakdown by Country Income Group

	Patent Rights Index			GIPC Index (Overall)		
	1990–2004	**2005–2015**	***%Change***	**2016–2020**	**2021–2024**	***%Change***
High Income (H)	3.37	4.10	*21.8*	0.72	0.74	*2.0*
Upper Middle Inc (UM)	2.20	3.24	*47.2*	0.39	0.44	*13.0*
Lower Middle Inc (LM)	1.87	2.78	*49.2*	0.32	0.37	*17.9*
Low Income (L)	1.78	2.45	*37.9*			

Note: Country Income Groups are based on World Bank Classification.

that controls for inflation and smooths out exchange rate fluctuations over a three-year (moving average) period.[22]

Over time, the average patent rights level has increased in each income group, but the greatest percentage increases have been in the middle-income countries. For high-income countries, their patent regimes and IP levels were already fairly high, so it was the middle-income countries that had to ratchet up their standards to be in compliance with TRIPS. Lower-income countries have a lower percentage increase in the strengthening of their patent rights than middle income countries for two reasons: first, some had relatively high levels to begin with, as former U.K. and French colonies (for example, the African countries), and second, some of the least developed countries were granted extensions and transition periods that allowed them to delay the implementation of the TRIPS provisions.

2.3.3 *Enforcement in Practice*

This section examines the correlation between the patent rights index (PRI) and previous survey measures of enforcement in practice. The focus is on the ratings produced by the World Economic Forum (WEF), Economist Intelligence Unit (EIU), and Institute for Management Development (IMD),

[22]For example, in 2024, the breakdown is: Low income countries have a Gross National Income (GNI) of less than or equal to \$1,135, Lower Middle Income: \$1,135 $<$ GNI $\leqslant$ \$4,465, Upper Middle Income: \$4,465 $<$ GNI $\leqslant$ \$13,845, and High Income: GNI $>$ \$13,845.

and a more recent enforcement index developed by Papageorgiadis and Sofka (2020). The WEF, EIU, and IMD are presently discontinued. Their indexes were based on questionnaires sent to experts, and their responses were aggregated into a single rating for each country. Country comparisons are not straightforward since different groups of experts judged different countries. This creates not only much subjectivity but also inconsistency, since experts in different countries are likely to have different standards and expectations.

The Papageorgiadis and Sofka (2020) index — referred to as ENF below — is based on enforcement data. Its components include quality of patent administration, patent litigation decisions, border controls, cultural and societal attitudes towards purchasing infringing goods, among others.[23]

Table 2.17 indicates a high, but imperfect, correlation between the patent rights index and various measures of enforcement in practice. In general, strong patent laws and enforcement correlate, but there are cases where enforcement falls short in strong patent systems. The indexes of IP enforcement in practice all correlate very highly with one another.

Table 2.18 shows the correlation between PRI and indexes of IP enforcement in practice, broken down by income group. It helps identify where the discrepancy in laws and practice actually arises.

As Table 2.18 suggests, it is in the lower-middle-income (LM) countries where the greatest differences between statutory laws and the carrying out of laws are observed. This group of countries was, like other signatories

Table 2.17. Correlations of Patent Rights Index (*PRI*) with Measures of IP in Practice

	PRI	***WEF***	***IMD***	***EIU***	***ENF***
PRI	1.00				
WEF	0.660	1.00			
IMD	0.610	0.900	1.00		
EIU	0.734	0.874	0.789	1.00	
ENF	0.677	0.950	0.923	0.884	1.00

Notes: *WEF*, World Economic Forum; *IMD*, Institute for Management Development; *EIU*, Economist Intelligence Unit; *ENF*, Enforcement Practice (Papageorgiadis & Sofka (2020).

[23]The authors conduct a validation exercise where IP experts evaluate the link between firm decisions on litigation and enforcement in practice.

Table 2.18. Correlations between *PRI* and IP Practice, by Income Group

Breakdown by Country Income Group				
Income Group	***WEF***	***IMD***	***EIU***	***ENF***
H	0.382	0.213	0.580	0.158
UM	0.242	0.263	0.435	0.440
LM	0.073	0.094	0.227	−0.098
L	0.231	0.443	0.205	0.607

Notes: H denotes high income group, UM upper middle income, LM lower middle income, and L low income group.

to TRIPS, required to raise their standards of IP protection. But these countries are also compelled to achieve economic growth and raise living standards (not just IP standards). This would require them to lean on imitation and the copying of advanced technologies from abroad — and thus for IP authorities in these countries to exercise more discretion in implementing strong IP enforcement measures.

2.3.4 *IP Provisions and Country Characteristics*

This section digs deeper into the nature of countries that provide stronger or weaker levels of IP protection. Consider the following country characteristics:

- Research and development as a percentage of GDP.
- GDP and per capita GDP are measured in constant 2015 U.S. dollars.
- Trade Openness is the sum of exports and imports to GDP.
- Freedom to trade and property rights are indexes.
- Economic Freedom Index is an aggregate of multiple variables.
- Political Freedom Index comprises civil liberties and political rights.
- Human capital Index is based on years of schooling and returns to education.
- Gini is an index of income equality, and the poverty rate is the percentage of the population living below the national poverty line.

Indexes on economic and political freedom, human capital, and freedom to trade are developed by organizations cited in Appendix 2A. Data on gross

Table 2.19. Economic Characteristics of Countries by Levels of Patent Rights: 1990–2015

PRI Quintile	Bottom	Fourth	Middle	Second	Top
R&D/GDP	0.19%	0.25%	0.37%	0.82%	1.79%
GPD (billions $)	83.9	65.0	114.0	328.0	1,590.0
GDP per capita	3,140.5	2,720.7	5,554.7	14,436.2	35,786.0
Trade Openness	65.9	62.2	76.7	85.3	92.8
Freedom to Trade	5.1	5.7	6.7	7.6	8.5
Property Rights	3.3	3.5	4.5	6.0	8.3
Economic Freedom	5.2	5.5	6.2	7.0	7.8
Political Freedom	32.3	38.6	49.5	68.0	84.7
Human Capital	1.8	1.8	2.1	2.7	3.2
Gini Coef.	0.42	0.43	0.44	0.42	0.33
Poverty Rate	38.6	44.5	40.8	23.4	17.3

Note: Sources of variables are explained in the text. Sample = 122 countries.

domestic product (GDP), exports, imports, poverty, and income inequality are from the World Bank. The Gini coefficient ranges from zero (representing perfect equality) to one (representing perfect inequality).

Table 2.19 groups countries into five groups (quintiles) according to their average levels of patent strength (based on the PRI measure) over a quarter-century. For each quintile group, the table reports the mean values of each of the country characteristics.

It can be seen that countries that have stronger patent protection levels tend to be richer, conduct a higher rate of R&D investment, are more open to trade, have greater levels of economic and political freedom, and have high levels of human capital. They also have lower levels of poverty and income inequality. This is not to suggest any causal relationships between patent strength and these country characteristics (yet). The table merely points out the characteristics of relatively high versus low patent strength countries.

The same pattern can be observed with the overall GIPC index of IP protection, as shown in Table 2.20.

The key takeaway from Tables 2.19 and 2.20 is that some care has to be exercised when analyzing the effects of stronger IP protection on social, economic, and political outcomes. In many cases, countries that undertook

Table 2.20. Economic Characteristics of Countries by Overall GIPC Scores: 2016–2023

GIPC Quintile	Bottom	Fourth	Middle	Second	Top
R&D/GDP	0.62%	0.85%	0.82%	2.25%	2.64%
GPD (billions $)	588.0	1,240.0	1,510.0	1,010.0	4,120.0
GDP per capita	5,663.1	11,411.5	11,913.5	34,792.8	51,539.7
Trade Openness	61.1	75.0	72.2	82.5	105.9
Freedom to Trade	5.9	7.0	7.5	8.4	8.6
Property Rights	4.9	5.6	6.3	7.8	8.9
Economic Freedom	5.9	6.6	7.0	7.7	8.0
Political Freedom	47.2	50.5	54.3	84.5	88.6
Human Capital	2.5	2.8	2.9	3.5	3.6
Gini Coef.	0.38	0.40	0.44	0.34	0.33
Poverty Rate	16.7	20.6	20.0	17.5	16.2

Note: Sources of variables are explained in the text. Sample = 55 countries.

reforms in their IP systems were already relatively wealthy and technologically strong. They had the resources to undertake reforms or absorb the transition costs of reform. Countries experiencing high poverty rates and wide income inequalities are more constrained in implementing strong IP measures that affect prices of important goods, like medicines and food, or access to education. Their economic priorities substantially differ from those of wealthier economies. Thus, both theoretical and empirical research need to control for country differences such as these, among other factors.

2.4 Comparative North–South Analyses

This chapter concludes with some preliminary analyses of North–South innovation and technology transfer. "North" is commonly used as a shorthand or metaphor to refer to developed countries, and "South" to developing countries, including the least developed.[24]

The IP systems of countries have become stronger since 1995, with developing countries making relatively the most adjustments to their systems.

[24]While not geographically accurate — South Korea, for instance, is wealthier than many countries in the "North" — the distinction persists in discussions of global inequality.

How has this translated in terms of innovation outcomes in the South? This is best answered using careful, empirical analyses, in light of the confounding factors that were previously discussed, such as poverty, wealth, inequality, and prior human capital and technological development. Before turning to formal evidence, this section explores some raw descriptive statistics.

Can some changes in the technological potential of the developing world be detected? It turns out that the progress is mixed and that some useful lessons can be drawn from the diverse experiences.

As a measure of innovation, consider Table 2.21, which shows the top ten foreign nations obtaining patent grants in the U.S. in 2020.[25] Focusing on patents granted in the same patent office, such as the U.S. Patent and Trademark Office (USPTO), helps control for patent examination standards, which could vary across international patent offices. Moreover, the U.S. has relatively high standards so that relatively robust and high-value inventions are sought for protection in the U.S., particularly given the costs of patenting in the U.S., such as the filing fees, search and examination fees, and maintenance fees discussed in the previous chapter.

Table 2.21 then traces back to see where these countries ranked in 2015, 2005, and 1985. In 2020, the top nations included Korea, China, Taiwan, and India. Going back several decades, it becomes apparent how much these four countries leapfrogged their way up. China was ranked 56th in 1985, and Korea 23rd.

However, as for the rest of the developing world (i.e., excluding China and India), they account for less than 2% of all U.S. patent grants to foreign countries. That has remained consistent since 1985.

Next, Table 2.22 presents data on the technological balance of payments (BOP).[26] Like its international trade counterpart, this BOP indicates which countries export more technology than they import, as measured by international flows of licensing fees and royalties (in millions of real 2012 U.S. dollars). These flows encompass all types of intangible assets, including patents, copyrights, designs, and trademarks. Net technology importers are countries whose payments for the use of intangible assets exceed their receipts; net exporters are those with the opposite pattern. According to the table, the global strengthening of IPRs appears to be associated with rising BOP surpluses among net technology exporters (such as the U.S.,

[25]The data are from the U.S. Patent and Trademark Office's open data portal (https://data.uspto.gov/home).

[26]The data are from https://unctadstat.unctad.org/datacentre/.

Table 2.21. Number of Patent Grants in U.S.

Country of Origin	Grants in 2020	Rank 2020	Rank 2015	Rank 2005	Rank 1985
Japan	53,779	1	1	1	1
China	26,845	2	5	17	56
Korea	23,705	3	2	4	23
Germany	19,173	4	3	2	2
Taiwan	13,105	5	4	3	16
U.K.	8,470	6	8	5	3
Canada	7,914	7	6	6	5
France	7,614	8	7	7	4
India	5,984	9	10	18	36
Israel	4,844	10	9	12	15
Share of Grants					
Upper Mid-Inc, excl. China		1.48%	1.21%	0.83%	0.72%
Lower Mid-Inc, excl. India		0.20%	0.14%	0.11%	0.05%
Low Income Countries		0.003%	0.002%	0.001%	0.003%

Note: Share of grants per the same year as the rank of individual countries.
Source: U.S. Patent and Trademark Office, Patent Counts by Origin and Type.

Table 2.22. Technological Balance of Payments

Real 2012 dollars	2005	2010	2015	2020	2023
USA	46,107	66,399	72,589	62,304	66,225
Japan	3,411	8,224	18,556	12,994	17,387
Germany	−1,674	1,201	5,675	17,607	18,886
Low-Income Economies	−145	−264	−553	−498	−418
Mid-Income Economies	−3,515	−7,666	−10,339	−10,781	−16,347

Note: Licensing receipts minus payments, in millions of real 2012 USD.
Source: UNCTAD, Trade in Services, Charges for Intellectual Property.

Germany, and Japan), and growing BOP deficits among net technology importers (typically low- and middle-income countries).

There are two ways to interpret this pattern. On the one hand, increased payments of licensing fees and royalties could indicate greater access to IP assets, such as technologies, industrial secrets, medicines, seeds, and creative works, which would be a positive development. On the other hand, rising payments might reflect increased rents accruing to high-income countries, driven by stronger IPRs. In this interpretation, the growth in payments results from improved terms of trade or the ability to charge higher fees per transaction. The reality likely lies somewhere in between.

Interestingly, the technology BOP deficit is smaller for low-income countries than for middle-income countries. This can be accounted for by the fact that the levels of technology created and imported are small in the low-income countries. They have less to export, and they do not import as many technological inputs to power their innovation activities. To the extent that they are receiving licensing contracts from abroad, the fact that their deficits are small suggests that they are not transferring exorbitant rents abroad (or else much higher payments would have been observed).

2.4.1 *Explanatory Factors*

Why have innovation responses in much of the developing world remained relatively modest? Why do these countries continue to run deficits in their technological balance of payments? While these questions are examined in greater depth later in the book, several explanatory factors are worth considering at the outset:

1. The mixed experiences across countries suggest that intellectual property rights (IPRs) are not the sole determinant of technological potential. Other enabling conditions, such as good governance and high-quality institutions, must also be present.
2. IPRs tend to have a more significant impact on innovation once an economy reaches a threshold level of technological capability or absorptive capacity. These capacities include the ability to identify, assimilate, and apply valuable knowledge. However, such capabilities cannot be created by legal reforms alone. At best, stronger IPRs may create a more favorable environment for business investment and human capital accumulation, but they do not directly generate the underlying capabilities needed for innovation. This may help explain why certain developing (or former developing) countries, such as India, Singapore, and Taiwan, have been more successful in leveraging IP protections.
3. Another important consideration concerns the pace and sequencing of reform. Is swift, comprehensive reform preferable to gradual, incremental change? Some scholars emphasize the benefits of lighter forms of

protection, such as utility models, which offer a more flexible alternative to full patent protection. Utility models will be discussed in detail in Chapter 5.

4. A larger issue is whether IPR standards should be harmonized worldwide or differentiated according to a country's level of development. Adopting strong minimum standards modeled after those of high-income countries may be burdensome for low-income economies. Stronger IPRs may attract foreign direct investment (FDI), but they can also crowd out domestic innovation when local firms lack the technological capacity to compete with foreign entrants. This may explain why, in later chapters, stronger IPRs are often found to stimulate FDI and technology transfer, but not domestic innovation.
5. Strengthening legal rights is only part of the equation; making those rights accessible and affordable is equally important. The costs associated with obtaining and enforcing IPRs are often quite high, especially for small inventors and those in the least developed countries. As noted earlier, the patent application process is complex and resource-intensive. These barriers help explain why inventors from developing countries account for only a small share of U.S. patents granted. A vicious cycle may also emerge, where the lack of IP ownership weakens a country's bargaining power in international negotiations.
6. Lastly, it is worth asking whether developed countries have complied with their obligations under the TRIPS Agreement. Thus far, the attention has mostly been on whether developing countries are compliant. For example, developed countries are required under Article 66.2 to provide incentives for technology transfer to LDCs. Since 2003, they have been mandated to submit annual reports to the WTO documenting their progress. These reports are publicly available.[27] However, compliance has been inconsistent. Some countries have failed to submit reports in certain years or have filed only cursory one-page submissions. The activities reported are not always substantive (e.g., teaching English in Bangladesh) and are sometimes directed toward countries that are not among the least developed (e.g., upper-middle-income countries like the Slovak Republic).[28] There remains substantial room for improved compliance with Article 66.2 and more meaningful collaborations between the global North and South.

[27]https://e-trips.wto.org/En/Reports/TRIPSRelatedReportsSubmission.
[28]See Park (2017) for further examples.

2.4.2 *Policy Implications*

The data trends in this chapter motivate the following questions:

- How do IPRs influence economic growth, poverty alleviation, and social welfare?
- What is the relationship between IPRs and domestic innovation?
- To what extent do IPRs promote international technology transfer?
- How do the effects of IPRs differ across industries, sectors, and stages of development?
- How might emerging technologies, particularly artificial intelligence, affect the technological balance of payments?
- What alternatives or complements to formal IP systems are viable?

These questions guide the analysis throughout the book. Rather than providing definitive answers to these complex debates, the book surveys existing research and helps readers develop informed perspectives on the evidence and arguments that shape international IP policy.

Appendix 2A. Data Sources

1. Innovation and Creativity

Data Source	Description	Websites
U.S. National Science Foundation	Science and Engineering Indicators	https://www.nsf.gov/ https://ncses.nsf.gov/indicators
U.S. Patent and Trademark Office (USPTO)	Patents and trademark data Open Data Portal	https://www.uspto.gov/ https://data.uspto.gov/home
European Patent Office (EPO)	Patent information, Examination Guidelines PATSTAT Database	https://www.epo.org/en
World Intellectual Property Organization (WIPO)	Global patent/trademark data. Treaties and Laws.	https://www.wipo.int See IP-statistics and WIPO-Lex
Organization for Economic Cooperation and Development (OECD)	Main Science and Technology Indicators (R&D), Structural Analysis Industry Database	https://data-explorer.oecd.org/
United Nations Educational, Scientific and Cultural Organization (UNESCO)	Institute for Statistics. R&D expenditures and personnel	https://www.unesco.org/en http://uis.unesco.org/
U.S. Copyright Office	Annual Reports. Registrations data	https://www.copyright.gov/
International Union for the Protection of New Varieties of Plants (UPOV)	Pluto database. Statistics on Plant Breeders' Rights	https://www.upov.int/en https://pluto.upov.int

(*Continued*)

2. Economic Data

Data Source	Description	Websites
U.S. Bureau of Economic Analysis (BEA)	Interactive Tables. Foreign Direct Investment, Services, Price Indexes	https://www.bea.gov/ https://www.bea.gov/itable
United Nations Trade and Development (UNCTAD)	Technology Transfer, World Investment Report	https://unctadstat.unctad.org/datacentre/
Eurostat Database	Economy and Finance. General/Regional Statistics	https://ec.europa.eu/eurostat/data/database
Le Centre d'études prospectives et d'informations internationales (CEPII)	Database on trade, macroeconomics and finance, investment	https://www.cepii.fr/CEPII/en/cepii/cepii.asp
World Trade Organization (WTO)	Statistics on trade. Information on TRIPS Agreement, Council Decisions	https://www.wto.org/ https://stats.wto.org/
World Bank	World Development Indicators. GDP, Poverty, Gini	http://databank.worldbank.org
Design of Trade Agreements (DESTA)	Trade Agreement database	https://www.designoftradeagreements.org/
Penn World Tables (PWT 10.01 release)	Economic growth data, Human capital index.	https://www.rug.nl/ggdc/productivity/pwt/

3. Legal and Related

Data Source	Description	Websites
Lexis-Nexis	Matthew Bender & Co., Inc. *World Patent Law & Practice*, 2024 *World Trademark Law*, 2024 *Int'l Copyright Law & Practice*, 2025	https://www.lexisnexis.com/
Westlaw Precision	Thomson Reuters *Patents Throughout the World*, 2023 *Trademarks Throughout the World*, 2024 *Copyright Throughout the World*, 2024	https://1.next.westlaw.com/
TAPED Database	Trade Agreement Provisions on Electronic-commerce and Data	https://unilu.ch/taped
Global IP Estimator	Data on patent and trademark filing fees	https://www.quantifyip.com/

4. Institutions

Data Source	Description	Websites
Global Intellectual Property Center (GIPC)	International IP Indexes U.S. Chamber of Commerce	https://www.uschamber.com/intellectual-property
Property Rights Alliance	International Property Rights Index	https://propertyrightsalliance.org
Fraser Institute	Economic Freedom of the World Indexes, 1970–2024	https://www.fraserinstitute.org
World Economic Forum	Global Competitiveness Reports, 2000–2017	https://www.weforum.org/
Freedom House	Freedom in the World, 1973–2024	https://freedomhouse.org/
Economist Intelligence Unit	Intellectual Property Protection, 1994–2011	www.eiu.com
Institute for Management Development	World Competitiveness Yearbook 1995–2009	https://www.imd.org

5. Firm Level Data

Data Source	Description	Websites
Standard & Poor Global	Capital IQ database. Revenues, R&D, Balance sheet, etc.	https://www.spglobal.com/market-intelligence/en
Moody's	Orbis database (formerly a Bureau van Dijk database). Includes IP data linked to companies.	https://www.moodys.com/web/en/us/capabilities/company-reference-data/orbis.html

Appendix 2B. Quantitative Methods

The main quantitative tool used in the book is *derivatives*, a method for analyzing the effects of a change in an input on some output.[29] The relationship given by $y = f(x)$ posits that a variable y is a function of some variable x. For example, y could represent a company's profits per week and x could be hours of labor per week. The ratio, $\frac{\Delta y}{\Delta x}$, is often of interest, where Δy is the *change* in y and Δx the *change* in x. It shows how much y changes per some change in x. In the profit example, if $\frac{\Delta y}{\Delta x} = 10$, it suggests that expanding employment by one more hour per week (i.e., $\Delta x = 1$) is associated with a \$10 rise in profits per week.

That ratio can be found by taking the derivative of $f(x)$ with respect to x:

$$\frac{\Delta y}{\Delta x} \approx \frac{dy}{dx} = f'(x)$$

where dy, dx denote the differentials (the changes) in y, x respectively. In effect, the derivative is the slope of the function, $f(x)$, which varies depending on the value of x at which the derivative is measured. The slope precisely reveals how the value of y or $f(x)$ changes as x changes marginally.

Here are some common rules for taking derivatives:

- $f(x) = \alpha \Longrightarrow f'(x) = 0$
- $f(x) = \ln x \Longrightarrow f'(x) = \frac{1}{x}$
- $f(x) = e^{\alpha x} \Longrightarrow f'(x) = \alpha e^{\alpha x}$
- $f(x) = \alpha x \Longrightarrow f'(x) = \alpha$
- $f(x) = \alpha x^{\beta} \Longrightarrow f'(x) = \alpha\beta x^{\beta-1}$

[29] For more details on quantitative methods, see Hoy *et al.* (2022).

where α is a constant parameter. The derivative of a constant is zero, by definition, because it does not change.

Now, the function $f(x)$ need not be linear; it could be positively-sloped in some segments of $f(x)$, flat, or negatively-sloped in other segments. For example, the relationship between profits and labor hours could be nonlinear. Initially, more employment helps to produce more sales and profits. But too many labor hours per week could have a deleterious effect on profits. Workers do not get sufficient rest or time to recuperate. Their productivity diminishes, producing less output per hour as the hours pass, but they still require to be paid the same hourly wage. At some point, profits would decline because revenues do not catch up to the cost increases.

To find the optimal labor hours, or hours that maximize profits, take the derivative of profits with respect to labor hours and equate the derivative to zero. Solving for the labor hours that set the derivative to zero yields the profit-maximizing level of labor. To repeat in general terms, the optimal x^* which maximizes $f(x)$ is that level of x^* at which $\frac{dy}{dx} = f'(x^*) = 0$.

The intuition for this optimization condition is hill-climbing. A climber is at the top of a hill if the slope of the hill is flat (or equal to zero). If the slope is positive, and the climber wishes to reach the top of the hill, she should keep moving forward in the same direction; if the slope is negative, she should walk back or in the reverse direction. A positive (negative) slope means that she can feel the elevation rise (fall). Likewise, if x^* is the quantity that maximizes y, small deviations in that quantity should produce no change in $f(x)$, which is why the derivative $\frac{dy}{dx} = 0$ so that $\Delta f(x) = 0$. This is tantamount to being on top of the hill. No change in elevation is detected in movements around the peak. If increasing x beyond x^* results in $\frac{dy}{dx} > 0$, that means that y could increase, contradicting that x^* is the point that maximizes $f(x)$. On the other hand, if increasing x beyond x^* results in $\frac{dy}{dx} < 0$, that means that y can be raised by decreasing x, that is, by choosing a quantity lower than x^*. Again, the fact that $\frac{dy}{dx} \neq 0$ contradicts the assumption that x^* is the optimal x that maximizes $f(x)$. It is not the case that at that point, $f(x^*)$ is at its peak value.

Here is a profit maximization example: suppose that $y = 2\sqrt{x} - \frac{1}{3}x$ is the profit equation.[30] The goal is to find the optimal labor hours, x, which

[30]Profits equal revenues minus costs. Revenues are given by price per unit times the number of units produced and sold. Here, the price per unit is 2 and the quantity produced is the square root of labor hours, x, reflecting diminishing marginal productivity of labor. Hence, revenues are $2\sqrt{x}$. Costs are given by $\frac{1}{3}x$ where $\frac{1}{3}$ is the wage per hour. Hence, costs are wage per hour times the number of hours employed.

maximizes profits, y. The solution is obtained from:

$$\frac{dy}{dx} = x^{-0.5} - \frac{1}{3} = 0$$

which holds when $x^* = 9$ hours. At this level of employment, the maximal profits are $y^* = f(x^*) = 3$.

The condition for optimization $\frac{dy}{dx} = 0$ is called the *first-order condition (F.O.C.)* for finding the critical x^*. However, the critical x^* could correspond to either a maximum or a minimum of $f(x)$; in other words, a hiker could be at the bottom of a valley rather than the top of a hill. To decide which, it is necessary to consider the *second-order condition (S.O.C.)*, which essentially involves taking the derivative of $f(x)$ a second time. That is, take the derivative of $\frac{dy}{dx} = f'(x)$ with respect to x again. Let the notation for the second derivative be $f''(x)$.

- If $f''(x^*) < 0$, then x^* maximizes the value of $f(x)$
- If $f''(x^*) > 0$, then x^* minimizes the value of $f(x)$

The intuition can be seen in the figure below. Note that $f'(x)$ tracks the slope of $f(x)$, and $f''(x)$ tracks the slope of $f'(x)$.

In the left figure, as x starts from zero and moves rightward, the slope of $f(x)$ is initially very steep and highly positive, then gets flatter and flatter, hits a zero slope, and then turns negative and becomes even more negatively sloped. Thus, throughout, its slope, f', is decreasing in value. Hence, the reason $f'' < 0$ and $f(x)$ is shaped like a hill. In the right figure, as x starts from zero and moves rightward, $f(x)$ is initially very steep and negatively sloped, and then becomes less negatively sloped, and hits a zero slope before turning slightly positively sloped and then increasingly positively sloped. Thus, throughout, its slope, f', is increasing in value. Hence, the rate of change of its slope is positive ($f'' > 0$) and $f(x)$ is shaped like a valley.

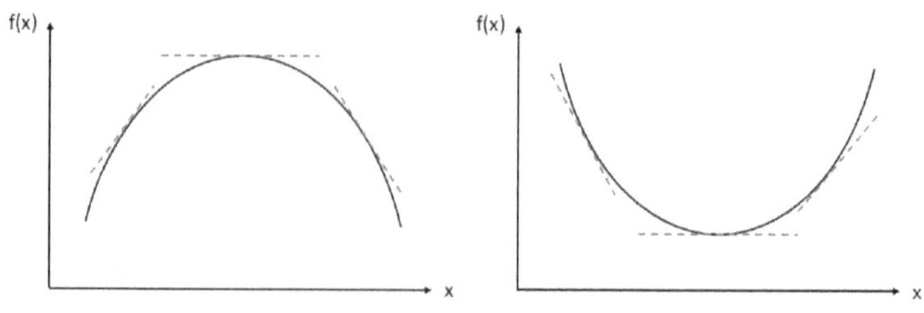

$f''(x) < 0$ $\qquad$ $f''(x) > 0$

Lastly, some remarks on notation. Until now, a two-variable relationship, $y = f(x)$, has been studied. But y may be a function of many inputs; for example, profits depend upon not only labor, but also the stock of equipment and machinery, taxes, interest rates, and regulations, such as those on industrial property:

$$y = f(x_1, x_2, \ldots, x_n)$$

To find the optimal x_1 holding other factors constant, we take the partial derivative:

$$\frac{\partial y}{\partial x_1} = \frac{\partial f(x_1, \bar{x_2}, \ldots, \bar{x_n})}{\partial x_1}$$

where bars on top of variables mean that they are being held constant at their existing values. Note the important change in notation: a ∂ symbol is used rather than d to represent *differentials* or changes in the value of variables when dealing with multiple variables.

Appendix 2C. Empirical Methods

The empirical presentation in this book focuses on descriptive statistics and some *regression* analyses. Consider a random variable (r.v.) x. Suppose it has N possible discrete outcomes $(x_1, x_2, \ldots, x_N)$ and let p_i be the probability associated with outcome x_i. The probabilities sum to 1; that is, $\sum_{i=1}^{N} p_i = 1$, where Σ is the symbol for summation. Its

1. Expected value (or mean) is $E(x) = p_1x_1 + p_2x_2 + \ldots + p_Nx_N = \sum_{i=1}^{N} p_ix_i$
2. Variance is $\sigma_x^2 = \sum_{i=1}^{N}(x_i - E(x))^2$
3. Standard deviation is $\sigma_x = \sqrt{\text{Variance}}$
4. Correlation with another r.v. is $\dfrac{\sum_{i=1}^{N}(x_i - E(x))(y_i - E(y))}{\sigma_x \sigma_y}$

The correlation coefficient varies from -1 (perfect negative correlation) to zero (no correlation) to $+1$ (perfect positive correlation). Note that the variance of $x + c$ where c is a constant is the same as the variance of x since c by definition has no fluctuation. But the variance of cx is c^2 times the variance of x as c when multiplied by x magnifies the latter's volatility.

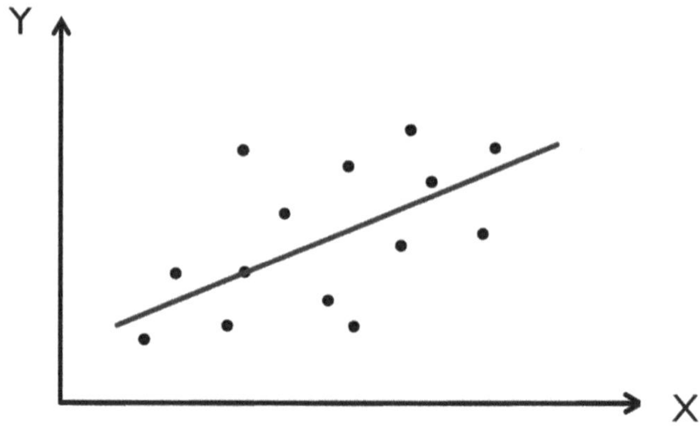

Figure 2C.1. Scatter Plot

For continuous random variables, the expected value is given by

$$E(x) = \int_a^b xp(x)dx$$

where $p(x)$ is a probability density function, which shows the probability of observing realizations of x in any specified range, and where $p(x) \geq 0$ and $\int_a^b p(x)dx = 1$. The integral $\int$ is analogous to the Σ symbol for continuous variables, such as real numbers (as opposed to integers). The limits of integration $[a, b]$ depend on the range or space of x. It could be $[0, 1]$ or $[-\infty, +\infty]$.

2C.1 *Regression Analysis*

The objective is to find an equation (or model) that best fits the data. Consider a two-variable linear relationship between x and y, namely $y = f(x) = \alpha + \beta x$. The multivariable linear case has analogous insights.

This equation will not exactly capture real-world data on x and y. See Figure 2C.1. Assume the solid line is the equation (or the hypothesized model). The 14 dots in the figure represent observations on x and y. Clearly, there are errors. The points in the scatter plot do not all land on the solid line. Therefore, rewrite the model with a random error term tacked on: $y = f(x) = \alpha + \beta x + \varepsilon$. For a good model, the errors should have a mean of zero ($E(\varepsilon) = 0$) and be unpredictable, or the researcher should have taken predictable patterns into account in building the model.

Let $\hat{y} = \hat{\alpha} + \hat{\beta}x$ be the estimated model, where ^ indicates estimated value. Consequently

$$\underbrace{y}_{\text{Actual}} = \underbrace{\hat{y}}_{\text{Predicted}} + \underbrace{\hat{\varepsilon}}_{\text{Residual}}$$

The $\hat{y}$ is the value of y predicted by the solid line, and $\hat{\varepsilon}$ is the measured vertical gap between the actual y and predicted y. The goal of regression analysis is to find the best line that goes through the data with the least errors (to be made specific shortly). Rewrite as

$$y = \underbrace{\hat{\alpha} + \hat{\beta}x}_{\hat{y}} + \varepsilon$$

Define the sum of the squared residuals (SSE) to be

$$\text{SSE} = \sum_{i=1}^{N} \hat{\varepsilon_i}^2 = \sum_{i=1}^{N} (y_i - \hat{\alpha} - \hat{\beta}x_i)^2$$

The residuals are squared so that the deviations are all preserved. Had they not been squared, a positive deviation of say +5 would cancel out with a negative deviation of −5, such that their sum gives the incorrect impression of accurate fits. The goal then is to find those values of α and β which minimize SSE. How is that done? Use the method of partial differentiation discussed in Appendix 2B. Calculate the first-order conditions (F.O.C.):

$$\frac{\partial \text{SSE}}{\partial \alpha} = 0, \quad \frac{\partial \text{SSE}}{\partial \beta} = 0$$

The solutions to the F.O.C. are the pair $(\hat{\alpha}, \hat{\beta})$. This can be accomplished using software packages, such as R, STATA, or EXCEL. The above two-variable case provides the intuition for working with a multi-variable model like:

$$y_i = \alpha + \beta_1 x_{1i} + \beta_2 x_{2i} + \ldots + \beta_n x_{ni} + \varepsilon_i$$

2C.2 *Interpreting Results*

Researchers focus on, among other things:

1. The **sign** of each β_j. Qualitatively, a positive (negative) sign indicates a positive (negative) association between y and the x variable, controlling for other factors.

2. The **magnitude** or coefficient value of β_j. This is the value of the partial derivative (slope) of y with respect to x_j, $\frac{\partial y}{\partial x_j}$. If, for example, $\hat{\beta}_j = -3$, this means that for an increase in x_j by 1 unit (however x is measured, whether in meters or dollars), y would decrease by 3 units (however y is measured, whether in meters or dollars). Note that if the variables were measured in natural logarithms, such as $\ln y$ and $\ln x_j$, the coefficient estimate β_j represents percentages; for example, a 1% change in x_j is associated with a β_j% change in y.
3. The **significance** of each β_j. This depends on the coefficient value of β_j relative to its standard error (s.e.). The larger $\hat{\beta}_j$ is relative to its s.e., the more reliable the estimate and the more influential the x_j variable is deemed to be. Intuitively, suppose someone predicts the price of eggs to be \$10 per carton, but thinks the forecast error is plus or minus \$8. In that case, that person is not very confident of her prediction, given that the error in absolute value is about 80% of the expected price. In contrast, someone who thinks the forecast error is plus or minus \$1 is far more confident, since the forecast is only ten percent of the expected value.[31]

As a guide, the following *significance levels* are usually referenced:

Symbol used	Significance at	Ratio of $\frac{\beta_j}{s.e._j}$
*	10% level	≥1.645
**	5% level	≥1.960
***	1% level	≥2.576

Note: These are for sufficiently large observations ($N > 1000$).

The significance level of β_j is about rejecting the (null) hypothesis that x_j has no effect on y — that the true value of β_j is zero. Researchers want to be confident that β_j is not zero.[32] The significance level is a chosen standard as to whether to reject the null hypothesis that $\beta_j = 0$. Many

[31]Another analogy is the case of dart throwing. Players aim for the center of the board. If a player misses by 5 inches, is that good or bad? That cannot be answered in absolute terms, as it depends on the circumference of the board. If the diameter is 2 feet, the player made a very accurate throw, but if the diameter is 1 foot, not so. This is why the mean is normalized by the standard error and judged by how large the standard error is relative to the mean value.

[32]This is akin to the practice of law where it is desired to know beyond a reasonable doubt that something is significant, so by default it is assumed that there is no significant effect unless the data show sufficiently otherwise.

studies cited in this book choose a 5% level of significance. At this level of significance, the probability of wrongly rejecting the null hypothesis is 5%. Other researchers prefer a stricter standard, such as the 1% level of significance.

Alternatively, instead of using the significance guideposts shown in the table above, other researchers report the *p-value*. This is the probability of observing a non-zero coefficient value as large as the researcher estimated if the null hypothesis ($\beta_j = 0$) were true. Essentially, the above 10%, 5%, and 1% significance levels correspond to p-values of 0.10, 0.05, and 0.01, respectively. By reporting only the p-values, the researcher informs the audience what the significance level of the coefficient estimate is. This has the advantage of not rigidly following the significance asterisks ($*$, $**$, and $***$) ratings.[33]

It is important to remember that the discussion has been about statistical significance and not quantitative significance. The significantly estimated coefficient differs from zero in a statistical sense; that is, one can strongly reject that it is zero. Now that could include an estimate like $\beta_j = 0.000001$. However, from an economic point of view, the effect is trivial. For example, a study could find that wearing masks all day reduces lung cancer rates by 0.000001%, but this is a fairly minor benefit, even if it is truly non-zero from a statistical perspective.

Another important regression result to report relates to the estimation equation as a whole. How well does the estimated model (line or curve) fit the data? A common goodness-of-fit statistic is the *R-squared*:

$$R^2 = \frac{\text{Explained Variation}}{\text{Total Variation}} = \frac{\sum_{i=1}^{n}(\hat{y}_i - \bar{y})^2}{\sum_{i=1}^{n}(y_i - \bar{y})^2}$$

which shows the proportion of the total variation in the data, defined as the variation about the sample mean, $\bar{y}$, that is explained by the model ($\hat{y} = \hat{\alpha} + \hat{\beta}_1 x_1 + \ldots + \hat{\beta}_n x_n$).

However, the R^2 is susceptible to being raised by adding more variables to the model, even if they are statistically insignificant. The adjusted R-squared accounts for that:

$$\text{Adj } R^2 = 1 - \frac{N-1}{N-K}(1 - R^2)$$

[33]For example, if the p-value of the coefficient estimate of variable x_j were 0.051, the coefficient would not have merited $**$, but it was very close to being significant at the 5% level.

where N denotes the number of observations and K the number of explanatory variables. The formula for the adjusted R-squared penalizes increases in K.

2C.3 *Empirical Strategies*

1. Randomized Control Trials: These are experiments that compare the effect of an intervention on a treated group and a control group. Participants are randomly assigned to these groups. For example, young entrepreneurs can be randomly assigned to receive managerial training or to a control group that does not receive such training. The researcher can then study the differences in outcomes between the two groups.

2. Natural Experiments: This is a form of research design in which the researcher exploits a naturally occurring event to study the effects of the event on outcomes. Natural experiments rely on external events for the variations in exposure to a treatment or intervention. The researcher does not control the randomization. For example, changes in IP laws that create variations in the level of protection can be assessed for their impact on an outcome without the researcher directly manipulating the experiment. A case in mind is the *America Invents Act* in 2011, which changed the U.S. patent system from "first-to-invent" to "first-to-file." Researchers can compare the differences in innovation and patent filing behavior under the two regimes.

3. Difference-in-Differences Approach: This is an econometric method that helps estimate causal relationships when random assignment is not possible. The method evaluates the impact of a treatment or policy intervention by comparing the changes in outcome over time (post-treatment versus pre-treatment) and between groups (treatment group and control group). It is assumed that, were it not for the intervention, the mean outcomes for both groups would follow a *parallel trend* over time. An application might be a copyright reform that enhances protection for digital media. The treatment group could be firms in the digital content industry, such as online publishing. The control group could be firms in a similar industry that are not reliant on digital content, such as traditional publishing.

The treatment effect can be identified as follows:

$$\Delta = \overbrace{\underbrace{[y^{\mathrm{T}}_{\mathrm{Post}} - y^{\mathrm{T}}_{\mathrm{Pre}}]}_{\text{One difference}} - \underbrace{[y^{\mathrm{C}}_{\mathrm{Post}} - y^{\mathrm{C}}_{\mathrm{Pre}}]}_{\text{Another difference}}}^{\text{This is the }\textbf{Difference}\text{ in Differences}}$$

- $y_{\text{Post}}^{\text{T}}$ = Outcome in the Treatment Group after the intervention
- $y_{\text{Pre}}^{\text{T}}$ = Outcome in the Treatment Group before the intervention
- $y_{\text{Post}}^{\text{C}}$ = Outcome in the Control Group after the intervention
- $y_{\text{Pre}}^{\text{C}}$ = Outcome in the Control Group before the intervention

The Δ difference-in-differences effect can be estimated using the following regression model:

$$y_{it} = \alpha + \beta_1 \text{TREAT}_i + \beta_2 \text{POST}_t + \beta_3 \text{TREAT}_i \times \text{POST}_t + \ldots + \varepsilon_{it}$$

where TREAT $= 1$ if the subject is in the treatment group and TREAT $=$ 0 if it is in the control group. POST $= 1$ in the period after the intervention and POST $= 0$ before. The subscript i indexes subjects and t time. Once the equation is estimated on data, the outcome for the treated group is

$$\Delta^{\text{TREATMENT Group}} = \underbrace{(\hat{\alpha} + \hat{\beta}_1 + \hat{\beta}_2 + \hat{\beta}_3)}_{\text{TREAT=1,POST=1}} \quad - \quad \underbrace{(\hat{\alpha} + \hat{\beta}_1)}_{\text{TREAT=1,POST=0}} \quad = \hat{\beta}_2 + \hat{\beta}_3$$

and for the control group is

$$\Delta^{\text{CONTROL Group}} = \underbrace{(\hat{\alpha} + \hat{\beta}_2)}_{\text{TREAT=0,POST=1}} \quad - \quad \underbrace{\hat{\alpha}}_{\text{TREAT=0,POST=0}} \quad = \hat{\beta}_2$$

Therefore, the measured effect of the intervention would be

$$\Delta = \Delta^{\text{TREATMENT Group}} - \Delta^{\text{CONTROL Group}} = \hat{\beta}_2 + \hat{\beta}_3 - \hat{\beta}_2 = \hat{\beta}_3$$

In other words, it is the coefficient of the interaction term, $\text{TREAT}_i \times \text{POST}_t$.

2C.4 *For Further Reading*

Bailey, Michael (2016). *Real Stats: Using Econometrics for Political Science and Public Policy*, Oxford: Oxford University Press.

Glaister, Stephen (1984). *Mathematical Methods for Economists*, 3rd edition, Oxford: Blackwell.

Hoy, Michael, Livernois, John, McKenna, Chris, Rees, Ray, and Stengos, Thanasis (2022). *Mathematics for Economists*, 4th edition, Cambridge: MIT Press.

Huntington-Klein, Nick (2022). *The Effect: An Introduction to Research Design and Causality*, CRC Press, Abingdon: Taylor & Francis Group.

Chapter 3

R&D and Economic Growth

3.1 Introduction

R&D is widely argued to be a critical input into knowledge creation, which in turn is a key determinant of firm production and economic growth. There are different kinds of R&D, such as basic research which builds fundamental knowledge (like the foundations of natural science or social science), and applied research which focuses on the applications of knowledge (such as engineering solutions, medical treatments, or social and community policy interventions). Developmental research involves the development of a product from, say, a blueprint or design that emerges from an R&D lab. A critical next step for economic impacts, such as productivity, employment, or trade, is the commercialization process in which the R&D outputs are marketed, sold, or licensed for use.

R&D innovations can yield not only new products but also new processes for production. The former can yield new sources of revenue for a firm, whereas the latter can help lower the cost of production. Of course, knowledge creation can occur as a by-product of some activity or discovery, or it can be the outcome of intentional R&D activity in pursuit of market profits or other incentives.

This chapter begins by providing a conceptual framework for economic growth and identifies the role of research and development, and discusses other interesting aspects of R&D, such as how the benefits from it can spill over to other laboratories or companies, or across borders to knowledge creators in other regions and countries.

3.2 Production Possibility Frontier

Broadly speaking, economic goods and services are produced using resources and technology. Technology can be thought of as devices or methods of utilizing resources to manufacture goods and provide services. Given the state of technology and the resource constraints, society is capable of producing finite combinations of goods. Figure 3.1 shows a *production possibility frontier* for the case of two goods. Of course, in the real world, there are N different kinds of goods, but for diagrammatic simplicity, let us assume a 2-good world.

Figure 3.1 shows all the feasible combinations of good 1 and good 2, denoted by Y_1 and Y_2 respectively, that can be produced with the available resources and available technology. The production possibility frontier provides an upper bound on what can be produced. The frontier has a negative slope, indicating that the only way to produce more of one good is to produce less of the other, since if society is on the frontier, all resources are being utilized. To produce more of say good 1, resources need to be withdrawn from facilities that produce good 2 and redeployed in facilities that produce good 1. The production possibility frontier here has a concave shape. In this case, it is assumed that there are rising opportunity costs

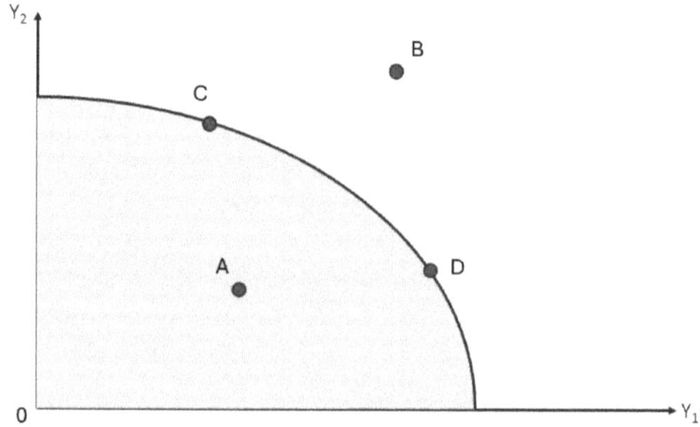

Figure 3.1. Production Possibilities Frontier

of increasing the production of either good. This means that successively more of one good needs to be given up in order to produce a unit more of the other good. This is because resources tend to be specialized (better at one activity than another). For example, those that are better suited to making good 2 are diverted to making good 1, but that could cause a big reduction in good 2 but not a big increase in good 1 since the production of good 1 uses other specialized resources.

Note that the feasible combinations of goods that can be produced include zero units of good 1 and 2. In other words, a society could choose not to produce anything or be prohibited from producing anything. Another combination of Y_1 and Y_2 that is feasible for the economy to produce is point A, but note that point A represents a case where not all resources are fully utilized. Points inside the frontier indicate an underutilization of resources or the "unemployment" of resources. For example, producers are not hiring workers or installing and operating machines. Points C and D are feasible and represent points of full employment. All resources are utilized. It can also be said that all points on the frontier, like C and D, represent efficiency, since no resources are wasted.

However, consider point B. Is this feasible? No, because there are not enough resources to produce that combination of Y_1 and Y_2. If society tried to produce that combination, what would occur? Typically, prices will rise or wages will rise because the demand for resources to produce goods and services exceeds the supply of resources. Hence, society will experience inflation. In this simple model, a tradeoff between inflation and unemployment emerges. Aim to produce beyond the frontier, inflation occurs; underutilize resources, and then unemployment results. The study of business cycles is about two key phenomena: episodes of inflation and unemployment, and economic booms and recessions. A goal of an economy is to steer clear of both inflation and unemployment through the use of *stabilization policies*; that is, the use of government policies to keep economies on the frontier or to avoid or dampen deviations around the efficient frontier. Whether to keep an economy specifically on a point like C or D requires other criteria, such as social welfare and equity considerations.

Now that business cycles have been explained, turn next to economic growth. This is the study of the expansion in production possibilities. Two key mechanisms have been identified: either society needs more resources (for example, the discovery of more minerals, or an increase in the labor force, in capital such as machinery and equipment, or land), or society

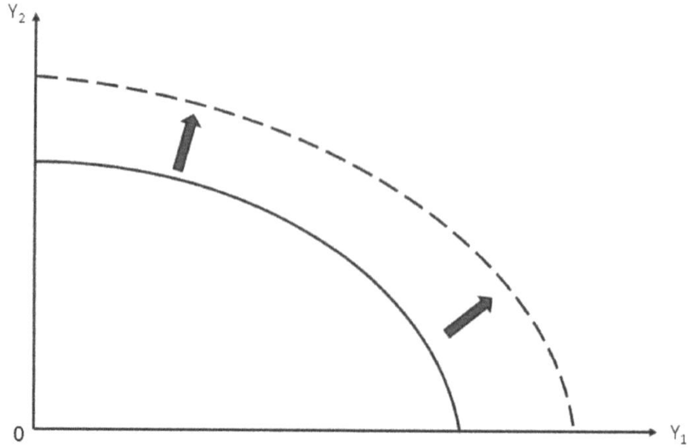

Figure 3.2. Depiction of Economic Growth

has more and better technology, made possible through R&D and inventive and other creative activity. Figure 3.2 shows that economic growth is represented by an outward shift in the production possibilities frontier.

The connection to intellectual property (IP) is that the system of intellectual property protection shapes the nature and direction of creative and innovative activity. An appropriate IP policy gives rise to new resources for production and improves the efficiency of existing resources. Much of the research and debate centers on what constitutes appropriate IP policy — the strength of IP rights and the design of IP protection.

3.3 Determinants of Economic Growth

It is helpful to use a few symbols and equations to organize ideas around R&D and economic growth. In actuality, the production possibility set is N-dimensional (not 2-dimensional as in Figures 3.1 and 3.2). If Y_i denotes the output (or value added[1]) of sector or industry i, total real gross domestic product (GDP) is given by

$$Y = Y_1 + Y_2 + \cdots + Y_n = \sum_{i=1}^{N} Y_i$$

[1]Value added is output minus intermediate inputs. This is important because different industries can use one another's output as a production input. To avoid the double-counting of industry output, only the value added contributions of each industry are added.

where Σ is shorthand for the sums.[2] Next, a *production function* is introduced that relates the output of goods and services to the inputs used to make them. The inputs become essentially the determinants of economic growth or the expansion in the production possibility set. In principle, production functions could be modeled for each sector, but for purposes of getting a general understanding of the role of R&D in growth, a production function shall be posited for a nation as a whole. It can be referred to as the **Aggregate Production Function**:

$$Y = Af(K, L) \tag{3.1}$$

where Y denotes output, K capital, L labor, and A technical efficiency. The f refers to a function, like a black-box, where inputs are fed into a system to generate output. Equation (3.1) captures the fact that output depends on both resources and technology. (This total supply Y is then divided up among aggregate demand: by consumers, businesses, governments, and their foreign counterparts.) Where innovation and IP come in is through the technology channel (A). Nonetheless, resources such as capital (K) and labor (L) are also important determinants of economic growth. Capital expands via physical investment activities, which in turn depend upon national savings. Economic growth is typically higher when consumers are more patient and save for the future, with their savings routed through the financial system to fund capital accumulation. Labor size and competencies are enhanced through population change, education, and training.

The economic growth rate here is defined as the percentage growth in output: $\frac{\Delta Y}{Y}$, namely the change in output (numerator) expressed as a percentage of the output level (denominator).[3]

Mathematically, the process of total differentiation can be used to decompose the growth in output among its constituents:

$$\frac{\Delta Y}{Y} = \frac{\Delta A}{A} + \alpha_K \frac{\Delta K}{K} + \alpha_L \frac{\Delta L}{L} \tag{3.2}$$

According to (3.2), economic growth is the sum of the growth in technical efficiency and the weighted average growth of capital and labor, where the

---

[2]By "real" is meant inflation-adjusted; else, the term "nominal" GDP is used. It is important to adjust for changes in the price level over time if society wants to track the true progress of economic growth — the growth in real output — not just the same units of goods and services produced, which simply got more expensive over time.

[3]In practice, one would calculate the growth rate of trend output, or the long run average output, to smooth out the cyclical fluctuations in output. Recall that deviations of potential output around the production possibility frontier are business cycles. The goal here is to try to measure the shifting of the frontier itself.

weights α_K and α_L are the capital income and labor income shares in total income, respectively.[4]

Earlier, Solow (1957) found that the growth in technical efficiency, $\frac{\Delta A}{A}$, accounted for almost half of the growth rate, but the earlier economic growth literature treated $\frac{\Delta A}{A}$ as *exogenous*, meaning that a growth rate for it was specified as given in models of the economy. It was not until the late 1980s and early 1990s that researchers allowed the technological growth rate to be *endogenous*, meaning that instead of being treated as given, the growth rate had to be solved for among all the other unknown variables in the model of the economy. By endogenizing this growth rate, it was possible to hypothesize and study the determinants of changes in technical efficiency, whether they are research policies (such as R&D taxes and subsidies), intellectual property rights, financial and market regulations, market size effects, and so forth. Until then, the focus had been on capital investment, via $\frac{\Delta K}{K}$, or human capital investment, such as educational policies, that affect skilled labor growth.

This framework — Eqs. (3.1) and (3.2 — can show where R&D fits into economic growth. Consider a knowledge production function:

$$A = A(R) \tag{3.3}$$

where the level of technology is a function of research and development investments, denoted by R. In some empirical studies, researchers use patent counts as a proxy for A, but one can think of A more broadly to include knowledge that goes beyond patented inventions, since not all knowledge goods are patentable (such as mathematical ideas, surgical procedures, games, and others mentioned in the laws) and some inventions are kept as trade secrets rather than patented. R&D can broadly include both private sector and public sector research investments, as well as research knowledge developed by foreigners. For simplicity, many other important factors that contribute to creating technological knowledge, A, are omitted, such as the institutional environment, human capital, infrastructure, fiscal policy, regulations, culture, and the existing stock of knowledge.

In the knowledge production function (3.3), it is plausible for the cumulative stock of R&D investments to account for the level of technology, A,

[4]For example, α_K could be about one-third and α_L about two-thirds, depending on the region, industry, or time period.

rather than contemporaneous one-time flows of R&D spending. The following identity helps to connect the stock of R&D to the flow of R&D:

$$R_t = I_t + (1 - \delta)R_{t-1} \tag{3.4}$$

which states that the stock of R&D knowledge capital at time t equals the flow of R&D investment (I) conducted at time t added to the stock of R&D knowledge capital as of time $t - 1$, which is the stock that remains after depreciation or some obsolescence, where $0 < \delta < 1$ is the rate of depreciation.

The available stock of R&D knowledge from (3.4) is responsible then, via (3.3), for enhancing technical efficiency A, which in turn should help boost the production of firms and thereby contribute to economic growth, via (3.1) and (3.2).

3.4 R&D Decisions

R&D decisions are made with a long-run view of profitability. If successful, research and development investment may yield improved ways of producing goods and services. It may also create new products for the market or enhance existing product quality. Those products can be marketed to consumers (medicines) or other firms as inputs into production (such as fertilizers) or innovation (scientific instruments).

Figure 3.3 shows the central role of the R&D sector: The figure shows that R&D is conducted deliberately in that the research sector responds to market needs. Consumers or producers demand new or improved outputs and inputs, respectively. Researchers then create knowledge goods which they sell (or license) to intermediate goods producers in the form of blueprints or designs. The latter producers, in turn, commercialize those blueprints/designs by creating goods and services embodying them, test the prototypes, and then sell (or license) them to the final goods sector. In addition to all these market transactions, the knowledge that the research sector creates also flows freely to all sectors and adds to the stock of social knowledge. For example, the public can observe and learn from the new intellectual goods and services that they bought. This is what is special about intellectual goods. The product is distinct from the underlying knowledge

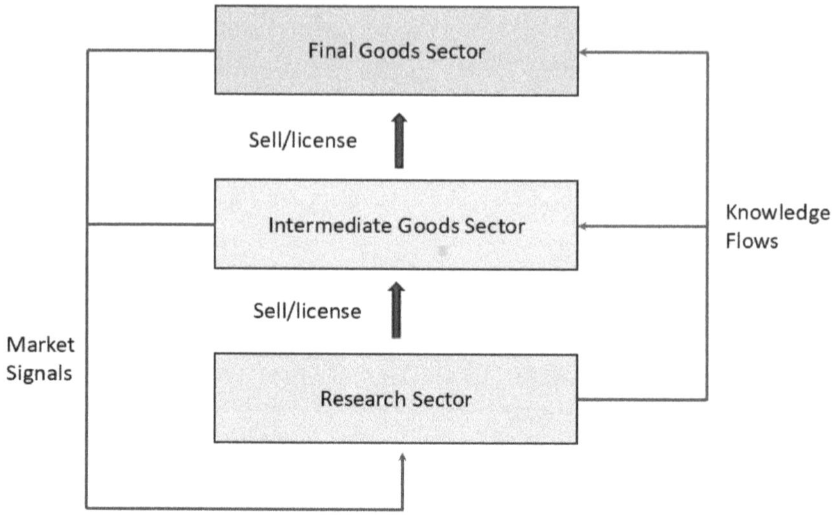

Figure 3.3. R&D Schema

upon which it is built.[5] The research sector is not able to capture the whole value of the knowledge created. It can only charge for the blueprints directly and for the final good indirectly, but it would not be compensated for its contribution to the general body of knowledge. These are what are known as knowledge *externalities* — benefits that accrue to society beyond the market participants in a transaction.[6]

Indeed, the patent system is built around this dichotomy between knowledge diffusion and commercialization. In exchange for obtaining patent protection, the party that is granted a patent is required to disclose the knowledge underlying its invention in a way that a person skilled in the art can replicate the invention. This knowledge is then available to the general public to build upon. The patent only excludes others from practicing the invention (or commercially exploiting it) but does not prohibit others from using the knowledge in their follow-on research. The same principle applies to other areas of IP, like plant variety protection. So, it is in this sense that the patent system implicitly contains a bargain: it protects the inventor in

[5]A laptop that is purchased provides value for the services and functions it has for the user, but it can also reveal knowledge about its technical creation and construction, and more information can be extracted through reverse engineering.

[6]Another example of a positive externality is that of a homeowner who tends to a beautiful garden that not only beautifies his own home but also the homes of his neighbors. The homeowner is not compensated for those external benefits.

the marketplace but leaves the knowledge free for further R&D, whether in the private sector, public sector, or academia.

3.4.1 *Firm Value*

In the short run, a firm incurs R&D costs upfront while it earns its investment returns (or profits) over time. Excluding the R&D experimental and developmental costs, a firm's profit per period is the difference between revenues and costs. Revenues are sales (typically price times the quantity of goods and services sold), and costs include wages and salaries, rent on land, rental on capital, and any royalties and licensing fees paid.

Given the time dimension (i.e., short versus long run), it is useful to compute the *present discounted value* of profits, and then conduct the analysis with a longer-term time frame in mind. Future profits need to be discounted by $(1 + r)$, where r is the real interest rate, because people prefer a dollar (or any other source of income) today rather than tomorrow. Therefore, a future source of income needs to be expressed in current value terms.[7] The focus is on profits because ultimately they capture the returns on current R&D and drive incentives for innovation and commercialization.

The present discounted value of the stream of current and future profits for a firm is given by:

$$V = \pi_0 + \frac{\pi_1}{1+r} + \frac{\pi_2}{(1+r)^2} + \frac{\pi_3}{(1+r)^3} + \cdots + \frac{\pi_T}{(1+r)^T}$$

where π denotes profits and r the real interest rate. The subscripts {0, 1, 2, ...} denote time. It is assumed that this is observed at time period zero, $t = 0$. Even the above expression is simplified. It ignores taxes on profits and risk and uncertainty. It also assumes that the interest rate is fixed and not variable. Here, time T is the duration of the profit flow. It could be that by period T, the company is displaced by a rival, or its technology or core business becomes obsolete in T periods. However, one could easily assume that T is infinite, that the business lasts forever, or one could model T as a random variable. In any case, the same qualitative insights will apply.

[7]For example, if \$1 is saved and earns interest at the rate of 10% per annum, it will be worth \$1.10 next year. Thus, the present discounted value (PDV) of \$1.10 next year is \$1 today, using the formula $\frac{\$1.10}{1+r} = \frac{\$1.1}{1+0.1}$. If the \$1 is saved for 2 years in a row, the \$1.10 earned after year one will be compounded, so it will be worth $\$1(1+r)(1+r) = \$1.10(1+r) = \$1.10^2 = \$1.21$ after 2 years. Hence, the present discounted value of \$1.21 in year 2 is \$1 $(= \frac{\$1.21}{(1+0.1)^2})$. Thus, the value of \$1.21 2 years from now equals \$1 today. This is the underlying basis for the PDV formula.

One can simplify further by assuming that the profit flow is the same every period ($\pi_t = \bar{\pi}$)[8]

$$V = \Big(1 + \frac{1}{r}\Big)\bar{\pi}\Big(1 - \frac{1}{(1+r)^T}\Big) \tag{3.5}$$

If the company is long-lived, then $V = (1 + \frac{1}{r})\bar{\pi}$, as $T \to \infty$. In the economics and finance literature, V is referred to as *firm value*. Firm value is higher if T is greater, since the owners of the firm get to enjoy profits for a longer period. Firm value is greater if r is lower since future profits are not discounted as heavily. And of course, firm value is greater if the steady flow of profits, $\bar{\pi}$, is greater. Otherwise, if future competitors are expected to enter the market and dissipate profits, the present discounted value of V would decline.

Indeed, this is closely relevant to the stock market. The market valuation of a firm is based on the stream of current and expected future profits, and so V can be thought as the company's market capitalization. The share price of a firm is essentially V divided by the number of outstanding shares (N): $q = \frac{V}{N}$, where q is the equity price. The rate of return (R.O.R.) to acquiring a share of this company is dividends per share (DIV) plus capital gains as a percentage of the equity price:

$$\text{R.O.R.} = \frac{\text{DIV} + \Delta q}{q}$$

Note that capital gain (loss) is given by the change in equity price, Δq. Investors have a choice of investing in a share of this company or in a bond that yields a rate of return of r. Hence, the arbitrage condition is $r = \text{R.O.R.}$, or else if one asset's rate of return is greater than the other's, investors will switch funds around from stocks to bonds or vice versa.

Back to R&D decisions. The firm compares its expected firm value to the upfront research and development cost of the technology, denoted by F. If this were a new company, it would assess whether it is worth spending the amount F on invention and commercialization. The benefits are that, if a technological breakthrough occurs, the firm can enjoy V, which captures the stream of future expected profits from marketing the new technology.

---

[8]The sum of the geometric sequence $S_n = 1 + x + x^2 + \ldots + x^T$, where $0 < x < 1$, can be shown to be $S_n = \frac{1-x^{n+1}}{1-x}$. In the firm's case, $x = \frac{1}{1+r}$. Substituting this into S_n and rearranging a bit will yield the formula (3.5).

Hence,

$$\begin{cases} \text{Invest in R\&D} & \text{if } V \geq F \\ \text{Don't Invest} & \text{otherwise} \end{cases}$$

Now, if the firm already exists, then it would compare the change in firm value to the upfront research and development cost, for if the R&D does not yield a sufficient marginal boost in the future stream of profits, it would continue to produce using the existing technology or sell its existing product lines.

$$\begin{cases} \text{Invest in R\&D} & \text{if } \Delta V \geq F \\ \text{Don't Invest} & \text{otherwise} \end{cases}$$

The role of IP protection gets rather nuanced from here, as will be explored in the rest of the book. As a first pass, IP enables the firm to better appropriate the returns to innovation represented in V or ΔV. Innovation, however, typically arises in an environment of interdependent firms. Innovation occurs within an ecosystem of other innovations, some of which are also protected by IP. Thus, IP rights also affect a firm's cost of development, F. This could contain licensing fees for the rights to use patented or copyrighted material in the commercialized product. Stronger IP rights grant licensors greater bargaining power over licensees. Moreover, the inputs that are priced into the cost, F, are not competitively supplied if they are under IP protection. The suppliers of inputs each have exclusive rights and so can price above marginal cost (or the competitive level).

In the analyses thus far, the R&D costs, F, were upfront. The next sub-section analyzes the case where some of these costs are spread out over time.

3.4.2 *Time-Cost Tradeoffs*

Suppose that the present discounted value of development costs is given by[9]

$$C^{PV} = C_0 + \frac{C_1}{1+r} + \frac{C_2}{(1+r)^2} + \cdots + \frac{C_T}{(1+r)^T}$$

For a more rapid discovery, these costs are expected to be concentrated in the early stages (i.e., the costs are front-loaded). A firm will also likely

[9]This analysis is due to Barzel (1968).

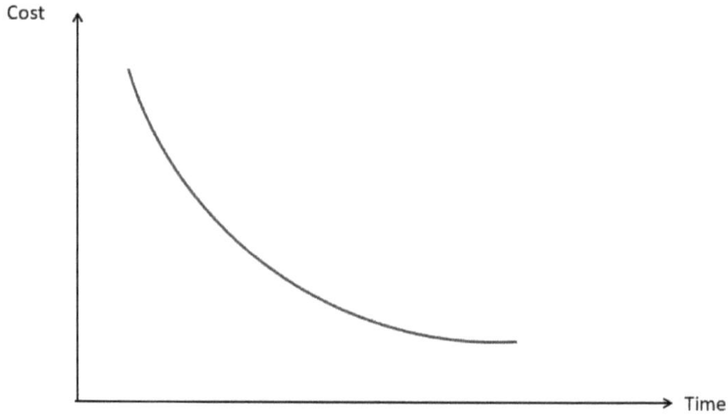

Figure 3.4. Development Time-Cost Tradeoff

conduct multiple, parallel experiments (such as clinical trials) until a technological breakthrough arises. Research expenses that are spread out to later periods would be discounted. Therefore, the cost C^{PV} would decline with time, as shown in Figure 3.4. The total development costs have this shape because, all else being equal, extending the development timeline reduces $CPVC^{PV}$ since future costs are more heavily discounted.

The benefits of technological development are also spread out over time:

$$B^{PV} = B_0 + \frac{B_1}{1+r} + \frac{B_2}{(1+r)^2} + \cdots + \frac{B_T}{(1+r)^T}$$

The present discounted value of it too falls with the time of technological development because delaying development pushes the arrival of profits to a more distant future, and those profit flows will be discounted from the current perspective. Moreover, the firm risks having another company develop the technology first or developing something similar, in which case future profits would not be as high. In the figure below, the B^{PV} curve is drawn linearly for simplicity, and above the development cost curve, or else it would not be profitable to consider developing the technology. According to Figure 3.5, the optimal innovation date is T^* as that is where the present discounted value of benefits exceeds the present discounted value of costs the most. (On a technical note, this maximum gap occurs at that date at which the slopes of B^{PV} and C^{PV} are the same.)

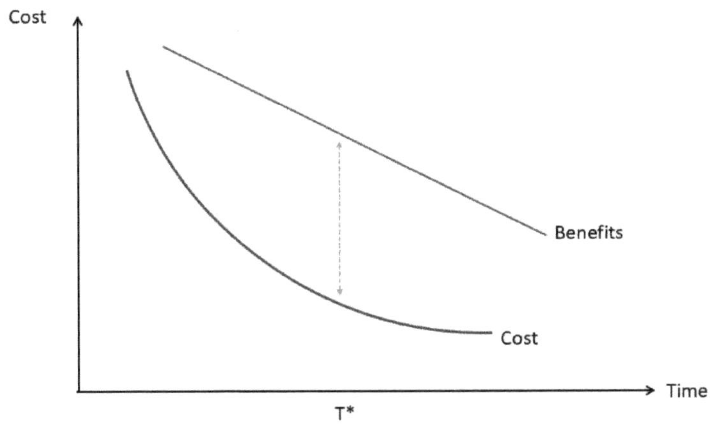

Figure 3.5. Optimal Innovation Date

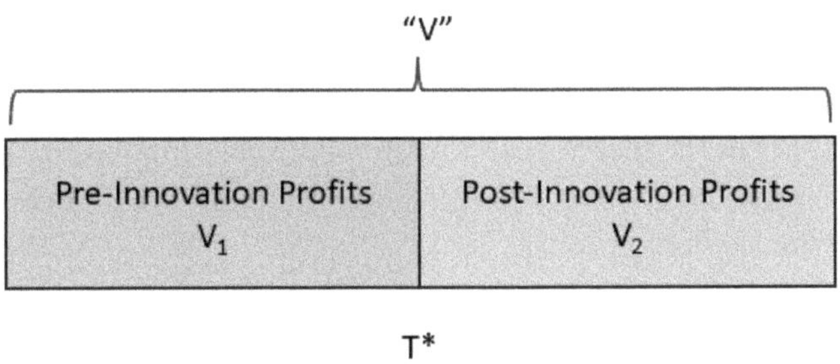

Figure 3.6. Firm Value Before/After Technology Development

The optimal date of technological development, though, will strategically change in response to imitation risk.[10] Consider Figure 3.6.

The rectangular box represents the size of firm value, V, seen from the perspective of the current period. It can be divided into two parts — before and after the date of technological development, T^*. Let the value attributable to the existing technology be denoted by V_1. This comes from the stream of pre-innovation profits from time 0 to time T^*, appropriately discounted. The second part of firm value is attributable to the new technology, denoted by V_2, which comes from the stream of post-innovation profits from time T^* to the end of the firm's life.

[10]The analysis here is from Park (1997).

Suppose the firm is competing against imitators. Imitation, whether before or after technological development, will lower firm profits and firm value. That is, either way, V_1 and V_2 will decline. However, they may not decline proportionately or evenly over time. The imitation of the current technology may be easier, more probable, intense, or severe than the imitation of the future technology, or vice versa.

If the imitation risk is greater with the future technology, the decline in post-innovation profits and firm value will likely be greater than that of pre-innovation profits and firm value, associated with the current technology. As Figure 3.7 shows, the firm has an incentive to postpone technological development; that is, delay innovation, such that T^* increases. This allows the firm to exploit its current technology longer. The greater losses from the future technology will be discounted in present value. Too early a technological development results in a greater risk of the future new technology being imitated during the life of the firm. Hence, postponing innovation reduces the lifetime hazard of imitation of the future innovation.

On the other hand, if the imitation risk is greater with the current technology, it is in the interest of the firm to expedite innovation. Figure 3.8 shows the launch date of technological development to be sooner. The firm is induced to switch more quickly to the new technology. This way, the firm can avoid the greater expected losses associated with the current technology.

Therefore, the time-cost tradeoff that was analyzed vis-à-vis technological development needs to be modified in the presence of imitation risk. The analysis also suggests that stronger IP protection could either delay or expedite innovation, depending upon whether IP protection is more effective at alleviating current imitation risk or future imitation risk. If IP protection, on balance, causes the imitation risk to be lower for the existing technology relative to the future technology, it will lead to a delay in innovation, as the firm can enjoy greater returns from the current technology longer.

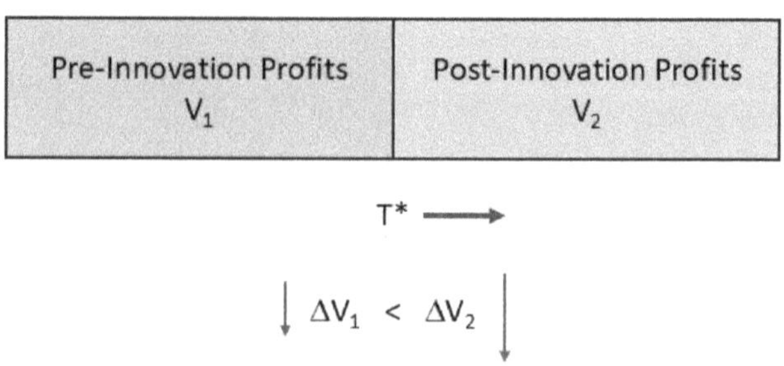

Figure 3.7. Imitation Risk Greater Post-Innovation

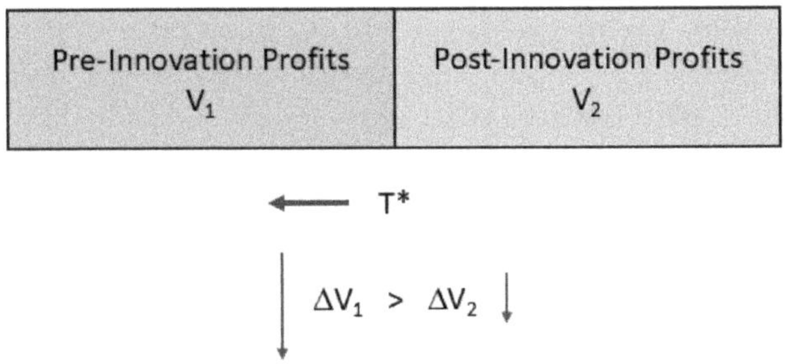

Figure 3.8. Imitation Risk Greater Pre-Innovation

But if future imitation risk is made to be lower, IP protection will expedite innovation so that the firm can capitalize on returns from the future technology.

3.4.3 *Market Failures and Innovation*

No guarantee should be expected that the free market rate of innovation is the socially optimal rate. Arguments exist as to why private R&D investment may fall short of, or exceed, the socially desired level. While R&D can result in a commercialized innovative output, the innovation contributes to the stock of knowledge which raises the productivity of future researchers. However, the innovator does not receive compensation for boosting the productivity of others. Consequently, the innovator does not take into account the benefits to future researchers when choosing its privately optimal R&D effort level.

This uncompensated benefit is referred to as a positive *externality*.[11] The R&D activity of one agent indirectly affects the production or innovation of another agent, other than by influencing the latter's input or output prices. External effects like this operate beyond price. The price or licensing fee of an innovative output does not reflect the full value of that

[11]The term "external" refers to the fact that third parties are affected by a transaction in which they were not directly involved. The externality can be either positive or negative. An example of a positive one is where party A purchases an air purifier from party B, but then party C, who lives with or near party A, benefits from the purer air. An example of a negative one is where party A purchases an electric generator from party B, but the noise bothers party C. In neither case is there any compensation. The party that benefits from an air purifier does not chip in for the cost of the product. The party that suffers from the noise does not collect damages or receive a free noise suppressor (or headphone). The price system fails in both cases because the price of neither the purifier nor the generator accounts for the external effects. However, if the price were adjusted sufficiently, say, lowered for the purifier and raised for the generator, or if adequate compensatory payments between parties A and C were allowed, the externality would vanish.

output. It does not capture the benefits of the knowledge created that spills over to other parties. So, when the innovator decides how much to invest in innovation, it only compares the price that it actually receives from a new innovation to the cost of producing it. If only it were fully rewarded with a higher price that appropriates the value to others, it would produce more. From that benchmark, it can be said that the private sector amount of innovation falls short of the socially optimal amount.

The above discussion needs to be modified when technological changes are manifested in the *quality* improvements of existing goods, for in this situation, *creative destruction* can arise whereby a newer quality version of a good displaces the existing quality version of the good. In this case, the private rate of innovation could be higher *or* lower than the socially optimal rate, depending on how radical the quality shift is. For either small quality jumps or large quality jumps, the private rate of innovation may be above the optimal; that is, the rate is too high. Society would be better off if innovation were to slow down. For intermediate jumps, the private rate of innovation may be below the optimal, or too slow, and society would gain if the pace of innovation could quicken.

The intuition is that innovations in product quality have two important impacts:

1. Innovations create benefits for consumers and knowledge externalities for future researchers.
2. Innovations destroy the profits of existing producers — a "business-stealing effect" — and even hurt households that own shares of existing firms and derive dividend income.

Moreover, innovators who enter the market and destroy existing profits anticipate that they may one day be displaced, but due to time discounting, they weigh their losses less than the profits of others that they destroy. It is because of the presence of these opposing effects that the private rate of innovation may be too high or too low from a social welfare point of view. If the quality improvement is incremental, the benefits to consumers and knowledge externalities are modest; for example, a new version of a smartphone with limited new features generates a marginal increase in consumer satisfaction and a marginal contribution to knowledge creation. In this situation, the business-stealing effect will likely dominate (i.e., outweigh the marginal benefits), and innovation would be deemed too rapid for society's benefit. Society could institute a tax on innovation to slow it down. Likewise, if the quality improvement is quite radical, whatever consumer benefits and knowledge externalities are generated, the big quality shift will leave behind a bigger creative destruction effect on existing products. Once again, the free market produces technological change that is too rapid for society.

It is when quality improvements are intermediate that the business-stealing effect will not outweigh the benefits to consumers and future researchers. In this case, the private sector rate of innovation may be too slow for society. A case for subsidizing private innovation may be made.

3.5 R&D Spillovers

The knowledge externalities that were discussed in the previous section can be called knowledge *spillovers*. The previous section discussed how R&D spillovers can occur between or among researchers, but they can also arise across firms, industries, and countries, to varying degrees. Firms that operate in the same or similar fields of technology, such as materials science, chemistry, or physics, are more likely to enjoy R&D spillovers from one another than from firms in distant fields or regions.

One firm's R&D can augment not only the knowledge production of the firm but also the knowledge production function of another firm, and the technological innovations of one firm can expand not only its production possibilities but also those of other firms. Those firms may be in other regions or countries. Figure 3.9 shows a few of the directions of uncompensated benefits that can flow across activities and organizations:

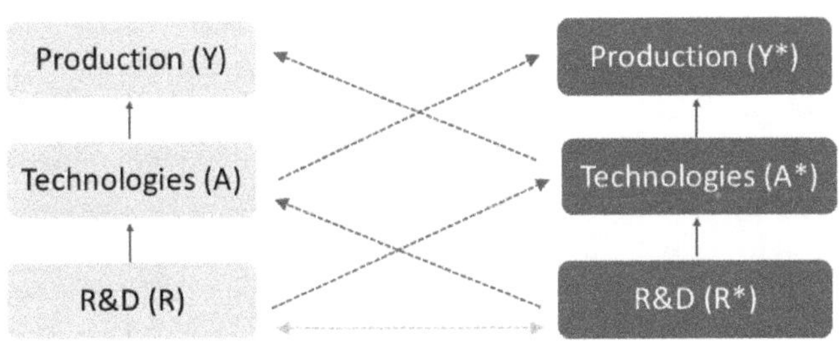

Figure 3.9. Nature of R&D Spillovers

Various sources of spillovers exist, from the dissemination of knowledge at conferences, trade shows, reports, journal articles and books, worker migration, job mobility, to corporate espionage and gossip among inter-company employees. And spillovers can also arise, where possible, via reverse engineering, whereby another entity can reconstruct a design or infer the solution to a technical problem by taking a product apart.

R&D spillovers can therefore affect the nature of competition and rivalry among firms, given that the benefits of R&D investments cannot always remain confined within the boundaries of a firm. Firms have opportunities to free ride off the R&D efforts of other innovators, as discussed in the next example.

3.5.1 *Spillover Example*

The following numerical example shows how R&D spillovers from one firm to another can raise the profits of the other.[12] In some cases, particularly in the case of free-riding, the other firm's profits can be greater than those of the firm conducting the R&D.

For ease of analysis, consider two firms in a market. The market demand is $P = 100 - Q$ where P denotes the price and Q the total quantity. The total quantity demanded by consumers is supplied by both firms; hence, $Q = q_1 + q_2$ where q_1, q_2 are the quantities supplied by firms 1 and 2, respectively. Let r_1, r_2 be the research *outcomes* of firms 1 and 2, respectively. In this example, the outcome will be a process innovation that helps lower the unit cost of production. But to attain the research outcome, it is costly. Let the cost of R&D for firm i be given by

$$C(r_i) = \frac{r_i^2}{2}$$

for $i = 1, 2$. The quadratic cost function indicates rising costs. Each additional unit of an R&D output raises the cost of conducting research at an increasing rate. The source of this is the diminishing returns to R&D expenditures. Each additional spending is less impactful than the previous spending at creating new knowledge, so a firm needs to do more spending to get the same impact. This assumption of rising costs may not always hold with technology like artificial intelligence (AI), but in this example, this particular feature of the R&D process puts some constraints on R&D capacity,

[12] The analysis here builds on d'Aspremont and Jacquemin (1988).

and thereby compels the firm to prioritize its best projects or experiments first.

Then, what does the outcome, r_i, achieve for the firm? In this case, it is assumed that it helps lower the costs of producing each unit of a good, as follows:

$$c_1 = 50 - r_1 - \gamma r_2 \tag{3.6}$$

$$c_2 = 50 - r_2 - \gamma r_1 \tag{3.7}$$

In the absence of R&D, each firm's unit cost of production is 50. Firm 1's R&D helps to lower its unit cost by r_1. Not only that, its R&D helps to lower the unit cost of production of firm 2 via a knowledge spillover effect, but not in an identical way. The γ parameter measures the degree of knowledge spillovers, where $0 \leq \gamma \leq 1$. When $\gamma = 0$, no spillovers occur, and when $\gamma = 1$, spillovers are perfect. For all values between those two extremes, knowledge imperfectly spills over between firms.

Thus far, the two firms are symmetric. They are the mirror image of each other in terms of the cost of production and revenue. For that reason, the focus here will be on solving firm 1's profit maximization problem and then inferring the solution for firm 2. Firm profits are given by the difference between revenue and costs:

$$\pi_1 = Pq_1 - c_1 q_1 \tag{3.8}$$

$$\pi_2 = Pq_2 - c_2 q_2 \tag{3.9}$$

Revenue is quantity sold times market price. Cost is quantity produced times the unit cost. There are two stages to the profit maximization process. The firm needs to decide on its R&D investment in the first stage. Then, in the second stage, it needs to decide how much output to produce. As was discussed earlier, R&D decisions are made in a forward-looking manner. Thus, start with the production decision, find the market outcomes, and then work backwards to determine the optimal R&D choice.

The optimal level of output to produce must satisfy this condition: $\frac{\Delta \pi_1}{\Delta q_1} = 0$. Imposing this condition and the analogous one for firm 2 (i.e., $\frac{\Delta \pi_2}{\Delta q_2} = 0$) delivers the following optimal levels of quantity produced:

$$q_1^* = \frac{100 - 2c_1 + c_2}{3} \tag{3.10}$$

$$q_2^* = \frac{100 - 2c_2 + c_1}{3} \tag{3.11}$$

Next, to see the effects of R&D spillovers, plug in Eqs. (3.6) and (3.7) into the optimal quantities (3.10) and (3.11):

$$q_1^* = \frac{50 + (2-\gamma)r_1 + (2\gamma - 1)r_2}{3} \tag{3.12}$$

$$q_2^* = \frac{50 + (2-\gamma)r_2 + (2\gamma - 1)r_1}{3} \tag{3.13}$$

Therefore, the outcomes of R&D have a cost reduction effect, allowing firms to produce more efficiently. For example, in equation (3.12), an increase in r_1 raises q_1. An increase in r_1 also increases the other firm's output, q_2, but only if $\gamma > \frac{1}{2}$ — see equation (3.13). The degree of spillovers must be high enough. Otherwise, if spillovers are small, firm 1's R&D boosts its own output in a way that it crowds out firm 2's market share of output.

Overall profits can be determined by substituting (3.12) and (3.13) into the expressions for firm profits (3.8) and (3.9) and then subtracting the cost of R&D development from each firm's respective profits:

$$\Pi_1^* = \frac{(50 + (2-\gamma)r_1 + (2\gamma - 1)r_2)^2}{9} - \frac{r_1^2}{2} \tag{3.14}$$

$$\Pi_2^* = \frac{(50 + (2-\gamma)r_2 + (2\gamma - 1)r_1)^2}{9} - \frac{r_2^2}{2} \tag{3.15}$$

Case 1: Non-cooperative Case

The net profit formulas in (3.14) and (3.15) can be used to trace the impact of spillover R&D under varying cases. Assume that firms do not coordinate their research investments even though they can affect each other's cost of production. Throughout, firm 1's research outcome is $r_1 = 10$. Firm 2 can also invest so that $r_2 = 10$ or conduct no research at all so that $r_2 = 0$. Two extreme values of the spillover parameter are examined: either perfect spillovers ($\gamma = 1$) or no spillovers.

- Version 1 ($\gamma = 0$, $r_2 = 0$): firm 1's net profits are then given by $\Pi_1 = \frac{(50+2r_1+0)^2}{9} - \frac{10^2}{2} = 494$. Meanwhile, firm 2's net profits are $\Pi_2 = \frac{(50+0-r_1)^2}{9} - 0 = 178$.
- Version 2 ($\gamma = 0$, $r_2 = 10$): both firm 1 and firm 2 earn net profits of 350.
- Version 3 ($\gamma = 1$, $r_2 = 0$): firm 1's net profits are 350 and firm 2's are 400.
- Version 2 ($\gamma = 1$, $r_2 = 10$): both firm 1 and firm 2 earn net profits of 494.

Table 3.1. Summary of Payoffs: Non-cooperative Case

Throughout $r_1 = 10$

		$r_2 = 0$	$r_2 = 10$
Degree of	$\gamma = 0$	$\Pi_1 = 494,\ \Pi_2 = 178$	$\Pi_1 = 350,\ \Pi_2 = 350$
Spillover	$\gamma = 1$	$\Pi_1 = 350,\ \Pi_2 = 400$	$\Pi_1 = 494,\ \Pi_2 = 494$

Table 3.1 summarizes the results.

The interesting case is version 3, where firm 2 is a free-rider. Its net profits are higher than firm 1's because firm 2 gets to enjoy the exact same R&D outcome but without incurring the development cost. In fact, under version 3, firm 1's net profits are lower than under version 1 where no spillovers occur. This is because the spillovers from firm 1 to firm 2 help boost the latter's competitiveness in the market and crowd out firm 1's market share.

Of course, firm 2 could do better by doing some of its own R&D. That is shown in version 4, where both firms are better off, as they each earn net profits of 494. This indicates that complete free-riding does not pay off. And the fact that both firms could be mutually better off suggests that R&D cooperation would be better. This is the next case.

Case 2: Cooperative Case

The optimal decision of both firms is to choose levels of r_1 and r_2 to maximize the joint profits:

$$\Pi = \Pi_1 + \Pi_2 \tag{3.16}$$

Substituting (3.14) and (3.15) into (3.16) and applying the same profit-maximization criteria yields[13]

$$r_1^* = r_2^* = \frac{50(1+\gamma)}{4.5 - (1+\gamma)^2}$$

Thus, in a world of no spillovers ($\gamma = 0$), the optimal research outcomes are $r_1^* = r_2^* = 14.3$, which yield net profits of 357 for each firm, or joint net profits of 714. In a world of perfect spillovers ($\gamma = 1$), the optimal research outcomes are $r_1^* = r_2^* = 200$ and joint net profits would be 5,000, to be split evenly between the two firms. Thus, going from no spillovers to

[13]The criteria are to find those levels of r_1 and r_2 such that $\frac{\partial \Pi}{\partial r_1} = 0$ and $\frac{\partial \Pi}{\partial r_2} = 0$.

perfect knowledge spillovers results in more than a fourteen-fold increase in R&D output and a seven-fold increase in net firm profits.

3.5.2 *Public Sector R&D*

The attention thus far has been on private sector R&D. But the government sector can also perform and fund research, as was discussed in Chapter 2. Government R&D can indeed be a source of knowledge spillovers for the private sector (and other sectors, such as academia and non-profit institutions) by contributing to a pool of public knowledge from which researchers can freely draw. Government R&D can also be a direct input into private sector research if the government provides resources for private R&D. To capture the influence of knowledge spillovers and funding from the public sector to private sector technological development, the knowledge production function (3.3) can be modified as

$$A = A(R, R^g) \tag{3.17}$$

where R^g denotes the stock of government R&D. As discussed in Chapter 2, government R&D tends to be functionally different from private sector R&D. It is more basic R&D and less commercially applicable, such as defense or space technology. The public sector, in general, invests in economic activities that the private sector has limited incentives to perform. The important aspect is that, though the outputs or objectives of government R&D tend to be different from those of the private sector, the knowledge that is created may be utilized or adapted in company research. The private sector may develop applications of fundamental public sector research.[14]

Now the R&D conducted in the public sector should also be subjected to a cost-benefit test. The benefits of government R&D to private sector economic growth and social well-being ought to be balanced against the costs. For example, the cost of funding it, whether by debt or tax-financing, may produce distortionary impacts on private savings and investments or work effort. Public sector research may directly crowd out private via the diversion of human capital from the private sector to the public. Human capital is also employed in two other sectors: academia and the non-profit sector. An expansion in R^g may lead to the withdrawal of researchers,

[14]Examples of technological knowledge developed in government research labs that influenced industrial R&D include the science of particle accelerators, satellites, semiconductors, lithography, biotechnologies, among others.

creators, scientists, and engineers from those other sectors. Theoretically, there should be some optimal level of government R&D that balances the marginal costs against the marginal benefits. Another way to put it is that the relationship between economic growth (ultimately) and the rate of government R&D investment may be nonlinear, positive up to a critical point and negative thereafter.

Another aspect is that government R&D spillovers may be international, spreading across the globe but not proportionally across foreign countries. In other words, the degree of international R&D spillovers, γ, may vary by trading partner, by geographical proximity of the foreign country to the domestic, or by the similarity in industrial and technological structure. Nevertheless, like our numerical example showed, government R&D has the potential to benefit both domestic research activities and foreign. Due to international spillovers, foreign governments may have an incentive to free ride on the R&D of other countries, but not as completely as to ignore the benefits of conducting some of their own R&D on their national productivity growth. This does suggest that the scale of government R&D can be potentially lower when the nation can enjoy knowledge spillovers from abroad; specifically, if $\frac{\hat{R^g}}{Y}$ is the optimal government R&D to GDP ratio that maximizes national social welfare, then to the extent that R&D spillovers flow into the country, R^g need not be as high. The government need not pursue the same level of R&D spending. International knowledge spillovers allow the size of the government research sector across countries to be smaller than they otherwise would be, thus saving their taxpayers some resources and tax burdens.

Figure 3.10 captures, first, the nonlinear relationship between economic growth and the domestic rate of government research, measured as the ratio of government R&D to GDP. Second, it shows how that relationship, the curve, shifts up or down as the foreign rate of government research varies. (This too is measured as the ratio of foreign government R&D to foreign GDP.)

In Figure 3.10, the various optimal domestic government R&D to GDP ratios are ordered as follows: $g_1 < g_2 < g_3$, while the foreign government R&D to GDP ratios are ordered as $h_1 < h_2 < h_3$. Suppose the foreign government chooses h_1. The domestic government's optimal choice is g_3. Due to global knowledge spillovers, if the foreign government increases its R&D investment rate to h_2 and then to h_3, the domestic government reacts and lowers its own investment rate to g_2 and then to g_1. This is because, again, the foreign R&D spillovers allow the domestic government to economize

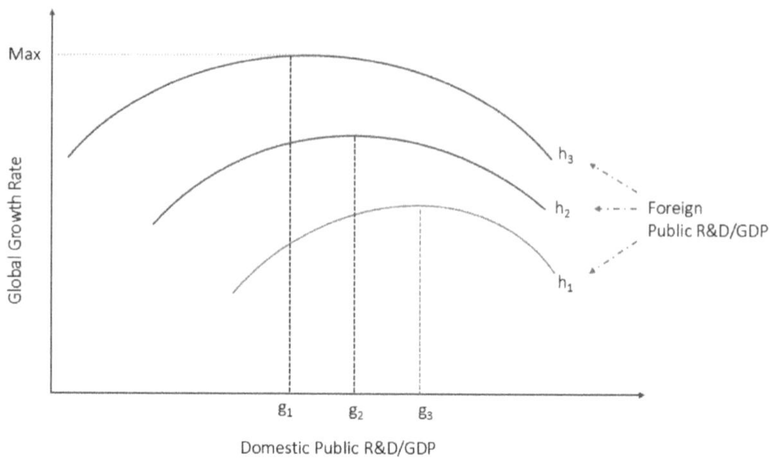

Figure 3.10. Global Public R&D and World Balanced Growth

on resources. But there is a limit. Even if the foreign government continues to expand its R&D, it is not in the interest of the domestic government to further contract its own R&D because it forgoes the national benefits of conducting its own research. The foreign government's R&D might not be a perfect substitute for its own R&D. The needs and priorities of domestic and foreign residents may differ regarding health, technology, climate, and so forth. Moreover, the degree of international spillovers is likely to be imperfect ($\gamma < 1$).

Assume in Figure 3.10 that the combination (g_1, h_3) maximizes the world's economic growth rate. Further decreases in g_1 will shift the curve back down (not shown in the figure to avoid clutter). The intuition as to why that would happen is that the foreign country benefits from spillovers from domestic R&D. Reducing domestic government R&D will then reduce knowledge spillovers to foreign R&D and thereby reduce foreign R&D. That, in turn, will mean lower spillovers from foreign research to domestic research. Hence, a cycle of cutbacks in public sector R&D is inefficient and self-defeating. So, again, from a global perspective, there is an optimal overall rate of government R&D to GDP in each country, deviations from which will lower the world balanced growth rate. Achieving these rates will require international policy coordination, since decentralized R&D decisions across countries will not likely attain that desired optimum.[15]

[15] A detailed analysis can be found in Park (1998).

3.5.3 *Evidence on International R&D Spillovers*

Do R&D expenditures in one country affect innovation and productivity in other countries, above and beyond the price channel? For the contribution to count as a spillover, it must be uncompensated. The good or service was not exported nor was it transferred abroad via market-mediated mechanisms with remuneration.

The typical empirical framework for estimating spillovers is to quantify the linkages in Figure 3.9. Moreover, the research investigation also involves determining the vehicle for spillovers. How does knowledge spread from a firm in one country to a firm in another? This is challenging. It is difficult to trace all the human touch points where knowledge is communicated at trade shows or conferences, or revealed through documents such as blueprints, publications, or preliminary drafts thereof, or obtained through reverse engineering a product or its earlier prototype. Research has had to make assumptions about the manner in which opportunities for knowledge spillovers arise.

Coe and Helpman (1995) posited that R&D spillovers are conveyed via trade flows and tested whether spillovers of foreign R&D can affect domestic productivity. Specifically, the outcome variable of interest is *total factor productivity (TFP)*, which differs from labor productivity (namely, output per worker), in that output is divided by a weighted average of capital and labor. This helps to measure technical efficiency, A. As an example of how to isolate that, see equations (3.1) and (3.2) from earlier.[16] The relationship to estimate is

$$\mathrm{TFP}_{it} = \mathrm{TFP}(R_{it}, R^*_{it})$$

where R denotes domestic R&D stock and R^* foreign R&D stock. Subscript i indexes country and t time. The foreign stock of R&D is, from the domestic country's point of view, an import share weighted average of the domestic R&D stocks of the trading partners:

$$R^*_{it} = \sum_{j=1}^{n} \mu_{ijt} R_{jt}$$

where j indexes the trading partners (of which there n countries) and μ_{ijt} is the bilateral import share between the domestic country i and the foreign country j; for example, $\mu_{ijt} = 0.09$ if country j accounts for 9% of imports of country i at time t.

[16] From (3.1), $A = \frac{Y}{f(K,L)}$, where f is some aggregation of capital and labor.

Using a sample of 22 countries over the period 1971–1990, Coe and Helpman (1995) find that both domestic and foreign R&D stock have a statistically significant positive impact on a country's total factor productivity. Among other interesting results, the study finds that a 1% increase in the stock of R&D in the U.S. can raise the TFP of other countries by 0.04%, and a 1% increase in the stock of R&D in Japan can raise other countries' TFP by 0.01%.

However, Keller (1998) questioned the robustness of the results in Coe and Helpman (1995). Recall that the latter assumed that international spillovers were facilitated by international trade — from more business contacts and exposure to foreign ideas and practices. Keller (1998) created randomly matched trading partners in that the study replaced actual bilateral trade data with randomly generated trade relationships. Surprisingly, the study found that the randomly assigned trade share also showed that spillovers affected TFP. Indeed, the random assignments produced stronger spillover R&D effects than those based on actual bilateral trade data. This casts doubt on whether trade is the key vehicle for transmitting knowledge spillovers. Some other channels must be at play; for example, the activities of multinational corporations and their affiliates and subsidiaries around the world, reverse engineering, or informal international knowledge flows, aided by labor mobility, conferences, workshops, academic seminars, social networks, open source communities, online forums, and international exhibitions.

Geography also matters. Keller (2002) finds that geographic distance conditions the degree of spillovers. Using a sample of 14 countries and 12 manufacturing industries over the period of 1970–1995, the study focuses on the source of foreign R&D spillovers from the G5 countries: U.S., U.K., Germany, France, and Japan, which account for the bulk of the R&D in the sample. A similar model is estimated (omitting country, industry, and time subscripts for convenience):

$$\hat{\text{TFP}} = \text{TFP}(R, R^{G5})$$

where $\hat{\text{TFP}}$ is relative total factor productivity,[17] and R denotes domestic R&D and R^{G5} a weighted sum of R&D from the G5 countries:

$$R^{G5} = \sum_{j=1}^{5} \omega_j R_j$$

[17]That is, where capital and labor are relative to the industry mean across countries.

where ω is a weight that is a function of the geographic distance of a G5 country to the domestic country — from capital city to capital city — measured in kilometers.

The main finding in Keller (2002) is that knowledge spillovers are strongly localized. Domestic R&D has a quantitatively larger impact on domestic TFP (raising it by 7.8%). Foreign (G5) R&D is 84% of the magnitude of domestic research and development if the domestic country is nearby. This contribution of foreign R&D is halved upon a distance of more than 160 kilometers and absent if the distance is more than 648 kilometers. However, in the second half of the sample period, the role of distance diminishes somewhat. Some R&D spillovers can travel almost 2,000 kilometers away. This could be due to increased globalization over time.

The empirical studies reviewed thus far all pertain to spillovers from private R&D. Park (1995) introduces government R&D to the analysis and quantifies how public and private research can generate cross-national spillovers. In this study, the degree of international R&D spillovers depends upon the technological similarity between countries. The more alike they are technologically, the more they will find the R&D of each other relevant and the more they will benefit from knowledge spillovers. The technological similarity between any two countries is measured by a comparison of their industrial composition of GDP (or value added). Specifically, the degree of spillover is constructed as follows. Let $Y = (Y_1, Y_2, \ldots, Y_J)$ and $Y^* = (Y_1^*, Y_2^*, \ldots, Y_J^*)$ be the percentage composition of GDP by industry in the home and foreign country, respectively, where J is the number of industries. For example, Y_2 or Y_2^* could be the share of the chemical industry in their country's overall production. All the shares in each country add up to 100%. An index, θ, can be constructed that measures the degree of overlap between the vectors Y and Y^*, such that θ varies from zero to one. If it is one, the two countries are perfectly similar technologically; if zero, they are completely dissimilar.[18] The foreign stock of R&D is then given by

$$R^* = \sum_{j=1}^{n} \theta_j R_j$$

where R_j's are the stocks of R&D in countries $j = 1, \ldots, n$, each of which may spill into the domestic economy imperfectly if $0 < \theta_j < 1$.

[18] Mathematically, θ is based on the angle between vectors Y and Y^*: cosine $\Theta = \frac{Y \cdot Y^*}{\|Y\| \|Y^*\|}$ where $\cdot$ denotes dot product and $\|.\|$ is the distance of a vector from the origin. The weight assigned by the domestic country to country j's research is $\theta_j = \cos(\Theta)$.

Park (1995) finds that private sector research is a more important determinant of private sector productivity growth than is government research. But government research does generate international spillovers into research so that government research can contribute to productivity growth indirectly by stimulating private R&D capital accumulation. A key reason why private research can affect productivity growth directly while government research affects it indirectly by influencing private R&D is that government R&D is largely basic research, making it quite conducive to research spillovers, while private sector R&D is largely applied and developmental, making it more connected to private sector production activities. Moreover, research investments add to the productive stock of R&D with a lag, and the lag for fundamental research is longer than that for applied and developmental research. The policy implications of this study are that international economic policy coordination in science and technology is worth pursuing as national R&D activities create positive global externalities. Policies such as subsidies could be coordinated to optimize global R&D efficiency, as some private firms may underinvest in R&D due to the inability to fully appropriate the benefits of their research.

International knowledge spillovers should also help developing economies catch up to the rest of the world, as long as companies in the developing world undertake some research, for otherwise they would not be able to enjoy the spillovers into research or augment local, indigenous knowledge with foreign knowledge.[19] Furthermore, countries with a weak R&D base may not have the absorptive capacities to utilize the foreign knowledge spillovers.[20] Firms need to conduct their own R&D in order to avail themselves of external knowledge, or that knowledge will be abstract or serve no purpose.

Coe *et al.* (2009) examine how institutions can condition the degree of international knowledge spillovers. For example, this study finds that stronger patent protection is associated with larger international knowledge spillovers. This is interesting because it shows that IP does not necessarily block the leakage of knowledge. IP protection could stimulate domestic R&D, so that with a larger volume of private sector research conducted,

[19]Implicit in the index of technological similarity is that foreign knowledge has to have relevance for domestic research; for example, physics research conducted abroad may not be as fully helpful if no physics research is undertaken locally. See also Park and Brat (1996).

[20]See Aghion and Jaravel (2015) and Cincera and van Pottelsberghe (2001).

more knowledge is created for cross-border spillovers. Keller (2022) highlights the expanded role of inward and outward foreign direct investment (FDI) in facilitating knowledge flows worldwide and the importance of absorptive capacity in enabling local firms to benefit from the positive externalities generated by foreign-owned companies. Spillovers from abroad enable local agents to access new business-relevant knowledge. However, to implement this knowledge, the local agents will need to undertake some additional investment and effort — namely, to build the capacity (skill set) to absorb knowledge. The net gain from knowledge spillovers comes after deducting the costs of that investment and effort.

Chapter 4

Economic Theories of IPR

4.1 Introduction

This chapter discusses the economic rationale for intellectual property rights (IPRs) and examines their optimal design. It begins by framing the underlying problem: knowledge is a public good — non-rivalrous and non-excludable — which means that, in the absence of legal protection, private markets will underinvest in innovation. The public-good nature of knowledge explains why exclusivity is granted through IPRs, particularly patents, trademarks, and copyrights. These rights serve as tools to correct market failures and promote innovation, creativity, and commercialization. The exclusive rights are usually for a temporary period, after which the work falls into the public domain. Allowing rights to expire and works to enter the public domain is one way to strike a balance between incentivizing innovation and ensuring its broad diffusion.

The chapter uses analogies (recipes, niches) to convey how IPRs help solve appropriation problems and incentivize investment in R&D, quality, and marketing. It also introduces some core economic concepts, ranging from consumer surplus to monopoly pricing and marginal revenue, so as to show the trade-offs inherent in IPR regimes. Stronger protection can create dynamic gains by stimulating innovation, but can also entail static losses through reduced output and higher prices. This trade-off is at the core of the IPR debate.

To explore when and how IPRs are effective, the chapter develops a simple framework linking R&D costs, imitation lags, and the duration of protection. It presents stylized cases where commercialization may or may not occur depending on whether firms can break even before imitation sets in or before their legal protection expires.

Next, the chapter introduces the Schumpeter versus Arrow debate: do monopolies or competitive markets better spur process innovations? Using numerical examples, the chapter shows that while monopolists can reap higher profits from innovation, competitive firms may have stronger incentives because they can license their innovation broadly and capture market-wide returns. A key lesson is that IPRs should be designed with attention to industrial structure.

The chapter then introduces the notion of optimal IPRs, recognizing that stronger rights can stimulate or stifle innovation depending on the level of existing protection. This leads to the inverted-U relationship between innovation and IPR strength. Both the duration and breadth of rights affect innovation incentives, often in nonlinear ways.

A further dimension is added with the measurement of patent value and quality. Merely counting patents is misleading. Metrics like forward citations, family size (weighted by GDP), renewal rates, and stock market reactions offer more robust indicators. The chapter draws from recent empirical research to show how patents vary widely in value and how quality matters for legal robustness and economic performance.

Finally, the appendix to the chapter discusses prize systems as an alternative or complement to patents, comparing their advantages and limitations.

4.2 Rationale for IPR

Markets for technologies, in the absence of IP protection, experience market failures. They typically fail to provide knowledge goods efficiently. Knowledge has the characteristics of a public good — a good that is neither excludable nor rivalrous. Non-excludability means it is difficult to prevent someone who does not pay from consuming the good. Non-rivalry means that one person's consumption does not detract from another person's ability to consume the same good.

A simple example is the light in a typical classroom. It is hard to exclude any one person or group from enjoying the light. Everyone in the room shares the same amount of light, regardless of how many people leave or enter. These public good characteristics make it challenging to charge a fee for lighting. Anyone can free ride on the payment of others. Then, if nobody pays for the lighting, it will not be provided; a market will not arise.

Also, if there is lighting, the marginal (i.e., extra) cost of allowing one more person to benefit is zero. So why charge a fee? Efficiency dictates that prices should reflect marginal cost, but here the marginal cost is zero! If no fees are charged, how can lighting be provided by the private market — namely, to cover the cost of lighting?

Like light, knowledge is a public good. Take a cooking recipe, as shown in Figure 4.1. It contains instructions for making a food item. Without the recipe, it would take a bit of trial and error to replicate the item.

This recipe is non-excludable and non-rivalrous. It was posted on the internet, where anyone can freely download it, and one person's download does not diminish anyone else's ability to download and use the recipe.[1]

Instructions range from the simple (a cupcake recipe) to the more sophisticated (a formula for making a pharmaceutical drug, as in Figure 4.2).[2]

Figure 4.1. Public Good Example: Recipe

[1]https://thepurpledoorkitchen.blogspot.com/2013/01/nutella-cupcakes-this-seasons-flu-remedy.html.

[2]https://en.wikipedia.org/wiki/Diazepam.

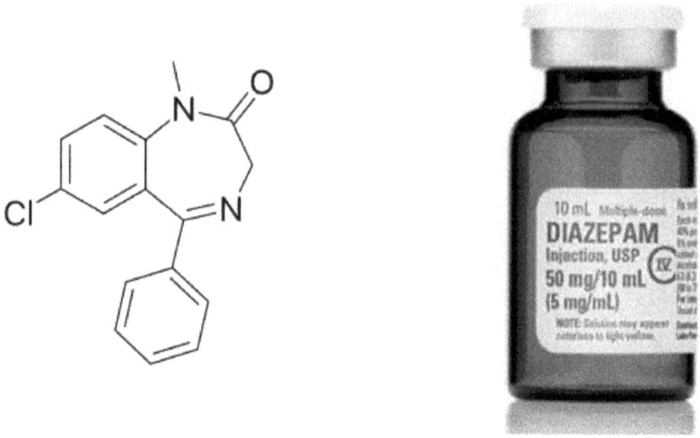

Figure 4.2. "Recipe" for Pharmaceutical Drug

Indeed, technology is like a "recipe" in that, to replicate it, one needs knowledge of how to mix the ingredients and how to apply established principles and techniques to achieve the intended result. Romer (1990) also employs the analogy of "instructions" in his theory of economic growth. In this view, technological change represents improvements in the instructions for combining raw materials to produce innovative goods. While the raw materials themselves have remained unchanged since prehistory, scientific progress has yielded increasingly sophisticated instructions for their use. Furthermore

> "... instructions for working with raw materials are inherently different from other economic goods. Once the cost of creating a new set of instructions has been incurred, the instructions can be used over and over again at no additional cost. Developing new and better instructions is equivalent to incurring a fixed cost. This property is taken to be the defining characteristic of technology" (p. S72).

Romer (1990) draws an important distinction between knowledge itself and the innovative outputs derived from that knowledge. As discussed in earlier chapters, IPRs protect the innovative outputs while leaving the underlying knowledge in the public domain. Technological creation and knowledge accumulation occur in tandem, producing, for example, instructions for manufacturing new and improved capital goods. While such goods can be made excludable through IP institutions, the underlying instructions remain non-excludable. They generate knowledge spillovers that benefit present and future researchers.

4.2.1 *Illustrative Example: Drug Development*

The following is a canonical example illustrating the public good aspects of knowledge and the rationale for IPRs. Suppose there is a disorder that is treatable by a drug. Assume the following conditions:

- Upfront R&D cost = \$100 million
- Manufacturing cost per unit (C) = \$10/pill
- Population affected = 20 million
- Need price $P > C$ for the innovator to recoup the upfront R&D cost

It costs a hundred million dollars to develop the drug (inclusive of clinical trials, testing, and experimentation). That is the *fixed* cost. Once the drug is developed, it costs a constant ten dollars per pill to manufacture it. That is the *variable* cost. The total variable cost depends on how many pills are made. Demand comes from twenty million people. For simplicity, assume that everyone needs one pill to be cured.

What price should the pharmaceutical firm charge to break even? The answer is \$15 per pill. At that price, the firm's per-unit profit is \$5, since $P - C = \$15 - \$10 = \$5$. With twenty million pills sold, the firm would earn total profits of \$100 million, which exactly covers the upfront, fixed cost of drug development.

The problem is that the R&D is incurred before commercialization. Once a technological breakthrough has occurred, imitators can make copies of the drug because knowledge is a public good. Before the research and invention, few might have known the cure for the disorder. But once a cure is discovered and the "recipe" revealed, knowledge becomes non-rival and non-excludable. Free-riders can come along — having done none of the R&D — and manufacture and market the pill. The free-rider only incurs the variable cost of ten dollars per pill. If the free-rider charged just one dollar less than the original innovator, it would earn a profit of \$4 per pill. But if the original innovator matched that lower price — or tried to — it would not be able to recoup its \$100 million in development costs. It would fall \$20 million short by charging a dollar less to each of the twenty million consumers.

The story does not end there. Another free-rider or producer can come along and charge an even lower price than \$14. In fact, with free entry, many competitors will outbid one another for the consumers' business, and the price of the pill will be driven down to marginal cost — namely, \$10 per pill. Thus, in a competitive equilibrium, firms make zero economic profits, as $P = C$. The original innovator, however, is out one hundred million dollars. But again, this is not the full story. In anticipation of this outcome, the original innovator would not have invested in the drug in the first place, and there would not be a pill to purchase or imitate.

This is the logic of IP protection — particularly patent protection (with the copyright case being similar) — to avert a market failure in which the demand for a good (i.e., treatment for a medical disorder) exists, but no supply emerges. By granting the innovator (or creator) a period of market exclusivity, society protects the innovator from immediate competition and allows it to charge a price above the marginal cost of production, thereby earning positive economic profits to help recoup its development costs. After the IP right expires, the invention enters the public domain, and the market can then become (more) competitive.

IP protection must also be credible. After an invention occurs, society has an incentive not to honor the IP. In this illustrative example, the question arises: why charge \$15 for a pill when the marginal cost is only \$10? An opportunistic government could promise the innovator that it will be allowed to charge \$15 after the invention, but then, ex post (after the invention), it could renege on that promise and make the drug available to society for \$10 per pill — or at least fail to rigorously enforce IP rights in the face of imitators.

This temptation for a government not to carry out its policy commitment is known as the time inconsistency problem. It typically arises in dynamic or multi-period settings, when decisions for the future are based on promises or announcements made in the current period. Once the future arrives, bygones are bygones: after one player has already made its decision (e.g., invent a drug) and cannot undo it, the other player may take advantage and deviate from its earlier announcement (e.g., make the drug available at cost).

In a repeated game situation, the credibility of the IP system can be sustained over time if governments remain committed to protection and enforcement and fulfill the expectations of innovators. However, under unstable political regimes or in environments of regulatory uncertainty, assurances of IP might be less credible and effective in influencing innovation and commercialization.

4.2.2 *The Case of Trademarks*

Trademark protection provides firms with incentives to invest in promotion and product quality. The owner of a trademark takes better care if it owns the mark as property. For example, if anyone could use the McDonald's arches, the company would have little incentive to invest in its fries and hamburgers or to advertise them, because people would not link those menu items to the McDonald's name and symbol. Worse yet, if another fast food restaurant served poor-quality food under the same symbol, consumers might mistakenly attribute that to the original McDonald's. This is the logic behind granting exclusive rights to use a distinct name and mark.

Brands allow firms to gain some market power and charge a price above marginal cost, even when there are no significant taste or style differences. Even when product differentiation is real, the price markup may exceed what the quality or cost difference would justify, simply due to the consumer's preference for the branded name. For example, Rolex watches or Bentley cars are priced at a premium above their competitors, even though the differences in cost and quality may not be as great. That is, $P \gg MC$ because the branded name carries recognition and status.

Are consumers' preferences for brand names rational? On the one hand, such preferences enable firms to exercise market power over their customers. On the other hand, brands convey information about a firm's reputation and the expected quality of its products. For instance, a business traveler in Dubai — someone who may never return there — might choose a brand-name hotel such as the Ritz-Carlton, knowing that the company has a reputation to protect. Even if the guest never visits Dubai again, they may stay at a Ritz property in other cities around the world. By contrast, a lesser-known hotel, lacking a recognizable brand, may have weaker incentives to maintain consistently high service standards. In this way, consumers obtain valuable signals about product quality from brand-name firms.

4.2.3 *Qualifications*

Intellectual property is a complex subject. The following points provide some important qualifications to what IPRs are. Some of these have been emphasized earlier, and some will be revisited later.

1. The term *monopoly* appears frequently in the IP and economics literature, but it is typically used to describe the pricing *behavior* of an IP holder. IP rights such as patents and copyrights do not create monopolies

in the traditional sense of a single firm dominating an entire industry. Rather, it is more accurate to say that IP rights grant the holder the right to exclude others from commercially using the protected idea, creation, or mark. They do not prevent other firms from entering the industry itself.

Often, the IP right pertains to a specific technological product or variety, not to an entire class of products or technologies. Rivals can enter and offer alternative product varieties. For example, in the mobile phone industry, Samsung, AT&T, MetroPCS, Sprint, T-Mobile USA, and Verizon Wireless each offer their own types of smartphones. Because of this variety competition, it may be more accurate to describe IP-intensive industries as *monopolistically competitive*, a structure that captures industries characterized by product differentiation.

Monopolistic competition refers to a single industry within which differentiated products exist. See Figure 4.3, where the larger circle represents the industry as a whole (e.g., ice cream). The smaller circles represent the market shares of different varieties (chocolate, pistachio, or some blended flavors). Market sizes vary, as some varieties are more popular than others. Competition exists within the industry, but it is

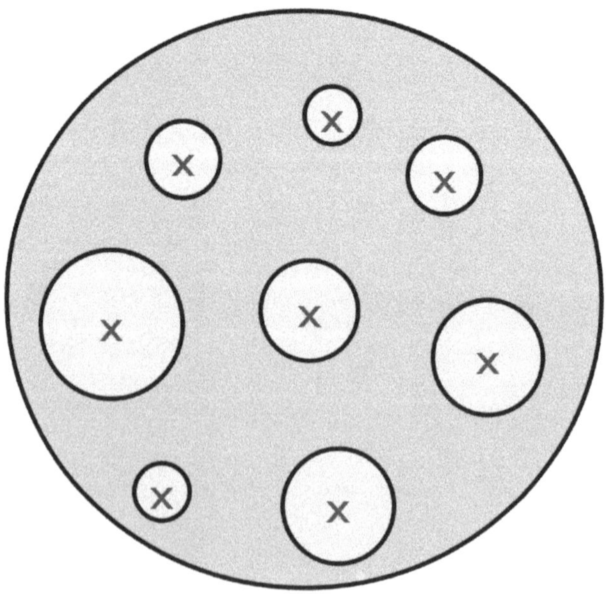

Figure 4.3. Idea Behind Monopolistic Competition

imperfect because the varieties are not perfectly substitutable for each other in consumption.

Each firm has a "niche" — selling a particular variety of ice cream. Within that product space, the firm behaves like a monopolist, exercising market power due to consumers' preference for its variety. But the varieties still compete with one another. While they are not perfect substitutes, if the price of one rises sufficiently, consumers may switch (e.g., from strawberry to cherry flavor).

2. Just because inventors have recouped their upfront R&D costs in their own domestic markets does not necessarily mean they no longer need exclusive IP protection in foreign markets. It is tempting to argue that output should be competitively supplied abroad — especially in less developed countries — and even more so if the innovator has already earned sufficiently large profits to recover development costs.[3]

   This creates a kind of time-inconsistency problem. Some inventors engage in innovation with the expectation of selling commercially in global markets. After the fact — once the invention is made and R&D costs are recouped — should they then be required to sell their products at marginal cost?

   First, inventors may seek access to global markets precisely because their inventions require a large customer base to recover high development costs. Second, knowing that they can serve a broader market influences the scale of their research projects. If it is only possible to recoup R&D costs from smaller domestic markets, inventors may limit the scope of their investment (i.e., choose less ambitious research projects). This could result in a loss to global welfare, as potentially valuable technologies might never be developed — technologies that could have brought benefits across many national economies.

3. IPRs are by no means the only way that innovators or creators can appropriate the returns to their innovation or recoup their development costs. They can also rely on:

   - **First-mover Advantages:** A firm can enter the market and commercialize its product immediately, before imitators have a chance to make copies. Obtaining an IP right takes time (search and examination) and incurs costs (filing fees, attorney fees). In some cases,

[3]Of course, this wades into a heated debate: What counts as "sufficient" profits? When is enough "enough"? IP holders may be incentivized to underreport or conceal profits for fear of losing their rights. As discussed in Chapter 8, the IP holder can also resort to differential pricing between developed and less developed countries.

relying on first-mover advantages may be more expedient, especially when combined with strategic advertising and publicity.[4]

- **Brand Loyalty:** A firm can gain market power through brand recognition, which imitators and knock-offs struggle to replicate. With careful monitoring for pirated versions and counterfeits, a firm can protect its branded goods from substitutes and avoid the costs and delays involved in securing formal IP rights.
- **High Set-up Costs:** In industries where production is highly capital-intensive, the equipment and infrastructure required to manufacture a product can serve as a natural barrier to entry. Imitators would need to invest in the same costly infrastructure to compete, which may deter them from attempting to do so.[5] Industries with high set-up costs, therefore, tend to be less reliant on formal IP protection.

Furthermore, some innovators and creators may not be primarily driven by financial rewards. They may be motivated by non-monetary compensation mechanisms, such as peer recognition, public praise, or professional networking. Others may possess complementary assets whose value rises as more users adopt their work; for example, a software company may distribute its program for free but charge for consulting services or training sessions.[6]

It is not surprising to see such individuals forgo or forfeit formal IPRs and engage in collaborative work. They have other ways to be rewarded for their innovations and creativity. Later chapters will explore their roles in greater depth.

4.3 Conceptual Tools

This section presents some basic tools used in the economic analysis of intellectual property. Two market structures will be studied: a competitive economy and a monopoly. Both represent extreme cases.

[4]Blockbuster films can generate substantial revenue in the first few months of release through aggressive marketing and word-of-mouth.

[5]Examples include aircraft manufacturing plants, telecommunications satellites, or multilingual AI foundation models.

[6]The popularity of a song may boost attendance at live performances by the artist or increase sales of paraphernalia, such as T-shirts or jewelry.

In a competitive industry, there are many (identical) firms producing the same homogeneous good. The industry allows for free entry and exit — there are no barriers to firms entering or shutting down. In equilibrium, price (P) equals the marginal cost (C) of producing the good. This convergence of P and C arises from intense competitive pressure. Any firm charging a price above C will be undercut by others; any firm charging below C will incur losses. With so much competition, firms treat P as given. They cannot influence it. The price of a good is ultimately determined by market demand and market supply.

In this example, assume that the average cost of production is constantly equal to C; that is, the cost per unit does not vary with the volume of output produced.[7] In this case, average cost (i.e., total cost divided by output) equals marginal cost (i.e., the cost of producing one additional unit).

Figure 4.4 shows the market demand curve.[8]

The demand curve shows the quantity demanded at different price levels. It is downward sloping for intuitive reasons. A lower price makes the good

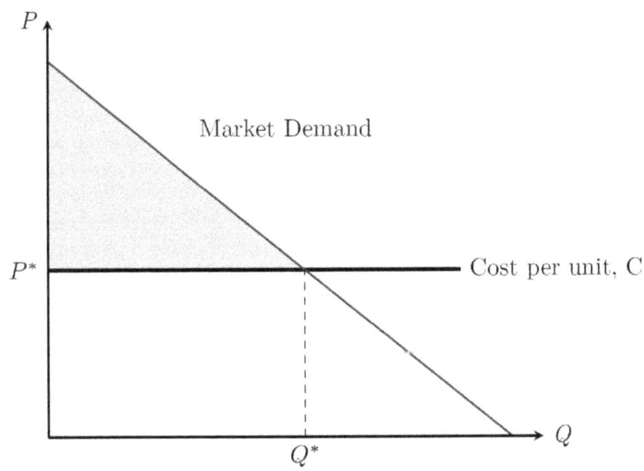

Figure 4.4. Market Demand and Consumer Surplus

[7]This assumption is not always realistic. At low output levels, a firm's average costs may decline as it gains production experience and spreads fixed costs — such as plant set-up costs or operating licenses — over more units. At higher volumes, however, firms may encounter diminishing returns to inputs due to longer working hours or resource constraints. In this more general case, the average cost curve is U-shaped with respect to output, rather than flat at C.

[8]This is derived by horizontally summing the individual demand curves of all consumers.

more attractive. Consumers are likely to switch from substitute goods to this good. Even holding income constant, a lower price increases the real value of income, enabling consumers to purchase more of the good.[9]

In a competitive market, the equilibrium price is $P^* = C$, and the equilibrium quantity is Q^*, which producers collectively supply. At this price, the market clears because supply equals demand. The consumer side of the market demands Q^* when $P = P^*$, and the producer side is willing to supply that quantity at the same price.

One way to measure the welfare gains to consumers is through *Consumer Surplus*, or CS for short. Pick any quantity between zero and Q^* in Figure 4.4, and imagine drawing a vertical line between the demand curve and the cost-per-unit line. This vertical distance represents $P-C$, or equivalently, $P - P^*$. The length of that line measures the CS from purchasing one additional unit at that quantity.[10]

Here is the reasoning: the price P on the demand curve represents the marginal valuation of the good by consumers; that is, what they are willing to pay for an additional unit. Through the price, consumers are "communicating" how much they value that extra unit. But they do not actually pay that price. Instead, they pay P^*, which is the prevailing market price. Thus, consumers enjoy a surplus — since $P - P^* > 0$ — when they purchase an additional unit of the good. (Imagine a consumer sees a desirable sweater in a store and is willing to pay up to \$50 for it, but discovers it is on sale for just \$20. By purchasing it, the consumer gains a surplus of \$30.)

To recapitulate, the vertical line between the demand curve and the equilibrium price represents the consumer surplus for the marginal unit at a given quantity. Suppose this process of measuring the vertical distance is repeated at each quantity level between zero and Q^*, and those values are all added up. The resulting sum is the *total* consumer surplus associated with the equilibrium quantity purchased, Q^*. A simpler way to calculate total CS is to find the area of the shaded triangle in Figure 4.4.

From the consumers' perspective, this represents their overall gains from trade. Had fewer goods been purchased (i.e., less than Q^* at the price P^*), the total consumer surplus would have been lower. The shaded area in Figure 4.4 would have been smaller. On the other hand, if consumers

---

[9]This could, of course, lead consumers to buy more of other goods as well, potentially offsetting the substitution effect, but this complexity will not be addressed in this book.

[10]For instance, if $Q = 10$, the vertical gap at that point reflects the CS from acquiring the 10th unit.

purchased more than Q^*, consumer surplus would also be lower. This is because additional units would be bought for which marginal valuations fall below P^*, the cost of each unit. Doing so is not rational. (For example, paying \$20 for a sweater that is only valued at \$12 results in a consumer deficit of \$8.) Therefore, purchasing beyond Q^* — equivalent to buying goods that consumers do not truly value at the market price — only detracts from the positive consumer surplus gained up to the point Q^*.

The analysis now turns to the case of a monopoly, which is the relevant benchmark when considering intellectual property rights. By granting exclusivity, IP rights enable a firm to behave monopolistically. To illustrate this, it is helpful to use a simple numerical example. Consider Table 4.1, which presents the market demand for different quantities of a good.

The data in the first two columns of Table 4.1 are plotted in Figure 4.5.

How might a monopolist behave? An important intermediate tool in the analysis is the *marginal revenue* (MR) curve. The third column of the table shows the total revenue associated with each quantity, calculated as price multiplied by quantity. Marginal revenue is the change in total revenue resulting from the sale of one additional unit. For example, if the price falls from \$50 to \$40 and consumers purchase one more unit, total revenue increases from \$50 to \$80. Therefore, marginal revenue is the increment: \$30.

Note that $MR < P$ because each additional unit sold fetches less than the listed price. To sell 3 units, the firm must lower the price to \$30. However, it could have sold the first two units for \$40 each. By reducing the price to \$30, the firm sacrifices \$10 on each of the first two units, resulting in a total loss of \$20. Thus, the benefit of selling the third unit is the price it receives for that unit minus the revenue lost on the earlier units. In this case, $MR = \$30 - \$20 - \$10$ for the third unit.

Table 4.1. Market Demand: Example

Quantity	Price (\$)	Total Revenue (\$)	Marginal Revenue (\$)
1	50	50	50
2	40	80	30
3	30	90	10

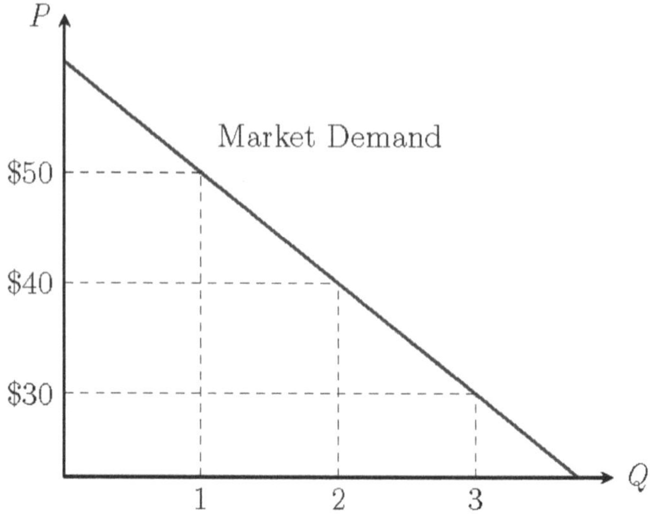

Figure 4.5. Monopoly Analysis: Step 1

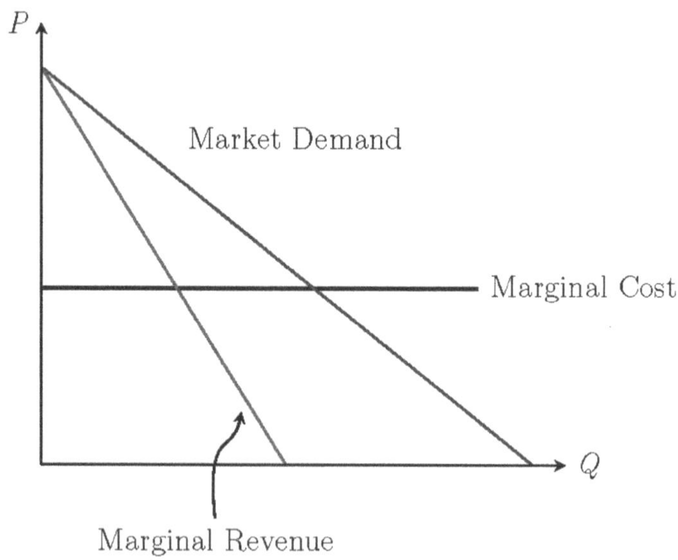

Figure 4.6. Monopoly Analysis: Step 2

A monopolist maximizes profit by producing at the output level where marginal revenue (MR) equals marginal cost (MC).

Suppose $MR \neq MC$. If $MR > MC$, the monopolist should produce one more unit, as doing so would increase profits. The marginal gain from selling the additional unit exceeds the marginal cost of producing it. Conversely, if $MR < MC$, the monopolist should have produced one less unit. In that case, reducing output would have increased profit, since the firm would save more in marginal cost than it would lose in forgone marginal revenue.

A couple of important points are worth noting. First, MR always lies below the price (i.e., beneath the demand curve), except at $Q = 0$. At that point, the first unit sells for the full price of the good, so total revenue and marginal revenue are equal.

Second, the monopolist charges whatever price corresponds to the profit-maximizing quantity on the demand curve. While it could charge marginal cost — and doing so would be generous, since MC reflects the true cost of producing the last unit — there is little reason to do so if consumers are willing to pay more for that quantity.

Refer to Figure 4.6. At the point where MR intersects MC, draw an imaginary vertical line upward. The corresponding point on the demand curve shows the consumers' marginal valuation of that quantity. In effect, the market is "speaking," revealing what it is willing to pay. Therefore, the monopolist charges the price indicated on the demand curve, not the marginal cost.

Figure 4.7 shows that the profit earned by the monopolist is given by the rectangle: $(P^M - P^*) \times Q^M$.

A few key points become transparent. Under a monopoly, prices are higher and the quantity sold is lower than in a competitive market. Furthermore, consumer surplus is reduced. This is illustrated by the smaller right-angled triangle formed between the vertical intercept of the demand curve and the monopoly price P^M, with base Q^M. Part of the consumer surplus that existed under perfect competition is transferred to the monopolist — namely, the latter's revenue.

But there is a shaded triangle that remains unaccounted for. This area is known as the *deadweight loss* (DWL). It represents unrealized gains from trade. At quantity Q^M, the marginal valuation of the good, as revealed by the price on the demand curve, exceeds the marginal cost of producing the good. This signals that additional units should be produced until the quantity Q^* is reached.

There are still consumers who are willing to pay more than the cost of production, meaning their marginal valuations exceed marginal cost. (As an analogy, consumers are willing to pay more for a sweater than it

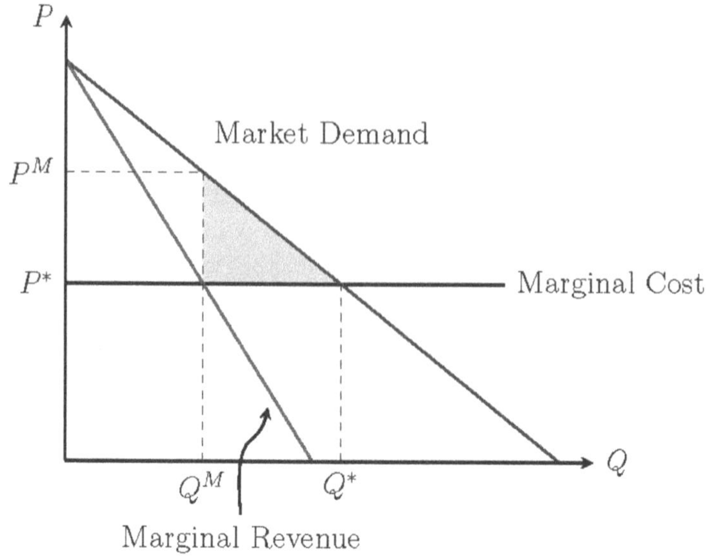

Figure 4.7. Monopoly Analysis: Step 3

costs to produce it.) Yet, the market does not supply those additional units. Although it would be socially optimal to expand output, it is not privately rational for the monopolist to do so. From the monopolist's perspective, profit is maximized at Q^M, not at Q^*.

This is the sense in which monopoly pricing leads to *static inefficiency.* At a given point in time, society incurs a deadweight loss (DWL). However, intertemporally, dynamic gains may accrue as innovators are motivated by the prospect of earning economic profits. In this sense, DWL can be viewed as the price society pays for maintaining an intellectual property rights (IPR) system, an inefficiency tolerated in exchange for a sustained flow of innovation over time.

4.4 Market Power

This section provides a numerical illustration of the conceptual tools developed thus far. The motivation for the analysis is the hypothesis attributed to Schumpeter (1942): that a positive relationship exists between innovation and monopoly power. The underlying rationale is that the opportunity to capture monopoly profits serves as a powerful incentive for innovation.

Given the risk and uncertainty inherent in innovation, firms often rely on internal financing rather than external capital, since outside lenders may be reluctant to fund projects whose outcomes are unpredictable.[11] To mitigate this uncertainty, firms may pursue multiple innovation projects simultaneously, employing teams of creators and engineers in parallel, with the hope that at least one project succeeds. Only a well-resourced firm — typically a large firm with market power — can afford such an approach.

Arrow (1962) challenged the *Schumpeterian hypothesis*, showing that in the case of process innovations, competitive markets may offer stronger incentives to innovate than monopolies. In what follows, the objective is to compare innovation incentives under monopoly and perfect competition.

4.4.1 *Case 1: Monopoly*

- Assume market demand is given by $Q = 100 - P$
- Assume a constant cost of production per unit: 30
- Total revenue $(TR) = PQ = 100Q - Q^2$
- Marginal revenue $(MR) = 100 - 2Q$

A monopolist maximizes profit by producing the quantity of output at which marginal revenue equals marginal cost.[12] Setting $MR = 100 - 2Q = 30$ yields $Q^* = 35$. The monopolist charges $P^* = 65$, as shown in Figure 4.8.

The monopolist's profits are \$1,225, equal to $(65 - 30) \times 35$.

Now suppose a process innovation — such as a more efficient method of production — lowers the marginal cost of production to 20. Re-solving the monopolist's optimization problem (i.e., setting MR equal to the new MC) yields an optimal quantity of $Q = 40$ and a price of $P = 60$, as shown in Figure 4.9.

The monopolist's new profits are $(60 - 20) \times 40 = 1{,}600$. Hence, the **gains from innovation** are given by $\Delta\text{Profit} = 1{,}600 - 1{,}225 = 375$. This \$375 increase in profit represents the monopolist's incentive to innovate.

What about a competitive industry?

4.4.2 *Case 2: Competitive Industry*

- Recall: market demand is $Q = 100 - P$

[11]The firm possesses asymmetric information relative to external funders; it knows more about its potential to achieve a breakthrough than do the external observers.

[12]The marginal revenue equation is derived by taking the first derivative of the total revenue function. See Appendix 2B in Chapter 2.

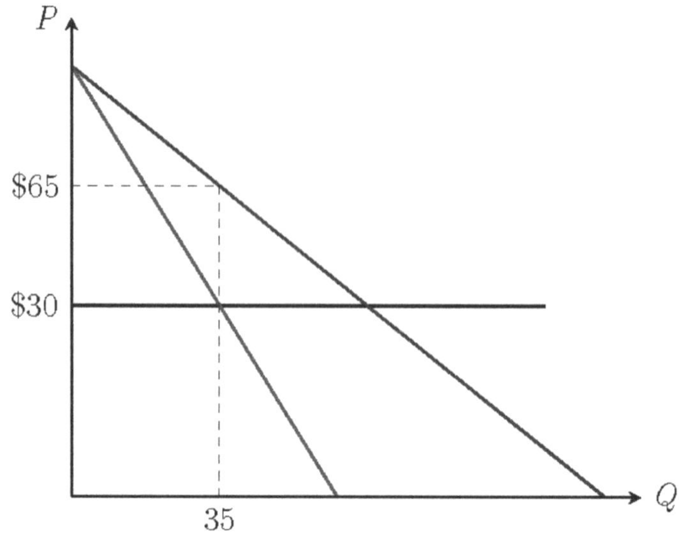

Figure 4.8. Monopoly Innovator: Pre-Innovation

- Again, the new marginal cost of production per unit is 20

The competitive industry initially sells 70 units at a price of 30. Zero economic profits are earned; that is, any accounting profits are exactly offset by opportunity costs.[13]

Now suppose that one innovator among the many competitive firms achieves a technological breakthrough and discovers how to manufacture the good more efficiently, reducing the marginal cost to 20, as shown in Figure 4.10. Assume the innovator obtains a process patent for this new method. The innovator cannot feasibly charge a monopoly price. As shown in Figure 4.9, the monopolist (with the new cost) would charge a price of 60, but there are still competitors capable of charging 30 using the old technology. Remember, the good is identical; it is simply produced by different methods.

Alternatively, the innovator could license the new technology to all other producers and charge a royalty of 10 per unit. In that case, the total cost of production for each firm would remain at 30: the new marginal cost (20) plus the unit royalty (10). The competitive market would continue to produce 70 units, sell at a price of 30, and earn zero economic profits.

[13]For example, the accounting profits may just offset the salary that entrepreneurs forgo to go into business.

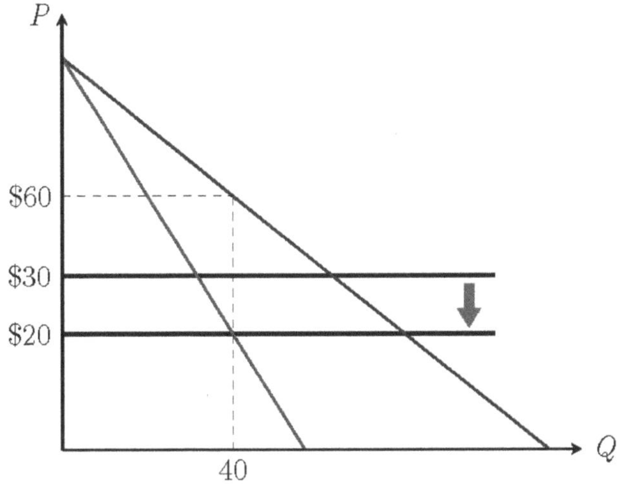

Figure 4.9. Monopoly Innovator: Post-Innovation

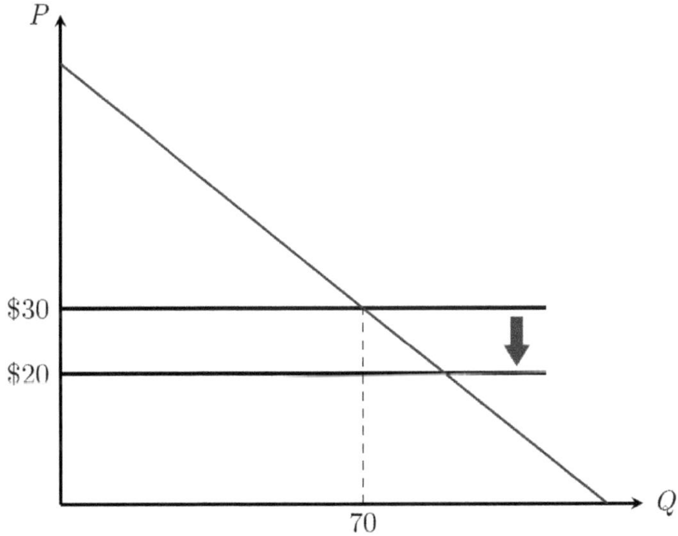

Figure 4.10. Innovation under a Competitive Industry

However, the licensor earns \$700 in royalties, calculated as 10×70. This amount represents the innovator's reward for developing a more efficient production process. Rather than earning zero economic profits like the rest of the industry, the innovator earns \$700 in licensing revenue.

Since the gains from innovation in the competitive industry (ΔProfit = 700) exceed the gains under monopoly ($375), Arrow (1962) concludes that a competitive industry may have stronger incentives to innovate.

4.4.3 *Limitations of the Illustration*

- **Applies Only to Process Innovations:** Product innovations that lead to new or improved varieties of goods typically involve markup pricing ($P > MC$) and may require exclusivity to be profitable.
- **Ignores the Cost of Innovation:** This example abstracts from the upfront R&D costs required to achieve the technological breakthrough. Larger, monopolistic firms may have a cost advantage in performing research and development.
- **Overlooks Innovation Races:** In practice, multiple firms may race to develop a breakthrough, with only one ultimately receiving the patent. This winner-take-all scenario leads each firm to incur development costs, potentially resulting in excessive or duplicative R&D investment.

4.5 Imitation and Commercialization

This section analyzes when patent duration is adequate and when it creates excess rent.[14]

Consider the following parameters. For simplicity, assume an interest rate of zero, so as to abstract from present discounted value computations:

- Let M = monopoly profits per year
- Let R = upfront (fixed) R&D cost
- Let $B = \frac{R}{M}$ = number of years required to recoup the R&D cost (i.e., the breakeven point)
- Let L = imitation lag (the number of years it takes for imitation to occur)
- Let T = duration of IP protection

IP protection is not always necessary for commercialization. Whether it is depends on the timing of three key variables: imitation (L), breakeven (B), and the expiration of IP protection (T). The IP holder seeks to recoup the development cost R. If it earns M per year, it takes B years to recover this cost, where $R = B \times M$. The innovator will commercialize the invention only if it expects to break even.

[14]This example is adapted from Eaton *et al.* (2002).

IP protection is effective if the duration of protection exceeds the time it takes for imitation to occur. Otherwise, without protection, imitators may undercut the IP holder, and monopoly profits may dissipate.

Case 1: $T > B > L$. In this case, IP protection leads to commercialization and is necessary. Imitation would occur before the firm has recouped its R&D cost ($B > L$). However, since IP protection lasts long enough ($T > B$), it effectively protects the innovator and encourages commercialization.

Case 2: $T > L > B$. Commercialization occurs, but IP protection is not necessary. The firm breaks even before imitation occurs ($B < L$), so the innovation would have been commercialized even without IP protection.

Case 3: $L > T > B$. IP protection is not needed. Imitation does not occur until after the protection expires ($L > T$), and the firm breaks even beforehand ($B < T$). Thus, the innovation is commercialized regardless of IP protection.

Case 4: $B > L$ and $B > T$. IP protection is ineffective. The firm does not have enough time to recoup its costs before protection expires ($B > T$), and imitation occurs before breakeven ($B > L$). Commercialization is unlikely in this case.

Case 5: $L > B > T$. Commercialization occurs despite weak IP protection. While protection expires before the firm breaks even ($B > T$), imitation does not occur until after breakeven ($L > B$). Therefore, the firm still has an incentive to introduce the innovation.

Of course, these scenarios assume perfect foresight. In practice, the actual values of T, B, and L vary across industries, technologies, and countries.

4.6 Optimal IPR

IPRs involve tradeoffs. On the one hand, benefits exist in the form of incentives for innovation, creation, investment, commercialization, and risk-taking. On the other hand, costs exist in the form of higher prices, lower output, and deadweight losses. A balancing act is required. In the absence of IPR, underinvestment in innovation may result. But in the presence of IPR, excessive investment in innovation may arise, for example, through *patent races* — races to be the first to obtain a patent right and exclude others. As pointed out in the previous section, such races could result in duplicative investments with only one winner (the patent awardee). Therefore, because stronger IPR can have both positive and negative effects, social welfare has a nonlinear relationship with IPR. Some optimal level of IPR trades off the marginal benefits of protection against the marginal harms of it on social welfare.

Furthermore, the rate of innovation can vary positively or negatively with stronger protection, depending on the existing level of protection, whether it is currently strict or lenient. This possibility gives rise to an inverted-U relationship between innovation and strength of IP protection, as shown in Figure 4.11. A mixture of the duration of protection and the breadth of protection determines IP strength. Duration refers to the life of the IP right. Patent protection, for example, can be for twenty years from the date of filing (or from the earliest priority date, as in the case of the U.S.), and copyright protection can last for the life of the author plus 70 years. The breadth of protection refers to how wide the IP owner's intellectual territory is. For example, a patent right makes claims about its inventions. The more the claims and the more extensive the claims, the greater the breadth of a patent right. The breadth of IP determines how dissimilar competing uses, variations, or adaptations of the protected work must be to avoid constituting infringement. A broad IP right, therefore, has a greater reach in preventing others from developing similar works, technologies, or methods. For instance, a broad patent might cover any use of the new screen technology across all smartphones, whereas a narrow patent might only cover the specific smartphone model or a very particular method of manufacturing the screen.[15]

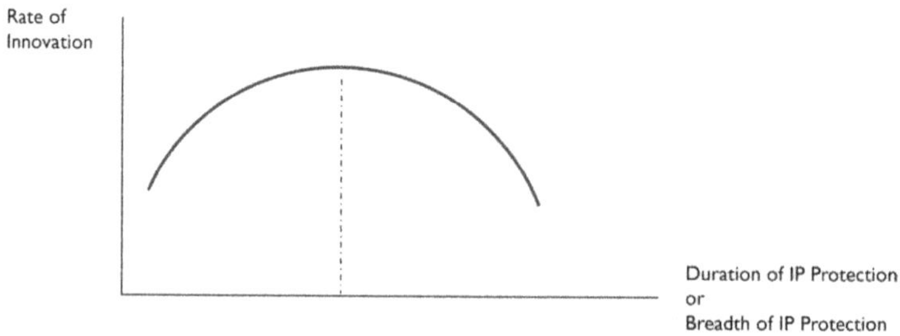

Figure 4.11. Nonlinear Relationship

[15]Patent scope and patent breadth are sometimes used interchangeably; however, some nuanced differences exist. The scope of protection is more general and comprehensive. Scope defines the legal range of IP protection. It involves not just the breadth of IP claims but also the interpretation of those claims under legal contexts, including judicial rulings. How courts interpret the language of the claims — whether broadly or narrowly — determines the boundaries of what the patent right excludes others from doing.

An inverted-U relationship between the rate of innovation and patent life rests upon market pressures to innovate. While longer patent life enhances the ability of a firm to recoup its R&D investments, it can also delay the entry of competitors and reduce the firm's will to generate new products — products that might only cannibalize the firm's existing ones. The latter effect dominates after patent life reaches a critical length.

The inverted U-relationship between innovation and patent life is also shaped by the size of innovations and their frequency.[16] Longer patent duration could encourage firms to produce radical innovations (i.e., increase the size of an innovation jump) yet reduce the frequency of innovations, for the reason just mentioned, which is that in the absence of rival entry, little incentive exists for the firm to displace its own existing innovations in the marketplace, and no competitive threat is present to spur the continual churning out of new innovative outputs. Let the rate of innovation equal the size of innovation multiplied by the frequency of its occurrence. The size (or economic importance) of an innovation is a positive function of the length of patent life, say T. If imitation does not occur until after a patent fully expires, the frequency of innovation is $\frac{1}{T}$. Hence, a longer patent life has two opposing effects on the rate of innovation: it increases the size of jumps but causes jumps to occur less frequently. Initially, the first effect dominates the second, but when patent duration is very long, the quality distance between a patent holder's good and that of generic producers is so large that further increases in T have only incremental effects on the incentives to innovate.

This inverted-U relationship in Figure 4.11 can also exist between the rate of innovation and patent breadth. Broad IP rights can encourage investment in R&D by providing exclusivity, but they can limit the entry of substitute goods or technologies and lead to monopolistic behavior. Narrower IP rights may promote competition and innovation by allowing others to build upon existing goods or methods, but may not provide sufficient protection to incentivize initial innovation. Thus, when protection is broad, the incumbent enjoys strong market power. New entrants must wait for their turn (after the existing rights of incumbents expire) to enjoy a broad scope. Therefore, under broad IP protection, payoffs are backloaded. Increasing breadth from low levels raises R&D incentives, but from high levels it reduces the time value of payoffs and diminishes R&D incentives. This again suggests that the optimal breadth of protection is an intermediate one.

[16]For a classic model of this, see Horowitz and Lai (1996).

To develop that insight further, it would be useful to distinguish between lagging breadth, which determines the range of inferior products that infringe, and leading breadth, which determines the range of superior products that infringe.[17] For example, if a patent holder has a patent on a good with quality level λ^*, a leading breadth of κ means that any future innovations with quality $\lambda \in [\lambda^*, \kappa\lambda^*]$, for $\kappa > 1$, would infringe upon the patent holder's right. Increasing leading breadth, κ, has two opposing effects on R&D incentives. On the one hand, the patent holder enjoys larger markups and has greater incentives to do R&D. On the other hand, the new patent holder has a weak bargaining position vis-à-vis incumbent patent holders early in the life of a patent. The new patent owner's innovation is likely to step on existing patent rights, requiring various licensing fees to be paid. It is only later in the life of a patent, when the patent rights of competing inventions expire, that the patent holder is in a stronger bargaining position with respect to the next generation of patent owners. In this sense, the payoffs to a patent are backloaded, arriving later in time. Thus, a larger κ increases the bargaining power of incumbent patent holders and weakens that of new patent holders, reducing the latter group's R&D incentive. Overall R&D increases only if the payoffs to a patent are not excessively backloaded. Hence, R&D may have an inverted-U relationship with respect to leading breadth (rising initially and falling after κ reaches a certain point).

These theoretical insights suggest that at very strong levels of IPR, innovation may be adversely affected. The challenging factor in designing effective IP systems is to know where the optimal IPR level is. The overall shape of the relationship between IPR and innovation is likely to be industry-specific or product-specific — or country-specific. Factors like innovative capacity or imitative capacity, market structure, market size, incomes, the quality of legal institutions, and enforcement effectiveness will vary across products, industries, and economies. Yet the IPR regime is typically established at the national level (as discussed in Chapter 1). Furthermore, the optimal design of an IPR system may be time-specific, depending on a nation's stage of economic development — whether it is still industrializing or already highly advanced.

4.6.1 *Patent Life, Breadth, and Costly Imitation*

The optimal patent policy has been discussed with respect to the breadth and length of patent protection. However, this policy should take into

[17] See O'Donoghue and Zweimuller (2004) for a detailed model.

account the costs of imitation, which are neither zero nor infinite. If the costs of imitation are prohibitively high, imitation is absent, and the optimal patent policy can be set without the consideration of imitators. If, on the other hand, the costs of imitation are zero, imitation is always a threat to the innovator. In either case, imitation activities are independent of patent duration. When, however, imitation costs are positive but not prohibitive, the incentive to imitate will depend on patent life. As explained in Parker (1974), the longer the patent life, the longer that imitators have to wait for a patent to expire, and the less patient or more anxious they become to try to invent around the patented product. Thus, optimal patent design needs to take into consideration that imitation is a function of patent life.[18]

Increasing patent life, as discussed earlier, might be viewed as enhancing a firm's ability to appropriate the returns to R&D by giving it more time to do so. However, that creates incentives for imitators to invent around the patent. The increased influx of imitators (and competing products) then reduces the effectiveness of patent protection. Policy and legal authorities could then compensate by increased the *breadth* of patent protection so as to preserve innovation incentives.[19]

Figure 4.12 maps out the decisions of patent holders and imitators based on the combination of patent life T and imitation costs K.

The shaded area represents combinations where patenting is not profitable. For example, if patent life is too short, the innovator cannot recoup the costs of R&D investment. Or if imitation costs are below some threshold level, imitation is too easy. This discourages the innovator from patenting and disclosing its invention. It would instead turn to trade secrecy if it invents at all. The non-shaded area shows the combinations of patent life and imitation costs where patenting occurs. The curve shown is the point of indifference, where an imitator is indifferent between entering or not entering the market. It is where the present discounted value of profits to the firm from innovation (and patenting it) — say V^{PAT} — just equals the imitation cost K.[20]

[18]See Gallini (1992) for a classic analysis of the optimal patent policy under costly imitation.

[19]Alternatively, as Gallini (1992) demonstrated, patents could be made very broad so as to preempt imitation and then patent life adjusted down just enough to achieve the desired patent reward (in terms of the firm value V, or the discounted present value of profits).

[20]And the derivative $\frac{dV^{PAT}}{dT} > 0$ holds because a longer patent life gives the firm more time to earn profits.

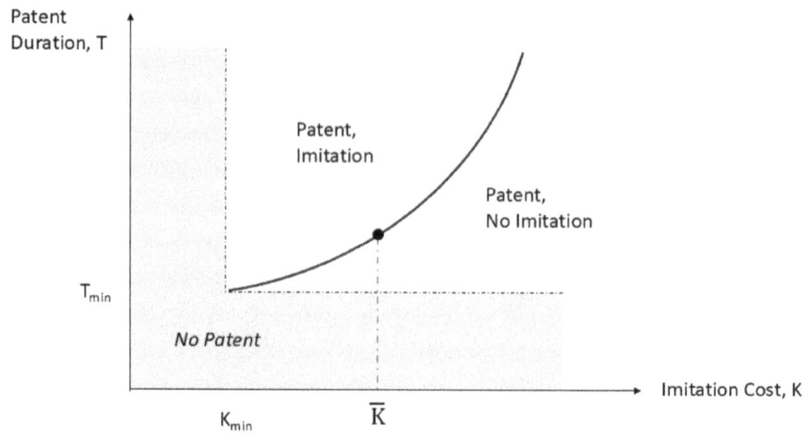

Figure 4.12. Patent Life and Imitation

Note that at some given level of imitation costs — say $\bar{K}$ on the curve — raising patent life T will encourage imitation, for the reason given earlier. Imitators do not want to wait for a patent to expire. It desires to share in the market opportunities. But at the same level of imitation costs (on the curve in Figure 4.12), a reduction in patent life discourages imitation. The gain from imitation is not as profitable with an earlier patent expiry date, as the technology will be in the public domain sooner, and the imitator can avoid incurring the costs of imitation given by $\bar{K}$.

It may well be optimal to keep patent life relatively short (say $T = 20$ rather than $T = 100$) and patent breadth relatively broad, making K relatively high rather than relatively low, say through tight non-obviousness and novelty requirements or broad judicial claims interpretations — measures that would increase the cost of developing imitations.[21]

4.6.2 *Product Innovations and Process Innovations*

The instruments of patent policy pertaining to the duration and breadth of protection can also be utilized to shape the direction of technological

[21]Later, it will be discussed how copyright protection is relatively long (life of author plus 50–70 years) and the breadth or scope is relatively narrow. This is in part due to copyrights protecting "expression" and not "ideas," the presence of independent creations, derivative or secondary works, where it would be socially beneficial to permit a greater freedom to use ideas, themes, and common artistic expressions without infringing on copyright. The relatively long duration helps compensate for the narrow scope of protection.

change. Some innovations result in new products while others introduce new ways of producing existing products. New products will largely compete on the basis of product differentiation. Their attraction is their distinctiveness and their meeting of some hitherto unfilled market needs. The innovator and existing firms will compete to the extent that some consumers are not (yet) willing to pay a higher price for the new product. New process innovations will likely lead to head-to-head competition between the new process innovator and the pioneering firm, with a cost advantage going to the process innovator and a head start advantage going to the incumbent. They will likely share the market. Another way to distinguish product and process innovation is to conceptualize product innovation as a horizontal differentiation among products, whereas process innovation could be viewed as a vertical improvement in a product, providing, say, a faster, lighter, and cheaper version.

The private market may be biased towards more product innovations or towards excessive production differentiation compared to the socially optimal ratio of product and process innovations. This is a well-known concern that in markets characterized by product diversity, there tends to be excessive entry. This is because when a new firm invents a new variety and enters the industry, it only takes into account its private benefits and costs, not the costs imposed on other firms. When it enters a crowded market, all firms' share of the market is smaller and their average costs of production higher (since their total costs are spread among fewer units of output). Hence, the lack of regard for external costs results in excessive entry in the private sector.[22] As Eswaran and Gallini (1996) put it: "Since process innovation reinforces competition, too little is done, and since product innovation relaxes competition, too much is done" (p. 724).

One policy solution to help correct the bias towards product innovation is to increase the breadth of patent protection for process innovations. This has the effect of raising the standard for a process innovation. It makes the entrant become a more formidable competitor. The entrant faces the prospect of larger profits from a bigger process innovation "jump" and is motivated to switch away from investing in product innovation. Eswaran and Gallini (1996) find that when the pioneer firm's R&D costs are low, the optimal policy should spur competition by encouraging process innovations, but if the pioneer firm's R&D costs are high, the optimal policy should

[22]Brand proliferation can be observed in the various brands of toothpastes, juices, over-the-counter medicines, TV channels, podcast stations, and automobiles.

dampen competition by encouraging more product innovations and product differentiation. The intuition is that when the R&D costs of the pioneer are low, its competition with the entrant is viable. But if those costs are very high, post-innovation competition would reduce the pioneer's ability to recoup its R&D investments, in which case product innovations should be promoted through the use of broader product patent protection and narrower process patent protection.

A few qualifications could be made. In the developing world, where innovative capacities are not as strong, indigenous firms tend to specialize in process innovations, so the bias towards product innovation is not as strong. In India, for example, product patents for pharmaceuticals were not recognized between 1972 and 2005. Indian firms specialized in process innovations, and a burgeoning generic drug industry grew during that period. Developing a new product often requires significant investment in research, testing, and development. In contrast, improving processes — such as in assembly lines, manufacturing techniques, or agricultural production methods — can often be achieved with less investment in high-level research. Process patents allow firms in developing countries to adapt and innovate in production methods without infringing on the product patents held by companies in developed countries. This fits with the incremental nature of innovations, rather than groundbreaking product inventions, in the developing world. Process patents allow for continuous improvement in industries like manufacturing, agriculture, and mining. For example, improving the efficiency of chemical processing might yield a new process patent but not necessarily require a completely novel product.

Another factor is that governments are not particularly able to customize protections, such as a broad or narrow scope. The laws on patentability tend to be one-size-fits-all; that is, they apply at the national level and not by industry or by product. However, patent examiners may adjust patent scope with their decisions on allowable patent claims and prior art.

For some firms, process innovations and product innovations are not substitutes but complements. Both kinds of innovation may not only be part of a firm's strategy but also a response to shifting market conditions.[23] Product innovations will enhance a firm's demand, and process innovations will reduce its costs of production so that the firm can produce larger quantities to satisfy the enhanced demand. Research capabilities in both product and

[23] See Athey and Schmutzler (1995).

process dimensions also complement each other. Increased process flexibility increases the marginal returns from product flexibility and vice versa. Developing countries with more advanced manufacturing and R&D sectors may choose this kind of complementary strategy to use product innovations as a way to gain entry into global markets and to use process innovations as a way to gain a competitive edge via a pricing advantage.[24]

4.7 Patent Value and Quality

The discussions thus far on measuring innovation and designing intellectual property policies have abstracted from patent value and patent quality. Merely comparing the counts of patented inventions across firms, industries, or countries does not fully capture the true levels of innovation. The counts ought to be weighted by some measure of economic value, such as market impact or the degree to which the patent covers valuable, innovative, and useful technologies. This section will discuss some methods for doing so. While patent value relates to the economic worth of a patent, patent quality concerns the validity of the patents granted. Do they satisfy the criteria for subject matter eligibility? Are they novel and non-obvious? Are their claims clear and sufficiently described? Patent quality is important to optimal patent policy design, as it helps strike a balance between creating incentives for high-value innovations and minimizing deadweight losses, particularly those stemming from low-value patents or invalid patents that stifle competition or clog the IP system. A well-designed IP system should elicit high-value innovations and grant legally robust IP rights capable of withstanding legal challenges and providing clarity in enforcement.

4.7.1 *Patent Value*

The value of patents is not easily observed. Patent rights are not frequently or widely traded like financial instruments, such as equities. Large, international exchange institutions for providing markets for patent rights are few

[24]For instance, South Korea became a leading player in consumer electronics and automobiles, focusing on both product patents and process improvements. Brazil's *Embraer* became a major player in the aviation industry by developing new aircraft models (particularly regional jets as its niche) and improving its production processes to compete against larger players like Boeing and Airbus.

and far between.[25] Few firms publicly disclose details about their patent transactions or technology transfer agreements. Furthermore, not all patent rights have a steady cash flow, since some (if not many) patented inventions are not commercialized, or are not "worked" (put into practice).

Consequently, patent valuation is largely based on observing the characteristics of a patent or the behavior of a patent holder that may *reveal* information about the underlying value. Table 4.2 provides an example of indicators used to measure patent value.

The first two approaches in the table have been the most common. The logic behind patent citation counts is that the more valuable patents are cited more heavily by later inventors or in later patents (hence the term "forward" citation, as opposed to backward citation, which refers to the citations of a patent to previous innovations).[26] Typically, the forward citations need to be counted within a specific time frame — say, in the first 5 years or 8 years after a patent is published for the method to be comparable across different patents, since the older the patent or the longer that time passes,

Table 4.2. Patent Valuation Methods

Method	Description
Citations	Forward citations (count of citations by subsequent patents)
Renewal Decision	Length of time patent kept in force and amounts paid to do so
Family Size (Raw)	Number of countries in the patent family
Family Size (Weighted)	Weighing countries in patent family by market size
Opposition Challenge	Incidence of opposition
Number of Claims	Claim counts in a patent
Technology Scope	Number of technology classes covered by a patent
Stock Market Response	Observed stock price reaction to patent grants

[25]Patent rights are tradable at auctions, held for example by *Ocean Tomo*, an intellectual property merchant bank. Or at a secondary patent market like *IAM*, which will be analyzed in Chapter 10.

[26]See Jaffe and Trajtenberg (2002) for a full treatment of the patent citation method.

the more opportunity a patent has to be cited. In many cases, though, citations tend to drop substantially after 6–8 years of publication.[27]

Patent rights need to be renewed (unlike physical property rights). In the U.S., in order to maintain a patent right, the patent holder is required to make three scheduled renewal payments: 3.5 years after a patent grant, 7.5 years, and then 11.5 years. At the European Patent Office, renewal payments are required annually from the third year after the application filing date. In both cases, the fees have generally been non-decreasing over time.

Given the costs of maintaining patent rights, the relatively most valuable patents will be selected by patent holders for renewal. For example, a patent holder would compare the change in firm value $\Delta V = V^{\text{Renew}} - V^{\text{Lapse}}$ against the renewal fee, ϕ.[28] Patents would lapse because the patent holders might assess that the economic value of the patent no longer justifies the cost of maintaining it. In practice, the majority of patents are not held to the full term (say 20 years after filing). Hughes (2024) shows data on patent renewal rates by grant year cohorts (from 1985 to 2010) at the USPTO, finding that roughly 85% of patents are renewed once, 65% twice, and 40% thrice. Thus, by the eleventh year, 60% of patents are not maintained. This is consistent with evidence from Lanjouw and Schankerman (2001) that approximately 60–70% of patents are not renewed by the 11th year, particularly for patents in fields where innovation is fast-paced, resulting in patents becoming obsolete or less valuable.

Another approach to gauging patent value is to examine patent family size (see Harhoff *et al.*, 2003). Patent family size refers to the number of countries in which an invention is protected by a patent; that is, the priority filing and the subsequent filings that emanate from it. Given the costs of acquiring patents in multiple jurisdictions, rights holders would reserve their more valuable technologies for international patenting.

However, the raw family size does not take into account the potential market size of the protected areas. For example, suppose patent X covers three countries A, B, and C, while patent Y covers three countries D, E, and F. Patent X and Y need not be equally valuable since the market sizes of countries A through F vary. Kabore and Park (2019) developed a method of patent valuation that weighs patent family size by the GDP (real gross domestic product) of the countries in the family. Several reasons exist as to why it is more useful to consider market size. Larger markets

[27]This can be determined from the *PATSTAT* database.

[28]V^{Renew} is the firm value of continuing to have patent protection and V^{Lapse} is the firm value after letting the patent right lapse. The firm renews a patent if $\Delta V > \phi$.

are more attractive to patent holders and firms. More developed economies offer greater rivalry not only from other innovators but also from imitators who are all more technologically capable of posing a competitive threat. Hence, the value of patent protection is greater than in a region where the threat of rivalry is less. As discussed in Chapter 1, the costs of patenting and the costs of maintaining patents are greater in larger markets. Thus, only those patent holders whose patent values are sufficiently high would find it economical to seek patent protection in those markets.

Patent valuation based on raw family size is a count:

$$V_j = \sum_{n=1}^{N} I_{jn}$$

where V_j denotes the patent value of a *priority* patent j. (When a patent for the same invention is filed in multiple other countries within the one-year period per the *Paris Convention*, those applications are referred to as *subsequent* filings.[29]) I_n is an indicator function which equals one if priority patent j is patented in country n and zero otherwise, and N is the total number of countries (including the country of priority filing). The market size-weighted family size is then given by

$$V_j = \sum_{n=1}^{N} \omega_n I_{jn}$$

where $\omega_n = GDP_n$ (real gross domestic product of country n). This measure takes into account the composition of the international patent family in terms of the market size of countries.

One distinct advantage of the family size measures of patent valuation is that they are ex ante. Information about a patent's citation and its renewal is known ex post. Furthermore, patent citations are not distinguished by how much impact the cited patents have on an invention; for example, patent X may cite prior patents A and B, but A may be more important to X's function than B. Moreover, the reason patent X may cite A and B is to indicate that they are alternative products or methods of production, so that X is not infringing on them, rather than that patent X builds on them. Renewals are also observed later in the life of a patent. Another limitation is that renewal choices provide rough measures of patent values and it may be

[29]The patent family consists of the priority patent and the subsequent filings. For purposes of measuring patent value, one needs only focus on priority patents since the subsequent ones are essentially duplicates (same invention).

difficult to tell if changes in renewal rates are due to changes in patent value or changes in the cost of renewing or maintaining patents. The limitation of patent family size is that it cannot be used to value domestic patents.

There are other potential indicators of patent value, such as whether a patent has faced an opposition challenge (Harhoff and Reitzig, 2004), with the premise being that more valuable patents are challenged, or the number of claims in a patent (Tong and Frame, 1994), signifying that more impactful inventions have more claims. Patent value may also be inferred from the stock price reaction to the grant of patents (Kogan *et al.*, 2017). The stock price of the firm would increase if the market expects the patent to result in profitable innovations and products. Kogan *et al.* (2017) employ event study analyses (to observe a firm's stock price over a short window surrounding the event of a patent grant). One limitation with the stock market approach is that only publicly traded firms' patents can be studied. Furthermore, stock price shifts can consist of noise, bubbles, and speculative fever, not just movements in firm fundamentals.[30] While the method provides early insight into the valuation of a patent, it leaves open the question of how to track its valuation later in the patent's life. Hughes (2024) also points out that when multiple patents are granted to the same firm on the same day, the stock market approach cannot determine the valuation of individual patent grants.

Table 4.3 provides some descriptive statistics about the various indicators of patent value. Table 4.3 shows that the average patent lasts for about 12–13 years, as measured from the date of application to the date of last non-renewal, and has about 16–17 forward citations during the first 5 years of its life. The average patent family size is around 6 countries and covers a market with a total GDP of nearly 11 trillion real (2005) U.S. dollars. Published patents contain around 13–14 claims on average.[31] It is interesting to see that university patents have the highest mean values in all of these indicators of patent value. This reflects well on the nature of open and critical research in academia.

In Table 4.3, the focus is on *characteristics* related to patent value, but not on the value of patents. Hughes (2024) builds on the patent renewal framework to calculate patent-level estimates of lifetime patent value.

[30] However, Kogan *et al.* (2017) do attempt to control for noise by calculating a signal-to-noise ratio for stock returns.

[31] For data on opposition proceedings, see Harhoff *et al.* (2003) and Harhoff and Reitzig (2004). Both studies find that around 8% of patent grants are challenged or opposed.

Table 4.3. Aspects of Patent Grants, by Applicant Type

Group (% group share)	Duration (Years)	Citations First 5 Yrs	Family Size	Weighted Family Size	Patent Claims
Company	12.8	16.1	6.0	10.90	13.4
(75.1%)	*(4.2)*	*(29.7)*	*(5.5)*	*(4.4)*	*(10.9)*
Gov Non-Profit	12.8	16.3	6.0	10.69	13.4
(1.5%)	*(4.1)*	*(39.0)*	*(4.6)*	*(4.2)*	*(10.1)*
Individual	12.2	18.1	5.4	10.86	14.5
(22.0%)	*(3.6)*	*(33.7)*	*(5.7)*	*(2.7)*	*(11.7)*
University	13.3	25.6	6.2	10.92	17.8
(1.4%)	*(3.8)*	*(46.1)*	*(5.5)*	*(3.5)*	*(14.9)*
Total	12.6	16.7	5.9	10.9	13.7
N = 1,354,926	*(4.1)*	*(31.1)*	*(5.5)*	*(4.1)*	*(11.1)*

Note: The table shows the means, with standard deviations in parentheses, for five countries: U.S., U.K., France, Germany, and Japan.
Sample period is 1982–2012.

Source: Kabore and Park (2019).

His approach differs from earlier work by modeling the idiosyncratic, patent-specific depreciation rates — namely, the rate at which patent value or the revenue flow depreciates over time. This can happen due to the forces of creative destruction caused by any combination of the arrival of new technologies, technological obsolescence, imitation or displacement by firm rivals, or market and industrial shifts.

In the conceptual framework of Hughes (2024), the probability that a patent holder will maintain a patent right depends on not just the renewal fee but also the patent's age, the years of patent term remaining, and the patent's depreciation rate.[32] The rate of depreciation, in turn, is a function of patent characteristics, such as the forward citations received, the timing of forward citations, the number of claims, and other indicators.

[32] An ordered choice model is embedded into the methodology. Since patent holders face three sequential decision points (when renewal fees are due at the USPTO), their decisions result in an outcome of 0, 1, 2, or 3 renewals paid. This sequence of decisions, combined with the assumption of constant depreciation in patent value and the real dollar amounts paid (or not paid) by the patent holder, reveals the patent's value. The patent holder decides to continue maintaining the patent if the future value exceeds the renewal cost.

Hughes' (2024) sample consists of over 3.3 million patents granted by the U.S. Patent and Trademark Office (USPTO) between 1983 and 2011. As mentioned earlier, renewal payments on U.S. patents are due at 3.5, 7.5, and 11.5 years after a patent is granted. Failure to pay these fees causes the patent right to lapse. Table 4.4 shows estimates of the real lifetime value of patents, value at patent grant, and the depreciation rate of patent value by

Table 4.4. Patent Values for U.S. Patents Granted, 1983–2011

Selected Technology Field	Statistic	Lifetime Patent Value	Patent Value at Grant	Depreciation Rate of Patent Value (%)
	Mean	16.99	7.88	44.10
Pooled	Std Dev	25.28	11.80	4.40
	Median	0.80	0.39	44.43
Analysis of Biological Mat.	Mean	14.94	6.72	43.52
Audio-Visual Technology	Mean	20.4	10.25	48.15
Biotechnology	Mean	15.52	7.18	44.71
Chemical Engineering	Mean	9.72	4.35	42.74
Civil Engineering	Mean	7.55	3.27	41.67
Computer Technology	Mean	23.63	10.07	40.90
Digital Communication	Mean	39.34	17.44	43.12
Electrical Machinery ...	Mean	13.67	6.4	44.69
Furniture, Games	Mean	4.49	2.05	44.19
Machine Tools	Mean	8.36	3.78	43.16
Medical Technology	Mean	16.76	6.7	39.57
Micro-Structural & Nano-Tech	Mean	32.02	16.64	49.94
Optics	Mean	33.76	17.72	50.33
Organic Fine Chemistry	Mean	7.7	3.59	44.48
Pharmaceuticals	Mean	10.28	4.55	42.62
Semiconductors	Mean	26.72	11.74	42.07
Telecommunications	Mean	31.85	15.55	47.05
Transport	Mean	9.88	4.77	45.96
Correlation with Depreciation Rate:		0.40	0.53	1.00

Notes: Patent values are in millions of real 2020 U.S. dollars.
Number of observations = 3,374,423 patents.

Source: Hughes (2024).

selected technological fields.[33] The patent values are in millions of real 2020 dollars and are calculated under the assumption that all renewal fees were paid. The lifetime value captures the value from the time of patent grant to the patent's expiry date. The depreciation of value is calculated from the date of patent grant — not the date of application nor the completion date of the R&D project.

The lifetime value of patents and the value of a patent at the time of grant are heavily skewed. The mean lifetime value is about \$17 million, but the median value is only \$800 K. This confirms that a minority of patents have high commercial value. Also noteworthy are the high patent values associated with AI-related industries, which will be discussed in Chapters 11 and 12 — industries such as digital communications, semiconductors, and computer technology. The depreciation rates are also considerably high; on average, across all technological fields, 44% of a patent's value erodes annually. This suggests a high degree of technological churning (or creative destruction).

Interestingly, there is a positive correlation between the depreciation rate and the patent value at the time of grant.[34] One reason might be that high patent values attract imitators, rivals, or new entrants to target their innovation efforts in similar invention spaces where markets signal high demand. Another possibility is that patent protection is more valuable when technologies are at greater risk of displacement or disruption. If technologies face little or no competitive threat, innovators may not bother to seek patent protection and incur the costs of filing and maintenance.

4.7.2 *Patent Quality*

Patent valuation and patent quality are distinct concepts but interconnected. Patents with suspected validity issues are likely to have lower value, all else equal. The same characteristics of a patent — citation counts and longer patent duration — can be markers of patent quality and patent value. This section discusses the need for a symmetric perspective on patent quality.

[33] Note that the table is an abridged version of Hughes (2024), which provides more technological fields than shown in Table 4.4.

[34] The correlations in Table 4.4 were calculated for all the technology fields reported in Hughes (2024), not just the ones shown in the table.

A report by the *Sunwater Institute* (2024) evaluates the legal robustness of U.S. patents granted.[35] The study assesses two types of errors: a *Type 1* error, where a patent is granted despite containing *invalid* claims, and a *Type 2* error, where a patent is rejected despite containing *valid* claims. The results show that the Type 1 error rate is under 9% while the Type 2 error rate is significantly higher. The implications of this study are that it refutes the oft-cited assertion that "bad patents" are clogging the U.S. patent system.

The Type 1 and Type 2 errors vary by technological field, as shown in Figure 4.13.

The rate and variance of Type 2 errors across technologies are clearly higher. Of the patent applications in Computer Networks that were denied, 30% are deemed to be false rejections. Of the patents granted in Semiconductors, 11% are deemed invalid.

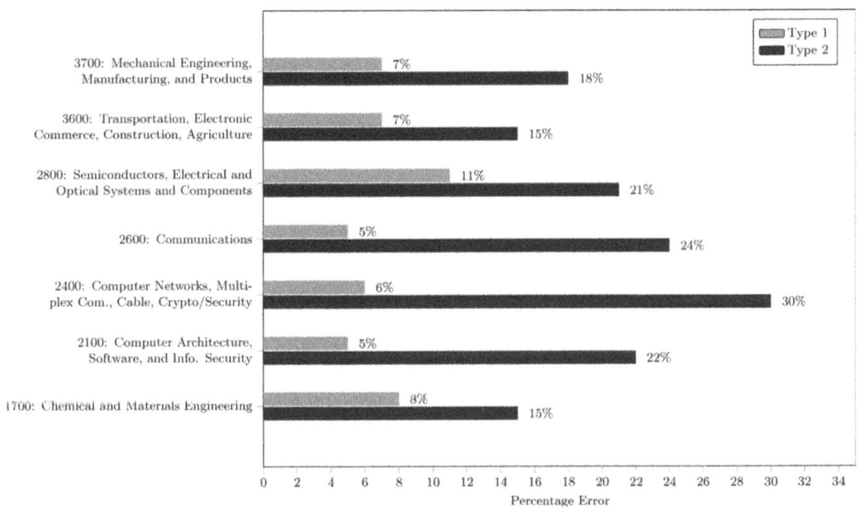

Figure 4.13. Error Rate across Technology Centers
Source: Sunwater Institute.

[35]See Harutyunyan *et al.* (2024).

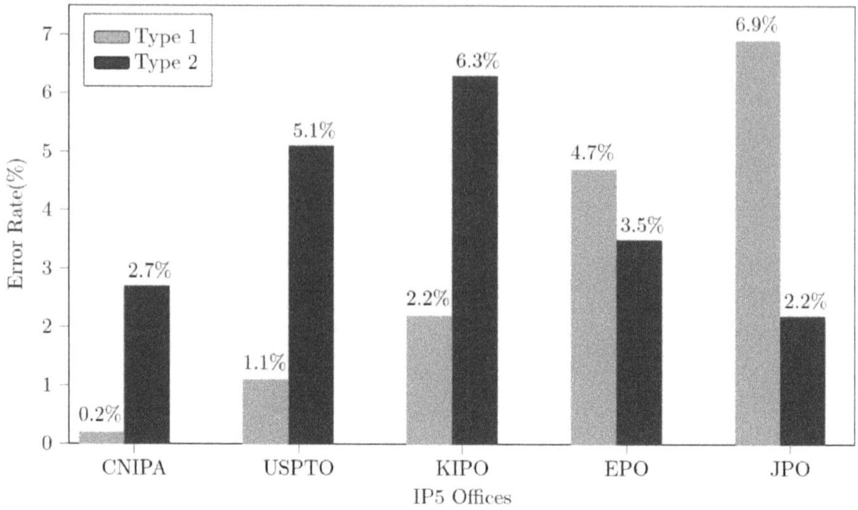

Figure 4.14. Error Rate across Global Patent Offices
Source: Sunwater Institute.

The error rates also vary by patent office. The five major IP offices (called IP5 group) process approximately 80% of worldwide patent applications. The IP5 consists of the USPTO, EPO, the JPO (Japanese Patent Office), KIPO (Korean Intellectual Property Office) and the National Intellectual Property Administration of the People's Republic of China (CNIPA). As Figure 4.14 shows, the USPTO, CNIPA, and KIPO commit a higher rate of Type 2 errors than they do of Type 1 errors. In contrast, the EPO and JPO have the reverse situation.[36]

Overall, policymakers should minimize both types of errors in a balanced way. The harm to a Type 1 error is the deadweight loss associated with the temporary "monopoly" (exclusive) rights granted to an invalid patent holder and the costs associated with legal challenges. The harm of a Type 2 error is that useful innovations may not be commercialized, and any R&D sunk costs remain unrecovered, which may discourage future innovation.

[36]The data for the global comparison in Figure 4.14 are from an earlier period than the data used to calculate the U.S. patent validity rates.

Appendix 4A. Prizes for Innovations

As an alternative to an IP system, prizes can be awarded to an innovator.[37] Prize mechanisms already exist to foster research and development. The *America COMPETES Reauthorization Act* of 2010 provides a framework for the U.S. government to implement innovation prizes. The non-profit organization *XPRIZE* hosts public competitions to incentivize technological breakthroughs.

The advantage of a prize system is that the innovation can be put into the public domain, and the deadweight losses associated with monopoly pricing can be avoided. A prize system could be run in the following way, with different variations:

- Announce the prize, the technological objective sought, and the award value, V.
- Fund the reward through philanthropy, corporate sponsorship, or the tax system.
- An innovator develops the innovation if the prize value V exceeds the cost of development, F.
- The innovator receives the award and waives IP rights, and the innovation is put into the public domain.
- Competition to manufacture and distribute the good or service based on the innovation should drive prices down to, or close to, the marginal cost of production, $P = MC$. (No need for $P > MC$ over time to help recoup the sunk cost F since the public sector or the sponsors paid for it.)

At the outset, there is no inherent reason why a prize system and an IP system cannot coexist. The debate centers on whether innovation contests or prize systems should replace the patent system altogether. A prize system could incentivize innovations that are not patentable, such as discoveries, mathematical ideas, algorithms, and other fundamental knowledge. It could also be used to sponsor one-off innovations aimed at addressing major social challenges, like neglected tropical diseases or climate change, where the private market may underinvest due to low expected profits but high R&D costs.

[37]See Chapter 3 of Spulber (2021) and Chapter 14 of Hall and Helmers (2024) for a survey of the literature.

However, as a replacement for patent rights, a prize system has several limitations. First, it is a top-down, centralized approach, where the prize announcer sets the agenda. In contrast, the patent system is more bottom-up, allowing researchers and the organizations they are affiliated with to pursue their own agendas, often guided by market demand. In academia, both top-down and bottom-up research occur. For example, academics might respond to a call for proposals from a foundation looking to sponsor a specific research project (e.g., Ethics of AI). Alternatively, academics often pursue their own research interests and seek funding either internally or externally. Sometimes, a coincidence of interests occurs: a government agency, like the National Institutes of Health, may express interest in sponsoring research on an oncology project that an academic team has been working on.

Second, the prize system operates on a winner-takes-all model. The announcement of sponsored research may prompt multiple parties to compete, each conducting potentially duplicative research. This resembles patent races and introduces inefficiency. While one firm or innovator ultimately receives the prize, the non-winners cannot recoup their investments. As more innovators enter the competition, the prize value (V) may need to increase to offset the low probability of winning.

Third, innovations are not always discrete breakthroughs, such as cures for major diseases or new green technologies, but are often adaptations, refinements, extensions, or hybrids of existing technologies. In this sense, innovation is a continuous journey. Patents, for instance, rarely cover entire products but rather the individual components that make up a product. As such, organizing contests for every technological component or improvement would be impractical. Breakthroughs can take years to materialize, and prizes tend to favor firms that have already begun their research.[38]

Fourth, it is not clear that a prize system is devoid of deadweight welfare losses (DWL). If the public sector sponsors the competition, the government would fund the prizes through taxes, which would create DWL. In addition, there are administrative costs associated with running the prize system and overseeing the commercialization and licensing of innovations.

---

[38]These firms likely anticipated filing for a patent, meaning the patent system initially motivated their research. While a prize announcement could encourage a firm to expedite its project, the prize system, in its abstract form (without a specific problem focus), may not be enough to sustain ongoing research unless researchers know in advance what future prize-worthy topics will be. Only with this knowledge could they steer their research in that direction. To maintain engagement, some form of IP protection is necessary, which is why a prize system would need to be supported by an IP system, or else firms may be less motivated to conduct early-stage R&D.

Chapter 5

North–South Models of Innovation

5.1 Introduction

This chapter explores aspects of innovation in a globalized world, focusing on the interactions between the technologically advanced economies of the *North* and the developing economies of the *South*.

The chapter begins by developing a partial equilibrium model to illustrate the core trade-offs. In this model, a Northern firm's investment in research and development (R&D) can be either protected or imitated by a Southern competitor. The analysis shows how IPR protection, such as trade secrecy, alters R&D incentives and the distribution of profits between the two firms. Without protection, the Southern firm can free-ride on the North's innovation, yet the Northern firm is still better off innovating than not.

The chapter then turns to general equilibrium models, which incorporate product cycles, international trade, and foreign direct investment (FDI). These models provide a richer understanding of how Southern IPR regimes can feed back to affect the pace of innovation in the North. The effects are not always straightforward; for example, stronger IPR in the South could paradoxically reduce Northern innovation by shifting manufacturing jobs back to the North, thus consuming labor resources that could have been devoted to R&D. Conversely, stronger IPR in the South can also stimulate

Northern innovation by shifting production abroad, freeing up Northern resources for innovation.

After examining the theoretical frameworks, the chapter turns to a critique of these models and a review of the empirical evidence. The empirical literature reveals complex, non-linear relationships between IPR and innovation. A central lesson is that the benefits of stronger IPR are conditional on a country's existing innovative capacity and level of economic development.

The final sections explore the economics of IPR harmonization, presenting a model that shows why differential, rather than uniform, standards are often optimal for countries at different stages of development. This leads to a discussion of utility models, or petty patents, as a less stringent and more flexible form of IPR. The experience of nations like South Korea suggests that such systems can effectively encourage minor, adaptive innovations that are useful for building technological capacity in the early stages of industrialization, serving as a stepping stone to a more robust patent system.

5.2 North–South Framework

5.2.1 *Partial Equilibrium*

Partial equilibrium analysis studies a single market or sector in isolation, holding other markets constant. It contrasts with general equilibrium analysis, which takes into account the interactions and interdependencies of all markets in an economy.

Assume two countries, North and South, and two firms, one from each country. Both firms produce a homogeneous good at constant marginal cost, c. Let the world market demand be given by $P = 1{,}000 - Q$, where P denotes the price of the good and Q the total quantity. Now $Q = q_N + q_S$, where q_N is the quantity supplied by the Northern firm and q_S the quantity supplied by the Southern firm.[1]

However, only the Northern firm engages in R&D, resulting in a process innovation that lowers its marginal cost of production. The Northern firm attempts to keep the innovation a trade secret, but the secret may leak to the Southern firm, allowing it to lower its marginal cost by the same amount.

[1] This model is adapted from Chin and Grossman (1990).

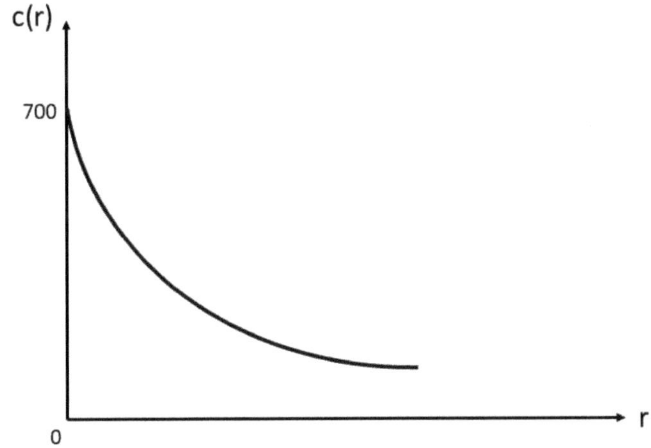

Figure 5.1. Marginal Cost Function

Assume the (constant) marginal cost of production is related to R&D investment (r) in the following way:

$$c(r) = 700 - \sqrt{r}$$

According to this equation, investments in research and development reduce the marginal cost of production, $c(r)$, but at a diminishing rate, as depicted in Figure 5.1.[2]

By default, the marginal cost of production is 700 when no R&D is invested. Three cases will be examined: (i) no trade secrecy protection, (ii) trade secrecy protection, and (iii) strategic R&D. The lessons are as follows: in the absence of trade secrecy protection, the Southern firm can free ride on the Northern firm's R&D investment, earning greater profits than the Northern firm because it does not incur the investment spending to develop the cost-cutting technology. However, the Northern firm is still better off investing in positive amounts of R&D, rather than investing nothing. With trade secrecy protection, which prevents the Southern firm from free-riding, the Northern firm is incentivized to invest more in R&D, gaining a competitive advantage and earning significantly higher profits than the Southern firm. In the third case, under trade secrecy protection, the Northern firm may invest so much in R&D that its cost advantage drives the Southern firm out of the market, allowing the Northern firm to be the

[2]That is, the first derivative is negative, $c' < 0$, and the second derivative positive, $c'' > 0$.

sole producer. However, this costly strategy leaves the Northern firm with zero economic profits.

Case 1: No Trade Secrecy Protection

Consider the output stage first, where r is treated as a parameter. Each firm chooses its output to maximize profits:

$$\pi_i = Pq_i - c(r)q_i, \quad i = N, S \tag{5.1}$$

Substitute $P = 1{,}000 - (q_N + q_S)$ into the above equation and use the method of optimization to get:[3]

$$q_i = \frac{1{,}000 - c(r)}{3}, \quad P = \frac{1{,}000 + 2c(r)}{3}, \quad \pi_i = \frac{(1{,}000 - c(r))^2}{9}, \quad i = N, S \tag{5.2}$$

Next, consider the R&D stage. Knowing what to expect in the output stage, the Northern firm can choose the optimal research and development expenditure, r. The net profit is the gross profit less the R&D expenditures:

$$\pi_N = \frac{(1{,}000 - c(r))^2}{9} - r \tag{5.3}$$

The optimal R&D is $r^* = 1{,}406.25$.[4] From this investment in R&D, a process innovation results which lowers the constant marginal cost of production from 700 to 662.5 (i.e., $c(r^*) = 700 - \sqrt{1{,}406.25}$).

The Southern firm's profit is $\pi_S = 12{,}656.25$ (using the formula in (5.2)). The Northern firm's net profit is the amount of the Southern firm's profit less the R&D expenditure, $\pi_N = 11{,}250$. Though the Southern firm is a free-rider, as it contributed no resources to the process innovation, the Northern firm still benefits from conducting the research solely. Had it chosen $r = 0$, the constant marginal cost of production would have been 700. Then, from (5.2), it can be seen that both firms' profits would have been lower: $\pi_N = \pi_S = \frac{(1{,}000-700)^2}{9} = 10{,}000$.

[3]As discussed in Appendix 2B of Chapter 2, the optimal level of output is derived by taking the partial derivative of π_i with respect to q_i and setting it to zero. For example, for the Northern firm, $\pi_i = (1{,}000 - q_N - q_S)q_N - c(r)q_N$. Calculate $\frac{\partial \pi_N}{\partial q_N} = 0$ to derive the "reaction function" $q_N = \frac{1{,}000-c(r)-q_S}{2}$. By an analogous process, another reaction function $q_S = \frac{1{,}000-c(r)-q_N}{2}$ is derived. Solving those two reaction functions for the two unknowns q_N, q_S yields the optimal output levels shown in the text.

[4]To derive this, first substitute $c(r) = 700 - \sqrt{r}$ into the net profit function 5.3 and then find the level of r that solves $\frac{\partial \pi_N}{\partial r} = 0$.

Case 2: Trade Secrecy Protection

Consider again the output stage first, where r is treated as a parameter. Because of the trade secrecy protection, the Southern firm is not privy to the cost-cutting innovation of the Northern firm. Hence, the profit functions are asymmetric:

$$\begin{aligned} \pi_N &= Pq_N - c(r)q_N \\ \pi_S &= Pq_S - 700q_S \end{aligned} \tag{5.4}$$

By applying the same profit maximization methods as in Case 1, two equations are derived for the two unknowns, q_N and q_S. Solving for them yields

$$q_N = \frac{1{,}700 - 2c(r)}{3}, \quad q_S = \frac{c(r) - 400}{3} \tag{5.5}$$

Substituting these into the demand equation ($P = 1{,}000 - q_N - q_S$) yields the equilibrium price, $P = \frac{1{,}700+c(r)}{3}$. Given the equilibrium price and outputs, the profits can be written as

$$\begin{aligned} \pi_N &= \frac{(1{,}700 - 2c(r))^2}{9} - r \\ \pi_S &= \frac{(c(r) - 400)^2}{9} \end{aligned} \tag{5.6}$$

Next, consider the R&D stage. The Northern firm chooses r to maximize its net profits. The solution is[5]

$$r^{**} = 14{,}400$$

and the resulting constant marginal cost of production is $c(r^{**}) = 580$. Substituting these into (5.6) yields the following profits of the Northern and Southern firm, respectively: $\pi_N = 18{,}000$ and $\pi_S = 3{,}600$. Compared to the case of no trade secrecy, the Northern firm is better off and the Southern firm worse off.

Case 3: Strategic R&D

Here, the Northern firm engages in predation to make the Southern firm exit the market. Recall from (5.5) that the Southern firm's output is $q_S = \frac{c(r)-400}{3}$,

---

[5]First, substitute $c(r) = 700-\sqrt{r}$ into π_N in (5.6) to get $\pi_N = \frac{[1{,}700-2(700-\sqrt{r})]^2}{9} - r$. The first-order condition (F.O.C.) is $\frac{\partial \pi_N}{\partial r} = \frac{1{,}200+8\sqrt{r}}{18\sqrt{r}} - 1 = 0$. The solution to this is $\sqrt{r} = 120$.

so that $q_S = 0$ if the constant marginal cost, $c(r)$, equals 400. Thus, an alternative strategy for the Northern firm is to invest $r = 90{,}000$, which would achieve a constant marginal cost of production of 400.[6]

With the global market to itself, the Northern firm's output is $q_N = 300$ using 5.5. From the demand curve, the equilibrium price is $P = 1{,}000 - q_N = 700$, which equals the original default marginal cost of production. Essentially, though it is a monopolist, the Northern firm acts "competitively," pricing at the Southern firm's marginal cost. Its gross profits are $\pi_N = 90{,}000$ using (5.6). But after subtracting its R&D investment cost of 90,000, its net profits are zero.

Table 5.1 summarizes all the cases that have been examined.

Trade secrecy allows the Northern and Southern firms to compete as *duopolists*, with the Northern firm being compensated for its process innovation by capturing the lion's share of world profits. This simple model offers an initial look at the North–South distribution of payoffs, both with and without IP protection.

5.2.2 *General Equilibrium Analysis*

Next, consider models that integrate consumers and producers, incorporate budget identities and resource constraints, and allow price variables — such as prices, wages, and interest rates — to adjust endogenously to achieve market equilibrium.

Imagine two countries (Figure 5.2):

1. Resources in North are allocated between R&D and manufacturing.
2. The South has lower labor costs.

Table 5.1. Summary of Outcomes

Scenario	**R&D (r)**	**N's Profits (π_N)**	**S's Profits (π_S)**
Pre-Innovation	0	10,000	10,000
No Trade Secrecy Protection	1,406.25	11,250	12,656.25
Trade Secrecy Protection	14,400	18,000	3,600
Strategic R&D	90,000	0	n/a

[6]That is, $c(r) = 700 - \sqrt{r} = 700 - \sqrt{90{,}000} = 400$.

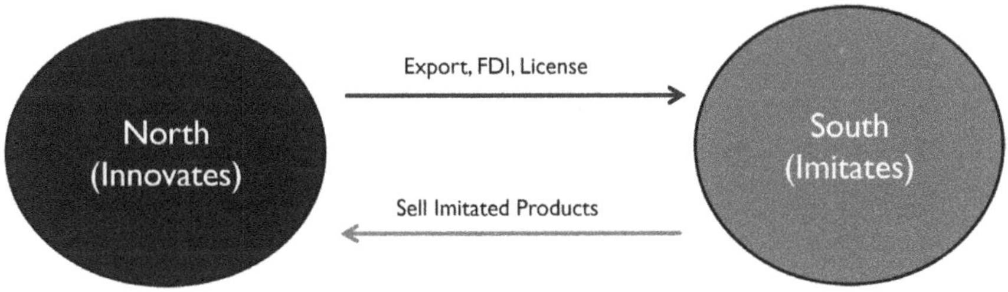

Figure 5.2. North–South Overview

3. Global IPR affects Northern innovation incentives to innovate, and Southern IPR determines technology diffusion from North to South.

These North–South models of trade are a central framework and have become the workhorse for researchers in the field.[7] Typically, innovation is assumed to occur in the North (N) and imitation in the South (S). The models exhibit product cycles where initially N exports a good and then S imitates it and takes over the exporting of the good. It is assumed that S has lower wages, an advantage which enables the Southern firm to undercut the price of the Northern firm and hence displace Northern production.

In this model, researchers have studied how IPRs in the South affect not only the volume of technology transfers and the composition (among licensing, exports, and FDI), but also the pace of innovation in the North.

Box 1. Summary Details of N–S Model

- **Product cycle:** A Northern firm has a monopoly over a good (with price equal to a markup over cost) until the South imitates, in which case the good is produced competitively (i.e., price = marginal cost) and the South displaces the Northern firms as producers of the good.
- **Total number of goods:** $n = n^N + n^S$ = original + imitated.
- **Market demands:** Demands exist for all n goods in each country. All firms (from N and S) compete for the same consumers.
- **Imitation risk:** This risk is inversely related to the strength of IPR.

[7]For early original work, see Grossman and Helpman (1991).

- **Resource constraints:**
  - ❑ In the North, finite resources are divided between R&D and manufacturing;
  - ❑ In the South, finite resources are divided between local (imitative) production and foreign companies (if any)

As Box 1 indicates, when the Southern economy successfully imitates and then takes over the manufacturing of the product, the Northern monopolist is displaced in the production of that good, and the good is supplied competitively worldwide. The total number of goods consists of the original (not yet imitated) goods and goods that have been imitated.[8] The share of imitated goods is a function of IPR levels in the South.

The impact of IPR on Northern innovation can be explained with the aid of the following *resource constraints*. In the North, resources are allocated between R&D and manufacturing. Hence, there are tradeoffs: if the North does more manufacturing, that negatively affects R&D in the North because more resources go into manufacturing than into R&D (and that is the intuition as to how stronger IPR could negatively affect innovation in the North). In a way, the South does Northern innovators a favor if it does a greater share of manufacturing. In the South, resources are allocated between imitation activity and foreign affiliate activity. The South will not suffer much loss of employment if stronger IPR shuts down local imitation because it may attract MNCs that can then employ local workers.

5.2.2.1 Predictions

What is the impact of stronger IPRs on innovation in the North? The answer depends on the type of innovation — whether it involves the creation of new product varieties or improvements in product quality — and on whether multinational firms operate in the South.

Before examining these outcomes, some further details are needed. Once innovation occurs in the North, technologies diffuse to the South either through imitation by firms in S or via formal technology transfer mechanisms, such as licensing or foreign direct investment (FDI). Profits earned in the South, in turn, influence Northern incentives to innovate. Innovation

[8] Technically, since n is continuous, it should be referred to as the measure of goods, not the number of goods. But for ease of exposition, the term "numbers" is used.

may take the form of expanding the variety of goods or improving the quality of existing goods. The equilibrium rates of innovation and technology transfer depend on underlying incentives (e.g., firm value maximization) and the available stock of economic resources (hence, the resource constraints discussed above). In many models, labor is assumed to be the sole factor of production, allocated between research and manufacturing.

On the demand side, consumers solve a two-stage budget problem: a dynamic one and a static one. The dynamic problem is to choose the time profile of their overall expenditures, E. The static optimization problem is to spread their expenditures E either among differentiated goods (in the case of variety-growth models) or among a fixed continuum of goods of different quality levels (in the case of quality-ladder models).

On the production side, producers all face a constant returns technology in which one unit of labor is needed to produce one unit of a good. Some goods are produced in the North and others in the South. Recall that the total number (measure) of goods is $n = n_N + n_S$. Consumers in each region consume quantities of each of the goods available in the world. It is not the case that consumers in one region consume goods produced only in that region (as in location models). Northern and Southern firms all compete for the same consumers. The exposition below presents some classic models of IPR in a North–South framework. First, some contrasting results are shown on the effects of IPR in variety-growth models. Next, similar analyses are shown for quality-ladders models. Throughout, the focus is on the economic intuition behind the results. Table 5.2 provides an overview of the key results in the models.

(i) Variety-Growth Models and IP

Helpman (1993) develops a model in which stronger IPRs in the South could lower the long-run rate of innovation in the North via a *production shifting effect*. To see this, consider the Northern labor-market resource constraint:

$$\bar{L} = L_R + L_M$$

where $\bar{L}$ denotes the fixed supply of labor in the North, L_R the labor employed in the research sector, and L_M the labor employed in manufacturing. Goods produced in the South result only from the imitation of Northern goods. Stronger IPRs, indexed by θ, reduce imitations (i.e., $\frac{dn_S(\theta)}{d\theta} < 0$). Thus, a tightened IPR regime shifts production back to the North. As a result, labor in manufacturing, L_M, increases. Given a fixed supply of Northern labor, wages in the North rise, thereby increasing the

Table 5.2. Impact of IPR in South on Innovation in North

Scenario	Impact
No Multinationals (Exporting Only)	**Negative:** Production shifts back to N and fewer resources for R&D in N.
Multinationals (FDI)	**Positive:** Attracts FDI and frees up resources for R&D in N and diverts employment away from imitation to affiliate production in S.
Multinationals (FDI) (with Imitation Costs)	**Negative:** Imitators in S incur greater resources to invent around Northern goods, raising labor costs. Less FDI occurs, shifting production back to N and reducing resources for R&D.
Licensing	**Positive:** More resources are available for R&D in N, as returns to licensing in S increase. Fewer resources in N are used in licensing negotiations to protect against misappropriation.

cost of research and reducing resources available for innovation, L_R. Hence, the rate of innovation in the North would decline.

Lai (1998) modifies the above model to allow some Northern firms to become multinational firms that produce in the South. In this case, stronger IPRs in the South attract FDI from the North. This enables production to occur in the South within local subsidiaries of Northern firms. Importantly, this possibility reduces the demand for manufacturing labor in the North and frees up resources for innovation. To see this, consider the Southern labor-market constraint:

$$\bar{L}^S = L_I + L_F$$

where $\bar{L}^S$ is the endowment of Southern labor, L_I the labor used in imitation, and L_F the labor employed by multinational firms. A Northern firm benefits from becoming a multinational because wages are lower in the South, but imitation risks are higher in the South. Thus, stronger IPRs in the South reduce risks of imitation and increase the expected returns to being a multinational firm. As a result, more production is transferred from the North to the South. Production shifting to the South relieves pressure in the Northern labor market, and more labor is available in the North for innovation. In other words, L_I decreases, L_F increases, L_M decreases, and L_R increases. Hence, in this model, stronger IPRs are associated with higher rates of long-run innovation and technology transfer.

(ii) Quality-Ladder Models and IP

The previous two models assumed negligible costs of imitation. In Glass and Saggi (2002), imitators incur fixed costs in order to imitate successfully, and multinational firms face additional costs of adapting their technologies to the South. Imitators in the South target both Northern firms' goods and multinational firms' goods for imitation. The Northern labor-resource constraint is similar to that in the variety-growth models, while the Southern labor-resource constraint is

$$\bar{L}^S = L_I + L_F + L_A + \alpha(\theta), \quad \frac{d\alpha}{d\theta} > 0$$

Here, L_A is the labor absorbed by multinational firms to adapt Northern goods to the Southern market, and $\alpha(\theta)$ is the labor used to make imitations of foreign goods and is a positive function of the stringency of IPR. For instance, the stronger the IP rights, the greater the costs of inventing around existing IP rights, so that more labor is needed.

An increase of θ reduces incentives to imitate but raises the total resources devoted to imitative activities. Because Southern imitators incur greater resources to invent around foreign goods, stronger intellectual property protection in the South results in greater resource scarcity. Less FDI occurs due to the higher costs of production and adaptation. With less FDI, Northern workers manufacture more goods since less production is transferred to the South. Consequently, less labor is available for innovation, and this model predicts a decline in Northern innovation and FDI.

In contrast, Yang and Maskus (2001) develop a model in which stronger IPRs increase long-run innovation and technology transfer via licensing. Stronger IPRs in the South increase Northern incentives to license in two ways. First, the contractual costs of license negotiation and enforcement are reduced. Second, due to reduced imitation risk, the Northern licensor can command a larger share of the rents; that is, have greater bargaining power. Under weaker IPRs, the licensor would have yielded a higher share to deter imitation or defection.

The Northern resource constraint is

$$\bar{L}^N = L_R + L_M + L_C(\theta), \quad \frac{dL_C}{d\theta} < 0$$

where L_C denotes the labor employed in licensing negotiations. Stronger IPRs in the South reduce contracting costs, so that the North can employ fewer workers to do contracting. In the South, goods are produced under Northern licensing agreements. Stronger IPRs in the South increase the returns to licensing there so that more production is transferred there. As a result, production labor in the South rises while Northern manufacturing employment, L_M, falls. Furthermore, fewer resources are absorbed in licensing negotiations so that L_C falls. Hence, more resources are available for innovation (i.e., L_R increases). Thus, both steady-state licensing and innovation are higher when IPRs are stronger.

One aspect not captured in the models above is that Southern IPR may influence not only the level of resources allocated to research but also the nature of Northern R&D. Consumers in the North and South have different technological needs and preferences, but Northern firms possess greater innovative capacities. Therefore, there is potential for the IP system in the South to influence Northern firms to develop technologies that are more appropriate to Southern needs, related to health, food security, or the environment.[9]

5.3 Critiques of North–South Models

The main critiques of North–South models include the following:

- N–S models ignore Southern innovation. This is important since one of the goals of IPRs reform is to encourage local innovation and risk-taking.
- Northern firms may engage in multiple modes of entry — export, FDI, and licensing — simultaneously, rather than individually or sequentially. This matters because stronger IPRs in the South could reduce FDI while increasing licensing, or vice versa, potentially raising the overall volume of technology transfer. The models surveyed in this chapter examine one mode at a time.
- The Southern market may be too small to affect Northern innovation incentives significantly.

Figure 5.3 demonstrates that global market shares are indeed asymmetric.[10] The N–S models examine how the strength of IPR in the South feeds back to Northern innovation. As Figure 5.3 depicts, however, the Southern

[9]See Diwan and Rodrik (1991) for a formal analysis.

[10]Shares are calculated from World Bank *World Development Indicators*, 2021.

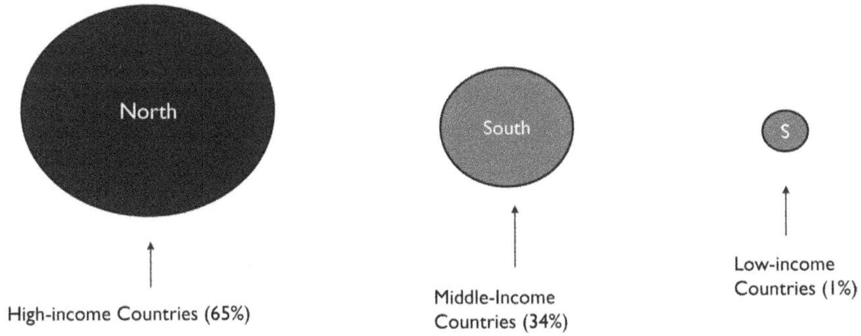

Figure 5.3. North–South Asymmetric Market Sizes

market constitutes a relatively small share of the world market from the perspective of the North. Low-income countries constitute approximately one percent of the world market. Thus, the contribution of their IPR to overall Northern incentives to innovate is likely to be very small.[11]

Some empirical evidence exists regarding the feedback of Southern IPR on Northern R&D. For example, Park (2012) studies the effect of foreign patent rights on the R&D of U.S. multinational firms using a unique micro-survey of parent firms and their foreign affiliates during 1982 to 2004. On average, U.S. firms' export market shares across the world were as follows: other developed countries (78%), upper-income developing countries (17%), and lower-income countries (5%). Their shares of outward FDI were similar: other developed countries (87%), upper-income developing countries (11%), and lower-income countries (2%).

Consider the following regression equation for testing the influence of foreign IPR on domestic R&D:

$$R_{ijt} = \beta_0 + \beta_D P_{jt}^D + \beta_N P_{jt}^N + \beta_S P_{jt}^S + \beta_X \tilde{X}_{ijt} + \varepsilon_{ijt}$$

where P_D is domestic patent rights, P_N is a weighted average of patent rights in Northern countries, P_S is a weighted average of patent rights in Southern countries, and $\tilde{X}$ is a vector of control variables, such as firm sales and income tax rates. Lagged export shares are used as weights.[12]

The abridged results are in Table 5.3.

The results show that domestic patent rights affect U.S. R&D, as do patent rights in other developed countries, such as Japan, the EU, Australia,

[11]This point is made in Chin and Grossman (1990) and Deardorff (1992).

[12]That is, if foreign country X had accounted for 5% of past U.S. exports, then country X's strength of patent rights receives a 5% weight.

Table 5.3. Influence of Domestic and Foreign Patent Rights on R&D

Dependent Variable: U.S. MNC R&D				
Select Variables	**(1)**	**(2)**	**(3)**	**(4)**
Domestic Patent Rights	0.891***	0.939***	0.887***	0.946***
Foreign Patent Rights in Other Developed Countries	1.808***	1.765***	1.872***	1.727***
Foreign Patent Rights in Developing Countries	−0.108			
Foreign Patent Rights in Upper-Income Developing Countries		−0.061		
Foreign Patent Rights in Lower-Income Developing Countries			−0.136	
Patent Rights in Brazil, India, China, Korea				0.074

Note: *** indicates statistical significance at the 1% level.

and Canada. However, the patent rights of developing economies consistently have an insignificant influence on U.S. R&D. The significance of this result is that N–S models need to account for asymmetric country sizes. A policy implication is that claims of weak Southern IPRs adversely affecting Northern innovation are not empirically supported. However, the South's share of the world market has been growing, and hence the findings may differ with a more updated sample.

Sharma (2015) finds somewhat different results. This study uses data on 78 developing countries from 1990 to 2010. It finds that patent protection in the South can positively affect innovation in the North. The sample of Northern countries includes the U.S. and other developed countries. The regression analysis examines how the patent strength of a middle-income (MI) country affects a weighted average of the R&D intensity of high-income (HI) countries, where the weights for each MI country are defined as the share of FDI flows from a particular HI country.

The mechanism uncovered in this study is that FDI flows from high-income countries to middle-income countries, with greater flows occurring when the host country's patent rights are stronger. The FDI in turn stimulates R&D in the North due to the production shifting effect. That is, resources are freed up for R&D in the North when more manufacturing is conducted in the South. While the study shows that Southern IPR has a statistically significant influence on Northern R&D via FDI, the *quantitative* impact is potentially small, as it is distributed among several high-income countries.[13]

5.4 Empirical Studies on North–South Innovation

This section reviews a few empirical studies on the relationship between domestic innovation and patent protection.[14] The studies find mixed evidence for developing countries, and that the effects are conditional on the presence of other factors related to innovative capacity.

5.4.1 *Non-linearities*

The theory thus far suggests a tradeoff: stronger patent protection improves an innovator's ability to appropriate the investment returns but also limits rivalry and competition. The former likely dominates when patent protection levels are not too strict, but once they are at high levels, the latter effect dominates. This inverted-U relationship likely applies in an industry setting, but when the data are evaluated across countries, the relationship is more U-shaped; that is, the relationship between innovation and IPR tends to be negative (downward sloping) for developing countries but positive (upward sloping) for developed countries.

The following describes empirical studies using international data. The first study by Allred and Park (2007) considers two measures of innovation: national-level residential patent data and firm-level R&D. Consider the following abridged Table 5.4.

The results above are obtained from a sample of 100 countries over the period 1965–2000 (every five years).[15] The index of patent rights used

[13]That is, the coefficient estimate of 0.06–0.12 must be divided among the countries comprised in the weighted average of the R&D of developed countries.

[14]The next chapter will focus on the relationship between IPR and technology transfer.

[15]The results were derived using a regression method suitable for patent count data.

Table 5.4. Residential Patenting and the Patent Rights Index

	All Countries		Developed Economies		Developing Economies	
	(1)	**(2)**	**(3)**	**(4)**	**(5)**	**(6)**
Patent Rights Index	0.109	−0.744***	0.238**	−0.746*	−0.256**	−0.158
(Patent Rights Index)^2		0.158***		0.147***		−0.022
Other Controls Included	Yes	Yes	Yes	Yes	Yes	Yes
Sample Size	491	491	184	184	307	307

Note: ***, **, * denote significance levels at the 1%, 5%, and 10% levels.
Source: Allred and Park (2007).

here was described in Chapter 2 (namely, the PRI index or GP index). Residential patents are essentially domestic patents.[16] Table 5.4 explains whether there is an association between that measure of innovation and the strength of patent protection, controlling for other variables, such as market size, WTO membership, and year effects. For the pooled sample of all countries, no statistically significant relationship can be detected between residential patenting and the strength of patent protection (see column 1). However, when the square of the patent rights index is included, the index has a statistically significant negative coefficient and its square has a statistically significant positive coefficient (see column 2). This suggests a U-shaped relationship between residential patenting and the strength of patent rights.[17]

In contrast to the theoretical analysis of the previous chapter, an inverted-U shape between innovation and IP strength is not observed. The explanation is that cross-country data are being analyzed. Across countries, innovation rises if the strength of patent rights is relaxed (or weakened). The "left-side" of the U-shaped curve[18] captures the benefits to developing

[16]The slight nuance is that some local affiliates of foreign MNCs file as residents.

[17]As discussed in Appendix 2C to Chapter 2, these sign configurations indicate that the second partial derivative of innovation with respect to the patent rights index is positive — hence the U-shape.

[18]Which can be imagined as having residential patenting on the vertical axis and the patent rights index on the horizontal axis.

countries (the South) of having limited patent protection so as to facilitate imitation and learning, and adaptive innovations. Indeed, the results confirm that strengthening patent protection for the less developed economies might actually impact Southern innovation negatively by raising the cost of innovation due to higher (monopolistic) prices of technological inputs and higher licensing fees for the use of IP. But beyond some critical level of patent rights, raising the strength of patent protection is associated with an increase in residential patenting. This is the "right-side" of the U-shaped curve, where the data capture the wealthier, more developed economies. For this group, stronger patent rights enhance the ability of innovators to appropriate their returns to innovation and therefore spur residential patenting activity.

Columns 3 and 5 show that when the sample is split between developed and developing countries, a positive association between patenting and patent rights is detected for the sub-sample of developed countries and a negative one for the sub-sample of developing countries. The results in columns 3 and 5 can explain why the patent rights index is insignificant in column 1 (the pooled sample); namely, because the positive coefficient for the developed countries and the negative coefficient for the developing countries largely offset each other.

Columns 4 and 6 fit a nonlinear relationship between residential patenting and patent rights to the split samples. The U-shape relationship is still present in the developed country sample, but it is not as robust; the coefficient of the patent rights index is statistically significant at only the 10% level. And for the developing country sample, no U-shaped (or inverted-U shape) is detected.

Table 5.5 turns to firm-level data and R&D investments by firms as the measure of innovation.

The above models were estimated for firms headquartered across countries over the period 1990–2000. The control variables include firm sales and industry dummies. The results are qualitatively similar to those for residential patenting. Column 1 shows that the strength of patent protection has a significantly positive relationship with the R&D investments of firms operating in developed countries; however, as column 3 shows, no statistically significant relationship exists between firm R&D and patent protection in developing countries. Patent protection levels are relatively low during this period in the developing world, and so they had no real influence on firm incentives to innovate. In columns 2 and 4, a nonlinear equation is fitted to the data, but a weak U-shaped relationship exists only

Table 5.5. Firm Level R&D Spending and the Patent Rights Index

	Developed Economies		Developing Economies	
	(1)	(2)	(3)	(4)
Patent Rights Index	0.912**	−4.389*	0.361	0.517
(Patent Rights Index)^2		2.051**		−0.073***
Other Controls Included	Yes	Yes	Yes	Yes
Sample Size	2143	2143	303	303

Note: ***, **, * denote significance levels at the 1%, 5%, and 10% levels.
Source: Allred and Park (2007).

in the developed country sample. Neither the patent rights index nor its square is statistically significant in the developing country sample.

The interpretation of the results is that patent protection has been primarily a driver of innovation in the developed world. It appears to be ineffective at stimulating innovation in the developing world, or it is not conducive to the kind of incremental, adaptive, or imitative research that firms in emerging economies engage in. Other empirical studies support this. Using the same index of patent rights, Falvey *et al.* (2006) find that patent protection is positively and significantly related to the economic growth of low-income and high-income countries but negatively with that of middle-income countries. It is this group that depends for its economic development on utilizing foreign technologies and being able to imitate them. The low-income countries hardly perform much innovation, so their IP protection serves primarily to attract imports and foreign direct investment. The high-income group does heavily engage in R&D and patenting, and thus patent protection is relied upon to secure innovation returns.

Chen and Puttitanun (2005) provide a theoretical basis for why a U-shaped relationship should arise between the optimal strength of IP protection and economic development. In choosing the strength of IPR protection, a government weighs two factors. First, if protection is weak, high-quality foreign innovations can be more easily copied and diffused via local imitation. Second, if protection is strong, local innovators have stronger incentives to engage in research and innovation. In less developed economies, the first factor is more prominent since the quality of local innovation is low; hence governments choose weaker IPR protection. In more developed economies, the quality of local innovation is higher and therefore governments choose stronger IPR protection.

Papageorgiadis and Sharma (2016), however, find both a U-shape and an inverted-U shape relationship between innovation and patent protection. This study uses two different measures of patent protection. The first is the Ginarte and Park (GP) index, representing the strength of patent statutes and case laws. The other index is a measure that captures enforcement-related aspects of the IP system. Patent owners face transaction costs when seeking to enforce their rights. Hence, the enforcement index employs three transaction cost constructs: (i) monitoring costs of public authorities; (ii) property rights protection costs relating to judicial enforcement; and (iii) servicing costs related to public administration.

Employing the natural log of patent filings P as the measure of innovation, Papageorgiadis and Sharma (2016) estimate the following equation on 48 countries over the period 1998–2011:

$$\ln P_{it} = \beta_0 + \beta_1 PRI_{it} + \beta_2 PRI_{it}^2 + \beta_3 ENF_{it} + \beta_4 ENF_{it}^2 + \beta_5 \tilde{Z}_{it} + \varepsilon_{it}$$

where PRI denotes the patent rights index, ENF the enforcement-related index, $\tilde{Z}$ a vector of controls, and ε the error term, with subscript i indexing countries and subscript t time. The study estimates $\beta_1 > 0$ and $\beta_2 < 0$, indicating an inverted-U relationship between patenting and the patent rights index, and $\beta_3 < 0$ and $\beta_4 > 0$, indicating a U-shaped relationship between patenting and the enforcement-related index. Tighter enforcement may initially deter follow-on innovation if it allows incumbents to better assert their patent rights, but as enforcement strengthens more broadly, entrants may put in more capital and invest more heavily in innovation.

In these previous studies, a quadratic model was fitted to the data. Hudson and Minea (2013) provide a more flexible approach of letting the data determine the form of the *polynomial* equation that connects innovation to IPRs. The authors employ an econometric method that determines thresholds and nonlinear slopes endogenously. The technique is known as *Panel Smooth Threshold Regression* or PSTR. The study finds that the effects of IPR on innovation is heterogeneous along two dimensions: the initial level of IPR and the level of economic development of a country.

A *Panel Threshold Regression* (PTR) model originally appears as

$$\mathrm{INNOV}_{it} = \beta_1 \mathrm{IPR}_{it} + \beta_2 \mathrm{IPR}_{it} \Gamma(Q_{it}, \bar{Q}) + \cdots$$

where Γ is a transition function, Q a transition variable (say, IPR or GDP per capita), and $\bar{Q}$ a threshold:

$$\Gamma(Q_{it}, \bar{Q}) = \begin{cases} 0 & \text{if } Q_{it} < \bar{Q} \\ 1 & \text{if } Q_{it} > \bar{Q} \end{cases}$$

But this does not generate a smooth transition. Countries can go abruptly from one regime to another; that is, suddenly the coefficient of IPR can jump even for a country whose value of Q is just slightly below $\bar{Q}$ at one moment and slightly above $\bar{Q}$ the next. This gives the impression that innovation makes a sudden change.

To allow for a smooth transition, the PSTR model replaces the transition function above, Γ, with a more flexible equation that is a function of a key parameter, γ: $\Gamma(Q_{it}, \bar{Q}, \gamma)$. Γ is normalized to be between zero and one and has a *logistic* specification.[19] When $\gamma = 0$, the transition function is constant and the PSTR corresponds to a linear model. When $\gamma \to \infty$, the PSTR corresponds to the original PTR model. The intermediate case $0 < \gamma < \infty$ allows for a smooth transition between regimes. The regimes could be, for example, weak IP regimes, moderate IP regimes, and strict IP regimes.

Hudson and Minea (2013) estimate the PSTR model on 62 countries — developed and developing — for the period 1980–2009. The measure of IPR is the GP index, and economic development is proxied by GDP per capita. The dependent variable is patents per capita, where the patenting measure is U.S. patents granted to residents of a country. As mentioned before, using U.S. patents granted allows a study to suppress differences in patent-granting standards across national patent offices. Furthermore, given that it is relatively expensive to file in the U.S., firms tend to apply for U.S. patents for their high-quality innovations.

Hudson and Minea (2013) find that the estimated relationship between the derivative of innovation with respect to IPR and the levels of IPR is nonlinear, as depicted in Figure 5.4. The method, in essence, lets the data reveal where and how relationships change. The outcome is a combination of inverted-U and U-shape aspects. Either high levels of IPR or low levels are associated with a rise in innovation. At low levels of IPR, raising the strength of patent protection can help kick-start some innovation, but at

[19]That is, $\Gamma = [1 + \exp(-\gamma \Pi_{j=1}^{J}(Q_{it} - \bar{Q}))]^{-1}$ and γ is a slope parameter that determines the smoothness of the transition. J is the number of regime switches.

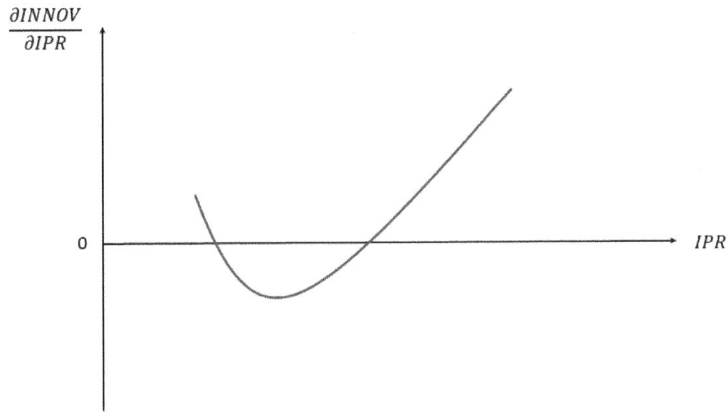

Figure 5.4. PSTR and Innovation-IPR Nonlinearity

intermediate levels, stronger patent rights may hinder imitative and adaptive learning and experimentation, thereby reducing innovation activity.

Note that Figure 5.4 assumes an identical relationship for all countries. Hudson and Minea (2013) extend the analysis by allowing the relationship between innovation and IPR to vary with the level of economic development, incorporating an additional transition function based on per capita GDP into the PSTR model. In effect, the curve depicted in Figure 5.4 becomes conditional on a country's per capita GDP. Higher per capita GDP shifts the curve to the right and dampens it because of synergies between IPR and economic development that prevent over-attribution of innovation outcomes to IPR alone. For countries above a certain income threshold, the curve may also rotate upward, indicating stronger innovation effects at higher levels of development.

The significance of the PSTR approach lies in its ability to capture both cross-country and temporal heterogeneities. For instance, although Ecuador and Singapore began with similar initial levels of IPR, their differing levels of GDP per capita resulted in contrasting effects: the elasticity of innovation with respect to IPR was positive for Singapore but negative for Ecuador. Elasticities also vary over time. In Egypt, for example, the elasticity was positive in the early 1980s but turned negative as the country moved up the middle-income ladder by the mid–1990s. These findings underscore a key lesson for IPR reform: a "one-size-fits-all" approach is not appropriate. Yet the TRIPS Agreement imposed uniform minimum standards on all countries — a tension this book will revisit.

In concluding this section on nonlinearities, it is important to exercise caution in interpreting movements along U-shaped or inverted-U-shaped curves. Briggs (2010) observes that these movements are primarily driven by cross-sectional variation rather than longitudinal dynamics. This is a valid concern, especially in light of TRIPS and other global or national reforms that have raised IPR levels across most countries. Consequently, the observed nonlinear relationships should not be read as time-series predictions; i.e., that innovation will necessarily rise or fall in the future in response to current IPR reforms. Rather, the nonlinearities reflect how differing economic characteristics across countries and regimes condition both the positive outcomes and normative assessments of IP reform.

5.4.2 *Economic Complexity*

Sweet and Maggio (2015) employ an alternative measure of innovation as the dependent variable of interest — namely, the Economic Complexity Index (ECI). This index is designed to capture both a country's capacity to generate knowledge and its ability to apply that knowledge productively. Two critical concepts provide the thematic structure of the ECI:

- *Diversity*: The number of distinct products a country can produce. This serves as an indicator of its innovative and productive capacity.
- *Ubiquity*: The number of countries capable of producing a given product. A lower ubiquity implies higher complexity, as fewer countries possess the knowledge and capabilities to produce the good.

Sweet and Maggio (2015) argue that the ECI offers a useful alternative to traditional measures of innovation, such as R&D spending and patent filings, both of which have some limitations. R&D data are often skewed toward large firms, excluding much of the innovative activity that occurs in smaller enterprises or informal sectors. Patenting data, meanwhile, do not capture the full universe of inventions, as many innovations are either not patentable, such as mathematical theorems, scientific principles, naturally occurring plant or animal varieties, and game rules, or are deliberately kept as trade secrets. Moreover, observed changes in patent filings raise an identification problem: are they driven by changes in actual innovation or merely by shifts in the propensity to patent?[20]

[20] See Kortum and Lerner (1999).

To clarify, suppose the number of patent filings is given by $P = \rho I$, where I denotes the volume of innovation and ρ the proportion of innovations that are patented. If P rises following IPR reforms, is the increase attributable to a rise in I or simply in ρ? Empirical researchers often struggle to disentangle these two components. The ECI helps sidestep this challenge by capturing a country's embedded productive knowledge. Overall, Sweet and Maggio (2015) find that ECI has a 0.64 correlation with R&D and a 0.81 correlation with patent grants.

The authors estimate a model in levels:

$$\text{ECI}_{it} = f(\text{IPR}_{it}, \text{Controls, including fixed effects})$$

as well as a dynamic model (with a lagged dependent variable):

$$\text{ECI}_{it} = f(\text{IPR}_{it}, \text{IPR}_{it-1}, \text{Controls, including fixed effects})$$

where subscript i refers to country and t to time. The measure of IPR is the GP index. The regression analysis is conducted on a panel of 94 countries over the period 1965–2005.[21] The results are consistent: the ECI is positively associated with IPR at conventional levels of statistical significance.

However, when the sample is split by income level or ECI, the positive association between IPR and economic complexity holds only for countries above the mean. For observations below the mean income or mean ECI, the coefficient on IPR is statistically insignificant, and in the dynamic model, even negative. Furthermore, when the analysis is limited to the post-TRIPS period, the results persist: the coefficient on IPR remains negative for the lower-income group but is positive for the higher-income group.

In Sweet and Eterovic (2019), the dependent variable of interest is productivity growth — specifically, the growth in total factor productivity. The model is

$$\text{GTFP}_{it} = f(\text{ECI}_{it}, \text{IPR}_{it}, \text{Controls, including fixed effects})$$

If ECI is not controlled for, IPR's coefficient can be positive (except when IPR is treated as endogenous). Once ECI is controlled for, the coefficient of ECI is positive and statistically significant, but the coefficient of IPR is not significant. Thus, the takeaway point is that patent protection has no direct role in productivity growth. What matters more to total factor

[21]For the dynamic panel data model, the study uses the *Generalized Method of Moments* (*GMM*), a regression technique that addresses endogeneity and corrects for the correlation between the transformed regressor and the transformed error term.

productivity growth is not laws *per se* but the adoption of frontier technologies, the acquisition of newer technologies, and the absorptive capacity of firms to make use of them.

This finding is reminiscent of an older study by Park and Ginarte (1997), which found that IPRs do not directly affect economic growth but indirectly by stimulating R&D and capital accumulation. Laws are important to markets, but there are some reasons why they may not appear to have a direct impact on productivity growth:

1. Changes in laws and institutions can be regarded as low-frequency events, as they do not change frequently or rapidly, whereas productivity growth can exhibit high-frequency fluctuations. It may well be that regressions better pick up relationships among variables that are more temporally aligned, or when both institutions and productivity are measured over extended periods (e.g., decades).
2. Productivity growth is also influenced by cyclical factors such as business cycles, demand conditions, mark-ups, imperfect competition, and regional heterogeneity, all of which may obscure the long-run influence of legal institutions.
3. Productivity is essentially defined as output over inputs. Either more output can be produced with the same quantity of inputs, or the same output can be produced with fewer inputs. These efficiency improvements depend critically on the application of technological innovations. While production responds directly to available resources and know-how, laws and institutions operate more indirectly by shaping the environment in which innovation and production occur. That said, laws and institutions can directly influence *inputs* such as technology and capital by affecting the expected returns to investment. For example, IPRs regulate whether firms can charge royalties or license fees for their intellectual property and whether they can exclusively exploit their innovations or must share them under certain conditions. IP laws determine how long economic profits can last before competitive entry can occur.

5.4.3 *Natural Experiment*

The studies reviewed thus far have been on aggregate innovation data. Qian (2007) focuses on the world pharmaceutical sector, an industry that tends to be highly dependent on patent protection due to the relative ease of replicating drug innovations. A century ago, few countries provided IP protection for drugs.[22] Many countries either completely excluded drugs and medicines from patent protection or had significant restrictions on pharmaceutical patents. The rationale had been that medicines were too important for public health to be subject to patent monopolies. Countries in Europe had policies that prevented or limited the patenting of pharmaceutical products, though they might have allowed patents on methods of production or on manufacturing processes. After World War II, the concept of protecting pharmaceutical innovations gained traction in international agreements and treaties. The push for stronger pharmaceuticals IP accelerated in the 1980s and 1990s with agreements like TRIPS.

Qian (2007) exploits a natural experiment in which some countries introduced pharmaceutical patent protection for the first time (or at least product patents for drugs for the first time). The ideal experiment would have been to randomly assign countries without a pharmaceutical patent system to implement one, but this is not feasible in practice, as institutions like the WTO or WIPO lack the authority to impose randomized policy changes. Instead, Qian (2007) constructs two control groups: (1) those countries that do not protect pharmaceutical patents and (2) those that have always provided pharmaceutical patent protection. Next, Qian (2007) matched them to a country that newly introduced pharmaceutical patents (or product patents). This matching was done for four time intervals: 1978–1982, 1983–1985, 1986–1990, and 1991–1995. The sample consisted of 92 countries, of which 26 adopted such patents for the first time. Qian (2007) then investigated the drug innovation behavior of this treatment group (i.e., the ones that adopted pharmaceutical patent laws) compared to the control groups, focusing not on immediate effects but on outcomes a decade later, to capture long-term structural shifts in pharmaceutical innovation.

The dependent variable is U.S. patents granted, weighted by citations to adjust for patent quality. The key independent variables are IPR and IPR squared (where the measure of IPR is the GP-index) and indicator variables for whether pharmaceutical patent law is implemented (e.g., yes/no). The results are that, relative to the control group, no statistically significant effect on drug innovation is detected ten years later upon the introduction of pharmaceutical patents. This confirms that the mere adoption of product patent laws does not induce pharmaceutical innovation. However, the interaction between the implementation of pharmaceutical patent laws and other measures like economic development, economic freedom, and human

[22]For a history, see Gaudillière (2006, 2008).

capital does have a positive effect on pharmaceutical innovation. This shows that countries that have high levels of economic development, markets, educational attainment, and innovative capacities are better able to leverage laws on IP.

Qian (2007) also identifies an inverted-U relationship between pharmaceutical innovation and the strength of patent rights. This sector-level analysis suggests the existence of an optimal level of patent protection, beyond which further strengthening may reduce innovation. In the context of the pharmaceutical industry, this pattern likely reflects the tradeoff between incentives and competition: while robust protection can encourage investment in drug development, excessively strong patent rights may increase market power, reduce competitive pressure, and ultimately stifle the pace at which new drugs are introduced.

Other studies reinforce the finding that intellectual property protection is more effective at stimulating innovation and productivity when sufficient levels of innovative capacity are already in place. Like Qian (2007), Hu and Png (2013) introduce industries into an international dataset, but more than just the pharmaceutical industry. Specifically, they study 50 manufacturing industries across 70 countries from 1971 to 2000. This study also uses the GP-index and interacts it with a measure of legal enforcement effectiveness. The key finding is that effective patent protection is most important for industrial growth in high-patent-intensive industries and technologically advanced economies.

Chu *et al.* (2014) find that patent rights negatively impact economic growth in countries that are distant from the global technology frontier, but have a positive impact in economies closer to the frontier. This is because developed economies rely on original innovations to drive productivity growth, and such innovations require relatively strong IP protection. In contrast, developing countries rely more on reverse engineering foreign technologies, an activity that is better accomplished under a more relaxed and flexible IP system.[23] Chu *et al.* (2020) also find that financial development plays a key role: patent protection more effectively spurs innovation in countries with higher levels of financial development. This is consistent with patent rights being more effective when economic freedom is greater.

[23]See Chu (2024).

5.5 Harmonization

This section explores the economics of why developed and developing countries should adopt different standards of IPR protection and then discusses the social welfare effects of harmonization. The treatment below is an adaptation of the Grossman and Lai (2004) model.

Model features:

- Two Countries: North and South
- Both conduct innovation and imitation
- Let θ_i denote the strength of IPR and M_i the market size in country $i = N, S$
- Let μ_i denote country i's share of world profits from innovation (such that $\mu_N + \mu_S = 1$)

Case 1: Closed Economy

The optimal IPR balances the deadweight losses due to market power and the marginal benefits due to enhanced innovation incentives. The optimal θ^* solves the following equation: $\Delta\text{DWL} = \Delta\text{B}(\theta^*, M)$.

ΔDWL measures the loss in consumer surplus (CS) net of profits. Firms' profits from innovation add to social welfare. ΔB measures the gain in consumer surplus owing to new valuable products created because of the spur to innovation, benefits that potentially last into the future even after IPRs expire. Market size, M, positively affects B by raising the return to innovation. IPR positively affects B, but at a diminishing rate.

This theoretical model shows that the optimal strength of IPR should vary with economic development. For example, the less developed the country, the smaller its market and the lower its innovative capacity, and thus the weaker its IPR level should be — for example, offering shorter duration and/or narrower scope.

The following provides some intuition using the notation previously defined. Most likely $\mu_N > \mu_S$; that is, the North has a greater share of world profits from innovation because of its greater technological capacity. Changes in IPR strength involve trade-offs: the ΔDWL in terms of the lost consumer surplus (CS) and the marginal benefits in terms of stimulating innovation so that CS is gained in the present and discounted future as innovation provides benefits over time until it becomes obsolete.

Note that changes in DWL must net out domestic firms' profits because producer surplus is part of social welfare.[24] If ΔDWL $>$ ΔB, protection is too strong, and vice versa.

Suppose that ΔDWL $=$ ΔB. This condition can be used to analyze how the optimal level of IPR responds to changes in underlying parameters. For instance, an increase in M (market size) raises the expected returns to innovation and thereby increases the marginal benefit of stronger intellectual property rights. It can be reasonably assumed that $B(\theta, M)$, the benefit function of IPR strength, is concave: when IPR is already high, the incremental gain from further strengthening tends to diminish. This occurs because monopolists with strong protections often reduce their pace of innovation, having already secured market exclusivity. As a result, additional increases in IPR strength yield smaller marginal benefits compared to when market power is weaker.

Case 2: Open Economy

The key modification here is that ΔDWL is now a function of μ, a country's share of profits from world innovation. Recall that domestic firms' profits are deducted from DWL because they help offset the loss in CS.

The optimal IPR policy functions (or best-response functions) for the Northern and Southern governments are, respectively

$$\Delta\text{DWL}(\mu_N) = \Delta\text{B}(\theta_N, M_N; \theta_S, M_S)$$

$$\Delta\text{DWL}(\mu_S) = \Delta\text{B}(\theta_S, M_S; \theta_N, M_N)$$

These two implicit equations help determine the optimal IPR levels, θ_N and θ_S. They are called best-response functions because of the interdependence: the North's choice of θ_N depends on θ_S, and vice versa. Each country's deadweight loss from IPR protection is mitigated by its share of profits from world innovation. The reason is that increased firm profits due to stronger IPRs add to social welfare and thereby cushion the loss in consumer surplus due to IPRs.

Note that the North's DWL function depends only on μ_N, its own share, and not μ_S. The same applies to the South's DWL function. The intuition is that, while a world leader (or a global social planner) would care about the world economy's constituents, a national leader (or a national social planner) cares only about its share of the world's constituents. Thus, a

[24] Ultimately, the economy contains a circular flow, whereby dividends and profits from sole proprietorships or partnerships flow to households.

policymaker in the home country cares only about the profits of domestic firms. The higher the domestic firms' share of profits from world innovation, the lower a country's net deadweight loss (again, the profits help offset the loss in consumer surplus that arises from higher prices due to stricter IPRs).

Moreover, the best response functions reveal temptations to free ride. Because the gains in consumer surplus (given by ΔB) are functions of the other country's market size and IPR level, either country has an incentive to lower its IPR to reduce its DWL while free riding on the other country's market size and IPR strength. Another way to express this is that allowing the other country to provide increased IPR protection enables a country to enjoy the innovation without the burden of increased deadweight losses at home.

Indeed, this is what the model capitalizes on — that the optimal choice of IPR is an *inverse* function of the other country's IPR — and it uses this feature to show why harmonization is not efficient.[25]

Compared to IPR policy in a closed economy, a country's IPR policy in an open economy stimulates innovation less because it has a relatively smaller influence worldwide.

To see this, temporarily depart from the two-country model and consider a world of n countries.

Each country, if it represents a small share of the world market, knows that its IPR policy has only a small impact on world incentives to innovate (see Figure 5.5). In the extreme case, if countries 2 to n do not have IPR systems, and only country 1 does, then country 1 bears the burden of incurring a deadweight loss, while its own small market size is the primary factor

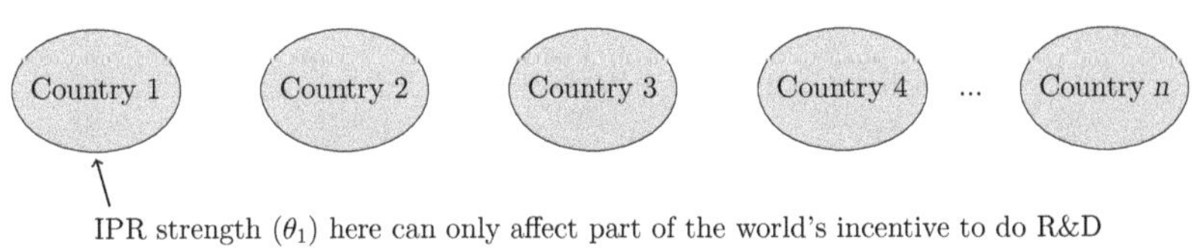

Figure 5.5. Multiple Countries of Symmetric Market Sizes

[25]The model's feature that a country has an incentive to free ride on the IPR of another country could be criticized for implicitly assuming that IPR lacks intrinsic value. For example, a culture where innovation is rewarded through IPR could motivate entry into high-tech careers, influence students' selection of STEM majors, build the capacity for original work, and foster trust around intellectual collaborations. These considerations, however, fall outside the scope of the model.

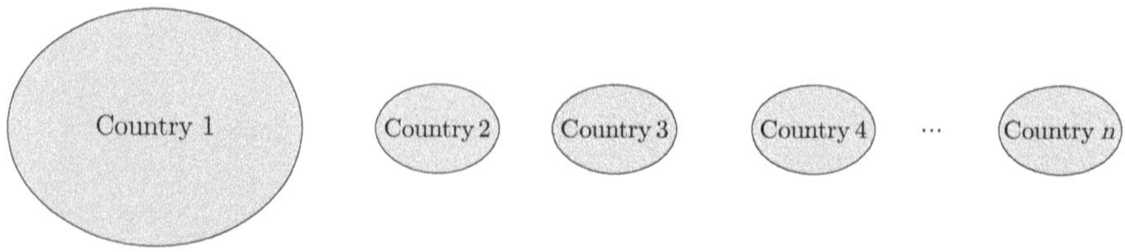

Figure 5.6. Multiple Countries of Asymmetric Market Sizes

that incentivizes innovators worldwide. For example, innovators from countries 2 to n would try to sell their goods/services in country 1 at a markup ($P > MC$) and recoup their fixed R&D investments there. But country 1's market is small, so it would motivate only a small R&D investment by innovators everywhere.

If country 1 is large, however, that makes a difference (Figure 5.6).

Hence, the index of IPR needs to be adjusted by market size. Incentives to innovate are zero if either $M = 0$ or $\theta = 0$. Therefore, let the effective market size-adjusted IPR strength be given by:

$$\theta_i \times M_i,$$

which equals the product of IPR strength and market size in country i.

5.5.1 *Equilibrium Protection*

Returning to the two-country case, the goal here is to find the equilibrium pair of IPR levels (θ_N^*, θ_S^*). First, the optimal IPR functions (or best-response functions) are downward-sloping. In other words, holding market sizes constant, an increase in θ_N leads to a decrease in θ_S, but the increase in θ_N is larger than the decrease in θ_S (or $\uparrow \theta_N > \downarrow \theta_S$), and vice versa.

The reasoning is that if $\Delta(\theta_N M_N)$ increases, then $\Delta(\theta_S M_S)$ decreases, but not one-for-one.

- If the market size-adjusted IPR level in the North rises, world innovation becomes less responsive to the South's IPR policy. The Southern government has less incentive to maintain strong IPRs (i.e., less marginal benefit to raising IPR standards).
- But the Southern government would not decrease its IPR strength proportionally (e.g., one-to-one) because it still wants to stimulate some domestic innovation. Hence, there is free-riding, but not complete free-riding.

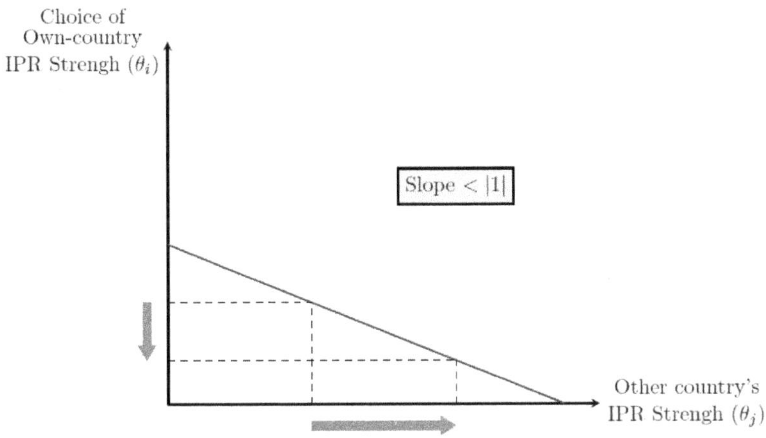

Figure 5.7. A "Best" Response Function

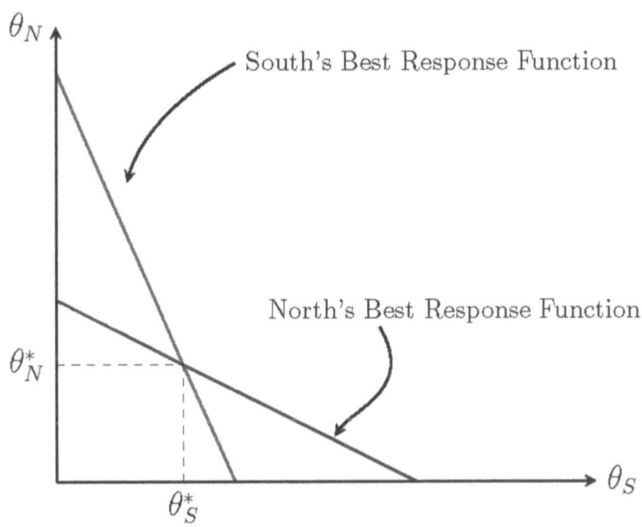

Figure 5.8. Equilibrium Protection under Symmetry

Hence, country N's IPR has an inverse relationship with the other country's IPR, but the slope of its best-response function is less than one in absolute value (see Figure 5.7).

Figure 5.8 shows the case of symmetry between North and South. The equilibrium IPRs are θ_N^* and θ_S^*.

In Figure 5.8, because both countries are symmetric, in equilibrium, they each provide the same IPR levels. Here, it is feasible to harmonize IPRs.

Consider an alternative scenario:

- *Suppose that* $M_N > M_S$: The larger Northern market means that the majority of innovation returns occur in the North. It is therefore more valuable to raise IPR in the North relative to the South. This condition indicates where to appropriate the returns to innovation.
- *Suppose* $\mu_N > \mu_S$: A greater share of world profits from innovation accrues to Northern firms. The majority of R&D is conducted by them. Their profits provide a greater offset to losses in consumer surplus in the North. Therefore, the North can tolerate a stronger IPR system than the South. This condition indicates who conducts the research and development.
- *Both conditions yield* $\theta_N^{**} > \theta_S^{**}$: Thus, differential IPR standards should emerge.

Both conditions — $M_N > M_S$ (a larger domestic market) and $\mu_N > \mu_S$ (a greater share of global innovation profits) — cause the North's best response function to shift upward (see Figure 5.9). Why? Because for any

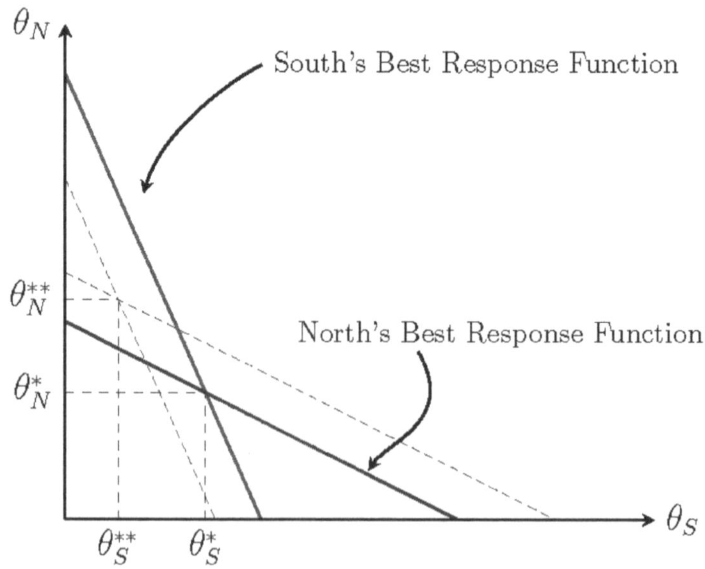

Figure 5.9. Equilibrium Protection under Asymmetry

given level of Southern IPR, a larger market and a greater appropriation of innovation rents make it optimal for the North to adopt a higher level of IPR protection.

In contrast, the same conditions shift the South's best response function downward (again see Figure 5.9). Why? Holding the North's IPR level constant, a smaller market and a lower share of global innovation profits reduce the South's incentives to enforce strong IPR, leading to a lower optimal IPR level.

This demonstrates why developing economies would and should choose lower levels of protection than developed countries.

5.5.2 *Optimal Protection*

The equilibrium IPRs derived thus far are most likely suboptimal from a world perspective. The reason is free-riding. Each country would prefer the other to bear some of the cost of IPR protection. In Figure 5.10, the outermost line given by $Q = \theta_N M_N + \theta_S M_S$ represents the line of efficiency. This occurs when all countries coordinate and act as one global economy, or when a global social planner can choose the optimal IPR levels. The planner

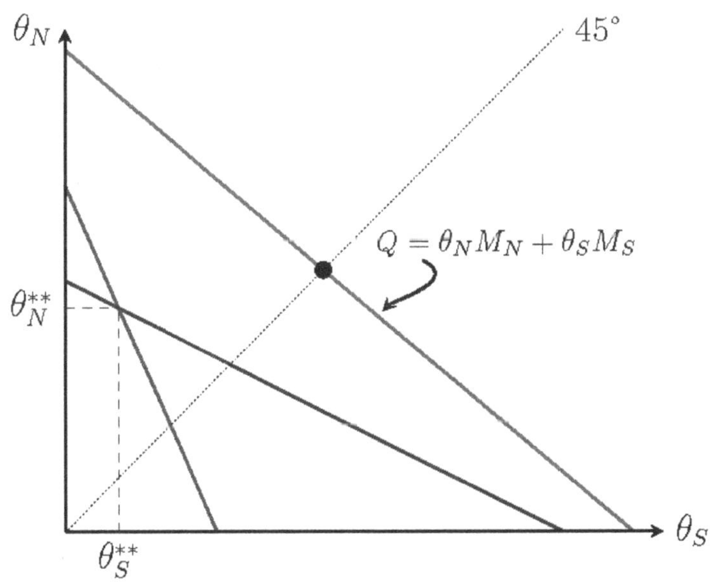

Figure 5.10. International Coordination: Global Protection

recognizes that there are innovators in each country who can sell and profit from markets anywhere. In that case, all that matters is the world level of IPR, or the world market size-adjusted IPR levels, Q. How Q is distributed between countries does not matter.

If the world market size increased, the Q line shifts outward and IPR levels would increase as well. The implication for harmonization is that harmonization is not necessary for optimal global IPR protection. The optimal pair (θ_N^*, θ_S^*) need not be on the 45° line. From an efficiency standpoint, any point on the Q line suffices.

To summarize:

- Under centralized, international coordination, what matters is the global **level** of IPR protection $Q = \theta_N M_N + \theta_S M_S$.
- In a decentralized equilibrium, a country would prefer the other country to raise IPR unilaterally, as this increases world innovation incentives without contributing to deadweight loss at home.
- Without international coordination, countries will provide weaker IPR protection than is optimal.
- Harmonization is not required from a global efficiency perspective. In a decentralized world, countries provide the same level of IPR protection only if they are symmetric.

5.6 Utility Models

The Grossman-Lai (2004) model implies that standards of intellectual property rights should be lower for developing countries. Indeed, in practice, some countries in the past have taken "baby steps" regarding IP systems — namely by adopting a system of utility models or petty patents. Table 5.6 shows a sample of countries that adopted these kinds of IP protection. Utility models encourage minor, incremental, and adaptive inventions, which are especially important to countries in the early stages of industrialization, as they are mostly imitators and importers of technologies at that stage.

The Grossman and Lai (2004) model would imply that the South should have IP standards that offer shorter duration, narrower scope, and greater flexibility. These are, in fact, the features of a utility model (UM) system.

South Korea provides a good case study. The country was extremely poor in 1960 with a per capita GDP of $158 in current dollars. Inflation-adjusted, that is equivalent to $1,028 per capita in 2015 dollars. In 2023,

Table 5.6. Sample Regions Protecting Utility Models

Japan	Germany	South Korea
Taiwan	China	Hong Kong
Argentina	Brazil	Chile
Mexico	Russia	ARIPO*

Note: * African Regional Intellectual Property Organization.

South Korea's per capita GDP reached $34,121 in 2015 dollars.[26] The source of South Korea's rapid economic development has been the subject of extensive scholarly study.[27]

During its rapid growth phase, South Korea was viewed as an "imitator" or even a "pirate" country. During the 1980s, the U.S. Trade Representative (USTR) had placed the country on its *Priority Watch List*, which identified countries it considered to have the most serious deficiencies in intellectual property rights protection and enforcement.[28]

But simultaneously, Korea specialized in minor, incremental, and adaptive innovations, which the UM system encouraged. That kind of innovation spurred the country to develop and strengthen its innovative capacity, enabling it to become a major R&D player and innovative nation, and then eventually adopt stronger patent laws. Korea's economic progress might have slowed had it adopted stronger patent protection initially or had no protection for minor innovations.

Box 2. Utility Models versus Patents

Highlights:

- Smaller inventive step (i.e., demonstrate a practical or functional advantage over prior art).
- Shorter duration (6–10 years).
- Do not require substantive examination; less expensive to acquire.

[26]Data are from the World Bank's *World Development Indicators*. See Appendix 2A of Chapter 2 for data sources.
[27]See Lee (2013).
[28]https://ustr.gov/sites/default/files/1989Special301Report.pdf.

Utility Models may be more suitable for Emerging Economies:

- Patents are most effective where innovative capacity exists.
- Patents create benefits and costs; for example, they raise the prices of knowledge inputs and thus the cost of conducting R&D.
- UM can facilitate reverse engineering, learning-by-doing, and serve as a stepping stone for further technological progress.
- Technologies with short life-cycles (e.g., electronics) especially benefit from UM protection.

Box 2 identifies the key differences between UM and regular patents and why they could be helpful for emerging economies. As Evenson and Westphal (1995) observed:

> "Strong IPRs can be a powerful instrument for encouraging many forms of investment at all levels of technological development if they are sufficiently focused on promoting those forms of investment which are respectively important at each level. ... Utility model protection, for example, is actively sought in the few countries, like Korea, that grant it. Moreover, the evidence suggests that it stimulates the kinds of minor, adaptive inventions that are important in the early to middle phases of technological development" (p. 2288).

Figure 5.11 plots the ratio of utility models to patents granted in South Korea, alongside the changes in patent protection levels (the dashed line), as measured by the GP-Index presented in Chapter 2. The figure illustrates Korea's initial dependence on utility models and then shows a dramatic shift: by the mid–1990s, Korea had switched to producing patentable innovations; the ratio of UM to invention patents falls precipitously, while its patent rights index (PRI) gradually increases.[29] This chart suggests a turning point: the technological maturing of Korean industries.

A structural transformation in indigenous innovative capacity preceded the patent reforms. By the mid–1990s, Korea's capacity to produce patentable inventions had developed, raising the demand for patent protection. During the 1960–1970s, this capacity was largely absent, and thus firms or inventors would not have been able to take full advantage of a patent system. There was low demand for patent rights (except by foreign MNCs). In that sense, the Korean patent system endogenously responded to an increase in innovative capacity. Firms demanded stronger patent protection as the nature of their R&D shifted from incremental to more

[29] Note that the GP-index increases in steps. This occurs because the index is constructed every 5 years.

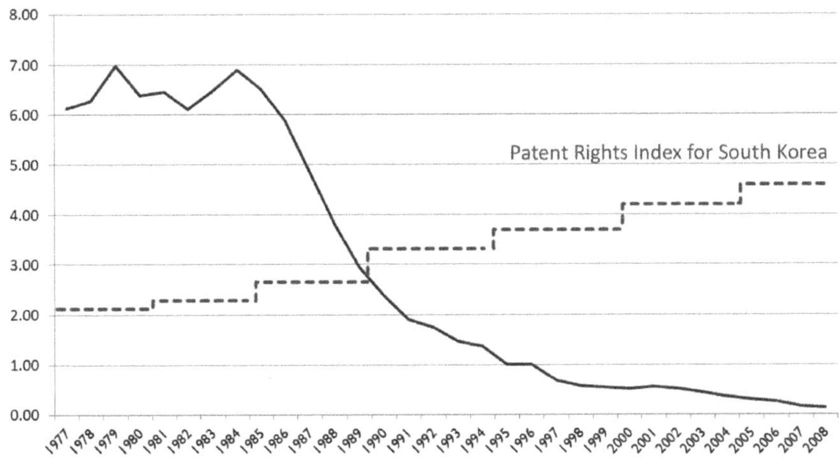

Figure 5.11. Ratio of Utility Models to Invention Patents in S. Korea

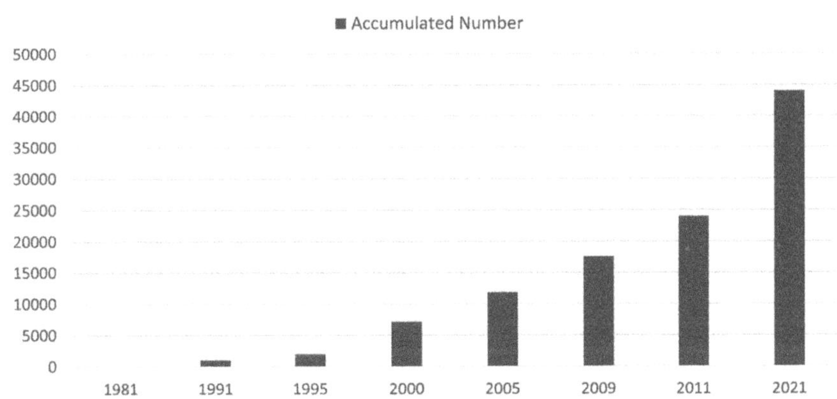

Figure 5.12. Corporate R&D Centers in S. Korea
Source: Korea Industrial Technology Association.

radical. In turn, the stronger patent system provided the environment for firms to continue pursuing more revolutionary research.[30]

This surge in innovative capacity is also reflected in the number of corporate R&D centers in South Korea. As Figure 5.12 shows, fewer than 50 R&D centers existed in 1981. By 1991, there were 1,000, and by 2021, there were upwards of 44,000 such centers. In 2009, approximately 45% of the centers operated in the electronics field, which is characterized by short product

[30]For examples of the research, see the annual reports of the *Korea Advanced Institute for Science and Technology (KAIST)*, https://kis.kaist.ac.kr/.

cycles, followed by machinery (20%) and chemicals (15%). However, by 2023, the distribution of R&D centers across industrial fields had become more balanced, due in particular to the growth of the services sector. About a quarter of the corporate R&D centers now operate in services.[31]

The rise in the number of corporate R&D centers indicates that Korean firms were, and are, able to fund their own internal R&D activities.

During its development phase, South Korea specialized in technologies with short product cycles. This strategy offered two advantages. First, when IPR protection is weak, shorter product cycles benefit if the imitation lag is sufficiently long, as obsolescence may occur well before imitation. As Lee (2013) argues, latecomers like Korean firms have less of a disadvantage against incumbents in short-cycle industries, as they do not have to rely on technologies dominated by the incumbents. Short product cycles disrupt incumbent technologies frequently enough to create opportunities for new players to emerge. In longer-cycle industries, such as pharmaceuticals, latecomers face greater challenges in acquiring skills, investing in facilities, and competing with technology leaders who may also have brand-loyal consumers. The second advantage is that suitable IP protection did exist for short-lived technologies — namely, utility models!

5.6.1 *Evidence*

The results in Table 5.7 draw on Kim *et al.* (2012), an empirical study of utility models (UM) analyzing a panel of 70 countries from 1970 to 2003. Innovation is measured by patent grants at the USPTO, and the growth rate refers to GDP per capita. A dummy variable $D = 1$ indicates a developed country and $D = 0$ indicates a developing (i.e., middle- and low-income) country.[32]

A stark asymmetry emerges: UM matters for growth and innovation in the middle- and low-income countries, but not for the developed countries. The pattern is reversed for patent protection. The index of patent rights matters for developed countries but not for the middle- and low-income countries.

[31] Data on R&D corporate sectors in Korea can be obtained from the Korea Industrial Technology Association (KOITA), see https://www.koita.or.kr/eng/ and https://www.rnd.or.kr/user/infoservice/coverage.do.

[32] The regressions control for variables like GDP per capita, R&D intensity, openness to trade, working age population, school enrollment, investment, population growth, and time dummies.

Table 5.7. Utility Model Regression: Country-Level

Variable	Innovation Equation	Growth Equation
Patent Rights Index (PRI)	0.088	−0.027
PRI × D	0.554**	0.095**
Utility Model Dummy	0.170*	0.091**
UM Dummy × D	−0.193	−0.075
Other controls	Yes	Yes

Note: ***, **, * denote significance levels at the 1, 5, and 10% levels respectively.

Table 5.8. Utility Model Regression: Firm-Level

Sales Growth Equation			
Variables	**Full Period**	**Pre–1987**	**Post–1987**
Patenting Intensity	0.025**	−0.019	0.053***
Utility Model Intensity	0.009	0.047**	0.005

Note: Other controls include firm age, firm size, and lagged sales (due to a dynamic specification). ***, **, * denote significance levels at the 1, 5, 10% levels, respectively.

Table 5.8 presents the next set of results, based on annual firm-level data for over 3,000 Korean firms.

The results show that before 1987, firm performance, as measured by sales growth, depended significantly on utility models and insignificantly on patentable inventions, controlling for other factors. A role reversal occurred after 1987: firm performance depended significantly on patentable inventions and insignificantly on utility models, controlling for other factors.

The year 1987 was chosen as the *break* year since major patenting reforms occurred that year, and since previous research on the Korean economy has focused on conditions before and after 1987. Overall, the results are consistent with the hypothesis that utility model protection is conducive to innovation and productivity in situations where innovative capacity is nascent.

Subsequent research by Prud'homme (2017) confirms that utility models allow developing countries to pursue a dynamic catch-up strategy. The study creates indices of utility model strength (strictness and appropriability) for four East Asian economies: China, Japan, South Korea, and Taiwan. It finds a co-evolution between utility model strength and technological capabilities. Early on, latecomers institute utility model regimes that are less strict and offer less appropriability. Then, as knowledge accumulates and technological capabilities strengthen, utility model protection becomes stronger. This strategy allows a country to transition from an imitative to a more innovative economy.

Chapter 6

North–South Models of Technology Transfer

6.1 Introduction

This chapter examines the role of intellectual property rights (IPRs) in shaping the international transfer of technology from developed (North) to developing (South) countries. As knowledge has become a critical driver of economic growth, the mechanisms by which technology crosses borders have taken on increasing importance in global policy debates.

The chapter discusses how different modes of technology transfer, including trade, foreign direct investment (FDI), and licensing, respond to variations in IPR protection across countries. It reviews empirical studies showing whether stronger IP can promote the international flow of technology-intensive goods, attract higher-quality FDI, and stimulate arms-length licensing transactions. However, these effects are not uniform. The responsiveness of technology transfer depends on sectoral characteristics, such as the ease of imitation and the longevity of product life cycles.

The chapter examines the technology transfer of patentable works as well as the international transfer of copyrighted works, assessing how multinational firms' transfer decisions are affected by the strength of IP protection abroad. It is through these transfers that host countries, particularly in the developing world, gain new technical knowledge.

The appendix to this chapter examines the profit-shifting motives behind international technology transfers, with a focus on how firms structure licensing arrangements to minimize tax liabilities.

6.2 Types (or Modes) of Technology Transfer

- Exports
- Foreign Direct Investment (FDI)
- Licensing
- Joint Ventures

One of the factors that firms consider when choosing a mode of technology transfer is the relative risk of technology misappropriation across different transfer modes. Exported goods can be reverse engineered by foreign firms, although doing so typically requires time and technical effort. Licensing arrangements pose greater risks, as licensees often gain direct access to blueprints, source codes, manufacturing processes, and trade secrets. In some cases, licensees may defect and establish their own firms, becoming rivals to the original licensor. Foreign direct investment (FDI), through the establishment of affiliates or subsidiaries abroad, can also lead to the leakage of proprietary information via employee mobility, as local personnel may leave to start competing firms. In addition, although less common today, firms face the risk of nationalization by host-country governments, which may result in the uncompensated expropriation of assets and technologies.

Thus, there is no perfect, risk-free mode of entering a foreign market. Each strategy entails trade-offs. An important implication is that firms must choose among different modes of entry — exports, FDI, and licensing — *jointly* rather than in isolation. Host-country conditions, such as intellectual property rights (IPRs), affect not only the overall volume of technology transfer but also the composition across different modes of entry.

In seminal work, Dunning (1977) provided an elegant framework for thinking about these decisions: the *Ownership, Location, and Internalization (OLI)* framework. The ownership factor influences a firm's decision to enter a foreign market. A firm selling a good abroad faces a disadvantage relative to local producers who better understand the domestic market; thus, to compete, the firm must possess some ownership advantage, such as a superior technology. The location factor influences a firm's choice between exporting and FDI. For instance, exporting may involve lower agency or setup costs compared to establishing a subsidiary abroad. To offset these costs, the foreign market must offer some location advantage, such as lower factor costs or proximity to final consumers. The internalization factor affects whether the firm produces the good internally via a subsidiary or licenses production to another party. Firms prefer to internalize production when controlling the production process reduces transaction costs, mitigates imitation risks, or improves coordination.

Stronger IPR protection in the host country can influence each of these factors: the value of ownership advantages, the attractiveness of locating production abroad, and the incentive to transact with external parties. As an illustration, suppose that ρ_{FDI} represents the imitation risk associated with establishing a multinational plant (in terms of the rate of dissipation of profits) and ρ_{LIC} represents the risk that a licensee defects to operate a rival business. Assume that $\rho_{\text{LIC}} > \rho_{\text{FDI}}$ because a wholly-owned or majority-owned affiliate can better control proprietary information. However, this does not mean that FDI always dominates licensing to unaffiliated parties. It is important to remember that establishing a plant abroad entails fixed *setup costs*. Let F denote these costs as a percentage of profits. Granting a local firm a license avoids these setup costs. Thus, a firm would be indifferent between FDI and licensing as a mode of entry if $\rho_{\text{LIC}} = \rho_{\text{FDI}} + F$. If the host country's IP system results in high imitation risks for licensing (i.e., $\rho_{\text{LIC}} > \rho_{\text{FDI}} + F$), the firm would prefer FDI. Moreover, if F is too large, the firm might even prefer exporting to the host country instead, since exporting avoids setup costs (and may be associated with low imitation risks if reverse engineering is very difficult). Essentially, exporters leverage existing domestic production infrastructure and platforms to serve foreign markets. These decision factors highlight the intricate trade-offs firms must evaluate when determining their international technology transfer mode.

Finally, it is important to distinguish between technology transfer and knowledge spillovers. A transfer of technology typically involves a market transaction; it is compensated. In contrast, a spillover refers to an externality: an uncompensated benefit that accrues to others. In practice, both paid and unpaid benefits may be transmitted simultaneously.[1]

[1]For example, consider the case of hiring a piano teacher. While the teacher is compensated for providing instruction on the instrument, the student may also receive additional, uncompensated knowledge, such as insights into the history of great composers, the workings of the music industry, or the career marketplace for musicians. Similarly, the export of a laptop involves the sale of a tangible good with associated software tools, but the purchaser may also gain, at no extra cost, new knowledge about the computer's underlying architecture and design.

6.3 Trends

Table 6.1 summarizes the level of global technology transfers, as measured by the stock of foreign direct investment (FDI), merchandise trade exports, and receipts of licensing fees and royalties, along with their distribution by major country or region.[2]

Table 6.1 shows that, in dollar terms, licensing remains the smallest form of international technology transfer, while the stock of foreign direct investment is the largest. Licensing, however, tends to involve highly specific contracts for the conveyance of technical know-how or the rights to manufacture and/or sell protected technologies. In contrast, FDI encompasses broader activities, including the establishment of subsidiaries, distribution networks, and local production facilities.

Among the regions, the European Union (covering 27 countries) accounts for the largest share of both FDI and exports. Among individual countries, the United States holds the largest share across the three modes, notably accounting for a greater share of global licensing receipts than the entire EU bloc combined. As of 2022, China surpassed Japan in its share of global FDI stock and merchandise exports, although it still trails Japan significantly in international licensing revenues. India, while currently holding a modest share among developing economies, is poised for growth over the next few decades, particularly as its innovation ecosystems continue to expand.

Table 6.1. World Technology Transfers and Distribution by Region, 2022

World Total (Trillions of USD)	FDI Stock (%)	Exports (%)	Licensing (%)
	$39.9	**$24.9**	**$0.45**
USA	20.1	8.0	28.2
European Union	31.8	28.5	24.2
Japan	4.8	3.0	10.7
China	7.3	14.5	2.9
India	0.6	1.8	0.3
Latin America & Carib	2.1	5.7	0.3

[2]The source of data is UNCTAD. See https://unctadstat.unctad.org/datacentre.

6.4 Previous Research

A substantial empirical literature has investigated how the strength of intellectual property rights (IPRs) affects international technology transfer, operating through trade, foreign direct investment (FDI), and licensing. This section reviews selected studies to highlight the state of the literature thus far and to draw lessons for conceptual understanding and policy analysis.[3]

Several dimensions distinguish these studies:

- *Sample Period*: Differences in timing (e.g., pre-TRIPS vs. post-TRIPS reforms)
- *Level of Aggregation*: Country-level, industry-level, or firm-level data
- *Mode of Technology Transfer*: Focus on a single channel (trade, FDI, or licensing) versus multiple channels
- *Host-country Classification*: Whether analyses pool all countries or distinguish between developed and developing economies
- *Controls for Industry Characteristics*: Whether studies control for sector-specific differences in R&D intensity, imitation risk, or product complexity

These dimensions, among others, help explain some of the variation in findings across empirical studies. As such, understanding the methodological choices embedded in each study is critical for interpreting the results and drawing policy conclusions.

6.4.1 *Trade as a Channel of Technology Transfer*

Early empirical work by Maskus and Penubarti (1995) identified two opposing effects of stronger IPRs on trade: a market-expansion effect and a market-power effect. Consider a firm in country A that exports patentable commodities to country B. Suppose country B strengthens its IPR regime. On the one hand, the firm's perceived market expands, as stronger patent rights reduce the risk of imitation by local firms. The demand curve it faces in country B shifts outward. On the other hand, stronger IPRs enhance the firm's market power by restricting the supply of competing goods, enabling the firm to establish higher prices. The market-expansion effect is likely to dominate in competitive environments, whereas the market-power effect

[3]For broader syntheses of this literature, see Park (2008b), Saggi (2016), and Maskus (2024).

may dominate where local competitors pose only a weak imitation threat. Using data on 47 countries and 28 manufacturing sectors in 1984, Maskus and Penubarti find a strong positive relationship between the strength of importing countries' patent rights and exports from OECD countries. Interestingly, they find that patent protection weakly attracts exports in the most patent-sensitive industries, suggesting that the market-power effect may outweigh the market-expansion effect in those cases. Another possibility is that firms substitute away from exporting toward other modes of technology transfer, such as FDI, when host-country patent protection is stronger.

Subsequent studies by Smith (1999) and Co (2004) further condition the effects of IPRs on exports by considering the imitative ability of the importing country. Intuitively, patent protection should matter more to exporters if destination countries have a greater capacity to reverse engineer and imitate foreign goods. Both Smith and Co use the share of R&D in gross domestic or national income as a proxy for the imitative ability of the importing country. Smith (1999), using cross-sectional data on U.S. state-level exports, finds that weak IP constitutes a barrier to U.S. exports when the destination country exhibits strong imitative capacity. Co (2004), using a panel dataset, finds that in countries where imitation risks are significant, stronger patent protection is associated with an increase in U.S. R&D-intensive exports but a decline in non-R&D-intensive exports. Thus, the market-expansion effect dominates for R&D-intensive sectors, while the market-power effect dominates for less technology-intensive sectors.

Ivus (2010) addresses a potential concern of reverse causality; that is, that developing countries may have strengthened their IP systems endogenously to attract trade and investment inflows. Ivus (2010) exploits the TRIPS Agreement as an exogenous shock to patent rights in a subset of developing countries. Specifically, Ivus (2010) classifies countries based on colonial origin: countries that were not colonized by Britain or France (non-colonies) are treated as the group affected by TRIPS, while former colonies are classified as the control group. The rationale is that pre-TRIPS, British and French colonies already had relatively stronger patent systems aligned with colonial legal traditions, whereas non-colonies did not.[4] Following TRIPS, it was primarily the non-colonial countries that substantially reformed their patent regimes. Using this treatment versus control setup,

[4]This distinction is evident in the Ginarte and Park (1997) patent rights index, particularly for Africa.

Ivus (2010) finds that stronger patent protection in developing countries significantly increased exports from patent-sensitive industries in developed countries. Notably, the effect is observed not only in the value but also in the volume (quantity) of exports.[5]

6.4.2 *FDI as a Channel of Technology Transfer*

FDI constitutes another major avenue for transferring technology internationally. Lee and Mansfield (1996) provide evidence from a panel of over 100 U.S. firms operating in 14 developing countries across six broad industries. The study finds that weak IPRs discourage foreign investment. The strength of IPR protection is based on a survey of managerial perceptions (see Mansfield, 1994). Moreover, the study shows that weaker IPRs affect not only the quantity but also the composition of FDI: firms are more likely to invest in sales and distribution outlets rather than in manufacturing plants or R&D facilities under weaker protection.

Nunnenkamp and Spatz (2004) similarly find that stronger IPRs are a significant determinant of U.S. outward FDI stocks, particularly in developing countries. A possible explanation is that in environments where technology protection is generally weak, incremental improvements in IPRs represent relatively major policy changes. In larger and richer countries, by contrast, FDI is often driven by other factors, such as market size, infrastructure, legal enforcement, and human capital, so the impact of IPRs may be less pronounced. This study also confirms that IPRs matter more when the host country exhibits significant imitative capacity, and that stronger patent rights affect not only the quantity but also the quality of FDI, as measured by the technology content of FDI.

Evidence from French multinationals provides a somewhat different perspective. Using firm-level data, Mayer and Pfister (2001) find that stronger patent rights have a negative influence on the location decisions of French multinational firms. When splitting its sample, the study finds that the strength of a developing country's patent laws has no statistically significant effect on location probability, while in developed countries, patent strength exhibits a quadratic (inverse-U) effect: initially encouraging FDI, but discouraging it after a certain threshold. It is important to note that Mayer and Pfister study location decisions (a yes/no outcome) rather than

[5] Research on the relationship between trade and IPRs continues to evolve. For example, Lin and Lincoln (2017) investigate the impact of stronger patent rights on the product variety of exports.

FDI flows or stocks. Thus, their results capture the initial entry decision but not the intensity or quality of technology transfer post-entry. Moreover, its findings can be consistent with either a market-power or market-expansion interpretation: greater market power may lead firms to open fewer affiliates, while expanded markets might prompt alternative entry modes such as licensing or joint ventures. A key limitation of focusing on single entry modes is that it constrains inference about the overall impact of IPRs on technology transfer.

Using firm-level data from Eastern Europe and the former Soviet Union, Javorcik (2004) finds that stronger patent rights significantly increase the probability of foreign investment in high-technology sectors, but have no statistically significant effect in other sectors. Moreover, across all sectors, weaker patent protection leads foreign investors to prefer investing in sales and distribution outlets rather than in manufacturing or R&D facilities. These findings align with those of Lee and Mansfield (1996) but differ from Mayer and Pfister (2001).

Bilir (2014) offers a novel perspective by incorporating the concept of product life-cycle lengths. Conducting a firm-level analysis of U.S. multinational FDI activity over 1982–2004, the study avoids confounding patent reforms with broader institutional or economic developments by exploiting within-country, cross-industry variation in product life cycles. The key insight is that the relevance of patent protection depends on the speed of technological obsolescence: for short-lived technologies, such as those in electronics, imitation is less threatening because products become obsolete quickly. Thus, strong patent protection may be less critical.[6]

Bilir (2014) measures product life based on the duration of patent citations. The assumption is that the length of time for which a patent is cited by subsequent patents is reflective of the lifespan of technologies embedded in products.[7] Controlling for other variables, the study finds an inverted-U relationship between the marginal effect of patent protection on MNC activity (such as market entry, number of affiliates, affiliate sales, assets, and employment) and product life-cycle length. Patent protection has a limited impact on FDI in sectors with very short product lifespans, and only a modest impact in sectors with very long product lifespans. The largest

[6]This insight resonates with the analysis in Chapter 5, where it was shown that emerging economies like South Korea in the 1970s and 1980s specialized in short-cycle technologies, often using utility models to incentivize incremental innovation.

[7]Specifically, for each industry, the mean forward citation lag is calculated to approximate the average product lifetime.

positive effects are observed in industries with intermediate product life lengths. This suggests that while stronger patent rights generally encourage FDI, their effectiveness depends critically on how rapidly technological innovations turn over.

6.4.3 *Licensing as a Channel of Technology Transfer*

Licensing agreements provide the licensee the right, and the technological knowledge, to manufacture, perform, or distribute goods and services protected by intellectual property (IP). Accordingly, IP protection affects the incentives for licensors to engage in licensing activities. Yang and Maskus (2001) identify an *economic returns effect*, whereby stronger IP protection reduces the risk of imitation (or defection by the licensee), thereby increasing the profitability of licensing. Stronger protection implies that licensing and royalty contracts can be better enforced and that the licensor gains greater bargaining power relative to the licensee. Under weak IP regimes, licensors may have to concede a larger share of rents to licensees to reduce the latter's incentives to defect. However, excessive strengthening of IPRs can also lead to *monopoly power effects*: where reduced competition dampens the incentive to upgrade existing technologies or develop new varieties. This could slow the pace of innovation and ultimately reduce the pool of technologies available for licensing. Thus, whether stronger IPRs encourage or discourage licensing is ultimately an empirical question.

Using a panel dataset of 23 countries from 1985 to 1995, Yang and Maskus (2001) examine the relationship between U.S. licensing flows (both affiliated and unaffiliated) and host-country patent rights. They find that stronger patent protection has an insignificant impact on affiliated licensing fees and royalties. One explanation is that since affiliated licensing occurs within multinational firms, these transactions are less sensitive to the external IP enforcement. Another possibility is that imitation risks are lower in affiliated transactions, and thus stronger IPRs merely increase the licensor's market power without significantly changing technology-sharing incentives. By contrast, for unaffiliated licensing, Yang and Maskus (2001) find a nonlinear (U-shaped) relationship with patent rights. At low levels of patent strength, the monopoly power effect dominates: weak enforcement in low-innovation environments lets stronger IP to consolidate market power without fostering much new licensing. At higher levels of patent strength, where destination countries have greater innovative capacity and pose higher imitation risks, the economic returns effect dominates, encouraging more licensing.

Using firm-level data, Branstetter, Fisman, and Foley (2006) offer complementary evidence on intra-firm licensing. Studying U.S. multinational companies and their affiliates in 16 countries, this study finds that patent reforms significantly increase technology transfer from parents to affiliates via affiliated licensing, particularly from parent companies that patent extensively. In contrast to Yang and Maskus (2001), who used aggregate data, this firm-level study captures how individual companies adjust their internal technology transfers in response to patent reforms. Moreover, Branstetter *et al.* (2006) investigate whether the observed rise in intra-firm licensing reflects a quantity effect (more technology flows) rather than solely a price effect (higher fees). They find that affiliate R&D activity and parent firm patenting both increase in countries undergoing patent reform, suggesting genuine technology transfer rather than mere rent extraction. Their timing analysis also finds no evidence of technology transfer preceding patent reforms, which addresses endogeneity concerns.

Park and Lippoldt (2005) study licensing as well, but differentiate among various forms of IP protection: patents, copyrights, and trademarks. Using U.S. firm-level data, they analyze unaffiliated (or arms-length) licensing flows and distinguish between developed and developing country recipients. Their regressions indicate that patent protection significantly promotes licensing, while copyright and trademark protections have weaker or even negative effects. In developed country markets, copyright protection has a positive effect, but in developing markets, both copyright and trademark protection appear to deter licensing, likely due to enhanced monopoly effects outweighing the economic returns effects.

Park and Lippoldt (2005) also find that patent reforms spur the growth of international licensing alliances between companies in developed nations and companies in developing nations. Overall, those developing nations that reformed their patent regimes the most enjoyed the greatest increases in licensing deals with developed nations. This was generally the case whether the developed partner nation was the U.S. or a non-U.S. country.

Santacreu (2025) shifts focus to the role of international trade agreements with IP provisions in fostering North–South technology transfer. Using licensing flows as a measure of technology transfer, Santacreu (2025) finds that between 1995 and 2012, technology transfers from developed to developing countries increased significantly more following the signing of regional trade agreements (RTAs) containing IP provisions than after RTAs without such provisions. To explain this, Santacreu develops a dynamic model calibrated for the United States (North), China (South), and the rest of the world. Unlike traditional North–South models, both regions engage in innovation. In the bargaining framework of the RTA, the North offers tariff reductions to the South in exchange for stronger IP enforcement.

As Santacreu emphasizes, it is not sufficient to compare steady-state outcomes; transitional dynamics must also be analyzed. During the transition, welfare gains are distributed unevenly: the North benefits both in the short and long run, as stronger Southern IP protection raises returns to innovation and tariff reductions lower intermediate input costs. The South eventually gains from increased innovation and productivity, but in the short run, it suffers welfare losses because higher royalty fees raise technology adoption costs. This creates a potential credibility problem: the South may be tempted to deviate from enforcement commitments to avoid short-run losses. Santacreu shows that with credible retaliation threats by the North, such deviation is deterred, making stable RTAs with IP provisions feasible. This analysis provides important lessons for the design of durable international agreements that link trade liberalization with intellectual property reforms.

6.4.4 *Cross-Cutting Themes*

Several important themes emerge from the empirical literature:

- Stronger IP protection has an inherently ambiguous effect on technology transfer. It can promote transfer through a *market-expansion effect* or an *economic returns effect*, but may also inhibit transfer through a *market-power effect* or a *monopoly power effect*.
- The impact of IP cannot be understood in isolation from host-country characteristics, particularly the destination's imitative capacity and sector-specific factors such as product life-cycle length.
- Analyzing modes of technology transfer — exports, FDI, and licensing — jointly rather than separately is critical, as firms may substitute strategically among these modes in response to changes in IP protection.
- Sectoral heterogeneity matters significantly. Industries differ in their vulnerability to imitation depending on technological obsolescence rates, the ease of product replication, setup costs, and the presence of natural barriers to copying.

- Transitional dynamics are important: while some gains from IP reforms accrue over the long run, short-run adjustment costs must often be absorbed by firms and countries.
- The role of control variables cannot be overstated. All the empirical studies reviewed here carefully control for factors beyond IP protection, such as market size, absorptive capacity, human capital, infrastructure, and other complementary policies (e.g., tax incentives, labor reforms, financial sector reforms, R&D subsidies, and public R&D investments), that also influence technology transfer decisions.

Thus, IPR reform should be viewed as one element of a broader strategy to promote international technology transfer, implemented in conjunction with other complementary policies. The prior empirical literature has identified key conceptual issues that guide an understanding of how IP protection influences global technology transfer. The subsequent sections of this chapter will examine more closely the specific channels through which IP affects technology transfer and the accompanying evidence.

6.5 International Technology Transfer and Patent Rights

Building on the insights of prior work, this section presents a conceptual framework for analyzing a firm's strategic choices among different modes of technology transfer and for assessing how changes in patent protection can alter those choices. It then reviews empirical evidence on the impact of patent rights on technology transfer decisions.[8]

The mode by which a multinational company enters foreign markets has important implications for knowledge diffusion and access to technologies — whether medicines, digital goods, or technical know-how. A key question is whether firms retain control of technical knowledge in-house or contract it out to local agents. Technological development in the Global South is shaped in part by how national patent policies influence both the scale and the composition of inward technology transfers.

This section builds on the internalization literature in the field of international business.[9] An MNC has to choose between transferring technologies

[8]The theoretical framework is based on Ivus *et al.* (2015), and the empirical study draws on Ivus *et al.* (2017).

[9]See Hill (2022).

to its subsidiary or engaging in arm's-length licensing. There are pros and cons to each. Keeping know-how internal prevents leakage and defection by a contractor who might set up a rival business. But arm's-length parties may have some local expertise, additional manufacturing capacities, and access to better distribution channels. From a host country's perspective, arm's-length licensing may be most valuable because it enables indigenous firms to access the technology and gain experience through learning-by-doing — even if this kind of licensing may entail greater risks for the MNC.

Simply comparing modes of technology transfer overlooks the critical role of the underlying technology and product characteristics. If either the technology or the product is complex, it may serve as a natural barrier to imitation. A technology is considered complex when it involves many interdependent components, as in the case of electronics, transportation systems, or scientific instruments. In contrast, discrete product industries — such as chemicals, pharmaceuticals, and biotechnology — tend to be easier to codify and communicate, making them more susceptible to misappropriation. A product is considered discrete when it is not divisible or modular, which allows outsiders to more easily understand how it is made. By contrast, examining isolated components of a complex product typically does not reveal how to replicate the whole product.

6.5.1 *Conceptual Framework for Patented Works*

Table 6.2 summarizes the choices to be discussed.

Table 6.2. Factors Determining Transfer Mode

Choice	Pros	Cons
Exports	Lower risk of technology leakage Existing production facilities are utilized	Higher labor costs
FDI	Lower labor costs abroad	Risk of imitation High establishment costs
Arm's-Length Licensing	Lower labor costs No set-up costs	Greater imitation risk Lack of direct control

All three major modes of technology transfer involve trade-offs, as illustrated above. Throughout, it is assumed that labor in the developing world is cheaper. Formally, let w_N and w_S denote wages in the North and South, respectively. The relative wage is then defined as $\frac{w_N}{w_S}$.

Let V^i denote firm value — that is, the present discounted value (PDV) of the stream of profits over time — associated with transfer mode i:

- FDI is preferred over exports if $V^F > V^E$
- Licensing is preferred over exports if $V^L > V^E$
- Licensing is preferred over FDI if $V^L > V^F$

where E, F, and L denote exports, foreign direct investment (FDI), and licensing, respectively. Exports generate income through direct sales or via intermediaries such as export agents. Under FDI, the firm earns revenue from the operations of its foreign subsidiaries. In the case of licensing, income derives from royalties paid by licensees who use the firm's intellectual property.

(i) Region of choice between Licensing and FDI

In Figure 6.1, the horizontal axis represents imitation risk, while the vertical axis measures the relative wage in the North compared to the South. Since both licensing and foreign direct investment (FDI) rely on Southern labor, relative wage differences do not affect the choice between these two modes. Instead, the key determinant is the risk of imitation; that is, the likelihood that a local licensee could appropriate the technology and establish a competing business. The vertical line in the figure indicates the threshold level

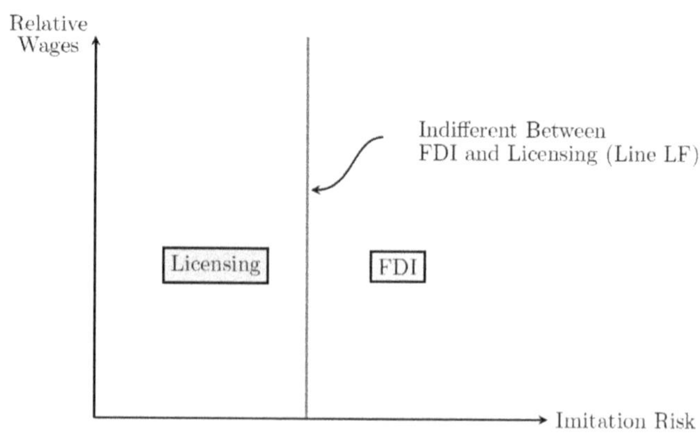

Figure 6.1. Choice between Licensing and FDI

of imitation risk at which the multinational corporation (MNC) is indifferent between licensing and FDI. If imitation risk falls below this threshold, the firm prefers licensing, thereby avoiding the fixed costs of setting up a foreign affiliate. Conversely, if imitation risk exceeds the threshold, the firm opts for FDI to retain greater control over the technology.

Imitation risk is closely associated with product complexity. In cases of high imitation risk — typically found in discrete product industries such as pharmaceuticals or chemicals — FDI is more commonly observed, as firms seek to retain tighter control over their technology. In contrast, when imitation risk is low — often the case with complex products like electronics or scientific instruments — firms are more likely to engage in arm's-length licensing. This theoretical prediction is supported by empirical evidence: pharmaceutical firms tend to rely on FDI and affiliate licensing, while electronics firms make greater use of unaffiliated, arm's-length licensing arrangements.

(ii) Region of choice between Exports and FDI

For comparing FDI and exporting, the indifference line in Figure 6.2 is upward-sloping. The intuition is as follows: an increase in imitation risk, ceteris paribus, makes exporting more attractive, since it avoids exposing proprietary knowledge to potential imitators near a foreign subsidiary. To maintain indifference between the two modes, the relative wage in the North must increase, making exporting less attractive by raising domestic production costs.

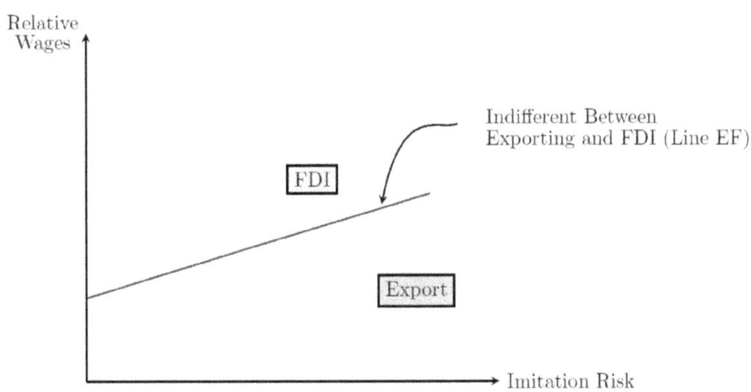

Figure 6.2. Choice between Exports and FDI

Holding the relative wage constant, if imitation risk rises above the level defined by the indifference line, the firm will choose to export, thereby insulating itself from local appropriation. Conversely, if imitation risk falls below this threshold, the firm will prefer FDI in order to benefit from lower labor costs in the South.

(iii) Region of choice between Licensing and Exports

As in the previous case, the indifference line in Figure 6.3 is upward-sloping. Holding the relative wage constant, a rise in imitation risk above the level defined by the indifference curve leads the firm to prefer exporting — producing at home to safeguard its proprietary technology. Conversely, a decline in imitation risk below the threshold induces the firm to license production to an agent abroad, thereby avoiding domestic production costs while accepting a greater risk of misappropriation.

(iv) Putting them all together

Let z index imitation risk.

In Figure 6.4, the Licensing–Export (LE) indifference line is steeper than the Export–FDI (EF) indifference line. This is because arm's-length licensing is riskier than FDI. Thus, the slope of LE is greater because a higher increase in the relative wage $(\frac{w_N}{w_S})$ is needed to maintain indifference for a given rise in imitation risk.

At very low levels of imitation risk (i.e., $z \approx 0$), the critical relative wage needed to induce entry is lower for licensing than for FDI. This is because licensing involves no fixed setup costs, and firms are keen on using cheaper Southern labor. By contrast, FDI requires an upfront investment, so the firm will only choose this mode if the Northern wage is sufficiently high to

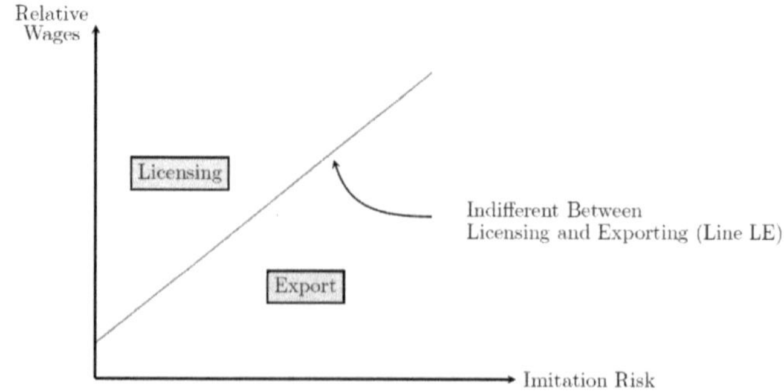

Figure 6.3. Choice between Exports and Licensing

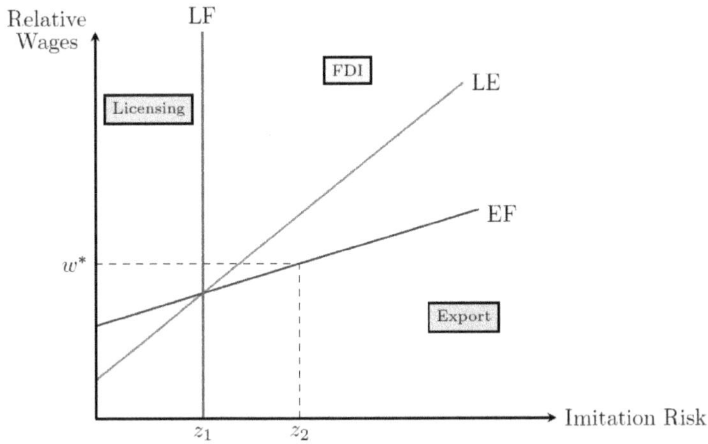

Figure 6.4. Full Choice

justify incurring those setup costs. Since no FDI occurs when $z < z_1$, the EF indifference line is irrelevant in that region and can be ignored.

Suppose the prevailing relative wage is w^*. Then, depending on the level of imitation risk (z), three distinct regions emerge:

- Arm's-length licensing if $0 < z < z_1$
- FDI if $z_1 < z < z_2$
- Exporting if $z_2 < z$

At $z = z_2$ and $w = w^*$, the firm is indifferent between exporting and FDI. Licensing is ruled out due to the high risk. The risk level, z_2, is too great to entrust technology to an unaffiliated partner. If the imitation risk rises above z_2, even FDI becomes too risky, as a foreign subsidiary operating in the South may be exposed to local imitators who gain proximity to proprietary technologies. Such high-risk scenarios are typical of discrete product industries.

Conversely, when $w = w^*$ and $z < z_1$, the firm is confident enough to license its technology to an external party. These low-risk situations are more characteristic of complex product industries, where imitation is difficult. For intermediate values of imitation risk ($z_1 < z < z_2$), the firm chooses FDI, transferring the technology internally within the MNC network. Thus, FDI is most likely in industries that are neither too discrete nor too complex.

(v) Strengthening Patent Protection

Assume that wages are exogenous. As long as the prevailing relative wage lies above the intersection point of all three indifference lines, the Licensing–Export (LE) line becomes irrelevant. In the range $0 < z < z_1$, licensing dominates. Beyond z_1, licensing is no longer viable, and the firm chooses between FDI and exporting.

Stronger patent protection reduces imitation risk and increases the bargaining power of the technology owner. As a result, the LE indifference line shifts to the right: licensors can now tolerate higher levels of imitation risk because improved IP enforcement offers better protection against misappropriation. At the same time, the Export–FDI (EF) indifference line rotates downward, reflecting the fact that, for each level of imitation risk, the threshold relative wage needed to make FDI preferable falls.[10]

With stronger IPRs, MNCs become more willing to engage in FDI even when the Southern wage advantage is reduced, and they also become more open to licensing technologies abroad. These effects are illustrated by the dashed lines in Figure 6.5, showing the new positions of the LE and EF boundaries.

At a given relative wage, these shifts cause firms to reallocate their mode of entry. Some firms switch from FDI to licensing. Others switch from exporting to FDI. The range of industries using licensing expands, while the

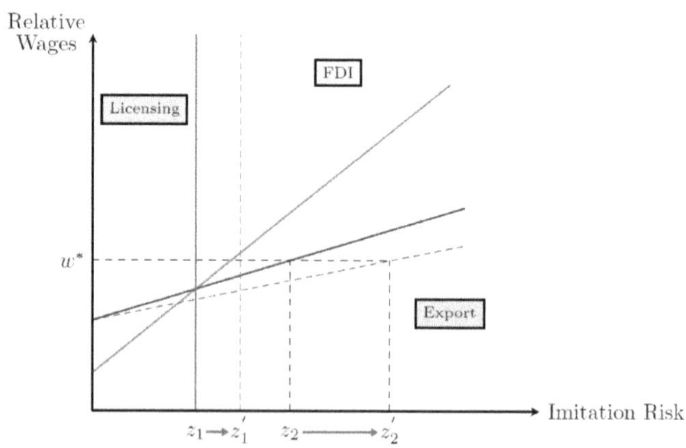

Figure 6.5. Increase in Patent Strength

[10]The EF line rotates because at $z = 0$, patent protection has no impact on the FDI–export decision, as imitation risk is already negligible.

range relying on exporting shrinks. The overall effect on FDI is ambiguous. It depends on whether the expansion of licensing displaces more FDI than the expansion of FDI displaces exports. This ambiguity helps explain why empirical studies might find mixed evidence on the relationship between IPR strength and FDI flows.

This analysis underscores the importance of studying technology transfer modes jointly rather than in isolation. The model predicts that stronger IPRs will lead more multinational corporations to operate outside firm boundaries through arm's-length licensing. The following section examines empirical evidence supporting this prediction.

6.5.2 *Evidence*

U.S. multinational corporations (MNCs) are the leading source of global technology transfers. This section examines licensing activity by U.S. MNCs in 44 developing countries over the period 1994–2009. The sample includes firms in relatively high-tech manufacturing sectors (i.e., excludes food, beverages, and textiles).

Two forms of licensing are analyzed: (1) *affiliate licensing*, which captures internal technology transfers between a parent company and its foreign affiliate (or subsidiary), and (2) *unaffiliated licensing*, which reflects arm's-length agreements with independent external firms. Patent protection in host countries is measured using the Patent Rights Index (PRI) or GP-Index discussed in Chapter 2.

The conceptual framework predicts that firms in complex industries are more likely to engage in unaffiliated licensing than those in discrete industries. It also predicts that stronger patent rights in host countries will facilitate arm's-length licensing, especially for technologies that are more easily imitated. In contrast, when patent protection is weak or uncertain, firms are more likely to internalize technology transfers; that is, to rely on intra-firm mechanisms such as affiliate licensing so as to maintain control over proprietary knowledge.

6.5.2.1 Complexity

Before proceeding, industries must be classified by their technological characteristics. Table 6.3 presents the classification used:

This classification follows Naghavi *et al.* (2015). Complexity is multidimensional and can be assessed based on (i) the number and diversity of

Table 6.3. Sample Discrete and Complex Industries

Discrete Industries	Complex Industries
Pharmaceuticals	Transportation
Non-Pharmaceutical Chemicals	Machinery and Equipment
Energy	Electronics and Components
Metals	

Table 6.4. Licensing by Type of Industry

	Unaffiliated Licensing % Share of Manufacturing	Affiliated Licensing % Share of Manufacturing
Discrete Industries		
Pharmaceuticals	1.01	8.35
Non-Pharmaceutical Chemicals	6.84	39.29
Energy	3.39	0.64
Metals	0.17	1.11
Complex Industries		
Transportation	24.49	18.65
Machinery & Equipment	25.96	13.95
Electronics & Components	37.88	13.30
Other Manufacturing*	0.24	4.52
Total	100	100

Note: *Includes a mix of discrete and complex products.

inputs, (ii) the degree of component integration, and (iii) the sociotechnical system required for production.

Table 6.4 presents the distribution of unaffiliated and affiliated licensing across the sampled high-tech manufacturing sectors in the 44 host countries.

The largest share of unaffiliated licensing is accounted for by the Electronics and Components sector — a complex industry — while the largest share of affiliated licensing occurs in the Non-Pharmaceutical Chemicals sector, which falls under the category of discrete industries.

Overall, licensing — whether affiliated or unaffiliated — is more prevalent in complex industries. These sectors typically involve integrated components or modular technologies that require coordination through cross-licensing or supply-chain cooperation. Table 6.4 shows that complex industries account for 88% of unaffiliated licensing in high-tech manufacturing, while discrete industries account for only 12%. In contrast, affiliated licensing is more evenly distributed, with both complex and discrete industries accounting for about half the total.

To preview the empirical results, Figure 6.6 shows the ratio of unaffiliated to affiliated licensing before and after a major patent reform in a host country.

As shown in Figure 6.6, the ratio increases by more than fourfold in discrete industries and by approximately 60% in complex industries. Although complex industries maintain a higher absolute ratio post-reform, the relative increase is larger for discrete industries. This supports the hypothesis that stronger patent rights facilitate arm's-length licensing, particularly where imitation risk is otherwise high.

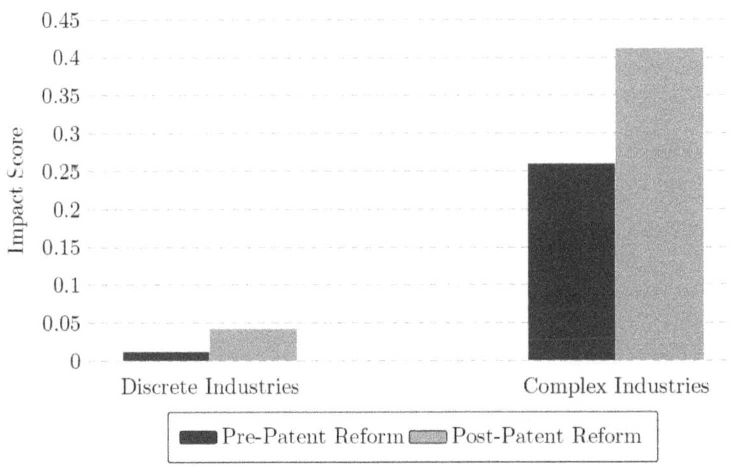

Figure 6.6. Ratio of Unaffiliated to Affiliated Licensing by Industry Complexity

6.5.2.2 Regression Framework

The outcome variable, T_{ijt}, denotes technology transfer, where i indexes the parent firm, j the host country, and t the year:

$$T_{ijt} = \beta_0 + \beta_1 P_{jt} + \beta_2 Z_i + \beta_3 (Z_i \times P_{jt}) + \cdots + \varepsilon_{ijt} \tag{6.1}$$

where P_{jt} is the patent rights index in the host country and Z_i the technological complexity index. The regression equation controls for several variables, including the parent firm's R&D intensity, host-country characteristics, and firm and year fixed effects.

The main regression results are presented in Table 6.5.

The coefficient on the patent rights index ($\ln P$) is significantly positive for both affiliated and unaffiliated licensing, indicating that stronger patent protection in host countries encourages technology transfer through both channels.

The technological complexity variable (Z) is positively associated with unaffiliated licensing and negatively associated with affiliated licensing, which is consistent with the earlier discussion: complex industries are more likely to license technology at arm's length, while discrete industries tend to internalize transfers.

In the first and second columns of Table 6.5, the coefficient of the interaction term ($\ln P \times Z$) is negative. This is consistent with the conceptual

Table 6.5. Technology Transfer, Patent Rights, and Technological Complexity

	(1) Unaffiliated	(2) Affiliated	(3) Ratio
Dependent Variable	$\ln L_U$	$\ln L_A$	$\ln\left(\frac{L_U}{L_A}\right)$
$\ln P$	0.311***	1.389***	−1.068***
Z	0.889**	−1.549**	2.498***
$\ln P \times Z$	−0.648*	−4.162***	3.500***
Other controls	Yes	Yes	Yes

Note: ln denotes natural logarithms. ***indicates significance at the 1% level, **5% level, and *10% level. Number of observations = 29,533.

framework. Lower technological complexity (i.e., lower Z) implies greater hazards of imitation. Thus, a rise in patent protection when imitation risk is higher induces more unaffiliated and affiliated licensing.

The third column of Table 6.5 shows that the interaction term has a positive coefficient. A combination of lower hazards of imitation (or higher Z) and stronger patent protection increases the ratio of unaffiliated to affiliated licensing.

An alternative measure of imitation risk is product life-cycle length, as discussed in Bilir (2014). Firms with longer product life cycles face greater hazards from imitation and are more reliant on strong IP protection, whereas firms with shorter product life cycles likely face technological obsolescence before imitation.[11]

As another perspective, the regressions in Table 6.6 incorporate product life-cycle length and its interaction with patent rights.

The coefficient on product life-cycle length is negative across all specifications, indicating that shorter product lifespans are associated with more licensing. This supports the view that short product cycles pose less of an imitation risk to firms than longer-lived products. The interaction between product life and patent protection has a positive and significant coefficient, indicating that patent protection is more effective in industries with a longer product life-cycle.

Table 6.6. Technology Transfer, Patent Rights, and Product Life Cycle

	(1) Unaffiliated	(2) Affiliated	(3) Ratio
Dependent Variable	$\ln L_U$	$\ln L_A$	$\ln\left(\frac{L_U}{L_A}\right)$
Product Life-Cycle Length	−0.367***	−0.494***	−0.530***
Product Life-Cycle Length × $\ln P$	0.135**	0.205***	0.257***
Other Controls	Yes	Yes	Yes
Number of Observations	22,576	19,831	15,361

***, ** denote 1% and 5% significance levels.

[11] Recall Chapter 4's discussion of breakeven periods and imitation lags.

6.5.3 *Summary*

1. The effect of patent rights on licensing depends on industry characteristics:
   - Imitation risk is greater in discrete industries and for longer-lived products; hence, arm's-length licensing is more common in complex industries.
   - Stronger patent rights in host countries increase both affiliated and unaffiliated licensing by MNCs.
2. It is important to examine not only the volume of technology transfer, but also the composition of intra-firm and arm's-length licensing.
3. This choice is relevant from an economic development perspective. External licensing facilitates the spread of knowledge and know-how beyond the boundaries of the MNC network to local firms.

While affiliated licensing is valuable in its own right, unaffiliated licensing is central to the diffusion of know-how and technology to indigenous firms. These knowledge transfers, in turn, raise the productivity and innovative capacity of local firms and support long-run economic development.

6.6 International Technology Transfer and Copyrights

The previous section examined the effects of patents on technology transfer in manufacturing industries. This section extends the analysis to the role of copyrights in facilitating technology transfer within the copyright and information industries and draws similar lessons regarding the impact of intellectual property rights (IPRs) on international knowledge diffusion.

Much of the existing literature on IPRs and global technology transfer has disproportionately focused on patent protection and manufacturing firms. This emphasis reflects the fact that the manufacturing sector historically accounts for the bulk of research and development (R&D) activity and that technological innovation has often been associated with inventions such as industrial machinery and chemical products. Copyright-based industries have sometimes been viewed as secondary to productivity growth, primarily producing cultural outputs, such as arts, music, and films, that are perceived to have a less direct connection to national productivity compared to scientific and industrial innovations.

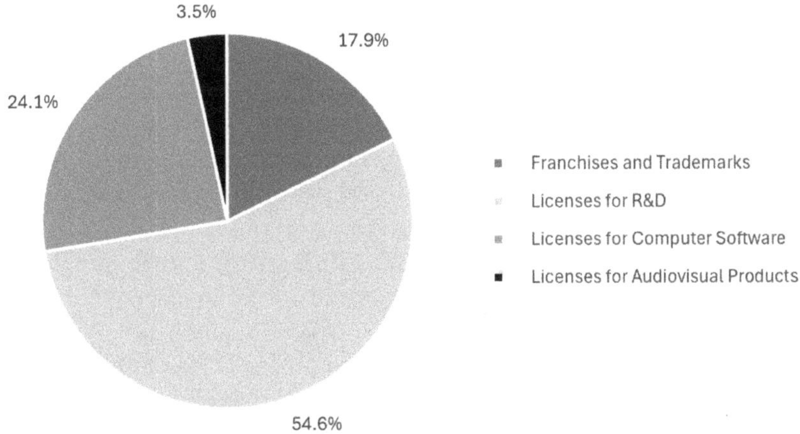

Figure 6.7. U.S. Outward Licensing, by Type of Service, 2023

Such a perspective, however, is unduly narrow. Certain copyrightable outputs, particularly software, databases, and digital tools and platforms, directly affect innovation and production activities across multiple sectors. When a broader view of knowledge goods is adopted, copyright industries emerge as major contributors to international technology transfer. In fact, through international licensing, the copyright sector accounts for a substantial share of global knowledge transfers. Figure 6.7 shows U.S. outward licensing revenues, broken down by type of service. The revenues are derived from payments received by U.S. companies from foreign entities for the use of their intellectual property.[12] In 2023, total U.S. outward licensing revenues amounted to $148.2 billion, of which 54.6% represented charges for the use of outcomes from R&D, including patents, trade secrets, and industrial processes. The next leading share, 27.6%, came from copyrighted works — the sum of licenses for the reproduction and/or distribution of computer software and audiovisual products.

How does the transfer of copyrighted works contribute to economic development? Two principal channels can be identified. First, the knowledge goods produced by creative activity — such as books, journal articles, software, databases, films, music, fine art, newspapers and periodicals, and digital works — contribute to human capital development. Human capital is a critical input into both public and private research efforts, as discussed in Chapter 3. Copyright laws, therefore, play a prominent, and sometimes

[12]Source: www.bea.gov, Interactive Tables, International Services, Table 2.1.

contentious, role in sectors devoted to education and information dissemination, including libraries, museums, and archives.

Second, copyright industries can generate spillovers into other sectors of the economy. The demand for creative works may stimulate the demand for goods and services produced by complementary industries, such as high-technology sectors. These supporting industries, in turn, produce technologies that enhance the value of creative works. The copyright regime, therefore, has the potential to influence the incentives of these complementary industries to invest in and disseminate new technologies. For example, computers, electronics, and communications equipment provide the means for delivering creative content. These technologies either improve consumers' ability to enjoy copyrighted works (e.g., better sound systems and visual quality) or enhance creators' ability to produce new copyrightable outputs (e.g., animation tools, photography equipment, tablets, webcams, and cloud storage). Consequently, the expansion of the copyright sector can motivate investment and innovation in these complementary industries.

Both channels — human capital formation and demand spillovers — operate in the international technology transfer sphere and can be described as direct and indirect effects. The direct effect arises because copyright protection influences the knowledge transfers originating from companies within the core copyright industries. The indirect effect emerges as the copyright sector expands in a host country, incentivizing firms in complementary industries to invest in new equipment, develop enabling technologies, and expand their operations, controlling for other factors. In this interconnected way, copyright protection can generate broader economic impacts that extend beyond the immediate, traditional domain of creative works, affecting industrial and technological development more generally.

6.6.1 *Core Copyright and Complementary Industries*

According to WIPO (2015): "Core copyright industries are industries that are wholly engaged in the creation, production, performance, exhibition, communication or distribution and sale of works and other protected subject matter." Core copyright industries typically include sectors such as:

- Publishing (books, newspapers, magazines)
- Music (recorded music, live performances)
- Motion pictures and video (film production, distribution)
- Radio and television broadcasting
- Software and databases

- Visual and graphic arts (photography, drawing, painting, sculpture)
- Advertising services
- Performing arts (theater, opera, dance)

WIPO has conducted a series of studies on the economic contribution of the copyright industries, surveyed across countries during the 2010s. Table 6.7 summarizes the share of the core copyright industries in the national economy, by income group.[13] These industries account for a significant share of GDP and national employment.

However, the term "contribution" is somewhat of a misnomer, as the chart does not suggest any direct connection between the production and employment of copyright industries and overall national GDP and employment. That is, the copyright industries' share measures relative magnitude but does not establish that these industries are responsible for generating a corresponding share of output or jobs. Establishing causal contributions would require a more detailed econometric decomposition analysis.[14]

Complementary industries that have a significant stake in the growth of the copyright sector include printing and related support activities; computer and peripheral equipment manufacturing; communications equipment; audio and visual equipment; semiconductors and other electronic components; navigational, measuring, and control instruments; magnetic and optical media; and electrical equipment. These industries primarily produce goods and services that either enhance the consumption of creative works or serve as inputs into the production of creative outputs.

Independent analyses of industry sales linkages confirm the strength of these relationships. For example, Ivus and Park (2022) show that the copyright sector ranks among the top customers for firms in complementary

Table 6.7. Core Copyright Industries' Share of the Economy

	Share of GDP	Share of Employment
Developed Countries	7.42	6.94
Developing Countries	4.60	4.56
All Countries (average)	5.54	5.78

Source: WIPO (2021).

[13] Based on WIPO (2021), Figure 6, p. 15.

[14] Comparable to analyses estimating the respective contributions of capital, labor, and technology to total factor productivity growth.

industries (that is, among the top ten industries of sale).[15] Thus, firms in complementary industries rely heavily on the copyright-based industries for their sales and growth.

Table 6.8 categorizes the two types of sectors along with their corresponding NAICS identification codes:

Table 6.8. Core Copyright and Complementary Industries by NAICS Code

NAICS Code	Copyright-Related Industries
5111	Newspapers, periodicals, books, and directories
5112	Software publishers
5121	Motion picture and video industries
5122	Sound recording industries
5151	Radio and television broadcasting
5152	Cable and other subscription programming
5161	Internet publishers
5171	Wired telecommunications carriers
5172	Wireless telecommunications (excluding satellite)
5173	Telecommunications resellers
5174	Satellite telecommunications
5175	Cable distribution
5179	Other telecommunications
5181	Internet service providers and web search portals
5182	Data processing and hosting
5191	Other information services
NAICS Code	**Complementary Industries**
3231	Printing and related support activities
3341	Computer and peripheral equipment
3342	Communications equipment
3343	Audio and video equipment
3344	Semiconductors and other electronic components
3345	Navigational, measuring, control instruments
3346	Manufacturing and reproducing magnetic/optical media
3353	Electrical equipment
3359	Other electrical equipment and components

[15]For example, nearly 48% of firms in the Communications Equipment industry reported the copyright industry as their second-largest customer, and 1.3% reported it as their top customer.

Before exploring the relationships between copyright industries and complementary sectors in greater detail, it is useful to analyze the theoretical foundations behind the impact of copyright protection on international technology transfer.

6.6.2 *Conceptual Framework for Copyrighted Works*

Consider two countries: a home country and a host country. Let the home country possess N^{Total} creative works whose owners (or firms) seek to commercialize them in the host market. The model examines how copyright protection in the host country affects both the number of works introduced and the volume of output per work. For simplicity, it is assumed that each firm owns a single creative work, so that N^{Total} also reflects the number of potential multinational firms operating in the host country. This assumption can be relaxed without loss of generality.

Each firm from the home country is modeled as a *dominant* firm facing a *competitive* fringe of copiers in the host country.[16] Depending upon the stringency of copyright enforcement in the host country or the flexibility of its laws on permitting uses without the owner's permission, a fringe of rivals can imitate or make copies of the copyrighted work. In this model, the copyright owner (as the dominant firm) will act as a monopolist over the *residual* demand; that is, the market demand net of the market taken by the copiers or imitators.

The model assumes free entry and exit of copiers, each of them behaving competitively as a price taker. For analytical tractability, the original and copied works are treated as perfect substitutes.

Market entry by the competitive fringe depends on relative cost structures. If the copyright owner enjoys a substantial cost advantage, fringe firms will not enter. Conversely, if fringe firms can produce copies at a lower unit cost, the copyright owner may be priced out. The analysis focuses on the intermediate and economically relevant case in which both the dominant firm and fringe coexist.

The copyright owner's objective is to maximize profits:

$$\Pi = p(m, q)q_o - c(q_o) - E(\lambda, \theta) \tag{6.2}$$

where $q = q_o + q_I$ is total market output, with q_o representing the output of the copyright owner and q_I that of the competitive fringe. The function

[16] This conceptual framework builds on Landes and Posner (2003) and Feinberg and Rousslang (1990).

$c(q_o)$ denotes the cost of production for the dominant firm. The variable m captures a demand-side parameter that varies by product type (e.g., films, databases, software) and reflects differences in consumer willingness to pay. This heterogeneity influences the size of the fringe and thus the relative importance of copyright protection across industries. As noted by De Vany and Walls (2007), pirated goods tend to concentrate in sectors characterized by high demand and large sales volumes.

Firms in the competitive fringe are assumed to price at marginal cost, such that $p = MC(q_I, \theta)$. Marginal cost is increasing in output due to diminishing marginal productivity, and also increasing in the strength of copyright protection, θ, as stronger protection raises the cost of producing additional infringing copies. Inverting the marginal cost function yields the fringe supply curve: $q_I = q_I(p, \theta)$.

In Eq. (6.2), E denotes the fixed cost of entering the host market. In many cases of international technology transfer, the creative work has already been developed in the home country. Nonetheless, introducing such works into a new economic or cultural environment may entail additional costs (see Jensen and Scheraga, 1998). These include adaptation costs such as translation (for books, training manuals, or software), contractual and collective licensing arrangements (particularly for music and films), infrastructural set-up (e.g., in media or publishing), and compliance with local copyright regulations. Cultural assimilation may also require content modification or localization.

In cases where the foreign affiliate is established to access local talent or contribute to local content, further creative development may be necessary so that the transferred work is both original and transformative. The entry cost function $E(\lambda, \theta)$ is modeled as decreasing in the adaptability parameter λ, such that $\frac{\partial E}{\partial \lambda} < 0$. That is, the more easily a work can be adapted to local conditions, the lower the cost of technology transfer.

Also, the entry cost is a positive function of the strength of copyright protection, θ. More stringent copyright laws and enforcement raise the level of originality and standards required for a work to avoid infringing on existing works. The key insight here is that strong copyright laws apply not only to local users in the host country but also to multinational companies and their affiliates operating within that jurisdiction. Under less stringent copyright regimes, firms have more flexibility to commercialize works that are adjacent to existing protected content or borrow more freely from existing expressions. Less stringent regimes indeed may have more flexible copyright limitations and exceptions. This makes it easier to transfer works into the host country. Under a more stringent regime, transfers are limited to more highly original and transformative works. Thus, stronger copyrights raise the adaptation requirements and increase the cost of entry, $\frac{\partial E}{\partial \theta} > 0$.

The multinational firm faces a two-stage decision problem. In the first stage, it determines whether to establish an affiliate in the host country to commercialize its copyrighted work. In the second stage, conditional on entry, it chooses the intensity of activity, such as the scale of investment, production, and creative research and development (R&D). The analysis proceeds by solving the problem backwards, beginning with stage two, where entry is assumed to have occurred.

Let Π denote long-run profits, abstracting from time discounting for simplicity. This assumption is justified by the extended economic life of most copyrighted works, which often persist for decades beyond their creation (e.g., the life of the author plus fifty to seventy years) and are less subject to technological obsolescence than many industrial products, aside from shifts in consumer taste or fashion.

The dominant firm maximizes *gross profits*, defined as $\hat{\pi} = p(m, q)q_o - c(q_o)$, by choosing its output q_o over the residual demand curve. The first-order condition for profit maximization equates marginal revenue (MR) and marginal cost (MC):

$$\underbrace{p + \frac{\partial p}{\partial q}\left(1 + \frac{\partial q_I}{\partial q_o}\right) q_o}_{\text{MR}} = \underbrace{\frac{\partial c}{\partial q_o}}_{\text{MC}} \tag{6.3}$$

Unlike a pure monopoly, the dominant firm's market power is reduced by the presence of the competitive fringe. Specifically, the gap between price p and marginal cost $\frac{\partial c}{\partial q_o}$ is narrowed due to the term $\frac{\partial q_I}{\partial q_o} < 0$, which reflects the inverse relationship between the output of the dominant firm and that of the fringe. When the dominant firm's output increases, the fringe reduces its supply.

Condition (6.3) implicitly gives the optimal output $q_o^* = q_o(m, \theta, c)$, where c denotes a cost parameter in the firm's marginal cost function. Substituting this solution into the gross profit expression gives $\hat{\pi}^* = \hat{\pi}(m, \theta, c)$. A key result of the model is that stronger copyright protection increases the dominant firm's output:

$$\frac{\partial q_o^*}{\partial \theta} > 0 \tag{6.4}$$

The intuition behind Eq. (6.4) is that a higher level of copyright protection (θ) raises the residual marginal revenue of the copyright owner, while leaving its marginal cost unchanged. This occurs because the term $\frac{\partial q_I}{\partial q_o}$ in Eq. (6.3) becomes less negative. In other words, as imitation becomes more costly, a marginal reduction in the fringe's output translates into a greater increase in the residual demand of the dominant firm.

As copyright protection increases, the fringe's marginal cost rises, reducing its output at each price level. This reallocation enlarges the residual demand and marginal revenue available to the copyright owner. Due to the downward-sloping market demand curve, the increase in the dominant firm's output is less than the decline in output from the fringe, leading to a reduction in total market quantity and a rise in price. Consequently, gross profits $\hat{\pi}^*$ increase with θ, i.e., $\frac{\partial \hat{\pi}^*}{\partial \theta} > 0$. These enhanced returns strengthen the firm's incentives to expand its technology transfer activities, including FDI, licensing, and creative research and development.

Nevertheless, it is important to acknowledge that the positive relationship between copyright protection and technology transfer may not be unambiguous. In particular, if multinational firms rely heavily on local knowledge inputs, stronger copyright protection in the host country could increase the cost of accessing those inputs. For example, the cost parameter c may rise due to higher royalty payments or licensing fees required to use intellectual property held by local firms or other multinational affiliates operating in the same market. This would erode the net gains from transferring copyrighted works, especially for firms that depend on third-party content.

However, if the copyright owner is a net exporter (or licensor) of intellectual property, or if licensing payments constitute a relatively small share of total production costs, the effect of copyright protection on c may be negligible. Additionally, the prediction in Eq. (6.4) does not apply in settings where no fringe exists, such as when the dominant firm enjoys overwhelming cost advantages that deter imitation entirely. These considerations indicate that the effect of copyright protection on output and profits is context-dependent and may vary by market structure.

Turning to stage one, a firm will enter the host market if the gross profit computed in stage two exceeds the entry cost; that is, if $\hat{\pi} \geq E(\lambda, \theta)$. From (6.2), this means that net profits, $\Pi > 0$.

This model is now used to characterize the total transfers of technology from the home country to the host. Let N denote the number of creative works in the home country available for sale in the host country. Recall that there is one MNC firm per work. For each of these works, the condition $\hat{\pi} \geq E(\lambda, \theta)$ must hold for the work to be marketed in the host country.

But entry costs are assumed to vary across works, reflecting differences in the degree of transformation or adaptation required. These differences depend on both firm-specific capabilities and the inherent characteristics of the copyrighted work.

Let λ represent the adaptability of a work to the local environment. The critical threshold λ^* corresponds to the marginal work for which entry is just profitable:

$$\hat{\pi} = E(\lambda^*, \theta)$$

Works with adaptability above this threshold ($\lambda > \lambda^*$) enter the market, while those below it do not. To characterize the distribution of these entry decisions, let $F(\lambda)$ denote the cumulative distribution function of λ across all potential works, where $F(\lambda^*)$ gives the fraction of works that fall below the entry threshold.[17] Accordingly, the fraction that enters the market is $1 - F(\lambda^*)$.[18]

The resulting number of works in the host market is therefore:

$$N = N(\hat{\pi}, \theta) = [1 - F(\lambda^*)]\, N^{\text{Total}} \tag{6.5}$$

where only those works with an adaptability index $\lambda \geq \lambda^*$ are successfully transferred to the host market.

The effect of an increase in copyright protection on the number of works in the host market is given by

$$\frac{dN}{d\theta} = N_{\hat{\pi}} \cdot \frac{d\hat{\pi}}{d\theta} + N_\theta \gtrless 0 \tag{6.6}$$

The net effect is theoretically ambiguous. On one hand, stronger copyright protection increases the market share and gross profits of the copyright owner, allowing more works to meet the entry cost threshold. On the other hand, the threshold itself is endogenous. More stringent copyright standards raise the cost of entry by requiring greater differentiation or originality.

[17] As a motivation for cumulative distributions, imagine a set of exam scores. A CDF answers questions like, "What fraction of students scored below 80%?" In general, the cumulative distribution function shows the total proportion of values that fall below a given point. For the grade example, the CDF starts at 0 (meaning 0% of the data is below the lowest value) and ends at 1 (or 100%) as it includes the entire distribution. For any number x, the CDF indicates how much of the distribution lies to the left of x. For example, the function $F(x) = 1 - e^{-x}$, defined for $x \in [0, \infty)$, is a CDF. It starts at $F(0) = 0$ and approaches $F(x) = 1$ as x becomes very large. This kind of function is often used in probability analysis because it makes it easy to find the likelihood of outcomes below a given threshold.

[18] Assume $F(\lambda)$ has support on $[0, \Lambda]$.

Works that are minor derivatives or insufficiently transformative may be excluded under tighter legal standards. As a result, firms must incur greater adaptation costs to legitimately transfer their works to the host market.

Finally, consider the overall *market size* for copyrighted works in the host country and its implications for supporting industries; namely, those that supply inputs into the production of creative goods or that provide complementary products consumed alongside them. Let S denote market size, defined as the product of the number of creative works and the total volume of output per work:

$$S = Nq = N(\hat{\pi}, \theta) \left[q_o(\theta, \ldots) + q_I(\theta, \ldots)\right] \tag{6.7}$$

Both the copyright owner's output and that of the copiers are included in S, since originals and copies are assumed to be perfect substitutes. The magnitude of this market directly influences the demand faced by firms in complementary industries. If S is too small, firms in these sectors may find it unprofitable to invest in facilities, infrastructure, or product development tailored to the copyright market. Conversely, if copyright reform leads to an expansion in S, it provides a channel through which copyright policy can generate spillover effects beyond the core creative industries.

As discussed earlier, an increase in copyright protection θ reduces imitative output (q_I) while expanding the copyright owner's output (q_o). However, because higher protection raises prices, the total quantity demanded q may decline overall. For firms in complementary industries, the distinction between originals and copies is largely immaterial; both create opportunities to supply complementary goods to the copyright sector.

From this perspective, complementary industries might prefer lower levels of copyright protection, which would increase the total volume of copyrighted goods. However, weaker protection may also reduce the number of works entering the market, N, and potentially diminish the average quality of those works. Although less stringent regimes may reduce adaptation burdens and thereby facilitate entry, the lower legal threshold may also incentivize the transfer of less differentiated or lower-value content. In countries where copyright laws are absent or extremely weak, the number of original works (N) introduced into the market is likely to be very small, leaving little for complementary industries to support or for local firms to imitate.[19]

[19]While the local market may be supplied with infringing imports, such scenarios typically do not attract multinational investment. The analysis here is concerned with legitimate market entry by copyright owners.

The market size of the copyright sector, as defined by S, is expected to expand primarily in response to major copyright reforms rather than marginal adjustments in protection. A significant shift in the legal regime can displace infringers and copiers while encouraging the entry of copyright-owning MNCs, thereby increasing the number of works available in the host market. This enlarged copyright sector is then likely to generate increased demand for complementary goods and services, thereby incentivizing U.S. parent companies in supporting industries to expand their investments in the host country.

6.6.3 *Evidence*

The conceptual framework highlights two distinct aspects of international technology transfer. The first is the decision of whether to enter a foreign market — referred to as the **extensive** margin. Conditional on entry, the second is the volume of investment or technology transferred — referred to as the **intensive** margin. Empirical analysis must distinguish between these two margins to avoid selection bias. Failing to do so can lead to either overstatement or understatement of the effects of copyright protection.

A useful analogy comes from labor economics. When wages are below some threshold level, some individuals may choose not to participate in the labor force. If analysis is restricted only to those employed, it may yield a biased estimate of the relationship between wages and hours worked. Similarly, in the context of technology transfer, a firm will enter a host market only if copyright protection is strong enough to offset entry costs. Among those that do enter, variation in the level of protection may then influence the intensity of investment or knowledge transfer. Distinguishing between these margins allows for a more accurate assessment of the role of copyright in shaping international firm behavior.

As discussed earlier, entry costs depend on firm-level setup costs and the ability to adapt production processes and brand identity to local market conditions. These costs are likely to vary across industries or types of creative works. Similarly, sensitivity to copyright protection is expected to be heterogeneous across sectors, much as it is in the context of patent protection.

Several studies, including USPTO (2012) and U.K. (2016), identify copyright-intensive industries based on revenue generation. Industries with higher domestic sales face greater risks under weak copyright regimes, as they have more to lose from infringement or market leakage. To capture this variation empirically, Ivus and Park (2022) use U.S. industry-level sales as a proxy for sensitivity to copyright protection. Because this measure is constructed from domestic sales data, it is exogenous to institutional and economic conditions in the host countries, making it a useful benchmark for cross-country analysis.

The empirical evidence draws on data from U.S. multinational companies operating in 69 countries between 1994 and 2011.[20] The sample comprises more than 200 firms in core copyright industries and over 600 firms in complementary industries. The figures below present trends in international technology transfer both before and after major copyright reforms, disaggregated by industry-level sensitivity to copyright protection.

To capture this sensitivity, copyright industries are grouped according to whether their U.S. domestic sales are above or below the median. Industries above the median are classified as relatively more sensitive to changes in copyright protection, under the assumption that firms with greater revenue exposure face higher stakes in protecting their intangible assets.

Figure 6.8 presents the ratio of each technology transfer outcome — FDI stock, unaffiliated licensing, and affiliate R&D — after a major copyright

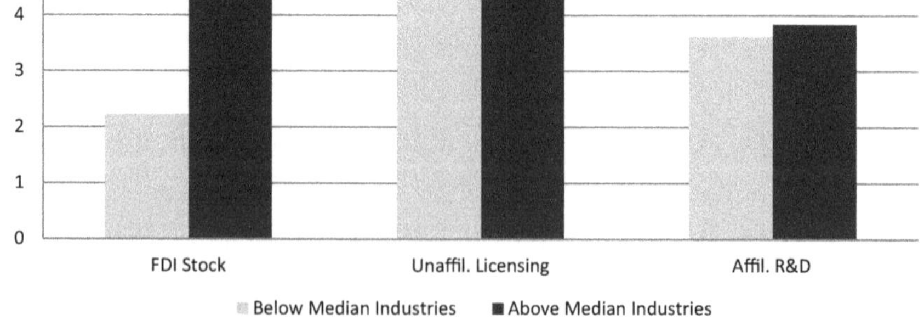

Figure 6.8. Technology Transfers by Type of Industry, Post/Pre-Reform Ratio

[20]See Ivus and Park (2022) and Park (2016).

reform relative to its pre-reform level.[21] The results indicate that technology transfer generally increases following reform, with larger gains observed in copyright industries with above-median domestic sales. This pattern suggests that firms in more copyright-sensitive sectors respond more strongly to improvements in legal protection abroad.

The increase in affiliate R&D, however, is only marginally greater in above-median industries than in those below the median. This limited differential is consistent with the fact that R&D activity in the copyright sector is relatively modest compared to the manufacturing sector and tends to be concentrated in software-related industries. As such, smaller post-reform changes in affiliate R&D are to be expected.

The regression analysis employs a two-step methodology to distinguish the effects of copyright protection at the extensive and intensive margins. Specifically, the model jointly estimates (i) a selection equation capturing the decision to enter a foreign market, and (ii) a conditional equation measuring the volume of technology transfer, investment, or licensing activity once entry has occurred. The probability of entry is modeled as a function of adaptation costs, which are proxied by the degree of similarity in creative outputs between the United States and the host country.[22] This similarity index serves as an exclusion restriction, influencing the entry decision but not the intensity of activity conditional on entry.

The first set of results, shown in Table 6.9, examines the relationship between host country copyright protection and unaffiliated licensing by U.S. multinational companies in copyright-related industries.[23] Unaffiliated licensees include both local firms and subsidiaries of non-U.S. multinationals. These licensing arrangements are particularly important from a development perspective, as they provide a channel through which indigenous agents can access foreign technologies and creative assets.

When entry costs are not accounted for, there is a positive relationship between copyright strength and licensing activity, and this relationship is

---

[21] Foreign direct investment stock is defined as the sum of the owner's equity and intercompany debt receivables, minus intercompany debt payables.

[22] For example, let $\mathbf{A} = (A_1, A_2, \ldots, A_n)$ represent the composition of creative goods in the U.S., and let $\mathbf{A}^* = (A_1^*, A_2^*, \ldots, A_n^*)$ represent the same for the host country. The cosine of the angle between these vectors measures the degree of dissimilarity. A value of zero indicates complete dissimilarity, and a value of one indicates complete similarity (or overlap). This approach was introduced in Chapter 3 in the context of international R&D spillovers.

[23] The dependent variable is measured as the value of licensing fees and royalties earned by the U.S. parent company from unaffiliated parties.

Table 6.9. U.S. International Licensing of Copyrighted Works

Dependent Variable: Licensing (Arms-length)		
Margin	**Intensive**	**Extensive**
Copyright Index	−0.129	−0.438***
Copyright Index × M	0.205**	0.261***
Observations	7,611	39,454
Adj. R-squared	0.778	

Notes: *** and ** denote 1% and 5% significance levels, respectively. M is a proxy for Industry Sensitivity. Control variables include host wages, tax rates, parent/affiliate sales, firm, country, year fixed effects.

stronger for industries that are more sensitive to copyright protection, such as software, broadcasting, cable television, and sound recordings.

However, once the entry decision is modeled explicitly, heterogeneous effects emerge, showing that copyright protection can exert market power effects for certain industries. For industries with relatively smaller sales, their business strategy likely relies on increased prices or increased licensing fees. This is accomplished by supplying less output or offering fewer licensing agreements, resulting in fewer technology transfers. But more technology transfers arise in industries that have greater market dependence on copyright protection. Firms in these industries benefit from stronger copyright protection because it enhances their ability to enforce licensing terms and to deter defection by licensees, who might otherwise seek to operate independently in the local market.

The analysis now turns to foreign direct investment (FDI). Copyright regimes may also influence firms' decisions to establish affiliates or subsidiaries abroad. In this case, the dependent variable is the number of FDI occurrences, measured as the count of U.S. multinational firm entries into host-country markets.

In Table 6.10, the coefficient on copyright protection is negative and statistically significant at the 10 percent level. This result suggests that stronger copyright regimes may advantage incumbent firms already operating in the host market. These firms are better positioned to assert their rights or to raise the prices and licensing fees associated with access to their protected goods and services. Holding other factors constant, a strong

Table 6.10. Copyright Protection and Episodes of Foreign Direct Investment

	(1) All Countries	(2) Exclude G6
Copyright Index	−0.418*	0.138
Copyright Protection × M	0.720***	0.412***
Control Variables	Included	Included
Observations	3,461	2,696
R-squared	0.676	0.396

Notes: ***, * denote 1%, 10% levels of statistical significance, respectively.
FDI episodes are measured by numbers of parent firms.
Controls: GDP, Host Wages, Income Tax Rate, and Institutional Quality
G6 countries: Canada, France, Germany, Italy, Japan, and U.K.

copyright regime in this instance may discourage new entrants, particularly smaller firms, from gaining a local presence. In such cases, firms may opt to serve the market through exports rather than through foreign direct investment.

However, the positive and statistically significant coefficient on the interaction between copyright protection and M — the U.S. industry-level market size — suggests that firms operating in sectors more reliant on copyright protection are more likely to establish affiliates or subsidiaries abroad. These firms have greater stakes in the enforcement of intellectual property rights and are better positioned to compete in host-country markets, including against other firms that may also benefit from stronger copyright regimes.

The discouraging effect of copyright protection on relatively smaller U.S. firms — those with a more limited presence in the domestic copyright market — disappears when the G6 countries are excluded from the sample. The G6 consists of Canada, France, Germany, Italy, Japan, and the United Kingdom. Column (2) in Table 6.10 reports results for U.S. FDI directed toward countries outside the G6. In this subsample, the coefficient on copyright strength is statistically insignificant, while the interaction term between copyright protection and industry-level U.S. market size remains positive and statistically significant at the 1% level.

These results indicate that enhanced copyright protection stimulates market entry across the copyright sector in non-G6 countries, with stronger effects in industries with greater sensitivity to copyright protection. One likely explanation for the difference is that G6 economies, along with the

United States, are home to many well-established copyright-intensive firms. As a result, smaller U.S. firms may face more formidable competition in these G6 markets following copyright reform, whereas they are more willing and able to expand into markets where local copyright producers are less dominant.

These findings are consistent with the conceptual framework. As discussed earlier, entry costs are likely to vary across countries, and it is typically more difficult for new creative works to enter highly developed markets where numerous high-quality creative expressions already exist. In such markets, especially within the G6, there is a greater burden on incoming works to differentiate themselves from existing content. This provides a plausible explanation for why the coefficient on copyright protection is negative in the full sample but not in the subsample that excludes G6 countries.

The final set of empirical results focuses on complementary industries. Expansions of the copyright market in a host country can create incentives for firms in related sectors to invest, transfer technologies, and undertake production or research and development activities locally. To the extent that copyright reforms enlarge the market for copyrighted works, firms in complementary industries may identify profitable opportunities to supply goods and services that enhance or support the consumption and production of creative content.

The data reveal inter-sectoral linkages between firms in copyright-related and complementary industries. U.S. parent companies in complementary sectors are observed to establish or acquire affiliates not only within their own industries but also in copyright-intensive sectors. The reverse is also true: firms based in copyright industries expand their operations into non-copyright sectors by acquiring affiliates in complementary industries.

Table 6.11 confirms that U.S. multinational parent companies frequently maintain affiliates across both copyright-related and complementary industries.[24] While most parent companies operate affiliates within the same industry, some diversify across sectors due to production needs or vertical integration strategies.

As shown in the table, before a major copyright reform, U.S. parent companies in the copyright industries had established 87 affiliates in complementary industries across 69 countries. Following reform (with timing varying by country), this number increased to 188 affiliates. Moreover, the

[24]For example, Sony Corporation owns affiliates operating in both electronics and film production.

Table 6.11. Cross-Industry Dependence

	Number of Affiliates in Complementary Industry	Mean FDI in Complementary Industry (relative to pre-reform)
Investors from the Copyright Industry		
Pre-Copyright Reform	87	1
Post-Copyright Reform	188	1.5
Investors from the Complementary Industry		
Pre-Copyright Reform	101	1
Post-Copyright Reform	356	2.8

Notes: Mean FDI is normalized by the pre-reform value.
The data are aggregated across 69 countries from 1994 to 2011.

average amount of FDI stock per affiliate in these sectors was 1.5 times greater after reform than before.

Similarly, U.S. parent companies in complementary industries expanded their acquisition of affiliates in copyright-related sectors following major copyright reforms. The average level of FDI stock invested by these firms in such affiliates nearly tripled post-reform. Table 6.11 illustrates a significant degree of interdependence between the copyright and complementary sectors, suggesting that expansion in one domain can generate investment spillovers in the other.

Table 6.12 presents estimated relationships between copyright reform and various measures of international technology transfer for a sample of U.S. multinational firms operating in complementary industries. Consistent with the high degree of cross-sectoral interdependence, the results suggest that copyright reforms encourage these firms, particularly those sensitive to copyright protection, to increase their FDI stock, unaffiliated licensing activity, and R&D conducted by their foreign affiliates.

To conclude, copyright protection can have both positive and negative effects on international technology transfer. On one hand, stronger protection may raise the cost of entry for firms facing higher production or adaptation costs, or allow incumbent firms to exercise greater market power. On the other hand, enhanced copyright regimes can strengthen a firm's

Table 6.12. Responses of Complementary Industries to Copyright Reform

	(1) FDI Stock	(2) Unaffiliated Licensing	(3) Affiliate R&D
Copyright Reform	−0.543	−0.249**	−0.369*
Copyright Reform × M	0.547**	0.208***	0.315**
Control Variables	Included	Included	Included
Observations	25,527	25,527	25,527
Adj. R-squared	0.465	0.406	0.372

Notes: ***, **, * denote 1%, 5%, and 10% significance levels. For firms in the complementary industry, M is based on *global* sales of copyrighted works.
Controls: GDP, Host Wages, Income Tax Rate, and Institutional Quality.

ability to safeguard its intangible assets, thereby encouraging foreign direct investment and licensing activity.

Importantly, the effects of copyright reform extend beyond traditional copyright-intensive sectors. As sales of copyrighted goods grow, they generate demand for complementary products and services, incentivizing investment in upstream and downstream industries. These intersectoral linkages illustrate how copyright policy impacts industrial development more broadly.

Appendix 6A. Transfer Pricing and Profit-Shifting

In this chapter, technology transfer was described as the movement of productive knowledge across borders — through FDI, trade, and licensing. However, when transfer pricing and profit-shifting are considered, these movements appear to be less about real technology diffusion and more about tax arbitrage strategies.

Multinational corporations (MNCs) can redistribute profits among affiliates in their network across different jurisdictions so as to minimize their overall tax burden. One way is to transfer the ownership of intellectual property (IP) — copyrights, trademarks, and patents — to an affiliate in a low-tax country or a tax haven country. The affiliate becomes the IP-holding entity, licenses the IP to the parent, other affiliates, and other companies around the world, and collects royalty payments. The IP-holding entity ends up paying little to no taxes on the income generated because it is domiciled in a low-tax jurisdiction or tax haven. Had the MNC retained ownership of the IP, it would have had to pay a higher tax on all the royalty income earned.

Transfer prices refer to the prices charged between related entities within an MNC for goods, services, or intangible rights. For example, transfer pricing applies not only to the initial sale of IP from the parent to an affiliate, but also to the royalties and fees that the affiliate — now the IP owner — charges the parent and other affiliates for the right to use that IP.

The internationally accepted standard for computing transfer prices is the *arm's-length principle*, which means that transfer prices between related entities should be comparable to prices that would be charged between "unrelated" parties under similar conditions. The challenge, however, with IP is its intangible nature and unique market, where such assets are not readily traded, making direct comparisons with unrelated transactions difficult. Hence, transfer prices can be manipulated to shift profits from a high-tax to a low-tax jurisdiction. Typically, companies might undercharge for tech transfers to affiliates in high-tax countries (to reduce taxable income there) while overcharging affiliates in low-tax countries where royalty fees can be tax-deductible.

What makes IP a candidate for global profit-shifting strategies? IP is a mobile asset which, unlike physical capital, can be transferred across jurisdictions with minimal transaction costs. Other characteristics that make IP favorable are as follows:

- *Non-rivalry*: IP can be used simultaneously in multiple markets without diminishing in use.
- *Scalability*: The marginal cost of deploying IP in additional markets is nominal.
- *Complex Valuation*: Determining the objective value of IP is challenging.

The following are the top 10 tax haven countries in recent years:

Tørsløv *et al.* (2023) found that in 2015, 36% of multinational profits had been shifted to tax haven countries. Bass *et al.* (2023) found that after 2000, there was a 0.41 correlation between transfers of patent assets from parent companies to affiliates and the corporate tax differential between the parent's jurisdiction and the affiliate's.[25]

[25]That is, where the differential was positive: $\tau_P - \tau_A > 0$, where τ_P is the corporate tax rate in the parent's jurisdiction and τ_A in the affiliate's.

Top 10 Tax Haven Countries	
1. Bermuda	6. Barbados
2. Cayman Islands	7. Switzerland
3. British Virgin Islands	8. Samoa
4. Gibraltar	9. Ireland
5. Luxembourg	10. Singapore

Source: Bass *et al.* (2023).

Global profit shifting has taken on a bewildering variety of schemes. One such scheme is known as the *Double Irish with a Dutch Sandwich*, as captured in the following diagram.

The example shows the lengths to which companies have exploited international tax loopholes. In Figure 6A.1, a U.S. parent company has a subsidiary in Ireland, called S_1, which is domiciled in Bermuda, a tax haven country. S_1 owns an Irish subsidiary as well, called S_2, which handles operations. The fourth player is a Dutch holding company, called N. The U.S. parent transfers ownership of an IP to S_1, who then licenses the asset to N. N in turn sub-licenses to S_2. Company S_2 then sub-licenses the right to the rest-of-the-world (ROW), where the IP asset contributes economic value. ROW then pays royalties to S_2, which then funnels the income to S_1, via N. Ultimately, S_1 books the income in Bermuda. Through various international tax reforms since 2015, this complex *Double Irish with a Dutch Sandwich* began to dissolve.[26]

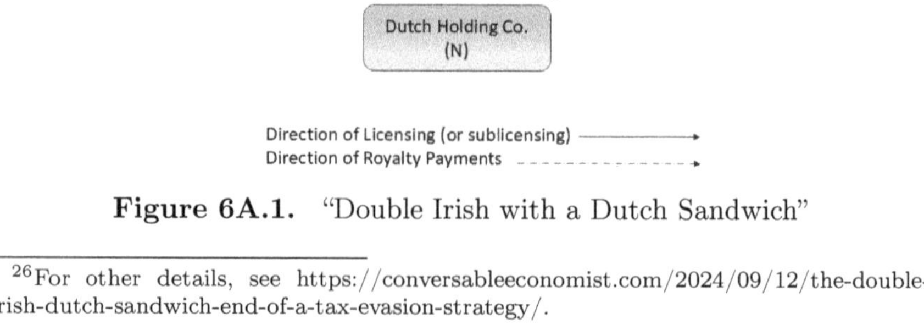

Figure 6A.1. "Double Irish with a Dutch Sandwich"

[26]For other details, see https://conversableeconomist.com/2024/09/12/the-double-irish-dutch-sandwich-end-of-a-tax-evasion-strategy/.

6A.1 *Implications for North–South Technology Transfers*

The occurrence of global profit shifting might lead to some skepticism about the empirical research: Are technology transfers even substantive? Should statistics on international licensing flows be distrusted? The short answer is no. While data cannot be taken at face value as a pure measure of international technology diffusion, technology transfers are happening and should be studied. The royalty payments are real and are documented financial transactions that have real effects on production and consumption. Where feasible, researchers could make econometric corrections to exclude tax haven countries or control for the tax incentives that might be driving royalty flows.

Tax haven countries are relatively few in number, with the U.S. being the top originating country of patent transfers by far, followed by the U.K. and Japan.[27] It is primarily intra-firm royalty and licensing payments that are affected by tax-motivated structuring. Tax authorities around the world have been clamping down on tax evasion. The profit shifting has led to significant losses of tax revenues from large corporations — income that could have funded public goods or reduced public debts. This fact has raised awareness. Profit shifting especially harms emerging economies, where R&D has occurred but where companies ship profits to tax haven countries, thereby depriving the emerging economies of tax revenues they worked hard to earn through technological investments.

From a measurement point of view, at the very least, it is awkward to observe tax haven countries being viewed as exporters of technologies — because they are the recipients of licensing fees and royalties — when in fact they did not conduct any of the R&D behind the technologies being exported, nor produce any of the creative content. The technological balance of payments (BOP) may also be misleading since it is quite feasible that a high-technology country (say, Germany) runs a deficit against a tax haven country (say, Luxembourg) because it pays more in fees and royalties than it receives, all due to the transfer of IP from one country to the other.

Foreign direct investment (FDI) data are also subject to measurement issues. FDI flows do not fully or solely represent the transfer of skills, capital, and technology — not when the main purpose is to establish an affiliate in a low-tax (or lower-tax) jurisdiction for purposes of transferring IP ownership to that company (or shell). An IMF study refers to this kind

[27] See Bass *et al.* (2023).

of FDI as *phantom FDI*, which during 2009–2017 outpaced the growth of genuine FDI.[28]

Santacreu (2023) provides rigorous theoretical and empirical analyses of how sensitive international licensing is to corporate tax differentials, controlling for other variables. The study uses OECD's *Balanced Trade in Services (EPOPS)* data from 1995 to 2012, covering 50 countries. The empirical findings confirm that MNCs in high-tax countries shift profits to lower-tax countries. The study conducts two policy simulations. The first is the implementation of a global corporate tax *minimum* (of 15%), as advocated under an OECD proposal. The second is a tax on IP held in foreign countries (akin to a policy under the U.S. *Tax Cuts and Jobs Act* of 2017). Both simulations are consistent. The policies would bring ownership of IP back to the home (parent) countries. However, interestingly, the simulations show that under these policies, firms' R&D intensity would have been lower relative to the baseline, as the additional royalty income would have been subject to higher effective tax rates. This suggests a tradeoff between raising tax revenue and preserving firms' incentives to invest in R&D.

On the other hand, the decline in R&D brought about by ending or reducing international profit shifting may be welfare-improving. The reason is that under a system of global profit shifting, companies might have been engaging in excessive R&D to create IP assets for purposes of a rent-seeking activity, like tax reduction or tax avoidance.

[28] See Damgaard *et al.* (2019).

Chapter 7

Creative Works

7.1 Introduction

This chapter examines the economics of copyright in the creative industries, particularly in the domains of film, music, publishing, and scholarly research. It evaluates the twin objectives of providing incentives for creative work and ensuring access to works. The chapter considers how copyright affects the commercial viability of creative outputs and the ecosystem of complementary industries that surround them, such as theatres, publishing houses, and digital platforms.

Two sections are devoted to piracy and to limitations and exceptions (L&E): the former involves unlawful copying and distribution, while the latter concerns authorized, lawful uses. Both piracy and L&E have more complex effects on creativity, sales, and access than is often assumed.

The final section concentrates on the case of academic publishing. This case highlights a friction between public funding of research and private appropriation of returns via journal pricing and paywalls. The chapter evaluates both the criticisms of current publishing models and the mechanisms, such as open access, price discrimination, and library subscriptions, that aim to expand access.

7.2 Creative Markets

Copyright issues are pervasive in the lives of creators, whether of books, music, films, paintings, sculptures, software programs, or scientific articles.

What do creators own, and what, if anything, do they owe others? What are consumers allowed or entitled to do with creative works, and what is prohibited? The stakes are high, given the immense commercial value of such works. According to a 2022 report of the International Intellectual Property Alliance, core copyright industries contributed $1.8 trillion in value added to the U.S. economy and accounted for nearly 6% of private sector employment in the U.S. The core copyright industries include book publishing, newspapers, sound recordings, motion pictures, radio and television broadcasting, computer software, video games, and periodicals and journals. These figures exclude indirect contributions from complementary industries, such as information technology and telecommunications, which target the creative goods market by supplying services and tools that either enhance the enjoyment of creative works (e.g., audio and video technologies) or serve as inputs in their production (e.g., digital tools and recording equipment).

Looming over the creative industries are potential pirates who threaten to appropriate the returns intended for creators. Although data on piracy are notoriously difficult to compile and interpret, some figures on software piracy are instructive. In 2017, the Business Software Alliance estimated that approximately 37% of software installed on personal computers worldwide was unlicensed. Piracy rates were as high as 90% in Libya, 89% in Zimbabwe, and 84% in Bangladesh. Even wealthy economies such as the European Union and the United States experienced software piracy rates of 28% and 15%, respectively.

The creative artist, therefore, operates under risks — not only the risk of piracy but also the uncertainty of the legal environment. The copyright system is complex and often lags behind new technological developments, such as digitization and the rise of social media. Over the past 100 years, copyright laws and regulations have evolved in a patchwork manner, comprehensible primarily to the cognoscenti — legal scholars and practitioners. The artist must navigate a labyrinth of copyright rules, limitations, and exceptions, all while undertaking the enterprise of producing valuable and fulfilling creative work.

7.2.1 *Copyrights Review*

A copyright owner acquires exclusive rights over her original literary, dramatic, musical, or artistic work. (Literary works include computer code.) Copyrights are limited in duration — although relatively long — typically extending for the life of the author plus 50–70 years, depending on the country. After this period of protection, the work enters the public domain, and anyone may use it freely without permission. Until then, the owner (or designated heir) can prevent others from commercially exploiting her work, or any work that is substantially similar, without authorization. She also retains control over derivative works, namely those that are adaptations of her original creation.

Copyright protection is automatic once the work is created. This stands in contrast to inventions, which require a formal application to obtain patent protection. If anything, the creator must take additional steps to permit others to use the copyrighted work freely. For example, the creator can grant a Creative Commons Attribution (CC BY) license, which allows others to distribute, adapt, or build upon the work and use it commercially, provided the licensee gives credit to the original creator (Figure 7.1).[1] Other Creative Commons license types contain similar provisions but may exclude derivative works; for instance, a creator could choose a CC BY-ND (No Derivatives) license, which requires others to give credit (BY) but does not allow them to alter the work (ND).

While the duration of copyright protection is long compared to patents and trademark protection, its scope is relatively narrow. For example, the term *original work* means that the work originated with the artist in question and was not copied from another source. In an extreme case, if someone else independently creates the same work, that person is also entitled to copyright protection, and the work would not be considered infringing.

Copyright protection applies to the expression of a work, not the underlying idea. A well-known example is the comparison between *Romeo and Juliet* and *West Side Story*. Both share a similar theme of star-crossed lovers, but represent different ways of expressing the theme. This idea–expression dichotomy is useful in scientific research, where multiple scholars

Figure 7.1. Copyright and Creative Commons Logos

[1] Logos are from https://logos-world.net/copyright-logo/ and https://logos-world.net/cc-creative-commons-logo/.

may arrive at the same idea independently. For example, Charles Darwin and Alfred Wallace both developed the theory of evolution. Isaac Newton and Gottfried Leibniz independently formulated calculus, though they expressed it differently. In economics, Robert Solow and Trevor Swan each developed the neoclassical growth theory model in 1956. Fortunately, none of these instances resulted in legal disputes that impeded the advancement of knowledge.

The protection of the specific expression, and not the underlying ideas, narrows the scope of copyrights. Economic considerations help explain why copyright protection is long in duration but narrow in scope. From the rightsholder's perspective, copyrights would be stronger if both the duration were longer and the scope of protection broader. But this comes with trade-offs. The ability to preempt independent creations or to claim rights over ideas would generate enormous transaction costs. It is infeasible to search the existing corpus of copyrighted works to detect infringement across variations in expression, including minute ones. The problem is even more acute with ideas, where exclusivity could result in excessive market power. Ideas are fundamental building blocks of artistic and scientific knowledge. Imagine a monopoly right over paintings of a night sky before dawn, or over the periodic table.

Copyright also comes with restrictions. For example, fair use permits the public — including other creators — to use portions of a copyrighted work without obtaining the author's permission. Transaction costs partly explain the rationale for fair use. The cost of locating and contacting the author(s), and negotiating fees and royalties merely to copy a portion of a work, can easily exceed the value of the intended use. In such cases, valuable uses would be forgone. Fair use is also in the vested interest of the author, as the value of her work may be enhanced through citations and broader utilization. Moreover, authors themselves are beneficiaries of fair use, since they likely built on prior work and will continue to do so in future work. Fair use also generates economic value, as will be discussed in a later section. Entire industries and companies, such as YouTube, TikTok, and others, have thrived because of it.

7.2.2 *Economics Review*

The economic rationale for the existence of copyrights is that knowledge goods, such as films, novels, and software programs, are public goods. They are non-rival and non-excludable. A song, for instance, enjoyed by one consumer does not detract from another's ability to enjoy it. Once composed and recorded, it is difficult to exclude others from listening. Returns to public goods are hard for a creator to appropriate in the marketplace. The optimal price is zero, given the low marginal cost of supply, and the accounting profits, if any, derived from a competitive market may be insufficient to cover the costs of creative development and commercialization. Hence, the government grants "monopoly-like" power to creators over their works for a limited time and with limited scope, allowing them to earn above-normal returns. Otherwise, few creative works would be produced if creators could not recover their costs. At some point, however, the monopoly distortion caused by copyright protection must end. Consumers should gain access to the work at a (lower) competitive price, and follow-on creators should be free to build upon it to generate additional knowledge goods for the benefit of society. Thus, copyrights involve a tradeoff: they tolerate static inefficiency (i.e., non-competitive provision of a good) in exchange for dynamic efficiency (i.e., incentives for investment and innovation).

7.3 Copyrights and Technological Development

As mentioned earlier, most people draw a clear connection between patents and technological development, since patents pertain to inventions such as machinery and equipment, chemicals and medicines, and computers and semiconductors. Moreover, firms in the manufacturing sector conduct the bulk of business R&D.

However, as discussed in Chapter 6, creative works contribute to technological development in several direct and indirect ways:

1. Artworks, music, films, books, and sound recordings are intellectual creations that contribute to the stock of human knowledge. Even in prehistory, humans recorded knowledge on cave walls. Cave paintings have enabled modern scholars to study aspects of ancestral life dating back some 30,000 years.
2. Software, databases, and journals are essential tools in scientific research and R&D. They serve as foundational inputs into the research process, enabling innovators to design and develop new machinery, equipment, building structures, and pharmaceutical products.

3. Demand spillovers can occur owing to the effects of market size. For instance, the expansion of copyright industries provides incentives for firms in complementary sectors to develop or invest in inputs and products related to the production or consumption of creative works.

7.4 Effects of Piracy

Pirates particularly target popular music, films, software, and books, viewing them as profitable arbitrage opportunities — copying and selling below the "monopoly" prices of creative works. In many regions, piracy is driven by poverty (the inability to afford market prices and the desire to access such goods), as well as by cultural attitudes or norms that regard the sharing or copying of intellectual goods as fundamentally different from taking or sharing physical property. Piracy is also facilitated by weak intellectual property protection or a lack of resources for IP enforcement.

First, it should be emphasized that estimating revenue losses due to piracy is challenging. Industry actors may be inclined to overstate such losses. Consider the demand curve in Figure 7.2.

Assume that pirated copies of the good are distributed for free. If the price is zero, 1,000 units are demanded. Absent piracy, suppose the price of the good is $10. Then only 100 units are demanded. At that price, industry revenues would be $1,000. However, the industry cannot credibly claim a

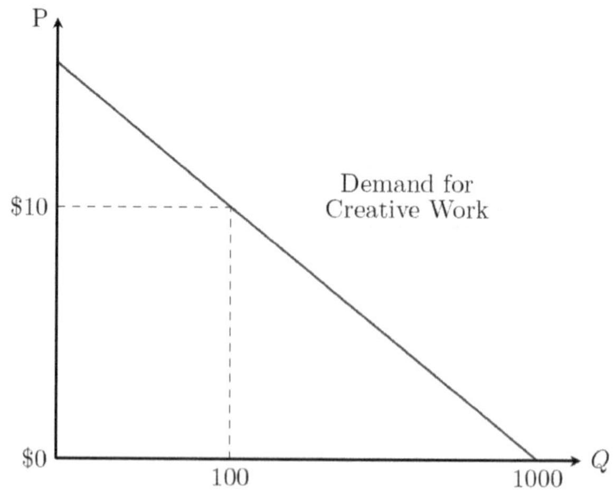

Figure 7.2. Demand for Creative Works

loss of \$10,000 in sales due to piracy (i.e., \$10 × 1,000) merely because 1,000 pirated copies are circulating. Such a claim ignores the fact that quantity demanded falls sharply as price increases from zero to \$10.

Second, piracy does not necessarily crowd out legitimate sales on a one-to-one basis. For example, if a pirate sells a copy of a Taylor Swift album, it does not follow that one album sale has been lost by the singer's authorized distributor. This is partly due to sampling effects. Buyers often sample goods before committing to a purchase or subscription. A pirated version may allow the consumer to learn more about a product — to sample an artist's work, an author's writing, or a software program. In some cases, for every five downloads, only one legitimate sale may be displaced. In fact, *sampling* may increase a consumer's desire to obtain the legal version, which may offer superior packaging, user manuals, or other materials. Access to a free novel by an author, for instance, may turn a reader into a lifelong fan of the novelist and purchase other books by the author.

Piracy or unauthorized copying can, in some cases, increase the value of complementary goods and services. For example, bootleg copies of music may raise the demand for live concerts. Before the era of digital streaming, video tapes — whether original or copied — increased the demand for video recording machines, such as VCRs and Blu-ray players. The concept of *indirect appropriability* refers to situations in which the copyright owner can appropriate some returns from copied materials (which they did not charge for directly) due to the added value that other paying customers derive from such copying. A classic case is free photocopying in libraries: journal publishers benefit indirectly because on-site copying increases the value of libraries, which in turn raises their willingness to pay for journal subscriptions.[2]

Because piracy is a function of multiple factors, such as poverty and social norms, there is not always a tight connection between the strength of copyright protection and the prevalence of piracy. Thus, strengthening laws and penalties may not fully eliminate piracy. The key implication is that robust copyright laws and enforcement alone are insufficient; they must be accompanied by efforts to shift social norms and promote economic development.

Fully eliminating piracy is not only infeasible; it may also be more strategic to find ways to accommodate it. A telling example comes from the case of iTunes in 2007. The platform allowed for paid digital access to content.

[2]See Liebowitz (1985).

Owing to a contractual disagreement, NBC Universal withdrew its content from the iTunes store, while broadcast networks ABC, CBS, and FOX did not.[3] Shortly thereafter, the pirating of NBC shows spiked. This episode illustrates that an all-or-nothing approach is ineffective. Consumers do not want to choose strictly between full-price access and piracy, but often prefer an intermediate option — such as subscription-based pricing — that allows them to pay a modest fee and still acquire content legally.

7.4.1 *Empirical Evidence*

Studies on the illegal file sharing of music and motion pictures are instructive. They help inform whether such activity displaces sales of legitimate goods or reduces incentives for creative work.

Empirical findings on the effects of piracy are mixed. Oberholzer and Strumpf (2007) found that music downloading had no measurable impact on the sales of copyrighted music. Their study focused on the behavior of German students and examined weeks when they were on holiday, as that was when they typically supplied files. A limitation of this study is that it examined piracy and sales contemporaneously, on a week-by-week basis. Piracy may have affected sales with a lag, which would not be captured by this design.

Rob and Waldfogel (2006), also using a college student sample, found that one album sale was crowded out for every five downloads. Hui and Png's (2003) cross-country study estimated a sales diversion rate of 42%. Together, these two studies suggest that the crowding-out effect of piracy is well below 100%, lending some credence to the possibility of sampling and indirect appropriation effects.

In 1999, Napster was launched as a peer-to-peer (P2P) file-sharing application that allowed users to exchange digital audio files. It sent major tremors throughout the music industry. Following a series of lawsuits, the denouement in 2001 was the shutdown of the Napster network.

Zentner (2006) finds that peer-to-peer (P2P) technology reduced the probability of purchasing music by 30%, and that, had downloading not been allowed, music sales in 2002 would have been just 7.8% higher. Thus, while Napster may have negatively impacted global music sales, it did not substantially destroy the music industry. There were signs of a downward trend in global music sales around that time.

---

[3]See Danaher *et al.* (2010) for an empirical study of this episode.

Table 7.1. Global Recorded Music Industry Revenues

		Percentage Distribution				
Year	**Total (Billions, Real 2017 Dollars)**	**Physical (%)**	**Streaming (%)**	**Downloads (%)**	**Performance (%)**	**Synchronization (%)**
1999	30.8	100.0	0.0	0.0	0.0	0.0
2004	23.9	93.7	0.0	1.6	4.8	0.0
2009	16.3	65.3	2.8	23.6	8.3	0.0
2014	13.3	40.6	14.1	29.7	13.3	2.3
2019	17.8	20.0	57.3	7.6	13.0	2.2
2024	23.6	16.3	69.2	2.7	9.8	2.0

Note: Nominal values converted to real using the GDP implicit price deflator (2017 = 100). https://www.bea.gov/.
Source: International Federation of the Phonographic Industry (IFPI), Global Music Report: State of the Industry 2025.

Table 7.1 shows the trend in global recorded music sales in the two decades following the launch of Napster.[4]

From a longer-term perspective, the global music industry did not collapse in response to new modes of delivering and consuming music. Table 7.1 shows that while there was a downward trend between 1999 and 2014, the industry began to recover thereafter. This recovery reflects a combination of accommodating new technologies and implementing novel business models. However, in real terms, global recorded music sales in 2024 remain only about three-quarters the size they were in 1999. In that regard, the ease of imitation and copying has taken some toll — at least in real terms.[5] Note the substantial displacement of physical recordings — such as albums, tapes, and compact discs — in favor of streaming.

Films have also been significantly affected by new technologies and piracy, particularly following the advent of BitTorrent, a peer-to-peer (P2P) file sharing protocol used for distributing large files over the internet.[6]

Piracy affects not only the artist, creator, or film studio, but the entire supply chain — including the agents who bring the product to market, sound engineers, costume designers, set builders, executives, promoters, and distributors. Danaher *et al.* (2014) studied the movie industry in Spain and

[4]In Table 7.1, synchronization refers to combining music with other media such as films, television shows, video games, and advertisements.

[5]In nominal dollars, which is the format in which the IFPI reports figures, the market size in 2024 appears larger than in 1999. However, from an economics perspective, it is necessary to adjust for price inflation over the period.

[6]See Zentner (2010) for an empirical analysis.

documented that rampant piracy there led producers in 2011 to withdraw from the Spanish market and refrain from releasing legal versions of their films at that time.

The lesson drawn from these experiences is that business models must evolve. Mechanisms that enable piracy, such as the internet or file-sharing technologies, are here to stay. Firms must adapt; they cannot expect to compete in the same way they did in the pre-digital era within a 21st-century, digital, global economy.

Businesses ought to adopt pricing and product differentiation strategies to compete with *free*. Firms should treat pirates who distribute goods at no cost as competitors and offer customers attractive alternatives through pricing and product variation. For example, they can offer convenience, complementary goods (such as high-quality packaging, booklets, and pamphlets about the artists or actors), customer service (especially protection against product defects, viruses, and so forth), and brand reputation — features that consumers typically cannot get from copiers or pirates.

They ought also to make legal digital distribution channels available. For example, consider offering consumers the options in Table 7.2.

Choice 2 offers an intermediate option between all-or-nothing; that is, between paying full price and obtaining the product for free. Some consumers are willing to pay a modest amount rather than obtain a pirated good at no cost. This requires that legal means of distribution (such as the digital option) be made available, and that consumers can find legitimate goods — songs, films, e-books, and articles — more easily than from pirated sites. Doing so fosters brand loyalty and trust. Many consumers, for instance, may wish to purchase just one song rather than an entire album, and are highly cost-conscious. This supports a business model that is both sustainable and capable of generating demand for complementary products. Indeed, modern digital services appear to have heeded the lessons from the piracy wave of the early 2000s. Many internet platforms now allow users

Table 7.2. Pricing Options amid Piracy

Choice Set 1	Choice Set 2
DVD (Pay Full Price)	DVD (Pay Full Price)
Pirate Version (Free)	**Digital Access (Half Price)**
	Pirate Version (Free)

to purchase music by the song, view films on a subscription basis, or even rent content à la carte for a reasonable fee. Product launch cycles have also accelerated. Prior to the 2000s, films typically premiered in theaters before being released on DVDs or VHS tapes. Today, films are available more quickly on home devices and televisions. Moreover, international release dates have converged; films are now launched in multiple countries simultaneously, whereas they once opened sequentially. The more impatient the consumer, the more likely they are to turn to pirated content.

7.5 Case Studies

This section presents two vignettes focusing on distinct forms of creative production: Bollywood films and Italian operas. By examining specific cultural products, these studies offer context-sensitive insights into the economic and institutional dynamics of creativity. They also incorporate a historical dimension, shedding light on how creative industries evolve.[7]

7.5.1 *Case of Bollywood*

Two key technological developments facilitated unauthorized movie distribution (piracy) in India during the 1980s and 1990s: (1) the VCR machine and (2) cable television. In response to increased piracy, India amended its Copyright Act of 1957 in 1994, with further reforms introduced in 1999. The 1999 reforms included provisions for injunctions against cable piracy.

Table 7.3 highlights the prolific nature of Bollywood's output. In 2010, Bollywood produced seventy percent more films than U.S. movie studios. However, total movie investments in India were only about one-twentieth of those in the United States, which has implications for film quality and global impact.

Piracy in India undermined investment in theaters. By crowding out the consumption of legal releases, piracy led to a decline in theater attendance. This, in turn, disincentivized the construction and maintenance of theaters, resulting in a shrinking number of venues. A vicious cycle emerged: with fewer places to watch films legally, piracy became more prevalent. The decline in attendance further deprived theaters of the revenues needed for reinvestment.

[7] The Bollywood case study is from Telang and Waldfogel (2018) and the opera analysis is from Giorcelli and Moser (2020).

Table 7.3. Bollywood vs. Hollywood

Year 2010	Indian Movie Production	U.S. Movie Production
Production	≈1,280	≈750
Investment	$479 million	$9,200 million

Source: Telang and Waldfogel, 2018.

Table 7.4. Indian Movie Revenues

Dependent Variable: Natural Log (Revenues)	
IMDb Rating	0.1635**
Dummy for 1985–2000	−0.5043**
No. of Observations	968

Note: ** indicates statistical significance at the 5% level.
Source: Telang and Waldfogel, 2018.

Table 7.4 is based on Telang and Waldfogel (2018), which presents regression evidence showing that movie revenues declined during the core period of piracy (1985–2000), even after controlling for film quality.

Film quality is measured using IMDb user ratings.[8] It is essential for the regression to control for quality; otherwise, changes in revenue could simply reflect shifts in audience preferences. The inference from the table is that piracy weakened the appropriability of returns for Bollywood film producers.

Shifts in movie production trends in India can be divided into two phases. The first is the piracy phase (1985–2000), during which filmmakers struggled to appropriate returns. The second is the recovery phase (2000–2010), strengthened. Telang and Waldfogel (2018) analyze four related indices of movie production in India. The first is the IMDb rating, while the other three pertain to output. *C.B.* denotes Census Board, the data source. The "C.B. aggregate" includes dubbed and recertified movies; the "C.B. movie-level data" excludes dubbed films; and "selected languages" refer to regional films. All measures show a decline following 1985 and recover after 2000.

[8]IMDb refers to the Internet Movie Database, a website that provides information about films and television shows. The IMDb rating captures the appeal of a film to its audience.

The recovery was also attributable to increased investments in shopping malls, which invigorated demand for theaters located within them. This development, in turn, enhanced the returns to movie-making. It illustrates a complementary or symbiotic relationship between shopping malls and theaters, in that each benefited from the presence of the other. Furthermore, the Indian government provided tax breaks for new multiplexes, incentivizing movie producers to cater to theater (and shopping mall) demand. Indeed, more than 50% of box office revenues came from these multiplexes. Coincidentally, this period also witnessed a global IT boom and a growing diaspora of Indian nationals. Indian professionals overseas had a strong demand for Bollywood films, triggering an export boost. Regions such as West Africa (in particular, Nigeria and the Ivory Coast) also have a high demand for Bollywood films.

The same period (2000–2010) witnessed significant growth in the television market and in multichannel systems. These multichannel stations were eager for additional content, including films. Over time, public, governmental, and private sector perceptions of the role of copyright appear to have improved.

The country-specific charts in Telang and Waldfogel (2018) indicate that the contraction in Indian movie production during the peak piracy period was not the result of a general slowdown in global demand for or supply of film production. Except for Hong Kong and Pakistan, most experienced an upward trend in film production between 1980 and 2020.

7.5.2 *Case of Italian Opera*

In a creative study, Giorcelli and Moser (2020) examine the effect of the introduction of copyright laws on the production of operas in Italy in the early 1800s. France, under Napoleon, invaded Italy in the late eighteenth century. Due to the timing of these invasions, two states — Lombardy and Venetia — adopted French-style copyright laws, while the remaining states implemented the French civil code but not copyright protections. The other states eventually introduced copyright protection, though not until after 1826.

It was the Northern Italian states of Lombardy and Venetia that adopted copyright law in 1801 following Napoleon's invasion of Italy. The staggered introduction of copyright laws across Italian states enabled the authors to study this historical episode as a natural experiment. Prior to the invasion and the adoption of copyright protection, opera piracy was widespread in Italy.

Table 7.5. New Operas per State and Period in Italy

	1780–1800 Range	1800–1820 Range
Lombardy & Venetia	≈1–3	≈4–8
Other States	≈1–2	≈1–4

Source: Giorcelli and Moser (2020).

Table 7.6. Average Number of New Operas, per State, Year

Time Period	Lombardy & Venetia	Other States
	All Operas ($N = 677$)	
1781–1800	1.575	1.350
1801–1820	4.550	2.083
	Historically Popular Operas ($N = 62$)	
1781–1800	0.125	0.083
1801–1820	0.600	0.158
	Operas of Long, Artistic Durability ($N = 42$)	
1781–1800	0.025	0.025
1801–1820	0.425	0.150

Source: Giorcelli and Moser (2020).

Table 7.5 shows that following the Napoleonic invasion, the supply of operas grew faster and became more numerous in the two states with copyright laws (Lombardy and Venetia) compared to states without such protection.

Table 7.6 presents the key differences in opera production between the treatment group (Lombardy and Venetia) and the control group of non-copyright-adopting states, before and after the Napoleonic invasion.

The average production of operas in the treatment group nearly tripled, while output in the control group increased by just over fifty percent. As shown in Table 7.6, this differential growth also extends to high-quality and durable operas. Opera quality is measured using assessments from the *Annals of Opera* almanac, and durability is proxied by the availability of opera sales on Amazon.com in 2014.

The table does not control for other variables, but the regression analyses in Giorcelli and Moser (2020) do. Overall, the key takeaway is that copyright reform stimulated creativity in the field of opera. However, the authors found that extending copyright protection beyond the life of the composer had no significant effect on opera output. The primary incentive effect arose from the availability of protection during the composer's lifetime.

7.6 Limitations and Exceptions

Copyright systems are founded upon a balance between exclusive rights and permissible uses. Copyright limitations and exceptions refer to legal provisions that allow the use of copyrighted works without the author's permission. These include doctrines such as fair use and fair dealing.

Both "rights" and "exceptions" might be viewed as competing. More and stronger rights for copyright owners may imply fewer and weaker exceptions for users, and vice versa. However, this section argues that the two can be complementary. The reason lies in the structure of the knowledge ecosystem, in which most individuals are simultaneously creators and users. Creation often depends on building upon the work of others or using existing works as inputs into new creative efforts. A balance between rights and exceptions is therefore in the mutual interest of both groups. Moreover, both the original copyrighted work and the derivative work created through permissible use can yield transformative and valuable economic contributions.

In the economics literature, patents have thus far dominated copyrights as a subject of study. Within the domain of copyright, another asymmetry exists: most economic analyses focus on the "rights" aspect, with relatively little attention paid to limitations and exceptions (L&E). As a result, few empirical studies are available on L&E. This section, therefore, concentrates mostly on the theoretical aspects.

Examples of copyright limitations and exceptions include the following:

- format-shifting and time-shifting,
- private use, non-commercial use, educational use,
- text and data mining,
- quotations and parodies.

Format-shifting refers to copying a protected work from one type of device to another, such as from a compact disc to an MP3 player. Time-shifting involves recording or downloading content for later viewing or listening, rather than consuming it at the time it is originally transmitted.

Time-shifting is generally not a problem for private, non-commercial use, but not if the content is pirated or shared beyond personal use.

Text and data mining (TDM) is the process of analyzing large volumes of text or data to identify patterns or relationships. Because TDM may involve copying copyrighted works, its legality depends on the existence of relevant limitations and exceptions, or on obtaining licensed access. Quotations refer to short excerpts from copyrighted works, while parodies mimic a work in a humorous or satirical way for purposes of social or other commentary.

The digital world has introduced several wrinkles into traditional copyright principles. In the physical world, a person who buys a book can later resell it. The *first sale doctrine* permits this, because once the book has been lawfully purchased, the copyright holder's control over its distribution is considered "exhausted." However, the first sale doctrine does not currently apply to digital transmissions, as these are not regarded as the resale of an existing product (like a book), but rather as the creation of a new copy. The nuance lies in the difference between distribution (selling a physical book) and reproduction (transmitting a downloaded book).

The new digital environment also prompted a rethinking of piracy. In the United States in 2011, media rights holders advocated for legislation entitled the *Stop Online Piracy Act (SOPA)*, which would have allowed rights holders and courts to block access to foreign websites accused of hosting pirated content. Search engines would have been required to remove links to such sites upon objection from copyright owners. SOPA was widely criticized for threatening internet freedom and undermining the open architecture of the internet. Critics also argued that SOPA ran counter to the principles of limitations and exceptions (L&E), which are an integral part of copyright systems and had enabled the emergence of platforms like YouTube. Massive protests in early 2012 — led by Wikipedia, Google, and user rights groups — ultimately led to the bill's defeat.

7.6.1 *L&E Regimes and Rationale*

It should be clear at the outset that limitations and exceptions (L&E) do not involve unauthorized copying or distribution. Rather, they constitute legally authorized freedoms established by statute or case law. Legal systems define permissible uses of copyrighted works through legislation and judicial interpretation. L&E delineate the rights and privileges of users

Table 7.7. L&E Systems

Fair Use	Fair Dealing
• U.S., Singapore, Taiwan, Israel	• Australia, Canada, U.K., India
• Flexible, general framework	• Specific, more detailed rules
• Principles-based	• Enumerated list of permitted uses

while at the same time imposing constraints on what rights holders can control, thereby placing limits on their market power.

There are two main types of limitations and exceptions (L&E) systems in place across countries (Table 7.7).

Under a principles-based system governing fair use, limitations and exceptions are evaluated qualitatively based on the purpose and character of the use, the nature of the work, the amount or portion used, and the effect on the potential market or value of the copyrighted work.[9] Fair use follows a case-by-case approach. By contrast, the fair dealing system is more explicit about what constitutes L&E. An enumerated list provides examples of works or activities that qualify as limitations and exceptions, such as private study, parody or satire, news reporting, research, criticism or review, judicial proceedings, or professional advice.

The Berne Convention's *three-step test* (Article 9(2)) sets the international standard for limitations and exceptions (L&E):

1. The exception must apply only in certain special cases.
2. It must not conflict with the normal exploitation of the work.
3. It must not unreasonably prejudice the legitimate interests of the author.

The three-step test is a legal requirement under both the Berne Convention and the TRIPS Agreement, and it provides the guiding framework for fair dealing systems. Although fair use is not explicitly framed around the three-step test, it is generally regarded as compliant in practice due to its balancing of rights and interests.

[9]See U.S. Copyright Act, Title 17, Section 107.

An economic rationale for limitations and exceptions (L&E) centers on the concept of transaction costs.[10] Transactions costs refer to the additional costs involved in facilitating a trade beyond the actual price or fee exchanged. These include the costs of negotiation, bargaining, drafting contracts, licensing, obtaining permissions, and enforcing rights. Legal exceptions can promote otherwise unfeasible exchanges by bypassing or reducing these transaction costs, particularly in cases where the costs of contracting exceed the value of the exchange. For instance, it is typically not cost-effective for a user to seek permission to quote a single paragraph or photocopy a single page of a textbook. Similarly, it would be inefficient for the author or publisher to enforce such minor uses through litigation. In these cases, no viable transaction would have occurred, and the exception facilitates socially beneficial uses without harming the copyright holder.

Another dimension to consider is the potential harm to the copyright owner, as illustrated in the following:

		Transactions Costs	
		HIGH	LOW
IP Profit Destruction	HIGH		Weak Case for Exceptions
	LOW	Strong Case for Exceptions	

The case for a copyright exception is strongest when two conditions are met: the transaction costs of obtaining permission are high, and the expected loss in profit to the copyright holder (from not charging a fee for the use of its copyrighted work) is low. In contrast, the case for an exception is weaker when transaction costs are low and the copyright holder stands to lose significant profits from uncompensated use.

7.6.2 *Costs and Benefits of L&E*

Limitations and exceptions (L&E) may carry potential risks. They can displace sales of copyrighted works or create confusion with original content. Adverse dynamic effects may arise if rights holders are less able to appropriate the returns on their investment.

[10]Of course, the justification for L&E extends beyond economics and commerce; they also serve important public interest purposes.

Table 7.8. L&E Example

Legal Shift	Format A (units)	Format B (units)	Price (per unit)
Before	100	100	$1
After	200+	0	>$1

On the other hand, L&E can increase the overall economic value of creative works. By permitting certain uses without prior authorization, they may expand the work's reach and utility. Table 7.8 offers a stylized example.

Suppose a consumer owns a Blu-ray movie but wishes to watch it on a tablet while traveling. Converting the movie into a digital file for personal use is an example of *format shifting*. For simplicity, assume that each format (Blu-ray disc and digital file) costs $1. At that price, there is a demand for 100 units of each.

Now, consider the introduction of a legal exception permitting format shifting. With this flexibility, a consumer can legally purchase the Blu-ray version and create a digital file from it for private use without needing to buy the same content twice. This makes the Blu-ray format more attractive, as it contains additional value because of lawful format shifting. Consequently, the demand for Blu-ray movies rises, as illustrated in Figure 7.3.

Thus, after the format-shifting exception, two outcomes are possible: an increase in the price of the copyrighted product and a rise in total sales. While the rights holder may forgo revenues from selling Format B (e.g., the digital version separately), these losses can be more than offset by higher revenues from increased sales of Format A (e.g., Blu-ray discs).[11]

Other exceptions could also raise the value of the original copyrighted work, such as quotations and parodies. For example, *MAD Magazine*, a satirical publication, frequently spoofed Hollywood films. These parodies often provided films with additional publicity and, in some cases, notoriety, thereby increasing public interest in the original works.

[11] An alternative option for the seller is to offer a *combo pack* — a bundled product that includes both the Blu-ray disc and a digital download code. The price of the bundle would be higher than that of a single-format product because of its appeal to the consumer.

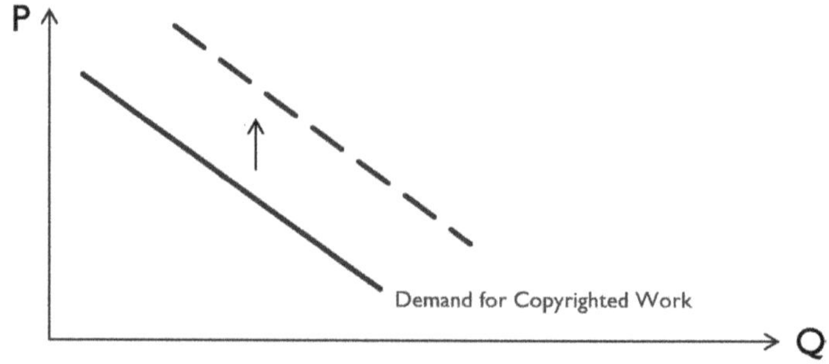

Figure 7.3. Copyright Flexibilities May Increase Demand

User rights, exceptions, and flexibilities may encourage transformative or derivative works, especially when rights holders themselves lack a comparative advantage in producing follow-on uses, as their expertise may lie in the creation of original works. Transformative derivatives can generate new industries and business models, stimulating investment and employment.[12]

In a landmark case, the rap group "2 Live Crew" created a parody in 1989 that borrowed the opening lines of Roy Orbison's song "Pretty Woman." The copyright owner sued for infringement, and the case ultimately reached the U.S. Supreme Court. The Court held that the use of the lyrics was transformative because it provided a cultural commentary on relationships, thus constituting a new expression.[13]

Another example is *Authors Guild v. Google*, a case concerning Google's book digitization project. Filed in 2005 and resolved in 2016, the court ruled that large-scale digitization for search and indexing can qualify as transformative fair use.[14]

7.6.3 *Empirical Work*

Empirical analyses of the economic effects of copyright limitations and exceptions remain limited.

Arai and Kinukawa (2014) examine the case of *Dojinshi*, fan-created derivative works in Japan. These self-published works, produced by amateur

[12]For example, reference guides to television series or film franchises such as *Star Trek, Mission: Impossible, James Bond,* or *Harry Potter.*

[13]*Campbell v. Acuff-Rose Music, Inc.*, 510 U.S. 569 (1994).

[14]*Authors Guild v. Google, Inc.*, 804 F.3d 202 (2d Cir. 2015). See also http://www.nolo.com/legal-encyclopedia/fair-use-what-transformative.html for more examples of transformative fair use.

artists, often incorporate characters and narratives from copyrighted anime or manga without explicit permission. Despite their derivative nature, copyright holders tend to ignore or tolerate the practice. One possible rationale is that *Dojinshi* enhances the value of the original works by deepening fan engagement. In some cases, rights holders have incorporated styles or narrative elements from *Dojinshi* into their productions.

In econometric work, Ghafele and Gilbert (2012) analyze the effects of Singapore's adoption of fair use. Their findings align with the international-level evidence presented in Chapter 6, which suggests that copyright regimes influence not only creative sectors but also complementary industries involved in the delivery and consumption of copyrighted content.

The authors examine three categories of industries: (i) core copyright industries (e.g., music, film, books, television, and radio); (ii) private copying technology industries (e.g., computers, optical media, DVD players) and (iii) a control group of unrelated sectors. The primary dependent variable is the growth in value added (VA). The study finds that, following the adoption of fair use, VA growth declined in the core copyright industries, increased in private copying technology industries, and remained statistically unchanged in the control group.

A few criticisms of the Ghafele and Gilbert (2012) study are worth noting. First, the classification of group (ii) — private copying technology industries — is arguably too broad. This category includes sectors whose growth could be driven by a host of unrelated factors, such as expansion into export markets, advances in patent-protected innovations, or labor cost advantages linked to multinational insourcing. Second, the study does not control for alternative determinants of value-added growth, which weakens causal inference. Third, the empirical analysis is based on a very limited sample: only 12 annual observations spanning 1999–2010. This small sample size reduces statistical power and raises concerns about the robustness and reliability of the findings.

A policy brief from the Lisbon Council (see Gibert, 2015) sought to empirically assess the scope of limitations and exceptions (L&E) and examine their relationship to industrial growth across eight developed countries. The study focuses on two sets of industries: (i) the core copyright sector, including publishing, audiovisual media, broadcasting, and information and communication technologies (ICT); and (ii) complementary industries, such as electrical and optical equipment, consumer manufacturing, wood and paper products, and construction.

The Lisbon Study constructs an index of L&E based on four dimensions: (i) whether the country adheres to the Berne Convention's three-step test (yes/no); (ii) the scope of L&E for public uses, such as criticism, parody, news reporting, and education, categorized as broad, narrow, or none; (iii) the scope of L&E for private uses, also classified as broad, narrow, or none; and (iv) the presence or absence of levies on private copying equipment, where the absence of levies is interpreted as a sign of greater flexibility.

Overall, the policy brief finds that a "flexible" regime of exceptions in copyright is associated with higher rates of growth in the overall economy, the information technology and services industry, and the traditional media industry. Workers also fared better, enjoying higher wages overall and in the communications and technology industries in particular.

The key problem for empirical research is that the constructed L&E index is highly correlated with the index of copyright strength discussed in Chapters 2 and 6 — namely, a correlation of 0.67. It also has a correlation of 0.74 with the U.S. Chamber of Commerce's GIPC Copyright Index. It is therefore challenging to disentangle the effects of exceptions from the effects of copyright protection on economic activity. Nonetheless, it is important to control for both shifts in copyright strength and shifts in exceptions, as both shape the copyright regime.

7.7 Publishing Industry

Creative activity occurs within economically interdependent innovation ecosystems. As pointed out earlier, creators build upon prior work. But that is only the tip of the iceberg. The commercialization, production, and distribution of creative works involve multiple complementary actors. For example, book production involves both the author and the publisher. Publishers contribute significant value-added services: editing, designing, printing, marketing, and more. Copyright protection (and fair use) must be considered in the author–publisher relationship, including how returns are appropriately shared. The publisher also assumes risks. It incurs up-front costs — such as paying advances to authors — before launching a book. Subsequent earnings may be positive or negative. Publishers invest in multiple titles, so a degree of cross-subsidization occurs: profits from bestsellers help offset losses from non-sellers.

The same ecosystem operates in other creative industries, in the sense that the commercialization of a good involves the coordination of complementary parties. A novel can be turned into a film for streaming or viewing at a theatre, a song into a concert performance, and a set of software codes into a business platform for customer relations management. Due to the input of multiple parties, the returns to a creator need to be shared with others who make things happen. Other parties that incur upfront investments may require some exclusivity in the market arrangement in order to recoup costs.

7.7.1 *Select Debates*

Does copyright protection impede the circulation of knowledge or does it facilitate its creation and availability? A look at the world of publishing is instructive.

A common refrain in the copyright research literature is the tradeoff between creativity and access. Copyrights that are too strong inhibit access to the work; copyrights that are too weak limit incentives to create. Copyrighted works take a long time to enter the public domain. During the period when a work is under copyright, it can be expensive to the general public due to non-competitive pricing. The rights holder may be unwilling to license the work widely or may disapprove of the intended use of the work by a party seeking a license. Hence, a common criticism of the copyright system is that it impedes the circulation of knowledge. A case that illustrates these issues is academic publishing. Academics depend heavily on journals and textbooks not only to learn but also to disseminate their research and seek tenure and promotion. They can circulate their findings through working papers, but these do not carry the imprimatur of peer review.

As with other creative output, textbooks involve a team effort beyond the author. Labor and material costs, and promotional expenses, comprise that effort. Similarly, team effort is behind journal production. Journal articles are relatively easy to copy or pirate. Levels of copyright protection should therefore be proportional to the ease of misappropriation as well as the development costs. Indeed, for journals, publishers often require that authors transfer the copyright to them. The publishers are then responsible for development and marketing.

But because of copyrights and the market structure of publishers, textbook prices and journal subscription fees tend to be quite hefty. Even a

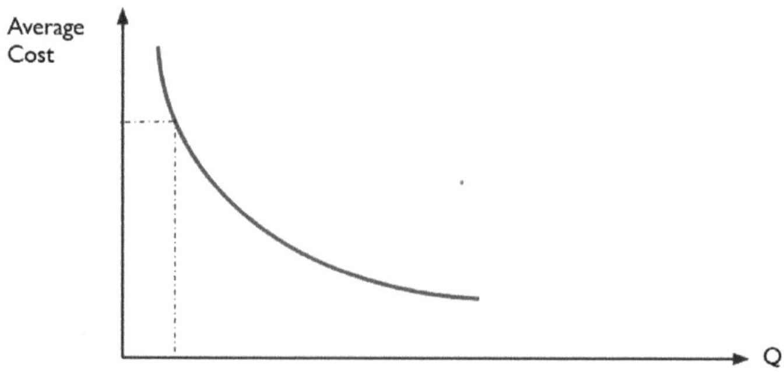

Figure 7.4. Economies of Scale in Academic Publishing, or Lack Thereof

single article from a journal can cost upwards of $39 to purchase. This puts scholarly works out of reach for most poor households and for researchers in poor countries. Academic books and journals are particularly expensive because of the lack of economies of scale (Figure 7.4). The market size is very small, consisting mainly of a tiny fraction of the world's population of researchers with advanced degrees. Chances are that only a few dozen people have ever read the average journal article. With this small customer base, academic publishers cannot spread their overhead costs as thinly as needed to reduce prices significantly.

How then are scholarly works made affordable? Several ways exist. First, the primary consumers of academic books and journals are employed in universities. University libraries purchase books and subscribe to journals on their behalf. (Government agencies and research institutes can also provide this service to their research staff.) Publishers like Elsevier, Wiley, Taylor and Francis, and Springer Nature produce multiple journals from multiple disciplines. Libraries typically contract to subscribe to the publisher's journals as a bundle. Faculty and students then access the articles for free. Second, publishers practice the art of price discrimination, charging different prices to different types of consumers depending on their elasticities of demand. Individual subscribers pay less than, say, libraries or research institutes do. Third, open-access journals are available. (Some journals provide open access options to authors.) Under open access, the author(s) retain copyrights and the readers access articles for free. How are open-access journals then financed if they do not charge readers? Largely, the authors pay the cost, and the authors obtain the funds from their research grants. Grant foundations and agencies do allow open-access fees to be budgeted.

While these measures help with affordability, there are gaps. Authors without sponsored research grants may not be able to pay the open-access fees. Researchers who are not affiliated with a university or a research organization, or who are affiliated with a university in a developing country whose library cannot afford the site license fees, will be precluded from free access. Price discrimination schemes can only go so far. For price discrimination to succeed, resale must be prevented. This is challenging to do with electronic copies, especially with pirate sites that can enable the evasion of market segmentation.

Indeed, a pirate site called Sci-Hub exists, which is the Napster equivalent for journal articles. Founded by a programming student from Kazakhstan, the site hosts downloaded copies of published articles and makes them available for free. Copyright authorities have tried to shut the site down, but it manages to re-emerge. How sites like this will impact the publishing industry has yet to be measured. It is also possible that book and journal prices rise due to piracy, as surviving publishers attempt to cover their costs.

A 2018 documentary film available on YouTube, entitled *Paywall*, levels highly charged criticisms against the oligopoly of journal publishing companies (see Box 1).[15] It laments the high prices of academic journals, the high profit margins of publishers, and the possible locking up of scientific knowledge due to monopoly pricing.[16]

Box 1. Paywall Documentary Highlights

- Academic publishers generate multi-billion-dollar profits.
- Profit margin is in the range 35–40% (greater than that of tech companies like Apple, Facebook, Google).
- Industry is oligopolistic and supplies a non-competitive amount of output.
- Claims of harm to libraries (i.e., by expensive books and journals) and to scientific research.

In addition to advocating for open-access journals and viewing Sci-Hub sympathetically, the film deplores the idea that publishers charge the public

[15]https://vimeo.com/273358286.

[16]A limitation of the profit margin data is that it could be cyclical; the film does not address that. Entry barriers and the oligopolistic structure could account for pricing, not just copyright protection. 232 Box 1. Paywall Documentary Highlights.

for journal articles based on research funded by taxpayer dollars. Much of the scholarship in science and the humanities is indeed funded by government grants; however, the economics behind this claim are more nuanced. Not all authors of journal articles have been funded through grants, whether from industry or government sources. When such funding does occur, it typically covers research-related expenses such as fieldwork, clinical trials, laboratory assistants, postdoctoral fellows, and conference travel. These research funds generally do not cover the cost of producing the journals, except in cases where they are earmarked for open-access fees. (Publicly funded grants may stipulate that awardees make their data and research findings available, but this is a separate issue.) The primary costs of journal articles arise from their production and dissemination, which are separate from the conduct of the research or the content creation itself.

7.7.2 *Are Scholars Hindered by the Cost of Books and Journals?*

As mentioned earlier, researchers rarely pay directly for access to journals; university or institutional libraries pay on their behalf. Moreover, journal articles are not always the most timely source of new ideas or findings. Given the publication lag — i.e., the time it takes for peer review and for articles to appear in print — researchers often depend on working papers or conference presentations for the most up-to-date knowledge.

7.7.3 *On Profit Margins and Circular Flow*

Why are academic publishers' profit margins relatively high? Consider the simple profit expression:

$$\text{Profit}(\pi) = \text{Revenue} - \underbrace{\textbf{Costs}}_{\Uparrow}$$

Publishers benefit because the primary intellectual laborer — the author — is unpaid. Bergstrom (2001) refers to this as "free labor for costly journals." The scientist-author's salary comes from the institution (university, institute, or other). In addition, authors often pay the journal for the cost of peer review. Nonetheless, authors derive non-monetary benefits from publishing an article in a journal, such as reputational enhancement, which improves their chances of promotion and winning prizes and grants.

Earlier, the affordability of journals and books was challenged. But some counter-criticisms of the affordability defenses can be made. First, journal subscriptions and books may be expensive for small academic institutions or for those in poor countries. Second, differential pricing may be circumvented by resale. (In the 2012 U.S. Supreme Court case, *Kirtsaeng v. John Wiley & Sons*, a Thai student attending college in the U.S. sold books in the U.S. that his friends and family had purchased more cheaply in Thailand and shipped to him.) Third, open access fees are not affordable if the scholar has no grant funding. Fourth, working papers are not fully peer-reviewed and therefore may not reflect established knowledge.

Fifth, there is no circular flow between journal sales and research. In other industries, such as the pharmaceutical or energy sectors, profits can be plowed back into R&D. But the profits from academic publishing and the research expenditures by academic scholars are separate and disconnected. That is, publisher profits do not typically fund the original research published in their journals, nor do they support university education. To generate a circular flow between them, a topic for future study and debate would be how to structure an alliance between publishers and academic networks. The relationship could be in-house or arm's-length. Research and publishing are complementary endeavors, so perhaps their organizations should be as well.

7.7.4 *Related Controversy*

If research is publicly funded, should private publishing companies charge the public for journal articles — knowledge created using taxpayer money? The comparison does not fully hold because public funding does not cover the costs of publication. While vaccine development can be taxpayer-funded, the publication costs — editing, typesetting, hosting platforms, and peer review coordination — as well as marketing expenses, are *not* taxpayer-funded. These public funds instead support the content of articles and books — the underlying research and creative pursuits.[17]

Even when taxpayer funds support research, some limits to public claims over downstream activities must apply. Consider an analogy: if a medical doctor's education is publicly financed, should the doctor be barred from charging fees for her private medical services later? Some quid pro quo may

[17]For taxpayer funds to fully support both research and publishing would require future academic grants to be larger, covering not just research expenses but also publication and dissemination costs.

be warranted — such as service in rural hospitals or underserved communities — but indefinite restrictions on income would be excessive. Regulating post-graduation earnings too strictly risks overreach. Similarly, just because public funds support the production of research does not mean that all subsequent stages — editing, publishing, and dissemination — must be free or nonprofit. The more appropriate question is what level of profit or markup is reasonable in light of the initial public investment.

In summary, copyright manages the relationships among scholars, readers (or students), educators, and publishers. Creativity and commercialization are team efforts; copyright regimes must reflect the needs of all participants in that ecosystem. Property rights help generate incentives for research and dissemination, but exclusivity also raises the market price of access to knowledge — that is, the paywall. Yet the paywall problem can be mitigated. In practice, various mechanisms lower the cost of access, including institutional library subscriptions, research grants, open-access publishing, tiered pricing based on income levels, and the circulation of working papers. Although these mechanisms have limitations, they nonetheless facilitate access to knowledge while maintaining incentives for knowledge creation and commercialization. Areas for further debate include the level of reasonable profits from publicly funded research, the creation of productive circular flows between research and publishing, and the potential for new organizational models to better serve innovation and access.

Chapter 8

Public Health

8.1 Introduction

This chapter examines intellectual property issues in public health, with particular attention to how patent protection in the pharmaceutical sector affects access to medicines in developing countries.

The chapter begins by exploring the distinctive nature of pharmaceutical innovation, where substantial R&D investments make firms heavily dependent on patent protection to recoup costs. However, this dependence on exclusive rights creates tensions when life-saving medications become financially inaccessible to those who need them most. These tensions became highly visible during the HIV/AIDS crisis in Southern Africa.

A conceptual framework for pharmaceutical pricing is developed and analyzed, along with the role of intellectual property flexibilities such as parallel importation and compulsory licensing.

Generic competition also receives attention, as the chapter investigates phenomena such as "evergreening" and patent thickets. The analysis extends to data exclusivity and the impact on delayed competition.

Two contemporary challenges receive attention: neglected tropical diseases, which affect over a billion people but receive insufficient commercial R&D investment due to limited market profitability, and the COVID-19 pandemic, which sparked intense debates about TRIPS waivers versus existing flexibilities. The chapter concludes with empirical evidence on how patent protection affects pharmaceutical R&D and technology transfer, particularly examining the transformation of India's pharmaceutical industry post-TRIPS.

An appendix on traditional medicines briefly considers indigenous knowledge systems and their relationship to modern intellectual property frameworks.

8.2 Nature of Pharmaceutical Innovation

Pharmaceutical innovation tends to be heavily dependent on IP protection due to the ease of copying drug innovations.[1] R&D is an expensive activity involving clinical trials and experimentation that is risky and uncertain in that all the research effort and clinical trials could still result in no breakthrough. Multiple trials, tests, and experiments are run in the hopes of a breakthrough. Another element of uncertainty is whether a drug discovery will obtain regulatory approval. The approval process could be lengthy and siphon significant time off the twenty years of protection that a patented drug is granted.[2]

Drug companies also spend heavily on sales and marketing — in some cases more than on R&D.[3] One argument for the marketing expenditures is that patents are time-limited so that drug companies aggressively market to recoup their R&D costs before generics or biosimilars enter the market. Third, even after a drug is approved for marketing, it may compete with follow-on drugs. To maintain market share, companies use marketing to differentiate their products from others, even if the product differentiation is marginal.

The high cost of pharmaceutical innovation and marketing creates incentives for international free-riding. Countries could rely upon others to conduct and pay for the research, while they enjoy the knowledge spillovers. Indeed, pharmaceutical drugs are frequent targets for imitation and counterfeiting.

All this is to say that the pharmaceutical sector is highly dependent on patent protection. At the same time, pharmaceutical innovations are critical to human health. And while it is acknowledged that pharmaceutical R&D

---

[1]See Acri (2024) for a thorough treatment of this sector.

[2]Effectively, if approval takes 8 years, a pharmaceutical company has only 12 years left to commercially profit from the drug.

[3]*Compustat* data for a sample of six companies (AbbVie, Bristol-Myers Squibb, Johnson & Johnson, Merck & Co., Pfizer, and Sanofi) over the period 2010–2025 show that R&D spending was approximately six times advertising spending. However, a broader measure of marketing, which includes selling, general, and administrative expenses, was roughly twice R&D spending. In *Compustat*, the variable identifiers for R&D, advertising, and this broader marketing measure are *xrd*, *xad*, and *xsga*, respectively. *Compustat* can be accessed via https://wrds-www.wharton.upenn.edu/.

can be very expensive and subject to extensive regulations, critics of high drug prices argue that much basic research is supported by public funding, creating an obligation on the part of the pharmaceutical industry to ensure reasonable access to resulting treatments. In exchange for the ability to price above marginal cost, society expects something in return: not just sustainable innovation but also for drugs to enter the public domain upon the expiry of a patent. Companies producing generic drugs or biosimilars can then supply the public with drugs at lower prices.[4]

While a drug patent is in force, some mitigating factors exist that limit price increases (above marginal cost). Pre-existing price controls may be in place. International price discrimination may be practiced. Or compulsory licensing can be used to enable more suppliers to provide a drug. Many drugs that are on the World Health Organization's list of essential medicines are off-patent — about ninety percent as of January 2020 — which should temper the cost factor.[5] However, that list may not include vital cancer drugs for patients.[6]

8.3 Case Study: HIV/AIDS

The HIV/AIDS crisis in Southern Africa provides a window into the complex relationship between patent rights and public health access. This case illuminates whether patent protections significantly impeded access to life-saving medications or whether other factors played the primary role in limiting treatment availability. This crisis, and later COVID-19, demonstrates that addressing health emergencies of such magnitude requires comprehensive solutions that extend beyond property rights reforms to include public goods investment and international cooperation.

In 1998, 39 pharmaceutical manufacturers filed a lawsuit against the South African government (Case No. 4138/98) to prevent the implementation of legislation designed to facilitate access to AIDS drugs at reduced costs. The case arose after South Africa passed the Medicines and Related Substances Control Amendment Act of 1997, which would have allowed

[4]Biologics are complex, large-molecule drugs made from living cells. Biosimilars are the counterpart of pharmaceutical generics; they are similar, but not identical, versions of biologics. Biologics are usually more expensive and involve lengthier clinical trials. See Acri (2024).

[5]Based on Schultz and McDole (2020).

[6]https://clarivate.com/life-sciences-healthcare/blog/implications-updated-essential-medicines-list/.

the government to import cheaper generic drugs and implement compulsory licensing provisions.[7]

During this period, antiretroviral therapy (ARV) cost between $10,000 and $15,000 per patient per year, making treatment financially onerous, if not impossible, for most affected populations.[8] Meanwhile, an Indian generic pharmaceutical company, CIPLA, offered to supply triple-therapy AIDS cocktails at approximately $350 per patient per year to developing countries.[9]

The pharmaceutical companies accused South Africa of infringing patent protections established under TRIPS. The companies were especially concerned that South Africa's legislation would set a precedent encouraging other countries to adopt similar measures, potentially undermining their global pricing strategies and ability to recoup R&D investments.

The stakes of this legal battle were enormous. South Africa had arguably suffered the most from HIV/AIDS globally, with infection rates approaching 20% of the adult population in some regions. Demographic projections at the time suggested that as many as half of teenagers in the hardest-hit countries of southern Africa would die of AIDS before reaching age 50.[10]

After much international pressure and widespread condemnation, the 39 pharmaceutical companies withdrew their lawsuit in April 2001.[11] The three years of legal proceedings generated significant negative publicity for the pharmaceutical industry.[12] The case highlighted tensions between intellectual property rights and public health needs in the developing world.

Consequently, in November 2001, the WTO adopted the Doha Declaration on the TRIPS Agreement and Public Health. The declaration established that public health considerations should take precedence over international patent agreements in certain circumstances.[13] It stated that the TRIPS Agreement "does not and should not prevent members from taking measures to protect public health" and that countries have the right to determine what constitutes a national emergency. The declaration also clarified that countries may employ *parallel trade* and *compulsory licensing* to deal with those emergencies — "flexibilities" that will be addressed in this

[7]https://pubmed.ncbi.nlm.nih.gov/12476916/.

[8]A provocative 2013 documentary traces the events during this period, called *Fire in the Blood*, https://www.youtube.com/watch?v=uMsseS_Lqs0.

[9]https://www.cipla.com/our-offerings/our-therapies/hiv-aids.

[10]https://pmc.ncbi.nlm.nih.gov/articles/PMC1173369/.

[11]https://pubmed.ncbi.nlm.nih.gov/11837037/.

[12]Particularly since Southern Africa accounted for a small percentage of global pharmaceutical sales.

[13]https://www.wto.org/english/thewto_e/minist_e/min01_e/mindecl_trips_e.pdf.

chapter. The declaration was also cognizant that not all developing countries have sufficient productive capacity to utilize the compulsory licensing option and that accommodations would be needed for those countries that lack domestic pharmaceutical manufacturing capabilities.

The Clinton Foundation played an important role in delivering AIDS treatment after the resolution of the South African lawsuit. Beginning in 2003, the Clinton Foundation HIV/AIDS Initiative negotiated significant price reductions with generic pharmaceutical manufacturers to produce antiretroviral drugs for the developing world.

During the actual period of the South African lawsuit (1998–2001), however, the Clinton Administration had a different stance. The U.S. Trade Representative placed South Africa on a trade watch list for IPR violations and applied diplomatic pressure to block the legislation that would have allowed South Africa to use parallel imports.[14] The Foundation's positive impact on access to AIDS treatment occurred after the organization was established in 2001.[15]

The HIV/AIDS epidemic led to important revisions in IP practice regarding public health needs. However, there are still ongoing challenges in translating these legal tools into practical improvements in access to essential medicines, particularly for the world's most vulnerable populations. Both the COVID-19 pandemic and the longer-term issues with neglected tropical diseases demonstrate these persistent challenges.

8.4 Parallel Imports

Explaining parallel imports requires understanding the concept of *exhaustion* in intellectual property (IP) law. IP control over a product is said to be exhausted after it is first sold by the IP owner (or someone authorized by the owner). Once exhaustion occurs, subsequent third parties are generally free to resell or distribute the goods without needing further approval from the IP owner — a principle known as the first sale doctrine. The key legal question is: "First sold where?" What is the relevant geographic unit?

Three geographic concepts of exhaustion are germane: national exhaustion, regional exhaustion, and international exhaustion.

Parallel importation is one of the key flexibilities under the TRIPS Agreement. It involves the importation of a product protected by a patent, copyright, or trademark from a country where the product was lawfully

[14]See the Washington Post article, "A Conflict of Health and Profit," May 20, 2000.
[15]https://www.clintonhealthaccess.org/south-africa/.

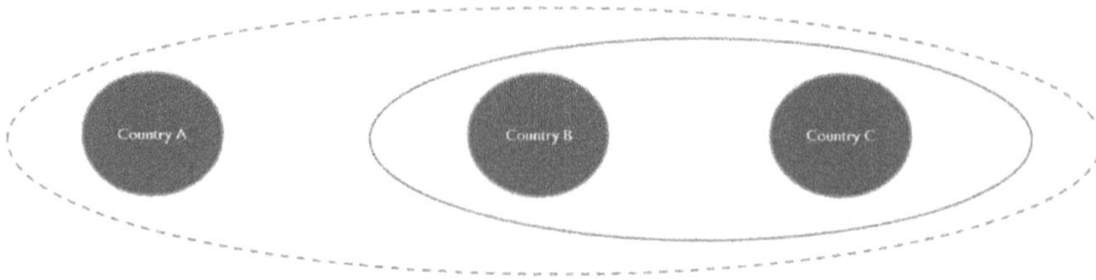

Figure 8.1. Parallel Importing

marketed — either by the rights holder or by an authorized party — but where the rights holder did not authorize its importation into another market. These parallel imports are genuine products; they are not counterfeits or pirated goods. The issue is not the legitimacy of the product itself, but rather the unauthorized transfer of that product across markets.

IP law is specific about the territorial reach of the rights holder's control. In a national exhaustion regime, that control is strongest. Once a product is sold domestically, others may resell it, but only within the same country. In Figure 8.1, a product first sold in country A can be resold within country A, but not in country B or C. Under this regime, parallel imports are effectively prohibited.

A regional exhaustion system allows resale within a group of countries that share a common exhaustion rule — such as the European Union — but not beyond it. In Figure 8.1, if countries B and C form a region with shared exhaustion, a product first sold in B may be resold in C, but not in A. This system permits parallel importation within the region but not from external markets.

An international exhaustion regime, by contrast, permits resale globally. Once a product is sold anywhere in the world, it may be resold elsewhere. In Figure 8.1, a good first sold in any of the countries A, B, or C may be resold in the others. This system fully allows parallel imports.

The TRIPS Agreement does not require member countries to adopt any specific exhaustion regime. Article 6 affirms that the issue of exhaustion is left to national discretion. Thus, countries may permit parallel imports if doing so aligns with their national interest.

From an economic perspective, exhaustion rules affect the ability of IP holders to engage in international price discrimination — that is, to charge different prices for the same product in different countries based on market demand conditions and purchasing power. A national exhaustion system facilitates such pricing strategies, which can help firms recover R&D costs. Consumers in high-price countries, however, may favor international exhaustion so that lower-priced imports can reduce local prices. Conversely, consumers in low-price countries may oppose international exhaustion, fearing that their affordable goods will be diverted abroad, reducing local availability and raising domestic prices.

8.4.1 *International Price Discrimination*

Recall that profits are the difference between revenues and costs, where revenue is the product of price and quantity: $R = P \times Q$. But since Q itself is inversely related to P, a monopolist cannot arbitrarily raise prices. At some point, the quantity demanded would fall to zero.

Internationally, firms can practice what economists call *Ramsey pricing*, where the price charged depends on how sensitive consumers are to price in different markets. In developing economies, incomes are lower, and drug expenditures take up a larger share of household budgets. In many cases, consumers pay out-of-pocket rather than through insurance. It is therefore not unreasonable to assume that consumers in low-income countries are more price-sensitive and should be charged a lower price. *Mutatis mutandis*, consumers in high-income countries, who are less sensitive to price, would pay more.

As a result, prices for the same drug may differ across countries depending on their level of economic development. If a multinational corporation (MNC) is forced to charge the same price in all markets, it may opt not to serve some of them at all, particularly those that detract from its global profits. In such cases, quantity supplied would fall to zero ($Q = 0$).

The higher the overall global profits the firm can earn, the more it can plow back into R&D. However, international price discrimination will not work if parallel imports can occur. In this scenario, consumers in the country where prices are higher benefit from accessing lower-priced drugs, but those in the country where drug prices are lower will observe drugs becoming scarcer and more expensive as they are exported abroad.

8.4.2 *Differential Pricing Example*

Imagine a global pharmaceutical monopoly firm. For simplicity, assume that it produces a drug at a constant cost (i.e., independent of volume). In that case, the marginal cost (MC) is also constant. Let $MC = \$6$.

Assume two countries: North and South, labeled markets 1 and 2, respectively.

- Demand curve in Market 1: $P_1 = 24 - Q_1$
- Demand curve in Market 2: $P_2 = 12 - \frac{1}{2}Q_2$

Market 2 is poorer, judging by the nature of the demand curve. Its consumers have a lower marginal willingness to pay for the drug.

Case 1: Price Discrimination

The monopolist serves both markets. In each market, the profit-maximizing level of output is determined where marginal revenue (MR) equals marginal cost (MC).[16] Those quantities are 9 in market 1 and 6 in market 2. Thus, the monopolist sells 15 units worldwide.

The monopolist, however, can price discriminate. It charges whatever the price consumers in each market are willing to pay for those quantities, and that information is on the demand curves. In market 1, consumers are willing to pay \$15 per unit for 9 units. In market 2, consumers are willing to pay \$9 for 6 units. Total (global) revenues for the firm are \$15 $\times$ 9 plus \$9$\times$6, or \$189. Total costs are the 15 units produced multiplied by \$6, which amounts to \$90. (Note that the MNC faces the same cost of production in both markets.) Hence, profits are \$189 $-$ \$90, which equals \$99.

This illustrates classic third-degree price discrimination. The firm charges a higher price in the less elastic (less price-sensitive) market. That aligns with economic intuition: inelastic demand permits higher markups.[17]

Figure 8.2 assumes no resale is allowed; that is, no parallel imports, or else prices converge because of arbitrage.[18]

Case 2: Uniform Pricing

In this case, the monopolist pools all the consumers and treats the global market as a whole. This requires coming up with a global demand curve. This is shown in Figure 8.3. Essentially, for each price level P, the market demands are summed horizontally.

---

[16]When demand curves are linear, the marginal revenue curve starts at the same point as the demand curve on the vertical axis and then intersects the horizontal axis halfway between $Q = 0$ and the quantity where the demand curve touches the horizontal axis when $P = 0$.

[17]Demands may be less elastic when consumers care about factors beyond price, such as specific features of the good, or when they face fewer substitute goods. Another reason for being less price sensitive is that the good is a small share of the consumer's budget.

[18]Traders buy the good where it is cheaper and sell it where it is more expensive. The supply of the good gets scarcer in the market from where it is withdrawn, which raises prices there, and gets more abundant in the market where it is placed, which depresses prices there.

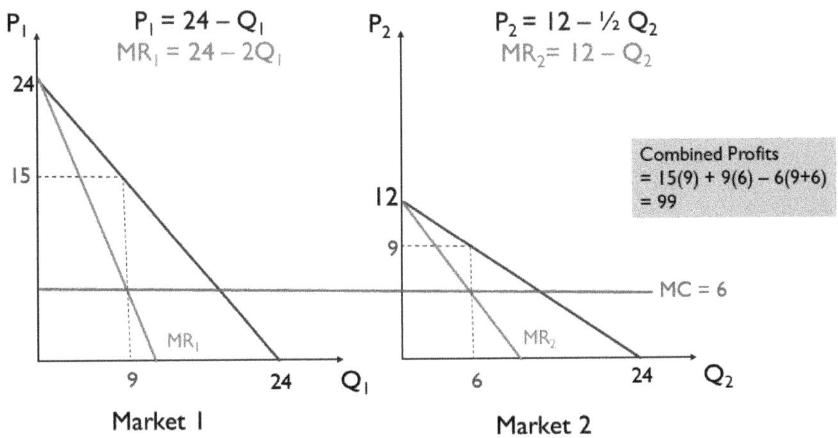

Figure 8.2. International Price Discrimination Example

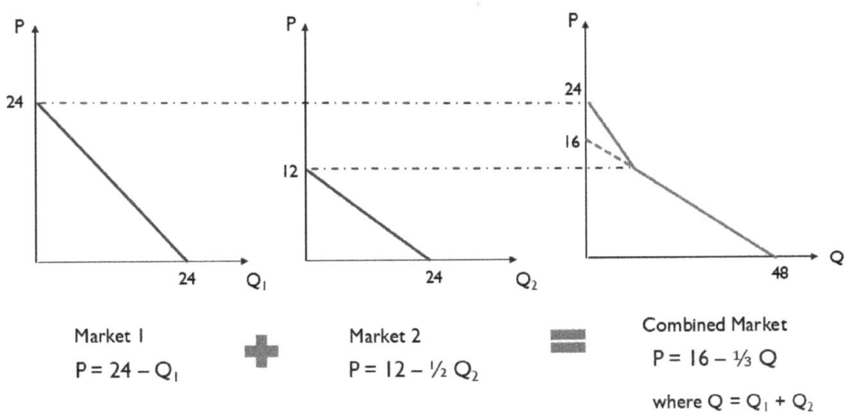

Figure 8.3. Combining Global Markets

The monopolist figures out the marginal revenue for the global market and equates that to marginal cost. This is shown in the third (right-most) panel in Figure 8.4.

The profit-maximizing level of output is 15. At that quantity, the monopolist charges \$11 per unit, found on the global demand curve. At that price, the individual market demand curves can be used to find the quantity that consumers in each market purchase. In market 1, at the uniform price of \$11, consumers buy 13. In market 2, they buy 2.

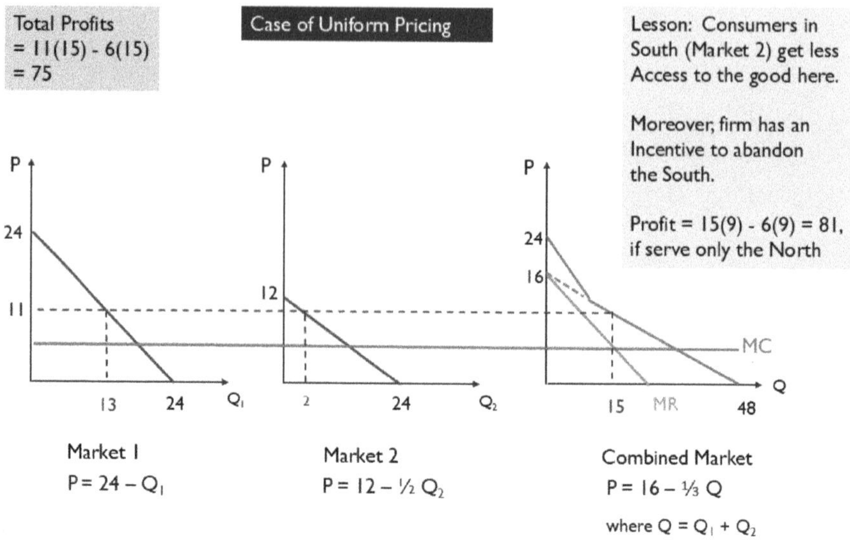

Figure 8.4. International Non-Price Discrimination

The market clears since 15 units are demanded and supplied. The monopolist makes a per-unit profit of \$5, which is the difference between price (\$11) and unit cost (\$6), or total profits of \$75 (= 15 × \$5).

But notice something interesting: the pharmaceutical MNC makes less profit than under price discrimination. Moreover, it has an incentive not to serve market 2 at all, and to serve market 1 only. Why? Return to Figure 8.2. By abandoning market 2, it can proceed to choose that level of output where market 1's marginal revenue equals marginal cost. The firm's optimal solution is to produce 9 units and charge \$15/unit. This yields revenue of \$135. The total cost of making 9 units is \$54 (= 9 × \$6). Hence, profits are \$81 (= \$135 – \$54), which is higher than \$75 (under uniform pricing)! This is the incentive for serving only market 1 if the firm is constrained from exercising international price discrimination.[19]

8.4.3 *Role of Price Controls*

The example thus far provided a flavor of how third-degree price discrimination works. Lower-income economies can benefit from comparatively

[19]This example depends on specific assumptions. For example, if marginal costs are not constant but rise with output, the monopolist might still serve both markets under uniform pricing.

lower prices if they do not allow for parallel imports. The analysis assumes that price discrimination arises as profit-maximizing firms charge prices (inversely) according to the price elasticity of demand. But international price differences may be due to variations in price controls.[20] This is the case in the European Union, where pricing regulations can vary for pharmaceutical products. International price differences create opportunities for international arbitrage. And parallel traders can exploit these differences — buying goods where prices are lower and selling them in markets where prices are higher — and bring about price convergence. As we saw in the example earlier, this would reduce the monopolist's global profits and thereby could reduce its innovation incentives.

But Grossman and Lai (2008) argue that this result may not hold true in a world of price controls — that parallel trade may (perhaps paradoxically) stimulate global innovation. The key insight here is that governments can choose the level of the price control; for example, they can choose a low price ceiling (a very strict price control) or a high price ceiling (a more relaxed price control). Consumers in markets where pharmaceutical prices are high would welcome the imports (or re-importation) of cheaper prescription drugs and medicines, which parallel trade allows to happen. The opponents of parallel trade, on the other hand, would point out the possible negative impacts on the innovation incentives of manufacturers if their global profits fall.

The Grossman and Lai (2008) model examines innovation incentives under parallel trade that is induced by differences in price controls across countries. The setup is the North–South model analyzed in Chapter 5. It is assumed that product development is mostly concentrated in the North. Previous analyses comparing innovation incentives under national versus international exhaustion regimes assumed given levels of price control. In contrast, this model treats price controls as endogenous to the exhaustion regime. The following are two motives for adjusting price controls:

- Under parallel imports, the Northern firm may avoid entering the Southern market if price controls are too tight. Arbitrageurs would buy the product in the South and sell it in the North. The Northern manufacturing firm would be better off selling the product only in the high price, unregulated Northern market. Understanding that possibility, the foreign government would relax the price control when it switches from a national

[20] Price differences across countries can also be due to cost-related differences, which are not explored here.

exhaustion regime to an international one to ensure that the Northern firm does not stay out of the Southern market.

- The optimal IPR policies tend to be strategic substitutes, as discussed in Chapter 5: a rise in the strength of IP protection in the North is associated with a decline in IP protection in the South. What matters to innovators is the overall global level of IP protection. The Southern government has an incentive to free ride on the North's IP system to provide sufficient innovation incentives, while it can set price controls at low levels to benefit its own consumers. But parallel trade, which takes goods out of the Southern market for sale in the North, would depress prices in the North and undermine the Northern firm's incentive to innovate. So, again, the Southern government would adapt and loosen its price controls so as to maintain world innovation incentives.

Specifically, if the Southern market is small, its free-riding on the North's IP protection has minimal impact on global innovation. However, once parallel trade is allowed, strict price controls become disadvantageous for the South. Goods may be diverted from the local market to neighboring countries in both the South and North. It behooves the South to set a more lenient price ceiling under international exhaustion.[21] By tolerating higher prices, the South enables innovative firms to earn greater profits and remain engaged in R&D. In this way, parallel trade does not harm innovation but may facilitate it in a world of price controls. It is the potential for arbitrage that acts as a mechanism for disciplining the South's free-riding behavior.

8.4.4 *TRIPS-Plus Free Trade Agreements*

As discussed in Chapter 1, TRIPS-plus agreements typically include provisions that go beyond the requirements of the WTO's TRIPS Agreement, often by imposing stricter intellectual property standards. Some of this increased strictness comes about by limiting parallel imports. For example, the U.S.-Chile FTA (2003) and the U.S.-Singapore FTA (2003) limit the ability of the partner countries to import goods without the permission of the patent holder. The U.S.-Australia FTA (2005) included provisions that gave patent holders the right to prevent parallel imports. The European Union has also negotiated several TRIPS-plus agreements that limit parallel imports. For example, the EU-South Korea FTA (2011), EU-Central

[21] Grossman and Lai (2008) cite evidence that the growth of parallel trade in Europe was accompanied by the loosening of price controls.

America FTA (2012), and EU-Peru and Colombia FTA (2013) also include provisions that require consent of the IP holder to import goods. The Trans-Pacific Partnership (TPP) (now the Comprehensive and Progressive Agreement for Trans-Pacific Partnership (CPTPP) after the U.S. withdrew) included tighter provisions on the importation of goods that infringe on IP rights.

On the whole, these TRIPS-plus agreements extend IP rights by preventing the unauthorized importation of goods or by raising the penalties for such imports. These agreements have been criticized for negatively impacting access to affordable medicines and other goods by restricting parallel imports that could otherwise help lower prices in the developing world.

Otherwise, at the multilateral level, TRIPS leaves countries room to permit parallel trade, provided it aligns with the exceptions and limitations allowed within the framework of international IP law. Public health considerations may be one of them — to promote access to affordable medicines. Parallel imports can be utilized to achieve this goal.

International law prohibits *unfair* parallel trade practices, such as the distribution of counterfeit goods or pirated products. Restrictions can be imposed by countries if evidence of such unfair practices exists, though these restrictions too must align with WTO rules.

8.5 Compulsory Licensing

TRIPS Article 31 provides international guidance on the issuance of compulsory licensing (CL for short). Firms or licensees seeking a CL must first try to obtain a voluntary license (VL for short) from the patent holder. A CL can be sought if the firm has been unable to obtain a VL on reasonable licensing terms in a reasonable amount of time. Article 31 requires that the patent holder receive *adequate remuneration* if it is compelled to give another party a license to its patented product. Moreover, goods produced under a compulsory license must be predominantly for the domestic market. This becomes an issue when local producers in a country lack the manufacturing capacity to produce the patented good. In this case, local producers would not be able to take advantage of acquiring a compulsory license. The local supply needs must be met through imports; that is, a foreign firm would need to apply for a CL and then export goods to that local economy. But Article 31 requires the firm to produce mostly for its own country, not abroad. Thus, following the *Doha Declaration*, a 2003 WTO decision modified rules to permit the exporting of pharmaceutical products under a CL to countries with insufficient production capacities. Per the TRIPS Amendment Article 31bis (2017), WTO members are permitted to import generic drugs manufactured under compulsory licensing in other countries, provided the importing country lacks manufacturing capacity and the TRIPS Council is notified.

8.5.1 *Compulsory License and Consumer Access to Patented Products*

The previous section showed that if a price ceiling is too low (or a price control too tight), the Northern firm might not serve the South. Here, the discussion focuses on the interactions of price controls and the compulsory licensing of a patent product. This provides for a richer analysis of issues pertinent to the access to medicines debate.[22] Bond and Saggi (2014) use game theory to analyze decisions of a multinational firm from the North and policies of a government in the South that seeks to provide access to patented drugs for its consumers. There are three stages to the game.

Stage	Player	Decision
1	Southern Government	Sets Price Control or Not
2	Northern Firm Chooses	(i) Market Entry (FDI) or, (ii) Voluntary License or, (iii) Staying Out of Southern Market
3	Southern Government	Issues CL or Not

Assume, for simplicity, that there is only one potential licensee in the South who has manufacturing capabilities. If the multinational firm from the North enters the Southern market — that is, engages in foreign direct investment (FDI) and sets up a subsidiary there — it incurs a fixed cost, F, to set up a distribution network and gain regulatory approval, and it produces a good of quality λ. If instead the local licensee produces the good, the good will be of a lower quality than λ because the licensee is assumed

[22]See Saggi (2024) for a more comprehensive treatment.

(reasonably) to be less technologically capable than the Northern firm, which originally developed the product and has some internal know-how. However, the local licensee has the advantage of being able to incur a lower fixed cost, F, to set up production. This is due (reasonably) to its existing distribution network and better knowledge of the local market.

As the table shows, in the third stage, if neither multinational entry nor voluntary licensing (VL) occurs, the Southern government has the option to issue a compulsory license (CL) to the local licensee to manufacture the Northern firm's patented product. However, the government must ensure that the licensee pays an adequate remuneration of R to the Northern company. And the CL is credible if the gains to the Southern government (that is, the combined consumer surplus and profits of the local licensee) exceed the setup cost and royalty R.[23]

Start with the case of no price control in Stage 1. Assume the Northern firm is forward-looking and assesses that CL is credible in Stage 3. It has to determine, in Stage 2, which of these outcomes is most favorable for it: enter and earn a present discounted value of profits (PDV) minus the setup cost, F, or license voluntarily. If Southern demand for the patent product is not very high or that consumers in the South are not as willing to pay a high price for it, then the difference between the PDV of profits and F would not be as large, tilting the Northern firm to offer the local producer a license to manufacture and sell the product in exchange for a licensing fee of ϕ. While it will not earn profits from producing directly in the South, the Northern firm can avoid the fixed cost, F. If ϕ exceeds the difference between the PDV of profits and F, the Northern firm will prefer to grant a voluntary license.

But whether the local firm will accept those terms, ϕ, depends upon whether the licensee can do better by rejecting the VL and applying for a compulsory license, CL, which the licensee can get with a delay.[24] Knowing that the licensee could do that strategically, the Northern firm might be induced to reduce the licensing fee somewhat under a voluntary license; that is, not charge as much for a VL. The reduction in the fee ϕ is a form of profit shifting (from the Northern firm to the Southern licensee). The threat of a CL, therefore, reduces the bargaining power of the Northern firm. In effect,

[23]Otherwise, the firm in the North would see that the South would be worse off to issue a compulsory license.

[24]Recall that under TRIPS, the patent holder should be given a reasonable amount of time, like 3–4 years, to work the patent locally.

the compulsory licensing option in the South expands the opportunities that Southern consumers have to access the patented good.

Now, if the Northern firm anticipates that a voluntary license will involve too much profit shifting, it could choose to enter the South instead and manufacture locally. The Northern firm may not earn as much lifetime profits as it would have had the South not had the power to grant a CL — as without CL, the firm would have chosen to do a VL — but the welfare of the South would be higher. Consumers there get to enjoy more consumer surplus. But Southern welfare would decrease if compulsory licensing were to displace voluntary licensing, since consumer access to the patented product (say, a drug) would be delayed. Of course, if the Northern firm found it to be unprofitable to either enter or grant a voluntary license, then compulsory licensing does raise Southern welfare. Consumers would get access to the patented good that they would otherwise not have. Moreover, the compulsory license makes the Northern firm better off too because it gets to receive some remuneration or income that it would otherwise not have (and avoid F!). In this specific case, a CL is win-win for both players.

Next, back to stage 1 and consider the case where a price control exists. Combined with the presence (or threat) of a compulsory license, the price control helps lower the price of the patented good for Southern consumers (closer to marginal cost) and reduces the transfer of rents to the Northern firm.

But if the Northern firm is discouraged from entering or voluntarily licensing, the price control must be relaxed enough to be set at a high level. The reason is that under a compulsory license, the Southern government must ensure that the Northern firm receives adequate remuneration, R. Otherwise, if the controlled price is too low, the local licensee may not earn sufficient profits to pay R, unless the Southern government subsidizes this loss, which negatively impacts its fiscal finances. But interestingly, if the price ceiling is set sufficiently high, the Northern firm might find it profitable to enter after all. This analysis demonstrates that the interaction of price controls and compulsory licensing can produce complex outcomes.

Historically, instances of compulsory licensing have not been common. For example, post-TRIPS, 24 episodes of CL arose during 1995–2011, as documented in Beall and Kuhn (2012). Their documented cases confirm that the threat of CL can lead to price reductions (discounts). Voluntary licensing (VL) resulted only in three cases, as the theoretical reasoning predicts, because the bargaining terms of VL are likely reduced.

The case of Thailand in 2006 is instructive. Its government issued a CL for drugs like Efavirenz, an antiretroviral drug used to treat HIV/AIDS, and Clopidogrel, a medication to prevent blood clots in heart disease patients.[25] The prices of these drugs declined sharply after compulsory licenses were issued (up to 90%). The presence of CL led companies to voluntarily lower their prices. For example, Merck lowered its price of Efavirenz to 72 cents per tablet (or 780 baht per bottle) in 2007, a price that was closer to what generic competitors had charged.[26]

8.5.2 *Compulsory Licensing and Innovation*

The previous discussion can be built upon to analyze how compulsory licensing affects the incentives of the Northern firm to invest in R&D.[27] First, assume a national exhaustion regime is in place. The Northern firm can practice international price discrimination. If the government in the South provides sufficiently strong patent protection, the Northern firm has an incentive to conduct R&D and enter the Southern market to manufacture and sell the patented good. However, if it has no incentive to enter, the government in the South would be better off allowing for imitation and not protecting the Northern firm's patent right. Why protect its patent when the firm is absent in the local market? Why allow it to preclude others locally from manufacturing and selling a similar or identical good?

Alternatively, instead of not protecting patent rights, the Southern government can issue a compulsory license to a local producer and require it to pay the adequate remuneration of R to the Northern firm. But the CL again is associated with a delay since the Northern firm must be granted a reasonable amount of time to work the patent locally.

How does the compulsory license affect innovation incentives?

(a) **Case 1: Southern entry is not profitable.** If the Northern firm's present discounted value of profits (PDV) falls short of the entry cost, F, a compulsory license (CL) still allows the firm to monetize its innovation in the South. Under CL, the firm receives a remuneration (royalties), R, that is proportional to product quality, q. This added revenue stream raises the marginal return to R&D.

[25] Wibulpolprasert *et al.* (2011).
[26] https://makemedicinesaffordable.org/chronology-of-access-to-medicine-campaign-in-thailand.
[27] See Bond and Saggi (2020) for details.

(b) **Case 2: Southern entry is profitable.** If PDV $\geq F$ absent CL, the firm would enter. With CL available, however, the firm may rationally delay entry — CL can flip the choice from entering now to waiting for a license. By staying out initially, a CL is triggered after a waiting period; the firm avoids the entry cost F and then collects R. The marginal return to increasing quality is lower under CL than under direct entry because: (i) the firm earns a smaller return per unit than it would by selling directly, and (ii) the waiting period for CL forgoes early-period earnings, reducing the present value of returns. Consequently, the firm chooses a lower research intensity.

In short, CL tends to raise R&D when it opens a market the firm would otherwise skip, but can reduce R&D when it displaces direct entry.

Next, consider the case where international exhaustion prevails. The Northern firm must practice uniform international pricing. Ordinarily, this would reduce innovation incentives as the firm's world profits would fall (as shown in the illustrative example earlier). The firm might even exit the Southern market. However, with the option of compulsory licensing, some degree of international market segmentation is restored, as a local licensee that obtains a CL would not be able to re-export the good back to the North. The Northern firm can then charge a monopoly price in the Northern market when a compulsory license is issued in the South. And in the case where the Northern firm serves only the North (say because the cost of entering the Southern market is too high relative to the PDV of profits), the option of CL can increase the Northern firm's incentives to perform R&D since its remuneration from CL would be higher if greater R&D results in higher quality products for sale in the South.

Box 1. Compulsory Licensing Case in India — *Bayer v. Natco*

This case illustrates how a compulsory license (CL) was granted after a voluntary licensing (VL) request failed. It was India's first CL and made India only the second country, after Thailand, to issue such a license for a cancer drug.

Bayer was granted a patent for its drug Nexavar (for treating liver and kidney cancer) in India in March 2008. Natco, a generic drug manufacturer, sought a VL from Bayer in December 2010. After Bayer refused, Natco applied for a CL in 2011 and obtained it in March 2012, four years after the patent grant. Bayer appealed in

March 2013 but lost. The Controller General of Patents required Natco to pay Bayer royalties of 6–7% of sales per quarter.

At the time, Natco priced a monthly dose of 120 tablets at 8,800 rupees (approximately \$176), while Bayer charged 280,000 rupees (approximately \$5,600), a 33-fold difference. The Controller and Appellate Board sided with Natco, citing the extremely limited access to Nexavar at Bayer's price. One witness testified that Bayer had recouped its R&D investment (incurred from 1994 to 2004) within a single year — namely, in 2005. In the model of Chapter 4, the breakeven period was $B = 1$.[i]

[i]For more details, see https://spicyip.com/page/12?s=natco+compulsory+licensing.

8.6 Generic Competition

As was discussed, pharmaceutical innovation is heavily reliant on IP protection, and during the period when a drug is under a patent, prices are above competitive levels. There are some mitigating factors, which are that the patent life is not always 20 years due to the time taken to get marketing approval. Or pressures from parallel trade, price controls, or threats of compulsory licensing may cause firms to forbear somewhat on charging monopoly prices. But during the life of a patented drug, some substitutability exists among therapeutic equivalents, which can better constrain price increases than if no substitutes are available. Also, competitors can produce a different version as long as it does not infringe.

Once the patent expires, competitors may enter the market to produce generic drugs and help to push drug prices towards competitive levels.[28] But some factors could delay generic entry. One phenomenon is referred to as *evergreening*, where the drug patent holder comes up with a new use for the existing medicine and files another patent for it, which protects some of the earlier intellectual territory, thereby effectively lengthening the duration of patent protection. The second deals with *test data exclusivity*, data that generic companies need to get their own marketing approval. The patent

[28]Assuming generic drug companies are sufficiently competitive. In some cases, they might be oligopolists.

owner has exclusive rights to the test data also for a temporary period, but the longer that period is, the greater the delay in generic entry.

8.6.1 *Evergreening*

Evergreening is not a formal concept in patent law. It refers to a situation where the drug company "obtains multiple patents that cover different aspects of the same product over a period of many years. This strategy effectively extends the patent term of the product" (Kilic, 2014, p. 42). A report by the advocacy organization I-MAK (Initiative for Medicines, Access, and Knowledge) (2022) attributes the practice of evergreening — of steadily marketing incremental innovations and improvements — to "blocking competition and keeping cheaper versions of medicines off the market." The Report analyzes twelve best-selling drugs and finds that 125 patent applications have been filed on their behalf, with 71 patent grants. Since 2012, the price of only one drug decreased while the prices of the rest increased by 68% on average.

Figure 8.5 depicts a potential timeline of the "evergreening" of a patent right. In Figure 8.5, a patent expires at time T, but like a relay race in which a baton is passed on, the next patent grant arrives at T, representing a new use of the previous patent. The patent owner of both the earlier and later patents, therefore, will enjoy a longer period of exclusivity. Evidence, however, is hard to generate since the new uses may be justified in terms of offering more variety. Incremental innovation can be vital to safeguarding public health when the new variety of drugs within a therapeutic class enables physicians to treat diverse patients more precisely. More dosing options may become available, and new physiological interactions may be uncovered. New uses for existing drugs may significantly improve upon the first-in-class drugs which, as Acri (2024) points out, are rarely optimal. The improvement innovations may fill the lacuna in the first ever-invented drugs of a therapeutic class and overtake them as the best-in-class and first-line therapies.

Re-purposing existing drugs may be a good solution, if not the only solution, when there are orphan drug cases. These deal with treatments

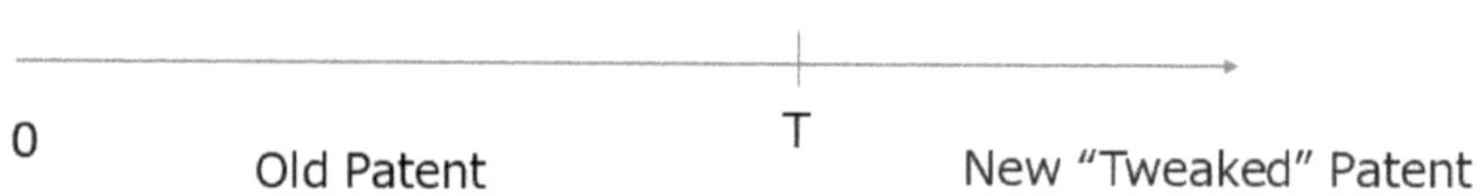

Figure 8.5. Sequential Patent Filings

for rare diseases or conditions affecting only a small population (say, fewer than one percent of the population). The market size is not large enough to justify the expense of R&D investments and clinical trials. This is similar for neglected tropical diseases — where the global market is also very small — which we address in the next section. In these cases, researchers look to see whether new uses for existing drugs can be found to cure a malady. A good example is the case of *Balamuthia*, an infection of the human brain caused by an invasive amoeba.[29] There are too few people with the disease to conduct a randomized controlled trial, and those afflicted by it do not survive long enough for a trial.[30] The eventual treatment for Balamuthia was a drug *Nitroxoline*, an antibiotic developed for urinary tract infection.

Moreover, when there is an extension of patent protection, it may be the result of some patent restoration that policy authorities allow to cover the time lapse due to regulatory approvals and lengthy clinical trials; for example, five additional years may be added on to the term of a patent.

Another aspect of the evergreening hypothesis is that pharmaceutical firms file multiple patents (contemporaneously or sequentially) to surround the core patent. By creating patent thickets, they can broaden the scope of their core patent right and block the entry of competitors who can produce near-alternative medicines or substitutes of the core patented drug. Figure 8.6 depicts that situation.

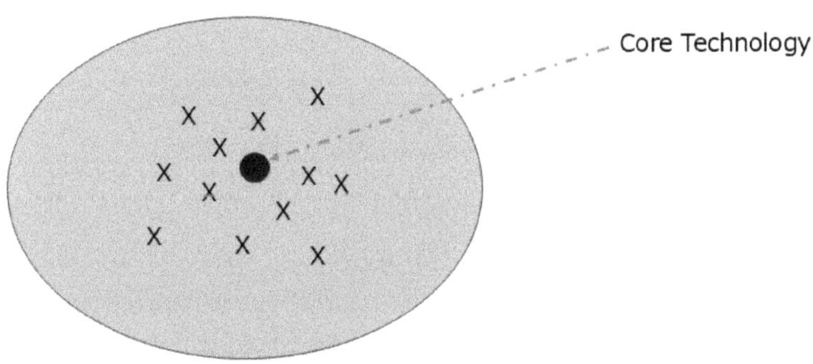

Figure 8.6. Patent Thickets around Drugs

[29] See https://www.cdc.gov/balamuthia/about/index.html?itid=lk_inline_enhanced-template.

[30] See the Washington Post story by Michael Lewis, March 13, 2025, https://wapo.st/4buoiLX.

Table 8.1. Patent Grants by Fortune 500 Firms

Industry Group	**Quarterly Mean 1990–2021**
Automobiles & Components	52.2
Capital Goods	31.6
Commercial & Prof. Services	5.4
Consumer Durables & Apparel	48.1
Consumer Services	6.2
Diversified Financials	4.7
Energy	21.7
Food, Beverage, and Tobacco	4.2
Health Care Equipment and Services	16.7
Household and Personal Products	21.2
Materials	13.2
Media and Entertainment	24.3
Pharmaceuticals, Biotech, and Life Sci.	10.3
Real Estate	3.9
Retailing	39.1
Semiconductors & Equip.	40.5
Software and Services	59.0
Technology Hardware and Equip.	60.7
Telecommunication Services	45.8
Transportation	3.9
Utilities	1.5
Overall Average	32.7

Note: Calculations based on data from Patents View, USPTO.

Claims of patent thickets around drugs may not hold up to scrutiny. Indeed, the literature has referred to patent thickets primarily in the field of information and communications technologies (ICT). Pharmaceutical companies do not patent as heavily as firms in the ICT sector, where innovations are modular (built on components working jointly with others) and where products feature short life cycles. Drug innovations are more discrete and are associated with longer product life cycles. Table 8.1 shows a cross-industry comparison.

The average rate of patenting by the pharmaceutical sector is below the industry average. This casts some doubt on whether pharmaceutical firms flood the market with patents. Moreover, when popular specific drugs are examined, such as *Lyrica* and *Xarelto*, there appears to be a discrepancy. I-MAK reported that 32 patents covered Xarelto and 68 covered Lyrica. But as discussed in Mossoff (2024), the USPTO reported three actual patent grants for Lyrica and five for Xarelto.

To the extent that more than a single patent covers a drug, this may be operationally related. The different patents surrounding a drug may be for different aspects of the drug, such as the active ingredient, the metabolite of the active ingredient, formulation, dosage and strength, method of administering, and manufacturing process. Thus, a single product can contain different *inventions*.[31]

Another oft-cited claim is that because of monopoly power, pharmaceutical companies can set prices at will. Figure 8.7 shows that this is not the case at all times.

The price points will be bounded by the consumer's demand curve. Where the demand curve intersects the vertical axis is the choke point where any price above it would cause the quantity demanded to vanish. Thus, even with exclusive IP rights, pharmaceutical companies face some market discipline. Moreover, monopolists can experience negative profits. Figure 8.7 shows that if the demand for its drug happens to be too

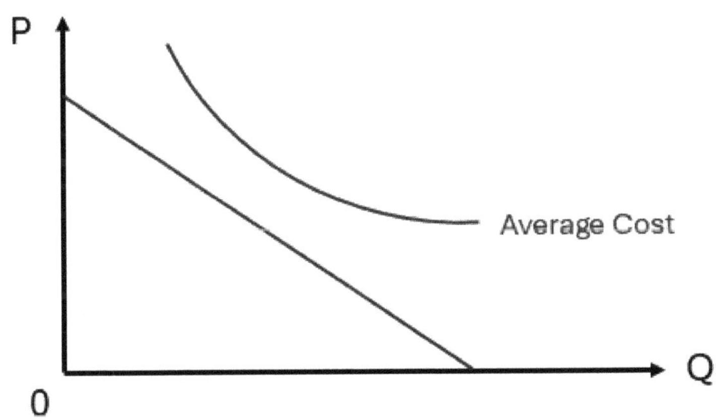

Figure 8.7. Monopoly Loss

[31]See Lietzan (2020). Moreover, these patents may not all expire at the same time. When the patent for an active ingredient does expire but a formulation patent remains in effect, a generic company may offer a therapeutically equivalent drug with a different formulation, provided it does not infringe on the existing formulation patent and complies with regulatory requirements.

low — that is, below the average cost curve — the monopolist will experience losses, which are not sustainable in the long run.

8.6.2 *Data Exclusivity*

This topic pertains to sharing clinical trial data with generic manufacturers, which allows them to gain regulatory approval without replicating the original studies after a drug's patent expires. In some legal regimes, the original patent owners — the innovative pharmaceutical companies — are granted exclusive rights over their clinical trial data for a specified period. This practice, known as test data exclusivity, delays the entry of generic competitors, who require the data to secure marketing approval. Consequently, consumer access to more affordable generic versions of off-patent drugs is also postponed. Test data exclusivity is a key provision in "TRIPS-plus" free trade agreements (FTAs). Lengthening and strengthening this exclusivity provides a clear advantage to the rights-holders. This raises a critical question: Does this enhancement of intellectual property rights (IPRs) foster innovation, or does it merely transfer greater economic rent to pharmaceutical patent holders?

This issue is of great importance to healthcare consumers facing costly medical choices. The high price of biologic medicines and therapies — for example, a cancer treatment can cost over hundreds of thousands of dollars per person annually — underscores the societal demand for the timely entry of generic alternatives. Moreover, clinical trial data represent a source of knowledge spillovers. Therefore, keeping this data proprietary for an extended period can adversely affect subsequent research and development.

The primary effect of test data exclusivity is not to prevent the entry of generics altogether, but rather to delay it, thereby postponing competition. In the larger context, pharmaceutical firms must recoup their substantial investments in both research and development (R&D) and clinical trials. They face the risk of failing to achieve this if their product becomes obsolete or if generic substitutes enter the market prematurely.

The debate over test data exclusivity can be illuminated by an indifference curve analysis, which is often used to model the trade-offs in intellectual property protection. To spur innovation, firms require a certain degree of appropriability from their IP. Policymakers can provide this protection through various combinations of measures, such as patent duration and patent scope. Patent scope influences how dissimilar a competing product must be to avoid infringement. While firms naturally prefer greater levels of both duration and scope, for any given level of appropriability, a trade-off exists. This conceptual framework can be extended to include data exclusivity. If policymakers choose to limit data exclusivity (i.e., reduce duration), they might need to compensate innovators through other means, such as a broader patent scope, to maintain the same incentive for innovation.

From a dynamic perspective, a longer patent duration combined with a narrower scope may be the lesser of two evils. A narrow scope of protection better assures the future entry of both innovative and generic firms. For instance, the doctrine of equivalents — which prevents competitors from making trivial changes to a patented invention to circumvent it — should not be interpreted so broadly that it stifles new entry. This doctrine establishes how functionally similar a competing product can be to an existing patent before it is considered infringing.

The model presented in Figure 8.8 cannot, however, determine the precise optimal length for a period of data exclusivity; for example, whether it should be eight years or twelve. This optimal duration depends on several parameters, including interest rates, fixed costs, and the expected flow of profits. Consequently, the ideal length may vary by firm, drug type, and the specific disease or illness being treated.

Finally, it is important to consider that the entry of generics does not abruptly displace originator firms, suggesting that current data exclusivity protections may be unnecessarily restrictive. Originator companies possess multiple competitive advantages that help them maintain market share even after patent expiration. First, major pharmaceutical companies benefit from significant brand-name loyalty that persists beyond generic entry. Second, these firms employ various strategies to extend their competitive position, such as seeking patent term extensions, developing new therapeutic uses for

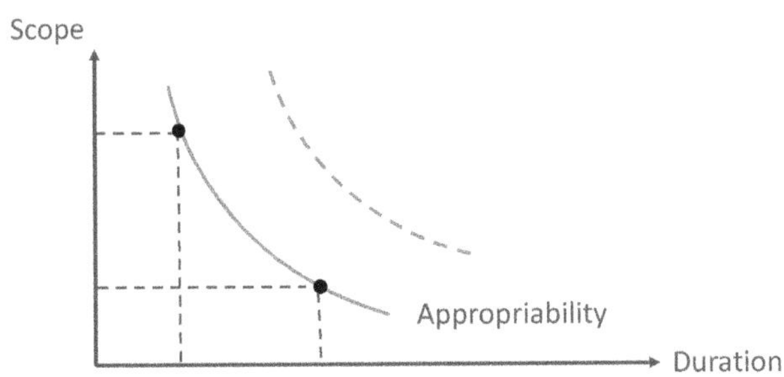

Figure 8.8. Scope and Duration Tradeoff

existing drugs, and engaging in strategic mergers and acquisitions. Third, particularly for biologics, the complexity of manufacturing processes creates natural barriers to entry that limit generic competition. Fourth, originator firms typically have robust product pipelines, allowing them to profit from new drug innovations while older products face generic competition. Given these inherent competitive advantages, originator firms appear sufficiently resilient to withstand increased generic competition without compromising innovation incentives. These considerations, therefore, favor making test data more openly available, as the policy benefits of faster generic entry likely outweigh the marginal risks to originator profitability.

8.7 Neglected Tropical Diseases

Neglected tropical diseases (NTDs) are infectious diseases that largely affect the underserved and marginalized populations in tropical and subtropical regions, and that have been significantly underfunded by pharmaceutical R&D due to limited commercial profitability.[32] The market size is by no means small. More than a billion people in those regions are affected by one or more of these NTDs.

The following are some examples of neglected tropical diseases (Table 8.2). Several factors explain the limited commercial R&D investment in NTDs. First, the diseases are specific to populations in low-income countries. The purchasing power of consumers there is not enough to stimulate the R&D of multinational companies.[33] Second, environmental factors are mixed in with the diseases, calling for a joint treatment; that is, treating the disease requires addressing the climate and environmental conditions that give rise to their spread, such as soil conditions, sanitary facilities, and water quality.

For the global system of IPRs, therefore, NTDs represent a significant challenge. A greater role is required of support from the public sector, non-profit foundations, and corporate volunteerism. And international coordination is crucial. In the case of *Advanced Market Commitments*, international sponsors need to collaborate to offer companies a binding commitment to cover the costs of vaccines or treatments at guaranteed prices.[34]

[32] https://www.who.int/health-topics/neglected-tropical-diseases.
[33] See Baker *et al.* (2017).
[34] See Kremer *et al.* (2020).

As shown in Table 8.3, the key funders of research on neglected tropical diseases are governments and non-profits, with the private sector having a small role.

Table 8.2. Neglected Tropical Diseases (NTDs) Examples

Disease	Sample Symptoms
Buruli Ulcer	Skin ulceration
Chagas Disease	Heart and digestive system damage
Dengue Fever	Joint and muscle pain
Dracunculiasis	Skin blisters
Human African Trypanosomiasis	Sleepiness sickness
Leishmaniasis	Anemia, weight loss
Leprosy	Nerve and limb damage
Lymphatic Filariasis	Disfigurement
Onchocerciasis (River Blindness)	Skin and eye problems
Schistosomiasis	Bladder damage, kidney disease
Soil-Transmitted Helminthiases	Intestinal worms; cognitive impairment
Trachoma	Blindness

Source: World Health Organization (WHO).

Table 8.3. Funders of Research on NTDs

Top Funders		Top Funding Organizations	
U.S.	$32.9	National Institutes of Health, U.S.	$21.2
Private Sector	$6.49	Bill and Melinda Gates Found.	$8.47
U.K.	$3.22	Aggregate Pharm/Biotech Co.	$6.5
EU	$1.66	European Commission	$1.66
France	$1.02	U.S. Dept of Defense	$1.47
Switzerland	$0.842	Wellcome Trust	$1.32
India	$0.688	U.S. Agency for Int'l Dev.	$1.26
Germany	$0.622	U.K. Foreign, Commonwealth and Dev	$1.04
Australia	$0.482	U.K. Medical Research Council	$0.631
Netherlands	$0.309	Indian Council of Medical Research	$0.496

Note: Billions of 2020 USD.

Source: G-Finder.

Specifically, the public sector provided 66% of the funding, the philanthropic sector 21%, and industry 12%.[35]

According to G-FINDER, during 2007–2023, about $70.8 billion was spent on NTD research.[36] This represents only a minuscule fraction of global GDP. From the World Bank's *World Development Indicators*, cumulative global GDP during those 17 years amounted to $1.36 quadrillion. Thus, total spending on neglected tropical diseases was 0.0052% of that. For perspective, that is $1 out of every $19,200 of global income. These figures suggest that funding challenges exist across all three sectors: private, public, and non-profit.

8.8 TRIPS Waiver and COVID-19

The battle against COVID-19 and the development of vaccines occurred under a very compressed timeline. It behooved firms and governments in the developed world to find the vaccines, since much of the developing world lacked local manufacturing capacity. And developing country access relied heavily on TRIPS flexibilities. However, during the recent pandemic, many developing economies did not think those flexibilities were enough. India and South Africa took the initiative at the WTO in late 2020 to propose a TRIPS waiver, whereby IP rights on COVID-19 vaccines would be suspended. Representatives from the global North advocated for the global South to use compulsory licensing instead, but the latter argued that it had been difficult to use compulsory licensing and other flexibilities, even before the pandemic. Thus, the world was divided on the TRIP waiver issue.

Kilic (2024) argues that TRIPS "was not crafted with a pandemic scenario in mind" (p. 445). Essential medical supplies, such as N-95 masks and ventilators, were in short supply. The experiences with compulsory licensing also had been riddled with bureaucracy. Consider the case of *Biolyse Pharma*, a Canadian pharmaceutical company that in 2021 sought to export a generic version of Johnson & Johnson's (J&J) COVID-19 vaccine to Bolivia, a country that lack sufficient manufacturing capabilities to produce and supply vaccines. J&J declined to grant Biolyse a voluntary license, so the company applied for a compulsory license under *Canada's Access to*

[35]The data are from G-FINDER, which stands for Funding of Innovation for Neglected Diseases. https://gfinderdata.impactglobalhealth.org/.

[36]https://gfinderdata.impactglobalhealth.org/pages/data-visualisations/allNeglectedDiseases.

Medicines Regime (CAMR). But a product is only eligible for compulsory licensing if it is added to Schedule 1 of the Canadian Patent Act. Even though Bolivia notified the WTO of its interest in importing vaccines from Biolyse, the Canadian government did not amend Schedule 1 to include COVID-19 vaccines. Thus, Biolyse was unable to obtain a compulsory license to manufacture and export the J&J vaccine to Bolivia. This example exemplifies the complexities and challenges in utilizing compulsory licensing during global health emergencies.

Eventually, the TRIPS waiver was adopted on June 17, 2022, during the WTO's 12th Ministerial Conference. It helped that the U.S. was supportive. In May 2021, the U.S. Trade Representative announced that the Biden-Harris Administration was behind the waiving of intellectual property protections for COVID-19 vaccines. This marked a pivotal shift in the negotiations. However, the waiver was not very timely since the height of the pandemic crisis was 2021. By 2022, incidences of COVID-19 decreased, and the demand for vaccination waned. Moreover, a lesson for future IP waivers, if any, is that it took two years for the WTO to come to a consensus after the proposal was initiated by India and South Africa. The waiver did not address the core of the problem, which was (and still is) that poor countries lack domestic manufacturing capacity. Not having to pay royalties or seek licensing agreements did not confer any advantages in vaccinating people in the developing world. Much dependence was on India's leading generics companies to supply generic vaccines, but they in turn could not scale up their production for the developing world, while managing their own domestic COVID-19 cases and variants during this period.

Of course, TRIPS waivers, or suspensions of IP, have impacts on incentives for future innovation, but the focus during the pandemic period was diffusion — ensuring people get tested and vaccinated. The U.S. International Trade Commission (2023) (USITC) conducted a study to evaluate the role of IP flexibilities and waivers during the pandemic. One of the study's many conclusions is that satisfying the global demand for COVID-19 diagnostics and therapeutics had been a moving target throughout the pandemic.

As the USITC study found, most of the manufacturers of COVID tests and therapeutics are in high-income countries. Likewise, supplies were concentrated in high-income countries or countries with manufacturing capacities like India and Brazil. A significant portion of COVID-19 therapeutics was distributed globally through donations and purchases based on publicly announced supply agreements.

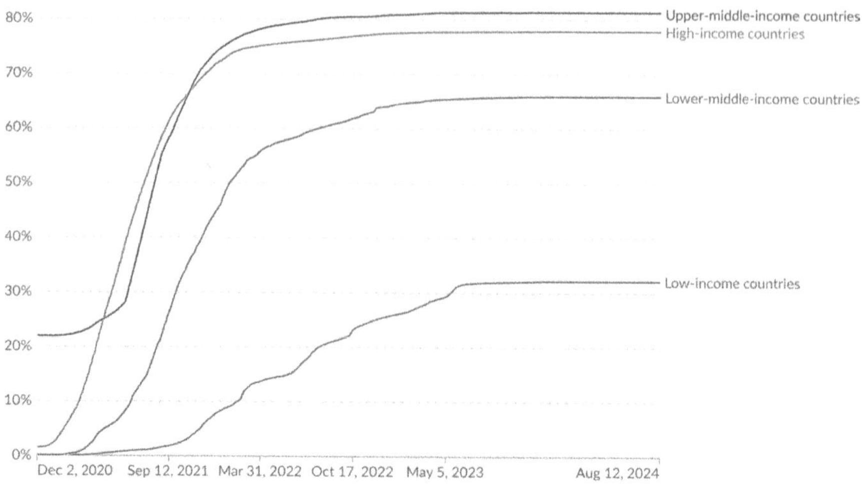

Figure 8.9. Total COVID-19 Vaccine Doses per 100 People
Source: Our World in Data (2024), World Health Organization; CC BY.

Figure 8.9 shows trends in COVID-19 vaccination by income group. The series plot total doses administered per 100 people, including boosters.[37]

As the figure indicates, populations in high-income and upper-middle-income countries received doses earlier and at higher rates. By August 2024, low-income countries had administered only about 45 doses per 100 people.

As an overall assessment, was the "waiver" justified? Here is a summary:

- The world was caught off guard by the pandemic. The price of medicines may not have been the main barrier to access. There were major problems with the supply chain, such as the availability of raw materials.
- As far as diagnostic tests were concerned, the COVID-19 testing tools were off-patent.
- Vaccines were not the only issue. Masks, ventilators, and gloves were in limited supply. Hospital beds, nurses, and physicians were also in short supply.
- Even with the waiver, vaccines have to be tested for safety and efficacy by proper regulatory authorities.

[37]Figure generated from https://ourworldindata.org/grapher/covid-vaccination-doses-per-capita.

- Waivers, if seen as a permanent, regular appearance, may discourage future innovation and preparedness.
- Waivers may also send a bad signal. They undermine TRIPS flexibilities, as they give the impression that flexibilities are only for public health emergencies.
- The approval process for a waiver is also slow; it took two years to obtain.

Even if a local producer obtains either a waiver or a license (compulsory or voluntary), certain fixed costs may need to be incurred in order to manufacture a vaccine or essential medicine, such as establishing manufacturing facilities and distribution channels. Depending upon the magnitude of these fixed costs, the local producer may be unable to price at marginal cost initially, since these fixed costs need to be recouped. In some cases, importing vaccines or medicines may be more practical so as to avoid substantial production setup costs.

Establishing vaccine manufacturing facilities requires substantial capital investment. Constructing a facility can cost between $50 million and $500 million per antigen, and building it can take 5 to 10 years before commercial viability.[38] These are factors that need to be accounted for when advocating for an IP waiver. The local manufacturer will need to rely on economies of scale to achieve cost-effectiveness in vaccine production.

8.8.1 *Vaccine Nationalism*

Vaccine nationalism on the part of developed countries may have affected developing countries' access to vaccines.[39] During late 2020, supply and demand imbalances existed around the world. Richer economies like the U.S., Canada, and EU had enough doses to immunize persons multiple times, while in South Korea, Taiwan, and Brazil, quantities supplied balanced quantities demand, but the rest of Latin America, Vietnam, Turkey, Egypt, and others experienced supply shortages.[40] There were speculations of vaccine hoarding in the North.

Vaccine nationalism is counterproductive and can generate a negative international externality. Immunizing only a small percentage of the world allows viruses to mutate. Prior vaccines or therapies may not protect against new strains arising from the mutations. In that sense, it would take longer

[38] See Plotkin *et al.* (2017).

[39] See Bollyky and Bown (2020).

[40] From the *New York Times*, Dec 15, 2020, https://www.nytimes.com/2020/12/15/us/coronavirus-vaccine-doses-reserved.html.

to combat COVID-19 when new variant growth is unchecked. Thus, a cooperative, balanced global strategy is needed for vaccination, rather than country-by-country independent actions.[41]

When countries act independently, racing to develop and vaccinate their own citizens first, duplicative R&D could result among firms competing against one another, along with patent races and hasty clinical trials (which could yield inferior vaccines with serious side effects). This undermines public trust. Global and local GDP would also be adversely affected. Incomes of people in the global South who are impacted by the disease decline, thereby affecting their import demand for goods from the global North. In addition, services trade and tourism would decline, further reducing world GDP. Thus, in an interdependent world economy, vaccine nationalism, which denies health protections in the rest of the world, backfires and harms interests in the global North.

8.9 Select Evidence on Pharmaceutical Innovation and Tech Transfers

Kyle and McGahan (2012) conducted a study of 192 countries from 1990 to 2006, focusing on the pharmaceutical sector. They find that patent protection significantly boosts R&D for diseases prevalent in high-income countries, but not for neglected diseases common in developing countries — such as malaria, tuberculosis, and river blindness. Using the number of new clinical trials per disease project as a proxy for R&D, they attribute this asymmetry to the underdeveloped science behind neglected diseases, limited prior exploration by innovators, and the low purchasing power of affected populations. Even substantial increases in patent strength would not sufficiently raise expected returns to cover the high R&D costs in these areas.

Dhanora *et al.* (2020) examined 168 Indian pharmaceutical firms from 2000 to 2013 and found that both product and process innovation, measured through patent stocks, significantly enhanced market power and profitability. Their analysis shows that TRIPS-compliant patent policy changes in 2002 and 2005 further strengthened firm performance, yet multinational enterprises retained superior market positions, with U.S.- and European-based firms particularly dominant.

[41] As the then UN General Secretary stated in 2020: "None of us is safe until we are all safe."

Cockburn *et al.* (2015) analyzed the launch of 642 new drug molecules across 76 countries between 1983 and 2002. They find that patent rights accelerate drug launches — which constitute the international diffusion of new medicines — whereas price regulations delay them. Product patents are more effective than process patents in promoting faster introductions.

Chaudhuri *et al.* (2006) examined the Indian market for quinolones, a class of antibiotics. They show that weak patent systems and price controls deter multinational investment in distribution networks. Although the introduction of product patents under TRIPS did not raise prices substantially (due to price regulations), it led to supply contractions. Foreign firms failed to fill the gap because their distribution infrastructure was underdeveloped. As a result, shortages emerged and prices rose. A key finding is that price regulation discourages MNCs from investing in distribution.

When domestic imitative supply contracted due to patent enforcement, consumers did not simply switch to foreign drugs with the same molecule. Instead, many substituted for different domestic molecules. This suggests that consumers value product variety, and that welfare analyses of product patents should consider variety, not just price effects.

Subsequent research by Duggan *et al.* (2016) confirms that the introduction of product patents in India did not lead to significant price increases of drugs. Large price increases may have been preempted by the prospect of price controls or compulsory licensing. On the other hand, the lack of large price increases could also have dampened profits for pharmaceutical companies in India and thereby limited the incentives of multinational companies to develop drugs specifically for the Indian market.

Arora *et al.* (2008), using firm-level data from India, describe how Indian pharmaceutical companies successfully entered global markets post-TRIPS. TRIPS had both a "stick" and a "carrot" effect. On the one hand, it curtailed imitation, pushing firms toward process improvements, adaptive innovation, and contract manufacturing. India emerged as one of the top ten patenting nations in the U.S. (see Chapter 2). On the other hand, the demand for affordable generics in industrialized countries — especially as blockbuster drugs came off patent — created export opportunities. Generics, for instance, account for about 90% of prescriptions in the U.S., 75% in Canada, and 70% by volume in Europe.[42] Additional trade liberalization through the

[42]See https://accessiblemeds.org/resources/reports/2023-savings-report-2, Canadian Generic Pharmaceutical Association report on *International Pricing and Canada's Generic Prescriptions Medicines*, November 2023. https://canadiangenerics.ca/, and https://www.iqvia.com/-/media/iqvia/pdfs/library/white-papers/iqvia-true-value-of-generic-medicines-04-24-forweb.pdf.

WTO and financial reforms under the IMF also helped Indian firms expand globally. Even generic production demands strong process engineering and sizable R&D investments. Importantly, India benefited from an extended transition period under Article 65.4 of TRIPS, delaying the requirement to grant product patents for pharmaceuticals until 2005, giving domestic firms time to adapt and upgrade technologically.

Appendix 8A. Traditional Medicines

WHO defines traditional medicines as "knowledge, skills, and practices based on the theories, beliefs, and experiences indigenous to different cultures... used in the maintenance of health and in the prevention... or treatment of... illness."[43]

In sub-Saharan Africa, demand for modern medicine is relatively low. Traditional medicine is more popular and may complement modern medicine. Currently, Gabon and Southern Cameroon are heavily reliant on traditional medicines. The Central African Republic is moderately to highly reliant, and Northern Chad is the least reliant.[44]

In some cases, traditional and modern medicine are substitutes. Indigenous people turn to traditional healers because they have doubts about modern medicine. Other times, according to field research, they may be complementary.[45] Traditional healers are often sought after when modern healthcare providers are expensive or unavailable, particularly in rural areas. But when they cannot treat their patients, traditional healers may cooperate with local health clinics.

8A.1 *Determinants of Traditional Medicine*

The following analysis is based on a study conducted by Lowes and Montero (2019) using data from Cameroon, the Central African Republic, Chad, Congo, and Gabon.

Table 8A.1 shows the determinants of various indices of traditional medicine use. The dependent variable is based on survey questionnaires. For the birth control index, respondents are asked a series of (yes/no) questions, such as whether they use traditional methods for birth control, know

[43]https://www.who.int/news-room/questions-and-answers/item/traditional-medicine.
[44]See Lowes and Montero (2019).
[45]*Ibid.*

Table 8A.1. Historical Correlates of Traditional Medicine Use

	Traditional Medicine Index			
	Birth Control (1)	**Pregnancy (2)**	**Advice (3)**	**Combined (4)**
Colonial Medicine Exposure:				
Share of Years Visited (1921–1956)	0.295***	0.0168	0.153*	0.293***
Colonial Variables:				
Atlantic Slave Exports	−8.140	3.733	17.89	−12.72
Distance to Closest Colonial Mission	0.484	−0.135	−0.601	0.710
Distance to Colonial Country Capital	0.504**	−0.0542	−0.041	0.173
Distance to Colonial District Capital	−0.143	−0.321	0.704	−0.481

Note: Asterisks denote significance at the 1% (***) and 5% (**) levels.

of at least one traditional method of birth control, and use traditional methods to delay pregnancy. The responses to these questions are then averaged per respondent. Likewise, for the pregnancy index and advice index, respondents are asked multiple (yes/no) questions, respectively, about their consultation with a traditional birth attendant or traditional practitioner (for coughs, diarrhea, fever), and their responses are then averaged across the questions, yielding an index score per respondent. The combined index is the average of the birth control, pregnancy, and advice indices.

Why do patients choose traditional medicines? The primary reason is a lack of trust in conventional medicine. Memories remain of treatments during the French military occupation. To seek a cure for sleeping sickness, the colonists had undertaken campaigns that forced treatments on locals that had severe side effects, including blindness and death.

Table 8A.1 shows regressions of the traditional medicine indices on colonial characteristics.[46] The results show that the farther away patients are

[46]To conserve space, the table provides only highlights of the research conducted by Lowes and Montero (2019). All regressions include geography and climate controls, disease suitability controls, and contemporary controls. Standard errors are in parentheses.

Table 8A.2. Traditional Medicine and Witchcraft

	Traditional Medicine Index			
	Birth Control (1)	**Pregnancy (2)**	**Advice (3)**	**Combined (4)**
Witchcraft Cause for HIV	0.0356***	0.00303	0.0342**	0.0389***
Observations	85,394	82,216	23,859	121,405
Clusters	219	219	219	219
Mean Dependent Variable	−0.152	−0.011	−0.006	−0.0001

Note: Asterisks denote significance at the 1% (***), 5% (**), and 10% (*) levels.

from the colonial missionaries or from the capital of the colonial country, the more dependent they are on traditional medicines for pregnancy and general advice. This is because the longer distance makes them less exposed to conventional medicine, such as conventional hospitals and service providers.

Traditional healers differ from conventional doctors in that they emphasize "social and emotional equilibrium" and community relationships. In some instances, the healers turn to witchcraft and identify supernatural origins as the diagnosis for an illness. Indeed, according to Table 8A.2, traditional healers attract patients who believe in the supernatural.

The positive coefficient on the Witchcraft variable indicates that those patients who believe that witchcraft causes HIV are more likely to turn to traditional healers for birth control, pregnancy, and general medical advice.

8A.2 *Case of Modern Day Taiwan*

Some supernaturalism appears to pervade traditional medicine in Taiwan as well. There, traditional medicine is practiced with a mixture of healing and spirituality.[47]

Taiwan's health care system is, in fact, a mixture of Western and traditional Chinese medicine. Traditional medicine is favored by indigenous communities (about 3% of the population), who are generally economically disadvantaged.

[47]The discussion here is based on a feature story in the *Washington Post* entitled "In Taiwan, new life breathed into traditional healing," Oct. 23, 2023, p. A14.

As the *Washington Post* profiled, Kula is a spiritual healer (or Sikawasay). In a ceremony, the healer performs rituals intended to communicate with ancestral spirits.[48] As one method of healing, Kula lights seven cigarettes and splashes rice wine into seven small plastic cups.

Healers like him tell the public: "If [Western] doctors say your body is fine and nothing is detected, but you still feel unwell, then you can come see us." According to him, traditional healing works by fostering strong ethnic identity and intercultural competence, which improves well-being by lowering depression and anxiety.

8A.3 *Should Traditional Medicines be Granted IPRs?*

To address that issue, consider the following questions:

- Is there a science to the medicine or practice, or is healing a pure spiritual exercise?
- Does the traditional medicine involve a commercial venture?
- What is the inventive step?
- Would IPRs have the perverse effect of turning traditional medicines into a trade secret?

Based on these questions, several challenges arise with regard to granting IP protection to spiritual healing. If there is a scientific basis to it, then the method could be eligible for IP protection, subject to examination standards for novelty, nonobviousness, and utility.

Typically, IPRs are granted to protect the returns from commercialization. Financial backers need to invest capital while facing risks and uncertainties about potential market demand. Such investors may not back the innovation without the security of an IP right. A related question is: how much investment went into developing the traditional medicines, and do the healers who developed the treatments need time to recoup their costs?

How much of the medicinal treatment is discovery versus invention? Was it clinically tested? Is the treatment obvious to a person who practices the art of traditional medicine? Is the knowledge (by definition) already in the public domain (if it has been practiced for many years by a community)? If so, are there other forms of IP that can protect traditional medicines?

[48]https://www.washingtonpost.com/world/2023/10/22/taiwan-indigenous-amis-tribal-traditional-healing/.

Perhaps a community right? The goal of the right may be a modest one: to pre-empt the treatment from becoming proprietary.

How should claims of the efficacy of traditional methods and healing practices be judged? Should the international public take the word of the indigenous group? Is there peer review, or should a community be relied upon to judge its own case? Advocates of traditional knowledge might say that only the local, indigenous groups are qualified to determine the claims and value, and assess the remedies for breach of rights.

Is there sufficient market demand outside Asia and Africa, where traditional medicine is practiced? This matters on two fronts. First, akin to piracy, there are greater risks of copying a popular treatment. Second, the larger market provides a greater venue for recouping the costs of converting a traditional medicine into a commercial product. But if traditional medicines are turned into a commercial venture, would the healers and practitioners turn to secrecy? That is, keep their knowledge a secret until they get an IP right, or keep it a secret to prevent exploitation of the traditional knowledge?

Chapter 9

Agriculture

9.1 Introduction

Agriculture presents distinctive challenges for intellectual property policy. Unlike mechanical inventions, agricultural innovations involve living systems that reproduce naturally, requiring corresponding adjustments to conventional IP frameworks. Seeds replicate themselves, genetic traits spread through pollination, and farmers have historically saved and exchanged varieties — practices that complicate IP systems based on exclusivity.

This chapter examines how intellectual property systems address agricultural innovation and their impacts on productivity, market structure, and technology transfer. Like other forms of IPRs, plant variety protection also involves tradeoffs between incentivizing research and ensuring broad access to improved varieties, particularly in developing countries where food security concerns are paramount.

The chapter traces the development from traditional plant breeding, which operated largely outside formal IP systems, to today's biotechnology sector protected by patents and plant variety rights. It explores the global expansion of plant variety protection and presents empirical evidence on how IP protection affects agricultural productivity across different crops and income levels.

The chapter also examines how market concentration in the seed industry has increased dramatically, driven partly by IP laws and merger activity among major agribusiness firms.

Finally, the chapter explores alternative innovation models, including open biotechnology initiatives that share research tools and genetic resources freely. These approaches offer lessons about how collaborative innovation can complement proprietary systems.

9.2 Agriculture and Economic Development

Agriculture occupies a special place in the global economy as it forms the foundation of the world's food supply. Currently, agriculture represents a smaller share of economic output and employment in the developed world than in developing countries, where it remains a dominant sector.

Food security remains a persistent concern in less developed countries, with haunting memories of famines in Bengal, India (1943), China (1958–1962), Ethiopia (1985 and 1999), Somalia (2011), South Sudan (2017), and other regions where food crises continue today. Global food crises occur episodically,[1] driven by weather extremes, armed conflicts, market disruptions, and other destabilizing factors.

Agricultural subsidies represent a major source of contention at the WTO. Subsidies in developed countries generally harm farmers in developing nations because excess production depresses world agricultural prices. In developing countries, declining world prices reduce farm incomes and worsen their terms of trade, since agricultural goods constitute a larger share of their exports. Lower farm incomes can force agricultural operations to shut down, potentially creating food shortages. Similar dynamics affect other sectors. Subsidies for cotton in developed countries, for example, depress global cotton prices and adversely impact cotton farmers throughout the developing world.

Technological innovation offers a key pathway to sustainable food security. Machinery innovations can augment labor productivity on farms or free workers for other economic activities. These innovations extend to improvements in transportation systems that deliver food more efficiently and preserve quality during transit. Biotechnological advances can yield higher-producing plant varieties or crops resistant to disease and drought. Process innovations enable farmers to better manage critical resources such as soil, water, pollinators, and fertilizers. Climate-related innovations also provide crucial support to the agricultural sector. In short, the intellectual

[1]See https://www.fightfoodcrises.net/.

property system plays a pivotal role in agriculture by influencing both the direction and accessibility of technological innovation in food supply, fiber, fuels, horticultural products, and biotechnology.

9.3 Agriculture and IPR

Intellectual property rights (IPRs) play a critical role in plant breeding. First, developing a new plant variety is a resource-intensive process involving years of research and field trials. Second, seeds are relatively easy to replicate — both biologically and commercially. Once released, competitors can reproduce and distribute the genetic material without bearing the R&D costs incurred by the original innovator. The biological nature of seeds, being self-replicating, makes agricultural innovation vulnerable to free-riding.

At the same time, overly restrictive IPRs can be counterproductive. Agricultural innovation can be sequential and cumulative: breeders frequently build upon existing genetic resources and traits developed by others. As a result, previous innovations must remain accessible to facilitate follow-on breeding. This tension — between the need to incentivize private investment and the need to preserve access for further innovation — underpins much of the global debate over IPRs in agriculture (see Campi, 2024).

Historically, intellectual property rights did not apply to biological innovations. For much of the 20th century, productivity growth in agriculture was driven primarily by public R&D institutions. Plant varieties were viewed as products of nature. Consequently, private innovation in seeds was limited. But developments in hybrid seeds were different. Hybrid seeds had a kind of natural protection against imitation, as they are difficult to repro duce (as this requires the parental line). The offspring of hybrid plants are not as productive as the parent hybrid.

Advances in biotechnology and the globalization of the IP system combined to increase the demand for IP protection. The establishment of the International Union for the Protection of New Varieties of Plants (UPOV) in 1961 marked a turning point. UPOV created a sui generis system of plant variety protection (PVP), granting breeders exclusive rights over the commercial use of novel varieties. The organization became operational in 1968. In some jurisdictions, patents were also granted for plant inventions.[2]

[2]For example, in 1980, the U.S. Supreme Court, in *Diamond v. Chakrabarty*, permitted the patenting of genetically modified organisms.

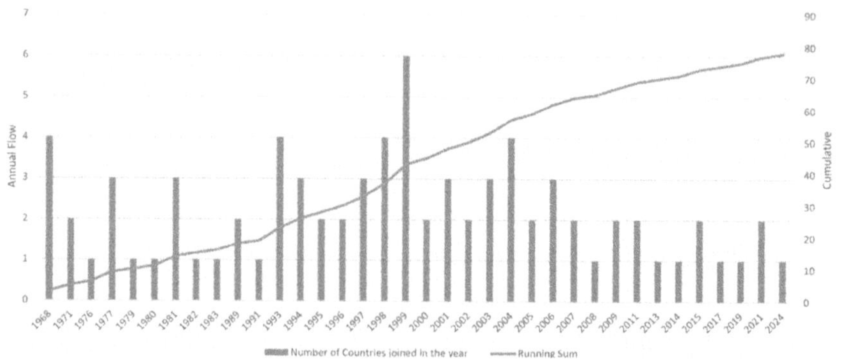

Figure 9.1. Membership in UPOV

UPOV is the key international institution supporting plant variety protection. In Figure 9.1, note the expansion in countries that became members and instituted PVP. There are 79 members as of 2024. The agreement of UPOV was revised in 1972 and 1978. The 1991 revision is the latest and most comprehensive.[3]

The TRIPS agreement also shapes IP rights in agriculture. Article 27.3(b) of the agreement stipulates that: "Members may also exclude from patentability . . . plants and animals other than micro-organisms, and essentially biological processes for the production of plants or animals other than non-biological and microbiological processes. However, Members shall provide for the protection of plant varieties either by patents or by an effective sui generis system or by any combination thereof." This clause permits countries to exclude plants and animals as subject matter for patents, but then are obliged to offer some other form of protection, such as Plant Variety Protection (PVP) or Plant Breeder's Rights (PBR). Now, while Article 27.3(b) allows countries the right to exclude plants and animals from patentability, it does not prohibit them from allowing it, as the U.S. and Japan have chosen to do. Under their general patent statutes, utility patents can be granted on transgenic varieties, animal breeds, and their propagating materials.

Plant breeders' rights (PBR), also known as plant variety rights (PVR), are rights granted to the breeder of a new plant variety that give the breeder exclusive control over the propagating material (including seed, cuttings,

[3]The 1991 Act is the standard for new UPOV members, and most existing members have either acceded to it or operate under the 1978 Act.

divisions, tissue culture) and, in cases of unauthorized use, harvested material (cut flowers, fruit, foliage) of a new variety for a number of years (say 20, or 25 for trees and vines).[4] A key difference between patents and PBRs lies in their requirements: patents must be novel, non-obvious, and industrially applicable, with an enablement requirement ensuring that a skilled practitioner can reproduce the invention. In contrast, PBRs are issued for varieties that meet the "DUS" criteria: Distinctness, Uniformity, and Stability. The enablement requirement is harder to fulfill for biological innovations (especially with mutations). Instead, it is required that there be uniformity and stability in reproduction (that the same essential characteristics in a plant be retained). Due to these differences between biological innovations and traditional industrial innovations, some countries, such as the United States, allow breeders to seek both a patent and a PBR for the same plant.

Under UPOV, plant breeder rights have been strengthened. Protection has been extended to harvested material and to *essentially derived varieties*, which are plant varieties that are predominantly derived from an existing protected variety and differ from the latter in a very minor way. This legal protection prevents cosmetic changes in existing varieties from circumventing plant variety rights.

The plant variety protection system has two important flexibilities:

- **Breeders' Exemption:** Plant breeders can use protected varieties for purposes of research and experimentation in order to breed other distinct and improved varieties.
- **Farmer's Privilege:** A farmer is free to save the seeds of a protected plant as long as they are for personal, non-commercial use.

Under the 1991 Act of the International Union for the Protection of New Varieties of Plants (UPOV), the breeders' exemption is mandatory (except in cases of essentially derived varieties). The farmer's privilege is optional; in other words, UPOV members may choose whether to allow farmers to save and re-use seed commercially.

Farmers' privilege is very important for developing economies where much of the land is planted with the seeds produced by the farmers themselves, since new quality seeds are not always readily available or are

[4]Varieties are variations within a plant species. Seeds are the reproductive unit of the plant. Varieties are plants that occur naturally, and their offspring will have the same characteristics as the parent. Cultivars are varieties that are selected and cultivated by humans.

expensive due to high royalties. New seeds would not necessarily cover all the market demand. Saved seeds could help fill the gap in market needs.

These flexibilities help balance breeders' rights with affordable access and ongoing research in variety development in both developed and developing countries.

9.3.1 *Trends*

UPOV issues the PVP certificates or titles: These data can be used as measures of new innovations or new technologies related to agriculture, like new varieties of soybeans, corn; or higher performing plant varieties, due to technological improvements in herbicide tolerance and in the insect resistance of crops.[5]

Tables 9.1 and 9.2 present some trends in plant variety innovations and their global diffusion. Total applications by residents more than doubled between 2016–2023, and China's share has grown tremendously in less than a decade, rising from just under a quarter to two-thirds of all applications. The count for Africa is the sum of resident filings in Kenya, South Africa, AIPO, Egypt, and Tunisia. Collectively, they account for less than one percent of all applications.

Table 9.1. Applications for Plant Variety Protection: By Residents

		Percentage Share (%)						
Year	**Total**	**U.S.**	**EU**	**China**	**Japan**	**Brazil**	**Africa**	**ROW**
2016	10,606	7.7	24.7	25.3	5.7	1.9	0.5	34.2
2017	12,566	6.5	22.0	31.9	4.9	1.6	0.5	32.7
2018	13,670	6.6	20.7	38.2	4.2	1.4	0.5	28.5
2019	15,623	5.8	18.3	46.9	3.6	1.0	0.5	24.0
2020	16,514	4.4	16.9	50.4	2.8	1.1	0.3	24.1
2021	18,908	6.6	13.8	55.7	2.5	1.0	0.3	20.1
2022	21,442	3.4	11.9	57.5	2.2	1.2	0.5	23.4
2023	23,684	2.3	9.4	65.6	1.7	1.2	0.4	19.4

Note: ROW = Rest-of-the-World.
Source: UPOV.

[5]https://www.upov.int/en/plant-variety-protection/pvp-statistics.

Table 9.2. Applications for Plant Variety Protection: By Non-Residents

		Percentage Share (%)						
Year	**Total**	**U.S.**	**EU**	**China**	**Japan**	**Brazil**	**Africa**	**ROW**
2016	5,222	15.2	13.0	4.5	7.0	2.4	7.6	50.3
2017	5,803	12.7	11.4	7.9	7.0	2.4	4.9	53.7
2018	6,011	11.8	12.0	9.0	5.2	2.3	4.1	55.6
2019	5,580	12.3	12.0	9.2	4.7	2.4	5.1	54.3
2020	5,957	11.8	10.8	10.6	4.3	2.6	5.7	54.3
2021	6,225	10.5	14.0	10.5	4.9	2.3	6.8	51.1
2022	5,747	11.4	11.3	12.1	3.8	2.4	6.6	52.4
2023	5,314	11.4	12.2	12.3	3.5	2.2	7.8	50.5

Note: ROW = Rest-of-the-World.
Source: UPOV.

Non-resident filings indicate the innovations of foreign inventors filed for protection in a country. They help gauge the international technology transfers. China does not engage as much international technology transfer to the degree that it files domestically, but it is on a par with the U.S. and EU Breeders from these six countries and region account for around half of all non-resident applications for plant variety protection, so they do account for a disproportionate share of the transferring of plant breeding technologies abroad. Despite accounting for a small share of all plant variety protection applications, the African countries appear to be more vibrantly holding their weight in transferring their plant innovations globally.

9.3.2 *Case Studies*

Innovations in agriculture have expanded and world trade in IP-protected agricultural goods has become more lucrative. Thus the stakes are high. Three high-profile disputes illustrate how firms and IP holders exerted their IP rights aggressively.

In 2005–2006, Monsanto held an EPO patent on a gene (called Roundup Ready, RR) but could not get it patented in Argentina. Exporters from Argentina tried to sell soybean-related products containing that gene in Europe. Monsanto sued to block those Argentine soy exports to Europe on the grounds that all *Roundup Ready* soy products, regardless of origin, embodied EU-patented gene traits. The Argentine firms were ordered to demonstrate that they had the licensing rights to sell. This challenge disrupted Argentina's soybean trade at the time, which accounted for over half the agricultural exports of Argentina.

In 2012, negotiations over the U.S.-Colombia Free Trade Agreement (2012) sparked a flash point when early drafts of the agreement threatened to abolish farmer's privilege. Colombian farmers would have lost the right to save or exchange seeds, and would have been mandated to make certified purchases each season. Smallholders subsequently organized nationwide protests, strikes, and farm blockades. Ultimately, negotiators restored a robust farmer's privilege, revealing how PVP provisions can ignite fierce political resistance when they imperil traditional seed-saving practices.

Another high-profile dispute unfolded in India after the introduction of Bt cotton in the early 2000s. Farmers' rights groups alleged that the high cost of genetically modified seed, royalty payments, and soil damage due to Bt cotton contributed to rural indebtedness and even suicides. Critics countered that the evidence did not support a direct causal link and that other factors, such as monsoon failure, access to credit, and preexisting debt, played more significant roles. Studies such as Gruère and Sengupta (2011) found that Bt cotton adoption was generally associated with higher yields and incomes, and that media narratives often oversimplified the complex socio-economic causes behind farmer distress.

Together, these cases illustrate both the promise and pitfalls of applying IPRs in agriculture. Strong IP systems can spur investment in improved seed technologies, but they can also undermine informal systems and provoke political backlash if not carefully tailored. The challenge lies in designing plant variety protection frameworks that align innovation incentives with public interest, especially in countries where agriculture remains the backbone of rural livelihoods.

9.4 Community Plant Variety Office

The formation of the Community Plant Variety Office (CPVO) is an important institutional development in the global intellectual property protection of agricultural and biotechnological innovations. CPVO was created by a European Union (EU) Council Regulation in 1994 and became operational in 1995. The Community Plant Variety Office grants plant breeders' rights (PBR) across the EU. CPVO is similar to other organizations like the EPO or WIPO, but it has its particular distinctions. It reviews, examines, and renders a decision on whether to grant a PBR. It provides a unified application process and has a single, standardized examination procedure, along with unified document requirements.[6]

The PBR gives the breeder of a new variety of plants exclusive control over the variety and the associated propagating and harvested material for a certain number of years, depending on the species. The vast majority of plant innovations is concentrated in agricultural and ornamental plants.

The CPVO's grant of PBR is legally valid throughout the entire EU. Yet, no harmonization of laws on PBRs has resulted, nor has the displacement of national offices. Individual EU nations retained their ability to grant PBRs that are valued only within their own borders. The same PBR cannot be valid both at a national office and at CPVO. Thus, if a firm has a PBR from a national office, say Germany, it will have to abandon that one in order to seek a CPVO-wide PBR.[7] The national level PBR and CPVO offer similar levels of legal appropriability. This split — national office PBR vs. a CPVO PBR — allows for some specialization. It allows larger EU-wide relevant innovations to be protected at the EU-wide level, which probably represent more valuable innovations, while the locally relevant varieties can be protected within a local market (or within a few others). Some varieties may only serve a small market and may only meet eligibility criteria in limited regions, in which case it is not economical to seek and enforce protection across the entire EU.

The CPVO member states consist of the 27 current European countries. In 1995, it began with 15 members, and then in 2004, it began gradually expanding to the present. Because of CPVO, more companies have switched from filing for a PBR in a country's office to filing at CPVO.

Figure 9.2 shows the dramatic decline in shares of PBR applications at national offices and a rise in CPVO's shares.[8] Table 9.3 shows both the level and distribution of applications at the home office, office abroad, and CPVO. The home or local office is where the breeder or company resides. The external office is the national office to which the breeder would apply for a PBR outside the home country. And the CPVO is the office serving the entire EU.[9]

As Table 9.3 shows, the introduction of CPVO led to a number of substitution effects. More breeders sought protection beyond their own countries,

---

[6]To learn more, see https://cpvo.europa.eu.
[7]See Würtenberger *et al.* (2021).
[8]The figure is from Prud'homme *et al.* (2022).
[9]CPVO is situated in Angers, France.

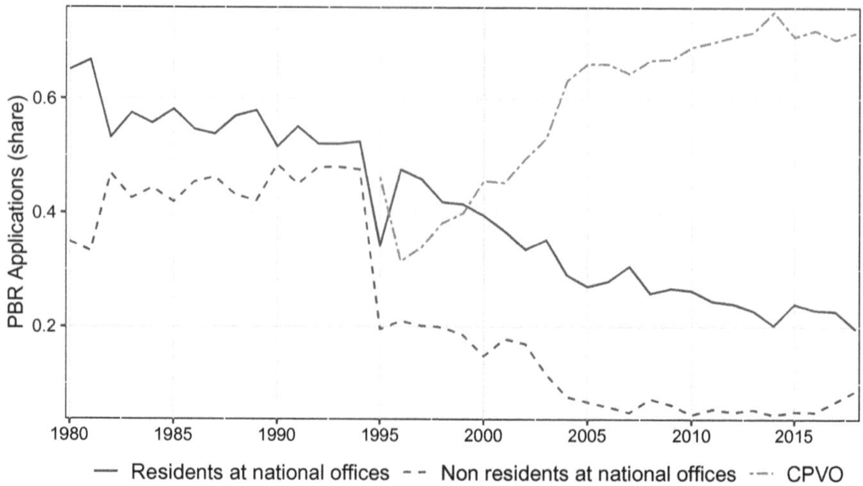

Figure 9.2. Evolution of PBRs upon CPVO Introduction

Table 9.3. Plant Breeders' Rights: Applications and Percentage Shares

Period	Local (Home Office)	External (Abroad)	CPVO Office
1983–1994	21,989	18,693	—
	54.1%	*45.9%*	
1995–2006	21,065	8,841	16,410
	45.5%	*19.0%*	*35.5%*
2007–2018	13,713	3,327	19,599
	37.4%	*9.0%*	*53.6%*

Note: Calculations based on PLUTO and CPVO plant variety databases.

switching away from filing at national offices to filing at CPVO. By the 2007–2018 period, more than half of plant breeder rights applications were filed at CPVO. The share of local offices decreased, and when breeders chose to apply across Europe, more chose to file at CPVO rather than at a foreign national office. The ability to do a single filing saves fees and other costs. Rather than go "door-to-door," filing in each national office for a plant breeder's right, firms can avail themselves of a centralized filing system. The savings can be used for other activities, such as more research, capital investment, or marketing.

Supranational institutions like CPVO are likely to have had a significant impact on the organizational structures of the agricultural or agribiotech firms, perhaps leading them to become more multinationalized as companies.[10]

9.5 Impacts on Agricultural Productivity

This section discusses evidence of the impact of plant variety protection (PVP) on agricultural productivity. First, a quantitative measure of PVP strength by country and time is needed. Such an index was created by Campi and Nuvolari (2015, 2021). The ingredients are given in Table 9.4.

The index varies from 0 to 5, with higher values representing stronger PVP regimes, and the index covers 104 countries from 1961 to 2018. Figure 9.3 shows the trend in the PVP strength of protection grouped by developed and developing countries.

Developing countries have increased their levels of PVP protection since 1975, while developed economies have increased theirs after 1995, largely because of the TRIPS agreement. While less developed countries were given transition periods to implement TRIPS, several of them adopted IP reforms well before the transition periods expired. By 2015, Figure 9.3 shows some convergence in PVP standards between the developed and developing countries.

Table 9.4. Index of Plant Variety Protection

Component	Normalized Score
Ratification of UPOV	0–1
Farmer's Privilege (absence)	0–1
Breeder's Exemption (essentially derived condition present)	0–1
Duration	0–1
Patent Scope	0–1
Overall Index	0–5

[10]It would be useful to conduct analyses on the economic impacts of CPVO on firm structure, firm investments, and growth.

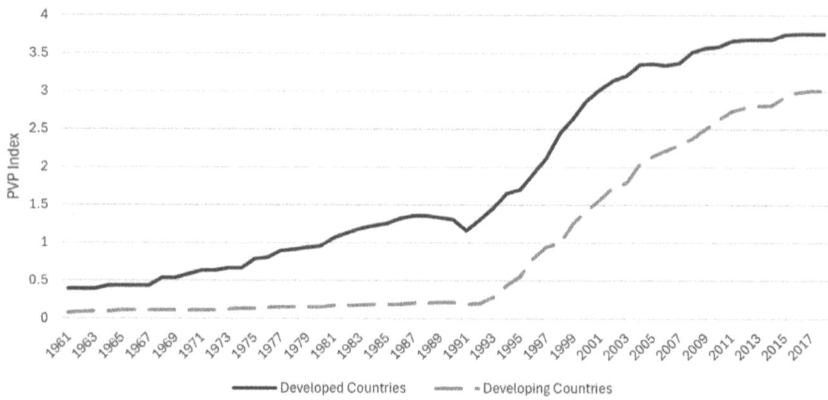

Figure 9.3. Trends in Plant Variety Protection Index
Source: Campi and Nuvolari (2021).

Table 9.5. Impact on Agricultural Output (Value Added): Case 1

Sample	Full	Developed	Developing
PVP Index	0.026***	0.033***	0.003

Notes: Other Control variables include Schooling, Irrigation, Population, Fertilizers, Area, Tractors (not reported); *** denotes statistical significance at the 1% level.

9.5.1 *Selected Evidence*

How did strengthening PVP affect agricultural production and productivity? Campi (2017) conducts a comprehensive analysis by type of crop and by country. Production is measured by value added and productivity by yields; specifically, the output per area harvested in hectares (or simply, output per hectare). The following tables show abridged results (that is, focusing on the main variables of interest and not all the control variables that are included in a regression analysis).

First, Table 9.5 focuses on the role of PVP while Table 9.6 observes the effects of patent protection as well, since some agricultural innovations can be protected by a patent or by a combination of PVP and patent, where each instrument covers different facets of an agricultural innovation.

PVP benefits production only in developed countries (North), not in developing countries, controlling for other factors. Once the patent rights

Table 9.6. Impact on Agricultural Output (Value Added): Case 2

Sample	Full	Developed	Developing
PVP Index	0.031***	0.024***	−0.014
Patent Rights	0.014	0.080***	0.004

Notes: Other Control variables include Schooling, Irrigation, Population, Fertilizers, Area, Tractors (not reported); *** denotes statistical significance at the 1% level.

Table 9.7. Impact on Cereal Yields

Sample	Full	High-Income	Middle-Income	Low-Income
PVP Index	0.050***	0.083***	0.001	0.081**

Notes: Other Control variables include Schooling, Irrigation, Population, Fertilizers, Area, Tractors (not reported); *** and ** denote statistical significance at the 1% and 5% levels, respectively.

Table 9.8. Impact on Yields of Maize

Sample	Full	High-Income	Middle-Income	Low-Income
PVP Index	0.114***	0.144***	0.079***	0.152***

Notes: Other Control variables include Schooling, Irrigation, Population, Fertilizers, Area, Tractors (not reported); *** denotes statistical significance at the 1% level.

index (i.e., the GP index) is controlled for, only PVP matters for agricultural production in the full sample. But in the sub-sample of developed countries, both instruments matter, with patent protection having a stronger quantitative effect. In the developing region, neither patent protection nor PVP protection has any significant impact on agricultural output.

The value-added regressions may be too aggregated. Tables 9.7–9.9 show the results by crop and focus on productivity: output per hectare, or yield. Yields can also reflect technical efficiency in agriculture.

On cereal yields, stronger protection for plant varieties is positively and significantly associated with agricultural productivity in the full sample, high-income sample, and low-income sample — but not in the middle-income sample. One possible explanation is that stronger PVP stimulates

Table 9.9. Impact on Yields of Wheat

Sample	Full	High-Income	Mid-Income	Low-Income
PVP Index	0.029***	0.051***	−0.025*	0.029

Notes: Other Control variables include Schooling, Irrigation, Population, Fertilizers, Area, Tractors (not reported); *** and * denote statistical significance at the 1% and 10% levels respectively.

agricultural innovation in high-income countries and attracts technology transfers in low-income countries. But in middle-income countries, stronger PVP may crowd out imitation, block access to seeds, and reduce the capacity to produce. Whatever technology transfer the middle-income countries receive does not compensate for the reduced ability to imitate innovations. Hence, the overall effect of PVP is neutral in the middle-income group.

Only for maize does PVP stimulate farm productivity for all income groups. Most maize seeds are hybrids that lose their traits in the next generation, limiting a farmer's ability to save and reuse seeds. In contrast, wheat is open-pollinated, so farmers can reuse harvested seeds while maintaining genetic characteristics. Thus, maize has a built-in natural protection. But as Campi (2017) notes, this creates a puzzle: maize should be less IP-dependent. One possibility is that PVP enables greater rents and profits to be captured on top of the natural barrier.

For wheat, PVP is negatively associated with productivity in middle-income countries and insignificant in low-income countries. Stronger PVP may allow producers and innovators to better exercise market power over wheat supply in the developing world, limiting technology transfers and the diffusion of innovations.

The result underscores the importance of IP flexibilities for low- and middle-income countries. As observed with utility models, imitation is central to the catching-up process of developing countries.

An extension of the above analysis is to examine the breakdown of the PVP Index by component and observe which aspect of PVP rights best contributes to agricultural productivity. The focus in Table 9.10 is on cereal yields:

Throughout, patent rights matter. They provide greater exclusivity and perhaps an incentive to innovate and invest in new technologies, including those that raise agricultural productivity. This raises the question of whether countries should reform the prohibition on the patenting of plants

Table 9.10. Impact on Cereal Yields, by PVP Component

Sample	Full	High-Income	Mid-Income	Low-Income
UPOV	0.070***	0.103***	0.053	0.108**
No Farmer's Privilege	−0.042	0.041	−0.228	n/a
Limited Breeder's Exemption	0.058***	0.077***	−0.063**	0.100
Duration	−0.015	0.026	0.105**	−0.065
Patent Scope	0.198***	0.185***	0.101**	0.292***

Notes: Other Control variables include Schooling, Irrigation, Population, Fertilizers, Area, Tractors (not reported); *** and ** denote statistical significance at the 1% and 5% levels, respectively.

and animals (other than micro-organisms), and on essentially biological processes for the production of plants or animals (other than non-biological and microbiological processes). This question is pertinent, especially if agricultural R&D is very costly. PVP may provide too little incentive to undertake it. Perhaps patents may provide the appropriate incentive. Further thought is warranted.

9.6 Genetically Modified Organisms

Genetic modification here refers to the biotechnology for introducing traits to increase yield, provide drought resistance, and insect resistance, among others. Innovation on genetically modified organisms (GMO) accelerated after TRIPS. In 1996, the global land area dedicated to biotechnological crops was 1.7 million hectares (Mha). By 2018, it was 191.7 Mha.[11] Table 9.11 shows the ten leading countries with biotech land and their share of the global land area, as well as a breakdown between industrialized and developing countries. Note that 91% of the global biotech land area is in the top five countries.

Another notable aspect is that many developing countries are engaged in GM/biotech production. Only two developed countries are on the top ten

[11]Data on GMO (biotech) crops are from the *International Service for the Acquisition of Agri-Biotech Applications (ISAAA)* Briefs. See https://www.isaaa.org/resources/publications/.

Table 9.11. Global Area of Biotech Crops, 2018

Leading Countries	**Million Hectares, Mha (Share, %)**
USA	39
Brazil	27
Argentina	12
Canada	7
India	6
Paraguay	2
China	2
Pakistan	1
South Africa	1
Uruguay	1
Industrialized Countries	46
Developing Countries	54
Global land area	191.7 Mha

Source: ISAAA (2018), Brief 54, Tables 1–3.

list: Canada and the United States. More than half of GMO-biotech production occurs in the developing world. This makes it all the more important that developing countries have a voice in the determination of global policy on GMOs, trade, and intellectual property.

By 2019, a total of 72 countries adopted biotech crops — 29 countries planted them and 43 additional countries imported them.[12] The top five biotech crops are shown in Table 9.12 along with their share of global biotech land. Half of GMO crops are in soybeans, and just under a third are in maize. Table 9.13 shows which countries are the top four leading producers in each type of biotech crop.

Biotech crops can be in one of three categories:

1. **Insect Resistance (IR):** Crop is modified to resist insect pests (for example, expresses Bt proteins). Examples include Bt cotton and Bt maize.
2. **Herbicide Tolerance (HT):** Crop is modified to tolerate specific herbicides (e.g., glyphosate). An example includes Roundup Ready soybean.

[12]https://www.isaaa.org/resources/publications/briefs/55/executivesummary/default.asp.

Table 9.12. Leading GMO Crops, 2018

Leading Crops	% of Global Area of Biotech Crops
Soybeans	50.0
Maize	30.7
Cotton	12.9
Canola	5.3
Alfalfa	0.7
Global land area	191.7 Mha

Source: ISAAA (2018), Brief 54, Table 31.

Table 9.13. Leading GMO Producers by Crop

Soybeans	Maize	Cotton	Canola
Brazil	USA	India	Canada
USA	Brazil	USA	USA
Argentina	Argentina	China	Australia
Paraguay	Canada	Pakistan	Chile

Source: ISAAA (2018), Brief 54, Table 30.

3. **Stacked Trait:** Crop contains both IR and HT, or other combinations of traits. An example includes maize with Bt (IR) + glyphosate tolerance (HT).

All stacked traits include multiple traits (for example, IR plus HT), but not all IR or HT crops are stacked. Globally, about 12% of the land area is IR, 46% is HT, and the rest (42%) are stacked traits.[13]

[13]Based on Figure 18, ISAAA (2018), Brief 54.

Proponents argue that GMOs are as follows:

1. Good for the environment in that society can rely less on pesticides and other chemicals because plants can be engineered to be resistant to diseases and drought.
2. Efficient because they produce higher yields: more food per unit of effort. This helps countries whose food supply is precarious, such as those in sub-Saharan Africa.
3. Nutritious because foods can be designed to be rich in vitamins. For example, Golden Rice is engineered to produce provitamin A, specifically β-carotene. It can combat vitamin A deficiency, a major public health matter in parts of Asia and Africa.
4. Advantageous for less developed countries, as this is their source of comparative advantage in trade (as they are rich in gene supplies). Biotech innovations can help them compete against agricultural subsidies in the developed world.

Critics of GMOs, on the other hand, have concerns about biodiversity and safety, the ownership of the food supply, corporate control of agriculture, and insufficient long-term testing. Environmentally, GMOs could lead to herbicide overuse and soil degradation, and insect-resistant crops could harm non-target species like butterflies or beneficial insects.

GMO regulations vary across countries along the following dimensions, as discussed in Smith (2024):

- Approval process (institutional oversight)
- Risk assessment (safety/biodiversity)
- Labeling (information to buyers)
- Traceability and Identity Preservation (origin)
- Coexistence of GMO and non-GMO crops
- International treaties: Cartagena Protocol, Codex Alimentarius

Smith's (2024) analysis finds that the regulatory environment widely varies even among GMO-adopting countries. Among countries with strong regulations — requiring labeling, assessing risk — are Spain, Australia, Brazil, and China. Countries with more lax regulations include the U.S., Canada, India, South Africa, the Philippines, Mexico, and Vietnam.

9.6.1 *GMO and IPR*

Innovation largely occurs in developed countries, but farmers in both the global North and South adopt GMOs. The unique features of GMOs are (i) self-replication and (ii) diffusion by nature. This creates challenges for IPR enforcement, as innovations can spread without authorization from the rights holder.

Self-replication makes it easy to reuse seeds. Diffusion by nature (wind) leads to cross-pollination, whereby GMO seeds can spread to non-GMO crops. Combined, these features affect the appropriability of the IP owner, not only domestically but internationally across borders.

The patent exhaustion discussion of Chapter 8 can be used to shed insights into some of the global IP aspects of GMOs. Consider the following game between two players — a farmer and a multinational company (MNC):[14]

- Farmer's Choices
  1. Pay license fee to use (or reuse) GMO seed
  2. Adopt GMO seed, but reuse without permission
  3. Adopt non-GMO seed
- Multinational Company's Choices
  1. Tech transfer to GMO country (with strong IPR)
  2. Tech transfer to GMO country (with weak IPR)
  3. Tech transfer to an intolerant GMO country

The patent owner's exclusive rights of the patented product are exhausted once a sale has been made. The issue here is whether farmers can reproduce patented seeds (i.e., plant and harvest without the patent holder's permission). Most countries say "no," unless it is unintentional.

Thus, suppose after adopting GMO seeds, the farmer saves them. The farmer can pay for it, not pay for it, or just use a non-GMO substitute. The farmer risks litigation if he does not pay for it, but is also possibly liable if GMO seeds arrive at his farm naturally from other plots. Although the GMO seeds arrive unintentionally on the part of the farmer, the legal liability in such cases is ambiguous.

---

[14]The analysis is based on Smith (2024).

		MNC transfers technology to		
		Country with Strong GMO patents	Country with Weak GMO patents	Country with No GMO patents
Farmer's Choices	GMO Adoption with license to re-use	Yes	No	No
	GMO Adoption with no license to re-use	Yes	Yes	No
	Adoption of non-GMO seed	Yes	Yes	Yes

Note: Non-licensed GMO seeds could diffuse.
Trade disputes could arise.

Figure 9.4. Patent Exhaustion Outcomes

Figure 9.4 captures the outcomes of the above game. The MNC can market its GMO products in one of three regimes. Under each GMO patent regime (or no regime), the farmer has three choices. The Yes/No refers to whether that choice will be taken. For example, in the top cell, if the MNC exports or sets up an affiliate in a strong GMO regime, the farmer will "Yes," adopt GMO seeds and license it. Or the farmer could also choose "Yes," adopt but not get a license to reuse the seed. Or, third, the farmer could choose "Yes" to adopt a non-GMO seed, particularly if the license fee for reusing seeds is too high.

In the top row, second column, if the MNC markets the seed in a weak GMO country, it is unlikely that a farmer will adopt the seed with a license to reuse the seed since patent enforcement is weak in the country. Hence, the first row and second column in Figure 9.4 show a "No." In a country with weak GMO patents, the farmer would either adopt the GMO seed without a reuse license or adopt a non-GMO seed.

If the MNC introduces the GMO product in a country that offers no GMO patents, then the farmer will not adopt (pay for) the GMO seed; he will either use a free version (a copy) or adopt a non-GMO seed.

The arrows in Figure 9.4 caution that the country without GMO patents could still get access to the GMO seeds, not by licensing, but by natural means (wind and pollination). For example, the seeds could diffuse from neighboring countries that have either a strong GMO patent regime or a weak one. That is, through natural causes, GMO seeds could eventually make their way to GMO-intolerant regimes. Farmers there could be seen as free-riding. Trade disputes could then ensue. This example identifies where the source of a global dispute could arise with biotech crops that have those two special features: self-replication and cross-border pollination.

9.7 Market Concentration in Seed Markets

Over the past decade, the global commercial seed industry has become markedly more concentrated, in large part due to mergers and acquisitions and stronger intellectual property regimes. This section explores the implications for market structure and innovation.[15]

As MacDonald *et al.* (2023) note, biotechnological breakthroughs dramatically increased both the cost and the risk of creating GM varieties. This drove stronger demand for IP protection, especially patents that require users to license proprietary seed traits. This shift, in turn, moved crop breeding from largely public-sector research into the private seed industry. Major seed firms now routinely cross-license one another's IP to gain access to key varieties and traits, and they have also used mergers and acquisitions to gain critical IP assets and find new distribution channels.

Rising concentration has prompted concerns about reduced competition, upward pressure on food prices, and weaker innovation incentives. When only a handful of buyers dominate purchasing, farmers can experience the effects of monopsony power, which compels them to sell their commodities at lower prices.[16] For example, coffee bean growers who must deal with just a few large multinationals (e.g., Sara Lee, Nestlé, Kraft, Procter & Gamble) typically receive less for their crop than they would in a more competitive buying environment.

In recent years, major mergers and acquisitions activities trimmed the "Big Six" agribusiness firms — such as Bayer (Germany), Monsanto (U.S.), Dow Chemical (U.S.), DuPont (U.S.), Syngenta (Switzerland), and BASF (Germany) — down to a "Big Four." Bayer's acquisition of Monsanto closed in 2018; Dow and DuPont merged in 2017, later spinning off their agriculture

[15]This section builds on two reports: OECD (2018) and a USDA report by MacDonald *et al.* (2023).

[16]Monopsony power occurs when a small number of buyers can reduce prices because sellers have few alternative customers.

Table 9.14. Agricultural Sales by Company

Year	Big Six	Total Sales in Billion U.S. ($)	Shares of Total Sales: Seeds & Traits (%)	Shares of Total Sales: Agricultural Chemicals (%)
2015	Monsanto (U.S.)	15.0	68.3	31.7
	Bayer (Germany)	10.6	13.4	86.6
	Syngenta (Switzerland)	12.8	22.0	78.0
	DuPont (U.S.)	9.8	69.2	30.8
	Dow Chemical (U.S.)	6.4	22.1	77.9
	BASF (Germany)	6.5	<0.01	99.9

Year	Big Six	Total Sales in Billion U.S. ($)	Shares of Total Sales: Seeds & Traits (%)	Shares of Total Sales: Agricultural Chemicals (%)
2021	Bayer (Monsanto)	22.6	49.4	50.6
	Syngenta Group owned by ChemChina	16.7	21.3	78.7
	Corteva Agriscience (DowDuPont spinoff)	15.7	53.7	46.3
	BASF (Germany)	9.7	20.4	79.6

Source: MacDonald *et al.*, 2023.

arm as Corteva Agriscience; and ChemChina acquired Syngenta in 2017. Table 9.14 summarizes their market sales before and after these consolidations.

The combined sales of the Big Six firms reached $61.1 billion in 2015, while the Big Four collectively reported $64.7 billion in sales by 2021. These companies differ in their relative emphasis on seed versus agrochemical production. Synergies are possible because seeds can be genetically modified for herbicide tolerance or coated with insecticides, enabling joint research and production of both seeds and chemicals to create cost and innovation advantages.

9.7.1 *Data on Seed Market Concentration*

Consider the four-firm concentration ratio (CR4). This equals the market share of the four largest companies in a defined market or industry. A limitation of CR4 is that it does not reveal the composition of sales among the largest four companies; for example, do they have equal shares of sales, or does the company with the largest sales dwarf the other three? For purposes here, it is adequate to know what share of sales is accounted for by the top four companies. The next chapter examines another measure of market concentration.[17]

Table 9.15 shows what percentage of the market for different types of seeds is accounted for by the four biggest firms in terms of sales. The table confirms what was mentioned earlier: agricultural markets are quite heavily

Table 9.15. Concentration in Seed Market, by Type

Country	Maize	Soybean	Wheat & Barley	— Rapeseed	Sunflower
Argentina	73	89	—	—	—
Brazil	97	82	—	—	—
Bulgaria	91	—	71	75	92
Denmark	98	—	83	95	—
France	73	—	—	81	77
Germany	66	—	44	72	—
Hungary	81	—	58	67	88
Mexico	81	—	98	—	—
Poland	57	—	47	62	—
Romania	74	—	60	71	85
Russian Fed.	67	—	38	70	78
Slovakia	75	—	57	59	85
South Africa	99	96	—	—	99
Turkey	89	—	51	—	93
United Kingdom	85	—	74	66	—
Ukraine	80	42	53	72	88
United States	82	69	—	—	—

Note: Each entry is the Four-Firm Concentration Ratio, CR4, market share.
Source: OECD (2018).

[17] For example, the Herfindahl-Hirschman Index (HHI).

Table 9.16. GM Events Approved for Cultivation, 1992–2018, by Firm

Seed	Maize	Soybean	Cotton
Total Events Approved for Cultivation	208	85	58
Syngenta (%) Share	30.8	3.5	5.2
Bayer/Monsanto (%) Share	37.0	65.9	74.1
Dow & DuPont (%) Share	31.3	25.9	15.5

Source: Calculations based on OECD (2018).

concentrated, not only in high-income countries like the U.S. and France but also in middle-income countries like Argentina, Brazil, and South Africa.

There are only a few cases where the set of four largest companies in a market captures less than half (50%) of sales. Table 9.16 shows the concentration in genetically-modified (GM) traits. As the OECD (2018) report noted, measuring the concentration of traits is challenging because of "stacking," the combining of two or more independently engineered traits (for example, herbicide tolerance plus insect resistance) into a single crop variety. If the crop has 100% of the market, should the herbicide-tolerant trait and the insect-resistant trait be allowed to have 100% of the market or 50% each? Consequently, market concentration will be indirectly measured by the "GM events approved for cultivation." Each event corresponds to a distinct GM line, and "approved for cultivation" means that it was legally authorized for commercial planting.

As the above table shows, three companies dominate the GM events. For GM events in cotton, approximately 95% of them are accounted for by the three companies. That said, the OECD (2018) report believes that the cultivation approvals understate the true degree of market concentration. The reason is that approvals count every single molecular event equally, regardless of how much it is actually planted. Thus, looking only at which events are approved tends to understate how much the market is really cornered by a handful of players. Even though dozens of cotton events are approved, farmers in fact only plant two or three of them on most of their acres, and those few top traits are almost all owned by Monsanto, Bayer, and Corteva. So, while Monsanto, Bayer, and Corteva account for about 95% of all approved cotton events, acreage-weighted data on the top ten commercial cotton varieties show that those same three firms control well over 90 percent of planted GM cotton seed sales (OECD, 2018).

Table 9.17 turns to the concentration of IP rights. The table shows how Plant Variety Protection (PVP) certificates (2001–2021) and U.S. plant

Table 9.17. Concentration in IP Rights, by Company

	Plant Variety Protection Certificates Issued 2001–2021			**Plant Patents Issued 1976–2021**		
	All Crops (%)	*GM* (%)	*Non-GM* (%)	All Crops (%)	*GM* (%)	*Non-GM* (%)
Total	8,407	4,092	4,315	17,208	12,117	5,091
Bayer	23.8	35.4	12.8	35.8	42.1	20.7
Corteva	26.3	47.4	6.3	29.7	37.8	10.0
Syngenta	7.6	7.6	7.6	5.4	6.1	3.7
Combined Share	57.7	90.4	26.7	70.9	86.0	34.4

Note: Calculations based on MacDonald *et al.* (2023).

patents (1976–2021) are distributed across all crops, and separately for GM and non-GM varieties. Three firms — Bayer, Corteva, and Syngenta — together hold the vast majority of GM-related rights, but their share of non-GM IP is much lower (around one-third).

9.7.2 *Effects of Market Concentration*

Mergers and IP rights have affected competition, with fewer firms in the industry. This raises concerns about the effect on prices. As Figure 9.5 shows, retail seed prices in the U.S. did increase during the period when market concentration in the seed industry increased. The average price for seeds increased by 270%, and that for GM seeds increased by 463%, during 1990–2020. For perspective, the commodity price inflation over this period was 56%.

However, mergers do not always lead to reduced competition and higher prices. They may also be the source of efficiency gains. Firms can exploit economies of scale by combining the volume of production. The decline in average costs of production can be passed on to consumers. Firms may be able to cut down on duplicative or redundant research, or leverage complementary technologies.[18]

[18]For example, in the DuPont and Pioneer merger of 1999, Pioneer Hi-Bred had hybrid germplasm expertise and DuPont had biotech platforms. These technological assets were complementary.

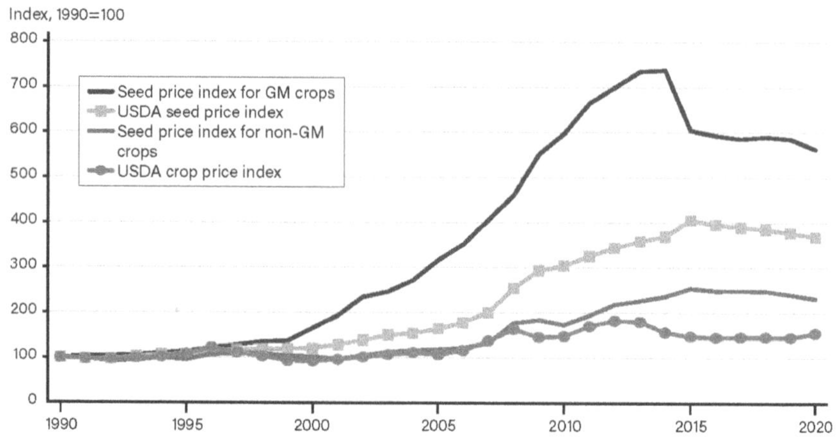

Figure 9.5. U.S. Retail Seed Prices
Source: MacDonald *et al.* (2023), Figure 2, p. 16.

Moreover, seed price increases must be weighed against the returns they provide on R&D and the productivity gains they generate. Higher seed prices (or licensing fees) reward firms for their investment in developing new varieties, while those varieties often reduce farming costs through greater agronomic efficiency, lower fuel, labor, and machinery requirements, and reduced chemical inputs. In many cases, these downstream savings may more than offset the initial price premium. A full cost-benefit analysis — rather than a focus on price alone — is therefore essential.

Figure 9.6 shows the changes in some of the measures of innovation, such as crop $\frac{R\&D}{Sales}$, plant patents, and plant variety protection certificates, where the values in 1990–1995 are normalized to unity.[19]

The R&D to sales ratio is fairly steady, while patents and PVP certificates fluctuate around a rising trend. In no case does it seem that market concentration was associated with harm to innovation. Indeed, Table 9.18 reports some regression results that market concentration had statistically insignificant impacts on seed prices and innovation, after controlling for other factors.

The model was estimated on a cross-section of EU countries in 2016. Innovation is measured by the median number of new variety listings per

[19]Specifically the $\frac{R\&D}{Sales}$ variable is the ratio of crop R&D spending to seed and chemical sales worldwide. It represents the rate of R&D investment of the world's seven largest seed companies.

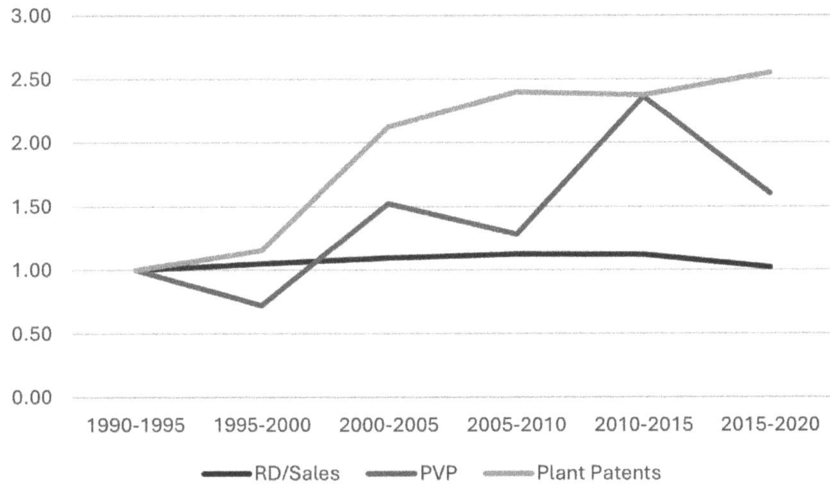

Figure 9.6. Innovation in New Crop Varieties
Source: Calculations based on MacDonald *et al.* (2023).

Table 9.18. Market Concentration on Prices and Innovation

	Dependent Variable			
	Log Average Seed Prices		**Log New Variety Listings**	
Log Market Size	0.140***	0.136***	0.470**	0.432**
Log CR4	0.052	−0.49	−0.035	−0.556
(Log CR4)^2		−0.589		−0.657
Other Controls	Yes	Yes	Yes	Yes
Number of Obs.	87	87	50	50
Adjusted R^2	0.98	0.98	0.35	0.33

Notes: Other controls include Public Breeders' share, Share of Farm-saved Seeds, Crop fixed effects, and Country fixed effects. ***, ** mark significance levels at 1%, 5% respectively.
Source: OECD (2018), Chapter 6.

market (each market being a country-crop pair). In the EU, seeds must be registered on a national list before they can be marketed; thus, the count of national list entries serves as a proxy for innovation, analogous to patent or copyright registrations.

The coefficient of the natural logarithm of CR4, the four-firm concentration ratio, is not significant at conventional levels. The regression models include a quadratic term for the market concentration variable. This is to check whether price changes occur more rapidly with market concentration and to check whether innovation might have an inverted-U relationship with market concentration; that is, initially an increase in market concentration might spur innovation as firms are better able to raise profits, but after some threshold level of market concentration, firms that face reduced competitive threats may lower their innovation efforts. But the quadratic terms are also insignificant. In short, no clear evidence exists that concentration has either boosted innovation (by giving firms bigger profits to reinvest) or stifled it (by letting firms rest on their laurels).

9.7.3 *Implications for Developing Countries*

Developing countries may be impacted by these developments in the market concentration of the commercial seed market with a lag. The reason is that farmers in the developing world mostly rely on informal markets for their seeds rather than on the commercial seed market. The OECD (2018) report indicates that 90 percent of seeds in Sub-Saharan Africa are obtained through informal local markets; for example, through saved seeds or seeds exchanged with neighbors.

But that is changing. Multinationals are steadily expanding into India and Sub-Saharan Africa by acquiring local seed companies. For example, in 2013, DuPont purchased South Africa's Pannar, and Syngenta later acquired MRI, Zambia's largest private seed firm.

As these shifts occur, more and better data are needed on market concentration in the developing and least developed countries in order to understand how global consolidation affects local seed prices, innovation rates, and technology transfer.

9.7.4 *Mitigating Market Concentration*

Several policy measures can mitigate the risks of excessive concentration and preserve an open, innovative seed sector:

1. **Antitrust Enforcement:** Competition authorities should continue scrutinizing large M&A deals and, when necessary, require structural

remedies, such as divestitures of assets or business units, that help maintain an adequate degree of competition.

2. **Public Oversight of Regulatory Science:** Governments or independent agencies should oversee the testing protocols and risk-assessment frameworks that all firms (large, medium, or small) use to demonstrate safety. These methods should be in the public domain to prevent any one company from controlling the demonstration of a product's safety.
3. **Licensing Opportunities:** Encourage the voluntary cross-licensing of essential traits under fair, transparent terms. Where parties cannot agree, mediation or arbitration can set reasonable royalty rates, and when absolutely necessary, compulsory licensing can ensure that critical innovations are accessible.
4. **Access to Germplasm:** Expand international seed-bank networks and support open-germplasm initiatives alongside commercial markets. While open source approaches alone may not fully recoup the high R&D costs of breeding, they can coexist with proprietary models to enhance genetic diversity and support small farmers. (The next section discusses ideas for open biotechnology).
5. **Public R&D Investment:** Public research institutions should continue to fund both fundamental and applied research, particularly areas that may be underinvested in by the private seed market, such as nutritional biofortification (e.g., zinc-rich wheat, iron-enriched beans, agrobiodiversity conservation, and climate-resilience traits). Furthermore, the public sector can take the lead to keep germplasm open at the early stages of research so that all innovators can benefit from shared discoveries and reduced duplicative efforts, and still allow private industry to seek IP protection for the final, marketable varieties.

9.8 Open Biotechnology

An intellectual property regime is not the only kind of system for stimulating innovation and technology transfer. An alternative system is open innovation, in which innovators share information within and between organizations, collaborate, and do not, in general, make their innovations proprietary. Open innovators utilize external resources and capabilities to source ideas. They share their innovative outputs freely, and organizations work collaboratively. IPRs are typically eschewed. Open innovation is applicable to software development, agriculture, biotechnology, and pharmaceuticals.

There are similar examples of collective invention from history — in the iron industry, machine tool industry, and scientific instrument industry.[20] They build on principles listed as follows:

- Free-revealing
- Collaborative Research
- Collective Invention
- User-driven innovation

What are the incentives for sharing and revealing information? For one thing, the opportunity cost of finding every solution to a problem by oneself is high. It is prudent sometimes to outsource that task to others; for example, an innovator can post online or in a community messaging board, a problem the innovator is interested in seeing solved and the attempts made thus far, allowing others working on the same problem to build on the innovator's efforts. Free revealing can indeed serve one's self-interest. Furthermore, from the point of view of the law of large numbers, it is useful to collaborate and work collectively so that ideas and designs can be tested by multiple parties, whether by many engineers working on a design problem or by many agricultural researchers working on a cultivation issue. The more who try out and test a *solution*, the greater the validity and robustness of the solution. Again, it pays to share and to let others have access to information. It is also useful to engage the users or consumers to partake in open development; end users know more about their own needs and can better communicate them to the developers. The more widely agents participate, the greater the odds of breakthroughs and the possibility of seeing a problem solved and adopted widely.

This section first discusses open innovation in general, then it discusses biotechnology in particular and how it relates to "open source" innovation, then examines some recent examples of open innovation in agriculture and biotechnology, and lastly addresses some policy issues, including the relevance of open innovation for developing countries.

9.8.1 *Open Innovation*

An open innovation system can be contrasted with a closed one, such as an IPR system. Under a closed system, the chief focus is on the expected payoff to R&D and on ensuring that it at least covers the upfront cost of R&D, which was the focus of chapters 3 and 4. Commercial laboratories precisely

[20] See Allen (1983).

seek IPR protection in order to achieve a net positive payoff. However, the IPR system relies on exclusivity and secrecy. Exclusivity helps prevent the competitive dissipation of expected profits. Secrecy is needed in order to preserve the novelty of the innovation. An innovation cannot be patented if it is not novel, and it is not novel if it is public knowledge. Yet, exclusivity and secrecy can impede knowledge creation and diffusion.[21] Breakthroughs in knowledge and technical solutions depend on people being able to make connections among hunches and ideas, to follow leads, to view the problem from different angles, and to get the broad perspectives of different individuals with various expertise and experiences. However, in the commercial laboratory framework, ideas, hunches, and leads tend to be heavily guarded. Firms do not want to lose their competitive advantage, and thus do their utmost to prevent the leakage of sensitive information, even within the same organization. As Johnson (2010) discusses, innovative breakthroughs arise when various pieces of the puzzle can be brought together, when ideas can be cross-fertilized or exapted (that is, where an idea developed for one problem is used for another), and when discoveries are made purposefully as well as serendipitously. Ridley (2010) develops a parallel theme about how ideas need to mate and produce new knowledge.

The point is that more open, collaborative innovation networks are conducive to fostering innovation breakthroughs. In some cases, the commercial model of innovation may stifle breakthroughs if it operates in a tightly closed environment where ideas are sequestered. For instance, two companies may each possess some piece of knowledge that the other lacks, but the combined knowledge could result in a technological breakthrough. In the case of Xerox Corporation, several of its rejected technologies became commercial successes. Other companies were able to find valuable uses for them, such as Synoptics, a company that specializes in Ethernet technologies. The value of these ex-Xerox technologies could not be realized within the confines of Xerox laboratories, but once they mixed with the ideas and knowledge bases of other companies, they proved to be useful. As another example, IBM struggled financially in the early 1990s, after many years of commercial success. The market for its mainframe systems was evaporating, and other companies were developing product niches in software and workstations. To survive, IBM had undergone a transformation from an essentially closed-innovation system to a more open one. It realized that it could not do everything on its own, and thus utilized the technologies of other companies and embraced open source software and open technology

[21] See Chesbrough (2003).

standards (such as the Linux operating system and the Java programming language).[22] Though IBM does not profit directly from these external technologies, those technologies help consumers derive more value from IBM products. Thus, while a closed commercial laboratory helps protect a firm's competitive advantage and prevent copying, ideas are less mobile and inhibited from "meeting" other ideas so as to contribute to technological improvements or breakthroughs.

Figure 9.7 provides a sense of the importance of open innovation from a historical perspective. The bar charts show a tally of major ideas and innovations by source. Was the innovation developed by an individual or a network of individuals? Was the innovation intended for the marketplace (where it could be sold or licensed) or allowed to flow freely into the public domain? An example of an individual's innovation that was developed for the market is air-conditioning; an example of an individual's innovation not developed for the market is X-rays; a network's innovation developed for the market is the internal combustion engine; and a network's innovation not developed for the market is the global positioning system (GPS).

Between 1400 and 1600, markets were not as well developed, and opportunities for networking innovations were limited. Technological breakthroughs were few, but what little was created was the result of individual efforts in a non-market setting. In the modern era (1800 to the present), there is an increase in market-driven innovations, but note that the innovative breakthroughs come predominantly from decentralized, non-market activity and are the result of group effort across organizations

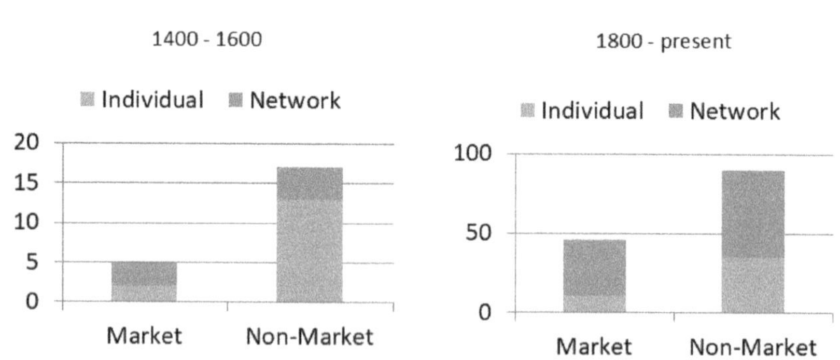

Figure 9.7. Count of Breakthrough Ideas and Innovations, 1400–Present
Source: Calculations based on Johnson (2010).

[22]These case studies can be found in Chesbrough (2003).

and regions. The inventor working alone in a commercial laboratory making a breakthrough does occur, but it is relatively uncommon. The reason for the high quantity of breakthroughs under open innovation is that it facilitates knowledge mobility and allows multiple parties to draw connections among clues and to exploit leads. This is not to argue that commercial innovation, along with IPRs, is not successful, for it is. The important lesson here is that innovation is not wholly dependent upon IPRs, and that in some cases, the proprietary system may inhibit innovation by reducing the communication of ideas. Open innovation can and should be utilized to complement commercial endeavors.

9.8.2 *Open Source Biotech*

According to the *UN Convention on Biological Diversity (CBD)*, "biotechnology covers any technological application that uses biological systems, living organisms, or derivatives thereof, to make or modify products or processes for specific use." The Green Revolution typifies early agricultural biotechnology innovation. Developing economies are seen as gene-rich in their biodiversity. When Heller and Eisenberg (1998) wrote about the anticommons effect of IPRs, the application was in biotechnology. Expressed sequence tags (EST) are an important research tool in gene discovery and sequence identification. Openness in research is a critical means of avoiding the high transaction costs of negotiation among diverse IP holders and preventing the underutilization of biotechnological innovations.

The OpenBio movement emulates the Free and Open Source Software (FOSS) movement. Free and open development is a process where innovations are shared freely rather than fenced off with IP claims. Distributions of modified technology may be controlled so that the modification also remains free and open. While IP recognition, like a patent or PBR, may be sought and granted, the license to use, redistribute, and modify the technology is provided gratis by the developer. It is typical of free and open development for users of innovations to be actively involved in the innovation process. FOSS is an example of free and open development, where the source code is readily available and freely redistributable.

Both software and biotechnology have some commonalities between software codes and genetic codes.[23] These codes are instructions behind a larger

[23]Dawkins (2004) draws an interesting analogy: "genes are software subroutines that perform cellular operations."

operating unit, whether it is a computer program or a cell. Some areas of biotechnology, such as computational biology or bioinformatics, are largely an extension of the FOSS movement.[24] In both fields, innovations can be cumulative and sequential, and constitute tools of research. Both the Open-Bio and FOSS movements were driven in large part by the proliferation of proprietary rights, whether patent rights or plant breeders' rights, and by concerns about the ability to use innovations and afford them. Another concern is that the subject matter may not be wholly appropriate for IPRs. Software, for example, involves mathematical algorithms, and life sciences involve scientific discoveries.[25]

9.8.3 *Examples in Agriculture and Biotechnology*

Analogous to the FOSS movement just discussed, a community has formed around open biotechnology and other open development projects in agriculture and the life sciences. These projects not only avoid some of the pitfalls associated with closed and proprietary innovation, such as the proliferation and fragmentation of rights, royalty fees, and the costs of procuring rights and enforcing rights, but they also foster and boost innovation.

These open innovation activities can be categorized in Table 9.19.

Table 9.19. Types of Open Activities

Types of Open Activities
Open Standards
Facilitate sharing of data (e.g., Clinical Data Interchange) Promote interoperability
Open Innovation
Share findings, participatory research and development.
Open Licensing
Non-exclusive, royalty-free. Share improvements and modifications under the same terms. Does not preclude commercialization and the seeking of IP rights (but with conditions).

[24]For example, computational biologists can use a public domain sequence search tool like BLAST.

[25]See Isaac and Park (2009) for more details.

What are the activities engaged in by "Open Development"? Open Bio includes setting technology standards to facilitate the sharing of data, platform development, and interoperability; e.g., clinical data interchange, standards, and tools for registering and exchanging biological data stored on multiple hosts.

Open innovation does not preclude commercial development. Technological improvements that arise from open innovation can be patented or commercialized. However, the licensees typically agree not to assert IP claims against other members of the *club*. The terms of licensing are designed to preempt modified open innovations from becoming proprietary and thereby encumbering research tools with proprietary claims.

Table 9.20 shows several examples of open innovation going on in agriculture and biotechnology, as it relates to medicines and food.[26]

Data from the International HAP MAP Project are public domain. Users agree not to inhibit access to the data to others and to share data with others who agree to the same conditions. Users may patent subsequent innovations but must not prevent others from accessing the project's data. The SNP Consortium also allows an SNP map to be freely accessible to all. The SNP example is illuminating because commercial interests, such as large pharmaceutical companies, joined with a charitable organization *Wellcome Trust* and academia to pursue open development in order to avoid a labyrinth of cross-licensing agreements and associated transaction costs.[27]

Food production and innovation benefit from collaborative research, owing to the dependence and interaction among upstream and downstream partners. All of these examples fit the definition of open innovation in biotechnology, especially in combining internal and external resources, having a vested interest in the sharing of knowledge, know-how, and resources, and maintaining resources.

9.8.4 *Policy Issues*

Several useful questions to close with are as follows:

[26]Genomics deals with the analysis of DNA sequences, while proteomics deals with the analysis of the set of proteins. Computational biology methods analyze complex biological data. SNPs are the most common type of genetic variation among people. They can act like biological markers for scientists to locate genes associated with disease.

[27]See Contreras (2025).

Table 9.20. Examples of Open Bio-tech

Bioinformatics	Computational Biology. Study genomics and proteomics.
International Hap Map	Map common patterns in the genome.
SNP Consortium	Database of single nucleotide polymorphisms that are important research tools.
CAMBIA (Center for the Application of Molecular Biology to International, Agriculture) Australia	Non-profit institute developing new technologies, paradigms and research tools; e.g., transgenic innovations. Oversees *Lens Project*, an open innovation platform for searching scholarly and patented knowledge.
Agro-Food Sector	Shared interest in natural resources, specific know-how, and combining external knowledge and internal innovation (e.g., secret recipes). Companies such as Heinz, Unilever, and Barilla have participated in open innovation platforms. Examples include the Hungarian wine industry, Dutch tomatoes.
Decorum Plants	Network of cut flower growers. Collaborative product development and branding.

1. Do open-biotechnology activities crowd out proprietary innovation or are they complementary to it?
2. Is Open Innovation sustainable?
3. Is it suitable for developing countries?

Some tentative thoughts are that open innovation probably does not crowd out proprietary innovation too significantly since open innovation tends to focus on more basic R&D, especially on research tools, that have wide public benefits. The share and the scale of research and development under proprietary innovation still dwarf those of open innovation. Saint-Paul (2003) develops an economic growth model to show that philanthropic innovation may displace proprietary innovation. But this happens in a case where the philanthropic innovation results in a good that is a *substitute* for the proprietary good. This reduces the sales and profits of the proprietor, and additionally, the philanthropic sector uses up human capital that could otherwise be employed in the proprietary sector. However, philanthropic innovation and proprietary innovation can also be complementary. Specifically, if the innovation resulting from philanthropy reduces the cost of private innovation, it can stimulate private innovation.

Is open innovation profitable? It may not be in the commercial sense, but it is rewarding. Otherwise, many people and organizations would not be participating in it voluntarily. Some researchers or creators engage in it for personal rewards, such as for one's reputation and for the satisfaction of finding solutions (e.g., software code-sharing on the web for programs such as R or Python, or the posting of medical commentaries and suggested treatments on blogs). Those take intellectual labor, but people do derive enjoyment. But most importantly, if what has been argued thus far is reasonable, then open innovation is practical: it facilitates innovation and development. It avoids some of the concerns with IPRs, such as the (high) cost of innovation and the blocking or impeding of innovation because some other party holds the rights to important inputs or competing outputs. Furthermore, it can actually be profitable in that participants can earn income from complementary assets. For example, a company that participates in seed varieties or disease treatment might sell equipment or consulting services, or have some other seeds and treatments that are proprietary. Open innovation may enhance the value of those complementary assets.

Regarding the impacts for developing countries, open innovation is beneficial since it eases their burdens from high royalties and licensing fees for the use of IP (foreign or local). Among the specific factors are reduced transaction costs, reduced litigation costs (since no one is asserting IP rights), increased knowledge spillovers, and reduced dependence on large companies, companies that possess market power due to their ownership of proprietary knowledge inputs. Also, as was seen earlier in the chapter, agriculture is still a relatively large share of the developing world's economies. Food security concerns are higher, and biotechnology serves a vital interest in this world. It makes sense for developing country research to be invested in OpenBio. Furthermore, at their stage of development, developing economy innovations are more incremental and adaptive. Those countries need access to basic science and research tools — the enabling technologies. Furthermore, participation and collaboration offer opportunities for learning by doing and learning by watching. Open innovation could foster skill development and human capital accumulation. Open innovation may serve as a good model for development projects in AI (artificial intelligence), particularly in providing access to technology and eliciting input from the global South on training AI, as well as mitigating risks.

It should be noted that the OpenBio approach has some disadvantages compared to intellectual property protection. This arises in fields of biotechnology that are inherently capital-intensive, where large labs and other physical capital investments are required. In addition, substantial sunk costs may arise from the need to comply with regulations (on health and safety) in order to get to market. Venture capitalists may have no incentive to fund biotech startups that cannot claim adequate proprietary rights in their innovations.

While user innovation has been important for research tools in bioinformatics and computational biology, it is much less plausible that consumers of biopharmaceuticals will propose improvements, and perhaps scarcely conceivable that even the most sophisticated consumer will be implementing improvements. This raises questions as to whether OpenBio really has a lot of prospects in biopharmaceutical development. End-user innovation appears minimal, modularity is low, and the costs of safety testing and regulatory compliance remain high. Prospects for OpenBio are therefore stronger in basic R&D or in projects centered on platforms and enabling technologies

While the OpenBio movement can expand developing-country access to the data and research tools essential for indigenous biotechnology efforts, it is unlikely, on its own, to generate the radical biopharmaceutical innovations urgently needed in the developing world; for example, to address neglected tropical diseases. Instead, OpenBio is likely to be most effective when complemented by targeted government research support.

Chapter 10

Organization and Markets

10.1 Introduction

This chapter examines a medley of topics concerning organizations that set standards for essential patents and markets for trading patent assets. From these topics, it becomes evident that the motivations for patenting extend well beyond the appropriation of returns to innovation. Firms view patents not merely as legal protections but as strategic business assets that can be leveraged through licensing, sales, or enforcement to generate revenue and maintain competitive advantages.

Why do companies sell patents? In part, sales reflect business restructuring. A firm may divest a particular division to focus on another, and thus unload intellectual property that is not a good fit with its new strategic focus. Selling patents can also generate immediate income and reduce costs, particularly the patent maintenance fees that must be paid wherever their patent rights remain in force around the world.

Why do companies buy patents? Acquiring patents offers a way to access technologies developed externally, without having to undertake the internal R&D. These acquisitions may complement their existing product lines or facilitate entry into new markets. Firms may also acquire patents for defensive purposes; that is, to build portfolios that can be used in cross-licensing negotiations or as bargaining chips in litigation.

Some companies acquire patents not to manufacture a product but to extract income through enforcement actions. These are often referred to as "patent trolls" — entities that maintain patent portfolios solely to profit from litigation or the threat of it, extracting royalties or damages from operating firms.

The rise in patenting activity — whether motivated by appropriation or strategic concerns — has fueled worries about a "patent explosion" and the emergence of "patent thickets." These thickets can raise barriers to innovation, as overlapping patent rights may require multiple licenses to practice a single invention. Additionally, the cumulative burden of multiple licensing fees — known as royalty stacking — can become a cost burden that hinders innovation. This chapter addresses concerns about patent thickets, patent hold-ups, and royalty stacking.

Patent ownership can turn over; patent rights can be reassigned and transferred. This chapter demonstrates how secondary patent markets enable firms to operate more effectively under uncertainty, provided they have access to such markets. Because patent resale makes patenting decisions reversible, it allows innovation and R&D investments to remain resilient amid uncertainty shocks. Through patenting, firms can acquire real options; that is, rights to expand a project, delay it, or abandon it at some future date. These options have value and are termed "real" because they involve tangible or intellectual property assets rather than purely financial instruments.

However, from an international perspective, secondary patent markets remain small and real options are limited. In developing economies that face substantial economic volatility, commodity price fluctuations, and market uncertainty, there should be greater consideration of adapting secondary patent markets as part of an IP-driven economic development strategy. Such markets could strengthen institutional capacity and enable these countries to better utilize intellectual property for economic growth. This approach is rarely considered in developing economies; consequently, lessons from secondary patent markets in advanced economies offer valuable insights for policymakers seeking to strengthen their innovation systems.

10.2 Case Study: Tale of Two Tech Companies

For many years, Apple and Samsung were longtime partners, with Apple outsourcing key components such as flash memory, screens, and processors to Samsung. The partnership extended well beyond simple outsourcing arrangements. Apple became one of Samsung's largest customers, at one point becoming its top customer. This partnership changed dramatically when Samsung developed its smartphone using Google's Android operating system that incorporated design elements similar to Apple's iPhone, including the front face layout and grid of icons.[1]

In October 2010, Apple approached Samsung to warn that the latter's phones and tablets were infringing on Apple's patents, demanding licensing fees of $30 per phone and $40 per tablet sold.[2] When Samsung refused, Apple filed suit in April 2011. Samsung responded with countersuits in multiple countries, including Japan, leveraging its ownership of 3G patents that were classified as standard essential patents (SEPs), which enable device compatibility and interoperability. Apple argued that these SEPs should be available under fair, reasonable, and non-discriminatory (FRAND) terms, a topic explored later in this chapter.

The litigation sprawled across multiple jurisdictions, including the United States, the European Union, Asia, and Australia, resulting in inconsistent rulings and awards. The overlapping intellectual property rights led to disputes over design patents (ornamental appearance), extent of damages (specific contributions versus total profits), standard essential patents, and licensing rates.[3]

The case study illustrates both the high stakes of IP litigation and the volatility of patent disputes: Apple won a $1 billion verdict in August 2012, only to see the USPTO question the validity of Apple's patents in December 2012, followed by a U.S. International Trade Commission ruling in favor of Samsung in June 2013.[4] The dispute was ultimately settled confidentially in June 2018.[5] The case highlights the massive resources that each side expended — resources that likely diverted time and attention away from productive innovation.

[1] https://quandarypeak.com/2013/09/smartphone-patent-wars-the-apple-vs-samsung-legal-battle/.

[2] https://www.cnet.com/tech/tech-industry/apple-offered-patent-licensing-deal-to-samsung-before-trial/.

[3] Even while litigation was underway, the two firms maintained their business relationship within the supply chain: Samsung continued to supply iPhone processors to Apple. Later, in 2014, Apple switched to doing business with Taiwan Semiconductor Manufacturing Company (TSMC). See https://www.investopedia.com/articles/markets/102714/how-apple-and-samsung-compare-and-coexist.asp.

[4] https://www.npr.org/2013/06/05/188812758/u-s-trade-commission-rules-apple-violated-samsung-patents.

[5] https://www.nytimes.com/2018/06/27/technology/apple-samsung-smartphone-patent.html.

A central issue that emerged was whether an infringer should pay damages only for the specific patented contribution to a multi-feature device or for the total profits from the device.[6] For example, if Apple's patented technology contributes only 30% of the value of Samsung's phone, should Samsung pay damages based on that contribution alone or on the entire phone's profits? Critics argued that limiting damages to specific contributions would encourage infringement, as violators could essentially treat patent violations as compulsory licensing arrangements with minimal financial consequences beyond what they would have paid for a legitimate license.

10.3 Patent Thickets

In high-technology industries, companies file extensive patent applications and engage heavily in cross-licensing due to the cumulative and sequential nature of their innovations and the modular architecture of their technologies. These companies produce complex products consisting of multiple components that must operate collectively to achieve functionality or desired properties. They have been the primary drivers of the patent boom since the emergence of the Internet era.

Concerns have emerged regarding the proprietary ownership of diversely held complementary inputs and the high transaction costs of negotiating across multiple parties. A potential anti-commons effect may arise when technologies become underutilized because fragmented ownership blocks access by different parties. Unlike a traditional commons problem where the absence of property rights leads to overuse (such as overgrazing on unowned farmland), patent thickets create the opposite problem: too many parties holding different rights and demanding fees leads to the underutilization of technologies. Moreover, decentralized, overlapping patents — where multiple patents cover the same invention or functional unit — result in wasteful duplication of licensing fees.

The patenting explosion since the early 1990s, led by technology giants like Apple and Samsung, has intensified concerns about patent thickets. These dense webs of overlapping patent claims create potential barriers to innovation and commercialization.

[6]https://www.lexology.com/library/detail.aspx?g=1435c64a-75b8-4b0d-abfd-33629ec34abd.

The primary concern is that users require permission to utilize patented technologies, necessitating license negotiations with patent holders. With numerous patents covering related technologies, users must pay multiple fees and negotiate with many parties independently. Absent a central coordinator (such as a standard-setting organization, discussed later), a new innovator might need licenses for patents X, Y, and Z, each owned by different firms.

A secondary concern arises because patents are often granted too broadly and build incrementally on existing technologies, making it easy to inadvertently infringe on prior art. When multiple patents cover overlapping technological ground, users may face duplicative licensing fees, effectively paying twice or thrice for access to the same underlying innovation.

These challenges have led to various institutional responses, including patent pools (consortia of firms that agree to cross-license patents to one another or third parties), mergers and acquisitions, joint ventures, and the development of firm reputations for reasonable licensing practices.

10.4 Defensive Patenting

Fears of overdependence on competitors' patents have led to *strategic patenting* behavior; namely, the accumulation of patent portfolios primarily to acquire bargaining chips in cross-licensing negotiations rather than to appropriate returns from innovation. This strategy ensures that if one company depends on another's patents, the dependent company can leverage its own patent assets to achieve more favorable licensing terms. Like the game of nuclear deterrence, each side can try to preempt conflict by possessing large patent portfolios.

This phenomenon explains the patent paradox identified by Hall and Ziedonis (2001): why do firms in the semiconductor industry patent heavily despite claiming in surveys that patent protection matters less for appropriating returns from innovation?[7]

The answer lies in defensive patenting strategies designed to preempt hold-up situations and avoid becoming a net importer of patented technologies (or net payer of licensing fees). Firms accumulate patent portfolios

[7] As discussed in Chapters 5 and 6, for semiconductors and other IT technologies, short product cycles often render patent protection less important than lead time advantages.

Table 10.1. Explaining the Patent Paradox

Dependent Variable: Patent Counts			
Period	**Before Major Patent Reforms (1979–1982)**	**During Major Patent Reforms (1984–1988)**	**After Major Patent Reforms (1989–1993)**
Log (R&D per worker)	0.457**	0.530**	0.041
Log (Capital per worker)	−0.030	0.128	0.574***

Note: Other Controls: Firm Size, Texas Instrument dummy, etc; ***, ** denote statistical significance at the 1% and 5% levels, respectively.

Source: Hall and Ziedonis (2001).

as defensive assets, which may partially explain the overall patent explosion. Without such defensive portfolios, firms risk paying substantial licensing fees while simultaneously facing infringement accusations. The costs of litigation are considerable, and injunctions can be devastating. A court-ordered shutdown during a trial and investigation can cost a firm millions of dollars per day.

Evidence for strategic patenting motives comes from Hall and Ziedonis's (2001) analysis of the U.S. semiconductor industry. The authors analyze 95 firms from 1979 to 1995, revealing a striking pattern. As Table 10.1 shows, after patent reforms, the R&D coefficient becomes statistically insignificant while the capital coefficient becomes substantially significant. A high stock of capital per worker indicates significant sunk costs, making firms more vulnerable to hold-up. The fact that capital per worker becomes significant after patent reforms suggests that semiconductor firms grew increasingly concerned about hold-up risks and responded by accumulating patent portfolios. Conversely, the insignificant R&D coefficient after reforms indicates that appropriating returns from innovation became a less important motive for patenting, supporting the defensive patenting hypothesis.

10.5 Standard Essential Patents

Some background motivation is first provided, and then some definitions and explanations for their relevance to IP.

10.5.1 *Network Effects*

A good is subject to network effects if the value of a good varies positively with the number of users of the good. Consider, for example, *WhatsApp*, the app for messaging and calling using a device's internet connection. Suppose only one person were on it. What is the value of the app to the consumer? Zero. Its value derives essentially from there being a large community of users. Likewise, an airline flight between any two cities enjoys network effects if either or both cities are a hub. Consumers also value an operating system like *Windows* for its large network of users. Moreover, consumers have the technological benefits of asking tech support-type questions to the many other users of a networked good (such as "how do I do this?" or "why does my system do that?"). The enlarged market motivates innovators to target their efforts on creating inputs, accessories, or complementary goods that work well with the networked good (for example, developing software programs to run on Windows).[8]

Network effects create *positive feedback* loops: success breeds success, failure breeds failure. This occurs in elections too, where the leading candidate gets more supporters and financial backers. Other politicians see a greater probability of being selected for a cabinet position or ambassadorship by aligning with the leading candidate than the lagging candidate. Campaign donors see greater odds of having their causes fulfilled and thus anticipate a higher return on their contributions from backing the leading candidate. Then, with more funding and political support, the leading candidate's lead widens.

Under positive feedback effects, history matters. Outcomes exhibit *path dependence*, whereby a current outcome is shaped by past decisions or events. For example, a university may be established on a farmland for purposes of peace and quiet. Once it establishes a strong science and engineering program, high technology companies begin clustering around the university to engage in university-industry R&D collaborations. Soon, the university attracts more top students and faculty, and subsequently, the industrial area around it expands, providing even more resources for joint research. Other complementary firms, such as IP firms and venture capitalists, settle in the area. Over time, memories fade as to why the university was located there in the first place.

---

[8]This explains why more tech savvy gadgets are installed on cars than on small planes, like the "bush planes" in remote areas like Alaska. Innovators can better recoup their investments in a larger market.

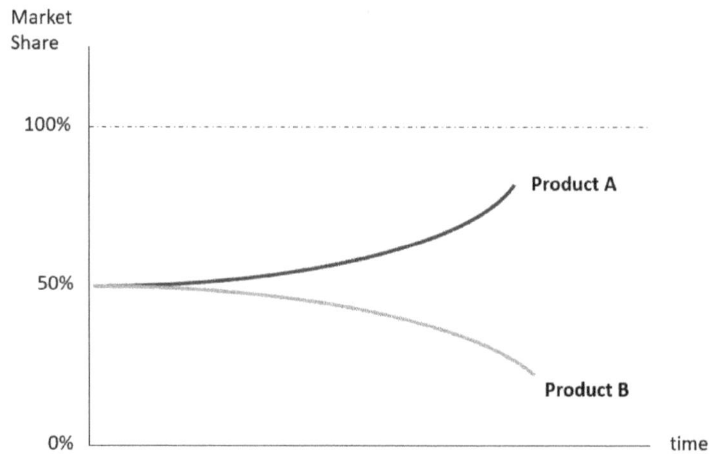

Figure 10.1. Tipping Point

Once a critical mass of users (or sponsors) is reached, network effects may lead to a tipping point where a product achieves market dominance, or where the market "locks in" to a particular technology, as illustrated in Figure 10.1.

Examples include the VHS pushing out Beta Max, two different types of video recording formats.[9] Or Blu Ray ousting HD DVD (recording disks), or the Qwerty keyboard winning over the Dvorak. In the end, whether the technologically superior (or inferior) good emerged is an open debate. Regardless, the path-dependent outcome is the result of network effects more than product quality.

Several lessons that emerge from network effects for business strategies are listed as follows:

- Importance of an early start for companies.
- Building up the customer base. Keep the price point reasonably low.

[9]Neither the VHS or Beta Max tapes were compatible in each other's video players. Initially, VHS products had the advantage of slightly more users. Consequently, more VHS players were sold than Beta Max players. Video stores, like *Blockbuster*, then stocked more movies in VHS format than in Beta Max format as more customers were renting VHS tapes. Gradually, it was costly for movie rental stores to stock duplicates in different formats, and therefore, they chose to go with the VHS format. Simultaneously, consumers were purchasing more VHS players since VHS options were more abundant at stores, and so on.

- Inclusiveness of network.[10]
- Importance of product and technical standards

It is the standards that will be emphasized here. The value of a good is enhanced with adoption, but two or more different standards in the marketplace will limit network effects since the market will be divided, and will remain so as long as products are not interchangeable; for example, an android app cannot be used on an i-phone and an iOS app cannot be used on an android phone. Companies should have an incentive to set a standard and produce a good that is essential for other products and uses, be they an operating system, a communications protocol, a file format, a container design, codes for banking, a programming language, infrastructure, and so forth.

10.5.2 *Standards*

As Maskus (2012) indicates, "a standard is a precise technical statement offering the engineering specifications of how a particular technology works and how ... other technologies may connect to it." Standards enable interoperability, whereby the systems and devices of different manufacturers can communicate and interact; for example, WiFi standards allow WiFi-enabled products, like phones and tablets, to connect and communicate regardless of brand. Email protocols like SMTP, IMAP, and POP3 allow different email services like GMAIL, Yahoo, and Outlook to exchange messages. Standards ensure product compatibility with existing goods and infrastructure, such as electrical plugs fitting into power sockets, toilet tanks connecting to toilet bowls (and the flush valve and fill valves inside the tanks fitting into holes of known dimensions).

Time was when connecting peripheral devices, like an external drive, mouse, or speaker, to a computer was a jumble. Different kinds of connectors, serial ports, parallel ports, and different kinds of cables made mixing and matching products very difficult, if not impossible. Then, along came a standardized interface, the USB (Universal Serial Bus), developed by a consortium of technology companies (IBM, Intel, Microsoft, and Compaq), which unified industries. Now, the keyboard, mouse, and smartphone can

[10]America Online (AOL) long ago kept its instant messaging app for subscribers only, thereby losing the opportunity to build a wide network of users.

connect seamlessly to hardware, like laptops and desktops. Improved product compatibility and interoperability facilitated the building of networks and the generation of network effects.

This is not to suggest that different standards cannot coexist in competition, nor that complete consolidation of standards — akin to a full tipping point — is necessary. Globally, for example, electrical voltage standards vary between 220V (common in Europe and Asia) and 110V (common in the United States and Canada); paper sizes differ between the A4 and letter formats; and measurement systems are divided between metric and imperial. At the industrial level, competition exists between Microsoft Office and Google Workspace, between gasoline- and diesel-powered vehicles, and — prior to the adoption of 4G/5G — between GSM (Global System for Mobile) and CDMA (Code Division Multiple Access) technologies in the wireless telecommunications market.

Consumer preferences and switching costs (and producer supply constraints) may be at work to sustain different standards. A product cannot be viewed in isolation. Other products help to reinforce the standard; for example, a tape/disc and the player must be compatible. Or in the case of vehicles, cars must be compatible with roads: a left-wheeled car goes with roads where cars drive on the right side, and a right-wheeled car with roads where cars drive on the left side. The cost of switching standards must take into account a multitude of products that need to be swapped out.

On September 3, 1967, Sweden switched from driving on the left to driving on the right. That day is known as *Dagen H*, or H Day. As Figure 10.2 shows, the transition was a messy affair and captures the kind of gridlock that would happen under product incompatibility.[11]

10.5.3 *Relevance to IP*

Standards can be formed formally by institutions, such as governments that set safety requirements, or by industry consortia, such as *Standard Setting Organizations (SSO)*, which will be discussed in the next section. Or standards can emerge organically via market dominance or by the interplay of market forces. The issue is: what if a private company has a patent to the technology that is a standard? Refer to this as a *standard essential patent (SEP)*.

[11] Image is from https://en.wikipedia.org/wiki/Dagen_H.

Figure 10.2. Dagen H

Even a regular patent confers market power to the patent owner by granting the ability to preclude others from using the covered technology.[12] An SEP provides additional market power by making the patented technology essential for industry compliance, giving the firm significant competitive advantages over others.

Concerns about anticompetitive behavior stem from various examples. For instance, Amazon provides a platform for online marketplaces but can "self-preference," prioritizing its own private-label products over those of third-party sellers. Google Search may likewise prioritize its own services in search results. Meta's algorithms may favor content from its own platforms (Instagram, WhatsApp) over external links. Google's algorithms may push organic search results for Google competitors down, forcing competitors to spend more on ads to maintain visibility.

The App Store requires developers to use Apple's in-app purchase system for digital transactions. In 2020, Apple removed Epic Games, the maker of *Fortnite*, from its store because Epic bypassed Apple's payment system and avoided paying the 30% commission. The federal court largely ruled in favor of Apple, finding that Apple did not violate federal antitrust laws in

[12]The temporary exclusivity provided by patent protection may also give the firm more time to build a network of users and turn its technology into a standard. If the patent later happens to be found statutorily invalid, by that time, users may have already become accustomed to the firm's technology.

most respects.[13] However, the court found that Apple violated California's Unfair Competition Law by prohibiting developers from informing users about alternative payment methods outside the app (like Venmo or credit card purchases), and issued an injunction requiring Apple to allow such communications.

Thus, in the case of patents, the SEP holder could refuse to license to rivals or charge them exorbitant fees. Moreover, innovation and commercialization can be adversely affected in cases where innovation is cumulative and sequential. Technologies are functionally linked: later innovation A cannot function without earlier innovation B. This is a problem if B is an SEP. The problem is compounded when a product requires multiple inputs working in concert, each of which is covered by a patent that is deemed "standard essential." And if multiple companies developed these standard technologies, the ownership of SEPs is fragmented, and the claims of ownership are overlapping.

High transaction costs would result if every user or developer had to negotiate one-on-one with every owner of essential technologies. Failure to come to an agreement would be harmful to consumers and other producers who invested in a standard. They may have designed their operations or business practices around standards and thus face higher switching costs to shift to alternative standards, if any. If developers are forced to pay higher licensing fees, they will likely pass their costs on to consumers. In the final analysis, the goal of standardization — ensuring interoperability — is undermined when SEP owners block access to essential technologies.

10.6 Standard Setting Organizations

Standard-setting organizations, or SSOs, are industry consortia that develop and maintain technical standards to ensure the compatibility and interoperability of products across different producers. Examples include the MPEG (Motion Picture Experts Group) which developed standards for digital video and audio compression, IEEE (Institute of Electrical and Electronics Engineers) for WiFi and Bluetooth standards, ISO (International Organization for Standardization) for information technology standards, and ETSI (European Telecommunications Standards Institute) which develops

[13]See https://www.macworld.com/article/674839/apple-removes-fortnite-from-app-stores-epic-games-sues-apple.html.

standards in ICT (information and communications technology).[14] The core roles of SSOs are listed as follows:

- Define the technical specifications (e.g., WiFi, USB, 5G).
- Determine which technologies should be included in a standard, but the SSO does not itself declare which patents are essential.
- Review disclosures of SEPs. Standard essential patents are self-declared by patent holders. SSOs do not independently verify "essentiality."[15]
- Establish licensing rules, usually requiring SEPs to be licensed on fair, reasonable, and non-discriminatory (FRAND) terms (see below).

Disputes about SEP validity and the enforcement of licensing agreements are handled through courts or arbitration boards, and not with SSOs. The members of SSOs are mostly private companies (namely, large, global technology companies), some academic institutions, and some government agencies. Members are predominantly from the U.S., Europe, Japan, and China. Only 10% are from developing countries.[16]

10.6.1 *A FRAND to Lean on*

The purpose of FRAND licensing for standard essential patents is to strike a balance between competing interests. On one hand, SEP holders possess additional market power compared to regular patent holders; on the other hand, technology implementers need affordable access to essential technologies. The implementer who is granted a license must also accept the FRAND terms in good faith.

The tricky aspect of FRAND, needless to say, is determining what is fair, reasonable, and non-discriminatory. Details on this go beyond the scope of this book. Suffice it to say that fees and royalty rates are specific to the technology, industry, and market demand. Among the factors to consider are: (1) a baseline based on comparable technologies and the terms set in prior licensing agreements; (2) the technology's value added over existing alternatives; and (3) proportional contribution of an SEP to the total standard (i.e., whether it is a major, essential component or a minor element).

---

[14]ETSI is a partner in the *Third Generation Partnership Project (3GPP)* which developed the fifth generation of wireless technologies, 5G.

[15]See ETSI IPR Policy: https://www.etsi.org/intellectual-property-rights#mytoc0.

[16]See https://www.iso.org/about/members.

10.6.2 *Declarations of SEPs*

SSO deliberations can be high-stakes as companies vie to include their technologies in a standard or strategically withhold essential patents. Firms have motivations both to underdeclare essential patents and to overdeclare them. On one hand, firms may not disclose some truly essential patents, perhaps strategically to attract higher royalties after a standard becomes entrenched. They also avoid FRAND commitments on those patents; that is, they get to charge more than FRAND fees or rates.

On the other hand, a motive for firms to overdeclare their patents as essential even though they are not essential is that the firm is seen as more influential if it has a large share of SEPs. Its stature is elevated in the standards-setting process. The firm could also attract partners who want to be associated with industry leaders (and thereby work to create network effects). Overdeclaration seems prevalent. Using patent citation data, Stitzing *et al.* (2018) find that 10–50% of SEPs may not be truly essential.

10.6.3 *Select Challenges*

While SSOs help facilitate product compatibility and interoperability and implement FRAND pricing, the system presents significant challenges for participants. Three concerns are addressed: *royalty stacking*, *patent holdup*, and *patent holdout*.

With many SEPs involved in some standards, the sum of the royalties charged by each SEP owner may exceed a user's willingness to pay, creating an anti-commons problem in which the standard is underutilized. Hall and Helmers (2024) point out that royalty stacking can arise from a negative externality. Each SEP holder charges a royalty while ignoring its impact on other firms. It does not realize that the combined (across-firm) royalties would exceed the licensee's marginal valuation. If all SEP holders could internalize the externality, they could recognize that collectively lowering royalties would increase overall adoption.

Patent pooling could be a means to mitigate royalty stacking. Patent pools are organizations where member companies license patents to one another (either royalty-free or under some other favorable arrangement). The patent pool could also license patents to parties outside the pool for a single collective license.[17]

[17]Patent pools can also offer FRAND rates, albeit voluntarily, unlike SSO members, which are committed to providing FRAND terms.

Another type of concern is ex post hold-up by a patent holder who waits for a standard to be widely adopted and for manufacturers to invest heavily in the standard, then demands high royalties for a late-declared SEP. On the other hand, opportunistic behavior can also arise among implementers or licensees. They may refuse to take licenses for a portfolio of SEPs but use the standard commercially nonetheless. The strategy is to wait and see if patent owners will sue for infringement. The holdouts can use that time to challenge the validity of SEPs or their essentiality, counting on prolonged litigation to avoid paying royalties. They calculate that these benefits will exceed the expected damages if they lose an infringement suit.

These hold-up and hold-out problems could be addressed through patent pooling and through regulatory oversight and enforcement mechanisms to deter anti-competitive behavior. Standard-setting organizations also need strong internal monitoring to prevent the withholding of SEPs. Additionally, courts should provide injunctive relief for SEP holders whose SEPs are being willfully infringed.

10.6.4 *Implications for North–South Relations*

Before ending this section, it will be useful to think about how SSOs affect developing economy interests. As mentioned earlier, participation of the developing world in standards-setting is low. The few, usually large, multinational companies from the North tend to set global standards. From the South's perspective, developing economy firms and implementers may feel excluded because global standards were set without their input — without taking into account their particular technological needs, circumstances, and specializations. Consider, for example, even small details like programming codes which use Western alphabets, or interfaces that read left to right. The global South may aspire eventually to become standards leaders rather than just standards followers, and to end their persistent technological balance of payments deficits, as documented in Chapter 2.

The FRAND rates may be fair and reasonable in the North but be onerous in the South. The practice of international price discrimination (in licensing terms) may benefit the South. Courts have ruled that the non-discrimination provision of FRAND does not mandate identical pricing for all licensees in all countries.[18] Tiered pricing under FRAND can occur as long as a commercial justification for it exists, such as different market

[18]See https://www.finnegan.com/en/insights/articles/uk-supreme-court-holds-that-uk-courts-may-set-global-frand-terms.html.

sizes, lower purchasing power, volume discounts, and as long as the terms do not constitute anti-competitive behavior. It must still be the case that similarly situated implementers should be treated similarly, and that the tiered pricing is not part of a scheme to thwart competition. The extent to which SEP holders practice global price discrimination is difficult to observe since licensing agreements tend to be confidential.

Finally, standards may well have contributed to the international division of labor as manifested in global value chains and outsourcing.[19] The reason is that standards help to reduce transaction costs over long distances. Standards supplement the forces of globalization that have been driven by decreases in communication and transportation costs. By enhancing product compatibility and interoperability across borders, standards better enable the international coordination of production and division of labor. Companies that specialize in a component need not fear that their components will not be interchangeable with other parts in the global supply chain. Knowing that their output will stay relevant because of standardization, they develop trust and invest and expand accordingly. This allows for economies of scale in markets that are enlarged through standardization.

10.7 Patent Hold-Up and Royalty Stacking

It is puzzling to see limited evidence thus far of patent hold-up and royalty stacking, despite the patent explosion and proliferation of SEPs. Hold-ups and royalty stacking should have left their mark on reduced innovation.

Galetovic *et al.* (2015) conduct a test to determine whether SEPs slow down innovation. They examine data on quality-adjusted prices of manufactured products (audio-video equipment, computers, telephones, photographic equipment, watches, automobiles, etc.) They hypothesize that if innovation is hindered by SEPs, quality-adjusted prices should not fall, or should fall very slowly. Their study compares products heavily reliant on SEPs to products less reliant on them. A key finding is that quality-adjusted prices of SEP-reliant goods fall faster than those of less-reliant goods. Their interpretation of this finding is that the observations are not consistent with SEPs hindering innovation.

Recall that standard essential technologies are like essential infrastructural facilities. They are technologies that enable the interoperability of connected systems, such as smartphones, laptops, televisions, and audio-visual

[19]See Swann (2009).

systems. Firms that hold patents on these technologies can potentially exert significant market power over user firms. Users make pre-commitments to the technology, learning its interface and format, and adapting their work habits to it. An example would be committing to a particular operating system of a computer. The high licensing fee that a standard-essential patent owner can charge is attributable partly to the technical value of the invention and partly to the value of being a standard.

10.7.1 *Digression: Quality-Adjusted Prices*

The concept of prices adjusted for quality can be illustrated with an example. Assume smartphone A costs \$2,000 and smartphone B costs \$1,000. Smartphone A has 16GB of RAM and Smartphone B has 4GB of RAM. Even though A is twice as expensive as B, in terms of quality, it is effectively cheaper. Quality-adjusted price is simply price (P) divided by quality (λ). Smartphone A has a lower quality-adjusted price per unit of RAM than smartphone B.

Focus now on innovations in a product. Assume that an Android phone sells for p per unit and that its initial quality level is normalized to one. Consider an innovation that increases the amount of RAM in the phone, such that $\lambda > 1$. Let P be the price of the new and improved Android phone. However, the old version of the Android phone is still available for sale at p per unit. Because the new Android model is better, $P > p$.

To summarize the particulars:

- Let P be the price of an improved good
- Let p be the price of the original good
- Let λ be the size of the quality jump ($\lambda > 1$)

The effective price of the new and improved Android phone ($\frac{P}{\lambda}$) may be lower than the original phone's price (p) once its higher quality is taken into account, even though $P > p$ in nominal terms. Figure 10.3 shows the price path upon the introduction of the new and improved Android phone to the market.

This is why observing a decline in quality-adjusted prices reflects innovation. How fast or sharp the drop in quality-adjusted prices will be depends on how quickly the new innovation is adopted in the marketplace. The decline could be long and drawn out if the commercialization is slow due to market or technological barriers.

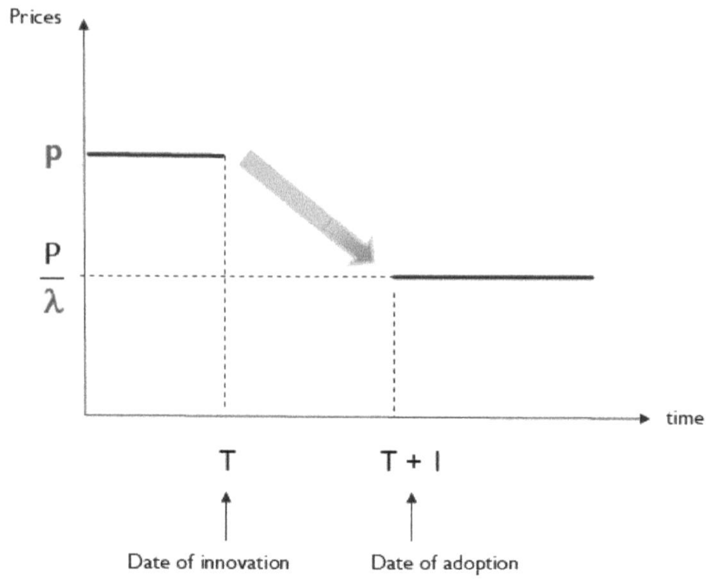

Figure 10.3. Path of Quality-Adjusted Price

Importantly, however, the new innovation — the new Android version — still competes with the original product. There is no guarantee that consumers will adopt the new and improved product, particularly if the quality jump is considered marginal. Consumers may stick to the original good if the price premium is not justified by the quality improvement. This explains why many consumers may hang on to their Samsung Galaxy S24 even though the S25 is available in the marketplace.

The consumer's decision is based on the following:

- If $P > \lambda p$, then stick to the old good
- If $P < \lambda p$, then switch to the new good
- If $P = \lambda p$, then there is indifference

10.7.2 *Quality-Adjusted Prices in Practice*

Turning to actual data, Galetovic *et al.* (2015) compare the quality-adjusted prices of goods that rely on standard-essential patents (SEPs) with those that do not — namely, automobiles. The latter serves as a useful benchmark because that industry is also patent-intensive but not dependent on SEPs.

Compared with non-SEP products such as automobiles, goods incorporating SEP technologies have experienced a steeper decline in prices over time. These are the very goods that prior literature has claimed to be subject to SEP holdup. As Figure 10.3 shows, innovation is generally associated with a downward trend in quality-adjusted prices. Hence, the finding of a steeper decline in the prices of SEP goods runs counter to the argument that standard-essential patents have impeded innovation.

10.7.3 *Policy Effect*

In eBay *Inc. v. MercExchange*, L.L.C., 547 U.S. 388 (2006), the U.S. Supreme Court stated that "a permanent injunction in patent infringement cases can be issued only if the plaintiff can show that the issue satisfies a four-factor test ... That test requires a plaintiff to demonstrate: (1) that it has suffered an irreparable injury; (2) that remedies available at law are inadequate to compensate for that injury; (3) that considering the balance of hardships between the plaintiff and defendant, a remedy in equity is warranted; and (4) that the public interest would not be disserved by a permanent injunction."[20]

This court decision weakened the patent rights of SEP holders by raising the standards required to obtain an injunction against infringers. Thus, a testable hypothesis is that, if SEPs hinder innovation, the ruling (which reduced the market power of SEP holders) should have stimulated innovation.

Consider the regression equation of Galetovic *et al.* (2015):

$$\textit{Quality-adjusted Price}_{it} = \alpha + \beta[\textit{SEP}_i \times \textit{Post 2006}_t] + \gamma \textit{SEP}_i + \cdots$$

where subscript i denotes industry and t denotes year. The "Post 2006" dummy variable captures the effect of the post-eBay *Inc. v. MercExchange* decision. If the hypothesis above is true, the data should show $\beta < 0$.

However, the regression result shows that $\hat{\beta} = 0.012 > 0$ and the coefficient estimate is actually statistically insignificant. Meanwhile, $\hat{\gamma} = -0.058$ and is statistically significant at the 1% level. The fact that $\gamma < 0$ indicates that SEPs are associated with a decline in quality-adjusted prices, which in turn is associated with a rise in innovation.

If the patent hold-up theory were true, increasing the number of SEPs should have hindered innovation. Conversely, weakening their rights should

[20] *eBay Inc. v. MercExchange*, L.L.C., 547 U.S. 388, 391 (2006).

have increased the pace of innovation or increased the rate at which quality-adjusted prices decline. Both SEP and *Post* 2006 are dummy variables, so the post-2006 effect of SEP is $\hat{\beta} + \hat{\gamma}$. If the combined coefficient were negative and larger in absolute value than $\hat{\gamma}$, the ruling would have been deemed to have a pro-innovation effect. If the ruling (which weakened SEP rights) had harmed innovation, the coefficient $\hat{\beta}$ should have been significantly positive, but it is not. It is not significantly different from zero.

10.7.4 *Effects of Royalty Stacking: Case Study*

Suppose N complementary inputs are used in the production of a mobile phone device. Each of these inputs is patent-protected. A license is needed for each input, which the manufacturer of the device dutifully obtains from the corresponding patent holder. Total royalties equal $R_1 + R_2 + \cdots + R_N$. The hypothesis is that high royalties could destroy an industry. Recall that Profit = Revenues – Costs (including licensing fees).

Four predictions that emerge are as follows:

1. Sales of devices should fall if high royalties are passed on to consumers in the form of higher prices for devices.
2. Average prices of devices should soar (as supplies shrink).
3. The device industry should become concentrated (as royalty stacking acts as a barrier to entry).
4. Profits of device manufacturers and SEP holders should suffer, as the device industry declines due to high royalties, which create a smaller market for licensing.

These predictions are evaluated using data from the *World Mobile Industry* between 1994 and 2013.[21] Contrary to expectations, none of the four predictions is supported by the evidence. There is no observed royalty stacking problem of sufficient magnitude to undermine the industry.

The royalty stacking concern is that multiple SEP holders, each acting in their self-interest and charging licensing fees, may collectively impose excessive costs on device manufacturers. The fear is that such uncoordinated behavior could destroy the final goods market, effectively "killing the goose that lays the golden egg," and thereby harming both manufacturers and SEP holders in the long run. However, the data tell a different story. The number of SEPs and SEP holders increased significantly during

[21]This case study is based on Galetovic and Gupta (2020).

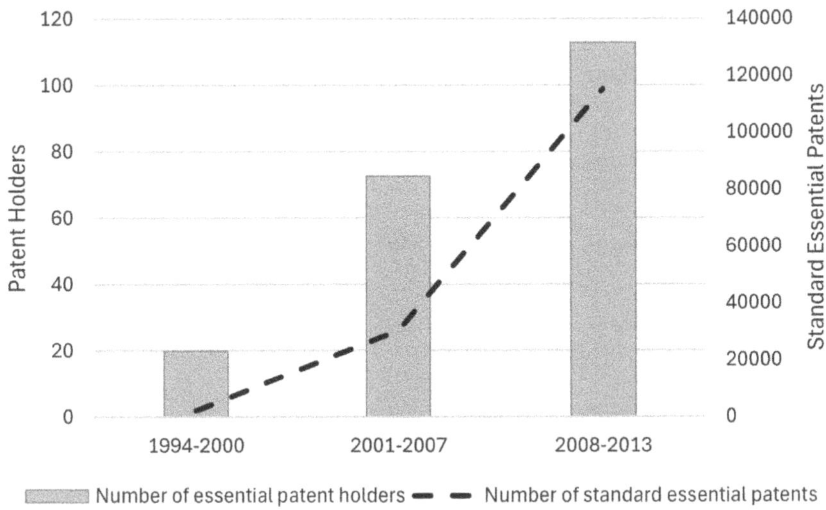

Figure 10.4. SEP Holders and Patent Trends
Source: Galetovic and Gupta (2020).

the study period, yet this did not correspond to deteriorating industry outcomes.

Figure 10.4 shows the growth in the number of standard-essential patents and SEP holders during the period of the case study, 1994–2013.

Table 10.2 provides operating statistics across wireless generations.[22] Despite the growth in SEP holders, several trends are notable:

- Global sales of devices have not declined. In fact, sales of 3G and 4G devices grew robustly.
- Average selling prices fell in real terms across generations, inconsistent with the stacking hypothesis.
- Gross margins for both SEP holders and manufacturers remained stable or even increased.

If royalty stacking were a significant burden, higher prices and falling margins would have been expected, yet these trends are absent. The data suggest that manufacturers were able to absorb or negotiate licensing costs without passing substantial burdens on to consumers or eroding profitability.

[22]In the table, 3GPP denotes Third Generation Partnership Project.

Table 10.2. SEP and Operating Data

Year	Number SEP Holders	Worldwide Sales of Devices, Millions			Avg. Selling Price 2013 Dollars			Avg. Gross Margin	
		2G	3G	4G	2G	3G	4G	SEP Holders	Rest of 3GPP
1995	4				800			97	102
1997	20	100			500			94	104
1999	35	300			350			92	106
2001	50	400			280	400		91	110
2003	65	200	500		200	550		88	113
2005	81	160	800		100	480		91	114
2007	92	120	1,100		50	350		93	115
2009	103	120	1,040		30	200		95	116
2011	118	80	1,200	1,780	30	120	380	97	114
2013	128	0	800	1,800	30	80	400	99	112

Source: Galetovic and Gupta (2020).

10.7.5 *Summary and Explanations*

The available evidence, while not definitive, is nonetheless revealing. The dire predictions surrounding royalty stacking and widespread patent hold-up have not materialized in the data. The continuous pace of technological progress, evident in successive generations of mobile technology (such as 5G), suggests that firms and standard-setting organizations (SSOs) have strong incentives to coordinate and avoid mutually destructive outcomes.

SSOs and market participants have demonstrated that coordination is possible. Blocking behavior is not always consistent with long-run profit maximization. Repeated interactions in the market induce licensing behavior that can conform to FRAND (fair, reasonable, and non-discriminatory) commitments. Cross-licensing arrangements, common among SEP holders, further reduce the risks of hold-up and facilitate product development.

Economic incentives are aligned to promote reasonable licensing. SEP holders benefit when their technologies are widely adopted and embedded in industry standards. This gives them strong motivation to offer licensing terms that encourage, rather than deter, adoption by device manufacturers.

Importantly, royalty rates are not set in a vacuum. The game-theoretic models that underpin the royalty stacking hypothesis often assume that each SEP holder sets its rate independently of others. In practice, however,

SEP holders are aware of the interdependencies among technologies. They can coordinate, whether through patent pools or informal cross-licensing arrangements.

10.8 Secondary Patent Markets

Thus far, this book has primarily examined the issuance of new patents. However, a distinct and increasingly important phenomenon in the intellectual property landscape is the emergence of secondary patent markets. In these markets, existing patents or bundles of patents are bought, sold, or licensed between firms. This section explores the economic rationale for participating in these markets and examines how secondary patent markets influence innovation behavior, particularly under conditions of uncertainty. It offers yet another lens through which to observe intellectual property markets in action.

The tradability of patents implies that innovation investments are not entirely sunk. Intellectual property assets, especially in sectors like digital technologies, can be repurposed and redeployed. Firms can use patents not only to protect inventions but also to store value, hedge risk, and potentially recoup R&D expenditures. In uncertain environments, the option to delay or accelerate investment becomes valuable. Secondary markets facilitate this flexibility by enabling firms to postpone, reverse, or reallocate innovation expenditures.

Importantly, the resale option — the ability to divest patent assets at a later time — only has value if firms initially acquire or generate those assets. This insight provides the foundation for applying real options theory to the analysis of patenting under uncertainty.

A key motivation for studying this topic is the counterintuitive empirical pattern observed during recent economic disruptions, such as the COVID-19 pandemic or the 2008–2009 financial crisis: patenting activity in certain sectors, particularly information and digital technologies, remained stable or even increased despite widespread economic uncertainty. A compelling case exists that secondary markets helped shape how firms in certain industries responded to uncertainty.

10.8.1 *Innovation Resilience*

Figure 10.5 illustrates how, during the early phases of the COVID-19 pandemic, output in IP-intensive industries declined less sharply and rebounded more quickly than in non-IP-intensive industries. Using normalized real

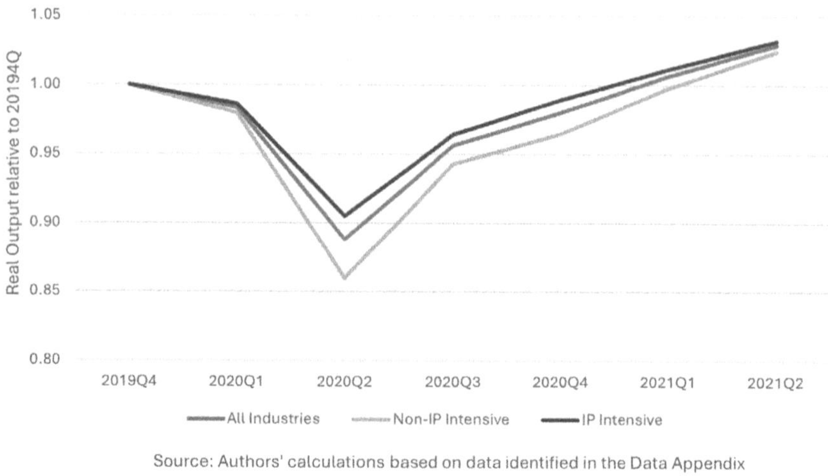

Figure 10.5. Growth in U.S. Real Gross Output by Industry, www.bea.gov.

gross output data, the analysis reveals that sectors reliant on intellectual property exhibited greater economic resilience during the shock period.[23]

This pattern suggests that intellectual property-intensive sectors behave differently from the broader economy, and that innovation, particularly in the form of knowledge capital, can exhibit resilience during economic shocks.[24]

To probe this idea further, Figures 10.6 and 10.7 display patenting behavior in two sectors: information technology and pharmaceuticals. These sectors differ markedly in their participation in secondary patent markets. Patent resales are more common in the information technology sector than in the pharmaceutical industry.

The data span two major economic disruptions: the dot-com crash of the early 2000s and the global financial crisis of 2008–2009. In each case, pharmaceutical patenting tends to decline with the business cycle, especially during the Great Recession. In contrast, information technology patenting appears relatively stable and even expands during downturns. Although not

[23]Figure 10.5 is based on data from the BEA's Interactive Tables and on the classification of IP industries defined by the U.S. Patent and Trademark Office and the Economics and Statistics Administration (2012), *Intellectual Property and the U.S. Economy: Industries in Focus*, U.S. Department of Commerce. Output values are normalized to 1 in 2019:Q4, the quarter prior to the pandemic.

[24]See also Buffington *et al.* (2021), Davis *et al.* (2021), and Dinlersoz *et al.* (2021).

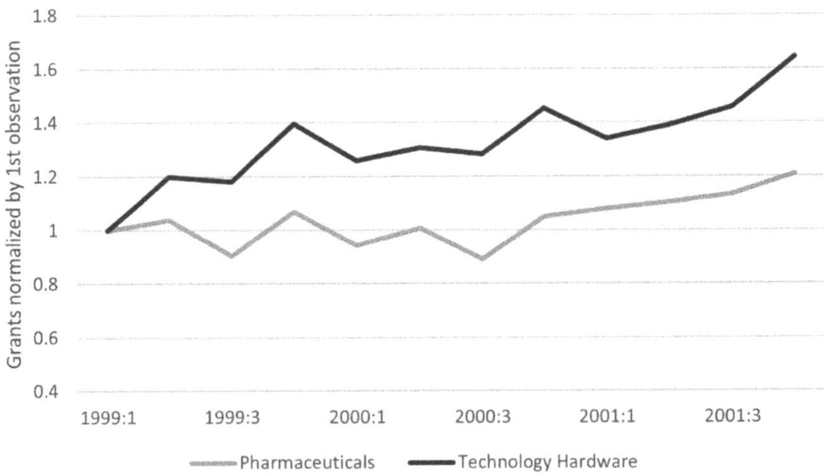

Figure 10.6. Patenting during the Dot-com Bubble

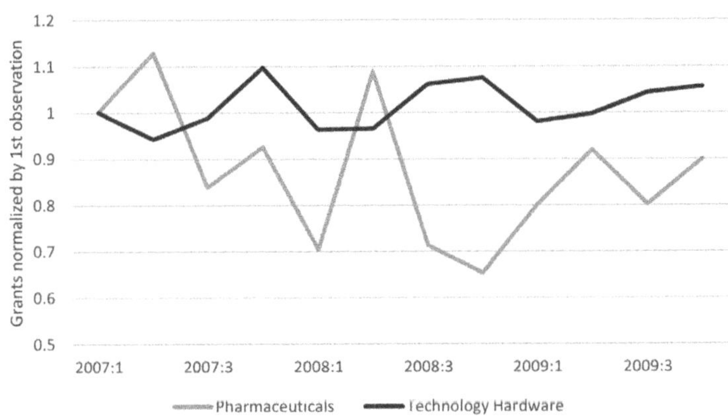

Figure 10.7. Patenting during the Great Recession

conclusive, these patterns are consistent with the hypothesis that access to secondary markets enhances the resilience of innovation activity.

10.8.2 *Secondary Market Deals*

As suggested above, participation in secondary patent markets varies by industry. Table 10.3 shows a sample of deals on the *IAM Market*. This online

Table 10.3. Secondary Market Deals in Patent Rights

Industry Group	Counts	Share (%)
Digital Economy	393	44.0
Health Economy	116	13.0
Automotive and Parts	65	7.3
Telecommunications	46	5.2
Manufacturing	46	5.2
Media & Entertainment	31	3.5
Electricity	27	3.0
Transport	27	3.0
Security & Defence	26	2.9
Household Goods	22	2.5
Chemicals	13	1.5
Food, Tobacco, and Beverages	13	1.5
Oil & Gas	10	1.1
Finance	10	1.1
Retail & Distribution	10	1.1
Construction and Building Materials	7	0.8
Test and Measurement	7	0.8
Support Services	6	0.7
Other	18	2.0
Total	893	100.0

Source: https://www.iam-market.com/.

listing platform brings "together people who see the commercial value of intellectual property and technology, and want to do business together."[25]

Table 10.3 presents a breakdown of recent transactions across industry groups. The data reflect the distribution of deals in which patents were listed for sale, licensing, or partnership.[26] The majority of transactions are concentrated in digital technologies and information sectors, where innovation tends to be modular and cumulative. These characteristics increase the likelihood of cross-licensing and make patents more easily tradable.

[25]The count of 893 transactions was obtained from the IAM Market portal, https://portal.iam-market.com/browse-iptech, accessed on March 21, 2022. The exact period of the transactions covered was not specified. Based on secondary sources (such as IAM's annual market analysis), that figure may represent a cumulative count over a multi-year period, likely spanning from around 2015 to 2022.

[26]The "Other" category in the table includes steel and other metals, utilities and mining, leisure and hospitality, printing, and education.

In contrast, industries such as chemicals account for a much smaller share of secondary patent market activity, and no deals specifically for pharmaceuticals are listed. This industry disparity may reflect differences in how easily intellectual property can be disaggregated and repurposed across firms and products.

In addition to the industrial breakdown, another perspective involves examining the technological fields involved in secondary patent market trading.

Table 10.4 shows the top twelve CPC sub-classes that appear in the traded patents. CPC refers to the *Cooperative Patent Classification System.* CPC codes are used to categorize patents based on the technology and inventions they cover. Just as a patent document can contain multiple claims, it can contain multiple technological fields identified by the CPC codes or symbols. CPC codes are alphanumeric, consisting of a letter followed by numbers. For example, A stands for "Human Necessities" and A01 denotes "Agriculture; Forestry; Animal Husbandry; Hunting."[27]

Table 10.4. Top 12 CPC Subclasses in the Share of Secondary Market Sales of Granted Patents

CPC Sub Class	**% Share Total Value**	**CPC_SubClass_Title**
H04	43.29	Electric Communication Technique
G06	27.20	Computing; Calculating; Counting
H01	6.62	Basic Electric Elements
G01	2.98	Measuring; Testing
H03	2.67	Basic Electronic Circuitry
G11	2.07	Information Storage
G02	1.69	Optics
G08	1.67	Signaling
A61	1.52	Medical or Veterinary Science; Hygiene
G10	1.50	Musical Instruments; Acoustics
H05	1.01	Electric Techniques not Otherwise Provided for
H02	0.90	Generation; Conversion, Distribution of Electric Power

[27]Table 10.4 shows invention-related CPC codes at the two-digit level of aggregation, as they are reflective of the underlying technology of the patent. Any further granularity of the CPC classification would result in too many categories to display effectively.

In Table 10.4, the leading technological field that appears in patents that are traded is *Electric Communication Technique*, code H04. Next is computing, calculating, and counting (G06), and the third is basic electric elements (H01). These three are technological fields that are typically utilized in information technology.

10.8.3 *Prior Research on Secondary Patent Markets*

Historically, the patent system has helped facilitate trade in technology, as Lamoreaux and Sokoloff (2003) document in their study of the U.S. during the late 19th and early 20th century. Patent agents and attorneys played the role of intermediaries to match inventors seeking capital and investors seeking to fund projects, as well as match the sellers and buyers of technologies. These intermediaries lowered the transaction costs of exchange and improved the division of labor between creators and commercializers.

Arora *et al.* (2022) discuss how markets for technology enable inventors to sell their inventions to firms better able to commercialize them. Similarly, Akcigit *et al.* (2016) argue that the trading of patents allows firms to keep innovations that are aligned with their business, sell those that are technologically distant from their core, and purchase those that are technologically closer to their strategic goals. Resales allow for the improved allocation of ideas across firms and promote economic growth and welfare.

Serrano (2018) finds that smaller firms gain from transferring patent rights to firms that are more effective at commercializing the innovations. In related work, Ma (2025) finds an interesting trend among U.S. industries, whereby production and innovation have separated; that is, some firms specialize in production and others in innovation, particularly the smaller firms. Ma (2025) traces this development to the patent trading market, which allows firms to find other ways to monetize their inventions, other than commercializing them and manufacturing the goods themselves.

Love *et al.* (2018) provide valuable insights on the scope of the brokered market for patents, finding that most of the packages of patents offered for sale were from product-producing technology companies, and that the vast majority of inventions pertain to technologies such as computers and telecommunications, with a few related to pharmaceuticals and life sciences.

10.8.4 *Index of Secondary Patent Market Exposure*

Firms vary in their exposure to secondary patent markets. The two sources of variation are that: (i) some technological fields are more involved than others in trading (for example, information technology innovations are traded more heavily than pharmaceutical ones) and (ii) firms vary in their fields of technological specialization. For example, a firm like *International Business Machines* specializes more in information technology hardware than in other fields, while a firm like *Pfizer* specializes more in pharmaceutical science than in other fields. These two variations can be exploited to design an index of secondary patent markets (denoted by ISE):

$$ISE_i = \sum_{j=1}^{N} Share_{ij} \times \frac{CPC_j}{\sum_j CPC_j}$$

- j indexes the technological field and N the total number of technological fields the firm innovates in during a given sample period.
- $Share_{ij}$ is the share of technological field j in the overall patent grants of firm i. For example, if this share equals 0.25, this indicates that 25% of the firm's patented innovations are in technological field j.
- CPC_j is the number of times technological field j is mentioned or listed in all the sold patent packages.[28]
- $\frac{CPC_j}{\sum_j CPC_j}$ is the share of technological field j in all the patent packages sold. For example, if this ratio equals 0.1, then technological field j accounts for 10% of all the technological fields that appear in the resale market.[29]

The index ISE measures the potential exposure of firm i to the secondary patent market. The higher the index, the greater the exposure. And exposure is greater the more the firm's innovation activities are specialized in those technological fields that are relatively most active in the patent resale market. Exposure increases if either the firm shifts to a technological field that is actively involved in the resale market or one of its existing fields of technological specialization becomes more attractive to patent

[28]The source of data is from Richardson Oliver Insights.

[29]Altogether, there are 116 CPC sub-classes at the two-digit level, i.e., letter plus two digits.

Table 10.5. Sample Indexes of Secondary Market Sales, by Industry

NAICS Code	Industry	Index of Sales Exposure
5182	Telecomm Data Process Services	0.3007
5112	Software publishers	0.2602
3342	Communications equipment manuf.	0.2062
3343	Audio and video equipment manuf.	0.1962
3341	Computer and peripheral equipment manuf.	0.1959
3344	Semiconductors and other elect. comp. manuf.	0.1209
5324	Commercial and Industrial Machinery ...	0.0720
3364	Aerospace products and parts manuf.	0.0347
3254	Pharmaceuticals and Medicines	0.0153
3251	Basic Chemicals	0.0059

traders — or both. The firm itself need not have bought or sold patent assets. The index measures its potential or prospects for finding trading partners. Table 10.5 shows some sample measures of ISE by industry.[30]

Table 10.5 shows the average exposure by industry. Indeed, the resale option is prevalent in the communications equipment, audio and video equipment, computers and peripherals, radio, TV, film, and cable broadcasting sectors. Note how the highly traded products are in complex industries, while the less traded ones are in the discrete industries. (Recall the discussion of complex versus discrete industries in Chapter 5.)

Table 10.6 groups firms into quintiles according to their index of secondary patent market exposure. The table helps to characterize the firms that utilize the secondary market. Much diversity exists. There are high R&D companies that access these markets as well as high R&D firms that do not. Those firms with greater exposure to such markets have a greater mean rate of patenting, but up to a point. For example, firms in the top quintile of exposure to secondary markets do not patent as much per quarter as do those in the second highest quintile and patent only slightly more than those in the middle quintile. One reason is that the firms in the top quintile tend to be relatively smaller firms, judging by their average sales and employment levels, and are highly specialized in particular technological fields. While firms of all sizes engage in trade, the relatively smallest

[30]NAICS stands for the North American Industry Classification System, which provides codes to identify the industry of firms.

Table 10.6. Types of Firms by Secondary Market Exposure

Quintile	Index Sec. Mkt Expo.	Patent Grants	Sales	R&D	Full-Time Employ.	Age (Years)	Tech Spec.
1	0.004	6.5	1,007.5	53.8	10,679	52	0.604
2	0.014	10.5	1,564.4	122.0	14,719	44	0.644
3	0.043	21.9	1,342.5	73.0	15,245	24	0.605
4	0.151	64.1	2,283.5	187.6	23,574	36	0.519
5	0.333	24.7	1,188.7	132.9	9,021	24	0.748

Note: Figures represent quarterly averages, unless indicated otherwise.

ones seem more prone to trade. The relatively older companies are in the bottom two quintiles, suggesting that the trading of patent rights occurs among relatively younger companies (based on firm age) or companies in relatively newer technological fields.

A firm's *technology specialization* is constructed by measuring the concentration of technological fields in a firm's patents granted (similar to the Herfindahl-Hirschman method for measuring industrial concentration): $HHI_{Tech}^{jt} = \sum_{j=1}^{M} s_{ijt}^2$, where M is the number of unique CPC class codes for firm i at time t and s_{ijt} is the share of each unique CPC class in all of firm i's patents in period t. Table 10.6 is consistent with previous work, which finds that specialized firms tend to engage more in technology markets (see Akcigit *et al.* (2016) and Ma (2025)).

10.9 Real Options Theory and Uncertainty

A real option gives an investor the right, but not the obligation, to make an investment decision in the future, such as to buy or sell an asset. These options are valuable under uncertainty. They provide managerial flexibility — specifically, the ability to defer, expand, contract, or abandon an investment as new information becomes available. Real options apply to both tangible and intangible investments, such as R&D or capital projects.[31] In the context of intellectual property, real options theory helps explain

[31] See the seminal work of Dixit and Pindyck (1994).

how patent resale markets can make innovation investments reversible and attractive under conditions of market uncertainty.

Investment decisions inherently involve the exercise of both reversibility and expandability options. The *reversibility option* reflects the value of being able to disinvest or liquidate capital assets in the future. This option encourages firms to undertake uncertain investments by reducing downside risk, since assets can be divested if market conditions deteriorate. In contrast, the *expandability option* captures the value of postponing investment until more information becomes available. This option discourages immediate investment by creating incentives to delay commitment.

10.9.1 *Conceptual Framework*

Investment is a decision made over time: firms can choose when to commit resources.[32] When future returns are uncertain, a firm that can purchase capital at a later date effectively holds a *call option*, while a firm that can resell capital at a later date (assuming investments are reversible) effectively holds a *put option*. Both options influence current investment incentives but in opposite directions. On the one hand, a higher value of the call option encourages postponement: firms may prefer to delay expansion when facing uncertainty. On the other hand, a higher value of the put option strengthens the incentive to invest now: only by acquiring capital in the present can the firm retain the right to sell it later if future returns disappoint. Consequently, greater future uncertainty has an *ambiguous* effect on investment incentives, as it raises the value of both the put and call options.

External factors can influence the relative value of these two options. In the case of patenting decisions, one such factor is the existence of secondary patent markets. These markets render patenting decisions more reversible by providing a venue for resale. Patent owners who face downside risk can transfer rights to another party, thereby enhancing the value of the put option. This reduces the risk of immediate investment and moderates the disincentive effects of uncertainty. As a result, firms with access to active secondary markets are likely to respond less negatively — or even positively — to increases in uncertainty.

It should be stated at the outset that the uncertainty facing the firm is firm-specific. If uncertainty were purely aggregate — affecting all firms

[32]This section is dapted from Abel *et al.* (1996) and Park *et al.* (2025).

equally — then a firm seeking to sell its patent might not find a willing buyer. The value of a patent depends on how well a given firm can commercialize the underlying innovation. A poor alignment between a firm's commercialization capabilities and the nature of the innovation may lead the firm to sell the patent, even if the innovation has high potential value for another firm. In this way, a decision to sell does not necessarily signal that the asset lacks worth.[33]

The remainder of this section presents a heuristic analysis to demonstrate how real options affect patenting behavior, with the following section turning to empirical evidence.

Consider a two-period model. In the first period, a firm chooses its patent portfolio, denoted by x. The second period is subject to uncertainty, such as fluctuations in market demand. Upon realization of the uncertainty, the firm may continue operating with x, expand its portfolio, or contract it. Let π_i denote profits in period $i = 1, 2$. The firm's value is given by

$$V(x) = \pi_1(x) + \phi\pi_2^e(x, \sigma) \tag{10.1}$$

where $\phi < 1$ is the discount factor and the superscript e denotes expected value, conditional on uncertainty. Second-period profits depend on a random shock σ, which will be discussed further below.

For simplicity, patents are the only factor of production considered. Let r denote the price of a patent (akin to wages for labor or the user cost for capital). The price could broadly include procurement and maintenance fees.[34] The value-maximizing firm chooses x to maximize $V(x) - rx$.

Assume that patented inputs, x, yield diminishing marginal returns to the firm; that is, each additional patented input increases output and profits at a diminishing rate. This may arise for several reasons. First, patented technologies require complementary assets. Without proportionate investments in these complements, additional patented inputs generate smaller incremental returns. Second, each patented input must be integrated into the firm's R&D and production processes. Coordination costs rise, and portfolio management may become overloaded. Third, there may be overlap among existing technologies in the firm's patent portfolio such that the incremental value of each new patent declines. Fourth, the incorporation of additional patented features in a product does not always translate into

---

[33]This reasoning aligns with Akcigit *et al.* (2016), who emphasize that an innovation must align well with a firm's existing line of business.

[34]All budgeted at the time of patenting. The imputed price of a patent could also include interest, depreciation, taxes, and an enforcement or risk premium.

a higher willingness to pay on the part of consumers or users. Once the core functionality of a product is established, contributions from additional patented technologies may become minor tweaks.

These diminishing marginal returns are reflected in a decline in the positive value of the marginal return to an additional patent in period 2 as successive acquisitions of patents occur.[35]

Uncertainty is represented by a firm-specific variable σ, which is not known in period 1. A high value of σ corresponds to high second-period profits, while a low value corresponds to low second-period profits. In other words, the shock σ can shift demand for the firm's product upward or downward, thereby raising or lowering the price it receives as consumer interest changes.

For simplicity, let σ take on any value along the real line — that is, from minus infinity to positive infinity. This wide variation is the source of uncertainty in period 2.[36]

It will be shown that when the realized shock σ is above a threshold σ_H, the firm will expand its patent portfolio in period 2. When σ is below a threshold σ_L, the firm will contract its portfolio. When σ lies between the two thresholds σ_L and σ_H, the firm will keep its patent portfolio intact.

In period 2, the choice of patent portfolio size x depends on the value of the uncertainty shock σ and the price of patents r. In particular, the choice is guided by the optimality condition: $\frac{\partial \pi_2}{\partial x}(x, \sigma) = r$, where the left-hand side is the marginal return to x and the right-hand side is the marginal cost of x. If $\frac{\partial \pi_2}{\partial x}(x, \sigma) > r$, it pays to increase x, and if $\frac{\partial \pi_2}{\partial x}(x, \sigma) < r$, it pays to decrease x.[37]

Figure 10.8 shows the relationship between patent portfolio size and uncertainty, holding the price of patents r constant.

The figure shows the locus of x and σ that keeps the marginal return to patents equal to $\bar{r}$. The line is upward-sloping because of diminishing marginal returns to patenting: as x increases, the marginal returns fall, requiring a higher σ to compensate. Recall that a rise in σ is positive news for the firm.

---

[35]That is, the first partial derivative, $\frac{\partial \pi_2}{\partial x} > 0$, and the second partial derivative, $\frac{\partial^2 \pi_2}{\partial x^2} < 0$, which signifies that the first partial derivative diminishes in value as x increases.

[36]Formally, the random shock σ is distributed according to a cumulative distribution function $F(\sigma)$, which has support over $\mathbb{R}$. $F(\bar{\sigma})$ equals the probability that $\sigma \leq \bar{\sigma}$. Hence, $F(-\infty) = 0$ and $F(+\infty) = 1$.

[37]Due to diminishing marginal returns to patenting, increasing patent holdings reduces the marginal return to patents, and decreasing them has the opposite effect.

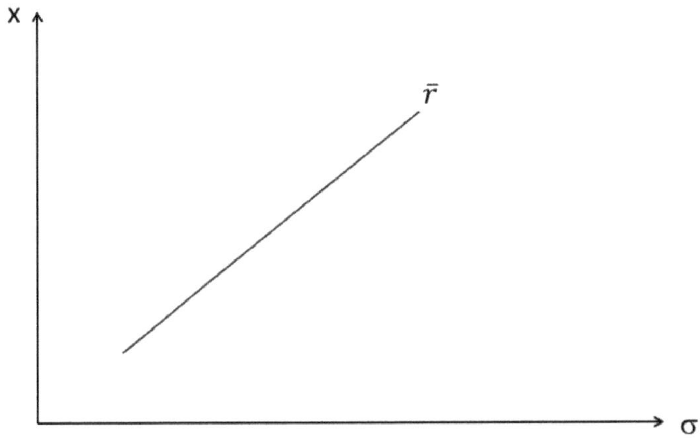

Figure 10.8. Patent Portfolio and Uncertainty

Now consider a secondary patent market. In this market, there are two distinct prices: one for purchasing a patent and another for selling a patent. Let r_H denote the purchase price of a patent (the ask price), and r_L denote the resale price (the bid price). A no-arbitrage condition requires that $r_L \leq r_H$. If this condition were violated such that $r_L > r_H$, an agent could realize limitless profits by instantaneously buying a patent at r_H and reselling it at r_L.[38]

Given these prices r_L and r_H, which are treated as exogenous, the two threshold values of σ can be determined as follows:

$$\frac{\partial \pi_2}{\partial x}(x, \boldsymbol{\sigma_L}) = r_L \quad \text{and} \quad \frac{\partial \pi_2}{\partial x}(x, \boldsymbol{\sigma_H}) = r_H, \tag{10.2}$$

Here, σ_L is defined at the margin where the firm is indifferent between selling a patent and retaining it, while σ_H is defined at the margin where the firm is indifferent between acquiring a patent and maintaining its existing patent portfolio. Note that acquisition can occur either through purchasing a patent from another firm or through patenting a new invention developed in the firm's own R&D lab.

[38]As an analogy, consider currency exchanges at the airport. Suppose a traveler from South Africa wishes to obtain U.S. dollars. If it costs 20 Rand to buy a U.S. Dollar and that same U.S. Dollar can be sold for 25 Rand, the traveler would make a 5 Rand profit by buying a dollar and immediately selling it, and could repeat this process at the booth. In reality, however, the resale rate would be lower than the purchase rate — for example, a U.S. Dollar might be bought for 20 Rand but sold back for only 18 Rand — eliminating the profit opportunity.

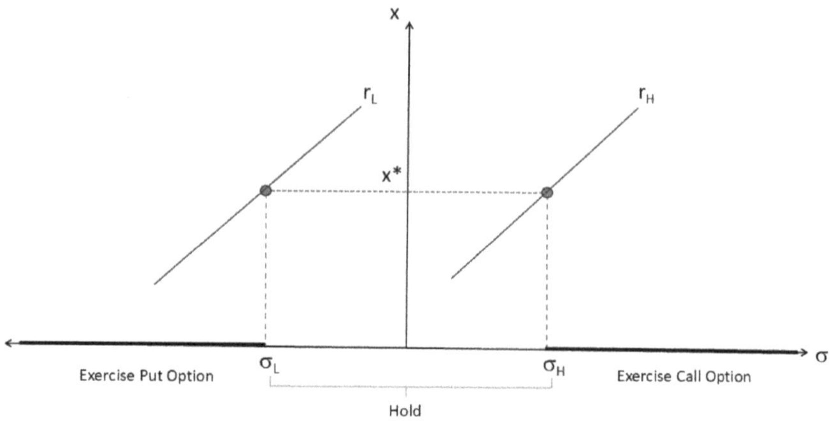

Figure 10.9. Real Options and Uncertainty

Figure 10.9 illustrates the options available to the firm in period 2, conditional on the realized value of the shock σ.

The figure depicts two lines: one where the marginal return equals r_L and another where it equals r_H. The first-period (optimal) patent portfolio is given by x^*. If the realized shock reflects pessimism — that is, a low value of σ — the marginal return to patents falls below the resale price r_L. In this case, the firm has an incentive to reduce its patent holdings. By selling a unit of x, it forgoes the marginal return but receives r_L in exchange.[39]

Conversely, if the realized shock reflects optimism — that is, a high value of σ — the marginal return to patents exceeds the purchase price r_H. In this case, acquiring an additional unit of x costs r_H but yields a marginal gain that is greater than the purchase price.[40]

When the uncertainty shock σ lies between the two thresholds σ_L and σ_H, it is not profitable to buy or sell patents. For example, adding another unit of x costs r_H, but the marginal return $\frac{\partial \pi_2}{\partial x}(x, \sigma)$ is lower. So, why buy? Reducing x by one unit fetches a price of r_L, but the marginal return is greater than r_L. So, why sell?

This explains why in Figure 10.9, there is neither expansion nor contraction in patent holdings when $\sigma_L \leq \sigma \leq \sigma_H$, but there is expansion when $\sigma > \sigma_H$ and contraction when $\sigma < \sigma_L$. In real option terms, when the

[39]As x is sold, patent assets become scarcer, and the marginal return to x rises back to r_L.

[40]As x is bought, patent assets become more abundant, and the marginal return to x falls back to r_H.

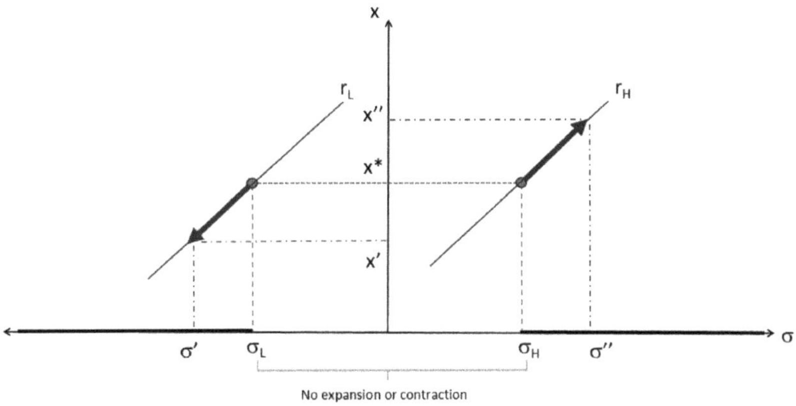

Figure 10.10. Exercise of Real Options

uncertainty shock exceeds σ_H, the firm exercises the call option to acquire more patents; when it falls below σ_L, it exercises the put option to sell patents. In all other cases, the firm maintains its patent holdings.

Figure 10.10 depicts the acquisition of patents when the realized shock is sufficiently high ($\sigma'' > \sigma_H$) and the disposition of patent assets when the shock is sufficiently low ($\sigma' < \sigma_L$).

The following table summarizes the different cases and action outcomes associated with each case, using the notation in Figure 10.10.

Real Options Scenarios		
Case 1	$\sigma < \sigma_L$	Exercise put option. Proceeds from sale equal $r_L(x^* - x')$, which are added to second-period profits, $\pi_2(x', \sigma')$.
Case 2	$\sigma > \sigma_H$	Exercise call option. Costs of acquisition equal $r_H(x'' - x^*)$, which are deducted from second-period profits, $\pi_2(x'', \sigma'')$.
Case 3	$\sigma_L \leq \sigma \leq \sigma_H$	Hold. No incentive to alter patent portfolio x^*. Second-period profits are $\pi_2(x^*, \sigma)$.

Overall, the analysis highlights the implicit advantages of a secondary patent market. The absence of such a market can be captured by $r_L = 0$ — that is, by the lack of any resale value. In this case, patenting investments are fully irreversible, leaving firms with only a call option. Under these conditions, shifts in uncertainty create incentives only to delay, postpone, or forgo patenting.

To recap: for a firm facing uncertainty, more valuable call options create incentives to postpone patenting in the current period, since the firm retains opportunities to invest later. More valuable put options motivate the firm to patent now, since the investment is reversible and the firm can dampen losses or profit from resales. An increase in uncertainty — as measured by the volatility of returns — has an ambiguous effect on patenting, since it raises the value of both the put and the call option, and the two have opposing effects on the incentive to patent. In the limiting case where reversibility is absent (i.e., no put option), uncertainty tends to depress current patenting. However, as secondary markets become more active and resale prices rise, this negative effect is attenuated. With sufficiently high reversibility, uncertainty might even spur patent filings.

10.9.2 *Some Evidence*

This section turns to the empirical evidence on whether exposure to secondary patent markets mitigates the effects of uncertainty on firm-level patenting. The reversibility of patenting decisions — enabled through such markets — entails important consequences for innovation and commercialization, which are summarized later in the section.

The dataset consists of a sample of 800 large companies operating in the United States over the period 1990–2021.[41] Together, these firms account for approximately one-third of all U.S. patents granted during the sample period. The dataset includes firms headquartered in fifteen countries, including the U.S., and spans 94 industries, classified according to the four-digit NAICS system.

In the empirical analysis that follows, the main outcome variable is the number of U.S. patent grants, measured by the date of application. The key independent variables are the Index of Secondary Market Exposure, ISE, previously described, and a measure of uncertainty. Following Czarnitzki and Toole (2011), uncertainty is proxied by the coefficient of variation in firm sales per employee, normalized by industry sales per employee. Denote this measure by UNC.[42]

---

[41]The data source is Park *et al.* (2025), based on information compiled from *PatentsView*, Standard & Poor's *Capital IQ* database, and Richardson-Oliver Insights.

[42]Specifically, the coefficient of variation for firm i at quarter t is given by: $UNCit = \frac{\sqrt{var(zit)}}{mean(z_{it})}$, where $z_{it} = \frac{\frac{sales_{it}}{employees_{it}}}{\frac{1}{N^{\iota}}\sum_{i=1}^{N^{\iota}}\frac{sales_{it}}{employees_{it}}}$. The mean and variance are computed over the preceding quarters of varying length depending upon data availability.

As a robustness check, an alternative measure of uncertainty is the volatility of a firm's stock market rate of return, net of industry and overall market volatility.[43] Denote this stock market based uncertainty measure by STK.[44]

Control variables in the analysis include the natural logarithm of the firm's R&D expenditures, the natural logarithm of firm sales, and a measure of industry concentration, HHI (Herfindahl-Hirschman Index). The HHI for industry j at time t is calculated as

$$HHI^{jt} = \sum_{i=1}^{N} s_{ijt}^2$$

where N is the number of firms in industry j and s_{ijt} denotes the sales share of firm i at time t. The HHI^{jt} is normalized to range from zero to one, with higher values indicating greater market concentration.[45]

The empirical results are supportive of the real options framework. In Table 10.7, column (1), the coefficient of uncertainty, UNC, is negative

Table 10.7. Patent Grants by Filing Date

	(1)	(2)	(3)	(4)
UNC	-0.157^{***}	-0.428^{***}		
$UNC \times ISE$		1.950^{***}		
STK			-0.006^{**}	-0.016^{***}
$STK \times ISE$				0.083^{***}
ln R&D	0.213^{***}	0.215^{***}	0.201^{***}	0.200^{***}
ln Sales	0.107^{***}	0.114^{***}	0.138^{***}	0.133^{***}
HHI	-0.197	-0.245^{*}	-0.232^{*}	-0.212
Other Controls	Yes	Yes	Yes	Yes
Observations	23,161	23,161	23,847	23,847

Note: ∗∗∗, ∗∗, ∗ denote significance levels of 1, 5, & 10% respectively.

[43]The methodology follows Bulan (2005).

[44]Specifically, the following regression model is estimated: $\rho_{i\tau} = \psi_{it} + \psi_{it}^{M}\rho_{M\tau} + \psi_{it}^{I}\rho_{I\tau} + \epsilon_{i\tau}$, where $\rho_{i\tau}$, $\rho_{M\tau}$, and $\rho_{I\tau}$ denote the stock market rate of returns of firm i, the market portfolio M (e.g., S&P 500), and the industry portfolio I, respectively. Trading days are indexed by $\tau = 1, 2, \ldots, n$. To ensure that the industry rate of return is uncorrelated (or orthogonal) to the market rate of return, $\rho_{I\tau}$ is obtained as the residual from a regression of industry returns on market returns. The *standard deviation* of the residuals $\epsilon_{i\tau}$ is then used to construct a measure of firm-level stock return volatility.

[45]Additional control variables include time fixed effects, firm fixed effects, firm age, cash flow, total assets, and the firm's technological specialization, as described earlier.

and statistically significant, indicating that uncertainty tends to depress patenting activity. However, in column (2), the coefficient of the interaction between the index of secondary patent market exposure and uncertainty, UNC, is positive and statistically significant. This suggests that firms with greater access to secondary patent markets are better able to offset the negative effects of uncertainty on their patenting behavior.

The critical threshold level of secondary market exposure, ISE^*, can be calculated as $ISE^* = \frac{-\beta_1}{\beta_2}$, where β_1 is the coefficient of uncertainty and β_2 the coefficient of the interaction term.[46] Based on the estimates in column (2), the critical value is approximately $ISE^* = 0.22$. Firms with $ISE < 0.22$ have relatively limited access to secondary markets, and for these firms, uncertainty exerts a net negative influence on patenting. In contrast, for firms with $ISE > 0.22$, patenting has a positive association with uncertainty, consistent with the theory that greater reversibility through secondary markets encourages innovation under uncertainty. Firms with sufficient levels of exposure to secondary patent markets experience the advantage of a "put option" to sell their patent assets later on.

Columns (3) and (4) replicate the analysis using the stock market-based measure of uncertainty, STK. The results are qualitatively similar to those obtained using UNC, reinforcing the robustness of the main findings. Across specifications, both R&D expenditures and firm sales exhibit positive and statistically significant effects on patenting, consistent with expectations.

The influence of industry concentration, measured by HHI, is mixed. In some specifications, concentration appears to have an insignificant effect on patenting, while in others it exerts a negative and statistically significant influence. Although concentration can, in theory, stimulate innovation by augmenting firm profits and internal resources, the evidence here does not support the view that greater industrial concentration promotes patenting.

The next set of results estimates the model by sector, focusing on information technology and biopharmaceuticals. As discussed earlier, these two sectors exhibit stark contrasts: information technology firms engage actively in patent resales, while biopharmaceutical firms largely do not.

The information technology sectors include public companies specializing in technology hardware, software, semiconductors, semiconductor equipment, and communications equipment. The biopharmaceutical group

[46]The threshold value of ISE is obtained by taking the derivative of the patent equation with respect to uncertainty and setting it equal to zero.

encompasses pharmaceutical manufacturers, life sciences firms, and biotechnology companies. The results in Table 10.8, column (1), indicate that uncertainty is negatively associated with patenting among information technology firms. However, once exposure to secondary markets is controlled for in column (2), a positive interaction effect emerges. Specifically, firms with an Index of Secondary Market Exposure (ISE) above a threshold of 0.23 exhibit a positive association between uncertainty and patenting. Approximately 49% of firms in the information technology sample exceed this threshold. For these firms, their relative resilience in patenting during periods of heightened uncertainty is plausibly explained by access to secondary patent markets.

By contrast, secondary market exposure plays a negligible role in mediating the effects of uncertainty in the biopharmaceutical sample (columns 3–4 of Table 10.8). Patent resales are not very common in the pharmaceuticals, biotechnology, and life sciences sectors. As a result, uncertainty exerts a negative influence on patenting (significant at the 1% level), and the $UNC \times ISE$ interaction term is statistically insignificant. These findings are consistent with the sectoral patterns observed earlier in Figures 10.6 and 10.7, where pharmaceutical patenting declined during economic downturns, while patenting in information technology remained comparatively robust. Thus, for firms in the biopharmaceutical sector, the predominant strategy

Table 10.8. By Select Sectors

	Patent Grants by Filing Date			
	INFO TECH	**INFO TECH**	**BIO-PHARM**	**BIO-PHARM**
	(1)	**(2)**	**(3)**	**(4)**
UNC	−0.192***	−0.914***	−0.622***	−0.739***
$UNC \times ISE$		4.056***		8.761
ln R&D	0.280***	0.276***	0.363***	0.368***
ln Sales	0.069	0.084	0.015	0.019
HHI	0.223	−0.114	−5.723***	−5.794***
Other Controls	Yes	Yes	Yes	Yes
Observations	8,999	8,999	2,962	2,962

Note: *** denotes statistical significance at the 1% level.

during times of economic uncertainty is to exercise the "call option" and delay, if not forgo, investment.

Consistent with expectations, firm R&D expenditures are a strong and statistically significant driver of patenting across sectors. Firm sales also have a positive, though statistically weaker, effect on patenting activity. Finally, industry concentration, as measured by the HHI, is strongly and negatively associated with patenting in the pharmaceutical sector, but shows no statistically significant relationship in the information technology sector.

10.9.3 *Reflections*

The analysis in this section highlights an important evolution in the economics of innovation: intellectual property rights are not just valued for their exclusionary power, but also for their tradability and liquidity in secondary markets. In a world of market volatility and uncertainty, the ability to repurpose, reallocate, and trade knowledge assets offers firms a mechanism to sustain innovation, even under adverse economic conditions.

The key takeaway points are listed as follows:

- **Empirical Implication:** Uncertainty is negatively associated with patenting activity, but access to secondary patent markets mitigates this effect. The mitigating effect varies by industry, reflecting differences in the extent to which firms engage in secondary market transactions.
- **Positive Implication:** The evidence helps explain the observed resilience of firm-level innovation under conditions of economic uncertainty.
- **Normative Implication:** Policymakers might consider facilitating opportunities for trading in secondary patent markets, particularly to assist innovators in the developing world to manage investment risks more effectively.

While financial markets for tangible assets are well-developed globally, resale markets for intangible assets remain relatively limited. Patent resale markets, in particular, are still largely localized and concentrated in a few high-income economies, such as the United States (through platforms such as IAM Market and Ocean Tomo), Europe (primarily via private brokers), and, to a lesser extent, Japan.

Although secondary market platforms are formally open to international participation, firms from developing economies are underrepresented. Several barriers contribute to this underutilization, including high transaction costs (related to valuation, legal, and brokerage services), limited familiarity with U.S. legal procedures, differences in patent quality and valuation practices, and the smaller size of patent portfolios among firms in emerging economies.

Thus, while secondary markets are accessible in principle, participation by developing-country firms remains low in practice. No major, organized secondary patent exchanges have yet emerged in developing regions. As a result, the mitigating effects of secondary markets on uncertainty-induced innovation shocks appear largely confined to firms operating within the established IP systems of advanced economies.

Chapter 11

Artificial Intelligence and IP

11.1 Introduction

The World Intellectual Property Organization (WIPO) describes AI as "a discipline of computer science that is aimed at developing machines and systems that can carry out tasks considered to require human intelligence, with limited to no human intervention."[1]

Another influential perspective comes from Russell and Norvig (2021), who categorize AI systems based on whether they think humanly, act humanly, think rationally, or act rationally — a framework that covers both cognitive processes and behavior. A key subset of AI is machine learning (ML), where algorithms learn and improve from data over time. Within ML, deep learning (DL) utilizes multi-layered neural networks capable of discerning high-level features from unstructured inputs like text or images.[2]

While many issues are interrelated, this chapter will concentrate on four topics: (1) AI authorship in copyright law; (2) AI inventorship in patent law; (3) the privacy implications of AI training; and (4) how restrictions on AI dataset disclosure affect knowledge sharing.

[1]See pp. 3–4 of WIPO/IP/A1/2/GE/20/1 Rev. https://www.wipo.int/edocs/mdocs/mdocs/en/wipo_ip_ai_2_ge_20/wipo_ip_ai_2_ge_20_1_rev.pdf.

[2]Appendix 11A provides a brief primer on artificial intelligence relevant for this chapter and the next.

Two main themes run throughout the analysis. First is the divergence between AI-assisted and AI-generated outputs. This distinction bears directly on whether the creator is a human or a machine — and hence, whether traditional incentives like copyright or patents serve any public interest purpose. Second is the importance of access: whether restrictions on training data, algorithmic transparency, or disclosure obligations enable or obstruct follow-on innovation.

The copyright section explores whether AI-generated works merit protection and whether training on copyrighted materials constitutes infringement. The patent section asks whether AI can or should be considered an inventor, and how legal standards like obviousness and enablement are affected when AI contributes to the inventive process. Subsequent sections examine the friction between data privacy and AI training and the evolving standards for disclosure.

One takeaway of the chapter is that the role of IP may lie not just in protecting creative and inventive outputs but in governing the ecosystems behind their development and commercialization. A second is the need for empirical evidence, not assumptions, to assess the impact of AI on creativity, investment, and access to knowledge.

11.2 State of AI

Figure 11.1 illustrates the global growth of AI-related publications and patents in recent years.[3] These indicators reflect both research intensity and innovation activity in the AI domain. While the number of publications appears to taper off slightly after 2021, patent activity shows near-exponential growth beginning around 2020 — a possible sign that AI is transitioning from exploratory research to commercialization and implementation.

Table 11.1 shows the distribution of AI publications by field and by sector. A disproportionate share of AI publications focus on machine learning, which has overtaken other subfields such as computer vision and pattern recognition since around 2016. Prior to that, algorithmic research dominated the field. Notably, the education sector accounts for over 80% of all AI publications, reflecting academia's continued leadership in foundational research, particularly in early-stage discovery and methodological development.

[3]See Maslej *et al.* (2024).

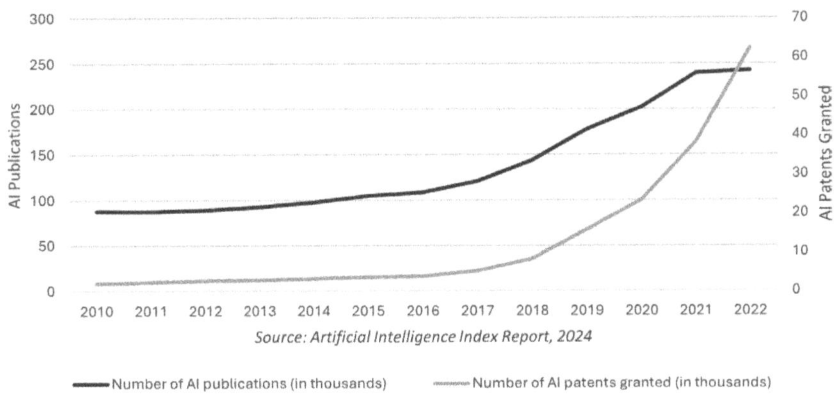

Figure 11.1. Global Growth in AI Research and Innovation

Table 11.1. AI Publications, 2022

Fields (Thousands)		**Sector (%)**	
Machine Learning	72.2	Education	81.1
Computer Vision	21.3	Industry	7.9
Pattern Recognition	19.8	Government	7.0
Process Management	12.1	Non-profit	2.6
Computer Networks	10.4	Other	1.5

Source: AI Index 2024 Annual Report.

As AI development accelerates, especially in proprietary contexts, the role of IP law becomes increasingly salient in determining how discoveries are shared, protected, or withheld.

Table 11.2 provides data on AI models and patents by country or region. Although China holds a substantial share of global AI patent grants (61.1%), this volume does not necessarily reflect the quality or impact of those patents. Patent counts alone may consist of single-claim filings or filings for status and peer recognition. This table does not capture patent citations or commercial relevance. By contrast, the U.S. leads in both the number of notable machine learning (ML) models and foundation models — categories that reflect functional deployment and economic influence.

A *notable ML model* refers to a machine learning system recognized for its technical significance or widespread adoption. Such models typically enable computers to learn patterns from data and perform designated tasks

Table 11.2. Regional Comparisons, 2023

Region/Country	AI Patent Grants (Percentage Share) (%)	Number of Notable Machine Learning Models	Number of Foundation Models
U.S.A.	20.9	61	109
China	61.1	15	20
European Union & U.K.	2.0	25	15
India	0.23	—	—
Rest-of-the-World	15.7	—	—

Source: AI Index 2024 Annual Report.

such as classification and prediction. A *foundation model*, by contrast, is a large-scale neural network trained on massive and diverse datasets. These models, such as large language models (LLMs), serve as platforms for a wide array of downstream applications, from image recognition to content generation.[4]

The U.S., China, and the EU–U.K. bloc are the dominant players in the development of both ML and foundation models. By contrast, the number of such models emerging from India and the broader Global South remains negligible or unreported, highlighting a growing asymmetry in AI innovation capacity.

Table 11.3 reports the number of foundation models released across sectors and organizations for specific periods. The majority of foundation models developed between 2019 and 2023 are open-access (approximately two-thirds), while the remainder are either limited-access or fully closed proprietary systems.

Although academia plays a central role in the publication of AI research, the development of foundation models is increasingly driven by private industry. As shown in Table 11.3, industry accounts for the overwhelming majority of foundation model development, with firms such as Google, OpenAI, Meta, and Microsoft leading the field. This reflects the high fixed costs and infrastructure demands associated with training these models,

[4]An example is a large language model (LLM) that uses trained parameters to generate human-like text or solve problems. Generative AI systems build upon these models to create novel outputs, including text, images, and audio.

Table 11.3. Foundation Models, 2019–2023

By Sector, 2023		**By Organization, 2019–2023 (Sum)**	
Industry	108	Google	40
Academia	28	OpenAI	20
Industry-Academia Collaboration	19.8	Meta	19
Government	12.1	Microsoft	18
Government-Industry Collaboration	10.4	DeepMind	15

Source: AI Index 2024 Annual Report.

which favor firms with access to advanced compute resources, proprietary data, and large engineering teams.

11.2.1 *Nature of the AI Market*

The market for artificial intelligence is currently dominated by a small number of large technology firms with substantial resources dedicated to research and development. Table 11.4 presents data on selected AI-focused companies, including their market capitalization over the past three years (adjusted to 2024 dollars), and their R&D-to-sales ratios.

Over three years, several firms saw dramatic real increases in market capitalization. NVIDIA's valuation rose nearly tenfold, while Palantir's more than quintupled.[5] The industry is heavily represented by a core group of U.S.-based technology firms, including Alphabet (Google), Amazon, Apple, Microsoft, and Meta, each of which commands hundreds of billions or trillions of dollars in market value.

R&D intensity is similarly noteworthy. Except for Apple and Tesla, most of these firms allocate double-digit percentages of sales to research and development. Meta and NVIDIA devote over a quarter of their revenues to R&D — investment levels that rival those seen in the pharmaceutical sector.[6] This pattern reflects an oligopolistic yet intensely rivalrous, innovation-driven AI market, where access to computational infrastructure, algorithmic breakthroughs, and data assets determines market leadership.

[5]In July 2025, NVIDIA became the first publicly traded company in history to reach a market value of $4 trillion.

[6]Recall Chapter 2 which showed the R&D to sales ratios by industry group.

Table 11.4. Market Capitalization and R&D Intensity of Leading AI Companies

	Market Capitalization (real 2024 billions of dollars)			R&D/Sales Ratio (percent)		
Firm Name	**Oct 20, '24**	**Oct 20, '23**	**Oct 20, '22**	**FY 2023**	**FY 2022**	**FY 2021**
Adobe Inc.	217.9	251.8	148.1	17.9	17.0	16.1
Alphabet Inc.	2,020.8	1,755.0	1,377.7	14.2	14.0	12.3
Amazon.com, Inc.	1,983.6	1,320.5	1,237.2	14.9	14.2	11.9
Apple Inc.	3,573.0	2,763.6	2,428.2	7.8	6.7	6.0
Arista Networks, Inc.	126.3	58.9	33.9	14.6	16.6	19.9
ASML Holding N.V.	261.2	220.7	190.2	14.4	15.4	13.7
Dynatrace, Inc.	16.3	13.9	10.2	18.8	16.8	15.8
Meta Platforms, Inc.	1,458.4	812.1	372.5	27.0	28.8	20.9
Microsoft Corporation	3,108.2	2,481.4	1,855.8	12.8	12.4	12.3
NVIDIA Corporation	3,385.1	1,045.3	319.8	27.2	19.6	23.5
Palantir Technologies	96.2	35.4	17.5	18.2	18.9	25.1
Tesla, Inc.	705.1	688.0	684.4	4.1	3.8	4.8

Source: S&P Capital IQ. Market capitalization deflated using the U.S. GDP Price Deflator.

The emergence of AI has raised fresh concerns about market power and concentration.[7] High concentration ratios in key AI markets precipitate these concerns. For example, NVIDIA controls approximately 92% of the data center GPU segment, according to IoT Analytics, which tracks data on the generative AI market (Table 11.5).[8]

In the global arena, AI confers competitive advantages for countries. Nations and companies with superior AI tools or greater access to data hold advantages over those without such resources, those constrained by stricter social regulations, or those facing higher royalty fees and more restrictive licensing arrangements. Low-income and least developed countries are particularly disadvantaged, as they often lack access to cutting-edge innovations and underlying knowledge, or must pay premium fees for technologies and products that incorporate these advances.

[7]See Ezrachi and Stucke (2017).
[8]https://iot-analytics.com/leading-generative-ai-companies/.

Table 11.5. Generative AI: Market Share of Leading Vendors

Datacenter GPUs (%)	Foundation Models & Platforms (%)	GenAI Services (%)
NVIDIA – 92	Microsoft – 39	Other – 76
AMD – 4	AWS – 19	Accenture – 7
Huawei – 2	Google – 15	Deloitte – 3
Intel – 1	OpenAI – 9	Capgemini – 2
Cerebras – 1	Other:	IBM – 2
	Anthropic – 4	McKinsey – 2
	Baidu – 4	BCG – 2
	Alibaba – 1	Cognizant – 2
	IBM – 1	EY – 1
		Bain & Company – 1
		TCS – 1
		NTT Data – 1
		Infosys – 1

Source: IoT Analytics Research.

U.S. firms dominate the AI landscape. As of 2024, U.S. companies account for roughly 34.6% of all AI-focused enterprises globally,[9] and nearly 60% of top-tier AI researchers are affiliated with U.S. institutions or firms.[10] Other nations in the top ten (as of September 2024) include China, the U.K., Israel, Canada, France, India, Japan, Germany, and Singapore. Leading companies such as Alphabet, Meta, Microsoft, and OpenAI possess significant advantages in access to talent, data, and computational resources, including GPUs (Graphics Processing Units), TPUs (Tensor Processing Units), and large-scale data centers required to train and operate AI models. These companies also benefit from relatively permissive regulatory environments. In the U.S., AI regulation has been characterized as lighter than in regions such as the European Union, allowing major tech firms to expand their AI capabilities with fewer regulatory constraints.[11]

[9]See Statista, "Distribution of Artificial Intelligence Companies Worldwide," 2024, https://www.statista.com/statistics/1452378/ai-distribution-by-country-worldwide.

[10]See https://snippet.finance/artificial-intelligence-2/.

[11]See Miller (2023).

11.2.2 *Trends in AI Patenting*

Between 2002 and 2018, the number of U.S. patent applications involving artificial intelligence technologies doubled, rising from approximately 30,000 to 60,000 filings. The share of patent applications incorporating AI-related subject matter has increased significantly over the longer term: in 1976, only 9% of patent subclasses included AI-related terms; by 2018, that figure had risen to 46%, indicating the growing diffusion of AI technologies across diverse fields.

The U.S. Patent and Trademark Office (USPTO) used a machine learning-based classification approach to identify and analyze AI patents across the entire corpus of filings. The methodology, described in detail by Giczy *et al.* (2022), involved the following steps:

- Creating a *seed set* of known AI-related patents based on expert classification;
- Training classification models — including neural networks — on both the seed set and a non-AI control group;
- Applying these models to the universe of U.S. patents to identify AI-related filings;
- Manually validating the outputs to refine accuracy.

Table 11.6 presents the AI components identified in the patent landscape.

Figures 11.2 and 11.3 present selected results from the USPTO's (2020) report. These charts illustrate trends in AI-related patent applications and the distribution of filings across different AI components.

Planning and control represents the most prevalent AI subfield in patent filings, followed by *knowledge processing*. However, since approximately 2012, *machine learning* and *computer vision* have experienced the most

Table 11.6. Components of AI Used in Patent Landscape

Planning and Control	Knowledge Processing
Vision	Speech
Machine Learning	Natural Language Processing
AI Hardware	Evolutionary Computation

Source: Giczy *et al.* (2022).

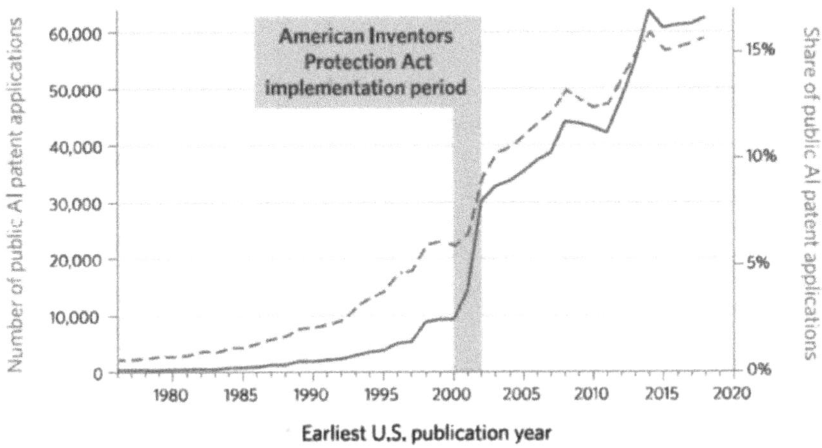

Figure 11.2. Share and Volume of AI Patent Applications (1976–2018)
Source: USPTO (2020), Figure 2, p. 5.

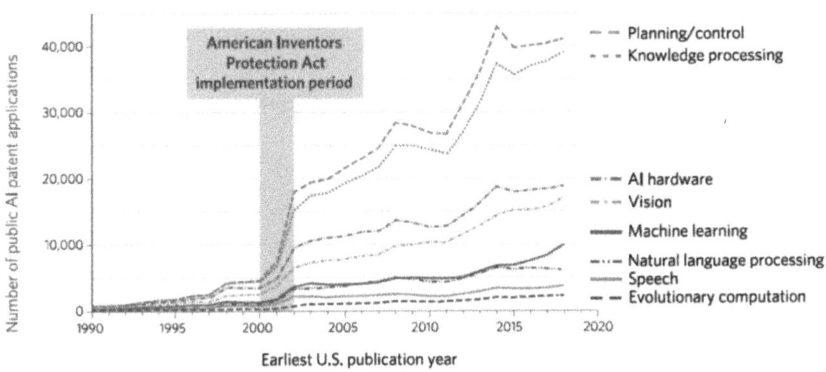

Figure 11.3. Volume of AI Applications by Component of AI
Source: USPTO (2020), Figure 3, p. 6.

rapid growth, reflecting their increasing importance in commercial applications and scientific research.

Company rankings for AI patents reflect a landscape in considerable flux.[12] In 2023, IBM led in generative AI patents, followed by Google, Microsoft, and Samsung. Generative AI patents accounted for more than

[12]IFI Claims is a database management company that tracks patent applications and grant data. See https://www.ificlaims.com.

one-fifth of all AI-related patents that year.[13] By mid-2025, however, Google had surged ahead to become the global leader in generative AI patents, followed by Samsung and Huawei. Within the U.S. market specifically, Google leads, followed by Microsoft and IBM.[14]

A significant development in AI patenting involves *agentic AI*, a type of artificial intelligence that makes decisions autonomously with minimal human input. Agentic AI accounts for approximately 5% of all AI-related patent applications globally and 7% in the U.S.[15] Google currently leads in agentic AI patenting, followed by NVIDIA. Notably, three Chinese universities — Tsinghua University, Peking University, and Zhejiang University — rank among the top ten patent holders in this field.[16]

The rapid rise in AI-related patent filings, spanning subfields such as machine learning, computer vision, and knowledge processing, reflects the growing ubiquity of AI as a general-purpose technology. This same technology enables non-human agents to contribute substantively to creative and inventive output. Their involvement challenges traditional doctrines of authorship and inventorship. The following sections examine how copyright and patent law are responding to these disruptions, with particular attention to the legal treatment of training data, disclosure standards, and the evolving status of AI-generated works and inventions.

11.3 Copyright Issues

At the core of copyright law is the concept of authorship. AI-generated works present doctrinal challenges. When an image, play, or musical composition is produced autonomously by a machine learning system, with minimal or no human creative input, is there an author behind the work? Under current doctrine, the answer is no. The U.S. Copyright Office has maintained that only works created by human beings are eligible for protection.[17]

[13]See https://www.ificlaims.com/news/ for news on the IBM, Microsoft, and Google race.

[14]https://www.axios.com/2025/05/15/ai-patents-google-agents.

[15]https://www.stanventures.com/news/google-takes-the-lead-in-generative-and-agentic-ai-patents-2710/.

[16]https://medium.com/@joycebirkins/top-15-pioneering-ai-research-institutions-across-china-and-the-us-companies-labs-and-f07f5a495b63.

[17]See U.S. Copyright Office reports on Copyright and AI, Parts 1–3, https://www.copyright.gov/ai/.

This section reviews legal scholarship that reinforces the view that copyright exists to recognize and reward human labor and expression, not machine outputs devoid of personal expression. Economic analysis supports this perspective. No underlying incentive problem exists for the legal system to correct. Unlike human creators, AI systems do not require motivation or compensation to produce output. Granting exclusive rights over AI-generated works risks overprotection and rent-seeking without any corresponding gain in creativity or innovation.

A practical ambiguity remains in edge cases: when a human user selects prompts and edits or curates AI-generated content, to what degree does that intervention constitute authorship? The copyright system will need to draw distinctions based on the degree of human control and originality. However, this threshold will shift as generative AI tools become more powerful, underscoring the importance of resolving these intellectual property questions proactively.

A more contentious issue concerns the use of copyrighted works as training inputs for AI models. Large language models (LLMs) often scrape materials from the open web without explicit permission, including copyrighted works. Does the ingestion of such material violate the exclusive rights of reproduction or adaptation? Or does it fall under fair use, text and data mining (TDM) provisions, or research exemptions?

Initially, it might appear that training AI does not constitute copyright infringement because the models do not reproduce copyrighted works directly. Texts are converted into numerical representations — token embeddings[18] — which serve as the model's internal vocabulary and do not resemble human expression. However, copyright law is concerned not with how data are encoded (text versus tokens) but with the use of copyrighted material. First, ingesting training data may involve copying, downloading, or scanning works, even if only temporarily. Second, information is stored in model weights and parameters, not as verbatim text. Third, the risk of regurgitation remains: AI outputs could reproduce copyrighted phrases, melodies, or images.[19] Conversely, weights and parameters represent the outcome of a machine learning process that encodes patterns and associations, which could support the argument that trained models constitute transformative use. These legal questions remain unsettled and depend on jurisdiction and context.

---

[18]See Appendix 11A.

[19]This risk varies significantly based on training data frequency and model size.

The stakes of this debate are high and are already playing out in litigation. In *Getty Images v. Stability AI*, the plaintiff alleged that its copyrighted photographs were used without authorization to train the Stable Diffusion model, which subsequently generated outputs that resembled Getty's distinctive style. Similarly, in *New York Times v. OpenAI and Microsoft*, the Times argued that LLMs' reproduction of its journalistic content undermines its subscriber base.

11.3.1 *Guiding Principles*

The preceding discussion highlights two fundamental questions that artificial intelligence raises for copyright law:

1. Should AI-generated outputs be considered copyrightable works?
2. Does the ingestion of copyrighted materials during training constitute infringement?

Craig (2022) argues that the answer is no on both fronts. First, works generated autonomously by AI do not meet the legal or philosophical definition of authorship and thus should reside in the public domain. Second, the use of copyrighted material for training does not itself produce a competing work, nor does it interfere with the creator's ability to benefit from their creation. In this view, training is more analogous to education or research than to commercial exploitation.

Historically, the copyright system has adapted to disruptive technologies — the printing press, phonographs, film, television, the internet — by refining doctrines rather than replacing them. AI represents the latest such technology, but with an added twist: it is not merely a tool or medium, but may increasingly act with agency, combining and generating expressive content beyond direct human control.

This dual role — AI as both input (tool) and output (creator) — complicates traditional categories of originality, fixation, and authorship. Courts, policymakers, and the public have been grappling with the implications for the copyright system. On this doctrinal question, Craig (2022) argues against creating new laws and rights specifically for machine-generated content. The law should be technologically neutral, not written for any specific invention or creation, yet it should not be oblivious to functional differences between new and existing technologies.

> "It is not appropriate for copyright law to respond to these technological developments in a formally tech-neutral way, treating alike AI and human activities and artefacts that are fundamentally different in nature. Nor is it sufficient to focus on their *functional equivalence*, analogizing between AI and human activities and artefacts without regard to the social values and public purposes that underpin the copyright system. Rather, it is the normative objectives of the copyright system and the values they reflect that should be regarded as technologically neutral."[20]

Thus, Craig's approach to technological neutrality seeks to achieve *normative neutrality* or *normative equilibrium*. This means interpreting and applying copyright law in ways that serve the law's fundamental purposes: incentivizing authorship and the dissemination of original works. These represent the normative objectives of the copyright system.

To the extent that AI disrupts society, the economy, and culture, maintaining technological neutrality may call for laws to be recalibrated in response to technological change. Adjustments may be needed, for example, to preserve equilibrium between the interests of users and authors. Consistency should be sought not in the application of the law "but rather in the steady pursuit of the law's purpose."[21]

Any new legal frameworks governing AI should therefore be informed by copyright law's fundamental aims. Copyright systems around the world, while varying in scope, strength, and specific provisions, generally seek to encourage creativity and advance social well-being. As noted earlier in the book, the intellectual property system is a publicly supported institution that exists to address market failures associated with knowledge as a public good. Administered by public agencies, its ultimate goal is to promote the public interest.

The following subsections address the issues of AI authorship and AI training data through the lens of this framework of technological neutrality aimed at normative balance. Rather than extending new rights to machines or imposing new liabilities on developers, the law's priority should be to safeguard the public interest, preserve the integrity of authorship, and ensure access to existing works without undue restrictions.

---

[20] Craig (2022), p. 31.

[21] *Ibid.*, p. 11.

(i) Authorship

AI systems are now capable of producing creative works with minimal or no human prompting. This raises a core legal and philosophical question: Who, if anyone, is the author? Is it the AI system itself, the human programmer, or some hybrid of the two? And what if the machine operates autonomously, with no specific direction or expressive contribution from a human being?

Traditionally, copyright law requires that a work originate from a human author. Absent human authorship, the work is ineligible for protection and enters the public domain. But legal ambiguity arises when a human trains, fine-tunes, or curates the model's behavior. Does facilitation count as authorship? If so, how much involvement is required to satisfy the originality threshold?

These doctrinal uncertainties also raise a larger policy question: Do AI-generated works even need copyright protection? That is, does extending protection to such works incentivize their creation, or incentivize the development and deployment of generative AI systems? If not, what is the rationale for granting exclusive rights?

Intellectual property rights exist to address specific market failures. They are justified when the absence of protection would deter investment in socially valuable creation. If an output would be produced anyway, without human authorship or creative risk, then copyright protection primarily creates economic rents.

The discussion thus far suggests that extending copyright to AI-generated works is neither an appropriate reward nor an effective incentive to promote the kind of authorship that advances the social purposes envisioned by copyright law. AI is not an author in either an ontological or teleological sense. It is not conscious of being an author, nor is it purposeful in the way that human creators are. An AI-generated output may resemble a work of authorship, but it lacks intentionality. A robot, for instance, may mimic a smile, but it is not expressing an emotional state; it has no feeling behind the gesture.

Creative expression protected by copyright is more than output. It is the embodiment of a human being's individual perspective, identity, and effort. The law protects that expressive effort, not merely the aesthetic or functional qualities of the final product. By contrast, an AI system is not a sentient, thinking entity. Denying copyright to its outputs does not impede its ability to generate content. The machine may be trained or programmed to produce works that appear expressive, such as melodies, paintings, or dance sequences. But these are simulations, not genuine expressions of thought or experience.

Human creations are typically intended to generate thoughts, emotions, perspectives, or public debate. As Buccafusco (2016) argues, a human author creates with the intention to produce mental effects in an audience — whether through a book, film, painting, or piece of music. This intentional, communicative dimension is central to the legal and moral conception of authorship.

Craig (2022) similarly contends that AI-generated works lack this communicative intentionality. Even if an AI's output is aesthetically or structurally equivalent to a human-authored work, it fails to "engage in authorship as a relational and communicative act."[22] The output may resemble human creativity, but its generative process is devoid of conscious thought, expression, or engagement with an audience.

Over time, AI systems may acquire more sophisticated capabilities to evoke emotional or intellectual responses, such as producing a provocative image about war and peace. But even these effects arise from engineered mimicry: machine learning algorithms, filters, and code designed to imitate human intention. The underlying system is optimizing for correlation, not expression.

Moreover, it remains an open question whether copyright protection is economically necessary for such works. If no human author or company has been denied compensation due to the absence of copyright, then the justification for exclusivity is weak. Machine learning systems will continue to generate outputs regardless of whether those outputs are eligible for protection. As non-sentient entities, they cannot suffer loss, indignity, or misappropriation in the legal or moral sense. They do not feel violated if their works are freely used or modified.

Craig (2022) suggests that extending copyright protection to machine-generated content might actually inhibit creativity rather than foster it. Machines may create a dense thicket of copyrighted outputs, many of which may be only minimally differentiated. This could chill follow-on creativity and limit access to basic creative building blocks. The analogy to the "anti-commons" is apt: just as excessive patent fragmentation can stifle innovation in biotechnology or software, a proliferation of overlapping copyrights in AI-generated outputs could burden human creators, especially given AI's

[22] *Ibid.*, p. 22.

ability to generate content at a far greater scale and speed than any individual author.

The concern is not limited to output saturation. As AI systems become more sophisticated, their "expressive" capabilities may increasingly resemble those of humans, potentially triggering claims for protection over millions of variations. If each AI-generated image, musical riff, or narrative thread is eligible for protection, the resulting IP landscape could become over-enclosed, making it difficult for artists, educators, and even other AI systems to reuse content without navigating complex and costly licenses.

Any resulting glut of AI-generated work could depress the market value of creative content and undermine incentives for human authorship. Copyright law is designed to stimulate creativity where it would otherwise be undersupplied, not to reward the mass production of derivative or indistinguishable works. In this sense, copyright risks being redirected away from its normative goal of rewarding and encouraging human expression.

(ii) Training Dataset

The training of artificial intelligence systems requires vast quantities of accurate and diverse data. When intellectual property rights are overly restrictive — requiring multiple permissions and licenses — they can impede access to essential training inputs. As a result, AI systems may develop with incomplete or skewed knowledge bases. This inaccessibility increases the risk of embedded bias, error propagation, or the amplification of noise, particularly when training datasets lack sufficient coverage of minority viewpoints, edge cases, or multicultural and multilingual diversity.

An instructive analogy is that of dart throwing, as depicted in Figure 11.4. Imagine that the goal of training AI is to hit a conceptual bullseye — a representation of some underlying truth, optimal solution, or fact yet to be fully observed (such as a vaccine formula, the blueprint for an energy-efficient engine, or a causal explanation of a historical event). Each throw of the dart represents an attempt to approximate that truth using available data. In the left-hand diagram, the thrown darts cluster around the bullseye. While not perfectly accurate, they demonstrate an unbiased pattern with low dispersion, suggesting that the dataset enables reasonably accurate generalizations.

However, the diagram on the right illustrates a different pathology: the thrown darts are tightly clustered, but they converge around a point that is far from the truth. In this case, researchers or AI systems may reach consensus, but the consensus is wrong. This outcome reflects a systematic

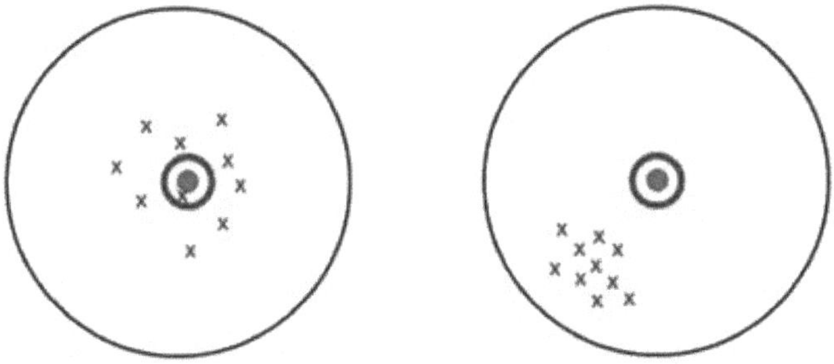

Figure 11.4. Illustration of Bias and Variance in Data Approximation

bias in the training data: the model is consistent but consistently inaccurate. The dataset is insufficient or skewed, leading to distorted inferences.

This scenario is particularly concerning in socially sensitive domains. Racial or gender bias may become entrenched when underrepresented groups are excluded from training corpora. Likewise, if the cultural or philosophical sources used to train an AI system draw exclusively from one tradition, such as Western or Eastern canons, it may reinforce a narrow worldview and marginalize alternative perspectives.

The moral of the analogy is clear: data quality matters. Good data are needed not only to offset bad data, but to enable systems to distinguish between true and false statements, relevant and misleading patterns. AI is only as robust as the diversity, accuracy, and completeness of its training datasets. When exclusivity and proprietary claims restrict access to high-quality content, they increase the likelihood that models will replicate or amplify bias — analogous to the right side of Figure 11.4. This strengthens the case for ensuring open or broad-based access to data in the training of AI systems, subject to appropriate safeguards.

When restrictions are imposed on access to training data — whether through copyright, trade secrecy, or contractual limitations — the result is often a smaller, less representative, and less efficient sample. The knowledge encoded into such constrained datasets may reflect existing power structures or dominant schools of thought, reinforcing bias and epistemic narrowness. What AI systems require, by contrast, are diverse and pluralistic inputs: multiple points of view, a wealth of facts, and competing theories. Only with such breadth can machine learning systems produce insights that are both accurate and socially responsive.

The challenge for policymakers is to strike an appropriate balance: to preserve incentives for creative production while ensuring that copyright law does not obstruct the socially beneficial development of artificial intelligence. Without sufficient legal flexibilities, such as fair use doctrines, text and data mining (TDM) exceptions, or collective licensing mechanisms, the development of representative and socially responsive AI systems may be compromised.

But why is the use of copyrighted works in training datasets not considered infringement? The prevailing legal rationale is that copyright protects expression, not ideas, facts, or functional use. The training process does not involve the enjoyment or appropriation of an author's expressive work in the conventional sense. AI systems are non-sentient; they do not experience, interpret, or derive meaning from creative content. As Craig (2022) emphasizes, training AI constitutes a non-expressive use of texts; that is, texts are used as data inputs to develop capabilities, not as works to be read, understood, or aesthetically appreciated.

A practical issue, though, is whether granting AI training datasets access to copyrighted materials has resulted in measurable market harm or diminished incentives for creative output and R&D. Under the WIPO three-step test, as well as many national fair use or fair dealing regimes, economic impact on the rights holder is a central consideration. However, empirical evidence on this point remains limited. Has the use of copyrighted materials in training datasets clearly displaced sales or licensing revenue? Has it deterred authorship or innovation? These questions highlight the need for empirical data to assess the economic impact of using copyrighted materials in AI training. Until more comprehensive studies are conducted, conclusions about market harm remain speculative.

In the meantime, challenges emerge when AI-generated outputs closely resemble the expressive structure or conceptual substance of copyrighted works. Consider a physicist who publishes a pathbreaking solution to a quantum gravity problem. A human author may later build upon or describe the same idea using different language, either with proper attribution or through independent reasoning. Copyright law accommodates this through its protection of expression, not ideas. But if an AI system, trained on the physicist's original text, produces content that mimics its explanatory structure or paraphrases core insights with minimal transformation, the original author may be deprived of recognition, royalties, or professional credit. In such cases, even if the use of the training material was non-expressive, the output could function as a market substitute and thereby trigger legitimate concerns about misappropriation, misattribution, and economic displacement.

The culprit here may not lie with AI training *per se*, but with the nature of the dataset. Large-scale generative models are often presumed to blend multiple sources into diffuse, hybrid outputs. Yet if a training dataset is narrow, skewed, or dominated by a single author or school of thought, the risk of disproportionate reproduction rises. The more homogeneous the inputs, the greater the likelihood that the outputs will essentially reproduce existing works with minimal transformation.

There is also a real cost dimension to the debate. If access to high-quality training data requires expensive licensing agreements, only well-funded researchers, firms, or institutions will be able to afford such content. This creates significant entry barriers in AI development, favoring incumbents with deep pockets and reinforcing concentration in both data ownership and model development. Smaller firms, academic institutions, and developers in low-resource settings may be effectively excluded from participating in cutting-edge AI research. As a result, the knowledge base underlying these systems could become increasingly biased, shaped by the priorities and perspectives of a narrow set of actors, precisely the outcome that is captured by the right half of Figure 11.4.

(iii) Potential Criticisms

- **Commercialization:** The discussion thus far has not fully addressed the commercialization side of creative production. Once works are generated, either entirely by AI or with human-AI collaboration, additional steps are required to bring them to market or put them into practical use. For instance, adapting a book like the *Wizard of Oz* into a film involves significant resources, investment, and specialized talent, from actors and directors to engineers and marketers. Chapter 6 established that the copyright industry operates in tandem with a complementary industry, which supplies essential inputs to the creative industry and enhances the value of creative outputs. This complementary sector may require the protection of intellectual property rights to provide these goods and services. Thus, beyond the traditional human author–audience relationship, a broader ecosystem of firms, platforms, and distributors plays a pivotal role in commercializing creative works. These intermediaries may depend on IP incentives to facilitate the production and dissemination of AI-generated works. Ultimately, empirical research is needed to illuminate how copyrights and AI jointly influence creativity and commercialization.
- **Over-Reliance on Intentionality:** AI lacks intentionality and consciousness. However, copyright has long protected works without inquiry

into the author's state of mind. For example, it protects corporate authorship, works-for-hire, ornamental designs, and pseudonymous publications. In practice, copyright focuses on the nature of the work, not the nature of the author, and rewards behavior, not deep cognition.

- **Perceived Risk of "Anti-Commons":** The concern about a potential AI-generated copyright thicket is well taken, given the volume of content AI systems can generate. But it cannot be assumed that copyrights in AI output would all be enforced. In practice, owners of copyrighted works may not find it cost-justified to enforce or register low-valued works. The copyright system may be able to prevent an anti-commons situation, despite an onslaught of AI works, through fair use or compulsory licensing.
- **Objection to Non-Expressive Use:** The argument that training AI on copyrighted works is "non-expressive" because the machine does not derive satisfaction from the work as a human would raises significant concerns. The entire goal of AI training on creative works is, in the end, to learn and replicate the expressive qualities. To argue that the use is non-expressive becomes problematic if AI generates output that extracts the expressive essence of the work, which then competes with the original work in the marketplace. From the machine's perspective, the use of copyrighted works may be non-expressive, but from a market perspective, the economic outcome might be quite expressive (or "market encroaching").[23]

11.4 Patent Issues

This section examines how artificial intelligence (AI) challenges core doctrines in patent law. Two critical questions emerge at the intersection of AI and patent protection: Can AI be recognized as an inventor? How should patent law evaluate standards such as novelty, non-obviousness (inventive step), and sufficiency of disclosure when AI significantly contributes to the inventive process?

At the outset, it should be noted that these issues pertain to AI-generated or AI-assisted innovations. The underlying hardware and software products and methods of AI systems, such as the application programming interfaces, foundation model architecture, and processing chips,

---

[23]See Comments of Benjamin L. W. Sobel submitted, December 15, 2019, regarding the U.S. Patent and Trademark Office's Request for Comments on *Intellectual Property Protection for Artificial Intelligence Innovation*, PTO-C-2019-0038.

remain eligible for intellectual property protection under existing frameworks. The applicable IP right — whether patent, copyright, trademark, design right, or trade secret — depends on what aspect requires protection (function, expression, branding, confidential information, or aesthetic design) and whether the legal criteria for that specific right are satisfied.

11.4.1 *AI as Inventor*

To date, AI has largely functioned as an assistive tool, augmenting human creativity and technical problem-solving. However, as AI systems grow in sophistication, capable of generating novel outputs without direct human intervention, their contributions increasingly resemble acts of invention. While AI lacks sentience and cannot qualify as an inventor in an ontological or legal sense, its role in generating technical solutions may be so substantial that it challenges the attribution of inventorship solely to a natural person. Most jurisdictions have affirmed that AI systems cannot be listed as inventors: they are not legal persons, and thus cannot own property or hold patent rights. Nonetheless, the operator or owner of the AI system, including its underlying models and training datasets, may have a claim to derivative rights or first possession.[24]

AI may, in some cases, be capable of autonomously generating inventions without meaningful human input or guidance.[25] The DABUS case spurred debate over AI inventorship and illustrates these tensions (see Box 1).

Box 1. Thaler and the DABUS Litigation

Stephen Thaler, a U.S. entrepreneur, filed patent applications in multiple jurisdictions listing an AI system named DABUS (Device for the Autonomous Bootstrapping of Unified Sentience) as the sole inventor. The applications covered a fractal beverage container and a flashing light beacon.

(*Continued*)

[24]See *Thaler v. Commissioner of Patents* [2021] FCA 879 (Federal Court of Australia). See also the discussion in de Rassenfosse *et al.* (2023).

[25]This mirrors debates in copyright law, where AI can produce outputs that resemble creative expression without exhibiting intentionality or communicative purpose.

Thaler argued that DABUS had independently generated the inventions and that excluding AI from inventorship would disqualify an emerging category of machine-generated innovations. He proposed that the human owner of the AI system should be permitted to hold the resulting patent rights.

Courts and patent offices in the United States, United Kingdom, European Union, and Australia rejected this claim, affirming that inventorship must be attributed to a natural person. However, they left open how to treat inventions generated by AI with human involvement.

One possible compromise is a hybrid attribution model, where the human acts more as a facilitator or supervisor — analogous to a jockey guiding a racehorse — rather than the sole originator of the inventive idea. Patent law could evolve to recognize derivative inventorship, allowing the human operator of the AI system to be named as the legal inventor.[i]

[i]See https://imagination-engines.com/dabus.html.

Thus, if an AI system autonomously generates an invention without human intervention or motivation, on what basis should patent protection be granted? Patents exist primarily to create incentives for innovation, rewarding the time, risk, and investment that human inventors incur in producing new knowledge. However, an AI system, as an inanimate object, does not require incentives: it performs tasks because it is programmed or trained to do so. Granting exclusive rights in such cases may confer economic rents to the owners or operators of AI systems, not as a reward for creative labor, but simply for possessing a machine capable of producing inventive outputs. In such cases, it would be argued that AI-generated inventions should fall into the public domain.

There is, however, a counterargument rooted in concerns about the appropriability of returns. Even if AI itself does not require incentives, its human developers and institutional backers (e.g., venture capitalists) may need protection to justify their investments in building, training, and deploying such systems. If AI-generated inventions can be easily copied, reverse engineered, and commercially replicated by competitors, the original developers may face reduced returns, potentially discouraging further investment. Yet this rationale blurs the line between protecting inventive labor and protecting capital investment. Policymakers must grapple with whether exclusivity is still justified when the inventive step is automated, and whether alternative mechanisms, such as trade secrecy, open licensing, or shorter patent terms, might better allow innovators and investors to capture their returns.

Trade secrecy presents a key tradeoff: it incentivizes investment in innovation without requiring public disclosure. However, if AI-generated inventions are increasingly withheld as trade secrets, the result could be a diminished public repository of technical knowledge, undermining the patent system's traditional quid pro quo.

Another complexity arises from the growing potential for *independent invention* by competing AI systems. In copyright law, independent creation is a defense to infringement; two individuals may coincidentally produce identical works without violating each other's rights. But patent law offers no such protection: an inventor who files second risks being blocked or liable for infringement. If AI systems are converging on similar inventive solutions, the likelihood of parallel discovery increases. This is especially true when suboptimal options have been exhausted and models converge on what may be the single best solution.[26] Thus, when AI models trained on large but overlapping datasets arrive at the same solution, it may reflect not copying or coordination, but the structure of the problem itself. But this convergence phenomenon also has implications for obviousness analysis: in domains such as engineering or the natural sciences, the frequency of independent invention may be a sign that the inventions are likely to be deemed obvious.

Commercialization likely remains a compelling case for granting exclusive rights over AI-generated inventions. Even when the inventive act is performed autonomously by an AI system, substantial human and financial resources are typically required to bring the resulting product to market. If the invention can be easily replicated — particularly by other AI systems trained on similar architectures — there is a risk of rapid imitation that erodes the original developer's ability to recoup the investment. In such cases, a temporary period of exclusivity, or a right analogous to patent protection, may be justified — not as a reward for creative insight, but as an incentive for downstream commercialization.[27]

[26]To paraphrase Tolstoy's *Anna Karenina*: all good solutions are alike, but each bad solution is bad in its own way.

[27]de Rassenfosse *et al.* (2023) also argue that the patentability of AI-generated inventions could encourage their commercialization and technology transfer.

Examples of downstream commercialization include pharmaceutical molecule generation; AI-designed engineering components for drones or autonomous vehicles; tax preparation or accounting software; AI-generated robotic systems that serve as instructors or caregivers; synthetic voices for media and branding; and AI-generated architectural or urban planning designs. Many other cases could be added. The important point is that even when the inventive task is performed by an AI system, value realization typically occurs downstream — in commercialization — and involves human labor, capital investment, and regulatory navigation. In such circumstances, temporary exclusivity may be justified not to reward creation, but to protect the substantial investments required to bring an AI-generated invention to market.

A useful analogy lies in the concept of derivative works under copyright law. Just as a filmmaker may seek exclusive rights to adapt a novel into a film, there is value in securing time-limited rights to exploit and scale the output of an AI system.

Patents may thus serve a secondary function: not to reward creativity *per se*, but to make the economics of deploying machine-generated inventions viable. Once created, such inventions often require active management, licensing, or inclusion in patent pools — particularly in fields where overlapping rights give rise to complex negotiations or blocking positions. The management of intellectual property remains a human task, even if AI tools can assist. The issue, then, is not whether machines require incentives, but whether the legal framework adequately supports the human and institutional infrastructure necessary for the commercialization of autonomous invention.

11.4.2 *Inventive Step*

The requirement of an inventive step, or non-obviousness, precludes the patenting of inventions that would have been obvious to a person having ordinary skill in the art (PHOSITA) at the time of the invention. The inventive step represents the "delta" — the difference between a new invention and existing knowledge. Patent law asks whether this delta would be obvious to a person having ordinary skill in the art. Artificial intelligence complicates this assessment in two major ways.[28] First, AI enhances the cognitive and technical capabilities of inventors, effectively raising the baseline of what is considered "ordinary skill." With advanced tools at their

[28]See Shemtov and Gabison (2022) for further discussion.

disposal, human inventors may be able to explore more complex problem spaces and generate more creative solutions. In this view, AI simultaneously raises the bar for obviousness and expands the frontier of what is technically achievable, enabling innovations that would not have emerged through human reasoning alone.

Second, AI also improves the capabilities of patent examiners, peer reviewers, and other skilled practitioners. As these evaluators incorporate AI into their assessments, the standard of what is considered "obvious" may rise in parallel. What might once have appeared inventive could now be deemed a routine extrapolation, especially when AI systems can autonomously identify optimal solutions from vast search spaces. But as AI-assisted techniques become increasingly common in technical fields, new ideas, creations, and inventions may appear more "obvious" than they would have before such tools existed. A priori, it therefore appears that AI can cut both ways: both raising the standard for inventiveness while simultaneously making higher-quality solutions more achievable.

The expanding use of AI also affects the stock of prior art. To the extent that AI assistance boosts human inventions or AI generates its own inventive outputs — especially alongside a rise in scientific publications produced with AI tools — the body of knowledge or prior art against which future inventions are measured will grow. This may disadvantage human-generated inventions that appear less sophisticated in comparison, or raise the bar for novelty. As a result, technologies may face a greater burden to differentiate themselves from existing art.

If the threshold for non-obviousness or novelty is raised due to benchmarking against machine capabilities, human ingenuity may be undervalued and under-incentivized. This has ramifications for human capital investments. Would individuals still invest in higher education knowing that AI could perform the bulk of the work or generate innovations autonomously — and that humans would merely need to *guide* AI, rather than be trained as experts themselves? Or would incentives for higher education increase in order to keep pace with AI development? While AI may endogenously increase in sophistication through self-supervised learning, human interventions often provide the impetus for better AI systems. Human managers and scientists provide the vision for AI development and design. In this case, AI may spur human capital development. Again, a priori, it appears that AI will have ambiguous effects on incentives for education. In the longer run, this could create an indirect effect on patenting, as a reduction in skilled professionals would translate into fewer R&D scientists and innovators.

Another critical dimension is disclosure. When AI is used in the inventive process, full disclosure may require explanations about the structure of the algorithms, the nature of the training data, and the way the AI system was prompted or configured to generate the inventive outcome. But black-box AI systems, especially those involving deep learning, can obscure the causal mechanisms underlying an invention. This makes it difficult for patent examiners and future researchers to verify how a particular result was obtained. This opacity, combined with the lack of access to training data, makes it difficult even for the PHOSITA to replicate the AI-generated invention. A later section of the chapter will address the disclosure requirement in more detail, particularly with respect to data sources.

Thus far, the attention has been on new inventions — whether AI-assisted or AI-generated. AI tools can also be used to optimize existing inventions, improving their performance or extending their longevity (i.e., making them less susceptible to technological obsolescence). If AI can systematically raise the quality of both existing and new inventions, the inventive "delta" can narrow as well as widen. This again introduces ambiguity about whether AI-enabled inventions will consistently cross the patentability threshold.

The inventive step has social implications. If the standard for the inventive step is set too high, only a few inventors will qualify for patent protection, markets may become concentrated, and innovators may become discouraged. This could lead to static product quality growth. If the standard is set too low, the result may be an overabundance of patents, including trivial or marginal improvements, which can lead to a flood of new filings and the emergence of patent thickets that stifle rather than spur innovation.[29] Once again, a nonlinear relationship can be visualized between the rate of innovation and the standard for the inventive step.

The problem of the anti-commons is a possibility here as well. If AI-generated technologies are subject to fragmented or conflicting rights, or if the training data that power them and the underlying machine learning processes are opaque, the development of downstream applications may be stifled. The result could be the underuse of valuable AI innovations, not because of technical constraints, but because of legal and institutional barriers to access.[30]

[29] See Rai (2019).

[30] See de Rassenfosse *et al.* (2023).

When the risk of patent rejection increases due to higher non-obviousness standards, firms may prefer trade secrecy over patenting, resulting in reduced public disclosure of new knowledge. This shift may contribute to a diminished ability to trace the source of innovations and draw connections among existing innovations.

Finally, the cost of development plays a critical role in a firm's decision to seek patent protection. This decision can be expressed as a simple inequality: a firm will apply for a patent if

$$\rho\Delta V > F$$

where F represents the fixed cost of development, including upfront R&D expenditures and patenting fees. The term $\rho\Delta V$ captures the expected incremental value of receiving a patent. Here, ρ is the probability of securing a patent, which depends in part on the patent examiner's judgment of non-obviousness, and ΔV is the difference in economic returns with and without protection. Specifically, $\Delta V = V^{PAT} - V^{NO\ PAT}$, where V^{PAT} is the firm's value with a patent and $V^{NO\ PAT}$ is its value without one. A rational innovator will pursue patent protection only if the expected benefit exceeds the cost; otherwise, the innovation is more likely to be retained as a trade secret.

The question is how AI affects that cost-benefit calculation. On the one hand, AI tools may reduce the cost term F by streamlining or automating key stages of the innovation process. For instance, in pharmaceutical development, AI may enable more targeted preclinical analysis by improving compound screening, reducing error rates, and identifying promising candidates more efficiently. These capabilities can reduce the number of clinical trials required and lower the probability of failure.

At the same time, AI could affect both ρ and ΔV. If patent examiners apply stricter non-obviousness standards due to widespread AI use, the probability ρ of a successful application may decline. Conversely, if AI tools allow competitors to imitate inventions more easily, the value of patent protection increases — and hence ΔV rises. But if an AI-embedded world leads to more rapid technological turnover — that is, faster obsolescence — product life cycles would shorten. The expected return from patenting falls, as the invention may become outdated before imitation even becomes viable. In such cases, innovators may rely more on lead-time advantages to commercially exploit the invention, avoiding the time and cost associated with patenting. Thus, the overall effect of AI on patenting behavior remains theoretically ambiguous and is sensitive to shifts in both legal thresholds and economic incentives. Table 11.7 summarizes these predictions.

Table 11.7. Possible Impacts on AI Patenting Incentives

Component	AI Impact	Mechanism
Probability of Patent Grant (ρ)	Ambiguous (↓ if stricter exams)	AI raises the baseline of obviousness, making patents harder to obtain in some fields
Patent Value (ΔV)	↑ if imitation risk is greater	Greater imitation risk increases the incremental value of patent protection
	↓ if product cycles more rapid	Increased turnover or technological obsolescence reduces demand for patents
Development Cost (F)	↓ due to automation	AI reduces R&D cost by automating discovery and accelerating prototyping

Many of the ambiguities behind these predictions can be clarified through more data and empirical analysis. For example, what are the true costs of developing general-purpose AI systems, such as large language models (LLMs) or artificial general intelligence (AGI)? These include not only direct costs — computing infrastructure, data acquisition, and personnel — but also indirect costs, such as licensing input technologies like pre-trained models, software libraries, or proprietary algorithms. In addition, AGI systems often rely on a broader technological stack that includes patent-protected or trade-secret components, further raising development costs. There are likely to be high fixed costs associated with AI development and low marginal costs of production and distribution to the extent that output generation is automated.

Furthermore, would firms underinvest in developing AGI systems if patents for AI-generated inventions were not available? Does the lack of protection for AI outputs discourage investment in the upstream tools that produce them? A related question concerns the downstream market: does the absence of patent protection over AGI outputs hinder commercialization — either because of weak appropriation mechanisms or because rival firms can easily replicate the outputs? If so, granting limited rights (patents, sui generis protections, or commercialization rights) may be necessary not to reward the AI itself, but to maintain a wider innovation ecosystem around it. These familiar questions in the IP literature require further empirical investigation in the context of AI markets.

11.5 Privacy

AI systems require massive amounts of training data. Concerns about data privacy are heightened, particularly because generative AI tools process and learn from vast datasets. These often include sensitive or personal information used as *inputs* during training, raising the risk that such data may reappear in *outputs*. Even anonymized data are vulnerable to hacking and other security breaches.

A difficult policy tradeoff arises between the data needs of AI systems and individual claims to privacy. AI innovations hold the potential to augment productivity growth and contribute to social welfare, but violations of privacy can generate significant social harm. These costs and benefits are heterogeneous not only across individuals and use cases but also in their degree and severity.

Tucker (2019) discusses how AI presents new or different problems for the law and economics of privacy:

- **Data Persistence:** Once created, digital information is difficult to erase.
- **Repurposing:** Data may be reused repeatedly, often for purposes beyond the original intent.
- **Data Spillovers:** Third parties may be affected by information exchanges between others. This challenges the traditional understanding of privacy as an individual's right to be left alone, since AI technologies can capture or divulge information from unwitting participants — through facial recognition, location tracking, and predictive modeling of groups and individuals, among other means.

King and Meinhardt (2024) also discuss the unique privacy risks posed by AI. These risks stem, among other things, from the surveillance and profiling that AI enables. Such practices threaten individual autonomy and offer little recourse for correcting inaccurate data or preventing the storage of personal information without consent. These risks jeopardize fundamental liberties and can affect opportunities for employment, housing, health care, and insurance when algorithms generate discriminatory profiles.

The authors argue that existing privacy laws and regulations on algorithmic decision-making offer insufficient data governance protections.

The authors provide three proposals for addressing data privacy challenges associated with AI. First, shift the data-sharing regime from **opt-out to opt-in**. Data on individuals should not be collected unless they explicitly consent; that is, unless they opt in. This would create a regime of privacy by default, replacing the current implicit system in which companies routinely collect personal data. One example comes from the genetic screening company *23andMe*, where customers were given the option to participate in surveys used for research.[31] These surveys asked questions about diet, exercise, preferences, and family history. Another example is *Apple iOS 14.5*, which prompted users upon opening an app to choose whether they wished to be tracked. A vast majority (about 70%) declined or did not opt in — an instructive sign that most users preferred to preserve their privacy.

A second proposal is to develop standards for the AI data development **supply chain**. The objective is to provide a holistic oversight of the entire training dataset pipeline. This includes documenting the provenance (or source) of data, limiting broad data collection in favor of purpose-specific use, improving the quality of data (e.g., removing "dirty" or erroneous inputs), and preventing the inadvertent disclosure of personally identifiable information (PII) in AI outputs. It would also be useful to document whether consent was given at any point along the chain where individual data were used. Were data subjects aware that their information was collected? Did they provide meaningful consent?[32]

A third proposal is to **flip the script** on how personal data are managed. In the current system, consumers' data are often scraped by firms without consent and used for data analytics. In some cases, consumers voluntarily provide personal information, such as contact or demographic data, in exchange for access to online services. In the flipped model, consumers would negotiate the terms under which firms access and use their data. This can be facilitated through data intermediaries that operate between data demanders (organizations) and data suppliers (individual consumers),

[31]The company filed for bankruptcy in March 2025 and underwent a court-supervised restructuring and asset sale process.

[32]This is analogous to the case of copyrighted material used in AI training: Were copyrighted materials included? Did their use fall under fair use or fair dealing, or did it require permission or consent? Did AI outputs inadvertently produce infringing content? A further policy consideration concerns whether data subjects should have the right to request deletion or exclusion of their data, and whether they can verify that such requests have been honored.

thereby enabling a system of personal data licensing. The intermediary would share data in accordance with the consumer's preferences, giving individuals more control over their personal information. This approach would replace the existing regime of data collection by default.

The question for further research is whether these proposals strike the right balance between society's technological needs and its desire to prevent harms. Would the strengthening of privacy rights disrupt AI training and future innovation? Or could it align the rate of AI innovation with the socially desired rate?

Implementation of these proposals is not without difficulty. Training datasets come from heterogeneous sources, making it difficult to disentangle ownership, obtain permissions, or attribute contributions. A one-size-fits-all approach to training data is unlikely to succeed, given the differing norms and sensitivities across sectors such as music, journalism, scientific publishing, and medicine.[33] Is it feasible to clear rights? In many cases, the sheer volume and diversity of data — combined with layered metadata and conflicting contracts among publishers, platforms, and authors — make comprehensive clearance prohibitively complex. On the other hand, the status quo of unchecked data scraping risks infringing rights, eroding trust in the AI ecosystem, and ultimately harming creativity and innovation.

More theoretical and empirical research will be needed to evaluate these and other proposals for balancing privacy rights and AI innovation. Clearer identification is also needed on the specific technological benefits of AI, as well as the privacy risks associated with AI training and outputs. Future work should prioritize high-impact benefits and high-risk uses, while applying proportionate attention to low-impact risks.

11.5.1 *Selected Empirical Studies on Impacts of Privacy*

The European Union's 2018 General Data Protection Regulation (GDPR) addresses growing concerns about the use of personal data.[34] The GDPR governs the collection, use, and storage of personal information. Organizations are required to serve as responsible data stewards: they must appoint a data protection officer and implement appropriate data security measures. The regulation applies to both consumers and businesses operating in the EU, whether foreign or local.

[33]See Love (2023).

[34]https://gdpr.eu/what-is-gdpr/.

More recently, the EU adopted the AI Act in 2024, becoming the first major jurisdiction to impose a binding legal framework on AI systems, including foundation models.[35] This section reviews selected studies that shed light on the economic implications of these regulations.

Goldfarb and Tucker (2012) review the empirical literature on innovation and privacy prior to 2012, highlighting two case studies. The first, on advertising, finds that privacy protections can reduce the effectiveness of targeted advertising. Privacy controls that prevent advertisers from tracking clicks and user data make it more difficult to learn about consumer preferences and behavior.

The second case study focuses on electronic medical records (EMRs). The adoption of EMR technology can generate network benefits among hospitals, allowing them to better exchange patient information. On one hand, strengthening privacy protections can build consumer trust, encouraging individuals to share more data and thereby increasing the value of EMRs. On the other hand, regulatory burdens associated with privacy rules can reduce that value. On balance, the empirical evidence suggests that strong privacy protections are associated with decreased adoption of EMR technology.

Demirer *et al.* (2024) analyze how privacy regulations, specifically the GDPR, affect firms' production choices. The study focuses on two specific inputs: data storage and computational services (e.g., those used to run applications). The analysis draws on firm-level data from a large cloud technology provider, covering over 37,000 customer firms. The dataset includes monthly observations spanning from 2015 to 2021.

In their framework, firms require "information" to produce goods and services. The following is a flexible formulation, agnostic as to whether information augments productivity generally or is specifically capital- or labor-augmenting:

$$Y = g(K, L, I)$$

where Y denotes output, K capital, L labor, and I information. Information, in turn, is modeled as a function of two inputs: computational resources, C, and data, D:

$$I = f(C, D)$$

[35] https://artificialintelligenceact.eu/.

In this model, the GDPR acts as a "cost shock" to a firm's inputs. On average, the privacy regulations increase the cost of storing data by 20%, due to compliance requirements and usage restrictions.[36]

The empirical results show that, on average, EU firms stored 26% less data than U.S. firms two years after the GDPR entered into force. EU firms also reduced their use of computational services by 15% relative to U.S. firms. The study further finds that the inputs C (computational resources) and D (data) are highly complementary. However, the elasticity of substitution between them — that is, the degree to which firms can swap one input for the other in response to changes in relative prices while maintaining output — is relatively low, estimated between 0.34 and 0.44. This implies that firms cannot easily substitute computational services for data storage when storage costs rise.

The significance of this study is that it provides early empirical evidence that privacy regulations impose measurable compliance costs on firms. However, these costs must be weighed against the broader benefits of privacy protections, including enhanced consumer data safety and autonomy.

In a complementary study, Frey *et al.* (2024) find that firms adjust their innovation strategies in response to privacy regulations. As in Demirer *et al.* (2024), the GDPR is viewed as increasing the cost of data storage. Websites can no longer outsource user data to third parties, such as digital marketing firms, without obtaining explicit consent. Companies are also required to encrypt or anonymize stored data, and EU residents are granted rights to access, delete, or transfer their personal information.

Frey *et al.* (2024) use data from *Patstat*, focusing on patent family applications as a measure of new inventions.[37] Their dataset covers 57 countries and 76 industries over the period 2010–2021. The findings show that the GDPR reduced overall patenting activity but also created incentives for firms to shift from data-intensive innovations to data-saving innovations. A sample of their regression results is in Table 11.8.

In the table, the dependent variable varies across specifications: in columns (1) and (4), it is the share of AI patents in the stock of patent

[36]The article cites studies indicating that compliance costs can range from $1.7 million for small firms to $73 million for large firms.

[37]Recall from Chapter 4 that patent applications for the same invention can be filed in multiple countries or patent offices. These multiple filings should not be treated as distinct innovations, as they typically represent a single invention. Collectively, they constitute a patent family.

Table 11.8. GDPR Exposure and AI Patenting

	(1) All AI	(2) Data-Saving	(3) Data-Intensive	(4) All AI	(5) Data-Saving	(6) Data-Intensive
GDPR Exposure × post-2018	−0.000	0.003	−0.004	−0.106***	−0.012	−0.016
GDPR Exposure × post-2018 × EU27	−0.011***	0.016***	−0.015***			
GDPR Exposure × post-2018 × Firm				0.175***	0.307***	−0.228***
Number of Observations	53,319	36,249	36,249	44,240	30,356	30,356

Notes: *** denotes significance at 1% level. Year and applicant fixed effects included.

families for an applicant; in columns (2) and (5), it is the share of data-saving AI patents within that AI stock; and in columns (3) and (6), it is the share of data-intensive AI patents. Exposure to GDPR regulations is based on the share of sales of Information and Communications Technology products and services (ICT) sold to EU final consumers.

The sample in columns (1)–(3) includes all applicants in the EU-27, including universities and individuals. The sub-sample in columns (4)–(6) is restricted to private companies. The key coefficient estimates of interest are those in which the GDPR exposure measure is interacted with applicant type. The main findings are as follows: among EU applicants exposed to the GDPR, patenting in data-saving AI technologies increases by 1.6% more than for non-exposed applicants, while patenting in data-intensive AI technologies decreases by 1.5% more. Private companies appear more responsive. Among them, GDPR-exposed firms increase their patenting in data-saving AI technologies by 30.7% more than others, and decrease their patenting in data-intensive AI technologies by 22.8% more. The quantitatively large increase in data-saving AI patenting among private companies suggests that privacy regulations may not suppress innovation outright but rather rechannel it toward less data-reliant technologies. These results imply that firms with greater commercial sensitivity to regulatory compliance costs are more likely to adjust their patenting portfolios in response to privacy laws.

Thus, increases in data storage costs resulting from the GDPR do influence the trajectory of AI innovation, though with a dampening effect overall. As Frey *et al.* (2024) note, an unintended consequence of the GDPR is that it may increase the market dominance of established firms, as they are better positioned to shift toward less data-intensive innovations. The issue of market concentration will be addressed in more detail in Chapter 12.

11.5.2 *Examples of Data-Saving Innovations*

As AI expands, the demand for data will grow (a so-called "thirst for data"). Data are needed to make AI more accurate and representative; however, more is not always better. Efficient methods exist to achieve comparable performance while using less data.[38] As the empirical evidence shows, firms are increasingly engaging in data-saving innovations in AI. This section concludes with examples of such innovations. The general goal of these innovations is to train AI systems to learn effectively without relying on a massive, indiscriminate dragnet of data — and in doing so, to become more privacy-respecting.

1. **Synthetic Data:** Artificially generated data that mimic real-world information to train AI models. For example, synthetic emails covering diverse topics can be used to train customer service agents. Simulated driving scenarios can be used to train autonomous vehicles in a safe, controlled environment.
2. **Federated Learning:** A model training approach that relies on decentralized data. Rather than aggregating data in a central repository, training occurs locally on devices or computers. The raw data never leave the devices; only the model updates are shared to improve a central algorithm.
3. **Transfer Learning:** A technique in which knowledge learned in one domain is applied to a different, but related, context. For instance, a model trained on internet images can be adapted for use in interpreting medical X-rays. Similarly, skills learned in bicycling can be applied to riding a scooter.

These approaches shift the emphasis from big data to smart data. Public policies can help incentivize firms to adopt more efficient, targeted, and privacy-preserving methods for training AI. For example, the use of financial incentives, such as tax credits for companies implementing federated learning or synthetic data generation; government procurement contracts that

[38] See Finck and Biega (2021).

require vendors to use privacy-preserving AI methods; and public research grants for AI projects that include data minimization or privacy by design.

11.6 Enablement Requirement and AI Training

The enablement requirement discussed earlier serves several important functions: promoting knowledge diffusion, fulfilling a public teaching function, and stimulating future innovation. From the perspective of economic growth and development, it helps developing countries learn and catch up, thereby reducing North–South gaps. This section focuses on the disclosure of details related to AI training, including the materials used, the provenance of data, and the training process and architecture.

What constitutes sufficient disclosure in AI patents? A major privacy concern arises if a patent application is required to divulge the AI training data, including the model's weights and parameters. What, then, should a patent reveal — and how much — in order to satisfy the enablement requirement while also respecting privacy rights?

11.6.1 *Source Codes and Algorithms*

For perspective, it is useful to draw lessons from software patents. Case law and statutes do not require the disclosure of source code in order for a software patent to satisfy the enablement requirement. The requirement can be met in other ways. Courts have held that no undue experimentation is imposed on a programmer skilled in the art who attempts to replicate the invention without access to the original source code. Instead, a patent may disclose alternative forms of technical detail, such as flowcharts, step-by-step descriptions in natural language, mathematical formulas, pseudocode, and other supporting documentation.

The underlying logic is that disclosure should focus on *functionality*, not specific source code. A patent should describe what the software program does, not what it is. The emphasis is on the underlying concepts and ideas, rather than the specific code used to express them. Moreover, a software invention can often be implemented in multiple ways while serving the same function. Some inventors argue that disclosing source code could unduly narrow the scope of protection to a single implementation, rather than covering the broader functionality. Over time, this could weaken patent protection, as implementation methods evolve with the emergence of new platforms, operating systems, and programming languages. Additionally, some inventors may prefer to protect source code as a trade secret.

For software patents, disclosure of the underlying algorithms and processes is generally required. For a person having ordinary skill in the art who is familiar with programming and algorithmic logic, a high-level description of the invention is typically sufficient to satisfy the enablement requirement.

AI patents are a developing area of law. As with software patents, the focus should be on enabling a PHOSITA to reproduce the invention without undue experimentation. To meet this standard, disclosure of the algorithm is typically necessary, along with the model architecture, key parameters, and an explanation of the model's functioning. In the case of neural networks, this includes details such as the number of layers and the activation functions used. By contrast, disclosure of AI training datasets is far less straightforward. Including the entire dataset is impractical due to its size, privacy concerns, and the proprietary nature of much of the data.

Rather than disclosing the full dataset, the patent must be transparent and sufficiently clear about the *black box* surrounding an AI invention. For example, neural networks function as input ⇒ output systems: the inputs are observable, as are the resulting outputs, but what occurs within the *black box* is often opaque. What is the reasoning behind the output? This question lies at the heart of the *explainability* issue; that is, understanding the AI's decision-making process. Accordingly, AI patents should describe how training was conducted, the relevant features of the inputs, and the methods used to generate the outputs.

11.6.2 *Case Study: EPO Guidelines on AI Training*

Aboy *et al.* (2024) provide an informative retrospective on the European Patent Office's treatment of enablement in AI patents. In 2020, the EPO's Board of Appeal (BoA), in decision T 0161/18, denied an AI patent application on the grounds of insufficient disclosure and lack of inventive step. The application in question (No. 06804383.5) concerned the use of artificial neural networks (ANNs) for determining cardiac arrest. The BoA ruled that:

> "... the claimed method differs from the prior art only by an artificial neural network, the training of which is not disclosed in detail. ... The training of the [ANN] cannot therefore be reworked by the person skilled in the art and the person skilled in the art can therefore not carry out the invention."[39]

The challenge during examination was that, without details about the specific input data, network type, and ANN architecture, the invention appeared overly general and insufficiently specialized. As Aboy *et al.* (2024) emphasize, an AI-related invention must not be merely *generic*, but rather *specialized*, in order to provide a technical solution to a concrete problem. Simply applying machine learning or deep learning to a given research domain is not sufficient. As they write, "Patents must not be mere 'hunting licenses' for future research endeavors or 'armchair inventions' obtaining monopolies for something they have not actually invented."[40]

Moreover, the lack of detail regarding the training of the ANN undermined the patent applicant's ability to distinguish the invention from prior art. Neural networks have long existed and have been used for similar diagnostic purposes. Without disclosure of the training dataset or methodology, the Board found it difficult to identify any specific technical effect attributable to the invention. In essence, a key component for evaluating the inventive step — the ANN's *specialization* — was missing. This omission gave the impression that a person skilled in the art could replicate the invention using only general knowledge.[41]

The key question is whether alternative methods exist for satisfying the enablement requirement in AI patents without disclosing the underlying training data. Indeed, the EPO examination guidelines do not require such disclosure. In March 2024, the EPO issued the following guidance:[42]

> "The technical effect that a machine learning algorithm achieves may be readily apparent or established by explanations, mathematical proof, experimental data or the like. ... If the technical effect is dependent on particular characteristics of the training dataset used, those characteristics that are required to reproduce the technical effect must be disclosed unless the skilled person can determine them

---

[39] See Aboy *et al.* (2024), p. 835.

[40] *Ibid.*, p. 838.

[41] The patent's claim that the invention worked with the help of an artificial neural network, "the weighting values of which are determined by learning," was not considered sufficiently specific.

[42] https://www.epo.org/en/legal/guidelines-epc/2024/g_ii_3_3_1.html.

> without undue burden using common general knowledge. However, in general, there is no need to disclose the specific training dataset itself."

Thus, in lieu of disclosing full AI training datasets, AI patents could instead include:[43]

i. the structure and architecture of an AI model (e.g., neural network);
ii. a complete description of the training process;
iii. a specification of the input data used for training;
iv. disclosure of at least one representative dataset;
v. validation data or performance results.

These guidelines provide a productive starting point, but there is room for refinement. Aboy *et al.* (2024) recommend that patent office guidelines include concrete examples and checklists to help clarify expectations. Improved disclosure practices could enhance AI transparency and facilitate the global diffusion of technical knowledge.

Looking ahead, one possibility is the creation of a data depository modeled after the *Budapest Treaty*, which governs the deposit of biological materials. An analogous system for AI could enable innovators to deposit training datasets, allowing the public and examiners to verify whether disclosure requirements have been met.

As AI tools assisting inventors become more sophisticated, the enablement requirement itself may need adjustment. In the future, it may be sufficient for a patent to disclose enough information for a person skilled in the art — *assisted by AI* — to replicate the invention. If AI reduces the burden of replication, the required level of disclosure could, in principle, be lowered.

Appendix 11A. Primer on Artificial Intelligence

Artificial Intelligence (AI) refers to computer systems designed to perform tasks that ordinarily require human intelligence.

Modern AI has evolved from simple rule-based systems, relying on explicitly programmed instructions, to sophisticated learning algorithms capable

[43]See Aboy *et al.* (2024), p. 838.

of generating new content (text, images, or audio) based on vast training data. This Appendix provides a high-level overview of AI to support Chapters 11 and 12. References for further study are provided at the end.

11A.1 *Key AI Concepts*

- **Foundation Models:** These are large AI systems trained on massive datasets. They form the foundation for more specialized models. Examples include Generative Pre-trained Transformer (GPT)-4 (language), Dall-E (image generation), and Contrastive Language-Image Pre-training (CLIP) (text-image alignment).
- **Large Language Models (LLMs):** A subset of foundation models focused on processing and generating natural language. LLMs are trained on extensive collections of text drawn from a wide range of disciplines. Examples include OpenAI's ChatGPT, Anthropic's Claude, Meta's LLaMA, and Google DeepMind's Gemini.
- **Machine Learning:** Machine learning (ML) is the process by which computers learn from data. Instead of following explicit programming instructions, ML systems analyze data to recognize patterns and make predictions. The systems learn by adjusting their internal parameters based on the performance of their predictions.
- **Deep Learning:** Deep learning (DL) is a type of machine learning that uses artificial neural networks with multiple layers, where a layer is a stage of computation. Inspired by the human brain, a neural network is a network of connected nodes (neurons) that are like intelligent sensors that receive and process data and control the transmission of information to other neurons. These connections and ways neurons process information are what allow the network to learn complex patterns from data.

11A.2 *AI Interfaces*

Users interact with AI systems in the following ways:

- **User Interfaces (UIs)** are the front-facing part of AI models, such as the ChatGPT website, Claude's chat window, or the voice interface of Siri. The UIs are the screens, the buttons, and the menus.
- **Prompting** is how users communicate what they want from an AI. Prompts can consist of questions or research tasks for AI.
- **Application Programming Interfaces (APIs)** enable software programs to communicate with one another. The user does not directly

engage with APIs. APIs are digital messengers who work behind the scenes. For example, when a user books a flight through a travel agent's website, the website communicates with the airline's database via the airline's API.

As a metaphor, consider ordering a car. The foundation model is the automobile factory. The LLM is a specific assembly line, such as an SUV (Sport Utility Vehicle). The API is analogous to the car dealership network. The UI is the sales representative and the showroom.

11A.3 *How the Sausage is Made*

Consider a user prompting a large language model to complete a task.

1. **Tokens:** Texts that are communicated to an LLM are broken into smaller units called tokens (words or parts of words); for example, "Where is the bank?" could be separated into "Where," "is," "the," "bank," "?."
2. **Embedding:** The tokens are then converted into numerical vectors (or lists of numbers), called embeddings, that represent semantic meaning. Tokenization and embedding are necessary because machines do not natively understand human language. They process numbers and symbols instead. The embedding is unique. It differentiates the word "bank" when used in a sentence about a financial institution from the word "bank" when used to describe nature, like a "river bank." Token embeddings act as a kind of "translation layer" that sits between human language and the binary code that computers understand. The AI model processes embeddings using its neural network.
3. **Transformer:** A transformer is a type of neural network architecture that enables the model to process all parts of a text in parallel, rather than sequentially. Think of it as reading an entire chapter at once and noticing how themes connect, rather than line by line.
4. **Generation:** The LLM uses patterns that it learned during training to generate a response, which consists of a new sequence of embeddings, which are then decoded back into human-readable text.

11A.4 *AI Frameworks and Development Tools*

AI developers need specialized software to build AI systems. These tools are called frameworks and provide the building blocks for creating AI models:

- **TensorFlow**, developed by Google, is a toolkit for the complex mathematics underlying AI development.

- **PyTorch**, developed by Meta, is a machine learning framework that provides the tools and libraries for building and training neural networks.
- **Other frameworks** include JAX (by Google), MXNet (supported by Amazon), which, like PyTorch, are also ML frameworks for providing neural network tools and libraries.

11A.5 *The Hardware of AI*

AI systems require enormous computing power. Different types of hardware conduct this computational work:

- *CPU (Central Processing Unit)* is the general-purpose "brain" of a computer. CPUs are, however, relatively slow for AI workloads.
- *GPU (Graphics Processing Unit)* is the workhorse of AI. GPUs perform thousands of simple calculations simultaneously.
- *TPU (Tensor Processing Unit)* is Google's custom-designed chip specifically for AI workloads.

The enormous computational demands of modern AI have made hardware a critical bottleneck in AI development. Training the largest AI models requires data centers with thousands of interconnected chips. Running these centers can cost hundreds of millions of dollars in computing resources. Moreover, data centers exact an environmental cost in terms of electricity usage for power and water usage for cooling.

11A.6 *The AI Computing Ecosystem*

The modern AI landscape consists of companies that develop foundation models and provide API capabilities and hardware infrastructure.

- **Foundation Models and LLM Developers:** Companies that create and train large language models include OpenAI (GPT models), Anthropic (Claude), Google DeepMind (Gemini), Meta (Llama), Microsoft (Copilot models), French company Mistral AI (Mistral Large, Le Chat), and Chinese companies like Baidu (ERNIE) and Zhipu AI (GLM). Most AI companies do not own all the hardware they need. Instead, they partner with hardware firms, such as cloud providers.

- **Hardware Infrastructure:** The physical capital of AI:
  - ❑ *Cloud Providers*: Amazon Web Services (AWS), Microsoft Azure, and Google Cloud provide the data centers where most AI models run.
  - ❑ *Chip Manufacturers*: NVIDIA presently dominates the AI chip market with its GPUs, while AMD, Intel are competitors.
  - ❑ *Semiconductor Foundries*: Major technology companies like Apple, NVIDIA, and AMD rely on semiconductor foundries to manufacture their chips. For example, Taiwan Semiconductor Manufacturing Company (TSMC) currently runs the world's largest independent semiconductor foundry. These foundries produce silicon wafers with complex integrated circuits that power everything from smartphones and computers to cars and AI accelerators.

Training data come from a variety of sources:

1. **Publicly Available Data:** This includes information freely accessible from the internet, such as webpages, open datasets (e.g., resources from LAION (Large-scale Artificial Intelligence Open Network), including billions of multilingual image-text pairs), books and articles in the public domain (such as non-copyrighted works), social media posts and shared data.
2. **Arrangements with Media and Publishers:** Licensing agreements that AI companies have with media organizations and publishers to use their copyrighted content for training. For example, OpenAI's deals with Reddit, NewsCorp, Vox Media, and the Atlantic.[44]
3. **Licensed Datasets:** AI companies can purchase or license specific datasets from data providers that have curated data for machine learning purposes.
4. **Proprietary Data:** Some companies use their own internally generated data for training models, which could include their user data (with appropriate consent and anonymization) or any internal research.

The ecosystem also includes application developers who build useful products for consumers and businesses by incorporating these AI models into software applications.

---

[44]https://www.fastcompany.com/91130785/companies-reddit-news-corp-deals-openai-train-chatgpt-partnerships.

11A.7 *Glossary of AI Terminology*

AI-Assisted Output: Human-produced output using AI as a tool.

Algorithm: A step-by-step procedure for solving a problem or performing a task.

Application Programming Interface (API): A connection point that allows different software programs to communicate.

Artificial Neural Network: A computer system designed to process information in layers, modeled after brain behavior.

Deep Learning: A subset of machine learning using neural networks with multiple layers to process data.

Embedding: A numerical representation of a word or token that captures its meaning in context, enabling AI models to process language mathematically.

Fine-tuning: Additional training of a pre-trained AI model.

Foundation Model: A large AI model trained on broad data at scale.

Generative AI: AI systems that can create new content such as text, images, or audio based on patterns learned from trained data.

Generative Pre-trained Transformer (GPT): A type of AI model developed by OpenAI that can understand and generate human-like text.

Large Language Model (LLM): A type of foundation model trained to understand and generate human language.

Machine Learning: Teaching computers to learn patterns from data rather than following programming instructions.

Model Weights: Numeric values that represent the strength of connections between neurons in a neural network. These values are adjusted during training to capture what the AI model has learned from the data.

Supervised Learning: Training an AI by using labeled data.

Tokens: The smallest units of input processed by language models, often words or sub-word segments.

Transformer: A neural network architecture that processes all parts of the input at once. It uses a technique called self-attention, which helps the model determine which words or tokens are most relevant to each other, regardless of their position. For example, in "She put lotion on her elbow because it was dry," the model uses self-attention to infer that "it" refers to "elbow."

User Interface (UI): The part of an AI system that users directly interact with, such as a prompt window.

Unsupervised Learning: Training an AI using unlabeled data, allowing it to discover its own patterns.

11A.8 *For Further Reading*

Bishop, Christopher and Bishop, Hugh (2024). *Deep Learning: Foundations and Concepts.* Switzerland: Springer.

Greenwood, Matt (2024). *Artificial Intelligence: An Introduction to AI for Teenagers.* Brisbane: Ochreland Publishing.

Japkowicz, Nathalie and Boukouvalas, Zois (2024). *Machine Learning Evaluation: Towards Reliable and Responsible AI.* Cambridge: Cambridge University Press.

Naudé, Wim, Gries, Thomas, and Dimitra, Nicola (2024). *Artificial Intelligence: Economic Perspectives and Models.* Cambridge: Cambridge University Press.

Russell, Stuart and Norvig, Peter (2021). *Artificial Intelligence: A Modern Approach*, Fourth Edition. New York: Pearson.

Theobald, Oliver (2021). *Machine Learning for Absolute Beginners.* London: Scatterplot Press.

Chapter 12

Artificial Intelligence, Innovation, and Diffusion

12.1 Introduction

This chapter examines the economic impacts of artificial intelligence (AI) on innovation, international technology transfer, productivity growth, and North–South development gaps. It highlights how AI can act as a general-purpose technology, not only revising production processes but transforming how scientific discoveries emerge. At the same time, the chapter discusses concerns about the uneven distribution of AI capabilities, market concentration, and environmental bottlenecks.

The chapter begins with an analysis of how AI facilitates innovation. Drawing on the idea of AI as a method of invention, it considers how machine learning and other AI learning systems affect the production of new knowledge. It emphasizes how AI can accelerate scientific discovery by enhancing predictive accuracy and enabling prioritized searches over vast hypothesis spaces.

The discussion then turns to AI and international technology transfer, showing how AI can facilitate trade, foreign direct investment, and licensing. However, it also points out the barriers to AI adoption due to infrastructure gaps, data access issues, and regulatory fragmentation. The chapter briefly discusses the role of the WTO and other multilateral institutions in managing data flows.

Next, the chapter reviews evidence on the productivity effects at both the firm and worker levels. Due to measurement lags, there may be delays in observing AI's impacts. Subsequent sections explore AI's role in widening or narrowing global inequality.

Finally, the chapter briefly addresses two structural bottlenecks that limit the scale and diffusion of AI: access to compute resources and environmental constraints. Because these costs are not fully internalized, market mechanisms alone are unlikely to resolve them. Overall, the chapter presents AI as both an engine of innovation and a source of global frictions.

12.2 Innovation

Griliches (1957) had long ago articulated an important distinction between inventions that yield new products and inventions that transform the very process of innovation. Griliches emphasized that "the invention of a method of invention" can have profound and long-lasting economic consequences.[1] Building on this insight, Cockburn *et al.* (2019) argue that artificial intelligence also represents such a transformative force, a meta-invention capable of reshaping how new technologies are discovered, evaluated, and commercialized.

Cockburn *et al.* (2019) delineate three technological domains within AI, each with varying implications for innovation:

- **Robotics**, encompassing computer vision, sensor networks, systems and control theory, and layered control architectures;
- **Symbolic systems**, including natural language processing, symbolic reasoning, pattern recognition, and image alignment;
- **Learning systems**, covering machine learning, deep learning, reinforcement learning, unsupervised learning, Bayesian networks, and knowledge representation.

Among these, learning systems such as deep learning hold the greatest promise for accelerating the innovation process itself. These systems can be used not just to solve well-defined technical problems, but also to generate new hypotheses and identify patterns in unstructured data.

[1] Griliches (1957) showed that hybrid corn was an example of an invention that changed the innovation process itself.

To conceptualize AI's impact on innovation, one can revisit the ideas production function introduced in Chapter 3:

$$\Delta A = \theta f(R, A)$$

where ΔA denotes the growth of the knowledge stock, A is the existing technological base, and R represents inputs into research and development. AI can lower the cost of R, enhance the productivity of researchers, and increase the spillovers from A by making tacit knowledge more accessible or reusable. The parameter θ captures the efficiency of transforming R&D into new knowledge, which AI can plausibly increase.

On the output side, the aggregate production function becomes

$$Y = AF(K, L, M)$$

where Y is total output, K is physical capital, L is labor, and M denotes AI-enabled machines and systems. Importantly, M is both a factor of production and a technological embodiment of one of the "blueprints" that comprise the stock A. AI systems are products of accumulated knowledge, and in turn, they can augment or automate the productivity of both K and L. In this framework, AI is not just another input. It is a recursive enabler of innovation, capable of improving the discovery process and feeding back into the system to accelerate technological growth.

Cockburn *et al.* (2019) supplement their conceptual framework with empirical data drawn from two sources: scientific publications (from the Web of Science) and U.S. patent grants. Their publication sample spans 1955–2015 and includes approximately 96,000 AI-related articles, 61% of which focus on learning systems, 21% on robotics, 12% on symbolic systems, and the remainder on other AI-related topics. Roughly 85% of these articles were authored by academics, and 44% appeared in computer science journals.

The patent sample, drawn from the same period, consists of approximately 13,600 AI-related U.S. patents. In contrast to the publication sample, 91% of these patents are held by private firms, while only 7% originate from academia. The distribution of technologies differs as well: 41% of AI patents are in robotics, 29% in symbolic systems, 28% in learning systems, and the remainder in other AI areas. Remarkably, while machine learning research was initially driven by academic institutions, by 2014, industry had become the dominant source of ML model development.[2]

[2]See also Gopinath (2023).

Table 12.1. Percentage Growth in Publications across Domains, by AI Field

	Biology	Physics	Medicine	Chemistry	Materials	Neurosci.	Comp. Sci
Learning Systems	133	13	123	51	105	258	18
Robotics	97	135	20	283	525	348	−8
Symbol Systems	13	84	−13	7	216	109	36

Note: Each figure is the percentage growth rate between 2004–2006 and 2013–2015.
Source: Cockburn *et al.* (2019), p. 138.

After 2010, patenting activity in all three AI subfields — learning systems, symbolic systems, and robotics — accelerates significantly, consistent with a general-purpose technology (GPT) diffusion pattern.

Table 12.1 illustrates the rising share of AI-related publications across a wide range of scientific disciplines. In particular, the most rapid growth occurs in the learning systems category, spanning fields such as biology, chemistry, physics, neuroscience, materials science, medicine, and computer science. This diffusion into diverse domains supports the characterization of AI as a general-purpose technology (GPT): one that not only improves productivity within its own sector but also enables innovation and problem-solving across a broad spectrum of knowledge-intensive fields.

Igna and Venturini (2023) dig deeper into what makes firms capable of leveraging AI. Using a large sample of 20,192 European companies (of which 409 are AI innovation firms) during 1995–2016, the study delves into the determinants of AI innovation. It finds that inventive success at AI is a function of some existing capabilities:

- Earlier experience in Information and Communications Technology (ICT) innovation
- Strong knowledge base; i.e., possessing existing internal competencies
- Scale of firm innovation

Firms with narrow technological competencies are not as successful at utilizing AI. These results can help explain the success of incumbent firms with an early lead or head start. The findings may help explain, as will be discussed later, why the data market is concentrated among a few large firms.

The study models two equations: one modeling the probability of achieving an AI innovation, and the other modeling patenting productivity. Estimates of the first equation show that the probability is indeed higher for companies that are active in ICT. Estimates of the second equation reveal strong learning effects or "dynamic returns," whereby patenting productivity is a function of past developments in AI innovation and of complementarities with ICT experience (for instance, in networks and communication, high-speed cognition, and imagery). Another interesting finding is that diverse competencies matter, not specialized or narrow ones, for producing AI innovations.

The significance of these findings is that Big Tech has a competitive advantage in generating AI innovations, and this will be reflected in future advances. As the study notes:

> "The results ... suggest that ... a small group of top innovators at the frontier of AI, which exploit their first mover advantage, as well as built-up competences, [could] strengthen their technological leadership and expand their market power." (p. 14)

In technological races in this sphere, the winners will tend to dominate, a theme that will be addressed later in the chapter.

Recall the earlier argument that artificial intelligence (AI) is more than a tool or a form of knowledge-embodied capital. Rather, it functions as a method of invention. In this spirit, recent scholarship has suggested that AI transforms the very process of scientific discovery and innovation. Agrawal *et al.* (2024) provide a theoretical foundation for this view by modeling how AI can guide innovators through a vast combinatorial space of potential ideas. Innovation often involves a search process, either sequential or parallel. In a sequential model, inventors experiment iteratively, learning through trial and error until a viable solution emerges, as in the development of a new vaccine or mechanical device. Alternatively, multiple projects may proceed in parallel, with some being abandoned and others pursued based on their promise. In either case, the innovation process involves prioritizing efforts under uncertainty.

AI has the potential to search for solutions from a vast space of possibilities more efficiently and cost-effectively. (For instance, in the domain of biomedicine, clinical trials are notoriously expensive and time-consuming.) Researchers often need to figure out if they are on the right path or need to switch paths. Using AI-based prediction models, researchers can better prioritize their search efforts. Agrawal *et al.* (2024) coined the term

Hassabis hypothesis to describe the idea that AI-based prediction models will enhance scientific discovery and innovation.[3]

Agrawal *et al.* (2024) employ a survival analysis framework to formalize the notion of prioritized search in innovation. Let H_z denote the hazard function, which refers to the conditional probability that the zth hypothesis will prove to be a technological breakthrough given that the previous $z-1$ hypothesis tests failed. Intuitively, the higher the value of H_z, the higher the chance of success at that stage, assuming no earlier successes have occurred. This analysis is called survival analysis because the search process ends (analogous to an organism's "death" in survival models) upon the first breakthrough. This analytical framework produces the following calculations:

(i) the overall probability of a breakthrough, given constraints on resources and budget
(ii) the expected duration of search
(iii) the expected profits

Now, if all experiments have the same payoffs and tests have the same costs, all the experiments can be ranked according to their success probabilities. A prioritized search strategy then involves beginning with the hypothesis that has the highest predicted probability of success and proceeding in descending order. Agrawal *et al.* (2024) also extend their model to account for heterogeneity in payoffs and outcomes. Overall, the model demonstrates that AI, by delivering higher fidelity predictions of success probabilities, can improve decision-making and efficiency across all three dimensions: (i)–(iii). By sharpening the prioritization process, AI reduces wasted effort and accelerates the rate of discovery.

Empirical examples of AI accelerating the scientific discovery process include *AlphaFold*, *AlphaDev*, and *GNoME* — all developed by *DeepMind*, a subsidiary of Alphabet (Google). *AlphaFold* enables researchers to simulate protein folding in a computer environment, reducing the need for costly and time-consuming wet lab experiments. *AlphaDev* uses AI to discover faster algorithms for fundamental operations such as sorting, which is critical for improving software performance. *GNoME* (Graph Networks for Materials Exploration) applies AI to the field of materials science; notably, it screened

[3]The term is derived from a keynote speech delivered by Demis Hassabis, CEO and co-founder of Google DeepMind, who — along with John Jumper — was awarded the 2024 Nobel Prize in Chemistry for the development of AlphaFold, an AI system that predicts protein structures with remarkable accuracy.

an enormous chemical compound space and predicted over two million new crystalline compounds in just 17 days.[4]

Another illustrative example is *FourCastNet*, an AI system developed by Anima Anandkumar (California Institute of Technology and NVIDIA) to simulate complex physical systems. One prominent application of *FourCastNet* is in weather forecasting. Another application lies in modeling plasma behavior in nuclear fusion experiments, a domain where high-fidelity simulations are essential but computationally expensive. Here, AI enables researchers to conduct a large number of virtual experiments with greater speed and efficiency.

In addition to enabling prioritized research, AI also facilitates interdisciplinary discovery. This argument has been advanced by Cheryl Cui, CEO of Bota Biosciences, who suggests that AI can serve as a bridge to scientific generalism. Human scientists are often constrained to narrow disciplinary silos due to the sheer volume of specialized knowledge required to master a single domain. In contrast, AI systems excel at aggregating and synthesizing vast bodies of knowledge across fields. This capacity enables researchers to identify opportunities that emerge at the intersections of disciplines, precisely where, as Cui notes, a lot of interesting findings happen.[5]

12.3 Technology Transfer

Artificial intelligence (AI) not only facilitates innovation but also plays an increasingly important role in international technology transfer. AI contributes to the development of new goods and services, as well as the enhancement of existing ones, for export, foreign direct investment (FDI), and cross-border licensing.

From a production standpoint, AI improves efficiency and product quality, supporting firms' ability to compete in foreign markets. From a diffusion standpoint, AI-related technologies can be transferred directly through exported products, indirectly through FDI and multinational supply chains, or via licensing agreements that enable foreign firms to adopt AI-driven processes. In this way, AI functions both as a form of innovation and as a mechanism for technological dissemination.

As a tool, AI can aid investors in conducting international market analysis, identifying profitable trade and investment opportunities, while

[4]See Maslej (2024).

[5]See https://www.weforum.org/stories/2024/07/technologists-ai-scientific-discovery/.

predictive models can help assess political and economic risks. Moreover, AI-powered platforms can assist businesses in navigating complex local regulatory environments.[6]

However, the international diffusion of AI also presents challenges for the developing world. In particular, AI-enabled automation in manufacturing and services in advanced economies may trigger a wave of reshoring, whereby production is relocated from the Global South back to the North. This shift would likely dampen foreign direct investment (FDI) flows to developing countries, undermining one of the key channels of technology transfer. In addition, the high cost of AI infrastructure and talent development may place developing-country firms at a disadvantage in acquiring licensing contracts from firms in the North. Further constraints could arise from the use of export controls by developed countries, particularly on advanced AI technologies and semiconductor components, which may inhibit access to critical inputs needed for domestic AI development in the South. Finally, concerns over weak intellectual property protection in some developing countries may make Northern firms hesitant to transfer technology or license AI innovations.

12.3.1 *Why Trade-Related?*

The WTO (2024) report provides a comprehensive analysis of the role of artificial intelligence (AI) in the global trading system. Among the ways that AI can affect international trade are as follows:

- **Serve as a General-Purpose Technology (GPT):** Unlike traditional digital goods, AI functions as a general-purpose technology with wide applicability across industries.
- **Reduce Trade Costs:** AI can lower trade costs through improved supply chain management and predictive analytics in logistics, and automation in customs procedures.
- **Transform Services Trade:** AI will help expand digital services.
- **Shift Composition of Trade:** The integration of AI into products will raise the demand for technology-intensive goods and services. Consequently, the composition of global trade is expected to shift toward higher-value, AI-enabled products.

[6]See https://www.scrut.io/post/ai-compliance for an example of an AI-enabled compliance platform.

- **Affect Comparative Advantage:** As AI adoption affects productivity across sectors and countries, it may lead to a reconfiguration of comparative advantages.
- **Need for AI Readiness in Developing Economies:** The report emphasizes the importance of digital infrastructure and human capital development in preparing developing countries to participate in and benefit from AI-enabled trade.

As AI is expected to usher in these changes, policies must be prepared to address challenges in data governance, intellectual property, ethics, and trustworthiness, and must be coordinated to prevent regulatory fragmentation in AI.[7] A divide has already emerged between economies that lead in AI innovation and those that primarily function as users or adopters of the technology. This asymmetry in technological capability raises concerns about unequal access to the benefits of AI and potential dependency on foreign-developed systems. In response, some countries may engage in a technological race, employing industrial policies to strengthen domestic AI capabilities and reduce reliance on foreign digital infrastructure.[8]

A central trade-related issue in the context of AI is the governance of cross-border data flows. These flows are critical for AI development, as training AI models requires access to vast and diverse datasets. As such, restrictions on data movement can act as significant barriers to innovation and digital trade. According to the WTO (2024), a scenario in which all cross-border data flows are restricted could result in a 5% decline in global GDP and a 10% drop in exports. At the same time, as discussed in Chapter 11, such openness must be weighed against legitimate privacy concerns surrounding the use of large-scale data in AI training.

International trade may also be shaped by emerging considerations that remain conceptually and empirically unsettled, such as the need to ensure trustworthy AI, and the possible re-evaluation of intellectual property rights associated with AI-generated innovations. Efforts to mitigate the risks posed by AI systems could introduce new layers of regulatory oversight. While well-intentioned, these measures risk increasing compliance burdens, particularly for smaller firms, and could lead to regulatory fragmentation that distorts or impedes cross-border trade. As noted in the

[7]See Goldfarb and Trefler (2019) for a survey of cross-border regulatory issues related to AI.

[8]Kilic (2025) argues that industrial policy can play a critical role for developing nations by mitigating dependence on Big Tech, fostering local innovation, and advancing long-term technological sovereignty.

WTO (2024) report, the economic cost of fragmented data regimes alone could exceed 1% of global GDP.

Regulatory divergence is not just a technical matter, but one with economic and strategic implications. Differing national standards can raise transaction costs, reduce interoperability, distort trade flows, and hinder innovation or technology transfer. Just as importantly, divergence may trigger regulatory arbitrage. Firms developing AI models and training datasets may migrate toward jurisdictions with weaker standards — those lacking strict privacy laws, localization mandates, or source code disclosure requirements. For example, suppose the European Union were to adopt stringent rules promoting AI safety and data protection. In that case, companies might shift operations to more permissive environments, such as the United States or China.

This mechanism risks a "race to the bottom," where regulatory authorities, anticipating capital flight, choose laxer standards to retain or attract AI firms. In game-theoretic terms, this can lead to a suboptimal global equilibrium, where no country enforces strong protections for safety, privacy, or accountability, even though all would benefit from more robust safeguards if adopted collectively.[9]

In this evolving landscape, the WTO has a critical role to play as the leading multilateral institution for coordinating the trade-related aspects of AI governance. Moreover, the WTO can help advance the interests of developing countries by identifying areas where differential treatment or technical assistance may be warranted to support their participation in AI-enabled trade and regulatory implementations.

12.3.2 *Case of Digital Services Trade*

Sun and Trefler (2023) provide an empirical analysis of how artificial intelligence innovations and cross-border data regulations interact to influence global data flows. The study uses mobile apps as a case study of digital services trade. Apps are commercially provided by multinational companies — TikTok (China), Facebook (U.S.), Spotify (Sweden), and Waze (Israel). When the user of the app and the developer of the app are located in different countries, this counts as digital trade. The share of mobile app users engaging in cross-border usage is quite large.

[9]Vogel (1995), however, challenges the simplistic notion of a universal race to the bottom, arguing that under certain conditions, trade reforms can lead to a *trading up*, where stronger regulations in one jurisdiction compel others to raise their standards.

The study finds that the deployment of AI in apps helps to augment trade in digital services. On average, AI-enabled apps see more than a tenfold increase in their number of foreign users. However, cross-border restrictions on data flows tend to significantly reduce digital services trade by limiting the number of foreign users of apps. Tracking regulations over time, the study documents a proliferation of restrictions on cross-border data flows between 2001 and 2019. The number of restrictions increased rapidly just as the mobile app industry was emerging globally (2008–2012).

AI deployment in mobile applications is measured by the patented technologies embedded within them, typically those related to AI algorithms. As discussed in Chapter 10, patents are classified by technological fields using the Cooperative Patent Classification (CPC) system. These technological classifications do not always align with standard economic product categories. Identifying the AI content of a product, such as a mobile app, therefore, requires several methodological steps. First, AI-related patents are identified via their CPC codes.[10] Second, each app lists the patents that protect it (usually by official patent number). Among these, AI-related patents can be isolated using the CPC classifications. The final step is to assess the degree to which each AI patent is deployed within the app. To this end, the study applies a textual matching technique based on *cosine similarity* between the app's product description and the corresponding AI patent description.[11] Let ρ_{ap} denote the similarity score between app a and patent p. A value of zero indicates no overlap, while a value of one indicates perfect overlap. Aggregating ρ_{ap} across the patents covered in an app yields the amount of AI innovations deployed in app a at time t:

$$AI_{at} = \sum_{p=1}^{P_{at}} \rho_{ap}$$

where P_{at} is the total number of patents associated with app a at time t.

The study then employs the above measure of AI deployment in apps to estimate its effect on cross-border digital trade. Specifically, it examines how AI intensity influences the number of foreign users of an app, a proxy for digital services exports, by estimating the following regression model:

$$\ln(\text{Foreign Users}_{at}) = \beta \ln(1 + AI_{at}) + \cdots$$

[10]The CPC code for neural networks, G06N 3/02, is used to represent an AI algorithm.

[11]This *cosine similarity* method was mentioned in Chapters 3 and 6. Here, the large language model (LLM) transformer converts the text into mathematical vectors called *embeddings*. The cosine of the angle between these vectors quantifies semantic similarity.

where the dependent variable is the natural logarithm of the number of foreign users of app a at time t, and the key independent variable is the log-transformed AI intensity measure, $\ln(1 + AI_{at})$. The transformation accommodates cases where $AI_{at} = 0$. The regression specification includes firm fixed effects to control for unobserved, time-invariant heterogeneity across app developers, and industry-year fixed effects to account for shocks or trends specific to particular sectors in given years. Moreover, the model acknowledges the endogeneity concern that AI deployment is a strategic choice by firms, potentially influenced by their existing or expected level of digital exports. The study addresses this by creating an *instrumental variable* that predicts the likelihood of AI adoption. It is constructed as the product of two components: (1) a country's AI abundance (the AI expertise in a country) and (2) the industry-specific AI intensity, defined as the typical degree to which AI technologies are embedded in apps within that industry. This interaction serves as a predictive proxy for the likelihood of AI adoption by a firm in a given country and sector. The instrument (the likelihood of AI adoption) is used to isolate the part of AI deployment that was due to AI adoption and not to other factors promoting digital trade. After determining how much the AI adoption environment increased AI deployment, and how much the growth in digital trade is attributable to the AI adoption environment, it is possible to infer more cleanly how AI deployment contributed to digital trade.

Data on commercially available apps is sourced from *Sensor Tower*. The dataset covers more than 1,200 firms and more than 35,000 apps spanning the period 2015–2020. The regression results show a statistically significant positive estimate of β, confirming that the deployment of AI spurs digital services trade.

In addition to examining the role of AI, Sun and Trefler (2023) investigate how regulatory barriers to data flows affect cross-border digital trade. Specifically, the study leverages the OECD's *Digital Services Trade Restrictiveness Index* (or Digital STRI), with a focus on two key components: (i) restrictions on data transfers across borders (e.g., data localization requirements); (ii) restrictions on data development (e.g., local presence requirements). To assess the interaction between AI deployment and regulatory frictions, the following regression model is estimated:

$$\ln(\text{Foreign Users}_{at}) = \beta \ln(1 + AI_{at}) + \Theta \underbrace{\text{Data}_{nt} \times \ln(1 + AI_{at})}_{\text{Interaction}} + \cdots$$

where Data_{nt} denotes the index of data flow restrictions in country n at time t. The interaction term captures whether such restrictions moderate the effectiveness of AI deployment. For both categories of data restrictions, the coefficient of Θ is negative and statistically significant, indicating that the restrictions counter the effects of AI deployment on spurring digital services trade. An additional insight from the study is that stringent restrictions on cross-border data flows are disproportionately enacted by authoritarian regimes, highlighting a geopolitical dimension to digital services trade.

Lastly, the study finds that AI deployment generates positive knowledge spillovers. Even developers whose own apps are not protected by AI-related patents can experience gains in digital services trade due to the deployment of AI in other firms. To quantify this effect, the study estimates the following regression on a restricted sample of app developers without any AI patents of their own:

$$\ln(\text{Foreign Users}_{at}) = \beta \ln(1 + AI^{e}_{at}) + \cdots$$

where AI^{e}_{at} denotes external AI deployment. By construction, the digital services exports of these developers depend on the corpus of AI developed by others. The results reveal that the coefficient β is positive and statistically significant at the 1% level. This indicates that AI deployment by others confers benefits even to non-AI-innovating firms.

In related work, Trefler and Sun (2022) examine additional outcomes and find that AI deployment increases app downloads by a factor of six, doubles the number of exported app varieties, and promotes creative destruction, as evidenced by the elevated rates of app entry and exit.

12.4 Productivity

This section reviews research on how AI contributes to productivity growth. By automating routine and repetitive tasks, AI reduces workloads and reallocates resources to higher-value activities. Workers may then concentrate on non-routine or creative tasks. At the firm level, AI tools can enhance the efficiency of labor, capital, and other inputs, while also supporting managers in organizational operations, business forecasting, and decision-making. In addition, AI can address complex problems, detect patterns in unstructured data, and, importantly, generate novel innovations of its own.

Despite these mechanisms, the productivity effects of AI have not yet materialized fully in national statistics. This mirrors an earlier puzzle famously noted by Robert Solow (1987): "You can see the computer age everywhere but in the productivity statistics." A similar concern was raised by Gordon (2016), who argued that the transformative impact of the internet had been overstated in light of modest post-1990s productivity gains.

One explanation is the so-called "J-curve" effect, as articulated by Brynjolfsson *et al.* (2019). When firms invest in a general-purpose technology like AI, they must first undertake substantial intangible investments in software, organizational restructuring, managerial practices, and workforce training. These preparatory efforts are typically unmeasured in national accounts. During this phase, measured total factor productivity (TFP) may fall even though real productive capacity is improving.

The resulting trajectory of TFP resembles a J-curve. In the early period, productivity appears artificially low due to under-accounted intangible inputs. Subsequently, measured productivity rises above the starting point as the unmeasured inputs contribute to productivity growth. Later measures of productivity growth will be above the true productivity growth because it will appear as if "the measured capital stock and employed workers have spiked and become much more productive."[12]

Recent studies by Corrado *et al.* (2021) and Brynjolfsson *et al.* (2019) assess whether the J-curve phenomenon is applicable to AI adoption. If TFP declines during periods of heavy AI investment, this may indicate that firms are engaged in unmeasured preparatory activities such as training, integration of new systems, and firm reorganizations. However, disentangling this effect from other macroeconomic shocks remains difficult. Factors such as the COVID-19 pandemic, trade policy disruptions, and changes in tax regimes also influence observed TFP trends and complicate causal attribution.

Corrado *et al.* (2021) caution that the empirical evidence remains ambiguous. The applicability of the J-curve to AI hinges on the depreciation rate of capital. Suppose the intangible capital associated with AI, such as data assets, algorithmic models, and organizational know-how, has a low rate of depreciation. In that case, the delay between investment and payoff will be longer, and the J-curve more pronounced. At present, the depreciation rate of AI-related capital remains poorly understood, and its

[12]See Brynjolfsson *et al.* (2019).

estimation poses challenges due to the proprietary and evolving nature of AI technologies.

Further empirical insight comes from Czarnitzki *et al.* (2023), who examine the relationship between AI adoption and firm-level productivity. Viewing AI as a general-purpose technology (GPT) that facilitates new methods of production, the authors investigate whether AI adoption is positively associated with productivity gains, controlling for confounding factors. Their empirical analysis draws on data from the German portion of the European Union's Community Innovation Survey, also known as the Mannheim Innovation Panel.

The authors construct two primary measures of AI use: a binary indicator for whether a firm has adopted any AI technologies, and a continuous variable capturing the intensity of AI integration in business processes. Their empirical framework centers around a production function of the form $Y = AF(K, L, AI)$, where output depends on physical capital (K), labor (L), and AI-enabled technologies as inputs. This contrasts with the innovation-oriented framework of Cockburn *et al.* (2019), who analyze AI's impact on the generation of new ideas and the acceleration of R&D processes. In Czarnitzki *et al.* (2023), AI enters the production function primarily by shifting the knowledge frontier, either by increasing the stock of ideas (the A term) or by enhancing the production of knowledge inputs (e.g., machine learning algorithms, natural language processing tools).

The estimation framework employed in Czarnitzki *et al.* (2023) takes the following functional form:

$$\ln Y_{it} = \ln A_{it} + \alpha_K \ln K_{it} + \alpha_L \ln L_{it} + \alpha_I \ln AI_{it} + \cdots + \varepsilon_{it} \tag{12.1}$$

where the dependent variable $\ln Y_{it}$ is the natural logarithm of firm-level output, measured either as gross sales or value added (i.e., sales net of intermediate inputs). The term $\ln A_{it}$ captures total factor productivity and includes unobserved firm-specific effects. The explanatory variables include the logarithms of capital input (K_{it}), labor input (L_{it}), and an AI-specific input term (AI_{it}), with corresponding output elasticities α_K, α_L, and α_I.

A key econometric concern is endogeneity: firms' input choices are potentially correlated with unobserved productivity components. In particular, more productive firms may be more likely to adopt AI technologies, thereby biasing the estimated coefficient α_I upward. To address this, the authors use instrumental variable techniques and fixed-effects models to control for firm heterogeneity and isolate the causal impact of AI adoption on productivity outcomes.[13]

The data are based on a survey of companies, which asks whether the enterprise uses AI methods and if so, which of the four methods (machine learning, image recognition, language understanding, and knowledge-based system) and for which of the five areas of application (products, services, automation, data analytics, communication with customers). Thus, there are $20(= 4 \times 5)$ combinations of methods and applications. The reference year is 2018. AI users account for about 7% of the nearly 6,000 observations. An AI user is defined as a firm that uses at least one AI method. AI intensity is measured as the number of method-application combinations used out of 20. The average AI intensity of a firm is about 13%.

Table 12.2 presents condensed regression results that estimate the relationship between AI adoption and firm-level performance, controlling for firm size, industry, and other factors.

The results indicate that both AI adoption and intensity of use are positively associated with firm-level sales. Using value added instead of sales as the dependent variable yields qualitatively similar results. Ordinary least squares (OLS) estimates do not account for potential endogeneity; that is, the possibility that more productive firms are more likely to adopt AI. To address this, the study employs two-stage least squares (2SLS), a method that first replaces the AI variable with a predicted (instrumented) value that reflects only the variation in AI adoption due to external factors

Table 12.2. AI and Firm-Level Performance

Dependent Variable: Sales				
Estimation Method	**OLS**	**2SLS**	**OLS**	**2SLS**
AI indicator	0.055*	1.179***		
AI intensity			0.271*	8.715***
R-squared	0.910	0.887	0.910	0.878

Notes: $***$ and $*$ denote statistical significance levels of 1% and 10%, respectively.
Source: Czarnitzki *et al.* (2023). Other variables are included.

[13]Their instruments are based on lagged local-level AI adoption rates within the same industry, which are presumed to be correlated with a firm's likelihood of adopting AI but exogenous to its current productivity shocks.

uncorrelated with firm performance.[14] The R^2 statistic reflects the model's explanatory power; i.e., how well the regressors explain variations in the outcome.

The key finding is that once simultaneity bias is mitigated through 2SLS, the estimated effect of AI on productivity is substantially larger. Overall, the study provides evidence that the adoption of AI can enhance productivity.

A study by Silva *et al.* (2024) adds a twist to previous research by showing how the effects of AI innovation on productivity depend on how far firms are from the technological frontier. Interestingly, it is the laggard firms that stand to gain more from AI to raise their efficiency levels. The study analyzes firm-level data from 2011–2019, spanning 15 European countries. Productivity is defined as *multi-factor productivity (MFP).*[15] Using a difference-in-differences approach, the study compares a group of firms that are active in AI innovation and a control group of firms that are not active in AI. The methodology accounts for potential reverse causality, recognizing that highly productive firms are more likely to engage in AI innovation.

The study estimates an equation such as

$$\ln MFP_{it} = \cdots + \beta_1 \ln AI_{it} + \beta_2 \ln DTF_{it} + \beta_3 \ln AI_{it} \times \ln DTF_{it} + \cdots \tag{12.2}$$

where the key variables are highlighted (and the control variables and fixed effects terms are suppressed). The subscripts i, t denote firm and year, respectively. AI is a binary variable which equals one in the year of the first filing of an AI patent and in the years thereafter. The variable equals zero in the years before the first filing. DTF denotes distance-to-frontier. It is measured as $\ln \frac{MFP_{ft}}{MFP_{it}}$, where MFP_{ft} is the multi-factor productivity level of the *frontier* company. The larger (smaller) DTF is, the farther (closer) the firm is to the frontier.

As Table 12.3 shows, the study estimates $\beta_1 > 0$, $\beta_2 < 0$, and $\beta_3 > 0$, which signify that AI innovations augment productivity, that lagging firms have lower levels of productivity, but that lagging firms enjoy a bigger boost to their productivity from AI innovation.

[14]The fitted AI variable is derived from a first-stage regression that uses instruments including past innovation expenditures per employee, pre-sample industry-level AI adoption, and a dummy for whether the firm reports facing innovation obstacles.

[15]In contrast to total factor productivity (TFP), MFP is more general. It divides output by a weighted average of a broad range of inputs, beyond just capital and labor.

Table 12.3. Distance to Frontier and AI Effects

Dependent Variable: Log of Multi-Factor Productivity		
	(1)	(2)
AI (post × treatment)	0.151*	0.190**
Distance to National Frontier (DTF_N)	−0.114***	
AI × DTF_N	0.027***	
Distance to Global Frontier (DTF_G)		−0.351***
AI × DTF_G		0.023***
Other Controls	Yes	Yes
Observations	7,076	7,076
R-squared	0.271	0.327

Notes: ***, ** and * denote statistical significance levels of 1%, 5% and 10%, respectively.
Source: Silva *et al.* (2024).

Distance to National Frontier means that the firm's MFP is measured against that of the national leader, while Distance to Global Frontier compares a firm's MFP to that of the global leader. The results show that AI innovations have a positive influence on productivity, but the gains are higher for companies that lag behind. This may occur because AI appears to help level the playing field, enabling lagging companies to expand their knowledge base and enhance their absorptive capacities. Estimates in both columns are consistent; however, the larger negative coefficient of −0.351 (associated with the variable DTF_G) indicates that lagging companies have greater difficulties catching up to global leaders than to national frontier firms.

Shifting from firm-level productivity to individual work performance, the next three case studies examine how AI affects the productivity of scientists and professionals, drawing on recent empirical evidence.

Hao *et al.* (2024) find that scientists who adopt AI tools exhibit significantly higher research productivity: they publish 67.4% more papers, receive an average of 3.16 more citations per publication, and ascend to team leadership roles approximately four years earlier than their non-adopting peers. However, this increase in output comes with a notable tradeoff; namely, a contraction in scientific focus. The use of AI tools is associated with a reduction in the diversity of scientific topics pursued, suggesting that AI may reinforce existing research trajectories rather than catalyze new ones.

The study draws on the *OpenAlex* dataset, which covers more than 100 million research papers published between 1980 and 2024 across six major disciplines: Biology, Medicine, Chemistry, Physics, Materials Science, and Geology. To identify AI-assisted research, the authors applied the BERT language model to classify papers, ultimately determining that only 1.57% of the sample exhibited signs of AI involvement. The study also distinguishes among phases of AI development, such as machine learning, deep learning, and transformer-based language models, and finds that across these phases, AI appears to augment existing lines of research rather than initiate novel ones.

A couple of criticisms could be raised about this study. First, the classification of AI-assisted papers relies on information in titles and abstracts. Although the model is validated by human experts with strong agreement (Fleiss' Kappa = 0.960), this method still risks false positives (non-AI papers misclassified as AI-assisted) and false negatives (AI-assisted work overlooked due to a lack of explicit keywords). Such misclassification could systematically bias the estimated productivity effects, particularly if researchers in high-impact, data-intensive fields are more likely to mention AI tools explicitly. In that case, the analysis may conflate *field effects* with *tool effects*, such that the observed gains in productivity reflect disciplinary advantages rather than AI adoption *per se*.

Second, regarding the finding of scientific contraction, the observed concentration of topics could reflect a productive convergence on high-value subfields (for example, structural biology following the advent of *AlphaFold*), rather than an inherent narrowing of research focus. Furthermore, by excluding interdisciplinary and social science fields, the study may overlook areas where AI, in fact, broadens research scope.

Noy and Zhang (2023) evaluate the productivity effects of generative AI through a randomized controlled trial on 453 college-educated professionals. Each participant was assigned two occupation-specific writing tasks, such as press releases, short reports, analysis plans, or sensitive emails, with performance incentives tied to quality. The output was evaluated by blinded reviewers. Participants were randomly assigned to either a treatment group, which was given access to ChatGPT, or a control group, which was not.

The results show that access to ChatGPT significantly increased productivity, both by reducing the time required to complete tasks and by raising the evaluated quality of output. Moreover, the treated group exhibited less dispersion in productivity, suggesting that generative AI tools can help lower-skilled or slower workers catch up to higher performers. By contrast, the control group not only performed worse on average, but also showed greater inequality in outcomes.

One limitation of this study, however, is that it focuses on individual-level productivity rather than market-level effects. Even if generative AI improves the performance of individual workers, it does not address whether the demand for those workers persists. For example, if generative AI reduces the need for certain kinds of programming or communication roles, then the skill-enhancing effect demonstrated in this study may not translate into improved labor market outcomes for affected workers.

Another limitation is that the observed productivity gains appear to result not from human-AI collaboration, but from direct substitution of ChatGPT output. A majority of participants in the treatment group reported either submitting unedited ChatGPT responses or making only superficial edits. This suggests that the gains stemmed primarily from task substitution rather than augmentation. This distinction is critical: if AI is evaluated as a tool to assist workers, then its value lies in complementing human skills. But if the tool effectively replaces workers, the short-run productivity improvements seen in controlled experiments may not translate into lasting economic gains.

Business school researchers conducted a more nuanced field study in collaboration with the Boston Consulting Group, a global management consultancy.[16] The participants were highly educated professionals whose assigned tasks closely resembled their actual job responsibilities. The researchers implemented two randomized controlled experiments to evaluate AI's impact on workplace performance.

In the first experiment, tasks were categorized as *inside the frontier*; that is, tasks that AI could capably perform, such as drafting client emails, brainstorming ideas, or analyzing structured data. In the second experiment, tasks were classified as *outside the frontier*, involving higher-order cognitive functions such as making critical business recommendations or solving complex, unstructured problems that exceed current machine capabilities.

Each participant first completed a baseline task without AI assistance to establish an initial performance benchmark. Participants were then randomly assigned to one of three conditions: (a) a control group with no AI access, (b) a group given access to GPT, and (c) a group given access to

[16]See Dell'Acqua *et al.* (2023).

GPT along with brief prompt engineering training. Outputs were evaluated by independent experts using standardized rubrics.

In the *inside the frontier* situation, participants with access to GPT demonstrated higher productivity (i.e., more tasks completed), faster completion times, and improved output quality. These effects were especially pronounced among lower-skilled participants. However, the untrained GPT group produced more uniform or homogenized outputs, a concern also raised in Hao *et al.* (2024). By contrast, those who received AI training generated more distinctive and higher-quality work.

In the *outside the frontier* situation, results were mixed. While GPT-assisted participants performed faster and delivered higher-quality business recommendations, their performance on complex problem-solving tasks declined relative to the control group. Surprisingly, participants who received AI training performed worse on those tasks than the untrained GPT group. In this experiment, human subjects appeared to rely excessively on AI, failing to exercise necessary skepticism or inject human judgment where AI still falls short. This highlights the critical need for skilled knowledge workers to recognize the limits of AI or where human insight is indispensable.

While the study is methodologically rigorous and conducted in a real-world setting, its external validity is limited by the highly selective nature of the participant pool. The 758 participants are drawn from a top-tier management consulting firm and may not be representative of the broader labor market, where educational levels, field expertise, and digital literacy vary widely.

Although the three studies reviewed focus on worker-level outcomes within organizational settings, they have broader macroeconomic implications. First, while AI is a powerful productivity-enhancing tool, its effective deployment depends on complementary investments in human capital, including robust education systems, vocational training, and continuous on-the-job learning. Policymakers should not regard AI as an autonomous solution operating on "auto-pilot." Rather, realizing its full social value requires human judgment and oversight.

For developing countries in particular, the appropriate response to AI's rapid advancement is not intimidation, but strategic engagement. These economies should recognize that AI's true utility emerges when it works in conjunction with human labor and human insight. With targeted investments in human capital, developing economies can not only be consumers of AI innovations but contributors to them.

For example, India's National Education Policy emphasizes digital literacy and coding skills as essential foundations.[17] In Africa, initiatives such as the African Union's Digital Transformation Strategy 2020–2030 support the integration of AI and digital skills into secondary and tertiary education.[18] Brazil and Mexico have also launched policy frameworks and initiatives aimed at improving AI readiness, training, and infrastructure.[19] These public initiatives represent an important first step in building the human capital needed to adapt to AI.

Ultimately, AI should be viewed not as a substitute for human development but as its complement. Its long-run impact on productivity, inequality, and growth will depend on the ability of countries, especially in the Global South, to invest in people as well as in machines.

12.4.1 *A Word on Automation*

As AI inputs become cheaper through technological progress or outsourcing to the developing world, the scale of production can expand. Figure 12.1 illustrates the effect.

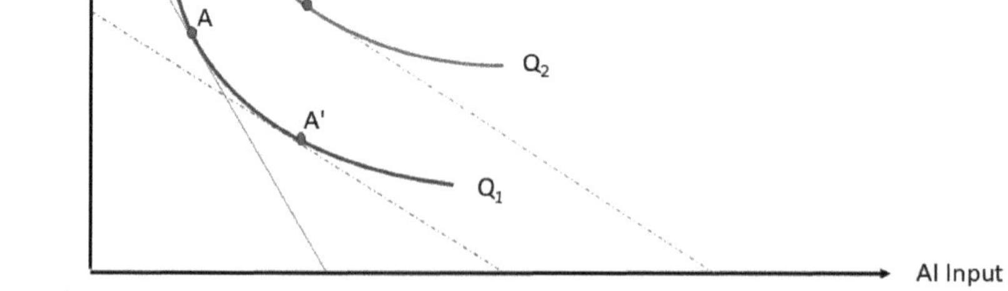

Figure 12.1. Substitution of AI Input for Other Inputs

[17]See https://prsindia.org/policy/report-summaries/national-education-policy-2020

[18]See https://au.int/sites/default/files/documents/38507-doc-dts-english.pdf.

[19]See https://investmentpolicy.unctad.org/investment-policy-monitor/measures/4930/launches-the-brazilian-artificial-intelligence-plan-2024-2028, https://www.cminds.co/_files/ugd/7be025_5b56471311f74346a6ad5faa1e7a8ec9.pdf.

The curve labeled Q_1 is known as an *isoquant* which shows combinations of AI and other inputs that can produce a given quantity of output denoted by Q_1.[20] Point A is the current point of cost minimization where the firm's budget is given by the triangle formed by the solid line; the slope of this line is the ratio of the price of the AI input to that of other inputs. When the price of the AI input falls, holding other factors constant, effectively the firm's budget expands, and the new point of cost minimization is B. A higher level of output, Q_2, is attained, and more of all inputs are employed. Point A' is the hypothetical point that shows the pure substitution effect; that is, had the price ratio been the dashed line initially, the firm would be operating with a higher mix of AI inputs relative to other inputs. The figure shows that there will be some input displacement (like labor inputs) due to artificial intelligence or automation, but that with an increased scale of production, employment levels could be higher. This is important for the South, where automation or AI can relieve workers of tedious, manual labor and redirect their employment, with appropriate training.

This illustration captures two key effects of automation: a substitution effect (AI replacing factors of production, like labor) and a scale effect (growth in total production and potentially more jobs overall). The net result depends on the pace of AI adoption, the extent of worker reskilling, and whether demand rises with productivity. For countries in the Global South, this underscores the importance of investing in complementary infrastructure — education, connectivity, and digital readiness — to ensure that automation translates into inclusive development rather than job loss. This analysis shows that, while displacement is possible, with sufficient reskilling and demand growth, aggregate employment and output can both increase.

It is also important to consider the demand-side drivers of automation and AI adoption. The uptake of AI is not merely supply-driven by technological advancement; it is also shaped by market demand, often in response to labor shortages, cost pressures, or a growing preference for leisure and quality of life. In many cases, automation emerges as a response to unfilled job vacancies or the desire to alleviate physically demanding, repetitive, or dangerous tasks. In lower-income countries, for example, automation can relieve workers from hazardous or exhausting forms of labor. Few, for instance, lament the arrival of washing machines, which replaced grueling

[20]The convexity of the curve is due to the diminishing marginal productivity of inputs.

manual laundry work, or the spread of digital learning platforms, such as McGraw-Hill's *Connect*, Pearson's *MyLab* or Cengage's *MindTap*, which lessen the burden of grading for educators.

These examples highlight that AI and automation are not inherently adversarial to labor. Understanding the demand-side motivations for automation provides a fuller perspective on its potential benefits as well as its risks.

12.4.2 *Singularity*

A natural segue from the discussion of AI and productivity is the concept of technological singularity: the hypothetical point at which artificial intelligence surpasses human intelligence, rendering human labor redundant in many domains. Theorists argue that such a threshold would unleash superintelligent innovation, driving unprecedented and possibly exponential economic growth. Nordhaus (2021) examines whether this frontier is being approached by identifying several empirical signals consistent with an economy nearing singularity. These includes the following:

- A high elasticity of substitution between capital and labor, indicating that machines are increasingly able to replace human workers across tasks;
- A rising capital share of income in national accounts, suggesting that returns to capital (including AI systems) are outpacing those to labor;
- Sustained increases in total factor productivity (TFP) growth, reflecting accelerated technological progress;
- An accelerating capital-to-output ratio, as more investment is channeled into machines and AI systems relative to output produced;
- A rising share of information capital in total capital stock — i.e., capital embedded in data, algorithms, and computing infrastructure rather than physical machinery.

These trends, if confirmed, would point toward a structural transformation in the sources of economic growth and the nature of production.

Singularity requires a high degree of substitutability between capital and labor, especially in the form of intelligent capital such as AI. As automation becomes more widespread, labor is displaced from an increasing number of tasks. The elasticity of substitution is critical: the greater it is, the more seamlessly AI can take over human functions. However, even if technological singularity is approaching, its effects on measured productivity may not yet be visible. As discussed earlier, measurement lags and intangible capital accumulation can obscure real gains, leading to underestimates of total factor productivity growth. Conversely, if intangible inputs are omitted from measurement, observed productivity may be overestimated in the long run.

Nordhaus (2021) also distinguishes between two key margins of technological progress: the intensive margin, where AI automates existing human tasks (task automation), and the extensive margin, where it enables the creation of new tasks (task evolution). The singularity hypothesis implies a tipping point at which automation exceeds task evolution. In such a world, AI systems would determine not just how tasks are performed but also which tasks matter, effectively becoming the principal drivers of innovation, organization, and strategic decision-making.

In the Nordhaus (2021) framework, singularity occurs at the point where the economic growth rate exceeds 20 percent per year, driven by machine-generated innovation. To evaluate the proximity of singularity, the study conducts six empirical tests. The findings are summarized in Table 12.4.

Of the six indicators, four are negative or inconclusive, and two are weakly positive. Nordhaus concludes that singularity is not imminent. The required economic conditions, such as a high degree of elasticity of substitution in consumption or production, and consistently high growth trajectories, are not observed in the data to date.

Table 12.4. Singularity Conditions

Test Type	Test Result	Time Until Singularity
1. Elasticity of substitution between capital and labor > 1	Ambiguous	
2. Rising productivity growth	Negative	
3. Rising share of capital	Positive	>100 years
4. Accelerating growth in capital-output ratio	Negative	
5. Rising share of information capital	Positive	>100 years
6. Rising productivity growth hidden due to mismeasurement	Negative	

Source: Nordhaus (2021), Table 7.

These results stand in contrast to the forecasts of several prominent thinkers who predict the emergence of an artificial intelligence (AI) singularity. Among these futurists, three figures are especially influential:

- Ray Kurzweil, *The Singularity is Near* (2005)
- Eliezer Yudkowsky, *Machine Intelligence Research Institute Writings* (2001–), https://intelligence.org/
- Nick Bostrom, *Superintelligence: Paths, Dangers, Strategies* (2014)

Kurzweil (2005) envisions a future in which the exponential growth of computing power enables machines to surpass human intelligence. He anticipates not only rapid innovation but also recursive self-improvement, whereby machines can design more capable successors.

Yudkowsky (2008) also argues that AI systems may undergo recursive self-enhancement. His focus is not on the celebration of scientific achievement but on existential risk: the possibility that uncontrolled machine intelligence could threaten human survival.

Bostrom (2014) likewise foresees the rise of "superintelligence"-AI systems vastly exceeding human cognitive skills. He emphasizes the difficulty humans would face in controlling or predicting such agents and warns that the transition to superintelligence could be irreversible.

These futurists base their long-run prognostication on technical potential, but Nordhaus (2021) argues that economic indicators, such as productivity, capital deepening, and input substitutability, must align with the singularity hypothesis. His findings, based on empirical metrics, suggest that these thresholds have not been met. While Kurzweil, Yudkowsky, and Bostrom emphasize computational capacity, Nordhaus emphasizes economic feasibility and valuation: growth must not only be rapid but valuable within an economic framework: "The economic perspective insists that the growth must be weighted by the economic valuation of the good or service."[21]

12.5 North–South Gaps

Here is an overview of the gaps:

1. **Technology Gaps and the AI Divide:** The rapid advancement of AI technologies has predominantly occurred in a select group of countries, leading to a widening technological gap between the Global North

[21]Nordhaus (2021), p. 326.

and South. This disparity, often referred to as the "AI divide," results from concentrated AI research, development, and infrastructure in developed nations, leaving developing countries with limited access to these transformative tools. To mitigate this divide, several strategies can be employed:

- *Capacity Building*: Investing in education and training programs to develop local expertise in AI and related fields.
- *International Cooperation*: Establishing partnerships between developed and developing countries to facilitate knowledge transfer and collaborative research.
- *Policy Frameworks*: Developing inclusive policies that promote equitable access to AI technologies and address ethical considerations.

2. **AI's Impact on Income Distribution and Employment:** AI can exert contrasting effects on global income distribution. On the one hand, it can boost productivity and economic growth; on the other, it can exacerbate income inequality and unemployment, particularly in regions lacking the skills and infrastructure to adapt to technological change. In developing countries, the lack of resources to implement AI solutions can lead to job displacement without the offsetting benefits of increased productivity. Conversely, advanced economies are more likely to experience job transformation rather than elimination, further widening global income disparities.
3. **Effects on Trade and Foreign Direct Investment (FDI):** AI influences global trade patterns and FDI flows by altering comparative advantages. Automation and AI-enabled processes reduce the relative cost advantages of low-wage labor, diminishing the appeal of outsourcing to developing countries and potentially leading to a decline in FDI in labor-intensive sectors. However, AI also opens new avenues for trade in digital services and can enhance supply chain efficiencies. Developing countries that invest in digital infrastructure and skills development are better able to attract new forms of FDI that are based on technology and innovation.
4. **Market Competition and Intellectual Property:** The AI industry is marked by significant market concentration, with a handful of major technology firms possessing substantial market power (further discussed in the next section). These firms control vast datasets and advanced AI models, creating high entry barriers for smaller competitors and for firms in developing countries. In addition, their ownership of AI-generated works and related intellectual property may further restrict competition.

It is important that those IP rights in the Global North not crowd out opportunities for creators in the Global South.

5. **Technological Balance of Payments:** The technological balance of payments, which tracks the flow of technology-related payments between countries, will be significantly affected by AI. Currently, most developing countries are net importers of AI technologies and remain heavily dependent on foreign innovations. Their deficits in the technological balance of payments are likely to widen with the spread of AI, worsening their international terms of trade. To mitigate this imbalance, policies that promote domestic AI research and development, together with regional collaboration, are essential. Encouraging local innovation is not merely about narrowing external deficits but about building resilient domestic industries and capturing greater economic value within national economies.

This overview suggests that the Global North is likely to widen its technological lead over the Global South, given that most AI innovations originate from and are owned by firms in advanced economies, especially the United States. While China, as a leading emerging economy, presents a significant challenge to U.S. dominance, most other developing countries risk falling further behind. Again, a key indicator of this growing divide is the technological balance of payments: developing economies are typically net importers of innovation, paying more in licensing fees than they receive.

As Table 12.5 illustrates, exports of licensed intellectual property, as measured by receipts of fees and royalties, remain heavily skewed toward

Table 12.5. Licensing Exports, by Select Years

Country Group	2005	2010	2015	2020	2022
A. Developed	209.4	273.2	323.6	348.8	346.9
B. Developing	3.1	5.4	17.7	25.4	31.8
Ratio A/B	68	51	18	14	11

Note: Billions of real 2017 U.S. dollars. Data are based on charges for the use of intellectual property.

Source: UNCTAD Data Center.

the developed world. Although the gap has narrowed over time, the asymmetry is still pronounced. In 2005, the developed world earned 68 times more in licensing fees than the developing world; by 2022, this ratio had fallen to 11. This trend suggests some convergence, possibly due to rising innovation in large emerging economies. However, the extraordinary growth of AI capabilities in the North, combined with any expansion of IP protections around AI, could reverse this convergence, worsening the terms of trade for the Global South and deepening the global skills divide.

Closing this gap will require more than passive diffusion of AI technologies. Proactive measures, such as international cooperation on AI standards, funding for education in computer science and machine learning, and policies that promote balanced IP frameworks, are preferable to prevent existing inequalities in the digital era from widening.

If AI does not diffuse more equitably across borders, the role of IP flexibilities becomes increasingly important. In particular, compulsory licensing may be warranted as a policy response to rising market concentration and patent control by a handful of multinational firms. This echoes earlier debates in pharmaceuticals and biotechnology, where access to essential innovations prompted exceptions to exclusive rights. These flexibilities may be required for AI training data and foundational models, the ownership of which is often proprietary and concentrated in a few high-income countries. Without sufficient open access or shared licensing mechanisms, the concentration of resources risks exacerbating global inequality.

The case for IP flexibility is particularly pressing in the context of AI training datasets and foundation models. These are not merely outputs but essential building blocks for production and innovation — akin to an *essential facility*, vital for businesses to operate (such as airports, telephone networks, and utilities). Just as access to vaccines or internet connectivity became global policy concerns, so too must access to AI capabilities be treated as an international policy objective.

Developing countries that lack access to high-quality, large-scale training datasets or the compute resources required to build foundation models may find themselves permanently disadvantaged. Introducing limited exceptions, such as fair use for non-commercial training, public-private open model consortia, or cooperative data-sharing frameworks, could help ameliorate this imbalance without dismantling the IP system altogether.

Open innovation and open science can therefore play an important role in bridging global disparities in AI capabilities.[22] Developing economies often gain critical knowledge through participation in open innovation ecosystems, enabling local researchers to avoid high licensing fees, adapt global innovations to regional needs, and engage in scientific exchange.

Open source AI frameworks, in particular, hold promise for empowering developers in the Global South to continue scientific progress on their own terms. However, most open source communities lack the resources to train large-scale generative AI models. These efforts require vast amounts of computing power, access to cloud infrastructure, and highly skilled labor — resources currently concentrated in a few large corporations. Overcoming this barrier will likely require targeted public investment. Governments, multilateral organizations, and philanthropic consortia could play a vital role in funding open source AI initiatives, especially those that prioritize inclusion and capacity-building for underrepresented regions and languages.

While the preceding discussion focused on global disparities in access to AI, similar concerns about concentration can arise *within* countries. Incumbent firms may enjoy enduring advantages from early access to data and AI infrastructure. Entrants, particularly in developing economies, face significantly greater barriers to accessing high-quality training data and compute resources.

12.5.1 *AI, Technological Progress, and Catch-Up*

Korinek and Stiglitz (2021) examine the development implications of AI and automation, arguing that without targeted policy interventions, these technologies are likely to exacerbate global inequality. Their analysis presents a compelling case for pursuing more inclusive outcomes from AI-driven technological change.

A key theme in their analysis is the potential shift in *comparative advantage*. AI is both resource-saving and labor-saving, undermining the two primary factors on which many developing countries base their specialization and export strength. As a result, AI innovations risk devaluing the very

[22]Emerging initiatives exemplify this shift. The *LAION* project offers large-scale, openly licensed image-text datasets used to train models such as Stable Diffusion. India's *Bhashini* mission, under the National Language Translation Mission, seeks to build multilingual AI tools for low-resource languages using public-private partnerships. The *AfricaNLP* and *Masakhane* projects similarly aim to enhance AI capacity and corpus development for African languages. See LAION (2023), https://laion.ai; Bhashini, https://bhashini.gov.in/vision-mission; and Masakhane, https://www.masakhane.io.

sources of comparative advantage that have historically enabled catch-up growth. Korinek and Stiglitz (2021) develop theoretical models to illustrate how AI can reshape comparative advantage. A consequence of this shift is downward pressure on the returns to natural resources and on wages in the developing world. As discussed earlier, the traditional low-wage advantage held by many countries in the Global South is eroded by advances in automation. Multinational firms may respond by reshoring labor-intensive production to advanced economies where AI systems can substitute for low-wage labor.

This trend could have broader implications for development. In particular, the product life cycle described in Chapters 5 and 6 may become short-circuited: new products developed in the North may no longer be easily imitated and scaled in the South if their production relies less on labor and more on advanced automation. In such a scenario, Southern firms lose the ability to displace Northern producers through cost advantages, thereby narrowing opportunities for their exporting and industrial upgrading.

Moreover, AI could lead to a deterioration in the *terms of trade* of developing countries. This is important because the terms of trade indicate, essentially, how much a country needs to export to other countries in exchange for a certain amount of imports. When a country's terms of trade become unfavorable, it has to export more in order to get the same amount of imports, which thereby reduces its bargaining position in global markets. This terms of trade deterioration can arise if developing countries continue to specialize in primary commodities or low-skill manufacturing while high-income countries gain further advantages in producing AI-intensive goods and services. The terms of trade depend on a host of factors, such as productivity differences between trading partners, relative consumer demands, currency values, and any trade interventions, such as quotas or tariffs.

A further concern, as noted earlier, is that AI may reinforce market power. Korinek and Stiglitz (2021) point to three mechanisms. First, information is non-rivalrous and has a near-zero marginal cost of distribution, allowing a single firm to serve large markets. Second, the high fixed costs of developing AI and machine learning (ML) systems create barriers to entry. Third, training datasets generate network effects. Better data attract more users and developers, reinforcing the advantage of incumbent firms. These factors collectively strengthen the market power of early movers.

AI could also increase the market power of firms outside the core AI industries. For instance, companies may deploy algorithms to engage in tacit or even explicit price fixing.[23] Real estate companies, insurance providers, law firms, and even universities may apply AI tools to monitor price dispersion and effectively maintain agreed-upon pricing structures. In addition, companies can use AI methods to study consumer behavior with much greater precision than in the past. By identifying patterns in individual preferences and purchasing behavior, firms may be able to charge different prices to different customers, as was discussed in Chapter 8. Perfect price discrimination occurs when the seller charges each consumer a price equal to his/her marginal willingness to pay, rather than offering a single price to all consumers or all units.

In Figure 12.2, consider an individual's demand curve, which is downward sloping due to diminishing marginal utility, the principle that each additional unit consumed provides less additional satisfaction. Suppose the market price of the commodity (e.g., tickets to an opera performance) is $30. At this price, the consumer chooses to purchase three units (or watch the opera three times). The consumer will not purchase the fourth unit because her marginal willingness to pay for it is $20, which is below the cost of purchasing it, and her consumer surplus (CS) would then be negative. But at three units of consumption, the consumer's total utility is $40. This surplus can be broken down as follows: on the first unit, she is willing to pay $60 but only pays $30, resulting in $30 of CS; on the second unit,

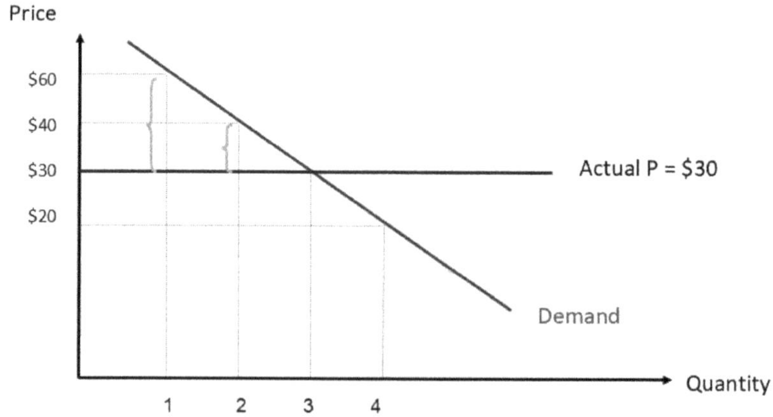

Figure 12.2. Price Discrimination and Consumer Surplus

[23] https://www.theatlantic.com/ideas/archive/2024/08/ai-price-algorithms-realpage/679405/.

her marginal willingness to pay is \$40, yielding \$10 of CS; and on the third unit, her willingness to pay equals the price, so she breaks even.

In a competitive market, the seller does not initially observe each consumer's demand curve. It only knows that the market price happens to be \$30, which is determined by the intersection of market demand and supply. However, with the aid of personalized advertising, predictive modeling, and deep learning tools, sellers can begin to infer the marginal willingness to pay (MWP) of individual consumers for each unit. In that case, why charge a flat \$30 for all units? Why not charge this consumer \$60 for the first unit, \$40 for the second unit, and \$30 for the third unit — and even \$20 on the fourth unit? Through AI's assistance, the seller can appropriate most or all of the consumer's surplus. While this form of perfect price discrimination is rarely achieved in practice, AI may enable sellers to improve their ability to extract consumer surplus.

Korinek and Stiglitz (2021) recommend policies that steer technological progress towards making AI *labor-using* innovations, rather than labor-saving, particularly in the developing world. The goal is to ensure that AI complements rather than displaces human labor. For example, AI tools can assist rather than replace workers or professionals by offering support in areas such as diagnostic decision-making (e.g., in radiology), precision farming, or tailored education plans. In human services, like social work, elder care, and early childhood education, AI systems could schedule appointments, manage records, or provide language translation. This frees up time for human caregivers to focus on the empathetic and interpersonal aspects of their job that AI cannot replicate. Collaborative robotics (or "cobots") could be designed to work alongside humans, enhancing productivity without replacing them. For instance, a cobot might assist with lifting heavy objects while a human focuses on assembly or quality control. AI can offer human resource tools for job matching and aid marginalized workers (e.g., refugees, the disabled, rural populations) to find employment that suits their skills and conditions.

Korinek and Stiglitz (2021) emphasize the importance of strengthening social protections for workers who are displaced or disrupted by AI. These protections may include redistributive policies, targeted investments in education and training, and expanded access to public goods that facilitate learning and skill development. While these social policies can be designed and implemented at the national level, a more difficult challenge arises at the international level. The global diffusion of AI may generate gains for some countries and losses for others. How can the gainers from AI, often high-income countries, compensate the losers, particularly in the developing world? Addressing this imbalance will require international cooperation, as echoed in the WTO (2024) report.

Korinek and Stiglitz (2021) also call for more inclusive growth policies; that is, policies that enable all countries to benefit from AI in a balanced and sustainable manner. At present, AI appears to disproportionately advantage developed countries, raising concerns about a "rich-get-richer" dynamic. While AI may not actually lower growth in the developing world or trigger a de-industrialization, the gap between North and South may still widen if AI augments productivity more in the Global North than in the Global South.

Equally important is the need to include developing countries more meaningfully in AI policy design. In areas such as data governance and digital regulation, the voices and concerns of developing economies have so far been underrepresented. Most AI models to date have been trained on datasets that originate from developed countries, raising risks of cultural misrepresentation and algorithmic bias. To ensure fairness and accuracy, AI systems must be trained on multicultural and multilingual data sources.[24]

The following comments consider a scenario in which AI technologies raise welfare in all countries, yet still contribute to a widening gap between the Global North and the Global South. In economics, a *Pareto improvement* refers to an outcome in which at least one party is made better off without making anyone else worse off.[25] If AI innovations raise living standards in both developed and developing economies, then, in principle, the world economy as a whole experiences a mutual gain.

As illustrated in Figure 12.3, both a leader nation and a follower nation ascend the technological or economic developmental ladder owing to advances in AI. For the follower nation, the diffusion of AI enhances its knowledge base and introduces new tools for productivity growth. However, since the leader nation is better able to exploit AI innovations and retains control of AI training datasets, it climbs much higher, thereby widening the technological gap. But though the follower never catches up to the leader, is it not better off than before?[26] After all, the process of economic catch-up

[24]See Liu (2024) and Globig *et al.* (2024) for discussions of cultural bias and misperceptions in AI systems.

[25]Named after the Italian economist Vilfredo Pareto (1848–1923).

[26]This situation is analogous to the *ultimatum game* in behavioral economics, where player 1 determines how to split a prize, say $100, and player 2 decides whether to accept the offer. Rationally, player 2 should accept any positive amount, but in practice, low offers (e.g., $1) are often rejected out of a sense of fairness or to incentivize Player 2 to be more generous in future games.

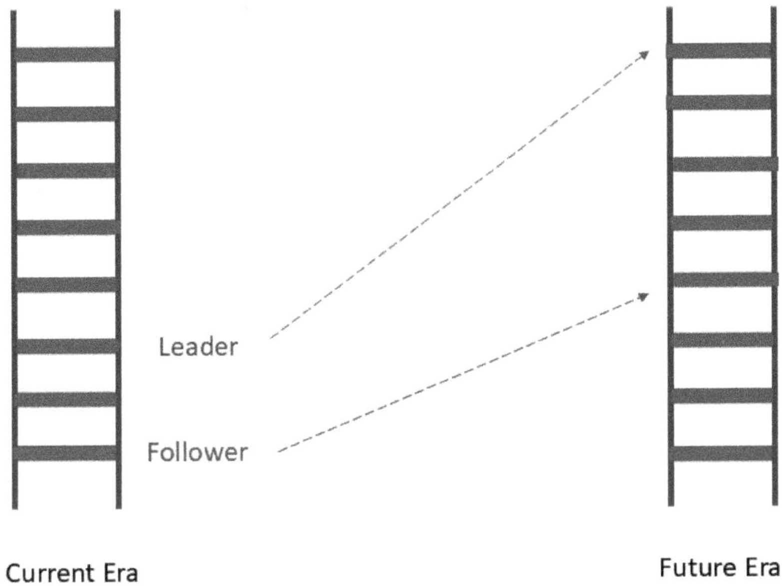

Figure 12.3. Technological Ladder

should not be viewed as an end in itself but rather as a means of achieving growth and development. The ultimate objective should be for developing countries to be better off than before.[27]

However, though the developing world achieves a higher standard of living, it still remains a technology follower. Its firms might never reach the global technological frontier, nor shape the direction of innovation in ways that reflect their unique needs, constraints, or cultural contexts. The terms of trade may continue to favor the Global North, reinforcing its bargaining power over key decisions on the global allocation of resources and on the design of international rules, standards, and institutions. In such a scenario, developed countries may continue to obtain better access to scarce global resources and exercise disproportionate influence over technological governance. These are, to be sure, speculative outcomes, but they highlight what persistent gaps in technological capacity and institutional voice might entail — even if all countries have climbed up the ladder. These concerns lend further support to the case for balanced and inclusive growth.

[27]Chang (2002) provides another type of ladder analogy. Once developed countries reach a certain level of advancement, they may attempt to "kick away the ladder" by erecting policy barriers or investment restrictions to maintain their lead.

12.5.2 *Policy Implications*

Korinek and Stiglitz (2021) propose reforms to intellectual property (IP) systems, such as reducing the length of patent protection. However, as discussed in Chapter 1, most patents are not held for the full statutory term of 20 years. Many are allowed to lapse within 5 to 7 years due to maintenance costs and the diminishing commercial value of the underlying inventions. In fast-moving sectors such as ICT and AI, firms often forgo patenting altogether for technologies with short life cycles, knowing that the innovation may become obsolete before it is imitated. Moreover, some firms may prefer to leverage first-mover advantages and commercialize AI technologies quickly, rather than wait through the patent examination process, which can take months or even years and may involve opposition or validity challenges.

A more pressing concern is the need to curb rent-seeking behavior in the patent system. Some firms file patents not to use them, but to hoard them, without actually manufacturing or commercializing any related products. These entities, often referred to as *patent trolls*, rely on litigation or the threat of litigation to extract royalty payments from others who independently develop and commercialize similar technologies. Reform efforts might focus on limiting such non-productive patenting practices. Patent scope should also be more closely aligned with the economic significance of the invention. Patents that make marginal contributions should not receive the same breadth of protection as those that generate substantial technological or market impact. Aligning patent protection with the value of inventions can help ensure that the system promotes innovation without distorting competition or hindering follow-on research.

Other relevant IP policies include efforts to encourage voluntary licensing of AI technologies. In cases where voluntary arrangements are not forthcoming or are offered on unreasonable terms, compulsory licensing (CL) may be invoked. However, CL is typically not immediate. Patent holders are generally allowed a period of three to four years to "work" the patent; that is, to develop, manufacture, or license the invention before compulsory measures can be considered. Even then, the licensee is required to pay reasonable compensation to the patent holder.

For either voluntary or compulsory licensing to be effective, however, the licensee must possess the technological and absorptive capacity to implement the patented invention. Without sufficient domestic expertise, infrastructure, or manufacturing capability, licensing alone will not lead to any meaningful transfer of technology. In this regard, a more fundamental policy priority for the Global South is to build indigenous technological and production capacity. This includes investing in education, R&D infrastructure, and skills development to enable local firms to absorb, adapt, and build upon licensed technologies. Licensing mechanisms, whether voluntary or compulsory, can only make a difference if recipients are capable of making productive use of the technology.

Other policy considerations pertain to algorithms and data, which are central to AI development. In most jurisdictions, software source code and algorithms are not required to be disclosed in patent applications. However, as discussed in Chapter 11, there are alternative ways to satisfy the *enablement* requirement so as to enhance transparency and provide instructional value to follow-on inventors, even without full code disclosure.

Finally, with respect to data exclusivity, the critical dilemma is how to balance privacy rights with the need to avoid monopolistic control over key information resources. Overly restrictive data controls risk producing anti-competitive outcomes by limiting access to the raw material needed to train AI systems or develop competing services. A useful parallel comes from pharmaceutical R&D, where test data exclusivity can delay the entry of generic or biosimilar manufacturers. Such restrictions reduce consumer surplus by limiting access to affordable drugs. A similar risk arises in AI markets, where concentrated control over proprietary datasets may hinder entry, reduce consumer choice, and raise costs for users.

12.6 Bottlenecks

The chapter began by exploring how AI can spur innovation and technology transfer, and ultimately contribute to productivity growth. It then examined the potential downsides; chief among them was the risk of widening disparities between technology leaders and laggards. This final section turns to some of the barriers that need to be addressed to close, or at least narrow, those gaps. These include market factors and resource constraints.

12.6.1 *Market Concentration*

As discussed earlier, the current structure of the AI economy reflects significant concentration among a small number of incumbent firms. Leading tech companies such as Google (Alphabet), Microsoft, Amazon, Meta, and

NVIDIA control a disproportionate share of the computational infrastructure, proprietary training data, and foundational models. These inputs are not easily replicable: training large language models requires billions of parameters and vast datasets of high-quality and computational resources that only a handful of firms currently possess.[28]

While a few foundation models have entered the industry, the market for chips on which these models depend for training is heavily concentrated.[29] Table 12.6 presents a select list of companies offering large language models (LLMs) and foundation model products. Among these providers, OpenAI holds the leading market share in terms of subscribers.[30]

Table 12.6. Foundation Model Providers

Country	Company	Foundation Model/Product(s)
USA	OpenAI	ChatGPT (GPT-4, GPT-4o)
USA	Microsoft	Copilot (via OpenAI models)
USA	xAI	Grok
USA	Anthropic	Claude (Claude 3 series)
USA	Google DeepMind	Gemini (Gemini 2.5)
USA	Meta (Facebook)	LLaMA 3
USA	Perplexity AI	Perplexity Ask
China	Alibaba Cloud	Tongyi Qianwen
China	DeepSeek	DeepSeek-VL, DeepSeek-Coder
China	Baidu, Huawei	Ernie Bot, PanGu
France	Mistral	Mistral, Mixtral
India	Sarvam AI, Krutrim	OpenHathi, Krutrim
South Korea	Naver	HyperCLOVA X
United Arab Emirates	TII (Abu Dhabi)	Falcon (Falcon 180B)
Germany	Aleph Alpha (Heidelberg)	Luminous
Germany	DeepL (Cologne)	DeepL Voice, DeepL Write Pro

[28]See the *Generative AI Market Report 2025–2030*, https://iot-analytics.com/product/generative-ai-market-report-2025-2030/.

[29]See Korinek and Vipra (2024).

[30]See https://menlovc.com/2024-the-state-of-generative-ai-in-the-enterprise/.

The foundation model industry includes a growing number of international players. However, it is not yet highly competitive in the traditional economic sense. It exhibits characteristics of significant first-mover advantage (notably OpenAI), strong network effects, significant fixed costs, and dependence on proprietary cloud systems that can create switching costs and lock-in effects. This is because foundation models are often tied to specific cloud computing platforms and lack portability across them.[31]

The upstream market for AI compute is far more concentrated than the downstream market for foundation models. Specialized hardware, particularly GPUs, is essential for training large models. Table 12.7 lists some of the primary chip providers in the AI ecosystem, along with their core areas of specialization.

The market for graphical processing units (GPUs) used in training AI models is dominated by NVIDIA, which in 2023 held an estimated 92% market share.[32] Meanwhile, in the third quarter of 2024, Taiwan Semiconductor Manufacturing Company (TSMC) dominated the global market for chip fabrication,[33] accounting for approximately 64% of the global

Table 12.7. AI Chip Providers

Country	Company	Specialization/Product(s)
USA	NVIDIA	GPUs
USA	AMD	GPUs
USA	Intel	CPUs, AI accelerator design, fabrication
USA	Google (Alphabet)	TPUs (Tensor Processing Units)
Taiwan	Taiwan Semicon. Mfg. Co.	Chip fabrication
South Korea	Samsung Electronics	Chip fabrication
China	Huawei (HiSilicon)	Chip design

[31]For example, OpenAI's GPT-4 is available exclusively through Microsoft's *Azure*, Google's Gemini is integrated into *Google Cloud services*, and Anthropic's Claude is deployed via *Amazon Web Services (AWS)*.

[32]See Korinek and Vipra (2024).

[33]Companies such as NVIDIA, AMD, and HiSilicon are considered *fabless*, meaning they design but do not manufacture their own chips. Instead, they outsource production to foundries like TSMC and Samsung.

pure-play foundry business.[34] A pure-play foundry specializes in manufacturing integrated circuits for other companies.

Korinek and Vipra (2024) identify two key sources of the high fixed costs associated with foundation models: i. the pre-training costs and ii. fine-tuning costs of adapting the models for specific use cases. These fixed costs give rise to both economies of scale (advantages of being able to spread the costs on a large volume of output) and economies of scope (cost savings of adapting a model to a variety of applications). The high costs and market conditions also create incentives for vertical integration — combining foundation models with data platforms or proprietary databases, or integrating foundation models and chips.[35] Mergers and acquisitions could likewise arise to exploit economies of scale and scope.[36]

Gans (2024) identifies three broad market domains where an incumbent's market power may be reinforced: (i) training data, (ii) input data, and (iii) AI predictions. Training data are subject to feedback loops: the more users a platform attracts, the more data it can collect, leading to better model performance, which in turn attracts even more users. Refusals to share, sell, or license this data can raise substantial entry barriers. Input data refer to information gathered from market interactions, such as consumer preferences or willingness to pay, which can be used to exercise market power through price discrimination or the tailoring of personalized products. Finally, control over AI predictions, such as matching algorithms in advertising, enables firms to extract greater consumer surplus through finely targeted advertising. The significance of this framework is that market power in AI does not stem solely from computational resources, but from the strategic control of data across the value chain.

Thus, the concern is that the market power of today's AI companies may reinforce their incumbency, leading commentators such as Korinek and Stiglitz (2021) to warn of potential "winner-take-all" scenarios. However, this concern is not unique to the AI era. Similar fears were raised

---

[34]See *Taipei Times*, January 14, 2025. https://www.taipeitimes.com/News/biz/archives/2025/01/14/2003830149.

[35]An example of data–model integration is xAI, trained on data from X/Twitter, and an example of model-chip integration is Google DeepMind, which developed Tensor Processing Units (TPUs) in-house.

[36]Over 300 AI deals were concluded in 2024, a thirty percent increase from 2023. For instance, AMD acquired Silo AI, Europe's largest private AI lab. NVIDIA acquired Run:ai, an Israeli platform company. See https://analyticsindiamag.com/ai-trends/who-bought-what-2024s-biggest-ai-mergers-and-acquisitions/.

during earlier technological waves, including the internet boom.[37] Yet, casual observations show that markets have historically experienced substantial turnover. For instance, persistent churning occurs among the top 25–30 companies in the *Fortune 500*, the S&P 500 stock index, and the *Dow Jones Industrial Average* since the 1950s.[38] The lesson is that AI companies, too, are not immune to market forces. They may rise, merge, divest, or fall, as creative destruction, innovation, and imitation continue to reshape industries.

Ultimately, to use the language of supply and demand, a major outward shift of the long-run supply curve is needed — both in AI outputs and the inputs into their production. This includes the expansion of foundation model providers, semiconductor chip designers, foundries for chip fabrication, and other critical elements of the AI supply chain, as well as the development of newer, more efficient AI technologies. However, in the short run, several bottlenecks constrain this growth. The remainder of this section addresses two particularly important ones: (i) access to compute resources and (ii) environmental limitations.

12.6.2 *Bottleneck 1: Compute Resources*

Among the most binding constraints is compute. Training large foundation models requires access to high-performance GPUs, which are not inputs that can scale elastically. They more closely resemble capital-intensive infrastructure.[39]

Bottlenecks extend well beyond GPUs. Data centers, server networks, and specialized AI engineering talent are likewise relatively inelastic.[40] None of these inputs responds quickly to price signals, and all involve long lead times. Major technology firms, such as Microsoft, Meta, and OpenAI, have secured preferential access to key components through long-term supply agreements. Yet such contracts do not expand overall capacity; instead,

[37]See Shapiro and Varian (1999) for an early treatment of industry dominance in the information economy.

[38]See S&P Global historical data and market reports, CNN Money: Fortune 500 archives, and the official S&P Dow Jones Indices website https://www.spglobal.com/spdji/en/.

[39]These resource constraints — compute, energy, bandwidth, and data — may all have relevance for the feasibility of *Singularity*, which presumes frictionless scaling.

[40]See, for example, https://www.rand.org/pubs/research_reports/RRA3572-1.html and https://www.mckinsey.com/featured-insights/artificial-intelligence/notes-from-the-ai-frontier-applications-and-value-of-deep-learning.

they allocate scarce resources to incumbents and may exacerbate shortages for others.

Under these circumstances, the market does not clear efficiently. Scarcity in compute resources does not automatically trigger a rapid supply response. Capital intensity, time-to-build, technical complexity, control over key inputs, and geopolitics (including export controls on high-end chips) all constrain expansion and limit new entry. In short, the foundation model market is shaped not only by algorithms but also by the hardware and infrastructure on which those algorithms depend.

12.6.3 *Bottleneck 2: Environment*

Compute resources are also constrained by energy availability and environmental cost. Training and deploying foundation models at scale depends not only on chips and data but also on access to affordable, low-carbon electricity. This adds a physical and ecological dimension to the economics of the AI market.

Every foundation model encounters physical constraints. "Cloud" is only a metaphor. Computations occur in data centers — in real facilities that require land, electricity, and cooling infrastructure. These demands are significant. According to the International Monetary Fund, the world's data centers in 2023 consumed as much electricity as France or Germany. Their electricity use could eventually rival that of India, currently the world's third-largest consumer.[41]

The electricity that powers these systems often comes from fossil fuels, though this varies significantly by geographic location and national commitments to renewable energy. According to the International Energy Agency (2025), the consumption of electricity by data centers has been growing at four times the rate of total electricity consumption since 2017.

Beyond energy, the physical infrastructure of AI relies on critical minerals: silicon for advanced chips, rare earth elements for electronic components, and lithium and cobalt for batteries that power data centers and mobile devices. Many of these inputs are extracted from regions that are environmentally fragile or geopolitically unstable.[42]

Another critical pressure point is water. Data centers consume billions of gallons of it annually, primarily for cooling. Much of this water is drawn

---

[41]See https://www.imf.org/en/Blogs/Articles/2025/05/13/ai-needs-more-abundant-power-supplies-to-keep-driving-economic-growth.

[42]See International Energy Agency (2021).

from stressed watersheds.[43] After use, cooling systems discharge wastewater, including effluent from condensation processes. These discharges often require on-site treatment facilities. At a time when the world faces mounting pressure to decarbonize and conserve water, improving the eco-efficiency of data centers is imperative.

The environmental burden is distributed unevenly. Advanced economies have built data centers near cleaner energy sources. By contrast, many countries in the Global South face fragile grids, water scarcity, and inadequate cooling infrastructure. Even when the economic case for AI adoption exists, the environmental cost may be prohibitive.

The sustainability of AI, therefore, requires building more energy-efficient systems, innovating in cooling technologies, and investing in environmentally responsible mining. Put simply, the future viability of AI might well rest on "Green AI."

Still, AI may be part of the solution, in that it can contribute to finding environmental solutions. Machine learning systems can help optimize energy use, reduce emissions, and monitor environmental degradation. Applications such as smart grids, dynamic energy pricing, traffic management, and precision agriculture illustrate how AI can help alleviate environmental costs. Whether AI proves a net benefit or cost to the environment will depend on economic choices in technological design.

[43]https://www.asce.org/publications-and-news/civil-engineering-source/civil-engineering-magazine/issues/magazine-issue/article/2024/03/engineers-often-need-a-lot-of-water-to-keep-data-centers-cool.

Chapter 13

Lessons for Economic Growth and Development

13.1 Introduction

The intellectual property system is one of several important influences on the development of economies. Indeed, few areas within the study of economic development remain untouched by innovation, creativity, and knowledge. Technology plays a vital role in addressing problems related to food supply, nutrition, health, climate change, clean water, education, income growth, and poverty reduction.[1] These technological solutions may originate from local research, be transferred from abroad, or arise through knowledge spillovers.

This final chapter synthesizes key themes developed throughout the book, aiming to draw lessons for economic growth and development. The chapter begins by recapping the basic framework for understanding intellectual property rights (IPRs), clarifying that the primary focus is not a simple trade-off between exclusivity and access, but rather how IPRs can be designed to foster innovation while ensuring the resulting benefits are widely shared.

The chapter then illustrates that the effects of IPRs are not uniform but are instead conditional on several factors. It delves into how the degree

[1]See van Marrewijk and Brakman (2023) for a comprehensive treatment of economic development.

of product market competition can interact with IP reforms to either stimulate or stifle research and development. Furthermore, it highlights that the impact of IPRs varies significantly across industries, with some sectors being more reliant on patents for appropriation than others. The analysis also considers firm-level productivity, showing how market expansion, driven by stronger IPRs, tends to benefit more productive, low-cost firms while potentially displacing less efficient local companies.

A principal argument of the chapter is the "stage-dependence hypothesis," which posits that the optimal level of IP protection is contingent on a country's technological maturity. This implies that a one-size-fits-all approach to global IP standards is suboptimal. Instead, policy should be flexible and potentially differentiated by industry or technological capability.

Building on these lessons, the chapter discusses the implications for both developing countries and the global IP reform agenda. Sections labeled Docket I and Docket II indicate key priorities for the global IP regime. They highlight two tender spots in the regime: the underutilization of TRIPS flexibilities during the COVID-19 pandemic and the underinvestment in capacity building. The chapter discusses the potential of Artificial Intelligence (AI) as one of the tools for capacity building.

The concluding section discusses areas for further research and policy debate.

13.2 Recap on Framework

Intellectual property rights (IPRs) are frequently framed as a tradeoff between exclusivity and access. However, this characterization requires important clarifications. Access is not binary; it exists along a continuum. The granting of exclusive rights does not necessarily eliminate access — it conditions access. Exclusivity inhibits access in cases where users do not pay a licensing fee or royalty. Access to the creative or technological output still exists, but it is not free and often not offered at a competitive price. This distinction is frequently overlooked. Consumers can still obtain a copyrighted book, a patented pharmaceutical, or a trademarked product, but only in exchange for a fee, typically priced above marginal cost due to the temporary market power conferred by IP protection.

The critical question is not whether exclusivity restricts access, but whether it leads to socially inefficient price increases or quantity decreases that reduce social well-being to a degree not offset by the innovation and creativity fostered by exclusive IP rights. A related concern is whether exclusivity permits the abuse of IP rights; for example, through anticompetitive behavior, excessive litigation, or strategic patenting that deters entry.

Under normal IP operations, however, access to new products should be expected, albeit at non-competitive prices. The dynamic versus static efficiency tradeoff further illuminates this relationship. In the short run, prices above marginal cost ($P > MC$) and the resulting static inefficiency are accepted in exchange for new and superior products over the long run. Without such dynamic incentives, there may be no access to certain new goods at all if innovation is suppressed. Consider that even goods developed through public funding rather than private markets under IP protection do not provide entirely costless access. Instead of paying license fees or market prices, consumers pay indirectly through taxes. Thus, regardless of the model of provision, access always entails some form of cost, whether explicit or implicit.

13.2.1 *Economic Development*

Policy debates concerning intellectual property rights (IPRs) should also not be framed in binary terms — whether IPRs are effective or ineffective for economic development. Rather, the focus should be on the appropriate design of IP systems and on whether they are suitably aligned with the economic and institutional context in which they operate.

Recall that economic growth involves the expansion of output, driven by two principal determinants: resources and productivity. Technological change, whether in the form of new products or improved production processes, affects both. Yet output alone does not capture the full meaning of development. Broader measures of well-being include health, environmental quality, education, and cultural life. Standards of living extend beyond material goods to encompass heritage, civil and political life, and social progress.

1. Essentially, development is supported when new technologies expand a nation's resource base — whether physical capital or human capital — or raise the productivity of existing resources. These technologies may be domestically produced or obtained through trade, investment, licensing, or knowledge spillovers.

2. Technological innovation does not arise in isolation, but emerges within an appropriate organization of markets and institutions, of which IPRs form a crucial component. Markets and institutions help create the incentives and opportunities for innovation and diffusion.
3. IPRs are not the sole means of promoting innovation and diffusion. Developing economies often rely on copying, imitation, and catch-up strategies. Additional mechanisms such as open innovation, trade secrecy, lead-time advantages, and complementary business models (e.g., providing free access to core technologies while monetizing services) also play important roles in fostering inventive activity.
4. Developing economies seeking to catch up may find foreign technologies prohibitively expensive or lack the capacity to innovate independently. They would benefit from greater freedom to imitate. While some copying may constitute outright infringement, other forms, such as reverse engineering, adaptation, and limited reproduction, represent legitimate learning mechanisms. Yet, concerns remain that IP definitions and enforcement standards imposed by higher-income countries may restrict even these learning channels, making access more difficult for developing countries.

The tradeoffs implied by these tensions are summarized in Figure 13.1. Properly designed, IP can stimulate economic development by increasing innovation, attracting investment, enhancing national competitiveness, and even fostering national pride. Yet the same systems impose significant costs. These include raising prices through restrictions on generic alternatives and limiting access to essential technologies and knowledge. IP systems may also block innovation through unreasonably high licensing fees or overly broad protections that cover fundamental knowledge. Disparities between developed and developing countries go beyond innovation capacity to encompass legal expertise and political influence. Moreover, IP systems operate within private markets, leading firms to prioritize high commercial returns. Consequently, the IP framework has not proven adequate for addressing neglected tropical diseases or climate change, necessitating continued public funding for technologies that are public goods.

Finally, caution is needed when interpreting empirical evidence on the effects of IP. Reverse causality and endogeneity are recurring concerns: IP enhancements may follow, rather than cause, economic development. Rising incomes may drive IP reforms through increased demand for protection and expanded resources for IP infrastructure, including patent offices,

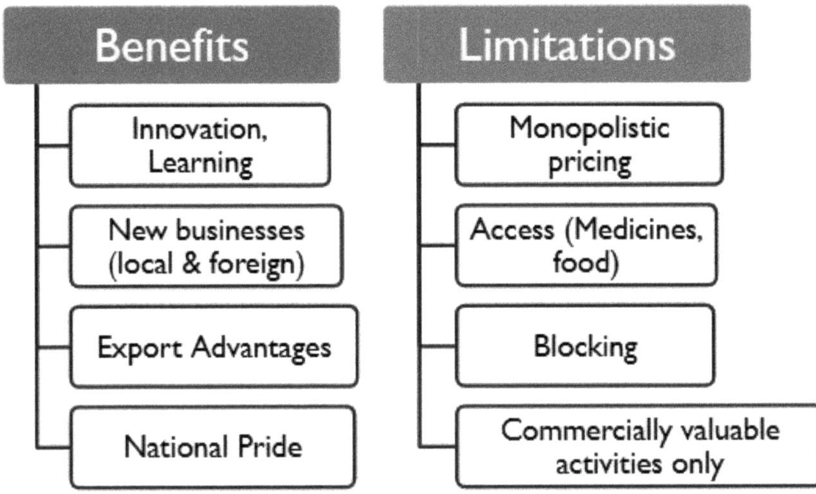

Figure 13.1. IP Tradeoffs

courts, and registry systems. As emphasized in Chapter 4's discussion of harmonization, differences in IP strength across countries largely reflect underlying disparities in innovative capacity and market size.

13.3 IP Effects: Varying Factors

This section reviews ways in which the effects of intellectual property rights (IPRs) are conditional upon the presence of complementary factors, such as:

- Degree of product market competition
- Firm productivity advantages

13.3.1 *Product Market Competition*

Aghion et al. (2015) conduct a study showing how innovation, as measured by R&D, is determined by the interaction between IP reforms and product market reforms. Their sample includes 17 countries in the European Union, spanning 13 industries over the period 1987–2003. A product market competition index is constructed from expert surveys and ranges from 0 to 100, capturing whether, for each country-industry pair, a reform improved competitive conditions. Countries are classified as having high or low IP regimes based on a patent rights index (GP-index) and actual legal developments.

The impacts of product market reforms were as follows: the ratio of R&D to value added rose significantly in the group of high-IP countries and changed only modestly in the group of low-IP countries.

The theoretical foundation for this result is the "Neck and Neck Competition" hypothesis. Firms are motivated to conduct R&D to escape competition. In a pro-IP regime, patent holders enjoy longer exclusivity and a broader scope of protection, allowing them both more time and a larger market to recoup their investments. From society's perspective, any anti-competitive effects of IP, such as monopoly pricing, are mitigated when product markets are open and competitive to begin with.

These predictions also vary across industries. Surveys show that firms differ in the extent to which they rely on patent protection, trade secrecy, or lead time advantages to appropriate returns on innovation. Table 13.1 below reports the mean percentage of product innovations for which each of these appropriation mechanisms is effective.[2]

For example, patents were effective in appropriating returns for 50.2% of drug innovations, whereas lead time was more effective for 61.5% of innovations in the steel industry. Based on the data in Table 13.1, industries

Table 13.1. Effectiveness of Appropriation Mechanisms, by Select Industry

Industry	Patents	Lead Time	Secrecy
Medical Equipment	54.7	58.1	51.0
Drugs	50.2	50.1	53.6
Computers	41.0	61.4	44.2
Basic Chemicals	38.9	38.3	48.0
Machine Tools	36.0	61.0	61.5
Aerospace	32.9	58.0	55.1
Communications Equip.	25.7	65.6	47.2
Steel	22.0	61.5	37.0
Electronic Components	21.4	45.6	34.0
Food	18.3	53.4	58.5

Source: Cohen *et al.* (2000).

[2]The table is an abridged version for illustration. For the full industry list, see Table 1 of Cohen *et al.* (2000).

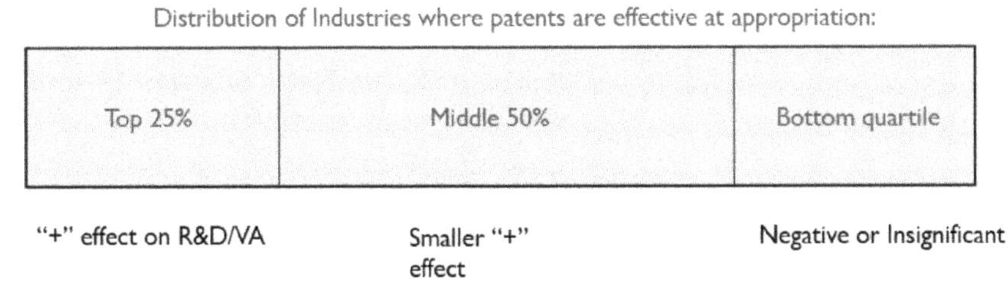

Figure 13.2. Effects by Industry Group

can be ranked according to their dependence on patents. In Aghion *et al.* (2015), separate regressions of $\frac{\text{R\&D}}{\text{Value Added}}$ on the interaction between product market reform and IP reform were conducted by industry. Figure 13.2 groups industries into the top quartile (where patents are most effective), the middle 50%, and the bottom quartile and summarizes the coefficient signs by industry group.

The interaction of IP and product market reforms has the strongest positive effect on innovation in the top quartile industries. In contrast, the effect is negative in the bottom quartile, where cumulative innovation is prevalent and patent blocking is a concern, such as in electrical and optical equipment. This effect is palpable: Galasso and Schankerman (2015) find that in such industries, patent invalidation leads to an increase in patent citations, suggesting that knowledge flows more freely when barriers to follow-on innovation are removed.

13.3.2 *Firm Productivity Advantages*

This section illustrates how low-cost producers are better positioned to benefit from IP protection by examining firm behavior under monopolistic competition. The model shows how market expansion can lead to more innovation and greater product variety, with these benefits disproportionately favoring firms with higher productivity (i.e., lower marginal costs).

Consider a monopolistically competitive industry (as introduced in Chapter 4) with many firms, each enjoying exclusive rights over a distinct product variety. The industry is characterized by free entry and exit.

Let price be $P(n)$ and average cost be $AC(n)$, where n is the number of firms and q the output per firm. Total cost equals the sum of fixed cost (F) and variable cost (cq), where c is the per-unit production cost.

Total cost (TC) and average cost (AC) are then:

$$TC = F + cq,\ AC = \frac{F}{q} + c$$

respectively. The fixed cost includes upfront investments in innovation, as well as items like factory space or rent. Typically, P and n are inversely related; that is, more competition lowers price. But average cost rises with competition, because each firm captures a smaller market share (holding total demand constant), reducing q and limiting economies of scale. Market size is given by $Q = nq$. These features are summarized in Figure 13.3.

The equilibrium conditions are listed as follows:

- If $P > AC$, Entry: more varieties.
- If $P < AC$, Exit: fewer varieties.
- If $P = AC$, long-run equilibrium.

The difference $P - AC$ represents per-unit profit. At P^*, the market reaches an equilibrium with n^* varieties.

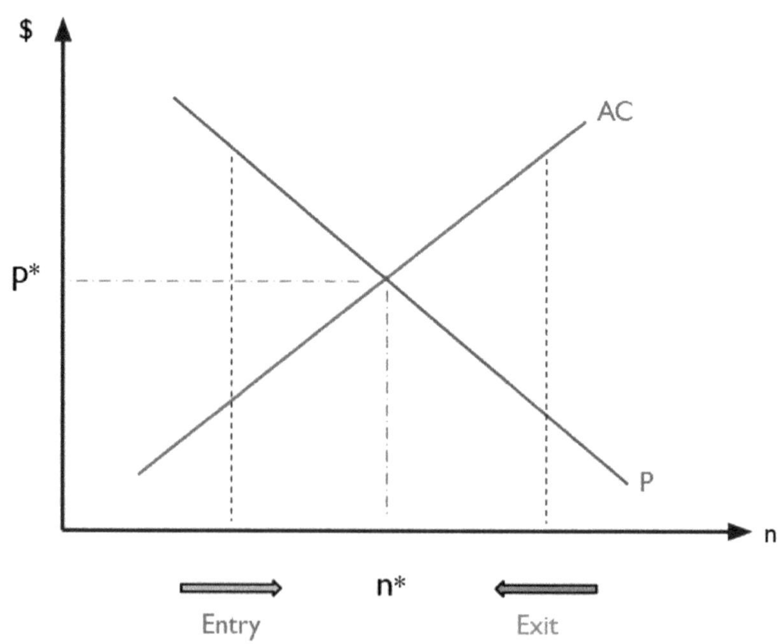

Figure 13.3. Price Average Cost Model

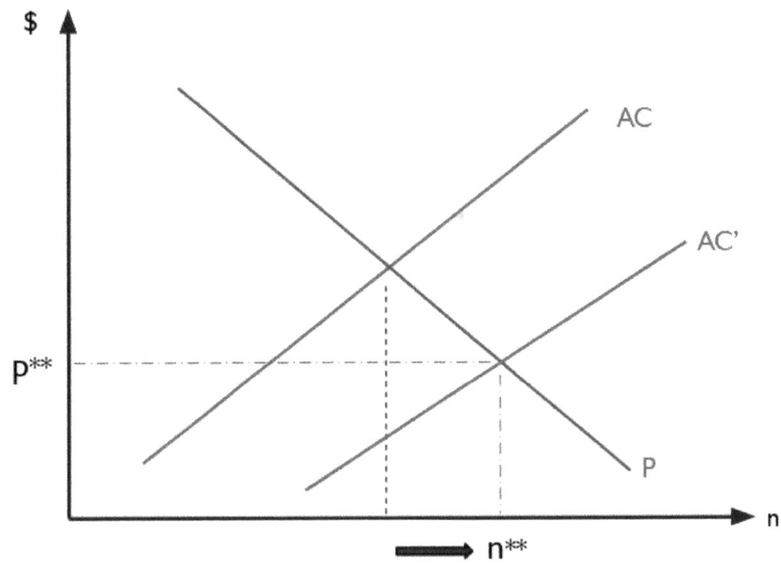

Figure 13.4. Shift in AC curve

When IP rights are strengthened, firms benefit from higher demand (as less is siphoned off by imitators). Holding n constant, each firm's output, $q = Q/n$, increases. As a result, fixed costs are spread over a larger quantity of output, shifting the AC curve downward, as shown in Figure 13.4.

At the initial level of n, $P > AC$. This encourages new entry, ultimately leading to more innovation and new varieties.

13.3.2.1 Cost Differences

Now consider cost differences across firms.[3] More productive firms have lower marginal costs, c. Let profits be a reduced-form function $\pi = \pi(c)$, with higher c implying lower profits:[4]

[3]This analysis is adapted from Melitz and Trefler (2012).

[4]Formally, $\frac{\partial \pi}{\partial c} < 0$. A "reduced form" expresses an endogenous variable (profit) as a function of exogenous ones (e.g., cost). In Figure 13.5, $\pi(c)$ is decreasing and convex in c; hence, all else equal, a firm that produces at a slightly lower marginal cost than its rivals earns disproportionately higher profits.

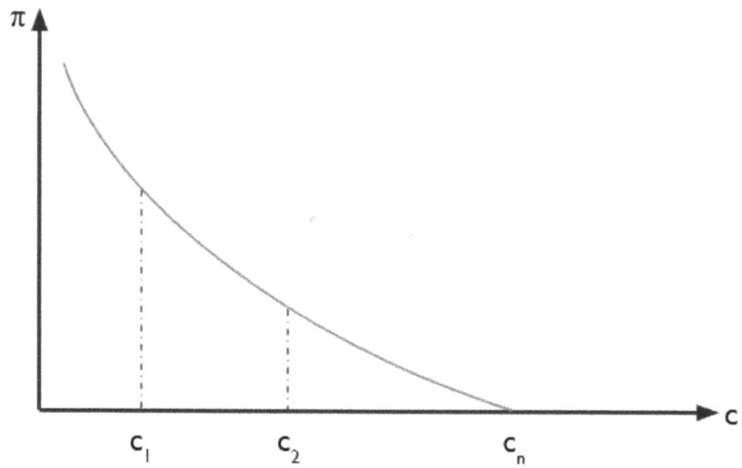

Figure 13.5. Profits and Marginal Cost, c

Firm 1, being more productive than Firm 2, earns higher profits. Firms with marginal costs exceeding a cutoff level c_n exit the market.

Now return to the case where IPRs expand market size and stimulate innovation. This results in entry and more competition, including from foreign multinationals. Firms differ in productivity, however, with some able to produce at much lower costs than others. More productive firms, with lower c, are much better positioned to survive increased competition from multinational entry. In contrast, higher-cost domestic firms will find themselves squeezed toward the exit threshold, where profits approach zero and continued operation is infeasible. Next, consider how these dynamics evolve when market size expands.

13.3.2.2 Impact of Market Size Expansion

Suppose that stronger IPRs expand trade, reduce imitation, and increase total market size Q. The larger market attracts more competitors, creating two opposing forces that affect each firm's output:

- Holding Q fixed, an increase in n lowers each firm's output $q = Q/n$.
- Holding n fixed, an increase in Q raises q.

Thus, market expansion creates both competitive pressure (reducing q) and growth opportunities (increasing q). Which effect proves stronger depends on the specific circumstances.

More productive firms, such as multinational corporations (MNCs), are better able to capture the growth in market demand. Their lower c enables them to either charge lower prices or accept lower markups. High-cost firms face the opposite situation. They lack this pricing flexibility and struggle to compete for the additional customers that market expansion brings. As a result, when markets expand, high-cost firms see their profits decline while low-cost firms see their profits rise. This creates a pivotal shift in competitive dynamics, as illustrated in Figure 13.6.

The figure shows how market expansion creates winners and losers based on production costs. Two critical thresholds emerge: c^* and c^{**}.

- Firms with marginal costs higher than c^{**} exit the market.
- Firms with marginal costs between c^* and c^{**} obtain lower profits.
- Firms with marginal costs lower than c^* enjoy higher profits.

Trade liberalization, IP reform, and market expansion tend to favor low-cost, high-productivity firms while penalizing higher-cost ones, ultimately forcing less efficient firms to exit the market. Though foreign MNCs may dominate local markets due to their cost advantages, consumers in lower-income economies benefit from greater product variety and lower prices. The main takeaway from this example is that efficient producers are better positioned to benefit from IPRs, potentially crowding out weaker domestic competitors. This underscores the importance of complementary policies

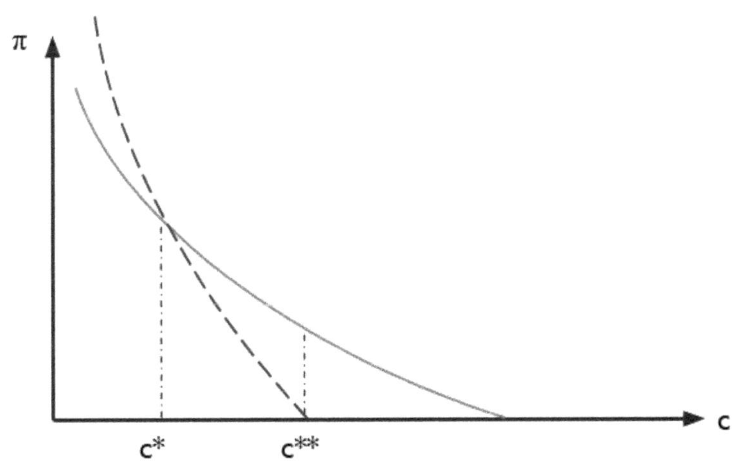

Figure 13.6. Low versus High Cost Firms

that improve local firm productivity before or alongside IP strengthening. Without such capacity-building, IP reform may inadvertently lead to market dominance by foreign multinationals.

13.4 Stages of Economic Development

This section discusses the inadequacy of a one-size-fits-all IP regime for promoting economic growth. The strengthening of IP systems across the world, particularly following the TRIPS Agreement, often occurred in countries that were net importers of technology. These same countries typically held relatively few intellectual assets and produced goods of comparatively lower quality.

This creates a fundamental tension. Exporting remains a vital pathway for developing economies to grow, earn foreign exchange, and manage international debt, whether incurred through development financing or balance of payments crises. To succeed in competitive export markets, especially those of wealthier countries, firms in the developing world must upgrade the quality of their products. Quality upgrading, in turn, requires R&D investment, which depends heavily on how a country's IP regime balances protection for innovators with access to existing knowledge.

What level of IP protection best supports such upgrading? This is the crux of the *stage-dependence hypothesis*, which posits that the optimal strength of IP protection depends on a country's level of technological development and different industry-specific capabilities. Research, as discussed in earlier chapters, demonstrates that uniform global IP standards are suboptimal.

Liu *et al.* (2021) provide evidence that the effect of patent protection on export quality varies not only across countries or products, but at the intersection of both. For example, South Korea's electronics industry in the 1980s was more technologically advanced than its chemical sector, yet still lagged behind Germany's electronics sector. These differences imply that policy should be sensitive to country-product combinations. Liu *et al.* (2021) identify a *critical quality threshold*: when a country's export quality in a given product is above this threshold, stronger patent rights enhance innovation and quality upgrading. Below it, the opposite holds.

Other studies support this stage-dependent perspective. Kim *et al.* (2012), discussed in Chapter 5, show that countries at different stages utilize different types of IPRs. While patents are more common in developed economies, *utility models*, which protect incremental innovations at lower cost, are prevalent in the developing world. Chen and Puttitanun (2005) argue that in countries with low indigenous innovative capacity, weaker IP rules facilitate imitation and technological catch-up, whereas stronger protection stimulates innovation in more technologically mature settings. Likewise, Chu *et al.* (2014) find a stage-dependent effect of IPRs on innovation and economic growth using a model inspired by the ideas of Joseph Schumpeter — particularly the notion that innovation and competition at the technological frontier are key drivers of long-run economic growth. In their analysis, the optimal strength of patent protection rises as a country advances toward the global technology frontier.

This section now turns to a case study of China's ballpoint pen industry to illustrate these factors at work.

13.4.1 *Case Study*

This case study illustrates a stage-dependent relationship between IPR protection and export quality. China is the world's largest exporter of ballpoint pens. In 2017, it exported 8.38 billion units (28.5% of global exports), with Japan ranking second at 14.3%.

The town of Fenshui, in Hangzhou, Zhejiang Province, serves as China's pen-manufacturing hub, accounting for roughly 40% of national output. Recognized as the country's export center for ballpoint pens since 2009, Fenshui hosted over 600 manufacturers and 379 supporting firms by 2017.

Pen production in Fenshui began in the 1970s, when China was still a low-income economy. With limited resources and R&D capacity, firms grew by imitating existing products and competing on price. Over time, some firms began undertaking limited R&D to differentiate their pens with minor quality enhancements. These improvements offered innovators only short-term gains before being rapidly copied in the absence of effective IPR protection. Nevertheless, competitive pressure and incremental innovation gradually raised the industry's average product quality.

As firms matured technologically, disputes over imitation became more common. A local administrative rule in the 1990s sought to curb unfair copying, and national IPR reforms soon followed. China revamped its patent system in 2000 and again in 2009, partly in response to TRIPS commitments. As protections improved, innovators increasingly pursued design patents and adopted quality differentiation strategies. At the same time, improvements in education, inward FDI, and trade deepened the local knowledge base and enabled partnerships with universities and design centers. These collaborations enhanced firms' capacity to innovate and capitalize on stronger IP rights.

A related development in upstream supply capabilities reinforced this transition. In 2016, the state-owned Taiyuan Iron and Steel Co. (TISCO) independently developed the high-grade stainless steel used in pen tips. These components were previously imported. Although TISCO was not itself a pen manufacturer, its breakthrough removed a critical bottleneck in the supply chain, enabling fuller vertical integration by Chinese pen producers.[5] This milestone illustrates how complementary innovations in adjacent industries can help move a sector past the threshold at which patent protection begins to reinforce rather than restrict innovation and quality upgrading.

In sum, the ballpoint pen industry highlights the dynamic role of IPR protection across stages of development. Early on, weak protection allowed imitation-driven, incremental quality growth. Later, with stronger technological capabilities and institutional support, robust IP enforcement enabled firms to pursue more substantial innovations and reap greater returns.

13.4.2 *Conceptual Framework*

The idea behind stage-dependent effects of IPR can be developed using a simple model of quality improvements.[6] Let q_{jn} denote the quality level of a product j in country n. Some products undergo significant quality upgrading over time — consider, for example, computer processors progressing from the Intel 386 to the 486, then to the Pentium series and beyond. The following expression captures the evolution of quality over successive product generations:

$$q_{jn}^{(m)} = \lambda^m q_{jn}^{(0)} \tag{13.1}$$

where $\lambda > 1$ represents the fixed size of the quality jump, and m denotes the number of successful innovation steps (or generations) since the initial product.[7] The initial product quality is normalized to $q_{jn}^{(0)} = 1$, so that:

$$q_{jn}^{(m)} = \lambda^m$$

[5]See https://www.chinadaily.com.cn/business/2017-01/18/content_27986240.htm.

[6]This section builds on Liu *et al.* (2021).

[7]The parentheses around m in the q variable signify that m denotes version, not an exponent. For the λ^m term, this is λ to the power of m.

That is, the product improves by a factor of λ with each successive innovation, resulting in exponential quality growth over time.

Now assume that the size of the quality jump depends positively on the strength of patent protection, denoted by θ:

$$\lambda = \lambda(\theta) \tag{13.2}$$

where θ represents the strength of patent rights, such that $\frac{\partial \lambda}{\partial \theta} > 0$. This captures the idea that stronger IP protection creates greater incentives for firms to pursue more substantial (or radical) innovations, as the rewards for leapfrogging in quality are enhanced.

In quality improvement models, the markup factor that a patent-holding firm can charge is tied to the size of the quality jump. For example:

$$\underbrace{p}_{\text{Price}} = \underbrace{\lambda(\theta)}_{\text{Markup factor}} \times \underbrace{MC}_{\text{Marginal Cost}} \tag{13.3}$$

The larger the value of θ, the greater the λ, and thus the more the price will exceed marginal cost ($p > MC$). This price-cost margin reflects the temporary market power conferred by patent protection and serves as an incentive to innovate.

On the other hand, the cost of conducting R&D or innovation is also influenced by the strength of patent protection. Let $\alpha(\theta)$ represent the resource cost of producing an innovation. The lower the value of $\alpha(\theta)$, the more efficient the innovation process.[8]

Assume that the innovation cost α is increasing in patent strength θ: $\frac{\partial \alpha}{\partial \theta} > 0$. That is, stronger patent rights raise the resource requirements (or cost) of innovation. Several mechanisms contribute to this effect. First, patent protection increases the cost of inputs into innovation. Suppliers of patented components or technologies may charge higher prices or licensing fees under a strong IP regime. Second, innovators face greater transaction costs when negotiating licenses, including the costs of cross-licensing, due diligence, and contract enforcement. Stronger patent rights enhance the bargaining power of licensors in these negotiations.

Third, stronger IP enforcement also expands the scope of patent coverage through legal doctrines such as the *doctrine of equivalents*. This doctrine can make it more difficult for subsequent innovators to avoid infringement, even when introducing differentiated products. As a result, developers

[8]The inverse, $\frac{1}{\alpha(\theta)}$, is a measure of innovation productivity. For example, if $\alpha(\theta) = 1/2$, then half a unit of resources is required to produce one innovation; equivalently, one unit of resources yields two innovations.

must expend more effort and resources to design around existing patents. These costs make innovation more difficult in environments with stringently enforced patent regimes.

In sum, while stronger patent rights increase the rewards to innovation by enhancing markups (via $\lambda(\theta)$), they also raise the cost of achieving those innovations (via $\alpha(\theta)$). The net effect on innovation incentives — and on product quality growth — thus depends on which of these two forces dominates.

Specifically, the growth rate of product quality is a *positive* function of the growth in the size of quality jumps and a *negative* function of the growth in the cost of innovation. Formally,

$$\frac{\dot{q}_{jn}}{q_{jn}} = f\left(\underbrace{\frac{\dot{\lambda}(\theta)}{\lambda(\theta)}}_{\text{“+”}}, \underbrace{\frac{\dot{\alpha}(\theta)}{\alpha(\theta)}}_{\text{“−”}}\right) \tag{13.4}$$

where $\frac{\dot{x}}{x}$ denotes the percentage growth rate of variable x, and $f(\cdot)$ is an increasing function in the first argument and decreasing in the second, respectively.

This formulation captures the fundamental trade-off: stronger patent rights (θ) may increase the incentives to innovate by enlarging quality jumps (λ), but they also raise the resource cost of innovation (α). The net effect on the quality growth rate $\frac{\dot{q}}{q}$ depends on which effect dominates.

If rising innovation costs are onerous and the potential for quality jump growth is low, then stronger patent rights may *reduce* the rate of product quality upgrading. That is, $\frac{\dot{q}_{jn}}{q_{jn}} < 0$, as firms find it unprofitable to invest in innovation. In this case, a less stringent patent system can facilitate quality upgrading by lowering the barriers to incremental improvement. Narrower interpretations of the *doctrine of equivalents* make it easier for firms to invent around existing patents. While the resulting quality jumps (λ) may be modest and the flow of monopoly profits limited, the relatively low innovation cost (i.e., lower $\alpha(\theta)$) enables a steady pace of incremental upgrades. This is the pattern observed in the early-stage development of China's ballpoint pen industry, where innovation occurred despite weak IP protection.

In contrast, when the potential for large quality improvements is high, stronger patent protection *encourages* innovation and quality upgrading: $\frac{\dot{q}_{jn}}{q_{jn}} > 0$. Robust IP rights provide firms with the incentives to invest in more radical innovation, even when such efforts require significant R&D outlays.

Because successful innovation yields substantial markups and firm value, higher development costs are justified by larger expected returns. In such settings, weak patent systems undermine incentives for substantial quality jumps by allowing competitors to quickly imitate high-value innovations.

These two contrasting possibilities underscore the role of *technological capacity*. In environments with higher technological capacity, firms are more efficient innovators. They require fewer resources to achieve innovation and can better absorb the transaction costs associated with patent-intensive regimes. Moreover, they are more likely to be capable of making larger quality improvements, which increases the returns to patent protection. In such settings, stronger IP rights amplify incentives to innovate. The opposite holds when technological capacity is low: higher innovation costs cannot be easily absorbed, and returns to innovation are limited by firms' inability to leap ahead. In these cases, a more flexible or weaker patent regime better supports quality upgrading.

Together, these insights yield two testable hypotheses:

1. Below a threshold level of technological capacity, the relationship between patent protection and product quality upgrading is negative.
2. Above a threshold level of technological capacity, the relationship between patent protection and product quality upgrading is positive.

These hypotheses have been tested using panel data on export quality, patent protection, and technological capacity, and are discussed in the next section.

13.4.3 *Empirical Testing*

To empirically test the stage-dependent effects of patent protection on product quality upgrading, Liu *et al.* (2021) construct a panel dataset covering 82 developing countries and 235 SITC 4-digit product categories over the period 1990–2010.[9] The key outcome variable is a granular export quality index derived from Henn *et al.* (2020), while the central explanatory variables include a closeness-to-frontier (CTF) measure and a patent rights index (PRI).

The PRI is an effective patent rights indicator that adjusts the GP-index discussed in Chapter 2 to account for the effectiveness of legal enforcement, using data from the *Fraser Institute*.

[9]SITC 4-digit products refer to commodity *subgroups* in the UN's Standard International Trade Classification.

The CTF variable is constructed at the product-country level and scaled from 0 to 100. It measures how close a given product in a specific country is to the global quality frontier. The methodology draws on the World Bank's *Doing Business* framework.[10] The CTF can be interpreted as a normalized position on a quality ladder: for example, if China's ballpoint pen industry has a CTF score of 50, this means it is halfway between the highest- and lowest-quality producers of that product globally. A score of 100 indicates frontier status, while a score of 0 indicates maximal distance from the frontier.

The main regression specification is as follows:

$$QLTY_{ijt} = \beta_1 \, PRI_{it} + \beta_2 \, (PRI_{it} \times CTF_{ijt}) + \beta_3 \, CTF_{ijt} + \cdots \quad (13.5)$$

where $QLTY_{ijt}$ denotes export quality of product j in country i at time t, PRI_{it} the effective patent rights index for country i at time t, and CTF_{ijt} the closeness-to-frontier index for product j in country i at time t. The ellipsis denotes additional control variables and fixed effects (e.g., country, product-year), which are omitted here for clarity.

The critical threshold of CTF — that is, the point at which the effect of patent protection on product quality shifts from negative to positive — can be derived by taking the partial derivative of $QLTY$ with respect to PRI:

$$CTF^* = -\frac{\hat{\beta}_1}{\hat{\beta}_2} \quad (13.6)$$

When $CTF_{ijt} > CTF^*$, the marginal effect of stronger patent rights on export quality is positive. Conversely, when $CTF_{ijt} < CTF^*$, the effect is negative.

The core regression results are summarized in Table 13.2. They confirm that the effect of patent protection on export quality depends on the proximity of the country-product pair to the global technological frontier. In the pooled sample (column 1), the coefficient on the patent rights index (PRI) is negative and significant ($\hat{\beta}_1 = -1.101$), while the interaction term with CTF is positive and significant ($\hat{\beta}_2 = 0.025$). This implies a critical threshold of $CTF^* = -\hat{\beta}_1/\hat{\beta}_2 = 44.0$, from the formula (13.6). That is, when a country's product quality is less than 44% of the global frontier, stronger patent rights are associated with *lower* export quality. Conversely, above this threshold, patent protection is associated with *higher* export quality.

[10] https://archive.doingbusiness.org/en/doingbusiness.

Table 13.2. Patent Protection and Export Quality

	Dependent Variable: Export Quality			
	Pooled (1)	Low Income (2)	Lower Middle Income (3)	Upper Middle Income (4)
PRI	-1.101^{***}	0.110	-1.368^{***}	-2.227^{***}
$PRI \times CTF$	0.025^{***}	-0.002	0.029^{***}	0.040^{***}
CTF	0.367^{***}	0.313^{***}	0.358^{***}	0.346^{***}
Observations (N)	160,662	28,231	69,057	62,655
Adj. R-squared	0.844	0.896	0.821	0.763
Implied Threshold	44.0	—	47.2	55.7

Note: $***$ denotes statistical significance at the 1% level.

The threshold value of 44.0 suggests that a significant share of country-product combinations fall below the level where patent protection supports innovation. The lower the threshold, the broader the range of quality levels that can benefit from stronger IP protection.

Columns (2)–(4) show estimates for sub-samples by income group. In low-income countries (column 2), patent protection has no statistically significant effect on export quality, consistent with the idea that these countries tend to produce goods near the bottom of the quality ladder. In contrast, for lower-middle and upper-middle income countries, the interaction term is positive and statistically significant at the 1% level. The estimated thresholds are 47.2 and 55.7, respectively, indicating that stronger IP rights support quality upgrading primarily among technologically more advanced country-product pairs. Overall, the results provide empirical support for the stage-dependence hypothesis: the effect of patent rights on product quality is conditional on a country's technological position relative to the global frontier.

To assess the broader policy implications of the threshold effects, Table 13.3 reports the distribution of country-product pairs across different ranges of *CTF*, the closeness-to-frontier index. This is important for evaluating whether, on balance, stronger effective patent protection is likely to spur or hinder export quality upgrading in developing countries. If most country-product combinations fall below the threshold, then patent reforms could inadvertently impede product quality upgrading across much of the developing world.

Table 13.3. Distribution of *CTF* by Income Group

CTF Range	(1) Pooled	(2) Low	(3) Lower Middle	(4) Upper Middle
	Percent of Country-Product Combinations			
0–10	1.2	4.9	0.7	0.2
10–20	3.7	14.7	2.0	0.5
20–30	7.4	25.9	5.2	1.2
30–**44**	17.8	31.5	22.5	6.2
44–50	11.6	9.4	17.1	6.4
50–60	22.8	7.8	29.8	21.9
60–70	22.1	3.3	17.1	36.2
70–80	10.2	1.3	4.2	20.7
80–90	2.8	0.8	1.0	5.8
90–100	0.6	0.4	0.3	0.9
% below threshold	30.1%	n/a	39.2%	24.7%
% above threshold	69.9%	n/a	60.8%	75.3%
Total Combinations	160,700	28,799	69,182	62,719

Notes: The threshold value **44.0** is for the pooled sample. The threshold for LM is **47.2** and for UM is **55.7**. All countries are non-high income. Threshold for L is not available (n/a) due to the statistical insignificance of patent rights. Total counts refer to the sum of country and product pairs.

Table 13.3 partitions the full sample of CTF scores into ranges of 10 points each, from 0 to 100, and reports the share of country-product combinations falling into each range. For the pooled sample, 30.1% of country-product combinations lie below the critical threshold of 44.0; these are instances where stronger patent protection is expected to reduce export quality. Conversely, the remaining 69.9% are above the threshold, where IP reforms are more likely to stimulate innovation.

The breakdown by income group reveals substantial heterogeneity. In low-income countries (column 2), most country-product pairs are concentrated in the lowest deciles of *CTF*, with 77% falling below 44. In contrast, upper-middle income countries (column 4) exhibit greater technological maturity: 75.3% of their combinations lie above the threshold. Lower-middle income countries occupy an intermediate position, with 60.8% of combinations above their own group-specific threshold of 47.2.

This distributional evidence complements the regression analysis by showing that the effect of patent reforms is highly varied. In countries or sectors closer to the global frontier, stronger patent protection may indeed foster vertical innovation. But for a sizable share of low- and lower-middle-income producers still far from the frontier, patent strengthening may raise costs and discourage quality upgrading.

What makes patent policy recommendations particularly complex is that it is not sufficient to simply propose that patent rights be strengthened in higher-income countries and relaxed in lower-income countries. The crux of the matter is that the appropriate level of protection is not determined at the country level alone, but at the *country-product* level. Within any given country, different products can lie on opposite sides of the critical CTF threshold. Likewise, a particular product may be ripe for innovation in one country but not in another, depending on the local technological capabilities.

Revisiting the earlier case study: when China undertook major patent reforms in 2000, it was still classified as a lower-middle-income country. Yet, the CTF score for Chinese ballpoint pens was classified as a high-IP intensity product; that is, it was above the critical threshold, making the industry well-positioned to benefit from stronger IP protection. In contrast, China's pharmaceutical sector, which is also high-IP intensive, was below the threshold at the time of reform.

A similar pattern was observed in India. When India introduced product patent protection for pharmaceuticals in 2005, its pharmaceutical sector remained below the relevant CTF threshold for lower-middle income countries. Meanwhile, India's telecommunications sector had reached the threshold and was more likely to benefit from stronger patent protection. It was not until 2010 that India's pharmaceutical industry surpassed the critical CTF value.

Comparable experiences are found in upper-middle-income countries such as Brazil and Chile. When Chile reformed its patent law in 1991 and Brazil followed in 1997, only Brazil's pharmaceutical sector had reached a technological level above the threshold. Other high-IP products in Brazil, such as telecommunications equipment, remained below the threshold at the time of reform. In contrast, some low-IP products, such as articles of paper and pulp, were already above the relevant threshold and stood to gain from stronger IP protection.

These differentiated experiences raise an important policy question: should patent regimes be uniform across industries, or should they reflect product- or sector-specific conditions? Currently, patent laws are applied nationally and uniformly, with few exceptions. However, the evidence presented here suggests that a more differentiated IP regime, tailored to the innovation potential of specific sectors, could better support dynamic quality upgrading and innovation.[11]

13.5 Lessons for the Developing World

Much of the preceding analysis shows that intellectual property rights (IPRs) tend to function most effectively when firms already possess some degree of innovative capacity and are close to the global technological frontier. IPRs also operate best when complementary institutions, such as competitive markets and efficient financial systems, are present. IPRs function within a second-best environment, where market imperfections pre-exist. Without IPRs, underdevelopment may result from weak incentives and insufficient protection of knowledge assets. Yet the effects of IPRs are quite nuanced, as the following points indicate.

1. IPRs protect knowledge assets and help create incentives for innovation and commercialization. However, they do not directly generate skills or capabilities. While an IP system may complement an innovation ecosystem, an education system, or a performing arts infrastructure, IPRs themselves are not instruments of skill formation. They may create incentives to acquire skills, but the process of skill-building, including learning-by-doing and experiential learning, is distinct. Policymakers should not lose sight of the need to promote such learning. Moreover, IP regimes must create space for domestic inventors and entrepreneurs to develop, commercialize, and market their innovations. If IPRs allow incumbent firms — especially foreign firms with a head start — to dominate, they risk foreclosing opportunities for local actors.
2. IPRs are not always necessary for innovation or diffusion. Several factors can naturally deter imitation or piracy. For example,
    - technological complexity may serve as a barrier;
    - tacit knowledge is often not codified and may remain inaccessible despite patent disclosures or reverse engineering efforts;

[11] Cho *et al.* (2015) discuss the possibility of industry-specific IP standards, and Acemoglu and Akcigit (2012) argue for differential patent protection for industry leaders and laggards.

- innovators often use alternative appropriation strategies such as trade secrecy, lead-time advantages, or complementary business models (e.g., offering a product for free but charging for associated services, as in the case of certain apps or platforms);
- not all inventors are driven by commercial motives. Academics, hobbyists, and open source communities often innovate for reasons such as curiosity, reputational gain, or the intrinsic satisfaction of problem-solving. This reflects the broader realm of Open Science and Collective Invention.

3. In some situations, the IP system may hinder innovation and commercialization:

   - over-assertion of rights may lead to excessive litigation and strategic lawsuits;
   - overly broad protection can privatize basic knowledge and impede follow-on innovation;
   - fragmentation of rights among too many owners can produce an anti-commons effect, where overlapping claims impede research progress; and
   - firms may engage in defensive patenting, obtaining patents not to exploit innovations but to deter litigation or to gain leverage in cross-licensing negotiations.

4. Innovation does not take place in a vacuum. It occurs within an *ecosystem* of research organizations (academia, government, non-profit organizations, and the private sector). Given the positive externalities associated with knowledge, the public sector especially has a role to play in undertaking or supporting socially valuable R&D through funding, subsidies, procurement contracts, and research grants. Public investment can also help preserve and expand the public domain.

What lessons emerge for latecomers pursuing economic catch-up? Proponents of relaxed IP enforcement often cite historical examples. A century ago, the United States, Switzerland, Japan, and Korea maintained weak IP systems and relied heavily on imitation. Some argue that these countries used piracy and reverse engineering as stepping stones to eventual innovation and growth.

This inference, however, is questionable for two reasons. First, it risks committing the "post hoc, ergo propter hoc" fallacy; the fact that economic growth followed imitation does not prove that growth was caused by technological imitation. Theoretical and empirical findings presented in prior chapters suggest a more complex relationship. Second, the relevant counterfactual is unknown: one cannot say with certainty whether growth might have been faster or more robust had stronger IP systems been in place. Furthermore, extensive copying and infringement might have provoked trade retaliation, reduced foreign direct investment (FDI), or discouraged innovation by foreign firms.

Instead of adopting weak or lax IP regimes, developing economies would benefit from *tailored* and *flexible* IP systems that reflect their level of development and institutional capacity. Earlier analysis has identified several such policy approaches. These include support for incremental innovation, the use of utility models, and the design of IP laws with built-in flexibility, such as broad limitations and exceptions (e.g., fair use, farmer's privilege, research exemptions, compulsory licensing with working requirements), narrower scopes of protection, and shorter durations.

Developing countries should also avoid "reinventing the wheel" and instead take advantage of technologies already available abroad through imports, inward investment, and licensing. An appropriately designed IP regime should motivate skill-building and human capital accumulation among the population. Without adequate rewards and recognition for creative and inventive work, few individuals will choose to pursue careers in science, engineering, or the arts.

13.6 Lessons for IP Reforms

The fight against global poverty is a defining goal of the modern era. IPRs are not peripheral issues in this endeavor. Because IPRs are pervasive throughout the economic development process, they play a critical role. A poorly designed IPR regime can exacerbate global inequality and lock developing countries into a state of technological dependency. Thus, the key theme here is for IP reforms to be pro-development oriented.

This requires IP policy design to take into account the special circumstances of developing countries: their lower purchasing power and more price-elastic demand; their constraints with health, literacy, and infrastructure; their reliance on informal markets and traditional knowledge; and their valuable cultural assets (art, music, film, storytelling) and geographical indications (wine, agricultural products, textiles, handicrafts) that could appeal to international markets.

Some key takeaways for IP policies are listed as follows:

1. **Avoid One-Size-Fits-All Solutions:** As the stage-dependent analysis in this chapter has shown, strong intellectual property protection tends to foster innovation only after a certain threshold of technological capability has been reached — a threshold that varies by country and by industry. Rather than adopting policies based solely on national income levels, policymakers should consider more flexible frameworks that differentiate the strength of patent protection across sectors, technologies, or product types.

   One option is to allow for sector-specific patent regimes, in which protection levels vary across industries based on their innovation potential and absorptive capacity. Another possibility is the use of graduated IP schedules, where countries progressively strengthen enforcement only as certain technological benchmarks are reached. The empirical thresholds identified in this chapter (e.g., CTF^* values) could serve as guideposts for such adaptive policymaking.

   In some respects, these principles have been built into the TRIPS framework. TRIPS sets minimum standards, allowing countries to exceed these minimums as they choose (although critics have argued that the minimum standards are the ones that need differentiating across income levels). TRIPS allows for transition periods for least-developed countries and provisions for compulsory licensing. The next step would be to make these flexibilities more tailored to national and sectoral readiness. Moreover, trading partners and international institutions might reconsider how IP-related conditionalities are imposed in trade agreements and aid packages, especially if such conditions are not aligned with a country's stage of technological development.
2. **Utilize IP Flexibilities:** These built-in flexibilities referred to above are core policy instruments that are available and particularly appropriate for countries with lower incomes and technological capacities. It is not unusual in market economies to routinely employ targeted interventions to address market failures or imperfections. In fact, this principle underlies the very foundation of IP systems, which grant temporary exclusivity to address the public goods problem of innovation.

   Baker *et al.* (2017) strongly advocate for flexibilities like the *Bolar exemption*, which allows generic drug companies to conduct the necessary clinical trials to get regulatory approval so that they can hit the ground running once a patent expires. Without this exception, their use of the patented drug for testing purposes may be deemed infringing.

3. **Utilize Patent Pools:** Recall that these are arrangements where multiple patent holders contribute their patents to a common pool, which then licenses the entire collection of patents as a package. The key benefits for developing countries are: (a) reduced transaction costs, as the pools reduce the costs of negotiating with multiple patent owners; (b) lower licensing fees when patent holders accept lower per-patent royalties in exchange for greater market access; (c) access to essential technologies, such as the *Medicines Patent Pool*, *COVID-19 Technology Access Pool*, and some green technology projects.
4. **Monitor Developed Country Obligations:** Given that least developed countries continue to run persistent deficits in their technology balance of payments, they clearly face ongoing barriers to acquiring foreign technologies. Developed countries should more fully implement their obligations under Article 66.2 of the TRIPS Agreement, which calls for the promotion of technology transfer to least developed countries. This includes not only undertaking substantive initiatives but also submitting comprehensive annual reports on their activities, as required under the Article. Developing countries could engage with the WTO to review compliance, evaluate the effectiveness of reported initiatives, and press for stronger enforcement of technology-transfer commitments.
5. **Invest in Capacity Building:** The empirical evidence shows that the benefits of IPRs are conditional on a country's absorptive capacity. A sound IP strategy should therefore include complementary investments in education, research infrastructure, and workforce development to enable domestic firms to absorb, adapt, and build upon technologies.

Each developing country may have a small market size and share of the global economy. It is tempting to waive IP protection in such a country on the grounds that it has a negligible impact on incentives for innovation in the North. This may be valid if it were only one country, but collectively, many of those countries could comprise a significant enough market size for a company to serve the combined market, particularly if its product is tailored almost entirely for that market, such as medicines, agricultural equipment, or culturally relevant creative content. Moreover, market size should not be treated as static. Through local innovation, entrepreneurship, and creative activity, a market can grow. Appropriately designed IPR systems can play a supportive role in that growth by stimulating local knowledge production and investment.

IP reforms or policies should not focus just on innovation but also on commercialization. Innovation is the initial phase. The next phase is to bring those innovations to the public. IPRs are important throughout the remaining process of bringing goods to market, whether the process involves moving a new drug from the lab to the pharmacy, adapting movie scripts based on novels for movie theaters, or transforming class notes into textbooks. Even when the original innovation is publicly funded or crowd-sourced, the commercialization process involves substantial intermediate steps. These include organization, contracting, distribution, quality assurance, and investment — steps that often require well-defined and enforceable property rights to ensure coordination and accountability.

The next two sections explore in greater depth two IP-related policy areas highlighted above, namely IP flexibilities and capacity-building. These remain the "tender spots" in the global IP regime to date.

13.7 Docket I: IP Flexibilities

This section reviews the COVID-19 pandemic as a stress test of the global IP regime. Many researchers and commentators have documented several structural shortcomings exposed by the pandemic, largely concluding that IP flexibilities proved inadequate in addressing urgent public health needs.[12]

During the pandemic, severe supply shortages arose globally in goods needed for emergency care: masks, diagnostic kits, PPE (personal protective equipment), ventilators, and vaccines. The economic system was marred by a combination of factors, such as a sudden surge in demand and global supply chain disruptions. Amidst all this, the supply response was not helped by TRIPS. The flexibilities under the agreement could not be effectively used to authorize the production and distribution of essential goods.

Compulsory licensing was hardly used, even in the face of a global health emergency. As discussed in Chapter 8, the TRIPS waiver proposed by South Africa and India in late 2020 took a long time to deliberate, prompting an editorial from *Nature* magazine in March 2022 warning that "Time is running out for COVID-vaccine patent waivers."[13] By the time a deal was struck in mid-2022, the pandemic was subsiding. Even then, the final

[12]See Kohler *et al.* (2022), Gleeson *et al.* (2023), Ferranna (2024), and Kilic (2024).
[13]https://www.nature.com/articles/d41586-022-00878-x.

decision was a watered-down version of the original proposal, removing IP barriers for COVID-19 vaccines, but not for treatments and diagnostics.

The core issue is that the TRIPS process for using flexibilities involves onerous procedural burdens that are ill-suited to a global emergency requiring rapid action.[14] For example, TRIPS requires compulsory licenses to be issued on a country-by-country and product-by-product basis, which is not conducive to timely, global distribution. A manufacturer must be found for each component of a product, or, if there is no domestic producer, a foreign supplier must be identified.

The case of Biolyse, discussed in Chapter 8, is instructive.[15] In April 2021, the Canadian generics company sought a voluntary license from Johnson & Johnson (J&J) to manufacture its COVID-19 vaccine and export approximately 15 million doses to Bolivia, which lacked the capacity to produce them domestically. J&J rejected Biolyse's offer of a 5% royalty and refused to negotiate further. Previously, in March 2020, the Canadian government had enacted the COVID-19 Emergency Response Act, allowing for the issuance of compulsory licenses during the pandemic. However, for Biolyse to obtain a compulsory license through Canada's Access to Medicines Regime (CAMR), J&J's vaccine first had to be listed in Schedule 1 of the Canadian Patent Act. That process dragged on for months, and ultimately, Biolyse was unable to export generic versions to Bolivia.

Germany and France both passed new legislation in March 2020 to permit compulsory licensing, but neither country issued a license during the pandemic. Two countries that did issue compulsory licenses were Israel and Russia. In Israel's case, it imported a generic version of AbbVie's drug Kaletra from an Indian company.[16] In Russia's case, a domestic company obtained a license from the government to manufacture a generic version of Gilead's drug Remdesivir.[17] Gilead filed a lawsuit against the Russian government but was unsuccessful. These cases remain rare. As Thrasher *et al.* (2023) note, many governments hesitate to issue compulsory licenses due to concerns about reprisals from trading partners or pharmaceutical firms.

---

[14]See Thrasher *et al.* (2023).

[15]See Lexchin (2023).

[16]See https://www.statnews.com/pharmalot/2020/03/20/abbvie-israel-hiv-kaletra-coronavirus-covid19/.

[17]https://www.statnews.com/pharmalot/2021/05/04/gilead-sues-russia-over-a-compulsory-license-issued-to-a-company-making-remdesivir/.

Two years into the pandemic, vaccination rates in low-income countries remained quite low. In March 2022, only 20 doses had been administered per 100 persons in low-income countries, compared to just over 100 in lower-middle-income countries and over 200 in upper-middle-income and high-income countries.[18] In wealthier countries, people were able to receive multiple booster doses. By August 2024, low-income countries still averaged about 50 doses per 100 people.

13.7.1 *Contributions from Other Sources*

The following are some key factors that supported innovation and diffusion during the COVID-19 pandemic and helped reduce the severity of the health crisis:

1. **Public and Institutional Support:** In the U.S., the *National Institutes of Health* contributed key mRNA technologies with C-TAP (the COVID-19 Technology Access Pool), a platform designed to facilitate the non-exclusive sharing of intellectual property and technical know-how among developers of COVID-19 health products. C-TAP also partnered with the Medicines Patent Pool. In parallel, the COVAX initiative — co-led by the Coalition for Epidemic Preparedness Innovations (CEPI), Gavi the Vaccine Alliance, and the World Health Organization (WHO) — was established to accelerate vaccine development and promote equitable access.[19] Gavi played a prominent role in procuring and delivering vaccines to lower-income countries and frontline health workers.[20]
2. **Patent Pledges:** These are voluntary commitments by IP holders to make their intellectual property freely available during public health crises.[21] The IP in question may cover vaccines, diagnostics, therapeutics, or medical devices. Pledges vary in their specific terms. Some require users to obtain a formal license, while others impose additional conditions. For example, licensees may be prohibited from asserting patent rights against the pledging entity, or they may be required to make any

[18]Data are available from WHO's *Our World in Data*, https://ourworldindata.org/. The doses refer to both initial doses and boosters.

[19]COVAX officially closed on December 31, 2023.

[20]Gavi is a global vaccine organization that raises donor funding from public and private sources to purchase vaccines for low- and middle-income countries in need, and also distributes supplies from its stockpile.

[21]See Contreras (2021) for further details.

Table 13.4. Examples of Pledged IP during COVID-19

Pledge	IP
Wellcome Trust Publisher's Group	Peer-reviewed publications on COVID-19
Medtronic	Ventilator design (e.g., Puritan Bennet 560 machine)
Moderna	mRNA vaccine patents
Open COVID Pledge	Patents and Copyrights

resulting products available to the public for free, at cost, or at a fair price. Some IP pledges, such as that of Medtronic, the ventilator equipment manufacturer, adopt a *GNU*-style license commonly used in the open source software community.[22] Under such licenses, users may modify or improve the technology, provided that any derivative works are made openly available to others under the same terms as the original pledge (Table 13.4).

While not a formal IP pledge, MIT's E-Vent project is an open source research initiative that provides free public access to designs for a low-cost emergency ventilator.[23] The designs were co-created by a team of engineers, physicians, and computer scientists.

IP pledges can be viewed as an intermediate approach between full IP enforcement and outright contribution to the public domain. The pledge allows the contributor to retain some control through licensing, and the scope of the pledge is typically limited to the duration of the health or other emergency.

While IP pledges help alleviate supply shortages, an important question is whether they also stimulate technological progress. de Rassenfosse and Palangkaraya (2023) provide empirical evidence that they do. Their study analyzes pre-pandemic data (2004–2017) on 1,213 U.S. patent pledges across various technological fields. Compared to a control group of non-pledged patents, pledged patents were more likely to spur follow-on innovations, as measured by forward citations.

[22]GNU stands for "Gnu's Not Unix."

[23]Normal ventilators can cost around $30,000. See https://news.mit.edu/2020/ventilator-covid-deployment-open-source-low-cost-0326.

The follow-on innovation effect was particularly strong for pledged patents with fewer restrictions. In contrast, pledged software patents did not receive more citations than the control group, possibly due to the limitations imposed by GNU-style licenses. Pledged patents of higher quality also generated more follow-on innovation, as did those owned by larger firms, though this may reflect the attractiveness of the technologies themselves rather than firm size alone.

3. **3D Printing or Additive Manufacturing:** During COVID-19, this industry played a remarkable role in responding to equipment shortages. The supply and utilization of 3D printers increased, enabling rapid prototyping and customization of medical devices.[24] The 3D maker community made design specifications freely available through file repository websites.

   How did the 3D-printer response come together?

   - Grassroots and open source communities, which shared PPE designs (face shields, ventilator adaptors, and swab accessories).
   - Volunteers, who donated time, materials, and expertise. These included hobbyists with home 3D printers and individuals working in university labs, all collaborating with hospitals to design solutions.
   - Crowdfunding efforts.
   - Industry support from leading companies such as Stratasys, 3D Systems, and MakerBot, which released free designs.
   - Public sector coordination, particularly from regulatory authorities that assisted with validation and logistics. In the United States, the Food and Drug Administration (FDA), under the Emergency Use Authorization (EUA) Act, streamlined the regulatory and registration process.[25]

   Open 3D-printing activity was not confined to the Global North. Colombia, Ecuador, Tanzania, and South Africa all experienced a "maker movement," where universities, businesses, and hobbyists contributed shared designs.[26] In Colombia, one technological specification was coordinated via a *WhatsApp* chat group. Start-ups such as Kenya's Kijenzi

[24]See Ishack and Lipner (2021) and Longhitano *et al.* (2021) for details.

[25]The FDA reviews medical devices under the 510(k) process, which determines whether a new device is substantially equivalent to a previously authorized predicate device. Medical device approvals are generally less cumbersome than drug approvals; no clinical trials are required except for the highest-risk products (Class III).

[26]https://www.undp.org/acceleratorlabs/blog/covid-19-how-we-tapped-local-innovation-and-maker-movement-address-ppe-shortage.

had built 3D-printing capacity by 2017, leaving them well placed to contribute when the pandemic hit. In addition, companies and organizations from developed countries also participated. Siemens allowed doctors and hospitals in need of medical devices to register for free access to its Additive Manufacturing Network. The U.S. National Institutes of Health created the NIH 3D Print Exchange program, an open, community-driven portal that provides freely downloadable, clinically vetted design files.

The open contributions of the 3D-printing industry are distinct from IP pledges. No IP waivers were involved. The contributions consisted of donated designs, shared knowledge, and acts of volunteerism — in other words, a public domain strategy.

The motivations for volunteerism and donations were multifaceted:

- A sense of social responsibility.
- Advertising and brand building. The 3D-printing industry viewed the pandemic response as an opportunity to showcase its capabilities; donations served as an investment in the industry's post-pandemic future.
- Opening doors. The actions of volunteers created future opportunities for them, including government contracts and connections with medical device manufacturers.
- Skill development. Increased production and innovation provided opportunities for learning by doing. Participants gained experience with new designs and methods that could enhance their future productivity.

The key takeaway from the COVID-19 pandemic is that TRIPS flexibilities largely fell short in practice. Other mechanisms played a vital role in alleviating shortages of essential medicines and supplies, such as IP pledges, 3D-printing initiatives, public funding, and global partnerships. A global pandemic treaty would be a step toward future preparedness (see Box 1). It could address several gaps exposed during COVID-19 pandemic, particularly the distribution of medicines to low-income countries and the need for stronger international coordination on emergency response, data sharing, and equitable access. However, such a treaty's effectiveness hinges on the implementation of access and benefit-sharing arrangements; for example, how are pathogen samples to be accessed and how are the resulting benefits to be allocated?

Box 1. Pandemic Treaty

In May 2025, the *World Health Assembly* — the decision-making body of the World Health Organization (WHO) — adopted a global *Pandemic Agreement* (often referred to as the "pandemic treaty") after 3 years of intensive negotiations following the COVID-19 pandemic.[i] Under the text adopted, the Agreement opens for signature and ratification only after the Health Assembly adopts a Pathogen Access and Benefit-Sharing (PABS) annex. Under the Agreement, participating manufacturers will provide "rapid access" to a share of real-time production of safe and effective vaccines, therapeutics, and diagnostics during a declared pandemic emergency.

PABS is contentious. Developing countries argue that it would promote equitable access and data sharing and help overcome the disparities experienced during COVID-19. Industry stakeholders, by contrast, contend that it could undermine innovation incentives by requiring access to materials and associated know-how or IP. A divisive point concerns tracking and tracing the origin of PABS materials and genetic sequence data (GSD).[ii] The idea is that a country that provides biological material or GSD should be entitled to share in the benefits.[iii] The benefits could be monetary (a share of profits) or in-kind (technology transfer, investment, or donated medicines). Drug companies, for their part, seek access without mandatory benefit-sharing. They argue that tracing the origins of GSD is technically difficult and that tracking requirements would slow innovation and development. Hence, their call to decouple access from benefit-sharing.

Beyond the PABS annex, many of the treaty's commitments are voluntary, which may limit their enforceability.[iv] In addition, if the United States withdraws from the WHO, the organization would lose a major funding source. Nonetheless, a U.S. withdrawal would not preclude private companies from participating in a PABS-like system, subject to resolution of the contentious issues described above.

[i]https://www.who.int/news/item/20-05-2025-world-health-assembly-adopts-historic-pandemic-agreement-to-make-the-world-more-equitable-and-safer-from-future-pandemics.

[ii]https://www.thinkglobalhealth.org/article/fate-unknown-pandemic-agreements-pathogen-access-and-benefit-sharing.

[iii]And not pay high prices to companies that manufacture drugs based on indigenous samples.

[iv]Nations may prefer voluntary commitments over binding ones due to concerns about sovereignty and domestic policy flexibility.

13.8 Docket II: Capacity Building

Recall that previous studies have argued that IPRs are more effective at boosting innovation or facilitating technology transfer when a firm or economy possesses a sufficient level of innovative or absorptive capacity. This then raises the question: how can such capacities be built?

Cirera and Maloney (2017) describe an "innovation paradox" in the developing world — namely, that "despite the vast potential returns to innovation, developing countries invest far less . . . than advanced countries" (p. xix). This is tantamount to leaving billions of dollars on the table in terms of forgone productivity growth. The authors point out that "innovation in the developing world faces barriers that are orders of magnitude more challenging than those found in the advanced world" (p. xxiv). These barriers stem from a combination of factors, including a lack of broad complementarities and limited managerial capabilities, that are not only confined to the private sector but also extend to government.

Another reason for the lack of investment in capacity building is the tension between short-run and long-run priorities. With limited resources, governments and societies may focus on urgent, immediate needs, such as responding to famine, disease outbreaks, environmental shocks (monsoons, droughts), housing crises, financial volatility, speculative attacks, unemployment, or political instability. Short-term demands often take precedence over long-term developmental goals, such as building an R&D sector, supporting an arts industry, expanding tertiary education, or developing a national information infrastructure (e.g., libraries, websites, and archives). Recognizing this trade-off helps put the task of overcoming structural barriers in a broader perspective.

Even when growth is prioritized, the key complementarities needed to support innovation are often absent. R&D factors operate jointly with physical and human capital. To make up for a human capital gap, formerly developing economies in East Asia (South Korea, Singapore, Taiwan), and now China and India, have sent students abroad for training. An alternative strategy is to attract foreign professionals — scientists, engineers, and artists — to help jump-start indigenous creative firms or institutions. Several Middle Eastern countries have followed this strategy by employing foreign academics to teach in local universities.

Moreover, it is not only science- and art-related human capital that is lacking for productivity and innovation, but also managerial and organizational skills: professionals who can lead, provide vision, develop organizational plans, manage human resources, oversee inventory, and monitor performance. Such learning can occur through exposure to and interaction with foreign affiliates of multinational companies, by observing their management practices and operational standards.

But a key barrier to attracting foreign knowledge workers and knowledge capital is the local institutional rigidities experienced in low-income economies. The market environment may not be business-friendly. The cost of doing business is high or onerous; for example, starting a new business could entail multiple procedures, an excess of permits required to do business, hurdles with registering property, difficulty of getting credit, tax burdens, cumbersome processes for enforcing contracts or collecting debt, and weak protection for minority investors.[27] In many cases, the very obstacle to improving the "doing business" environment is that there are persons (government workers and contractors) whose livelihoods depend on these existing rigidities. These rigidities provide economic rents to those who benefit from the status quo. Inefficient firms that should exit might be politically favored and are propped up with public subsidies or sheltered from competition. The overall lack of competitive pressure reduces incentives to innovate, improve quality, or provide strong customer service.

Governments themselves may suffer from organizational inefficiency. To promote innovation, they must be able to identify market failures and devise corrective solutions. For that, they need access to reliable data, effective analytic capacity, and sufficient implementation skills. Governments also need to earn credibility — that they will follow through on announced policies and not arbitrarily reverse course. Without that, they suffer from a problem of *time inconsistency*, where private actors no longer believe in long-term policy stability and refrain from making durable investments.

All of these are tall orders — but they are the harsh realities that many lower-income economies struggle with, and they severely impede technological progress. Beyond institutional reforms, the next topic considers how AI might serve as a tool for building innovative and absorptive capacities.

[27] See https://archive.doingbusiness.org/en/rankings.

13.8.1 *AI in Developing Countries*

This sub-section first outlines general ways in which AI can enhance innovative and absorptive capacities. It then presents examples of AI initiatives in the Global South, followed by a discussion of the challenges that developing countries still face in fully utilizing AI.

As a general-purpose technology, AI is applicable across multiple sectors — agriculture, health, education, finance, and public administration. It has the potential to address the many barriers to economic development discussed earlier.

- **Research:** For researchers in technological fields and the creative arts, AI provides access to global knowledge bases directly from a desktop or mobile device. Much of this content can be accessed in local languages through AI-powered translation tools. This access helps developing economies bypass traditional bottlenecks in expertise and training. Machine learning can complement limited human capital by detecting patterns and generating predictive insights. For hobbyists and local entrepreneurs, many AI tools are open source and free from licensing fees and proprietary restrictions. Google's TensorFlow, Facebook's PyTorch, and Hugging Face's Transformers are all freely available and form the tools needed for experimentation and application development.
- **Education:** AI language models, when adapted to local dialects and literacy levels, can significantly improve access to educational content. AI can facilitate the teaching of coding, math, and digital literacy. Personalized digital tutoring becomes especially valuable in situations where human teachers are scarce or unevenly distributed.
- **Government:** AI can assist with streamlining administrative procedures and reducing the costs of doing business discussed earlier. It can support data processing, evidence-based decision-making, and program evaluation. These tools help governments identify waste, reduce bottlenecks, and per the advice in every economics textbook, allocate resources optimally subject to budget constraints.

AI offers developing nations a chance to "leapfrog" — that is, to skip intermediate stages of technological development by directly deploying advanced digital tools. Agentic AI, in particular, is described by technologists as a "cognitive multiplier,"[28] one that can amplify scarce human and institutional capacities to enhance innovation and absorptive capability.

[28] https://www.publicissapient.com/news/3-waves-of-ai-transformation-in-industry, https://bigthink.com/business/why-2025-will-take-us-closer-to-the-turing-horizon/.

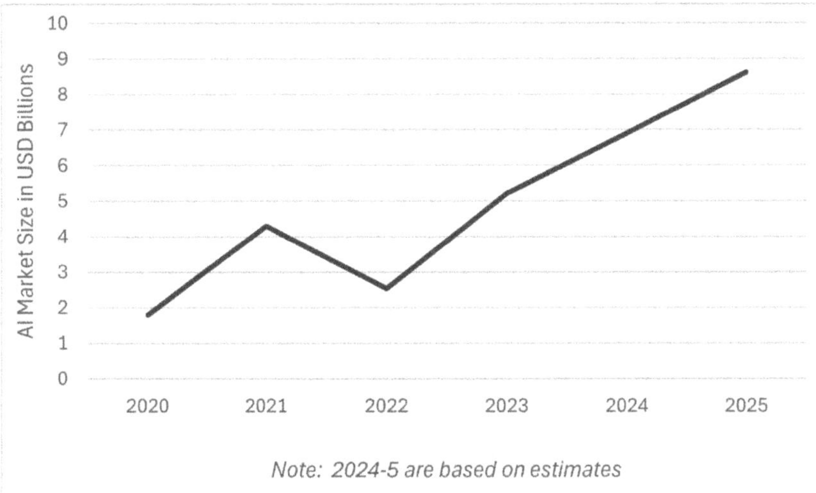

Figure 13.7. AI Market Size in Africa, 2020–2025.
Source: IT Edge News.

AI adoption is expanding across Africa. AI market size across Africa has grown substantially, as shown in Figure 13.7 (in billions of U.S. dollars).[29] Machine learning occupies the largest share of this market, followed by natural language processing. Across the continent, AI startups, tech hubs, research initiatives, AI institutes, labs, and national government strategies have emerged.[30] Partnerships have formed among universities, government ministries, the private sector, and global entities. These partnerships focus on areas such as agricultural innovation, healthcare delivery, and educational technology.

Table 13.5 presents selected examples of ongoing AI initiatives in the Global South.[31]

[29]Source: https://www.itedgenews.africa/unlocking-africas-ai-potential/.

[30]Signé (2025).

[31]Data compiled from various sources: Science for Africa Foundation (2025); Owoyemi *et al.* (2020); https://climateadaptationplatform.com/how-ai-supports-millions-of-small-scale-farmers-in-africa/; https://farmerline.co/farmerlines-darli-ai-recognized-on-times-list-of-the-best-inventions-of-2024/; https://www.lrfoundation.org.uk/news/ai-potential-to-reduce-pregnancy-deaths-bangladesh; https://www.wfp.org/wfp-drones; https://www.unido.org/news/jordan-presents-its-ai-strategy-and-implementation-roadmap; https://www.shaip.com/blog/building-inclusive-ai-for-india-shaips-role-in-project-vaani/; https://www.worldbank.org/en/news/feature/2021/07/07/prioritizing-the-poorest-and-most-vulnerable-in-west-africa.

Table 13.5. Examples of AI Initiatives in the Developing World

Region/Country	AI Application
Togo	Novissi platform for emergency cash transfers using ML
Nigeria	ML-based diagnosis of birth asphyxia
Zambia	Diagnosis of diabetic retinopathy
Kenya	Pathology Network: connecting patients and physicians
Tanzania and Zambia	AI-aided detection of pulmonary tuberculosis
Africa	AI research hub for maternal, sexual, and reproductive health
Africa	Darli AI: multilingual chatbot for smallholder farmers
Mauritius	National AI Strategy (Mauritius AI Council, MAIC)
India	Project Vaani: LLM capturing diverse Indian dialects
Bangladesh	Continuous pregnancy monitoring with AI integration
Jordan	AI strategy for public-sector efficiency and capacity building
UN WFP	AI-powered photo analysis for emergency response

These initiatives illustrate the breadth of AI applications, particularly in healthcare. Several projects directly target low-resource environments, while others focus on improving institutional efficiency. Despite their varied designs, a common thread among them is the reliance on multilingual tools, mobile infrastructure, and collaboration with international partners. These examples indicate that AI can help build indigenous innovation ecosystems.

Still, developing countries face significant hurdles in realizing AI's full promise. As discussed in Chapter 12, the global concentration of AI compute resources and the environmental costs of AI constrain downstream access for the Global South. But beyond these external limitations, many African and other developing countries also face serious internal obstacles. Urban–rural divides persist, national governance structures on AI remain underdeveloped, and mistrust of AI systems is common among local populations.[32] Legal frameworks also lag behind technological adoption. For instance, it is often unclear who bears responsibility when AI systems yield adverse outcomes.[33]

Gender equity remains an underaddressed issue in the design of local datasets and algorithmic outputs. Greater representation from Africa, South America, and Southeast Asia is needed in global AI forums, and international AI policy discussions must be more inclusive of their priorities and constraints. Domestic AI capabilities also require considerable development. As of 2025, Africa accounted for only 0.3% of global AI publications.[34] Inadequate infrastructure continues to pose barriers to development, and data quality issues remain widespread.[35] In the healthcare sector, for example, large clinical datasets are often unavailable, especially datasets with labels (i.e., annotations from experts). Existing datasets frequently over-represent populations from the Global North, embedding biases that negatively affect model performance when applied to African contexts, yielding inaccurate diagnoses and improper treatments.[36]

The costs of developing AI/ML solutions in healthcare — ranging from a few thousand to several million dollars — include expenses for data acquisition and preparation, hardware and computing resources, and system maintenance and upgrading.[37] In many least developed countries, these investments are further constrained by the scarcity of computers and smartphones, unreliable electricity, and poor internet connectivity. Thus, while the AI initiatives highlighted above offer promise, more progress is needed. Realizing the transformational potential of AI will require durable global partnerships, technology transfers, and long-term financing mechanisms.

13.9 Future Directions

This section identifies several important topics for further research and policy debate:

1. **Climate Change Technology and IP:** A crucial part of addressing climate change lies in the development and diffusion of green technologies. An open question remains: has IP been a major barrier to

[32]See Science for Africa Foundation (2025).
[33]See Owoyemi, *et al.* (2020).
[34]See Science for Africa Foundation (2025).
[35]See Victor (2025).
[36]See Owoyemi *et al.* (2020) and Victor (2025).
[37]See Owoyemi *et al.* (2020).

low-income countries accessing clean energy technologies, or are other constraints, such as limited financing, technical know-how, or infrastructure, more significant?

2. **IP and Competition Policy:** Significant policy debates sit at the intersection of competition law and IP, particularly in developing economies. These include how to address blocking patents, refusals to license essential technologies, mergers involving dominant tech firms, and anticompetitive conduct by digital platforms. The appropriate balance between IP protection and market competition warrants deeper study.
3. **Trademarks, Branding, and Development:** Although this book touches on trademarks, it does not fully explore how brand protection can assist developing country businesses. Strategic use of trademarks and branding could help local entrepreneurs differentiate their goods from those of global firms. Similarly, geographical indications (GIs) may support rural development, cultural heritage, and export competitiveness — topics deserving greater exploration.
4. **Trade Secrets and Data Ownership:** Trade secrets protect undisclosed know-how. While secrecy offers the advantage of indefinite protection, it may inhibit knowledge diffusion. AI development raises new concerns, as proprietary data and trained models are often treated as trade secrets. This creates barriers to transparency and competition. Future research should examine frameworks that promote responsible data sharing, such as data commons or data trusts, while maintaining incentives for data collection and curation.
5. **Informal Economies:** In many least-developed countries, large segments of the economy are informal. Entrepreneurs in these settings often innovate in ways that are not captured by the formal IP system, such as through new craft designs, recipes, or service delivery models, and often engage in mutual copying. What alternative forms of knowledge recognition or protection, such as community certificates or open source-like models, could support these innovators until they scale up or transition into the formal economy?
6. **New Frontiers — 3D Printing and Biotechnology:** Emerging technologies raise new IP challenges. With 3D printing, for instance, individuals can replicate IP-protected goods at home, echoing debates over digital piracy. In biotechnology, while fields like genetic engineering are not new, recent breakthroughs have pushed them to a new IP frontier. Tools like CRISPR have radically accelerated the pace of innovation and

lowered costs, while synthetic biology is rapidly maturing. These developments raise ethical questions and IP dilemmas, particularly about the patentability of foundational biological materials that could affect downstream innovation.

7. **Utilization of AI:** Developing economies should be able to leverage AI tools for capacity building. IP flexibilities will be essential to ensure that intellectual property rights on AI algorithms — or trade secrecy surrounding model architectures and weights — do not hinder the ability of local actors to adapt, customize, and develop locally relevant AI applications. In addition, training data must be representative and inclusive, reflecting local languages, social conditions, and cultural diversity.

In addition to these specific research areas, more general questions arise about the evolution of international institutions and global governance. How should global frameworks adapt to address the new technologies and the new markets?

There have been growing calls for new international treaties to supplement or update existing frameworks. For example, a potential treaty on access to knowledge could modernize IP rules for the digital era or help close the global knowledge divide. Proposals for a new treaty on pandemic preparedness have also advanced. In parallel, Europe has enacted legislation such as the Artificial Intelligence Act and the General Data Protection Regulation (GDPR), both of which shape the global regulatory environment.

A key institutional design question is whether global governance should proceed through multilateral treaties, regional pacts, or other models. While regional agreements may be quicker to implement, they also risk creating fragmentation. It is important to be mindful about *regulatory fatigue* or *regulatory confusion*, which can arise when multiple overlapping or conflicting agreements make it unclear which rules apply, undermining compliance and legitimacy.

In some cases, it may be more effective to work within existing frameworks, such as TRIPS, while gradually expanding or layering them into higher-order agreements. In other cases, a clean-slate approach may be warranted, involving sunset clauses for older frameworks. Regardless of the path taken, a patchwork of uncoordinated agreements is unlikely to deliver stable, development-friendly outcomes.

Bibliography

Abbott, Ryan (2022). *Research Handbook on Intellectual Property and Artificial Intelligence.* Cheltenham: Edward Elgar Publishing Ltd.

Abel, Andrew, Dixit, Avinash, Eberly, Janice, and Pindyck, Robert (1996). "Options, the value of capital, and investment." *Quarterly Journal of Economics*, 111(3): 753–777.

Aboy, Mateo, Lath, Aparajita, Minssen, Timo, and Liddell, Kathleen (2024). "The sufficiency of disclosure of AI inventions." *Journal of Intellectual Property Law & Practice*, 19(11): 834–840.

Acemoglu, Daron and Akcigit, Ufuk (2012). "Intellectual property rights policy, competition, and innovation." *Journal of the European Economic Association*, 10(1): 1–42.

Acri, Kristina (2011). "The economics of access to medicines: Meeting the challenges of pharmaceutical patents, innovation and access for global health." *Harvard International Law Journal*, 53: 25–43.

Acri, Kristina (2024). "Health and biopharmaceutical innovation." In Park, Walter (ed.), *Handbook of Innovation and Intellectual Property Rights.* Cheltenham: Edward Elgar Publishing, 396–416.

Aghion, Philippe, and Jaravel, Xavier (2015). "Knowledge spillovers, innovation and growth." *Economic Journal*, 125(583): 533–573. https://doi.org/10.1111/ecoj.12188.

Aghion, Philippe, Howitt, Peter, and Prantl, Susanne (2015). "Patent rights, product market reforms, and innovation." *Journal of Economic Growth*, 20(3): 223–262.

Aghion, Philippe, Jones, Benjamin F., and Jones, Charles I. (2019). "Artificial intelligence and economic growth." In Agrawal, Ajay, Gans, Joshua, and Goldfarb, Avi (eds.) *The Economics of Artificial Intelligence.* Chicago, IL: University of Chicago Press, 237–282.

Agrawal, Ajay, McHale, John, and Oettl, Alexander (2024). "Artificial intelligence and scientific discovery: a model of prioritized search." *Research Policy.*, 53(5): 104989.

Akcigit, Ufuk, Celik, Murat A., and Greenwood, Jeremy (2016). "Buy, keep, or sell: Economic growth and the market for ideas." *Econometrica*, 84(3): 943–984.

Allen, Robert (1983). "Collective invention." *Journal of Economic Behavior and Organization*, 4: 1–24.

Allred, Brent, and Park, Walter G. (2007). "Patent rights and innovative activities: Evidence from national and firm-level data." *Journal of International Business Studies*, 38(5): 878–900.

America Invents Act (2011). https://www.congress.gov/bill/112th-congress/house-bill/1249.

Appel, Gil, Neelbauer, Juliana, and Schweidel, David (2023). "Generative AI has an intellectual property problem." *Harvard Business Review.* https://hbr.org/2023/04/generative-ai-has-an-intellectual-property-problem.

Arai, Yasuhiro., and Kinukawa, Shinya (2014). "Copyright infringement as user innovation." *Journal of Cultural Economics*, 38(2): 131–144. https://doi.org/10.1007/s10824-013-9200-3.

Arora, Ashish, Belenzon, Sharon, and Suh, Jungkyu (2022). "Science and the market for technology." *Management Science*, 68(10): 7176–7201.

Arora, Ashish, Branstetter, Lee G., and Chatterjee, Chirantan (2008). "Strong medicine: Patent reform and the emergence of a research-driven pharmaceutical industry in India." Paper presented at NBER Conference on the Location of the Biopharmaceutical Industry.

Arrow, Kenneth J. (1962). "Economic welfare and the allocation of resources for invention." In Nelson, Richard (ed.), *The Rate and Direction of Inventive Activity: Economic and Social Factors.* Princeton, NJ: Princeton University Press, 609–626.

Athey, Susan, and Schmutzler, Armin (1995). "Product and process flexibility in an innovative environment." *RAND Journal of Economics*, 26(4): 557–574.

Baker, Dean, Stiglitz, Joseph, and Jayadev, Arjun (2017). *Innovation, Intellectual Property, and Development: A Better Set of Approaches for the 21st Century.* Center for Economic and Policy Research. https://cepr.net/images/stories/reports/baker-jayadev-stiglitz-innovation-ip-development-2017-07.pdf.

Barontini, Roberto, and Taglialatela, Jonathan (2022). "Patents and small business risk: Longitudinal evidence from the global financial crisis." *Journal of Small Business and Enterprise Development*, 29(2): 279–292.

Barzel, Yoram (1968). "Optimal timing of innovations." *Review of Economics and Statistics*, 50(3): 348–355.

Bass, Mickenzie, Santacreu, Ana Maria, and LaBelle, Jesse (2023). "Profit shifting in the 21st century: Multinationals' use of intrafirm patent transfers." Federal Reserve Bank of St. Louis *On the Economy Blog.* https://www.stlouisfed.org/on-the-economy/2023/sep/profit-shifting-multinational-use-intrafirm-patent-transfers.

Beall, Reed, and Kuhn, Randall (2012). "Trends in compulsory licensing of pharmaceuticals since the Doha Declaration: A database analysis." *PLOS Medicine*, 9(1): e1001154. https://doi.org/10.1371/journal.pmed.1001154.

Berger, Roland (2005). "A Study on the Cost of Patenting." Prepared on behalf of the European Patent Office. Munich: Roland Berger Market Research.

Bergstrom, Theodore (2001). "Free labor for costly journals." *Journal of Economic Perspectives*, 15(4): 183–198.

Bilir, Kamran (2014). "Patent laws, product lifecycle lengths, and multinational activity." *American Economic Review*, 104(7): 1979–2013.

Bloom, Nicholas, and Van Reenen, John (2002). "Patents, real options, and firm performance." *Economic Journal*, 112: C97–C116.

Bollyky, Thomas, and Bown, Chad (2020). "The tragedy of vaccine nationalism: Only cooperation can end the pandemic." *Foreign Affairs*, 99(5): 96–108.

Bond, Eric W., and Saggi, Kamal (2014). "Compulsory licensing, price controls, and access to patented foreign products." *Journal of Development Economics*, 109: 217–228. https://doi.org/10.1016/j.jdeveco.2014.04.001.

Bond, Eric W., and Saggi, Kamal (2020). "Patent protection in developing countries and global welfare: WTO obligations versus flexibilities." *Journal of International Economics*, 122: 103281.

Bostrom, Nick. (2014). *Superintelligence: Paths, Dangers, Strategies.* Oxford: Oxford University Press.

Branstetter, Lee G., Fisman, Raymond, and Foley, C. Fritz (2006). "Do stronger intellectual property rights increase international technology transfer? Empirical evidence from U.S. firm-level panel data." *Quarterly Journal of Economics*, 121(1): 321–349.

Briggs, Kristie (2010). "Intellectual property rights and development: The spatial relationships." *Journal of Economic Studies*, 37(5): 525-543.

Brynjolfsson, Erik, Rock, Daniel, and Syverson, Chad (2019). "Artificial intelligence and the modern productivity paradox: A clash of expectations and statistics." In Agrawal, Ajay, Gans, Joshua, and Goldfarb, Avi (eds.), *The Economics of Artificial Intelligence.* Chicago, IL: University of Chicago Press, 115–146.

Buccafusco, Christopher (2016). "A theory of copyright authorship." *Virginia Law Review*, 102: 1229–1295.

Buffington, Catherine, Chapman, Daniel, Dinlersoz, Emin, Foster, Lucia, and Haltiwanger, John (2021). "High frequency business dynamics in the United States during the COVID-19 pandemic." U.S. Census Bureau, CES Working Paper 21-06.

Bulan, Laarni T. (2005). "Real options, irreversible investment and firm uncertainty." *Review of Financial Economics*, 14: 255–279.

Campi, Mercedes (2017). "The effect of intellectual property rights on agricultural productivity." *Agricultural Economics*, 48(3): 327–339. https://doi.org/10.1111/agec.12337.

Campi, Mercedes (2024). "The complex landscape of intellectual property rights in agricultural research, development, and innovation." In Park, Walter (ed.), *Handbook of Innovation and Intellectual Property Rights.* Cheltenham: Edward Elgar Publishing, 330–341.

Campi, Mercedes, and Dueñas, Marco (2019). "Intellectual property protection, trade agreements, and international trade." *Research Policy*, 48(3): 531–545.

Campi, Mercedes, and Nuvolari, Alessandro (2015). "Intellectual property protection in plant varieties: A worldwide index (1961–2011)." *Research Policy*, 44(4): 951–964.

Campi, Mercedes, and Nuvolari, Alessandro (2021). "Intellectual property rights and agricultural development: Evidence from a worldwide index of IPRs in agriculture (1961–2018)." 57(4) *Journal of Development Studies*, DOI: 10.1080/00220388.2020.1817395.

Cardoso, Vitoria A., Lourenzani, Ana E.B.S., Caldas, Marcellus M., Bernardo, Cristiane H.C., and Bernardo, Roberto (2022). "The benefits and barriers of geographical indications to producers: A review." *Renewable Agriculture and Food Systems*, 37: 707–719. https://doi.org/10.1017/S174217052200031X.

Chang, Ha-Joon (2002). *Kicking Away the Ladder: Development Strategy in Historical Perspective.* London, UK: Anthem Press.

Chaudhuri, Shubham, Goldberg, Pinelopi K., and Jia, Panle (2006). "Estimating the effects of global patent protection in pharmaceuticals: A case study of Quinolones in India." *American Economic Review*, 96(5): 1477–1514. https://doi.org/10.1257/aer.96.5.1477.

Chen, Wantal, Yu, Xiang, and Yang, Wei (2024). "International trademark protection strength: 1990–2020." *World Economy*, 47(7): 3168–3198. https://doi.org/10.1111/twec.13579.

Chen, Yongmin, and Puttitanun, Thitima (2005). "Intellectual property rights and innovation in developing countries." *Journal of Development Economics*, 78(2): 474–493.

Chesbrough, Henry W. (2003). *Open Innovation: The New Imperative for Creating and Profiting from Technology.* Boston: Harvard Business School Press.

Chin, Judith, and Grossman, Gene (1990). "Intellectual property rights and North–South trade." In Jones, Ronald and Krueger, Anne O. (eds.), *The Political Economy of International Trade: Essays in Honor of Robert E. Baldwin.* Cambridge, MA: Basil Blackwell, 90–107.

Cho, Kyungchul, Kim, Changseok, and Shin, Juneseuk (2015). "Differential effects of intellectual property rights on innovation and economic performance: A cross-industry investigation." *Science and Public Policy*, 42(6): 827–840.

Chu, Angus (2024). "Macroeconomic effects of intellectual property rights." In Park, Walter (ed.), *Handbook of Innovation and Intellectual Property Rights: Evolving Scholarship and Reflections.* Cheltenham: Edward Elgar Publishing, pp. 13–26.

Chu, Angus, Cozzi, Guido, and Galli, Silvia (2014). "Stage-dependent intellectual property rights." *Journal of Development Economics*, 106: 239–249.

Chu, Angus, Cozzi, Guido, Fan, Haichao, Pan, Shiyuan, and Zhang, Mengbo (2020). "Do stronger patents stimulate or stifle innovation? The crucial role of financial development." *Journal of Money, Credit and Banking*, 52(5): 1305–1322.

Cincera, Michele, and van Pottelsberghe, Bruno de la Potterie (2001). "International R&D spillovers: A survey." *Cahiers Économiques de Bruxelles*, No. 169.

Cirera, Xavier and Maloney, William (2017). *The Innovation Paradox: Developing-Country Capabilities and the Unrealized Promise of Technological Catch-up*. World Bank, Washington, D.C.

Co, Catherine Y. (2004). "Do patent rights regimes matter?" *Review of International Economics*, 12(3): 359–373.

Cockburn, Ian, Henderson, Rebecca, and Stern, Scott (2019). "The impact of artificial intelligence on innovation." In Agrawal, Ajay, Gans, Joshua, and Goldfarb, Avi (eds.), *The Economics of Artificial Intelligence*. Chicago, IL: University of Chicago Press, 115–146.

Coe, David, and Helpman, Elhanan (1995). "International R&D spillovers." *European Economic Review*, 39: 859–887.

Coe, David, Helpman, Elhanan, and Hoffmaister, Alexander (2009). "International R&D spillovers and institutions." *European Economic Review*, 53: 723–741.

Cohen, Wesley M., Nelson, Richard R., and Walsh, John P. (2000). "Protecting their intellectual assets: Appropriability conditions and why U.S. manufacturing firms patent (or not)." National Bureau of Economic Research (NBER) Working Paper No. 7552. https://ssrn.com/abstract=214952.

Contreras, Jorge L. (2021). "The open COVID pledge: Design, implementation and preliminary assessment of an intellectual property commons." *Utah Law Review*, 833. https://ssrn.com/abstract=3780850.

Contreras, Jorge L. (2025). "The SNP Consortium: Background and context." University of Utah College of Law Research Paper No. 632. https://ssrn.com/abstract=5161427.

Corrado, Carol, Haskel, Jonathan, and Jona-Lasinio, Cecilia (2021). "Artificial intelligence and productivity: An intangible assets approach." *Oxford Review of Economic Policy*, 37(3): 435–458.

Craig, Carys J. (2022). "The relational robot: A normative lens for AI legal neutrality—commentary on Ryan Abbott, The Reasonable Robot." *Jerusalem Review of Legal Studies*, 25(1): 24–39. https://doi.org/10.1093/jrls/jlac003.

Czarnitzki, Dirk, Fernandez, Gastón P., and Rammer, Christian (2023). "Artificial intelligence and firm-level productivity." *Journal of Economic Behavior and Organization*, 211: 188–205.

Czarnitzki, Dirk, and Toole, Andrew A. (2011). "Patent protection, market uncertainty, and R&D investment." *Review of Economics and Statistics*, 93: 147–159.

Damgaard, Jannick, Elkjaer, Thomas, and Johannesen, Niels (2019). "The rise of phantom investments: Empty corporate shells in tax havens undermine tax collection in advanced, emerging market, and developing economies." *Finance & Development*, September. International Monetary Fund, Washington D.C.

Danaher, Brett, Dhanasobhon, Samita, Smith, Michael, and Telang, Rahul (2010). "Converting pirates without cannibalizing purchasers: The impact of digital distribution on physical sales and internet piracy." *Marketing Science*, 29(6): 1138–1151.

Danaher, Brett, Smith, Michael D., and Telang, Rahul (2014). "Piracy and copyright enforcement mechanisms." *Innovation Policy and the Economy*, 14: 25–61.

d'Aspremont, Claude, and Jacquemin, Alexis (1988). "Cooperative and noncooperative R&D in duopoly with spillovers." *American Economic Review*, 78(5): 1133–1137.

Davis, James, Holden, Diethorn, Marschke, Gerald, and Wang, Andrew (2021). "STEM employment resiliency during recessions: Evidence from the COVID-19 pandemic." National Bureau of Economic Research (NBER) Working Paper No. 29568.

Dawkins, Richard (2004). *The Ancestor's Tale.* New York: Houghton-Mifflin Co.

De Vany, Arthur S. and Walls, W. David (2007). "Estimating the effects of movie piracy on box-office revenue." *Review of Industrial Organization*, 30: 291–301.

Deardorff, Alan (1992). "Welfare effects of global patent protection." *Economica*, 59(233): 35–51.

Dell'Acqua, Fabrizio, McFowland III, Edward, Mollick, Ethan, Lifshitz-Assaf, Hila, Kellogg, Katherine C., Rajendran, Saran, Krayer, Lisa, Candelon, François, and Lakhani, Karim R. (2023), "Navigating the jagged technological frontier: Field experimental evidence of the effects of AI on knowledge worker productivity and quality." Harvard Business School Working Paper No. 24-013.

Demirer, Mert, Jimenez Hernandez, Diego J., Li, Dean, and Peng, Sida (2024). "Data, privacy laws and firm production: evidence from the GDPR." National Bureau of Economic Research (NBER) Working Paper No. 32146.

Dhanora, Madan, Sharma, Ruchi, and Park, Walter (2020). "Technological innovations and market Power: A study of the Indian pharmaceutical industry." *Millennial Asia*, 12(1): 5-34.

Dinlersoz, Emin, Dunne, Timothy, Haltiwanger, John, and Penciakova, Veronika (2021). "Business formation: A tale of two recessions." U.S. Census Bureau, Center for Economic Studies Paper No. CES-WP-21-01.

Diwan, Ishac, and Rodrik, Dani (1991). "Patents, appropriate technology, and North–South trade." *Journal of International Economics*, 30(1–2): 27–47.

Dixit, Avinash, and Pindyck, Robert (1994). *Investment Under Uncertainty.* Princeton, NJ: Princeton University Press.

Duggan, Mark, Garthwaite, Craig, and Goyal, Aparajita (2016). "The market impacts of pharmaceutical product patents in developing countries: Evidence from India." *American Economic Review*, 106(1): 99–135.

Dunning, John H. (1977). "Trade, location of economic activity and MNE: A search for an eclectic approach." In Ohlin, Bertil, Hesselborn, Per-Ove, and Wijkman, Per-Magnus (eds.), *The International Allocation of Economic Activity.* London: Macmillan, 395–418.

Eaton, B. Curtis, Eaton, Diane F., and Allen, Douglas W. (2002). *Microeconomics, 5th Edition.* Hoboken, NJ: Prentice Hall.

Eisenberg, Rebecca S. (2000). "Re-examining the role of patents in appropriating the value of DNA sequences." *Emory Law Journal*, 49(3): 783–800.

Eswaran, Mukesh, and Gallini, Nancy T. (1996). "Patent policy and the direction of technological change." *RAND Journal of Economics*, 27(4): 722–746.

Evenson, Robert E., and Westphal, Larry E. (1995). "Technological change and technology strategy." In Behrman, Jere and Srinivasan, T.N. (eds.), *Handbook of Development Economics*, Volume 3A. Amsterdam: Elsevier, 2209–2299. https://doi.org/10.1016/S1573-4471(05)80009-9.

Ezrachi, Ariel and Stucke, Maurice E. (2017). *Virtual Competition: The Promise and Perils of the Algorithm-Driven Economy*. Cambridge, MA: Harvard University Press.

Falvey, Rod, Foster, Neil, and Greenaway, David (2006). "Intellectual property rights and economic growth." *Review of Development Economics*, 10(4): 700–719.

Feinberg, Robert, and Rousslang, Donald (1990). "Economic effects of intellectual property rights infringements." *Journal of Business*, 63(1): 79–90.

Ferranna, Maddalena (2024). "Causes and costs of global COVID-19 vaccine inequity." *Seminars in Immunopathology*, 45: 469–480.

Finck, Michèle, and Biega, Asia (2021). "Reviving purpose limitation and data minimisation in data-driven systems." *Technology and Regulation*, 44–61. https://doi.org/10.26116/techreg.2021.004.

Frey, Carl B., Presidente, Giorgio, and Andres, Pia (2024). "Data-biased innovation: directed technological change and the future of artificial intelligence," Oxford Martin Working Paper Series on Technological and Economic Change. https://www.oxfordmartin.ox.ac.uk/publications/data-biased-innovation-directed-technological-change-and-the-future-of-artificial-intelligence.

Galasso, Alberto, and Schankerman, Mark (2015). "Patents and cumulative innovation: Causal evidence from the courts." *The Quarterly Journal of Economics*, 130(1): 317–369. https://doi.org/10.1093/qje/qju029.

Galetovic, Alexander, and Gupta, Kirti (2020). "The case of the missing royalty stacking in the world mobile wireless industry." *Industrial and Corporate Change*, 29(3): 827–853. https://doi.org/10.1093/icc/dtz074.

Galetovic, Alexander, Haber, Stephen H., and Levine, Ross (2015). "An empirical examination of patent holdup." *Journal of Competition Law & Economics*, 11(3): 549–578. https://doi.org/10.1093/joclec/nhv024.

Gallini, Nancy T. (1992). "Patent policy and costly imitation." *RAND Journal of Economics*, 23(1): 52–63.

Gans, Joshua S. (2024). "Market power in artificial intelligence." National Bureau of Economic Research (NBER) Working Paper No. 32270.

Gaudillière, Jean-Paul (2006). *La médecine et les sciences, 19ème–20ème siècles*. Paris: La Découverte.

Gaudillière, Jean-Paul (2008). "How pharmaceuticals became patentable: The production and appropriation of drugs in the twentieth century." *History and Technology*, 24(2): 99–106.

Gertner, Jon (2012). *The Idea Factory: Bell Labs and the Great Age of American Innovation*. London, UK: Penguin Books.

Ghafele, Roya and Gibert, Benjamin (2012). *Economic Value of Fair Use in Copyright Law: Counterfactual Impact Analysis of Fair Use Policy on Private Copying Technology and Copyright Markets in Singapore*. UK: Oxfirst.

Giczy, Alexander, Pairolero, Nicholas A., and Toole, Andrew A. (2022). "Identifying Artificial Intelligence (AI) invention: A novel AI patent dataset." *Journal of Technology Transfer*, 47: 476–505.

Gibert, Benjamin (2012). *The 2015 Intellectual Property and Economic Growth Index: Measuring the Impact of Exceptions and Limitations in Copyright on Growth, Jobs, and Prosperity*. Lisbon Council Policy Brief 9(2), Brussels.

Giorcelli, Michela, and Moser, Petra (2020). "Copyrights and creativity: Evidence from Italian opera in the Napoleonic age." *Journal of Political Economy*, 128(11): 4163–4210. https://doi.org/10.1086/710534.

Glass, Amy, and Saggi, Kamal (2002). "Intellectual property rights and foreign direct investment." *Journal of International Economics*, 56: 387–410.

Gleeson, Deborah, Townsend, Belinda, Tenni, Brigitte F., and Phillips, Tarryn (2023). "Global inequities in access to COVID-19 health products and technologies: A political economy analysis." *Health & Place*, 83: 103051.

Globig, Laura, Xu, Rachel, Rathje, Steve, and van Bavel, Jay (2024). "Perceived (mis)alignment in generative Artificial Intelligence varies across cultures." https://doi.org/10.31234/osf.io/suqa2.

Goldfarb, Avi, and Trefler, Daniel (2019). "Artificial intelligence and international trade." In Agrawal, Ajay, Gans, Joshua, and Goldfarb, Avi (eds.), *The Economics of Artificial Intelligence*. Chicago, IL: University of Chicago Press, 463–492.

Goldfarb, Avi and Tucker, Catherine (2012). "Privacy and innovation." *Innovation Policy and the Economy*, 12: 65–89.

Gopinath, Gita (2023). "Harnessing AI for global good: Policies and challenges." *Finance & Development Magazine*. Washington, DC: International Monetary Fund, 70–72.

Gordon, Robert (2016). *The Rise and Fall of American Growth*, Princeton NJ: Princeton University Press.

Griliches, Zvi (1957). "Hybrid corn: An exploration in the economics of technological change." *Econometrica*, 25(4): 501–522.

Grossman, Gene M., and Helpman, Elhanan (1991). *Innovation and Growth in the Global Economy*. Cambridge, MA: MIT Press.

Grossman, Gene M., and Lai, Edwin L.-C. (2004). "International protection of intellectual property." *American Economic Review*, 95: 1635–1653.

Grossman, Gene M., and Lai, Edwin L.-C. (2008). "Parallel imports and price controls." *RAND Journal of Economics*, 39(2): 378–402. https://doi.org/10.1111/j.0741-6261.2008.00019.x.

Gruère, Guillaume P., and Sengupta, Debdatta (2011). "Bt cotton and farmer suicides in India: An evidence-based assessment." *Journal of Development Studies*, 47(2): 316–337.

Guellec, Dominique, and van Pottelsberghe de la Potterie, Bruno (2007). *The Economics of the European Patent System*. Oxford, UK: Oxford University Press.

Hall, Bronwyn, and Helmers, Christian (2024). *The Economics of Innovation and Intellectual Property*. Oxford, UK: Oxford University Press.

Hall, Bronwyn, and Ziedonis, Rosemarie (2001). "The patent paradox revisited: An empirical study of patenting in the US semiconductor industry, 1979–1995." *RAND Journal of Economics*, 32(1): 101–128.

Hao, Qianyue, Xu, Fengli, Li, Yong, and Evans, James (2024). "AI expands scientists' impact but contracts science's focus." https://www.researchgate.net/publication/386948824.

Harari, Yuval Noah (2024). *Nexus: A Brief History of Information Networks from the Stone Age to AI*. New York: Random House.

Harhoff, Dietmar, and Reitzig, Markus (2004). "Determinants of opposition against EPO patent grants: The case of biotechnology and pharmaceuticals." *International Journal of Industrial Organization*, 22(4): 443–480.

Harhoff, Dietmar, Scherer, Frederic M., and Vopel, Katrin (2003). "Citations, family size, opposition and the value of patent rights." *Research Policy*, 32(8): 1343–1363.

Harutyunyan, Ani, Chervenak, Matthew, Schankerman, Mark, Matcham, William, and Shrestha, Nishant (2024). *Patent Quality in the United States: Findings and Suggestions for Policymakers.* North Bethesda, MD: Sunwater Institute.

Hausman, Jerry, Hall, Bronwyn, and Griliches, Zvi (1984). "Econometric models for count data with an application to the patents R&D relationship." *Econometrica*, 52: 909–938. https://doi.org/10.2307/1911191.

Hegde, Deepak and Luo, Hong (2018). "Patent publication and the market for ideas." *Management Science* 64(2): 652–672.

Heller, Michael, and Eisenberg, Rebecca (1998). "Can patents deter innovation? The anticommons in biomedical research." *Science*, 280(5364): 698–701.

Helpman, Elhanan (1993). "Innovation, imitation, and intellectual property rights." *Econometrica*, 61(6): 1247–1280.

Henn, Christian, Papageorgiou, Chris, Romero, Jose Manuel, and Spatafora, Nikola (2020). "Export quality in advanced and developing economies: Evidence from a new data set." *IMF Economic Review*, vol. 68(2): 421–451.

Hill, Charles (2022). *International Business: Competing in the Global Marketplace*, 14th edition. New York: McGraw-Hill.

Horowitz, Andrew W., and Lai, Edwin (1996). "Patent length and the rate of innovation." *International Economic Review*, 37(4): 785–801.

Hu, Albert G. Z., and Png, Ivan (2013). "Patent rights and economic growth: Evidence from cross-country panels of manufacturing industries." *Oxford Economic Papers*, 65(3): 675–698.

Hudson, John and Minea, Alexandru (2013). "Innovation, intellectual property rights, and economic development: a unified empirical investigation." *World Development*, 46: 66–78.

Hughes, Ryan (2024). "Examining U.S. patent values: Renewal choices, citation dynamics, and economic growth." USPTO Economic Working Paper No. 2024-5. Available at SSRN: https://ssrn.com/abstract=5051327 or http://dx.doi.org/10.2139/ssrn.5051327.

Hui, Kai-Lung, and Png, Ivan (2003). "Piracy and the legitimate demand for recorded music." *Contributions to Economic Analysis & Policy*, 2(1), Article 11.

Igna, Ioana and Venturini, Francesco (2023). "The determinants of AI innovation across European firms." *Research Policy*, 52(2): 104661.

I-MAK (2022). *Overpatented, Overpriced: How Excessive Pharmaceutical Patenting is Extending Monopolies and Driving Up Drug Prices.* https://www.i-mak.org/wp-content/uploads/2018/08/I-MAK-Overpatented-Overpriced-Report.pdf.

International Trade Center (2009). *Guide to Geographical Indications.* Geneva, Switzerland. https://www.intracen.org/resources/publications/guide-to-geographical-indications-linking-products-and-their-origins.

International Energy Agency (IEA) (2021). *The Role of Critical Minerals in Clean Energy Transitions*, IEA Report, https://www.iea.org/reports/the-role-of-critical-minerals-in-clean-energy-transitions.

International Energy Agency (IEA) (2025). *Energy and AI.* https://www.iea.org/reports/energy-and-ai.

Isaac, Alan and Park, Walter (2009). "Open development: is the 'open source' analogy relevant to biotechnology?" In David Castle (ed.), *The Role of Intellectual Property Rights in Biotechnology Innovation.* Cheltenham: Edward Elgar Publishing, 225–251.

Ishack, Stephanie and Lipner, Shari (2021). "Use of 3D printing to support COVID-19 medical supply shortages: A review." *Journal of 3D Printing in Medicine*, 5(2): 83–95.

Ivan Png (2017). "Law and innovation: Evidence from state trade secrets laws." *Review of Economics and Statistics*, 99(1): 167–179.

Ivus, Olena (2010). "Do stronger patent rights raise high-tech exports to the developing world?" *Journal of International Economics*, 81(1): 38–47. https://doi.org/10.1016/j.jinteco.2009.12.002.

Ivus, Olena and Park, Walter (2022). "All rights reserved: copyright protection and multinational knowledge transfers." *Economic Inquiry*, 60(3): 1064–1091.

Ivus, Olena, Park, Walter, and Saggi, Kamal (2015). "Intellectual property protection and the industrial composition of multinational activity." *Economic Inquiry*, 54(2): 1068–1085. https://doi.org/10.1111/ecin.12314.

Ivus, Olena, Park, Walter, and Saggi, Kamal (2017). "Patent protection and the composition of multinational activity: evidence from U.S. multinational firms." *Journal of International Business Studies*, 48(7): 808–836.

Jaffe, Adam and Trajtenberg, Manual (2002). *Patents, Citations and Innovations: A Window on the Knowledge Economy.* Cambridge, MA: MIT Press.

Javorcik, Beata (2004). "The composition of foreign direct investment and protection of intellectual property rights: Evidence from transition economies." *European Economic Review*, 48: 39–62. https://doi.org/10. 1016/S0014-2921(02)00257-X.

Jensen, Oscar W. and Scheraga, Carl A. (1998). "Transferring technology: costs and benefits." *Technology in Society*, 20: 99–112. https://doi.org/10.1016/S0160-791X(97)00031-6.

Johnson, Steven (2010), *Where Good Ideas Come From: The Natural History of Innovations.* New York: Riverhead Books.

Jones, Charles and Vollrath, Dietrich (2024). *An Introduction to Economic Growth.* New York: W.W. Norton.

Kabore, François and Park, Walter (2019). "Can patent family size and composition signal patent value?" *Applied Economics*, 51(60): 6476–6496. https://doi.org/10.1080/00036846.2019.1624914.

Keller, Wolfgang (1998). "Are international R&D spillovers trade-related? Analyzing spillovers among randomly matched trade partners." *European Economic Review*, 42: 1469–1481.

Keller, Wolfgang (2002). "Geographic localization of international technology diffusion." *American Economic Review*, 92(1): 120–142.

Keller, Wolfgang (2022). "Knowledge spillovers, trade, and foreign direct investment." *Oxford Research Encyclopedias: Economics and Finance.* https://doi.org/10.1093/acrefore/9780190625979.013.705.

Kilic, Burcu (2014). *Boosting Pharmaceutical Innovation in the Post-TRIPS Era*. Cheltenham: Edward Elgar Publishing.

Kilic, Burcu (2024). "Beyond intellectual property: Lessons on local manufacturing, collaboration, and policy from the pandemic era." In Walter G. Park (ed.) *Handbook of Innovation and Intellectual Property Rights*. Cheltenham: Edward Elgar Publishing, 440–452.

Kilic, Burcu (2025). *AI, Innovation, and the Public Good: A New Policy Playbook*. Center for International Governance Innovation (CIGI) Paper No. 318.

Kim, Yee Kyoung, Lee, Keun, Park, Walter G., and Choo, Kineung (2012). "Appropriate intellectual property protection and economic growth in countries at different levels of development." *Research Policy*, 41(2): 358–375.

King, Jennifer and Meinhardt, Caroline (2024), "Rethinking privacy in the AI era: policy provocations for a data-centric world." Stanford Human-Centered Artificial Intelligence (HAI) Institute, White Paper. https://hai.stanford.edu/policy/white-paper-rethinking-privacy-ai-era-policy-provocations-data-centric-world.

Klein, Michael and Sener, Fuat (2024). "Schumpeterian growth theory and the patent puzzle." In Park, Walter (ed.), *Handbook of Innovation and Intellectual Property Rights: Evolving Scholarship and Reflections*. Cheltenham: Edward Elgar Publishing, 102–119.

Kogan, Lev, Papanikolaou, Dimitris, Seru, Amit and Stoffman, Noah (2017). "Technological innovation, resource allocation, and growth." *Quarterly Journal of Economics*, 132(2): 665–712.

Kohler, Jillian, Wong, Anna, and Tailor, Lauren (2022). "Improving access to COVID-19 vaccines: An analysis of TRIPS waiver discourse among WTO members, civil society organizations, and pharmaceutical industry stakeholders." *Health and Human Rights Journal*, 24(2): 159–175.

Korinek, Anton and Stiglitz, Joseph (2021). "Artificial intelligence, globalization, and strategies for economic development." National Bureau of Economic Research (NBER) Working Paper No. 28453.

Korinek, Anton and Vipra, Jai (2024). "Concentrating intelligence: Scaling and market structure in artificial intelligence." National Bureau of Economic Research (NBER) Working Paper No. 33139.

Kortum, Samuel and Lerner, Joshua (1999). "What is behind the recent surge in patenting?" *Research Policy*, 28(1): 1–22.

Kremer, Michael, Levin, Jonathan, and Snyder, and Christopher M. (2020). "Advance market commitments: Insights from theory and experience." *American Economic Association Papers and Proceedings*, 110: 269–273.

Kurzweil, Raymond. (2005). *The Singularity is Near: When Humans Transcend Biology*. New York: Viking Press.

Kyle, Margaret and McGahan, Anita (2012). "Investments in pharmaceuticals before and after TRIPS." *Review of Economics and Statistics*, 94(4): 1157–1172.

Lai, Edwin (1998). "International intellectual property rights protection and the rate of product innovation." *Journal of Development Economics*, 55(1): 133–153.

Lamoreaux, Naomi and Sokoloff, Kenneth (2003). "Intermediaries in the U.S. market for technology." In S. Engerman, P. Hoffman, J-L. Rosenthal, and K. Sokoloff (eds.), *Finance, Intermediaries, and Economic Development*. Cambridge, UK: Cambridge University Press: 209–246.

Landes, William M. and Posner, Richard A. (2003). *Economic Structure of Intellectual Property Law*. Cambridge, MA: Harvard University Press.

Lanjouw, Jean and Schankerman, Mark (2001). "The quality of patents: If and when firms do and do not renew patents." *RAND Journal of Economics*, 32(1): 30–55.

Lee, Jeong-Yeon and Mansfield, Edwin (1996). "Intellectual property protection and U.S. foreign direct investment." *Review of Economics and Statistics*, 78(2): 181–186.

Lee, Keun (2013). *Schumpeterian Analysis of Economic Catch-up*. Cambridge, UK: Cambridge University Press.

Levin, Richard C., Klevorick, Alvin K., Nelson, Richard R., Winter, Sidney G., Gilbert, Richard, and Griliches, Zvi (1987). "Appropriating the returns from industrial research and development." *Brookings Papers on Economic Activity*, 1987(3): 783–831. https://doi.org/10.2307/2534454.

Lexchin, Joel (2023). "Canada and the pharmaceutical industry in the time of COVID-19." *International Journal of Social Determinants of Health and Health Services*, 53(4): 508–517.

Liebowitz, Stan (1985). "Copying and indirect appropriability: Photocopying of journals." *Journal of Political Economy*, 93(5): 945–957.

Lietzan, Erika (2020). "The evergreening myth." *Regulation*, Washington, DC: Cato Institute. https://www.cato.org/sites/cato.org/files/2020-09/regulation-v43n3-4.pdf.

Lin, Jenny and Lincoln, William (2017). "Pirate's treasure." *Journal of International Economics*, 109(C): 235–245.

Lippoldt, Douglas and Schultz, Mark (2014). *Uncovering Trade Secrets — An Empirical Assessment of Economic Implications of Protection for Undisclosed Data*. OECD Trade Policy Papers, No. 167, OECD Publishing, Paris. http://dx.doi.org/10.1787/5jxzl5w3j3s6-en.

Liu, Zhaoming (2024). "Cultural bias in large language models: A comprehensive analysis and mitigation strategies." *Journal of Transcultural Communications*, 3(2): 1–21.

Liu, Ming and La Croix, Sumner (2015). "A cross-country index of intellectual property rights in pharmaceutical innovations." *Research Policy*, 44(1): 206–216.

Liu, Yan, Park, Walter, and Fu, Dahai (2021). "Export quality and patent protection: Stage-dependent effects in development." *Review of Development Economics*, 25(2): 601–629.

Longhitano, Guilherme A., Nunes, Guilherme B., Candido, Geovany, and Lopes da Silva, Jorge V. (2021). "The role of 3D printing during COVID-19 pandemic: A review." *Progress in Additive Manufacturing*, 6: 19–37.

Love, Brian, Richardson, Kent, Oliver, Erik, and Costa, Michael (2018). "An empirical look at the 'brokered' market for patents." *Missouri Law Review*, 83: 359–407.

Love, James (2023). "We need smart intellectual property laws for artificial intelligence." *Scientific American*, August. https://www.scientificamerican.com/article/we-need-smart-intellectual-property-laws-for-artificial-intelligence/.

Lowes, Sara, and Montero, Eduardo (2019). "Traditional medicine in central Africa." *American Economic Association Papers and Proceedings*, 109: 516–520. https://doi.org/10.1257/pandp.20191095.

Ma, Yueyuan (2025). "Specialization in a knowledge economy." SSRN Working Paper No. 4052990. Forthcoming in *Journal of Political Economy Macroeconomics*.

MacDonald, James, Dong, Xiao, and Fuglie, Keith (2023). *Concentration and Competition in the U.S. Agribusiness*. U.S. Department of Agriculture, Economic Research Service, EIB-245.

Mann, William (2018). "Creditor rights and innovation: Evidence from patent collateral." *Journal of Financial Economics*, 130: 25–47.

Mansfield, Edwin (1994). *Intellectual Property Protection, Foreign Direct Investment, and Technology Transfer*. International Finance Corporation Discussion Paper No. 19. Washington, DC: World Bank.

Maskus, Keith E. (2012). *Private Rights and Public Problems: The Global Economics of Intellectual Property in the 21st Century*. Peterson Institute for International Economics, Washington, D.C.

Maskus, Keith E. (2024). "Intellectual property rights and international trade: Recent evidence and directions for research." In Park, Walter (ed.), *Handbook of Innovation and Intellectual Property Rights: Evolving Scholarship and Reflections*. Cheltenham: Edward Elgar Publishing, 27–47.

Maskus, Keith E. and Penubarti, Mohan (1995). "How trade-related are intellectual property rights?" *Journal of International Economics*, 39: 227–248. https://doi.org/10.1016/0022-1996(95)01377-8.

Maslej, Nestor, Fattorini, Loredana, Perrault, Vanessa, Raymond, Parli, Reuel, Anka, Brynjolfsson, Erik, Etchemendy, John, Ligett, Katrina, Lyons, Terah, James, Manyika, Niebles, Juan Carlos, Shoham, Yoav, Wald, Russell, Clark, Jack (2024). *The 2024 AI Index Report*. Stanford University. https://hai.stanford.edu/ai-index/2024-ai-index-report.

Mayer, Thierry and Pfister, Etienne (2001). "Do stronger patent rights attract foreign direct investment? Evidence from French multinationals' location choices." *Région et Développement*.

Melitz, Marc J. and Trefler, Daniel (2012). "Gains from trade when firms matter." *Journal of Economic Perspectives*, 26(2): 91–118.

Menell, Peter, Lemley, Mark, Merges, Robert, and Balganesh, Shyamkrishna (2023). *Intellectual Property in the New Technological Age: 2023, Vol. 1: Perspectives, Trade Secrets, and Patents*. Berkeley, CA: Clause 8 Publishing.

Merges, Robert and Duffy, John F. (2017). *Patent Law and Policy: Cases and Materials*, 7th edition. Durham, NC: Carolina Academic Press.

Merges, Robert and Nelson, Richard R. (1990). "The complex economics of patent scope." *Columbia Law Review*, 90(4): 839–916.

Milani, Sahar and Neumann, Rebecca (2022). "R&D, patents, and financing constraints of the top global innovative firms." *Journal of Economic Behavior and Organization*, 196: 546–567.

Miller, Audrey (2023). *Navigating the AI Regulation Debate*. https://www.tapestry.vc/insights/navigating-the-ai-regulation-debate-incumbents-startups-and-investors.

Mittelstadt, Brent (2019). "Principles alone cannot guarantee ethical AI." *Nature Machine Intelligence*, 1: 501–507.

Moon, Suerie (2008). "Does TRIPS Art. 66.2 encourage technology transfer to LDCs? An analysis of country submissions to the TRIPS Council (1999–2007)." Policy Brief No. 2, *UNCTAD–ICTSD Project on IPRs and Sustainable Development*, Geneva: UNCTAD–ICTSD.

Morin, Jean Frédérick and Surbeck, Jenny (2020). "Mapping the new frontier of international IP law: Introducing a TRIPS-plus dataset." *World Trade Review*, 19: 109–122.

Mossoff, Adam (2024). *USPTO Confirms Unreliable Patent Numbers by I-MAK in Drug Pricing Debate.* Hudson Institute, Policy Memo. U.S. Patent and Trademark Office (2024), Drug Patent and Exclusivity Study. https://www.uspto.gov/initiatives/fda-collaboration/drug-patent-and-exclusivity-study-available.

Naghavi, Alireza, Spies, Julia, and Toubal, Farid (2015). "Intellectual property rights, technological complexity, and the organization of multinational firms." *Canadian Journal of Economics*, 48(3): 881–902. https://doi.org/10.1111/caje.12161.

Nelson, Richard, Cohen, Wesley M., and Walsh, John P. (2000). "Protecting their intellectual assets: Appropriability conditions and why U.S. manufacturing firms patent (or not)." *NBER Working Paper 7552.* https://doi.org/10.3386/w7552.

Nordhaus, William D. (2021). "Are we approaching an economic singularity? Information technology and the future of economic growth." *American Economic Journal: Macroeconomics*, 13(1): 299–332. https://doi.org/10.1257/mac.20170105.

Noy, Shakked and Zhang, Whitney (2023). "Experimental evidence on the productivity effect of generative artificial intelligence." *Science*, 381: 187–192.

Nunnenkamp, Peter and Spatz, Julius (2004). "Intellectual property rights and foreign direct investment: A disaggregated analysis." *Review of World Economics*, 140(3): 393–414. https://doi.org/10.1007/BF02665982.

Oberholzer-Gee, Felix and Strumpf, Koleman (2007). "The effect of file sharing on record sales: An empirical analysis." *Journal of Political Economy*, 115(1): 1–42.

O'Donoghue, Ted and Zweimüller, Josef (2004). "Patents in a model of endogenous growth." *Journal of Economic Growth*, 9(1): 81–123.

Open Future Foundation (2024). *Democratic Governance of AI Systems and Datasets.* Open Future Foundation. https://openfuture.eu/publication/democratic-governance-of-ai-systems-and-datasets/.

Organization for Economic Co-operation and Development (OECD) (2015). *Frascati Manual 2015: Guidelines for Collecting and Reporting Data on Research and Experimental Development.* Paris: OECD Publishing. http://dx.doi.org/10.1787/9789264239012-en.

Organization for Economic Co-operation and Development (OECD) (2018). *Concentration in Seed Markets: Potential Effects and Policy Responses.* Paris: OECD Publishing.

Organization for Economic Co-operation and Development (OECD) (2021). *AI and the Future of Skills, Volume 1: Capabilities and Assessments.* Paris: OECD Publishing.

Organization for Economic Co-operation and Development (OECD) (2024). *AI, Data Governance and Privacy: Synergies and Areas of International Cooperation.* OECD. https://www.oecd.org/en/publications/ai-data-governance-and-privacy_2476b1a4-en.html.

Our World in Data (various years), Global Change Data Lab, https://ourworldindata.org/.

Owoyemi, Ayomide, Owoyemi, Joshua, Osiyemi, Adenekan, and Boyd, Andy (2020). "Artificial intelligence for healthcare in Africa." *Frontiers in Digital Health*, 2(6): 1–5.

Oxfam (2007). "All costs, no benefits: How TRIPS-plus intellectual property rules in the US-Jordan Free Trade Agreement affect access to medicines." Oxfam Briefing Paper. Oxford: Oxfam International. https://s3.amazonaws.com/oxfam-us/www/static/oa3/files/Oxfam_US_Jordan_FTA_Briefing.pdf.

Papageorgiadis, Nikolas and Sharma, Abhijit (2016). "Intellectual property rights and innovation: a panel analysis." *Economic Letters*, 141: 70–72.

Papageorgiadis, Nikolaos and Sofka, Wolfgang (2020). "Patent enforcement across 51 countries — Patent Enforcement Index 1998–2017." *Journal of World Business*, 55: 101092.

Park, Walter (1995). "International R&D spillovers and OECD economic growth." *Economic Inquiry*, 33: 571–591.

Park, Walter (1997). "A note on innovation and patents: Intertemporal imitation-risk smoothing." *Economics Letters*, 54(2): 185–189.

Park, Walter G. (1998). "A theoretical model of government research and growth." *Journal of Economic Behavior and Organization*, 34(1): 51–67.

Park, Walter G. (2005). "Do intellectual property rights stimulate R&D and productivity growth? Evidence from cross-national and manufacturing industry data." In Putnam, Jon (ed.), *Intellectual Property Rights and Innovation in the Knowledge-Based Economy.* Ottawa: Industry Canada, 9-1–9-51.

Park, Walter G. (2008a). "International patent protection: 1960–2005." *Research Policy*, 37(4): 761–766.

Park, Walter G. (2008b). "Intellectual property rights and international innovation." In Maskus, Keith (ed.), *Frontiers of Economics and Globalization*, Vol. 1. Amsterdam: Elsevier Science, 289–327.

Park, Walter G. (2010). "On patenting costs." *The WIPO Journal: Analysis of Intellectual Property Issues*, 2(1): 38–48.

Park, Walter G. (2012). "North-South models of intellectual property rights: an empirical critique." *Review of World Economics*, 148(1): 151–180.

Park, Walter G. (2016). "Multinational investments, technology transfers, and copyright protection." Conference Presentation, Western Economic Association, Lipsey Panel, Portland, Oregon.

Park, Walter G. (2017). "Averting a 'TRIPSxit' from the global intellectual property system." *George Mason Law Review*, 24(4), 883–906.

Park, Walter G. (2024) (ed.), *Handbook of Innovation and Intellectual Property Rights: Evolving Scholarship and Reflections.* Cheltenham: Edward Elgar Publishing.

Park, Walter G. and Brat, David (1996). "Cross-country R&D and growth: Variations on a theme of Mankiw-Romer-Weil." *Eastern Economic Journal*, 22(3): 345–354.

Park, Walter G. and Ginarte, Juan Carlos (1997). "Determinants of patent rights: A cross-national study." *Research Policy*, 26(3): 283–301. https://doi.org/10.1016/S0048-7333(97)00022-X.

Park, Walter G. and Lippoldt, Douglas C. (2005). "International licensing and the strengthening of intellectual property rights in developing countries during the 1990s." *OECD Economic Studies*, 40: 7–48. https://doi.org/10.1787/eco_studies-v2005-art2-en.

Park, Walter G., Torres, Gerard, Toole, Andrew A., and Hughes, Ryan (2025). "Real options in patenting: uncertainty and secondary patent markets." USPTO Economic Working Paper No. 2025-2. https://ssrn.com/abstract=5143769.

Parker, John E. S. (1974). *The Economics of Innovation: The National and Multinational Enterprise in Technological Change*, 2nd ed. New York: Longman.

Plotkin, Stanley, Robinson, James, Cunningham, Gerard, Iqbal, Robyn, and Larsen, Shannon (2017). "The complexity and cost of vaccine manufacturing — An overview." *Vaccine*, 35: 4064–4071.

Prud'homme, Dan (2017). "Utility model patent regime 'strength' and technological development: Experiences of China and other East Asian latecomers." *China Economic Review*, 42: 50–73.

Prud'homme, Dan, Campi, Mercedes, Dueñas, Marco, and Park, Walter (2022). "Institutional supra-nationalization and MNE's cross-border IPR strategies: Evidence from the Community Plant Variety Office." Paper presented at the Academy of International Business NE Conference, October 2022, Washington, D.C.

Qian, Yi (2007). "Do national patent laws stimulate domestic innovation in a global patenting environment? A cross-country analysis of pharmaceutical patent protection, 1978–2002." *Review of Economics and Statistics*, 89(3): 436–453.

Rai, Arti Kaur (2019). "Machine learning at the patent office: Lessons for patents and administrative law." *Iowa Law Review*, 104: 2617.

Rapp, Richard T. and Rozek, Richard P. (1990). "Benefits and costs of intellectual property protection in developing countries." *Journal of World Trade*, 24(5): 75–102.

de Rassenfosse, Gaétan, Jaffe, Adam, and Wasserman, Melissa (2023). "AI-generated inventions: Implications for the patent system." *Southern California Law Review*, 96(6): 101–126.

de Rassenfosse, Gaétan and Palangkaraya, Alfons (2023). "Do patent pledges accelerate innovation?" *Research Policy*, 52: 104745.

Reynolds, Taylor William (2003). *Quantifying the Evolution of Copyright and Trademark Law*. PhD thesis. Washington, DC: American University.

Ridley, Matt (2010). *Rational Optimist: How Prosperity Evolves*. New York: Harper Perennial.

Rob, Rafael and Waldfogel, Joel (2006). "Piracy on the high C's: Music downloading, sales displacement, and social welfare in a sample of college students." *Journal of Law and Economics*, 49(1): 29–62. https://doi.org/10.1086/430809.

Rodrik, Dani (2000). "Institutions for high-quality growth: What they are and how to acquire them." *Studies in Comparative International Development*, 35(3): 3–31.

Romer, Paul M. (1990). "Endogenous technological change." *Journal of Political Economy*, 98(5, Part 2): S71–S102. https://doi.org/10.1086/261725.

Russell, Stuart and Norvig, Peter (2021). *Artificial Intelligence: A Modern Approach.* 4th ed., Hoboken, NJ: Pearson.

Saggi, Kamal (2016). "Trade, intellectual property rights, and the World Trade Organization." In Bagwell, K. and Staiger, R. (eds.), *Handbook of Commercial Policy*, 1B, North-Holland: 433–512.

Saggi, Kamal (2024). "Compulsory licensing under the multilateral system." In Park, Walter (ed.), *Handbook of Innovation and Intellectual Property Rights: Evolving Scholarship and Reflections.* Cheltenham: Edward Elgar Publishing, 80–100.

Saint-Paul, Gilles (2003). "Growth effects of nonproprietary innovation." *Journal of the European Economic Association*, 1: 429–439.

Santacreu, Ana Maria (2023). "International technology licensing, intellectual property rights, and tax havens." *Review of Economics and Statistics*, https://doi.org/10.1162/rest_a_01382.

Santacreu, Ana Maria (2025). "Dynamic gains from trade agreements with intellectual property provisions." *Journal of Political Economy*, 133(4): 1133–1168.

Schankerman, Mark and Pakes, Ariel (1986). "Estimates of the value of patent rights in European countries during the post-1950 period." *Economic Journal*, 96(384): 1052–1077.

Schultz, Mark F. (2024). "Trade secrecy, knowledge sharing, and cooperation: The case of developing and manufacturing COVID-19 treatments." In Park, Walter (ed.), *Handbook of Innovation and Intellectual Property Rights: Evolving Scholarship and Reflections.* Cheltenham: Edward Elgar Publishing, 248–269.

Schultz, Mark F. and McDole, Jaci (2020). *Essential Medicines AND Patents: Recent Trend in the Latest Editions of the World Health Organization Essential Medicines List.* Switzerland: Geneva Network.

Schumpeter, Joseph (1942). *Capitalism, Socialism, and Democracy.* New York: Harper and Brothers.

Science for Africa Foundation (2025). *Governance of Artificial Intelligence for Global Health in Africa: A Review of Policy and Regulatory Frameworks.* https://scienceforafrica.foundation.

Scotchmer, Suzanne (2004). *Innovation and Incentives.* Cambridge: MIT Press.

Serrano, Carlos (2018). "Estimating the gains from trade in the market for patent rights." *International Economic Review*, 59(4): 1877–1904.

Shapiro, Carl and Varian, Hal (1999). *Information Rules: A Strategic Guide to the Network Economy.* Cambridge, MA: Harvard Business School Press.

Sharma, Ruchi (2015). "Influence of patent policy in the South on the research and development of the North: Exploration of the foreign direct investment channel." *Journal of World Intellectual Property*, 18(1–2): 29–40. https://doi.org/10.1111/jwip.12029.

Shemtov, Noam, Gabison, Garry A., and Abbott, Ryan (2022). "The inventive step requirement and the rise of the AI machines." In *Research Handbook on Intellectual Property and Artificial Intelligence.* Cheltenham: Edward Elgar Publishing, 423–442. https://doi.org/10.4337/9781800881907.00031.

Sherwood, Robert M. (1997). "Intellectual property systems and investment stimulation: The rating of systems in eighteen developing countries." *IDEA: The Journal of Law and Technology*, 37(2): 261–370.

Signé, Landry. "Leveraging AI and emerging technologies to unlock Africa's potential." In *Foresight Africa: Top Priorities for the Continent 2025–2030*. Africa Growth Initiative, Brookings Institution, Washington, DC: 138–167.

Silva, João S. and Tenreyro, Silvana (2006). "The log of gravity." *Review of Economics and Statistics*, 88(4): 641–658.

Silva, Larissa Marioni da, Rincon-Aznar, Ana, Venturini, Francesco (2024). "Productivity performance, distance to frontier and AI innovation: Firm-level evidence from Europe. *Journal of Economic Behavior and Organization*, 228: 106762.

Smith, Pamela J. (1999). "Are weak patent rights a barrier to U.S. exports?" *Journal of International Economics*, 48(1): 151–177. https://doi.org/10.1016/S0022-1996(98)00013-0.

Smith, Pamela J., Da'ar, Omar, Monroe, Kevin, Nunez, Fabricio, and Tuttle, Charlotte (2009). "How do copyrights affect economic development and international trade?" *Journal of World Intellectual Property*, 12(3): 198–218. https://doi.org/10.1111/j.1747-1796.2009.00360.x.

Smith, Pamela J. (2024). "Intellectual property protections of genetically modified organisms: Implications for technology transfers." In Park, Walter (ed.), *Handbook of Innovation and Intellectual Property Rights: Evolving Scholarship and Reflections*. Cheltenham: Edward Elgar Publishing, 342–373.

Solow, Robert M. (1956). "A contribution to the theory of economic growth." *The Quarterly Journal of Economics*, 70(1): 65–94. https://doi.org/10.2307/1884513.

Solow, Robert M. (1957). "Technical change and the aggregate production function." *Review of Economics and Statistics*, 39(3): 312–320. https://doi.org/10.2307/1926047.

Solow, Robert M. (1987). "We'd Better Watch Out," *New York Times Book Review*, July 12, p. 36.

Spulber, Daniel (2021). *The Case for Patents*. Singapore: World Scientific Publishing Co.

Stiglitz, Joseph E. (2008). "Economic foundations of intellectual property rights." *Duke Law Journal*, 57(6): 1693–1724.

Stitzing, Robin, Sääskilahti, Pekka, Royer, Jimmy, and Van Audenrode, Marc (2018). "Over-declaration of standard essential patents and the determinants of essentiality." https://ssrn.com/abstract=2951617.

Sun, Ruiqi and Trefler, Daniel (2023). "The impact of AI and cross-border data regulation on international trade in digital services: A large language model." National Bureau of Economic Research (NBER) Working Paper No. 31925.

Swann, Peter G. M. (2009). *Economics of Innovation*. Cheltenham: Edward Elgar Publishing.

Sweet, Cassandra M. and Eterovic, Dalibor (2019). "Do patent rights matter? 40 years of innovation, complexity, and productivity." *World Development*, 115: 78–93.

Sweet, Cassandra and Maggio, Dalibor (2015). "Do stronger intellectual property rights increase innovation?" *World Development*, 66(C): 665–677.

Telang, Rahul and Waldfogel, Joel (2018). "Piracy and new product creation: A Bollywood story." *Information Economics and Policy*, 43: 1–11. https://doi.org/10.1016/j.infoecopol.2018.03.002.

Thoma, Grid (2024). "Market valuation of international patenting using a real option approach: The moderating role of uncertainty." *Economics of Innovation and New Technology*, 1–22.

Thrasher, Rachel, Kaplan, Warren, Wirtz, Veronika J., Clear, Louise, Bodduluri, Shiva Priya, and Polaski, Sandra (2023). "Policy responses to COVID-19: Lessons for the global trade and investment regime." *Globalization and Health*, 19:66. https://doi.org/10.1186/s12992-023-00961-6.

Tong, Xuesong and Frame, J. Davidson (1994). "Measuring national technological performance with patent claims data." *Research Policy*, 23: 133–141.

Tørsløv, Thomas, Wier, Ludvig, Zucman, Gabriel (2023). "The missing profits of nations." *Review of Economics and Statistics*, 90(3): 1499–1534.

Trefler, Daniel and Sun, Ruiqi (2022). "AI, trade and creative destruction: A first look." National Bureau of Economic Research (NBER) Working Paper No. 29980.

Tucker, Catherine (2019). "Privacy, algorithms, and artificial intelligence." In Agrawal, Ajay, Gans, Joshua, and Goldfarb, Avi (eds.), *The Economics of Artificial Intelligence: An Agenda.* Chicago, IL: University of Chicago Press, 423–437.

U.S. Copyright Office (2024). *Copyright and Artificial Intelligence, Part 1: Digital Replicas.* Washington, D.C.

U.S. Copyright Office (2024). *Copyright and Artificial Intelligence, Part 2: Copyrightability.* Washington, D.C.

U.S. Copyright Office (2025). *Copyright and Artificial Intelligence, Part 3: Generative AI Training.* Washington, D.C.

U.K. Department of Digital, Culture, Media, and Sport (2016). *Creative Industries Economic Estimates.* https://www.gov.uk/government/statistics/creative-industries-economic-estimates-january-2016.

U.S. Department of Commerce (2013). *Copyright Policy, Creativity, and Innovation in the Digital Economy.* Internet Policy Task Force, Green Paper.

U.S. International Trade Commission (2016). *Trans-Pacific Partnership Agreement: Likely impact on the U.S. economy and on specific industry sectors.* Publication No. 4607, Washington, DC. https://www.usitc.gov/publications/332/pub4607.pdf.

U.S. International Trade Commission (2023). *COVID-19 Diagnostics and Therapeutics: Supply, Demand, and TRIPS Agreement Flexibilities.* Publication No. 5469, Washington, DC.

U.S. Patent and Trademark Office, Office of the Chief Economist (2020). "Inventing AI: Tracing the diffusion of artificial intelligence with U.S. patents." *IP Data Highlights*, 5: 1–17.

U.S. Patent and Trademark Office (2012). *Intellectual Property and the U.S. Economy: Industries in Focus.* Washington, D.C.: U.S. Department of Commerce.

van Marrewijk, Charles and Brakman, Steven (2023). *The Economics of Developing and Emerging Markets.* Cambridge, UK: Cambridge University Press.

Victor, Audêncio (2025). "Artificial intelligence in global health: An unfair future for health in Sub-Saharan Africa." *Health Affairs Scholar*, 3(2): 1–4.

Vogel, David (1995). *Trading Up: Consumer and Environmental Regulation in a Global Economy.* Cambridge, MA: Harvard University Press.

Wibulpolprasert, Suwit, Chokevivat, Vichai, Oh, Cecilia, and Yamabhai, Inthira (2011). "Government use licenses in Thailand: The power of evidence, civil movement and political leadership." *Globalization and Health.* 7(32): 1–8.

World Intellectual Property Office (WIPO) (2015). *Guide on Surveying the Economic Contribution of the Copyright Industries.* 2nd ed., Geneva, Switzerland.

World Intellectual Property Office (WIPO) (2021). *The Economic Contribution of the Copyright Industries: An Overview of the Results from WIPO Studies Assessing the Economic Contribution of the Copyright Industries.* Geneva, Switzerland.

World Intellectual Property Office (2023). *World Intellectual Property Indicators.* Geneva, Switzerland.

World Trade Organization (WTO) (2024). *Trading with Intelligence,* Geneva, Switzerland. https://www.wto.org/english/res_e/booksp_e/trading_with_intelligence_e.pdf.

Würtenberger, Gert, Ekvad, Martin, van der Kooij, Paul, and Kiewiet, Bart (2021). *European Union Plant Variety Protection.* Oxford, UK: Oxford University Press.

Yang, Guifang and Maskus, Keith E. (2001). "Intellectual property rights and licensing: An econometric investigation." *Review of World Economics*, 137(1): 58–79. https://doi.org/10.1007/BF02707600.

Yudkowsky, Eliezer. (2008). "Artificial intelligence as a positive and negative factor in global risk." In Bostrom, Nick and Ćirković, Milan M. (eds.), *Global Catastrophic Risks.* Oxford: Oxford University Press, pp. 308–345.

Zentner, Alejandro (2006). "Measuring the effect of file sharing on music purchases." *Journal of Law and Economics*, 49(1): 63–90.

Zentner, Alejandro (2010). "Measuring the impact of file sharing on the movie industry: an empirical analysis using a panel of countries." https://ssrn.com/abstract=1792615.

Index

A

Abel, A., 372
Aboy, M., 421–423
absorptive capacity, 109, 466, 500
academic publishing, 259
Acemoglu, D., 496
Acri, K., 266, 284
adaptation costs, 220
adequate remuneration, 277, 279
affiliate licensing, 209
Agentic AI, 510
Aghion, P., 108, 479
Agrawal, A., 435
agricultural innovations, 303, 314
AI Act, European Union, 416
AI
  as inventor, 405
  deployment, 443
  innovation, 435
  publications, 386
  readiness, 452
  safety, 440
  system, 406
  tools, 409–411, 443, 449, 515
AI training datasets, 402, 421, 459
AI-generated works, 395, 398
AIA, America Invents Act, 24
AIPO, African Intellectual Property Organization, 45
Akcigit, U., 368, 496
Allen, R., 332
Allred, B., 165
Amazon, 9
Anandkumar, A., 437
anti-commons, 29
Apple, 342
Apple iPhone, 5, 11
application programming interfaces, 424
appropriability, 91, 190, 289, 406
appropriate design of IP, 477

appropriately designed IPR systems, 500
Arai, Y., 256
ARIPO, African Regional Intellectual Property Organization, 45
arm's-length licensing, 207
Arora, A., 297, 368
Arrow, K., 112, 127
artificial general intelligence, 412
artificial intelligence, 389
artificial neural network, 422
Authors Guild v. Google, 256
automation, 453

B

Baker, D., 499
Baskin-Robbins, 9
Bass, M., 233
Bavarian Motor Works (BMW), 9
Beall, R., 280
Bell, Alexander Graham, 6
Berger, R., 30
Bergstrom, T., 262
Berne Convention, 16
best-response functions, 178
Biden, Joseph, 46th U.S. President, 293
Biega, A., 419
Bilir, K., 198, 213
Biolyse Pharma, 292, 502
biosimilars, 266
biotechnology sector, 303
BitTorrent, 245
Blue Mountain Coffee, 12
Bolar exemption, 499
Bollywood, 247
Bond, E., 278, 281
Bordeaux wine, 12
Boston Consulting Group, 450
Bostrom, N., 456
brand name, 117, 120
Branstetter, 200
Breeders' exemption, 307
Briggs, K., 172
Brynjolfsson, E., 444
Bt cotton, 310
Buccafusco, 399
Budapest Treaty, 423
Buffington, C., 364
Bulan, L., 379
burden of proof reversals, 28
business cycles, 83
Business Software Alliance, 238

C

call option, 372, 377
Campi, M., 305, 313, 316
capacity building, 457, 476, 508, 515
Cardoso, V., 13
Central Processing Unit (CPU), 426
certification marks, 54
Chang, H., 465
ChatGPT, 449
Chaudhuri, S., 297
Chen, W., 56
Chen, Y., 168, 487
Chesbrough, H., 333
Chin, J., 152
Cho, K., 496
Chu, A., 176, 487

Cincera, M., 108
Cirera, X., 508
climate change, 513
clinical trials, 266
Clinton Foundation, 269
closeness-to-frontier, 491–492
club good, 337
CNIPA, National Intellectual Property Administration of the People's Republic of China, 148
Co, C., 196
Coca-Cola, 10
Cockburn, I., 297, 432
Coe, D., 105, 108
Cohen, W., 480
collective invention, 332, 497
collective licensing, 402
collective marks, 54
commercialization, 130, 501
Community Plant Variety Office (CPVO), 310
comparative advantage, 460
competition policy, 514
competitive economy, 120
complementary industries, 217, 224, 230, 237
compulsory licensing, 277, 279, 281, 292, 466
compute resources, 432, 459
consumer surplus, 111, 122–123, 177, 462
Contreras, J., 503
contributory infringement, 28
cooperative patent classification system, 367, 441
copyright registrations, 48
copyrights, 7
  creative commons, 16, 239
  creative expression, 398
  creative works, 216, 237
core copyright industries, 216, 238
Corrado, C., 444
COVAX initiative, 503
COVID-19, 27, 292–293, 476, 501
Craig, C., 396, 399
creative destruction, 96
CRISPR, 12
cross-border data flows, 439
cross-licensing, 344
Cui, C., 437
Czarnitzki, D., 378, 445

D

3D printing, 505, 514
DABUS (Device for the Autonomous Bootstrapping of Unified Sentience), 405
Dagen H, 350
Danaher, B., 244–245
Darjeeling tea, 12
Darwin, Charles, 240
data
  centers, 471–472
  ownership, 403
  privacy, 413, 439
Davis, J., 364
Dawkins, R., 335
de Rassenfosse, G., 410, 504
De Vany, A., 220
deadweight loss, 125–126, 148–149, 177
Deardorff, A., 163

deep learning, 410, 424
DeepMind, 436
defensive patenting, 345
Dell'Acqua, F., 450
Demirer, M., 416
derivative (calculus), 70
derivative works, 408
Dhanora, M., 296
difference-in-differences, 78
differentiated IP regime, 496
digital learning platforms, 454
digital services trade, 440
digital services trade restrictiveness index, 442
Dinlersoz, E., 364
disclosure, 404, 411, 420
discovery, 29
discrete product industries, 203
distance-to-frontier, 447
distinctiveness, 11
Distinctness, Uniformity, and Stability (DUS), 307
Diwan, I., 162
Dixit, A., 371
doctrine of equivalents, 28, 289, 489
Doha Declaration, 268, 278
dominant firm model, 219
dot-com crash, 364
Double Irish with a Dutch Sandwich, 234
downstream commercialization, 407
Duggan, M., 297
Dunning, J., 192
duration of protection, 132
dynamic efficiency, 241
dynamic incentives, 477

E

economic
  catch-up, 478, 497
  growth, 1, 83, 85, 475
  rents, 398, 509
Economist Intelligence Unit, 50
Eisenberg, R., 29, 335
elasticity of substitution, 417, 454
embedding, 425
enablement requirement, 420, 467
Endogenous Growth Theory, 86
entry barriers, 403
entry costs, 220, 225
European Patent Office (EPO), 24, 141, 148, 422
essential facility, 459
essential medicine, 295
Eswaran, M., 137
Eterovic, D., 173
European Union, 194, 310, 440
Evenson, R., 186
evergreening, 283
exhaustion, 269, 282, 321
expandability option, 372
exporting, 207
extensive margin, 225
externalities, 88, 95
Ezrachi, A., 390

F

fair use, 240, 395
Fair, reasonable, and non-discriminatory (FRAND) licensing terms, 353, 355, 362
Falvey, R., 168
farmer's privilege, 307

FDI, foreign direct investment, 67, 158, 194, 197, 207, 228, 438
federated learning, 419
FEDEX, 9
Feinberg, R., 219
Fenshui, town in Zhejiang Province, China, 487
Ferranna, M., 501
Finck, M., 419
first sale doctrine, 252, 269
first-order condition, 72
flexibilities, 459, 476, 499, 515
format-shifting, 251
foundation models, 387, 424, 459
four-firm concentration ratio, 325
Frame, J. D., 143
Free and Open Source Software (FOSS) movement, 335
free-rider, 154
free-riding, 101, 115, 179, 183
Frey, C., 417–418

G

Galasso, 481
Galetovic, A., 356, 360
Gallini, N., 135, 137
Gans, J., 470
gender equity, 513
General Data Protection Regulation (GDPR), 415, 417–418, 515
general equilibrium, 156
general-purpose technology, 434, 438, 445, 510
generic, 8, 266
generic competition, 283, 290
genetically modified organisms (GMO), 317
geographical indications, 12
germplasm, 331
Gertner, J., 6
Ghafele, R., 257
Giczy, A., 392
Gilbert, B., 257
Ginarte, J., 51
Gini Index of Income Equality, 61
Giorcelli, M., 247
Glass, A., 161
Gleeson, D., 501
global financial crisis, 364
Global Intellectual Property Center (GIPC), 57–58, 258
global pandemic treaty, 506
Globig, L., 464
Goldfarb, A., 416
Gopinath, G., 433
Gordon, R., 444
GP Index, Ginarte and Park index, 166, 169, 173, 175, 479, 491
Graphics Processing Units (GPU), 391, 426
Green AI, 473
Griliches, Z., 432
Grossman, G., 152, 157, 177, 275
Gruère, G., 310
Guellec, D., 24
Gupta, K., 360

H

Hall, B., 149, 345, 354
Hao, Q., 448
Harhoff, D., 141, 143
harmonization, 177
Harris, Kamala, 49th U.S. Vice President, 293

Harutyunyan, A., 147
Hassabis hypothesis, 436
Heller, M., 29, 335
Helmers, C., 149, 354
Helpman, E., 105, 157, 159
Henn, C., 491
Herfindahl-Hirschman Index, 325, 379
Hermes, Birkin bag, 11
Hill, C., 202
HIV/AIDS crisis, 267
Honeycrisp Apple, 12
Hu, A., 176
Hudson, J., 169
Hughes, R., 141, 143–145

I

IAM, 140
Igna, I., 434
imitation, 130, 135, 478, 496
imitation risk, 94, 193, 205–206
imitative capacity, 134
inclusive growth policies, 464
independent invention, 407
index of plant variety protection, 313, 316
index of secondary patent market exposure, 369, 378
indirect appropriability, 243
industrial designs, 11
innovative capacity, 134
Institute for Management Development, 50
intellectual property rights (IPRs), 2
intensive margin, 225
internalization, 202
International Business Machines, (IBM), 333
International Intellectual Property Alliance, 238
International Monetary Fund, (IMF), 298
international price discrimination, 270, 281
international R&D spillovers, 103
international technology transfer, 215, 437
International Trade Center, Geneva, 13
International Union for the Protection of New Varieties of Plants (UPOV), 305
interoperability, 350, 356
inventive step, 26, 404, 408, 410
inverted-U relationship, 133–134, 165
Isaac, A., 336
Ishack, S., 505
isoquant, 453
iTunes, 243
Ivus, O., 196, 202, 217

J

J-curve effect, 444
Jaffe, A., 140
Japanese Patent Office (JPO), 45, 148
Jaravel, X., 108
Javorcik, B., 198
Jensen, O., 220
Jepsen, Carly Rae, 5
Johnson, S., 333
Jones, C., 13
Jumper, J., 436

K

Kabore, F., 141
Keller, W., 106, 109
Kilic, B., 284, 292, 439, 501
Kim, Y., 188, 486
King, J., 413
Kinukawa, S., 256
Korean Intellectual Property Office (KIPO), 148
Kirtsaeng v. John Wiley & Sons, 263
Klein, M., 10
knowledge capital, 14
knowledge production function, 86, 102
knowledge spillovers, 97–98, 193, 339, 475
Kogan, L., 143
Kohler, J., 501
Korinek, A., 460, 463, 466, 470
Kortum, S., 172
Kuhn, R., 280
Kula, spiritual healer, 301
Kurzweil, R., 456
Kyle, M., 296

L

La Croix, S., 52
Lai, E., 160, 177, 275
Lamoreaux, N., 368
Landes, W., 219
Lanjouw, J., 141
large language model (LLM), 388, 395, 412, 424
Lee, J., 197
Lee, K., 188
Leibniz, Gottfried, 240
Lerner, J., 172
Lexchin, J., 502
licensing, 158, 162, 194, 199, 331
  affiliated, 199–200
  unaffiliated, 199–200
Lietzan, E., 287
limitations and exceptions (L&E), 54, 237, 251, 254
Lin, J., 197
Lincoln, W., 197
Linux operating system, 334
Lipitor, 6
Lipner, S., 505
Lippoldt, D., 10, 200
Lisbon Council, 257
litigation costs, 32
Liu, M., 52
Liu, Y., 486, 491
Liu, Z., 464
logic of IP protection, 116
logos, 8
Longhitano, G., 505
Love, B., 368
Love, J., 415
Lowes, S., 298

M

Ma, Y., 368
machine learning, 387, 401, 424, 446
MAD magazine, 255
Maggio, D., 172
maintenance fees, 146, 341
Maloney, W., 508
Mansfield, E., 50, 197
marginal
  cost, 124–125
  revenue, 123–125
  utility, 462
market
  capitalization, 90, 389

concentration, 323, 327, 390
power, 390
size, 180
market-expansion effect, 195
market-power effect, 195
Maskus, K., 161, 195, 199, 349
Maslej, N., 437
Mattel, Hot Wheels, 11
Mayer, T., 197
McDole, J., 267
McDonald's, 117
McGahan, A., 296
Medicines and Related Substances Control Amendment Act, 267
Meinhardt, C., 413
Melitz, M., 483
mergers and acquisitions, 323, 470
Miller, A., 391
Minea, A., 169
minimum standards, 499
mobile app industry, 441
monopolistically competitive, 118
monopoly, 7, 117, 120
Monsanto, 12
Montero, E., 298
moral rights, 7
Morin, J., 19
Moser, P., 247
Mossoff, A., 287
multi-factor productivity, 447

N

Napoleon, 249
Napster, 244, 261
neglected tropical diseases (NTDs), 149, 290, 478
neighboring rights, 7
network effects, 347, 461, 469
neural network, 388
new plant variety, 305
Newton, Isaac, 240
Nexavar, 282
Nojima Co., 9
non-excludable, 241
non-obviousness, 408
non-resident filings, 42, 309
non-rival, 241
Nordhaus, W., 454
normative neutrality, 397
North–South, 63
gaps, 456
models, 157, 162
development gaps, 431
Noy, S., 449
National Science Foundation (NSF), 40
Nunnenkamp, P., 197
Nuvolari, A., 313
NVIDIA, 390, 469

O

Oberholzer, F., 244
obviousness, 407
Ocean Tomo, 140
Organization for Economic Cooperation and Development (OECD), 36, 236, 326
official fees, 31
open biotechnology, 336
open innovation, 331–332, 460
open source, 332, 460, 514
open-access journals, 260

original work, 239
overlapping patent claims, 344
Ownership, Location, and Internalization (OLI) framework, 192

P

Palangkaraya, A., 504
Panel Threshold Regression, 169
Papageorgiadis, N., 60, 169
parallel imports, 269, 275
Pareto improvement, 464
Paris Convention, 16, 25, 142
Park, W., 51, 107, 163, 200, 217, 372
Parker, J., 135
Parmesan Cheese, 12
partial equilibrium, 152
patent
  application, 23
  blocking, 481
  breadth, 132–133
  claim, 43, 138, 147
  enforcement, 22, 322
  family size, 142–143
  holdout, 354
  holdup, 354
  pledges, 503
  pools, 354, 408, 500, 503
  quality, 139, 146
  races, 131
  thickets, 285, 342
  trolls, 466
  value, 139
Patent Cooperation Treaty (PCT), 17, 24, 45
Patent Law Treaty, 17
Patent Rights Index (PRI), 53, 58, 166, 169
patentability, 25, 138
path dependence, 347
Pathogen Access and Benefit-Sharing (PABS), 507
Paywall, 261, 264
Penubarti, M., 195
person having ordinary skill in the art (PHOSITA), 408, 421
Pfister, E., 197
Pfizer, 6
pharmaceutical innovations, 175
pharmaceutical sector, 265
Pindyck, R., 371
piracy, 237, 242, 496
Plant Breeder's Rights, 11, 306, 336
plant variety protection, 11
Png, I., 10, 176
positive feedback, 347
Posner, R., 219
preliminary injunctions, 28
present discounted value, 89
price controls, 275
prior art, 138, 345, 409
priority, 24
priority patent, 142
privacy controls, 416
prize system, 150
procedural laws, 49
process innovation, 137
product
  complexity, 205
  cycles, 151, 213
  differentiation, 117
  innovation, 137
production
  function, 85, 433, 445

possibilities frontier, 82, 84
shifting effect, 160
profit-shifting, 232
proprietary innovation, 338
Prud'homme, D., 189
public
domain, 8, 111
good, 111–112
health, 265
put option, 372, 377
Puttitanun, T., 168, 487

Q

Qian, Y., 174
quality jump, 488
quality upgrading, 486
quality-adjusted prices, 357

R

Research and Development (R&D), 35, 37, 87, 98, 263
R&D spillovers, 100, 105
Rai, A., 410
Ramsey pricing, 271
Rapp and Rozek index, 51
real options theory, 342, 371
regression analyses, 73
Reitzig, M., 143
renewal fees, 8, 27, 31
research and development, 35, 151
resident filings, 42, 308
resident patenting, 167
reverse causality, 478
reverse engineering, 406, 478, 496
reversibility option, 372
Reynolds, T., 56
Ridley, M., 333
Ritz-Carlton, 117
Rob, R., 244
Rodrik, D., 162
Romer, P., 114
Roundup Ready Soybeans, 12, 309
Rousslang, D., 219
royalty, 128
royalty stacking, 342, 354, 360

S

Saggi, K., 161, 195, 278, 281
Saint-Paul, G., 338
sampling, 243
Samsung, 342
Santacreu, A., 200, 236
Schankerman, M., 141, 481
Scheraga, C., 220
Schultz, M., 10, 267
Schumpeter, J., 112, 126, 487
Schumpeterian hypothesis, 127
Sci-Hub, 261
search process, 435
second-order condition, 72
secondary patent markets, 342, 363, 367
semiconductor foundries, 427
semiconductor industry, 346
Sener, F., 10
Sengupta, D., 310
Serrano, C., 368
Shapiro, C., 471
Sharma, A., 169
Sharma, R., 164
Sherwood, R., 50
short-cycle industries, 188

Signé, L., 511
significance levels, 76
Silva, J., 447
Single Nucleotide Polymorphisms (SNP) Consortium, 337
singularity, 454
Smith, P., 196, 320
social welfare, 131, 178
Sofka, W., 60
Sokoloff, K., 368
Solow, Robert, 86, 240, 444
Sony Ltd., 9
Sony PlayStation, 11
South Korea, 184
Spatz, J., 197
Spulber, D., 149
stability, 11
stage-dependence hypothesis, 476, 486
standard essential patents, 343, 357
Standard Setting Organizations (SSO), 350
standard-setting organizations, 352, 362
static inefficiency, 241
Stiglitz, J., 460, 463, 466
Stop Online Piracy Act (SOPA), 252
Strumpf, K., 244
Stucke, M., 390
Sun, R., 440, 442
Sunwater Institute, 147
supply chain, 414, 471, 488
supranational institutions, 313
Surbeck, J., 19
Swan, Trevor, 240
Swann, P., 356
Sweet, C., 172
synthetic data, 419

T

tacit knowledge, 496
Taiwan Semiconductor Manufacturing Company (TSMC), 469
tax haven, 232
technological
  balance of payments, 235, 458
  complexity, 212
  Ladder, 465
  similarity, 107
technology transfer, 191
Telang, R., 247
Tensor Processing Units (TPU), 391, 426
terms of trade, 461
Tesla Cybertruck, 11
test data exclusivity, 283, 288, 467
text and data mining (TDM), 252, 395
TFP, Total Factor Productivity, 105, 444, 454
third-degree price discrimination, 272
Thrasher, R., 502
three-step test, 253
time inconsistency, 116, 119, 509
time-shifting, 252
tipping point, 348
tokens, 425

Tong, X., 143
Toole, A., 378
Tostitos, 9
trade
liberalization, 485
secrecy, 302, 333, 407, 480
secret, 10, 152
Trade-Related Aspects of Intellectual Property Rights (TRIPS), 18, 52, 59, 171, 268, 298
trademark, 8, 514
trademark protection, 117
traditional medicines, 298
Trajtenberg, M., 140
transactions costs, 254
transfer learning, 419
transfer pricing, 232
transformer, 425
translation costs, 33
Trefler, D., 439–440, 442, 483
TRIPS waiver, 292, 501
TRIPS-plus agreements, 19, 276
Tucker, C., 413, 416
Tørsløv, T., 233

U

U.S. Copyright Office, 394
U.S. International Trade Commission, 293
U.S. National Institutes of Health, 40, 506
U.S. Patent and Trademark Office (USPTO), 45, 64, 145, 148, 225, 392
U.S. Tax Cuts and Jobs Act, 236
U.S. Trade Representative (USTR), 185
UN Convention on Biological Diversity (CBD), 335
unaffiliated licensing, 200, 205, 209, 226
uncertainty, 371, 374, 382
uniformity, 11
user innovation, 340
user interfaces, 424
utility models, 184, 487, 498

V

vaccine nationalism, 295
van Pottelsberghe de la Potteries, B., 24, 108
Varian, H., 471
Venturini, F., 434
Vespa Scooter, 11
Vipra, J., 470
Vogel, D., 440
Vollrath, D., 13
voluntary license, 280

W

Waldfogel, J., 244, 247
Wallace, Alfred, 240
Walls, W.D., 220
Westphal, L., 186
WIPO Copyright Treaty (WCT), 16
WIPO Performances and Phonograms Treaty (WPPT), 16
working requirement, 43
World Economic Forum, 50

World Health Organization, 267
World Trade Organization (WTO), 15, 52, 67, 278, 298, 304, 438

X

XPRIZE, 149

Y

Yang, G., 161, 199
Yudkowsky, E., 456

Z

Zentner, A., 244–245
Zhang, W., 449
Ziedonis, R., 345

www.ingramcontent.com/pod-product-compliance
Lightning Source LLC
La Vergne TN
LVHW051054210926
848486LV00002B/106